DOUBLETAKES

Pairs of
Contemporary
Short Stories

T. Coraghessan
Boyle

*University of
Southern California*

with K. Kvashay-Boyle
University of Iowa

THOMSON
WADSWORTH

Australia   Canada   Mexico   Singapore   Spain   United Kingdom   United States

Doubletakes
Pairs of Contemporary Short Stories
T. Coraghessan Boyle

Publisher: *Michael Rosenberg*
Senior Editor: *Aron Keesbury*
Associate Production Editor: *Matt Drapeau*
Editorial Assistant: *Marita Sermolins*
Editorial Assistant: *Catherine Black*
Director of Marketing: *Lisa Kimball*
Executive Marketing Manager: *Carrie Brandon*
Manufacturing Manager: *Marcia Locke*
Compositor: *Lachina Publishing Services, Inc.*
Project Manager: *Ronn Jost*
Cover Designer: *Diane Levy, DFL Publications*
Printer: *Transcontinental Printing*

Cover Art: Werner Hoeflich, Untitled, 1996,
oil and Alkyd on canvas.

Printed in Canada.
1 2 3 4 5 6 7 8 9 10 07 06 05 04 03

For more information contact Wadsworth, 25 Thomson Place, Boston, Massachusetts
02210 USA, or you can visit our Internet site at http://www.heinle.com

For permission to use material from this text or product contact us:
Tel   1-800-730-2214
Fax   1-800-730-2215
Web   www.thomsonrights.com

ISBN: 0-15-506081-3

Library of Congress Control Number: 2003110008

Credits appear on page 655, which constitutes a continuation of the copyright page.

Contents

Alan Gurganus
Pam Houston

NO

Maybe

Preface

More than anything, what keeps me connected to the teaching of literature and writing after all these years — twenty-five and counting — is the astonishing pool of talent available to me each semester. I haven't done any genetic studies along the lines of Mendel into inherited characteristics, but it seems to me that the number of people with a great gift for writing and its appreciation is disproportionate to the number who develop the gift at its highest level and become the writers, teachers, and close readers of their generation. My job, as I see it, is to act as a coach, to help these (mostly young) writers and readers to realize their gift and develop it in their own way. There is no science to this, no formula, and despite what the credulous may believe, there are no rules, since art subverts any and all attempts to rope it in and regulate it.

Each writer approaches the world in an individual way — absolutely no one, among the billions now extant and all those gone down before us, has had precisely the same experiences — and this is what brings freshness and joy to each new generation of writers. Still, no artist creates *sui generis* — we are all an amalgam of our influences, of our deep reading and early mimesis, of our thoughts and emotions. The idea of this anthology, designed for use in writing workshops and contemporary literature classes, is to give some insight into what a story is and how it comes about, at the same time emphasizing, especially for undergraduates, that it is only through reading — reading for pleasure and analysis both — that one is enabled to write in the first place. The stories in this anthology are meant to serve as models, certainly, but beyond that to display a wide range of possibilities within the form. My hope is that these stories will awaken the writer's imagination in the students who study them. *So that's how it's done,* they will think. Or better yet: *I can do that.*

Reading for Enjoyment

Above all, what I hope to accomplish here is to give the neophyte writer and reader a sense of the joy the writer feels in composing a story that fires on all cylinders. Too often, students see fiction — novels, stories, poetry — as a subcategory of academic drudgery, as an assignment, a means to an end. My aesthetic, as writer and reader both, is to elevate the sense of enjoyment above all other literary considerations, to remind us all that literature is an art and that art exists to entertain.

With that goal in mind, on the first day of class each semester I ask my students to list their ten favorite works of fiction and the authors thereof. It's an instructive exercise. Many are unable to complete such a list; others have read only genre fiction or literary works assigned to them in their period classes. I then ask them if they can name their ten favorite CDs, movies, TV shows — no problem there. They take my point: To aspire to be a writer or a student of literature, you must read widely and enthusiastically, and you must especially be attuned to the work of the writers of your own time. When the notebooks are put away and the texts closed for the night, I want my students to indulge the private pleasure of reading as a way of getting the latest news, just as they might go to the Cineplex to take in a new release or download a tune from the Internet.

Interpretation for Enjoyment

All right. Fine. But students will say, "If literature is entertainment on the order of music or painting or film, why bother with interpretation at all? Why not just let it be?" Once or twice a semester, I will take that tack and simply read a story aloud for the pure delight of it, right at the end of class, without discussion. Out the door we go, but the students can't resist holding back, examining it among themselves, trying to gauge how the story has achieved its impact. *Did you hear that? Can you believe it? Well, you know what I think . . .* Yes, there is an essential mystery to the creation of art, which I will address in my Introduction, but that does not mean that the method of its creation is unavailable to analysis. What the reader must understand is that the process of entering a story — of being so swept away by the imagined world that one's senses essentially shut down — is precisely the process the writer has experienced on the other end. All writing is synthesis, but creative writing most often comes from an inner source, a discovery, an inspiration of the moment. The writers of the stories in this volume, I would guess, have not begun with a theme or statement — better save such for analytical writing — but with a single moment of inspiration that has come to them in the form of voice.

Narrative voice is the beginning, and voice controls the mode of the story — i.e., will this be narrated in the first, second, or third person and how will the tone color it — and gives rise to all the rest: development of character, theme, language, structure, and symbology. Even the most meticulously plotted stories are an accident of development, as are the most telling metaphors and richest characters (though, of course, in many instances, the characters derive from the author's own experience, sometimes presented in caricature, more often conflated into *sammel-persons*). Examine the opening lines of any of these stories — Richard Ford's "Rock Springs," for instance, or Annie Proulx's "The Half-Skinned Steer" — and you will see how voice reveals character and determines the tone and even movement of the piece as it progresses toward theme and discovery. The point is, one need not have a fully formed opinion on a given subject or even a worldview in order to produce a dynamic and engaging fiction: Follow the voice and the rest will fall in place. Over the course of a career, through the writing of story after story, the writer discovers whom he or she is and what his or her obsessions are. Then we have the beginnings of a worldview. And so, my advice to the student: Not to worry.

For the most part, this book is innocent of theory, because theory influences writers only peripherally, as a motive force that may require examination but not fealty — we are always looking for something new, but that something is more likely artistic or emotional than theoretical. This is not to say that trends or movements don't influence writers in the way that they influence everyone else in society — the elaborate, word-intoxicated postmodernist writing of the late sixties and seventies is represented here, for example, by Robert Coover and much younger writers such as David Foster Wallace and George Saunders, whose work builds on the experiments of that era. So too I include examples in the realist/minimalist mode that dominated North American writing in the eighties, as well as a strong representation of emerging writers who are synthesizing the influences of the past three decades into a new and widely divergent take on what a story is.

The Stories in This Book

The pieces collected in this volume are stories I have analyzed and enjoyed with the students in my fiction-writing and literature classes over the course of the years — and "enjoyed" is the cardinal word here. Literature is entertainment above all else, and too many students have been exposed to it as drill, as sociology, as text, as a sanctified house of signs and symbols available only to the theorist and critic, as homework, as drudgery. Stories can be good — can be entertaining — in a variety of ways, and the stories here reflect that variety, in their conception, style, structure, and technique. The approach is catholic: I want each student to find something here of interest, something new, something to stimulate his or her imagination.

Students will find the voices of these stories strong, compelling, and distinctive. They will begin to see how each author goes about solving the problem of how best to tell a given story, from Roald Dahl's reliance on intricate plotting in "Dip in the Pool" to Gabriel García

Márquez's creation of illusory worlds in his two stories for children and the allusive richness of Amy Hempel's "In the Cemetery Where Al Jolson Is Buried." How do these stories come about? What is the author thinking? What is the method? That is what this anthology seeks to uncover.

Finally, *Doubletakes* is intended to invite students into the realm of appreciation, enjoyment, analysis, and interpretation on a personal level. Each of us who has taught in high school, college, or the university would be able, I think, to construct our own anthology of stories that seem to our lights to be especially attuned to stimulating the writers and readers under our tutelage. *Doubletakes* is my own idealized congregation, an assemblage of stories that have worked particularly well in my workshop and literature classes over the years, and further, the book allows me to give a writer's take on each of the stories included here. I hope that the resulting text will be inviting, dispensing as it does with the impersonal academic apparatus that can be so intimidating to students who want only to discover what it is to read and to write.

Acknowledgments

There are a number of people I would like to thank for their help in putting this anthology together. Kerrie Kvashay-Boyle has been invaluable for her input on story selection and has been involved in this project from its inception, not only serving as a sounding board but as my co-editor as well. Aron Keesbury, my astute and stalwart editor at Wadsworth, has from the beginning given me the full benefit of his guidance throughout the process of composing the introductory matter and headnotes: Absent his creative spark, this project would never have come together. Next, I would like to express my gratitude to Bill Brisick, who first proposed to me the idea of an anthology drawing on my experience in the classroom, and Georges Borchardt, my agent, for making it happen. Finally, I want to cite the real and enduring professionals behind the scenes at Wadsworth: Matt Drapeau, the Associate Production Editor, and Ronn Jost of Lachina Publishing Services, Project Manager and Copyeditor, both of whom were a pleasure to work with and as certain and efficient as generals preparing for battle; my publisher, Michael Rosenberg, for his persistence in seeing this through; the Editorial Assistants, Catherine Black, who built the manuscript, and Marita Sermolins, who handled a lot of the little details that would have driven anyone else mad; Karyn Morrison, who cleared permissions (an equally daunting task); and, finally, all those who reviewed the manuscript, in its rawest form, for Wadsworth.

Introduction

My earliest experience of literature was, like many people's, the experience of an eager fan, a devourer of stories for the sheer pleasure of being privy to another world altogether. There were the stories my mother read me aloud when I was a child, and then the starter books and finally animal tales and nature books that I read on my own. In junior high, there were Shakespeare and Dickens, presented as artifacts by our teachers, and in high school, any pleasure I might have taken in the telling and reading of stories was subsumed in the compulsion to accumulate knowledge against the English Regents and the SAT exams. Senior year was more of the same, with a remote and pompous teacher reading aloud to us the great narrative and lyrical poems of English literature, but in a way that made them seem dead and remote — again, mere cultural artifacts. The early joy I'd taken in reading was gone.

Happily, it came back with a rush in the first literature class I took in college, a course in the short story. We read classics of the form — works of Guy de Maupassant, Anton Chekhov, James Joyce — but also more contemporary works by Ernest Hemingway, Conrad Aiken, Bernard Malamud, and Flannery O'Connor. I can still remember the frisson of recognition at the end of O'Connor's "A Good Man Is Hard to Find," in which the tragic mode is forced down the gullet of the comic in a way I never thought possible. This story was *entertaining* in a new way, and, like many first-time readers of O'Connor, I was taken completely by surprise. Here I was, enjoying a laugh-out-loud satiric piece about a conniving grandmother and the dreaded family vacation, when suddenly the story took the darkest turn possible. The work was ultimately tragic, shocking even, but I felt it and understood it in a way that forever reconfigured the way I felt about literature. There was a puzzle here — how was O'Connor able to pull it off? — and I was determined to take it apart and put it back together in order to find out.

Solving Puzzles

My next step was to enroll in a creative-writing class. There, in attempting my own stories, I began to see how even the most seamless piece evolves from an initial idea and the voice the author chooses, and

1

my pleasure in reading — in reading for entertainment, for news, for the aesthetic gratification the solving of that puzzle gives you — began to expand. People talked of a writer finding his or her voice, and that voice, as I discovered, referred to what makes each writer's work distinctive, in the way that the voice of a vocalist, combined with the texture of the rhythm and instrumentation behind it, makes a band instantly recognizable, even if you've never heard that particular tune. Turn on the radio, and there it is — you know that voice. Both my literature and my creative-writing classes suggested the way to discover that voice in myself — through wide reading, especially in my contemporaries, and the trial-and-error approach to the writing of my own stories. To know a story inside out, to know how it's put together, became a tremendous advantage, a key to solving the puzzle and making each story engaging in a whole new way.

Voice

All right. But what is it about the stories in this volume that make them unique, that make them entertaining on all levels? First, each has the distinctive voice we've spoken of, and you can see how elastic that voice can be if you contrast the two pieces by any of the authors included here. Black out the names and shuffle the stories, and you'll still hear the same tune playing. That said, there is a second shading of voice to consider, and that is not the authorial voice but the voice of the character or the third-person point of view closely identified with it. This is the voice that speaks to the writer in the first moment of inspiration and carries the story through all its complexities to its conclusion.

Thumb through the collection and examine the first lines only, because it is here that this voice is revealed. I can't speak for my fellow authors, but I can say that in all the stories I've written (and that must be about a hundred and fifty or so, as well as ten novels) I have begun with a voice and tone revealed to me in the first line and pursued the unfolding of the story from there. The act of creation *is* mysterious, no doubt about it, and most authors pursue it intuitively, waiting for the voice to begin whispering in their ears. Here is what Raymond Carver has to say about it in his essay "On Writing":

> I once sat down to write what turned out to be a pretty good story, though only the first sentence of the story had offered itself to me when I began it. For several days I'd been going around with this sentence in my head: "He was running the vacuum cleaner when the telephone rang." I knew a story was there and that it wanted telling. I felt in my

bones that a story belonged with that beginning, if I could just have
the time to write it.

Somehow, during the period of those "several days," the possibilities of
the story began to work themselves out on a subconscious level even as
the first line played like a mantra in his head.

Certainly, in given stories, authors will start with a structural idea
(Coover's "the convention," O'Brien's "The Things They Carried,"
Oates's "The Abduction") or even an ending that must be worked toward (Dahl's "Taste"), but the voice established in the opening line has
to carry all the rest. The first line of Richard Ford's "Rock Springs"
immediately establishes character and attitude through its word choice
and at the same time sets up the essential tension of the drama to follow ("Edna and I had started down from Kalispell, heading for Tampa-
St. Pete where I still had some friends from the old glory days who
wouldn't turn me in to the police."). Note "the old glory days." Note
"who wouldn't turn me in to the police."

So too, for example, Stacey Richter sets the table for us with this
from "The Beauty Treatment": "She smiled when she saw me coming,
the Bitch, she smiled and stuck her fingers in her mouth like she was
plucking gum out of her dental work." Immediately, we have a preju-
dice established ("the Bitch") and a character and an action spinning out
of it. This works just as effectively in the third person, as with Junot
Díaz's "The Brief Wondrous Life of Oscar Wao" ("Oscar de León was
not one of those Dominican cats everybody's always going on about.
He wasn't no player.") or Joyce Carol Oates's "Tick" ("She said, I can't
live with you under these conditions, and her husband said, But these
are the conditions. And moved out."). One of my own early stories,
"Descent of Man," begins with this line: "I was living with a woman
who suddenly began to stink." Well, why? the reader asks. And what
of it? Does it bother you? Why tell me? And the story then goes about
its business answering the reader's questions. (The answer to the first,
incidentally, is that she has been working as an animal behaviorist in
very close proximity to a chimp who could really be a bit more scrupulous as regards personal hygiene.)

Another example is the opening of the bonus story I've included
here as part of the Introduction (on page 7), Donald Barthelme's "The
School." The voice — in this case the monologue of a bewildered
teacher — helps establish both character and form from the outset: "Well,
we had all these children out planting trees, see, because we figured
that . . . that was part of their education, to see how, you know, the root
systems . . . and also the sense of responsibility, taking care of things,

being individually responsible. You know what I mean." The use of slang, the dilatory opening — "Well" — and the hesitation indicated by the pauses in the speech all indicate a character who is trying to work things out in his own mind. He is puzzled. And as he voices his perplexity, the form or structure of the piece begins to suggest itself. This is not quite a dramatic monologue, in that the person to whom this is addressed neither reacts nor plays a part in the piece, but it nonetheless develops a feeling of immediacy and intimacy as the speaker addresses a second person ("you know"; "see"; and further on in the piece, "But I think that the snakes — well, the reason that the snakes kicked off was that . . . you remember, the boiler was shut off for four days because of the strike, and that was explicable.").

Structure and Form

Which brings us to the next thing to consider: structure, that is, the way the story is put together temporally, how it selects the moment to enter the action and moves backward and forward in time to provide whatever setting and exposition are necessary. Think of it this way: You're sitting at a café or a bar, as Barthelme's narrator may be, telling your best friend about the bike accident you had yesterday when the misaligned front wheel struck the curb and you were hurtled like a missile into the hydrangea bush along with the bag of groceries in your backpack (a dozen eggs, whole wheat flour, oatmeal, one percent milk, and a package of chopped walnuts: Yes, you were going to make cookies). How do you structure your telling? Do you introduce yourself as a character, or is that unnecessary because your auditor already knows you? Do you begin with the purchase of the secondhand bicycle with its wobbly wheel? Or in the grocery store? Do you want to give us a history of the town and its sidewalks and crumbling curbs? Or would you prefer to start with the accident itself and work back from there?

Usually, the structure too is a byproduct of that first line, that voice, that agent of entry, revealing itself to the writer as he/she moves forward in an attempt to resolve the questions set up in the opening, but this is not always the case. Take, for example, Jorge Luis Borges's brilliant satire of the fusty academician, "Pierre Menard, Author of Don Quixote." The title alone gives us pause, because we know Cervantes as the author of *Don Quixote,* and that is a wonderful trick in itself, but with this story the form seems to precede and in fact dictate the voice.

Here we have a story in the guise of a scholarly article, and because of that structural innovation — this is an article, this is real, not fiction — immediate credence is given to even the most absurd statements, thus reinforcing the wicked humor of the piece. Another example is George Saunders's "I CAN SPEAK!™," composed in the form of a (Kafka-esque) letter to a dissatisfied customer. More often, in these stories, the plot will move forward in time from the point of departure in the opening line, with divagations for the necessary exposition, as in the two Ford stories, Cheever's "The Five-Forty-Eight," and Gaitskill's "Secretary." Some of the stories here invent new forms to contain them, most notably Tim O'Brien's "The Things They Carried" and Lorrie Moore's "How to Become A Writer," while others rely on the structure of the folktale, such as Calvino's "Marcovaldo" tales, García Márquez's fables, and, to a degree, Ellen Gilchrist's "Rich." In any case, it is instructive to examine the opening lines and ask why the writer has chosen to begin at that juncture of the narrative — you will see the structure revealed in the posing of the question.

Texture

The third thing that distinguishes these stories is what I'll call texture or color, the way in which the author employs the language of the narrator on a metaphoric or symbolic level. Obviously, the scholar of Borges's tale will speak differently from the streetwise narrators of John Edgar Wideman's "Doc's Story" and Junot Díaz's "The Brief Wondrous Life of Oscar Wao," and his diction will not be as colorful, but it is in the creative use of language that all these authors shine. One of the best examples here is Amy Hempel's deeply affecting story about the loss of a close friend, "In the Cemetery Where Al Jolson Is Buried." The story moves through an accretion and repetition of images rather than in the way of conventional plotting, giving it a depth and color a more traditional rendering might have sacrificed — thereby preventing it from slipping into the maudlin. How do you write about heartbreak and loss without staining the keyboard with tears? Hempel's solution is ingenious. As is the bright, chirpy narrative of Lorrie Moore's "People Like That Are the Only People Here: Canonical Babbling in Peed Onk," in which the narrator's loopy humor is used as a shield against the horror she feels.

To illustrate what I've been saying here, let's look at the text of "The School" for a moment.

Donald Barthelme

Donald Barthelme (1931–89) once served as a museum director, and many of the stories he produced in the sixties and seventies were abstracts, a body of work peculiarly skewed and nonrepresentational. His experiments with form led him to include graphics in some of his pieces, such as "Eugénie Grandet" or "At the Tolstoy Museum"; to order a story ("The Glass Mountain") in one hundred numbered sentences; or to interrupt his novel *Snow White* with a questionnaire for the reader. He is most often represented in anthologies with his early story "The Indian Uprising" (1968), which imagines the Comanches of movie lore invading a modern city while the narrator and his inamorata sit around languidly discussing art, music, and aesthetic arrangement ("Do you know Fauré's 'Dolly'?" "Would that be Gabriel Fauré?" "It would."). He is a master of the incongruous and of a kind of humor of juxtaposition, and his funniest work hearkens back to the absurdist playwrights of the fifties and sixties.

"The School" is a sly meditation on the limits of education in a universe ruled by mystery, accident, and death, and its humor builds through escalation to the absurd and symbolic final gesture.

DONALD BARTHELME

The School

Well, we had all these children out planting trees, see, because we figured that . . . that was part of their education, to see how, you know, the root systems . . . and also the sense of responsibility, taking care of things, being individually responsible. You know what I mean. And the trees all died. They were orange trees. I don't know why they died, they just died. Something wrong with the soil possibly or maybe the stuff we got from the nursery wasn't the best. We complained about it. So we've got thirty kids there, each kid had his or her own little tree to plant, and we've got these thirty dead trees. All these kids looking at these little brown sticks, it was depressing.

It wouldn't have been so bad except that just a couple of weeks before the thing with the trees, the snakes all died. But I think that the snakes — well, the reason that the snakes kicked off was that . . . you remember, the boiler was shut off for four days because of the strike, and that was explicable. It was something you could explain to the kids because of the strike. I mean, none of their parents would let them cross the picket line and they knew there was a strike going on and what it meant. So when things got started up again and we found the snakes they weren't too disturbed.

With the herb gardens it was probably a case of overwatering, and at least now they know not to overwater. The children were very conscientious with the herb gardens and some of them probably . . . you know, slipped them a little extra water when we weren't looking. Or maybe . . . well, I don't like to think about sabotage, although it did occur to us. I mean, it was something that crossed our minds. We were thinking that way probably because before that the gerbils had died, and the white mice had died, and the salamander . . . well, now they know not to carry them around in plastic bags.

Of course we *expected* the tropical fish to die, that was no surprise. Those numbers, you look at them crooked and they're belly-up on the surface. But the lesson plan called for a tropical-fish input at that point, there was nothing we could do, it happens every year, you just have to hurry past it.

We weren't even supposed to have a puppy.

7

We weren't even supposed to have one, it was just a puppy the Murdoch girl found under a Gristede's truck one day and she was afraid the truck would run over it when the driver had finished making his delivery, so she stuck it in her knapsack and brought it to school with her. So we had this puppy. As soon as I saw the puppy I thought, Oh Christ, I bet it will live for about two weeks and then . . . And that's what it did. It wasn't supposed to be in the classroom at all, there's some kind of regulation about it, but you can't tell them they can't have a puppy when the puppy is already there, right in front of them, running around on the floor and yap yap yapping. They named it Edgar — that is, they named it after me. They had a lot of fun running after it and yelling, "Here, Edgar! Nice Edgar!" Then they'd laugh like hell. They enjoyed the ambiguity. I enjoyed it myself. I don't mind being kidded. They made a little house for it in the supply closet and all that. I don't know what it died of. Distemper, I guess. It probably hadn't had any shots. I got it out of there before the kids got to school. I checked the supply closet each morning, routinely, because I knew what was going to happen. I gave it to the custodian.

And then there was this Korean orphan that the class adopted through the Help the Children program, all the kids brought in a quarter a month, that was the idea. It was an unfortunate thing, the kid's name was Kim and maybe we adopted him too late or something. The cause of death was not stated in the letter we got, they suggested we adopt another child instead and sent us some interesting case histories, but we didn't have the heart. The class took it pretty hard, they began (I think; nobody ever said anything to me directly) to feel that maybe there was something wrong with the school. But I don't think there's anything wrong with the school, particularly, I've seen better and I've seen worse. It was just a run of bad luck. We had an extraordinary number of parents passing away, for instance. There were I think two heart attacks and two suicides, one drowning, and four killed together in a car accident. One stroke. And we had the usual heavy mortality rate among the grandparents, or maybe it was heavier this year, it seemed so. And finally the tragedy.

The tragedy occurred when Matthew Wein and Tony Mavrogordo were playing over where they're excavating for the new federal office building. There were all these big wooden beams stacked, you know, at the edge of the excavation. There's a court case coming out of that, the parents are claiming that the beams were poorly stacked. I don't know what's true and what's not. It's been a strange year.

I forgot to mention Billy Brandt's father, who was knifed fatally when he grappled with a masked intruder in his home.

One day, we had a discussion in class. They asked me, where did they go? The trees, the salamander, the tropical fish, Edgar, the poppas and mommas, Matthew and Tony, where did they go? And I said, I don't know, I don't know. And they said, who knows? and I said, nobody knows. And they said, is death that which gives meaning to life? And I said, no, life is that which gives meaning to life. Then they said, but isn't death, considered as a fundamental datum, the means by which the taken-for-granted mundanity of the everyday may be transcended in the direction of —

I said, yes, maybe.

They said, we don't like it.

I said, that's sound.

They said, it's a bloody shame!

I said, it is.

They said, will you make love now with Helen (our teaching assistant) so that we can see how it is done? We know you like Helen.

I do like Helen but I said that I would not.

We've heard so much about it, they said, but we've never seen it.

I said I would be fired and that it was never, or almost never, done as a demonstration. Helen looked out of the window.

They said, please, please make love with Helen, we require an assertion of value, we are frightened.

I said that they shouldn't be frightened (although I am often frightened) and that there was value everywhere. Helen came and embraced me. I kissed her a few times on the brow. We held each other. The children were excited. Then there was a knock on the door, I opened the door, and the new gerbil walked in. The children cheered wildly.

※

We've talked a bit about the opening and the narrative voice and how it suggests the form. There is an intimacy between speaker and reader established right off, as the reader becomes the "you" sitting there beside the upset and confused narrator. He simply cannot figure what went wrong, when the lesson plan should have guided the class through all the little tremors and minor tragedies of a school year, but the beauty — and humor — of the story is that *we* can understand just what has gone wrong even if the narrator cannot. The lesson plan is meant to instruct the children in the richness and variety of life, but, of course, no lesson plan — no science or philosophy — can explain the essential mystery of the universe or the ineluctable wedding of life and death. This is what the story is getting at beneath the surface, on a thematic level — this is *what it's about.*

The texture of the story — its deep roots — is revealed when the reader poses the eschatological questions that no one, not even our teachers and parents, can answer, while Barthelme, ever playful and self-aware, even goes to the extent of putting those questions in the children's mouths ("They asked me, where did they go? The trees, the salamander, the tropical fish, Edgar, the poppas and mommas, Matthew and Tony. . . . And I said, I don't know. . . . And they said, who knows? and I said, nobody knows. . . . Then they said, but isn't death, considered as a fundamental datum, the means by which the taken-for-granted mundanity of the everyday may be transcended in the direction of — "). The fun here is that the author himself has supplied the meaning of the story in a naked and exaggerated way, thus poking fun at more ponderous treatments of the theme.

But this is only part of the way the story operates. Yes, it begins in voice and voice suggests form, but the most tricky terrain here is a further structural problem. You will have noticed that the story's comedy and payoff depend upon an almost-evolutionary progression in the nearness of the deaths. At first it's the insentient orange trees and herb gardens, escalating to snakes and fishes and then mammals and finally humans — and the escalation doesn't end there either but rather leaps from the orphan to the grandparents and the parents and ultimately two of the children themselves. The writer's problem here is how to get out from under the structure — it simply cannot escalate forever. Barthelme's solution is elegant, and it plays back into the voice and structure set up at the outset. Love — sex, reproduction — is the antithesis of death, and so the symbolic gesture of affection between the narrator and Helen, the teaching assistant, brings new life to the door.

This is a very funny story, its humor deriving from both situation/character and the mounting absurdity given release in the final lines. It is meant to be enjoyed and savored. And yet at the same time it presents a puzzle, as all good stories do, and the unlocking of that puzzle — the discovery of and use of the very key the author has had to discover on his end — makes that enjoyment all the deeper. All the stories in this volume should deliver the same sort of pleasure. Art is entertainment. Never lose sight of that.

What Else?

Look for the outrageous, the subversive, the shocking. Mary Gaitskill's stories take no prisoners, nor do Emily Carter's. They are artfully crafted, exquisite, yet naked and searing in their vision of contemporary mores. Look for beauty and humiliation, for intensely realized traumas of childhood and adolescence in the stories of Jamaica Kincaid and Isabel Huggan. These are stories that strike at the emotions, but there are humor and irony here aplenty as well. Again, great stories are as various as the writers who have composed them.

My method is to include two stories by each author in order to give you a better sense of a given writer's take on things than you might get in a standard, single-story anthology (I'd prefer three, but none of us here wants to further contribute to the epidemic of spinal curvature among American academics), and while I've incorporated some of the usual authors and stories because of their indispensability, I've tried to include a substantial proportion of work in various modes not generally found in other anthologies. Finally, the stories here don't have anything in common stylistically or thematically — the only common thread is in their persuasion, their beauty, and the force of their artistry. And, of course, in the joy of their telling.

T. Coraghessan Boyle, Ph.D.
University of Southern California

Ann Beattie

Ann Beattie's literary debut in 1976 was especially noteworthy in that her first two books — *Chilly Scenes of Winter,* a novel, and *Distortions,* a collection of nineteen stories — were published simultaneously. It was unusual in the seventies for a major commercial publisher to release a first book of stories rather than a first novel (Raymond Carver's luminous 1977 collection, *Will You Please Be Quiet, Please?* helped change all that, to a degree at least), and Beattie's publishers at Doubleday went out of their way to announce an extraordinary new talent in an extraordinary way. Her stories of this period, many of which first appeared in *The New Yorker,* were beautifully crafted, elliptical pieces that served to introduce a new generation — the hippies — and their tribal ways and mores to the literary world. She is a realist, with a fine comic touch, and her stories move through indirection or the tracing of a defining image rather than through the strong plotting that marked the short stories of the previous generation. Unlike many contemporary fiction writers, she seems equally at home in the novel and the short story, though most would agree that her major contribution has been in her short fiction.

"The Burning House" is the title story of her 1982 collection, and its loose structure, its use of the present tense, and its plunge into the shifting and chaotic scene of a gathering of friends are characteristic of her work. The opening lines are immediate and cinematic: "Freddy Fox is in the kitchen with me. He has just washed and dried an avocado seed I don't want, and he is leaning against the wall, rolling a joint. In five minutes, I will not be able to count on him." The story examines male/female relationships, as so many of her pieces do; its ending is as powerful and devastating as anything she's written. The second story here, "The Four-Night Fight," is from *Park City,* her 1998 volume of new and selected stories. It too is about a relationship, but here the structure is tighter, the humor broader, and the relationship a more familiar and mature one than that of "The Burning House."

The Burning House

Freddy Fox is in the kitchen with me. He has just washed and dried an avocado seed I don't want, and he is leaning against the wall, rolling a joint. In five minutes, I will not be able to count on him. However: he started late in the day, and he has already brought in wood for the fire, gone to the store down the road for matches, and set the table. "You mean you'd know this stuff was Limoges even if you didn't turn the plate over?" he called from the dining room. He pretended to be about to throw one of the plates into the kitchen, like a Frisbee. Sam, the dog, believed him and shot up, kicking the rug out behind him and skidding forward before he realized his error; it was like the Road Runner tricking Wile E. Coyote into going over the cliff for the millionth time. His jowls sank in disappointment.

"I see there's a full moon," Freddy says. "There's just nothing that can hold a candle to nature. The moon and the stars, the tides and the sunshine — and we just don't stop for long enough to wonder at it all. We're so engrossed in ourselves." He takes a very long drag on the joint. "We stand and stir the sauce in the pot instead of going to the window and gazing at the moon."

"You don't mean anything personal by that, I assume."

"I love the way you pour cream in a pan. I like to come up behind you and watch the sauce bubble."

"No, thank you," I say. "You're starting late in the day."

"My responsibilities have ended. You don't trust me to help with the cooking, and I've already brought in firewood and run an errand, and this very morning I exhausted myself by taking Mr. Sam jogging with me, down at Putnam Park. You're sure you won't?"

"No, thanks," I say. "Not now, anyway."

"I love it when you stand over the steam coming out of a pan and the hairs around your forehead curl into damp little curls."

My husband, Frank Wayne, is Freddy's half brother. Frank is an accountant. Freddy is closer to me than to Frank. Since Frank talks to Freddy more than he talks to me, however, and since Freddy is totally loyal, Freddy always knows more than I know. It pleases me that he does not know how to stir sauce; he will start talking, his mind will drift, and when next you look the sauce will be lumpy, or boiling away.

Freddy's criticism of Frank is only implied. "What a gracious gesture to entertain his friends on the weekend," he says.

"Male friends," I say.

"I didn't mean that you're the sort of lady who doesn't draw the line. I most certainly did not mean that," Freddy says. "I would even have been surprised if you had taken a toke of this deadly stuff while you were at the stove."

"O.K.," I say, and take the joint from him. Half of it is left when I take it. Half an inch is left after I've taken two drags and given it back.

"More surprised still if you'd shaken the ashes into the saucepan."

"You'd tell people I'd done it when they'd finished eating, and I'd be embarrassed. You can do it, though. I wouldn't be embarrassed if it was a story you told on yourself."

"You really understand me," Freddy says. "It's moon-madness, but I have to shake just this little bit in the sauce. I have to do it."

He does it.

Frank and Tucker are in the living room. Just a few minutes ago, Frank returned from getting Tucker at the train. Tucker loves to visit. To him, Fairfield County is as mysterious as Alaska. He brought with him from New York a crock of mustard, a jeroboam of champagne, cocktail napkins with a picture of a plane flying over a building on them, twenty egret feathers ("You cannot get them anymore — strictly illegal," Tucker whispered to me), and, under his black cowboy hat with the rhinestone-studded chin strap, a toy frog that hopped when wound. Tucker owns a gallery in SoHo, and Frank keeps his books. Tucker is now stretched out in the living room, visiting with Frank, and Freddy and I are both listening.

". . . so everything I've been told indicates that he lives a purely Jekyll-and-Hyde existence. He's twenty years old, and I can see that since he's still living at home he might not want to flaunt his gayness. When he came into the gallery, he had his hair slicked back — just with water, I got close enough to sniff — and his mother was all but holding his hand. So fresh-scrubbed. The stories I'd heard. Anyway, when I called, his father started looking for the number where he could be reached on the Vineyard — very irritated, because I didn't know James, and if I'd just phoned James I could have found him in a flash. He's talking to himself, looking for the number, and I say, 'Oh, did he go to visit friends or — ' and his father interrupts and says, 'He was going to a gay pig roast. He's been gone since Monday.' *Just like that.*"

Freddy helps me carry the food out to the table. When we are all at the table, I mention the young artist Tucker was talking about. "Frank says his paintings are really incredible," I say to Tucker.

"Makes Estes look like an Abstract Expressionist," Tucker says. "I want that boy. I really want that boy."

"You'll get him," Frank says. "You get everybody you go after."

Tucker cuts a small piece of meat. He cuts it small so that he can talk while chewing. "Do I?" he says.

Freddy is smoking at the table, gazing dazedly at the moon centered in the window. "After dinner," he says, putting the back of his hand against his forehead when he sees that I am looking at him, "we must all go to the lighthouse."

"If only *you* painted," Tucker says. "I'd want you."

"You couldn't have me," Freddy snaps. He reconsiders. "That sounded halfhearted, didn't it? Anybody who wants me can have me. This is the only place I can be on Saturday night where somebody isn't hustling me."

"Wear looser pants," Frank says to Freddy.

"This is so much better than some bar that stinks of cigarette smoke and leather. Why do I do it?" Freddy says. "Seriously — do you think I'll ever stop?"

"Let's not be serious," Tucker says.

"I keep thinking of this table as a big boat, with dishes and glasses rocking on it," Freddy says.

He takes the bone from his plate and walks out to the kitchen, dripping sauce on the floor. He walks as though he's on the deck of a wave-tossed ship. "Mr. Sam!" he calls, and the dog springs up from the living-room floor, where he had been sleeping; his toenails on the bare wood floor sound like a wheel spinning in gravel. "You don't have to beg," Freddy says. "Jesus, Sammy — I'm just giving it to you."

"I hope there's a bone involved," Tucker says, rolling his eyes to Frank. He cuts another tiny piece of meat. "I hope your brother does understand why I couldn't keep him on. He was good at what he did, but he also might say just *anything* to a customer. You have to believe me that if I hadn't been extremely embarrassed more than once I never would have let him go."

"He should have finished school," Frank says, sopping up sauce on his bread. "He'll knock around a while longer, then get tired of it and settle down to something."

"You think I died out here?" Freddy calls. "You think I can't hear you?"

"I'm not saying anything I wouldn't say to your face," Frank says.

"I'll tell you what I wouldn't say to your face," Freddy says. "You've got a swell wife and kid and dog, and you're a snob, and you take it all for granted."

Frank puts down his fork, completely exasperated. He looks at me. "He came to work once this stoned," Tucker says. *"Comprenez-vous?"*

"You like me because you feel sorry for me," Freddy says.

He is sitting on the concrete bench outdoors, in the area that's a garden in the springtime. It is early April now — not quite spring. It's very foggy out. It rained while we were eating, and now it has turned mild. I'm leaning against a tree, across from him, glad it's so dark and misty that I can't look down and see the damage the mud is doing to my boots.

"Who's his girlfriend?" Freddy says.

"If I told you her name, you'd tell him I told you."

"Slow down. What?"

"I won't tell you, because you'll tell him that I know."

"He knows you know."

"I don't think so."

"How did you find out?"

"He talked about her. I kept hearing her name for months, and then we went to a party at Garner's, and she was there, and when I said something about her later he said, 'Natalie who?' It was much too obvious. It gave the whole thing away."

He sighs. "I just did something very optimistic," he says. "I came out here with Mr. Sam and he dug up a rock and I put the avocado seed in the hole and packed dirt on top of it. Don't say it — I know: can't grow outside, we'll still have another snow, even if it grew, the next year's frost would kill it."

"He's embarrassed," I say. "When he's home, he avoids me. But it's rotten to avoid Mark, too. Six years old, and he calls up his friend Neal to hint that he wants to go over there. He doesn't do that when we're here alone."

Freddy picks up a stick and pokes around in the mud with it. "I'll bet Tucker's after that painter personally, not because he's the hottest thing since pancakes. That expression of his — it's always the same. Maybe Nixon really loved his mother, but with that expression who could believe him? It's a curse to have a face that won't express what you mean."

"Amy!" Tucker calls. "Telephone."

Freddy waves goodbye to me with the muddy stick. "'I am not a crook,'" Freddy says. "Jesus Christ."

Sam bounds halfway toward the house with me, then turns and goes back to Freddy.

It's Marilyn, Neal's mother, on the phone.

"Hi," Marilyn says. "He's afraid to spend the night."

"Oh, no," I say. "He said he wouldn't be."

She lowers her voice. "We can try it out, but I think he'll start crying."

"I'll come get him."

"I can bring him home. You're having a dinner party, aren't you?"

I lower my voice. "Some party. Tucker's here. J.D. never showed up."

"Well," she says. "I'm sure that what you cooked was good."

"It's so foggy out, Marilyn. I'll come get Mark."

"He can stay. I'll be a martyr," she says, and hangs up before I can object.

Freddy comes into the house, tracking in mud. Sam lies in the kitchen, waiting for his paws to be cleaned. "Come on," Freddy says, hitting his hand against his thigh, having no idea what Sam is doing. Sam gets up and runs after him. They go into the small downstairs bathroom together. Sam loves to watch people urinate. Sometimes he sings, to harmonize with the sound of the urine going into the water. There are footprints and pawprints everywhere. Tucker is shrieking with laughter in the living room. ". . . he says, he says to the other one, 'Then, dearie, have you ever played *spin* the bottle?'" Frank's and Tucker's laughter drowns out the sound of Freddy peeing in the bathroom. I turn on the water in the kitchen sink, and it drowns out all the noise. I begin to scrape the dishes. Tucker is telling another story when I turn off the water: ". . . that it was Onassis in the Anvil, and nothing would talk him out of it. They told him Onassis was dead, and he thought they were trying to make him think he was crazy. There was nothing to do but go along with him, but, God — he was trying to goad this poor old fag into fighting about Stavros Niarchos. You know — Onassis's *enemy*. He thought it was *Onassis*. In the *Anvil*." There is a sound of a glass breaking. Frank or Tucker puts *John Coltrane Live in Seattle* on the stereo and turns the volume down low. The bathroom door opens. Sam runs into the kitchen and begins to lap water from his dish. Freddy takes his little silver case and his rolling papers out of his shirt pocket. He puts a piece of paper on the kitchen table and is about to sprinkle grass on it, but realizes just in time that the paper has absorbed water from a puddle. He balls it up with his thumb, flicks it to the floor, puts a piece of rolling paper where the table's dry and shakes a line of grass down it. "You smoke this," he says to me. "I'll do the dishes."

"We'll both smoke it. I'll wash and you can wipe."

"I forgot to tell them I put ashes in the sauce," he says.

"I wouldn't interrupt."

"At least he pays Frank ten times what any other accountant for an art gallery would make," Freddy says.

Tucker is beating his hand on the arm of the sofa as he talks, stomping his feet. ". . . so he's trying to feel him out, to see if this old guy with the dyed hair knew *Maria Callas.* Jesus! And he's so out of it he's trying to think what opera singers are called, and instead of coming up with *'diva'* he comes up with *'duenna.'* At this point, Larry Betwell went up to him and tried to calm him down, and he breaks into song — some aria or something that Maria Callas was famous for. Larry told him he was going to lose his *teeth* if he didn't get it together, and . . ."

"He spends a lot of time in gay hangouts, for not being gay," Freddy says.

I scream and jump back from the sink, hitting the glass I'm rinsing against the faucet, shattering green glass everywhere.

"What?" Freddy says. "Jesus Christ, what is it?"

Too late, I realize what it must have been that I saw: J.D. in a goat mask, the puckered pink plastic lips against the window by the kitchen sink.

"I'm sorry," J.D. says, coming through the door and nearly colliding with Frank, who has rushed into the kitchen. Tucker is right behind him.

"Oooh," Tucker says, feigning disappointment, "I thought Freddy smooched her."

"I'm sorry," J.D. says again. "I thought you'd know it was me."

The rain must have started again, because J.D. is soaking wet. He has turned the mask around so that the goat's head stares out from the back of his head. "I got lost," J.D. says. He has a farmhouse upstate. "I missed the turn. I went miles. I missed the whole dinner, didn't I?"

"What did you do wrong?" Frank asks.

"I didn't turn left onto 58. I don't know why I didn't realize my mistake, but I went *miles.* It was raining so hard I couldn't go over twenty-five miles an hour. Your driveway is all mud. You're going to have to push me out."

"There's some roast left over. And salad, if you want it," I say.

"Bring it in the living room," Frank says to J.D. Freddy is holding out a plate to him. J.D. reaches for the plate. Freddy pulls it back. J.D. reaches again, and Freddy is so stoned that he isn't quick enough this time — J.D. grabs it.

"I thought you'd know it was me," J.D. says. "I apologize." He dishes salad onto the plate. "You'll be rid of me for six months, in the morning."

"Where does your plane leave from?" Freddy says.

"Kennedy."

"Come in here!" Tucker calls. "I've got a story for you about Perry Dwyer down at the Anvil last week, when he thought he saw Aristotle Onassis."

"Who's Perry Dwyer?" J.D. says.

"That is not the point of the story, dear man. And when you're in Cassis, I want you to look up an American painter over there. Will you? He doesn't have a phone. Anyway — I've been tracking him, and I know where he is now, and I am very interested, if you would stress that with him, to do a show in June that will be *only* him. He doesn't answer my letters."

"Your hand is cut," J.D. says to me.

"Forget it," I say. "Go ahead."

"I'm sorry," he says. "Did I make you do that?"

"Yes, you did."

"Don't keep your finger under the water. Put pressure on it to stop the bleeding."

He puts the plate on the table. Freddy is leaning against the counter, staring at the blood swirling in the sink, and smoking the joint all by himself. I can feel the little curls on my forehead that Freddy was talking about. They feel heavy on my skin. I hate to see my own blood. I'm sweating. I let J.D. do what he does; he turns off the water and wraps his hand around my second finger, squeezing. Water runs down our wrists.

Freddy jumps to answer the phone when it rings, as though a siren just went off behind him. He calls me to the phone, but J.D. steps in front of me, shakes his head no, and takes the dish towel and wraps it around my hand before he lets me go.

"Well," Marilyn says. "I had the best of intentions, but my battery's dead."

J.D. is standing behind me, with his hand on my shoulder.

"I'll be right over," I say. "He's not upset now, is he?"

"No, but he's dropped enough hints that he doesn't think he can make it through the night."

"O.K.," I say. "I'm sorry about all of this."

"Six years old," Marilyn says. "Wait till he grows up and gets that feeling."

I hang up.

"Let me see your hand," J.D. says.

"I don't want to look at it. Just go get me a Band-Aid, please."

He turns and goes upstairs. I unwrap the towel and look at it. It's pretty deep, but no glass is in my finger. I feel funny; the outlines of things are turning yellow. I sit in the chair by the phone. Sam comes and lies beside me, and I stare at his black-and-yellow tail, beating. I reach down with my good hand and pat him, breathing deeply in time with every second pat.

"*Rothko?*" Tucker says bitterly, in the living room. "Nothing is great that can appear on greeting cards. Wyeth is that way. Would 'Christina's World' look bad on a cocktail napkin? You know it wouldn't."

I jump as the phone rings again. "Hello?" I say, wedging the phone against my shoulder with my ear, wrapping the dish towel tighter around my hand.

"Tell them it's a crank call. Tell them anything," Johnny says. "I miss you. How's Saturday night at your house?"

"All right," I say. I catch my breath.

"Everything's all right here, too. Yes indeed. Roast rack of lamb. Friend of Nicole's who's going to Key West tomorrow had too much to drink and got depressed because he thought it was raining in Key West, and I said I'd go in my study and call the National Weather Service. Hello, Weather Service. How are you?"

J.D. comes down from upstairs with two Band-Aids and stands beside me, unwrapping one. I want to say to Johnny, "I'm cut. I'm bleeding. It's no joke."

It's all right to talk in front of J.D., but I don't know who else might overhear me.

"I'd say they made the delivery about four this afternoon," I say.

"This is the church, this is the steeple. Open the door, and see all the people," Johnny says. "Take care of yourself. I'll hang up and find out if it's raining in Key West."

"Late in the afternoon," I say. "Everything is fine."

"Nothing is fine," Johnny says. "Take care of yourself."

He hangs up. I put the phone down, and realize that I'm still having trouble focusing, the sight of my cut finger made me so lightheaded. I don't look at the finger again as J.D. undoes the towel and wraps the Band-Aids around my finger.

"What's going on in here?" Frank says, coming into the dining room.

"I cut my finger," I say. "It's O.K."

"You did?" he says. He looks woozy — a little drunk. "Who keeps calling?"

"Marilyn. Mark changed his mind about staying all night. She was going to bring him home, but her battery's dead. You'll have to get him. Or I will."

"Who called the second time?" he says.

"The oil company. They wanted to know if we got our delivery today."

He nods. "I'll go get him, if you want," he says. He lowers his voice. "Tucker's probably going to whirl himself into a tornado for an encore," he says, nodding toward the living room. "I'll take him with me."

"Do you want me to go get him?" J.D. says.

"I don't mind getting some air," Frank says. "Thanks, though. Why don't you go in the living room and eat your dinner?"

"You forgive me?" J.D. says.

"Sure," I say. "It wasn't your fault. Where did you get that mask?"

"I found it on top of a Goodwill box in Manchester. There was also a beautiful old birdcage — solid brass."

The phone rings again. I pick it up. "Wouldn't I love to be in Key West with you," Johnny says. He makes a sound as though he's kissing me and hangs up.

"Wrong number," I say.

Frank feels in his pants pocket for the car keys.

J.D. knows about Johnny. He introduced me, in the faculty lounge, where J.D. and I had gone to get a cup of coffee after I registered for classes. After being gone for nearly two years, J.D. still gets mail at the department — he said he had to stop by for the mail anyway, so he'd drive me to campus and point me toward the registrar's. J.D. taught English; now he does nothing. J.D. is glad that I've gone back to college to study art again, now that Mark is in school. I'm six credits away from an M.A. in art history. He wants me to think about myself, instead of thinking about Mark all the time. He talks as though I could roll Mark out on a string and let him fly off, high above me. J.D.'s wife and son died in a car crash. His son was Mark's age. "I wasn't prepared," J.D. said when we were driving over that day. He always says this when he talks about it. "How could you be prepared for such a thing?" I asked him. "I am now," he said. Then, realizing he was acting very hardboiled, made fun of himself. "Go on," he said, "punch me in the stomach. Hit me as hard as you can." We both knew he wasn't prepared for anything. When he couldn't find a parking place that day, his hands were wrapped around the wheel so tightly that his knuckles turned white.

Johnny came in as we were drinking coffee. J.D. was looking at his junk mail — publishers wanting him to order anthologies, ways to get free dictionaries.

"You are so lucky to be out of it," Johnny said, by way of greeting. "What do you do when you've spent two weeks on *Hamlet* and the student writes about Hamlet's good friend Horchow?"

He threw a blue book into J.D.'s lap. J.D. sailed it back.

"Johnny," he said, "this is Amy."

"Hi, Amy," Johnny said.

"You remember when Frank Wayne was in graduate school here? Amy's Frank's wife."

"Hi, Amy," Johnny said.

J.D. told me he knew it the instant Johnny walked into the room — he knew that second that he should introduce me as somebody's wife. He could have predicted it all from the way Johnny looked at me.

For a long time J.D. gloated that he had been prepared for what happened next — that Johnny and I were going to get together. It took me to disturb his pleasure in himself — me, crying hysterically on the phone last month, not knowing what to do, what move to make next.

"Don't do anything for a while. I guess that's my advice," J.D. said. "But you probably shouldn't listen to me. All I can do myself is run away, hide out. I'm not the learned professor. You know what I believe. I believe all that wicked fairy-tale crap: your heart will break, your house will burn."

Tonight, because he doesn't have a garage at his farm, J.D. has come to leave his car in the empty half of our two-car garage while he's in France. I look out the window and see his old Saab, glowing in the moonlight. J.D. has brought his favorite book, *A Vision,* to read on the plane. He says his suitcase contains only a spare pair of jeans, cigarettes, and underwear. He is going to buy a leather jacket in France, at a store where he almost bought a leather jacket two years ago.

In our bedroom there are about twenty small glass prisms hung with fishing line from one of the exposed beams; they catch the morning light, and we stare at them like a cat eyeing catnip held above its head. Just now, it is 2 A.M. At six-thirty, they will be filled with dazzling color. At four or five, Mark will come into the bedroom and get in bed with us. Sam will wake up, stretch, and shake, and the tags on his collar will clink, and he will yawn and shake again and go downstairs, where J.D. is asleep in his sleeping bag and Tucker is asleep on the sofa, and get a drink of water from his dish. Mark has been coming into our bedroom for about a year. He gets onto the bed by climbing up on a footstool that horrified me when I first saw it — a gift from Frank's mother: a footstool that says "Today Is the First Day of the Rest of Your Life" in needlepoint. I kept it in a closet for years, but it occurred to me that it would help Mark get up onto the bed, so he would not have to make a little leap and possibly skin his shin again. Now Mark does not disturb us when he comes into the bedroom, except that it bothers me that he has reverted to sucking his thumb. Sometimes he lies in bed with his cold feet against my leg. Sometimes, small as he is, he snores.

Somebody is playing a record downstairs. It's the Velvet Underground — Lou Reed, in a dream or swoon, singing "Sunday Morning." I can barely hear the whispering and tinkling of the record. I can only follow it because I've heard it a hundred times.

I am lying in bed, waiting for Frank to get out of the bathroom. My cut finger throbs. Things are going on in the house even though I have gone to bed; water runs, the record plays. Sam is still downstairs, so there must be some action.

I have known everybody in the house for years, and as time goes by I know them all less and less. J.D. was Frank's adviser in college. Frank was his best student, and they started to see each other outside of class. They played handball. J.D. and his family came to dinner. We went there. That summer — the summer Frank decided to go to graduate school in business instead of English — J.D.'s wife and son deserted him in a more horrible way, in that car crash. J.D. has quit his job. He has been to Las Vegas, to Colorado, New Orleans, Los Angeles, Paris twice; he tapes post cards to the walls of his living room. A lot of the time, on the weekends, he shows up at our house with his sleeping bag. Sometimes he brings a girl. Lately, not. Years ago, Tucker was in Frank's therapy group in New York, and ended up hiring Frank to work as the accountant for his gallery. Tucker was in therapy at the time because he was obsessed with foreigners. Now he is also obsessed with homosexuals. He gives fashionable parties to which he invites many foreigners and homosexuals. Before the parties he does TM and yoga, and during the parties he does Seconals and isometrics. When I first met him, he was living for the summer in his sister's house in Vermont while she was in Europe, and he called us one night, in New York, in a real panic because there were wasps all over. They were "hatching," he said — big, sleepy wasps that were everywhere. We said we'd come; we drove all through the night to get to Brattleboro. It was true: there were wasps on the undersides of plates, in the plants, in the folds of curtains. Tucker was so upset that he was out behind the house, in the cold Vermont morning, wrapped like an Indian in a blanket, with only his pajamas on underneath. He was sitting in a lawn chair, hiding behind a bush, waiting for us to come.

And Freddy — "Reddy Fox," when Frank is feeling affectionate toward him. When we first met, I taught him to ice-skate and he taught me to waltz; in the summer, at Atlantic City, he'd go with me on a roller coaster that curved high over the waves. I was the one — not Frank — who would get out of bed in the middle of the night and meet him at an all-night deli and put my arm around his shoulders, the way he put his arm around my shoulders on the roller coaster, and talk quietly to him until he got over his latest anxiety attack. Now he tests me, and I retreat: this man he picked up, this man who picked him up, how it feels to have forgotten somebody's name when your hand is in the back pocket of his jeans and you're not even halfway to your apartment. Reddy Fox — admiring my new red silk blouse, stroking his fingertips down the front, and my eyes wide, because I could feel his fingers on my chest, even though I was holding the blouse in front of me on a hanger to be admired. All those moments, and all they meant was that I was fooled into thinking I knew these people because I knew the small things, the personal things.

Freddy will always be more stoned than I am, because he feels comfortable getting stoned with me, and I'll always be reminded that he's more lost. Tucker knows he can come to the house and be the center of attention; he can tell all the stories he knows, and we'll never tell the story we know about him hiding in the bushes like a frightened dog. J.D. comes back from his trips with boxes full of post cards, and I look at all of them as though they're photographs taken by him, and I know, and he knows, that what he likes about them is their flatness — the unreality of them, the unreality of what he does.

Last summer, I read *The Metamorphosis* and said to J.D., "Why did Gregor Samsa wake up a cockroach?" His answer (which he would have toyed over with his students forever) was "Because that's what people expected of him."

They make the illogical logical. I don't do anything, because I'm waiting, I'm on hold (J.D.); I stay stoned because I know it's better to be out of it (Freddy); I love art because I myself am a work of art (Tucker).

Frank is harder to understand. One night a week or so ago, I thought we were really attuned to each other, communicating by telepathic waves, and as I lay in bed about to speak I realized that the vibrations really existed: they were him, snoring.

Now he's coming into the bedroom, and I'm trying again to think what to say. Or ask. Or do.

"Be glad you're not in Key West," he says. He climbs into bed.

I raise myself up on one elbow and stare at him.

"There's a hurricane about to hit," he says.

"What?" I say. "Where did you hear that?"

"When Reddy Fox and I were putting the dishes away. We had the radio on." He doubles up his pillow, pushes it under his neck. "Boom goes everything," he says. "Bam. Crash. Poof." He looks at me. "You look shocked." He closes his eyes. Then, after a minute or two, he murmurs, "Hurricanes upset you? I'll try to think of something nice."

He is quiet for so long that I think he has fallen asleep. Then he says, "Cars that run on water. A field of flowers, none alike. A shooting

star that goes slow enough for you to watch. Your life to do over again."
He has been whispering in my ear, and when he takes his mouth away
I shiver. He slides lower in the bed for sleep. "I'll tell you something
really amazing," he says. "Tucker told me he went into a travel agency
on Park Avenue last week and asked the travel agent where he should
go to pan for gold, and she told him."

"Where did she tell him to go?"

"I think somewhere in Peru. The banks of some river in Peru."

"Did you decide what you're going to do after Mark's birthday?" I
say.

He doesn't answer me. I touch him on the side, finally.

"It's two o'clock in the morning. Let's talk about it another time."

"You picked the house, Frank. They're your friends downstairs. I
used to be what you wanted me to be."

"They're your friends, too," he says. "Don't be paranoid."

"I want to know if you're staying or going."

He takes a deep breath, lets it out, and continues to lie very still.

"Everything you've done is commendable," he says. "You did the
right thing to go back to school. You tried to do the right thing by
finding yourself a normal friend like Marilyn. But your whole life
you've made one mistake — you've surrounded yourself with men. Let
me tell you something. All men — if they're crazy, like Tucker, if they're
gay as the Queen of the May, like Reddy Fox, even if they're just six
years old — I'm going to tell you something about them. Men think
they're Spider-Man and Buck Rogers and Superman. You know what
we all feel inside that you don't feel? That we're going to the stars."

He takes my hand. "I'm looking down on all of this from space," he
whispers. "I'm already gone."

The Four-Night Fight

The four-night fight began on Father's Day, June 20, but had nothing to do with the day. Her father had been dead for almost fifteen years; his father had left his mother and moved to Santa Barbara to spend his remaining years — so far, twelve had passed — golfing. Henry was not himself a father.

It had been a beautiful, sunny day. Lavender geraniums were in bloom, bordering the back porch. Inside the porch, yellow and red begonias blossomed, their flowers as large as their leaves. In one of the pots, a plastic parrot's one moving wing rotated as the wind blew. The summer before, Henry had gotten the other wing going, but this year he'd done nothing. Neither had he brought home plants for the porch, nor helped weed the geranium bed, to which he had added, against her objections, a dozen blue-black tulips, planting the bulbs the previous fall as she slept. First he refused to enlarge the flower bed. Then, when she did that, he "borrowed" bricks from the border to brace a rickety bookshelf. Then he ordered red tulips, was sent the bruise-colored ones instead, shrugged, ignored her dismay, and planted them while she was asleep. None of these things had anything to do with the fight.

The fight began in early evening, so that properly speaking, it was a four-night, three-day fight. The fight reminded her of hotel package deals: four nights, five days, in sunny Bermuda — but after you struggled to the hotel the pleasure of the first day would inevitably be shot: plane late; luggage delayed; rainstorm slowing the car to the hotel; a long line for check-in. They had taken a trip to Bermuda in October, to celebrate their anniversary. She had wanted to stay in a small hotel, he had insisted on staying at a sprawling resort. Like his father, he loved to golf. She had gone around on her moped alone, while he golfed, and though that might have made her feel bad, it had not, so why pretend to hold a grudge when actually she had quite enjoyed her freedom? She didn't pretend to hold a grudge. Nothing that happened in Bermuda had anything to do with the fight.

In fact, the reason the fight was so bad was that it snuck up on her. In the seconds preceding the fight, she had been perfectly happy, scooping the center out of a cantaloupe. Henry had become diabetic, so they no longer had cookies for dessert, only fruit. She kept a package of

Chips Ahoy hidden behind boxes of Tide in the laundry room, but she'd lost her taste for sweets, suddenly. Or maybe not so suddenly: she'd lost it when the cookies somehow absorbed, like a sponge, the smell of Tide. When she was a child, her mother had put milk of magnesia in chocolate milk to disguise the taste, but all it had done was make her cringe at the thought of plain chocolate milk, and also chocolate ice cream, or chocolate milk shakes. She was even wary of chocolate cake, and sniffed skeptically at Hershey bars. No matter: cookies and chocolate could easily be done without, and a person would be healthier because of it. So there she had been, scooping out the melon, looking forward to a made-for-TV movie the listing had said would be good, when suddenly Henry was standing in the kitchen doorway, looking at her in a peculiar way, contributing nothing toward fixing their dessert, having said not a word about the dinner she had just served. . . . Well: the thing was, the fight, in his mind, had already begun, but she had been slow to understand his sulking, mistaking it for simple fatigue, since before dinner he'd hauled out the trash and sprayed the lid with Clorox so that during the night the raccoon couldn't simply saunter up to the can and with a swipe of its paw crash the top of the trash can to the ground. Also, he had sawed off the broken limb of the lilac and dragged it into the woods, then gone inside and called his mother to give her some information she needed to pay her taxes. His mother was not the world's most pleasant person. Also, since it was Father's Day, she was in a bleaker mood than usual, despising Henry's father for leaving her and spending his retirement golfing in California. Maybe his mother's bad mood was contagious. Maybe Henry had done one too many chores. Maybe he harbored a grudge that she had made him spray the trash can with Clorox, which he continued to call "ridiculous," though it was the one thing that had ever deterred the tenacious, fat, garbage-can-toppling raccoon.

Standing in the kitchen doorway, he had said to her: "Sometimes I think this is all a huge fucking joke. Sometimes I think we're ants, and here in our anthill we scurry around, moving the dirt, building the anthill higher, eating our food, shitting it out, doing our humble chores for the fucking Queen Ant, foraging and accumulating, bringing things in, piling things up, moving the piles around, and all the while, in our little specks of ant brain, we hope a big rainstorm doesn't come and pound the whole fucking anthill into the ground, that we don't get washed down the hill, that we don't drown in the flood, but what would it matter if we did? What the fuck would it matter?"

It was so unexpected. So typical of Henry, though, who while having finally admitted, one night in Bermuda, as the sky was brightening from rose to crimson, that his obsessing about the deterioration of the ozone layer was really a way of not focusing on more immediate, personal problems that he might do something about . . . well: going on with this line of thought would give the mistaken impression she had been assessing the situation, seeing in it the seeds of similar situations — Christ! Did he think she'd gone to college to scoop the insides of melons into a garbage disposal? Could he really have thought that she would appreciate such a barrage of adolescent, ridiculous despair . . . had he been standing in the doorway with his weight thrown on one hip, in his loafers with their mashed-down backs, and his thumb hooked through a belt loop . . . was this miserable sight, this person she'd for some unfathomable reason married, so stupid as to think she'd appreciate being compared to an ant as she stood scooping pulp and seeds and fiber into the sink so that his diabetes wouldn't rage out of control . . . had they had what they agreed would be their last discussion of the ozone layer only to have him recast everything in terms of their pointless life inside an anthill?

"You're really insane," she said.

"I'm insane?" he said. And then he said something she didn't get — something about the Clorox. That didn't surprise her at all, because whenever she gave him a helpful hint he derided her or ignored it. The use of Clorox as a repellent hadn't been her own epiphany, by the way: it was something she'd read flipping through a tabloid in the supermarket, which was where she spent half her life, half of her pointless ant life, gathering food for Henry, because maybe Henry himself was the Ant King? After all, who was standing in the doorway, the picture of casualness, while her hair had fallen from her barrette to tickle her nose as she peered down into the messy abortion of melon pulp in the sink. . . .

She had apparently thrown the phone book at him. She saw that she had, because his hands flew up to protect his head, and certainly the phone book had not just animated itself to join in the fracas, surely she must have thrown it, accelerating the fight, which by that time had been going on for perhaps five minutes, of screaming and accusations, suspended only for troubled sleep, to resume the next morning.

The day after the fight he did not go to work, which did trouble her. If he had called to say he would not be at work, he would have had to do it while she slept — he didn't mind planting ugly tulips while she slept, for all she knew he had a complete private life. He told her about deficiencies in her character as he toasted an English muffin — one only; none for her — blaming her for trying to infantilize him with her air of superiority, banging his fist on the kitchen island and sending the nondairy creamer crashing to the floor, whatever he was saying about Clorox drowned out by the crashing glass. Then, insanely, completely insanely, as the muffin lodged in the toaster and began to burn, though it would be a cold day in hell if she ever again rescued any of his food, let him forage for it himself, ant that he was . . . Henry began to pick up the shards of glass and throw them, claiming the bits of glass were ants, or like ants — whatever he was saying. He was saying that he was scattering the anthill. Really, he was just a bully, uncivilized and out of control, wanting to lash out at who knew what, who could know who the designated Queen Ant was that morning, in his paranoia and rage. Black smoke poured from the toaster, and again the telephone book was animated, sailing through the air, smeared with cantaloupe juice, crashing way off course into the wall. She had wanted to paint the kitchen walls green; Henry had wanted them yellow. They had compromised on peach, which was good, considering the melon juice that was now smeared on the wall, though she resolutely did not care about that, did not care if the whole toaster erupted, did not care what he did with the rest of his day, did not care if he stood forever making analogies between broken glass and anthills, because he was cynical and unbalanced, she was not, she was — he was saying again — superior. Then he kicked the phone book as if he were making a final goal and looked around crazily, as if she represented a whole team who would cheer him. Looking over his shoulder, he asked if she had ever had a kind thought about his mother in her life. It did not deserve an answer.

The next day, he was gone when she woke up, but he was so agitated that he had left a message — a rant, really — on the answering machine. At the beginning, he taunted her by daring her to listen to the message all the way through, which she did intend to do, sitting at the kitchen counter, the air still redolent with the smell of burned bread, bits of glass scattered underfoot. "I did what the raccoon couldn't do," he screamed on the tape. "I turned over your fucking garbage can that the fucking garbage truck neglected to empty because they do not give a flying fuck if the whole world festers and deteriorates, if they can shorten their working day by ignoring the cans on the route. I turned it over and I was within one second, one millionth of an inch, of taking the lid and ramming it through the side window of your car. . . ."

At this, she got slowly off the stool and went out to the driveway, his voice fading in the background. She walked as if in a trance, but she was not really in a trance, she was just practicing being in a trance. What if he had really traumatized her, so that she had become a zombie? What if at this moment she was a zombie, looking at chicken bones, food-stained newspapers, all the detritus of their lives scattered in the street — not by the raccoon, but by the wild beast that was her husband? No: she would not let him drive her crazy. It was reasonable to be superior, and not a zombie. She could shuffle along, traumatized, and become what he would like her to become, but it was better simply to sidestep his expectations, just as she sidestepped the garbage. That night, a neighbor's boy would stuff most of it back in the can. She would see that from the bathroom window, getting up from the closed toilet seat where she was reading a mystery, preferring to be locked in the bathroom rather than downstairs, where Henry was silently watching the long-ago resignation of Richard Nixon on TV. It was not true that all teenagers were destructive and self-absorbed. The boy picked up almost everything, including soup cans with jagged edges and soggy coffee filters, then put the lid firmly on the trash can again. He could have been Sir Lancelot, he shone so in her imagination as what a man could be. Downstairs, she heard gunshots, and for a horrifying second she was so on edge that she had rewritten history and imagined Nixon being shot, then realized that Henry must have begun shooting at the teenager! Henry having a gun. Did he have a gun? Of course he didn't have a gun. And if he did have a gun, then she hoped he would use it on himself.

No, she didn't. She tried thinking that, to see how it would feel. It felt wrong. She was afraid she was beginning to forgive him. In saying she wanted him shot when she did not want him shot, she had begun to forgive him. And she might have, too, if he hadn't glared at her so coldly before pulling off the comforter and going to sleep on the sofa. Such histrionics, when there was a guest room. He was really out of control. Maybe he was actually cracking up. She tossed in bed half the night, and when she went down in the morning he was still there, the cover over the top of his body, including his head, his bare legs sticking out, one on the sofa arm, one on the floor. It was like finding the Elephant Man in a casual moment. She stood in the doorway, so fatigued she decided to forgive him, to try to get things back on track. If nothing else, he would certainly have to go back to his job soon. Perhaps he hadn't gone back yesterday. Perhaps she had assumed, incorrectly, that the hysterical message of the day before had been left from work — but how likely was that? He had probably not sat at his desk and simply raged, spitting his irrational thoughts into a telephone. He had probably called from . . . "Henry," she said, trying to keep her voice calm, "were you at work yesterday when you left that ridiculous message?"

He jumped up, tossing off the comforter with such force that she jumped back. He stood there, glowering at her, the comforter puddled around him like a collapsed parachute. His wild eyes made her think of someone who had just crashed into a dangerous jungle. He might have been wondering: Could this native be friendly? She tried to look friendlier by smiling, but the attempt to alter the expression of her mouth, she could tell, was only resulting in narrowed eyes. She could not smile. She did manage to unknot the frown that creased between her eyes. They stood there that way, gazing at each other, she barefoot in her long nightgown patterned with blue morning glories, he wearing a white sleeveless undershirt and nothing else, his knock-knees pathetic, his penis curved like a tiny fountain spout, and — she had been blocking it out because she really did not want to focus on it — on his arm, on his biceps, a terrible bruise, a terrible swelling: from doing battle with the trash can? From . . . God, it was a tattoo. It was a tattoo, and he saw that she saw it. Even the fountain spout seemed to recoil in dismay. Henry was standing there, staring at her with the We Are Ants expression on his face, and on his upper arm, the part of his arm she had grasped so many times as they made love, was MOM in red-inked script, and a circle inscribing it, a circle, she saw, upon closer inspection, that was not a conglomerate of ants, but swirls of small hearts and flowers, interspersed with skin puckered into scabs, an outer rim of flesh around the circle swollen and flecked with what seemed to be broken veins.

"Hurts," he said.

"Hurts?" she echoed. She was becoming the zombie whose role she had tried on for size. Numb. Unblinking. Who could blink looking at such a thing?

"I went drinking with Jim Cavalli, made a bet, guy couldn't pay up, we went to his tattoo studio, I got to choose from the fifty-dollar possibilities."

"Henry," she said, "what is this about your mother?"

"Cavalli chose."

"Cavalli had your arm tattooed MOM?"

"Cavalli wanted to beat him up. I was the one who agreed to settle on a tattoo."

"Cavalli . . . ," she said, searching her mind for a visual image of the man. The new, gawky kid from Princeton? Pink shirt, drank a lot of Dos Equis at the company picnic? Though she was not aware she'd been speaking, Henry began to respond to her sharpening mental image of Cavalli. "Went off the wagon himself because his Princeton girlfriend left him for her analyst," Henry said.

"So . . . what?" she said. "You and Cavalli went to a bar, and he told you his girlfriend had left him, you told him the human race, or you and I, how should I know? You told him we were ants, and then some guy who worked at a tattoo parlor sat down and you bet him . . . you bet what?"

"That the guy on TV would miss the shot."

"You bet that a guy would miss a shot, he said the guy would make it, the guy missed, and you ended up with MOM in majesty on your arm?"

"Hurts," he said quietly.

"Well, Jesus," she said. "I think we should go to the doctor and see if he can treat it, because I think your arm is infected." A headache came up inside her like rolling thunderclouds spreading across the sky. By the time she finished her sentence, electricity was crackling through her brain, a tooth-chattering wind had begun.

It was as if her pain made her transparent. Suddenly, he looked at her as if he could see the rain clouds inside. The pain piercings sinking into her jaw like lightning. "Your name is Angelina," he said. Her head hurt so much that she didn't mind this simple, neutral observation at all. Indeed she was Angelina. So true. He continued: "While I admit I hated you in that moment, it did occur to me that if I hadn't been angry, if I hadn't been angry when I was getting the tattoo, I could have had a tattoo of my wife's name, except that only three letters could be had for fifty dollars, because Cavalli was insisting on scrollwork. The part around the word is called scrolling. It's generic hearts and flowers and stuff."

This was too much to take in. Her head was pounding.

"They do it the way people doodle on a notepad when they're on the telephone, I guess." He had sunk into the sofa, pulling the comforter over himself. He looked like an ill, miserable child. He looked at her expectantly.

"I think we should go to the doctor," she said. She had begun to worry about the tattooist's needles. Why would Henry have done such a thing, when everyone was so worried about AIDS? How could he have been sure the needles were clean? Needles — Jesus Christ. He had someone take needles and scratch dye into his flesh. He had gone with some self-pitying moron named Cavalli. And yet, she was on the sofa beside him, snuggled under his good arm, the comforter around them both feeling soft and sheltering. At that moment the last thing she was thinking about was the fight. He had become, in her mind, a victim. Someone who had received far worse punishment than he deserved. Someone who needed medical attention, understanding, forgiveness. She envisioned herself driving him to the doctor's office — never mind that the doctor was sure to be horrified — going there, getting a prescription for antibiotics, perhaps topical creams, perhaps . . . perhaps the doctor would see that Henry was unbalanced and think of something to do. Though the more she thought about it, the more she disbelieved it. Unless she could walk right into the doctor's office with him, he would probably present it as regrettable, drunken madness.

She would have to go in and be a Greek chorus: *No, no, he was compar-ing life to being in an anthill; he's never cared if flowers are atrocious colors, he just plants them anyway, like flowers that would bloom in hell; his mother up-sets him, complaining about his father; our fight began on Father's Day, which can't be insignificant — either it's resentment of his own father spilling over into our life, or he's angry that people are procreating: he sees all these things as a personal affront, whether it's the holes in the ozone layer or clear-cutting the forest or people giving birth to a child. He's in a state of madness and despair, I tell you. He doesn't go to work anymore. Come to think of it, for days I haven't seen him eat.* She would have to say those things; no sitting in the wait-ing room reading *Good Housekeeping.* No information, today, about Kathie Lee's thoughts on how to parent. Cheese dips be damned.

The fight began again when, to her complete surprise, he refused to see the doctor. It was feeling better already, he suddenly said. He thought he had a bit of a fever, though, so he would — if she did not mind — nap for a bit.

"You're going to the doctor," she said.

"No," he said, "I am not."

Thus began a new day of fighting, which she had not been prepared for at all, having begun to forgive him. And, like anyone dragged into something unexpectedly, her reactions were not the best. Instead of focusing on his obviously infected arm, she found herself demanding an explanation of how, exactly, he would keep the raccoon out of the trash if he did not want to use her method. She twisted up her mouth and marched like a martinet, imitating his expression and his quick exit from the living room when the phone rang. The phone: news from the outside world. The doctor, by telepathic message having realized he should call? When she picked it up, it was Cavalli. The nerve! What did he want, she asked: to know if Henry would meet him for more drinks and then go out to a whorehouse? "No," Cavalli said evenly. "To know if he's coming to work." She hung up on him. Then the fight really swung into full gear. She was emasculating him again, it appeared. Again, he threatened her car windows. Couldn't he think of anything more original than that? Or, at the very least, admit that he wanted to hit *her*? "You'd like that, wouldn't you?" he said. It was not until three in the afternoon that she looked out and realized that neither of them had brought in the paper.

That night, he ate nothing. He sat with the remote control, flip-ping through channels, sentence fragments and incomplete sounds no doubt echoing the chaos of his brain. Once, he ran out the front door with the still-rolled newspaper, threatening a cat digging near a bush. He could have been heard miles away. If he did become violent, no one in the neighborhood would be surprised. Yes, they'd say, that guy was

really nuts. Nuts but wounded. She couldn't get the image of his infected arm out of her mind. It was as if the pain throbbed in her own
head. Of course, it was next to impossible to sleep. And when she was
at last almost asleep, what did he do but tear off in the car, going who
knew where, dressed — as she later found out — in the only clothes he
could find downstairs: a pair of madras bermudas with a ripped zipper
he'd taken from her sewing room and his flip-flops with the thongs
he'd glued back together in the basement, and her blouse. The nice
navy-blue blouse she'd ironed before the fight began and never taken
upstairs. He had left after cramming his body into her navy-blue
blouse.

She went downstairs and turned off the answering machine because
she did not want to hear whatever vicious message he might leave. She
did, though, make sure the ringer on the phone was on, so that if he —
or the police, God forbid — needed to reach her, they could. The only
phone call came from his mother, who had no sense of time, wanting
him to install a new bathroom sink for her at what she called "your
convenience." Wait until she saw the MOM tattoo. Let the two of them
discuss that.

Was he, in fact, headed for his mother's — and should she have
warned the woman that might be the case? Or to Cavalli's? Back to the
bar? Who knew where. Who knew how this was going to end, if it
ever did end. It was the longest fight she had ever been involved in,
and it was exhausting her and making her feel crazy herself. She took
aspirin and went back to bed.

In the morning, when she awoke, he was lying next to her. It was
not a dream, he was really there. The blue blouse was on the floor, the
madras bermudas discarded amid the thongs, his eyes squeezed shut so
tightly she wondered if he was only pretending to sleep. At first, barely
distinguishable in the tangle of white sheets, she didn't realize there
was a large gauze bandage on his arm. It was a thick pad of gauze,
wrapped entirely around his arm, and near the top were black stitches —
no: there was writing. On the gauze bandage, he had written, as best
he could, left-handed, because the tattoo was on his right arm, the
scratchy letters S O R R Y. There it was: the white flag of surrender, and
an added apology lest she mistake it. Propped on one elbow, she
frowned as she considered it: the wobbly O like a bubble being blown
from a bubble wand; the Y like a sprouting seed. It seemed to her the
sweetest thing he had ever done. Though he had done so many sweet
things in the time they'd been together. The four-night fight must
have been worse for him than for her, because he hated to carry a
grudge. "Let him golf. Forget him if you can't forgive him," he always
said to his mother. "Buy more flowers if that's what you want, honey,"

he had said to her when the garden bloomed that spring with its strange blossoms. She stared at the bandage. It was professionally done. He must have gone to the emergency room. On the night table she saw a glass of water and a bottle of medicine. It seemed to her a real salvation: the antibiotics that would cure the wound's infection, protecting his precious arm, that arm that had curled around her so many times, guiding her through crowds, protectively placed when he introduced her to a stranger. She stayed there, propped up, observing him, the way a person will look out a window and study the land after a storm, everything seeming greener, lighter, suddenly distinct. The familiar landscape was all there: from chin stubble to chest hair, from navel to knee, it was Henry, slumbering after the great storm. Henry, simply, no scrollwork needed to establish his importance, because when she saw him small hearts and flowers invisibly surrounded him always, an embellished border around the valentine of affection that was her love. What couple does not occasionally fight?

Aimee Bender

The stories of Aimee Bender meld the surrealism of writers like Barthelme, Coover, and Kafka with the archetypal elements of García Márquez — or better yet, Hans Christian Andersen and the Brothers Grimm. These are contemporary fairy tales, stories in which dream and magic intrude on the quotidian reality we perceive with our senses. In the title story of her first collection, *The Girl in the Flammable Skirt,* a daughter must take up her father's load in life — literally — in the form of a backpack made of stone ("It was solid rock. And dense, pushed out to its limit, gray and cold to the touch. Even the little zipper handle was made of stone and weighed a ton"). In another piece, a father's grief over the death of his own father manifests itself as a hole in his stomach. "What You Left in the Ditch," a fable about mutation and acceptance, begins with this line: "Stephen returned from the war without lips." There is a dark sense of humor at operation here, a fascination with the grotesque, but there is an airiness to the voice that keeps these stories from becoming morbid, while at the same time allowing for a real poignancy.

The first of the selections here, "The Rememberer," begins with this absurd proposition: "My lover is experiencing reverse evolution. I tell no one. I don't know how it happened, only that one day he was my lover and the next he was some kind of ape. It's been a month and now he's a sea turtle." As the story progresses, the lover dwindles away through the various stages of de-evolution until he's nothing more than a salamander in a pan of tap water. Ultimately, the piece becomes an allegory of a disintegrating relationship, one partner growing away from another as the primitive opposes the intellectual. The second story, "Quiet Please," deals with a familiar theme — grief over the death of one's father — in an equally fanciful way, avoiding sentimentality through the surreal image of the circus "muscleman" and his feat of elevation, and it bears comparison with Hempel's "In the Cemetery Where Al Jolson Is Buried" and Kincaid's "Figures in the Distance."

The Girl in the Flammable Skirt (1998) is Aimee Bender's first collection. She is also the author of a novel, *An Invisible Sign of My Own,* published in 2000.

The Rememberer

My lover is experiencing reverse evolution. I tell no one. I don't know how it happened, only that one day he was my lover and the next he was some kind of ape. It's been a month and now he's a sea turtle.

I keep him on the counter, in a glass baking pan filled with salt water.

"Ben," I say to his small protruding head, "can you understand me?" and he stares with eyes like little droplets of tar and I drip tears into the pan, a sea of me.

He is shedding a million years a day. I am no scientist, but this is roughly what I figured out. I went to the old biology teacher at the community college and asked him for an approximate time line of our evolution. He was irritated at first — he wanted money. I told him I'd be happy to pay and then he cheered up quite a bit. I can hardly read his time line — he should've typed it — and it turns out to be wrong. According to him, the whole process should take about a year, but from the way things are going, I think we have less than a month left.

At first, people called on the phone and asked me where was Ben. Why wasn't he at work? Why did he miss his lunch date with those clients? His out-of-print special-ordered book on civilization had arrived at the bookstore, would he please pick it up? I told them he was sick, a strange sickness, and to please stop calling. The stranger thing was, they did. They stopped calling. After a week, the phone was silent and Ben, the baboon, sat in a corner by the window, wrapped up in drapery, chattering to himself.

Last day I saw him human, he was sad about the world.

This was not unusual. He was always sad about the world. It was a large reason why I loved him. We'd sit together and be sad and think about being sad and sometimes discuss sadness.

On his last human day, he said, "Annie, don't you see? We're all getting too smart. Our brains are just getting bigger and bigger, and the world dries up and dies when there's too much thought and not enough heart."

He looked at me pointedly, blue eyes unwavering. "Like us, Annie," he said. "We think far too much."

I sat down. I remembered how the first time we had sex, I left the lights on, kept my eyes wide open, and concentrated really hard on letting go; then I noticed that his eyes were open too and in the middle of everything we sat down on the floor and had an hour-long conversation about poetry. It was all very peculiar. It was all very familiar.

Another time he woke me up in the middle of the night, lifted me off the pale blue sheets, led me outside to the stars and whispered: *Look, Annie, look — there is no space for anything but dreaming.* I listened, sleepily, wandered back to bed and found myself wide awake, staring at the ceiling, unable to dream at all. Ben fell asleep right away, but I crept back outside. I tried to dream up to the stars, but I didn't know how to do that. I tried to find a star no one in all of history had ever wished on before, and wondered what would happen if I did.

On his last human day, he put his head in his hands and sighed and I stood up and kissed the entire back of his neck, covered that flesh, made wishes there because I knew no woman had ever been so thorough, had ever kissed his every inch of skin. I coated him. What did I wish for? I wished for good. That's all. Just good. My wishes became generalized long ago, in childhood; I learned quick the consequence of wishing specific.

I took him in my arms and made love to him, my sad man. "See, we're not thinking," I whispered into his ear while he kissed my neck, "we're not thinking at all" and he pressed his head into my shoulder and held me tighter. Afterward, we went outside again; there was no moon and the night was dark. He said he hated talking and just wanted to look into my eyes and tell me things that way. I let him and it made my skin lift, the things in his look. Then he told me he wanted to sleep outside for some reason and in the morning when I woke up in bed, I looked out to the patio and there was an ape sprawled on the cement, great furry arms covering his head to block out the glare of the sun.

Even before I saw the eyes, I knew it was him. And once we were face to face, he gave me his same sad look and I hugged those enormous shoulders. I didn't even really care, then, not at first, I didn't panic and call 911. I sat with him outside and smoothed the fur on the back of his hand. When he reached for me, I said No, loudly, and he seemed to understand and pulled back. I have limits here.

We sat on the lawn together and ripped up the grass. I didn't miss human Ben right away; I wanted to meet the ape too, to take care of my lover like a son, a pet; I wanted to know him every possible way but I didn't realize he wasn't coming back.

Now I come home from work and look for his regular-size shape walking and worrying and realize, over and over, that he's gone. I pace the halls. I chew whole packs of gum in mere minutes. I review my memories and make sure they're still intact because if he's not here, then it is my job to remember. I think of the way he wrapped his arms around my back and held me so tight it made me nervous and the way his breath felt in my ear: right.

When I go to the kitchen, I peer in the glass and see he's some kind of salamander now. He's small.

"Ben," I whisper, "do you remember me? Do you remember?"

His eyes roll up in his head and I dribble honey into the water. He used to love honey. He licks at it and then swims to the other end of the pan.

This is the limit of my limits: here it is. You don't ever know for sure where it is and then you bump against it and bam, you're there. Because I cannot bear to look down into the water and not be able to find him at all, to search the tiny clear waves with a microscope lens and to locate my lover, the one-celled wonder, bloated and bordered, brainless, benign, heading clear and small like an eye-floater into nothingness.

I put him in the passenger seat of the car, and drive him to the beach. Walking down the sand, I nod at people on towels, laying their bodies out to the sun and wishing. At the water's edge, I stoop down and place the whole pan on the tip of a baby wave. It floats well, a cooking boat, for someone to find washed up on shore and to make cookies in, a lucky catch for a poor soul with all the ingredients but no container.

Ben the salamander swims out. I wave to the water with both arms, big enough for him to see if he looks back.

I turn around and walk back to the car.

Sometimes I think he'll wash up on shore. A naked man with a startled look. Who has been to history and back. I keep my eyes on the newspaper. I make sure my phone number is listed. I walk around the block at night in case he doesn't quite remember which house it is. I feed the birds outside and sometimes before I put my one self to bed, I place my hands around my skull to see if it's growing, and wonder what, of any use, would fill it if it did.

Quiet Please

It is quiet in the rest of the library.

Inside the back room, the woman has crawled out from underneath the man. Now fuck me like a dog she tells him. She grips a pillow in her fists and he breathes behind her, hot air down her back which is starting to sweat and slip on his stomach. She doesn't want him to see her face because it is blowing up inside, red and furious, and she's grimacing at the pale white wall which is cool when she puts her hand on it to help her push back into him, get his dick to fill up her body until there's nothing left of her inside: just dick.

The woman is a librarian and today her father has died. She got a phone call from her weeping mother in the morning, threw up and then dressed for work. Sitting at her desk with her back very straight, she asks the young man very politely, the one who always comes into the library to check out bestsellers, asks him when it was he last got laid. He lets out a weird sound and she says shhh, this is a library. She has her hair back and the glasses on but everyone has a librarian fantasy, and she is truly a babe beneath.

I have a fantasy, he says, of a librarian.

She smiles at him but asks her original question again. She doesn't want someone brand new to the business but neither is she looking for a goddamn gigolo. This is an important fuck for her. He tells her it's been a few months and looks sheepish but honest and then hopeful. She says great and tells him there's a back room with a couch for people who get dizzy or sick in the library (which happens surprisingly often), and could he meet her there in five minutes? He nods, he's already telling his friends about this in a monologue in his head. He has green eyes and no wrinkles yet.

They meet in the back and she pulls the shade down on the little window. This is the sex that she wishes would split her open and murder her because she can't deal with a dead father; she's wished him dead so many times that now it's hard to tell the difference between fantasy and reality. Is it true? He's really gone? She didn't really want him to die, that is not what she meant when she faced him and imagined knives sticking into his body. This is not what she meant, for him to actually die. She wonders if she invented the phone call, but she remembers the

41

way her mother's voice kept climbing up and up, and it's so real and true she can't bear it and wants to go fuck someone else. The man is tired now but grinning like he can't believe it. He's figuring when he can be there next, but she's sure she'll never want him again. Her hair is down and glasses off and clothes on the floor and she's the fucked librarian and he's looking at her with this look of adoration. She squeezes his wrist and then concentrates on putting herself back together. In ten minutes, she's at the front desk again, telling a youngster about a swell book on aisle ten, and unless you leaned forward to smell her, you'd never know.

There is a mural on the curved ceiling of the library of fairies dancing. Their arms are interwoven, hair loose from the wind. Since people look at the ceiling fairly often when they're at the library, it is a well-known mural. The librarian tilts her head back to take a deep breath. One of the fairies is missing a mouth. It has burned off from the glare of the sunlight, and she is staring at her fairy friends with a purple-eyed look of muteness. The librarian does not like to see this, and looks down to survey the population of her library instead.

She is amazed as she glances around to see how many attractive men there are that day. They are everywhere: leaning over the wood tables, straight-backed in the aisles, men flipping pages with nice hands. The librarian, on this day, the day of her father's death, is overwhelmed by an appetite she has never felt before and she waits for another one of them to approach her desk.

It takes five minutes.

This one is a businessman with a vest. He is asking her about a book on fishing when she propositions him. His face lights up, the young boy comes clean and clear through his eyes, that librarian he knew when he was seven. She had round calves and a low voice.

She has him back in the room; he makes one tentative step forward and then he's on her like Wall Street rain, his suit in a pile on the floor in a full bucket, her dress unbuttoned down, down, one by one until she's naked and the sweat is pooling in her back again. She obliterates herself and then buttons up. This man too wants to see her again, he might want to marry her, he's thinking, but she smiles without teeth and says, man, this is a one-shot deal. Thanks.

If she wanted to, she could do this forever, charge a lot of money and become rich. She has this wonderful body, with full heavy breasts and a curve to her back that makes her pliable like a toy. She wraps her legs around man number three, a long-haired artist type, and her hair shakes loose and he removes her glasses and she fucks him until he's shuddering and trying to moan, but she just keeps saying Sshhh, shhh and it's making him so happy, she keeps saying it even after he's shut up.

The morning goes by like normal except she fucks three more men, sending them out periodically to check her desk, and it's all in the silence, while people shuffle across the wood floor and trade words on paper for more words on paper.

After lunch, the muscleman enters the library.

He is tan and attractive and his arms are busting out of his shirt like balloons. He is with the traveling circus where he lifts a desk with a chair with a person with a child with a dog with a bone. He lifts it up and never drops anything and people cheer.

He also likes to read.

He picks this library because it's the closest to the big top. It's been a tiring week at the circus because the lion tamer had a fit and quit, and so the lions keep roaring. They miss him, and no one else will pet them because they're lions. When the muscleman enters the library, he breathes in the quiet in relief. He notices the librarian right away, the way she is sitting at her desk with this little twist to her lips that only a very careful observer would notice. He approaches her, and she looks at him in surprise. The librarian at this point assumes everyone in the library knows what is going on, but the fact is, they don't. Most of the library people just think it's stuffier than usual and for some reason are having a hard time focusing on their books.

The librarian looks at the muscleman and wants him.

Five minutes, she says, tilting her head toward the back room.

The muscleman nods, but he doesn't know what she's talking about. He goes off to look at the classics, but after five minutes, follows his summons, curious.

The back room has a couch and beige walls. When he enters the room, he's struck by the thickness of the sex smell; it is so pervasive he almost falls over. The librarian is sitting on the couch in her dress which is gray and covers her whole body. Down the center, there is a row of mother-of-pearl buttons and one of them is unbuttoned by accident.

The thing is, the muscleman is not so sure of his librarian fantasies. He is more sure that he likes to lift whatever he can. So he walks over to her in the waddly way that men with big thighs have to walk, and picks her up, couch and all.

Hey, she says, put me down.

The muscleman loves how his shoulders feel, the weight of something important, a life, on his back.

Hey, she says again, this is a library, put me down.

He twirls her gently, to the absent audience and she ducks her head down so as not to collide with the light fixture.

He opens the door and walks out with the couch. He is thoughtful enough to bring it down when they get to the door frame so she doesn't bump her head. She wants to yell at him but they're in the library now.

Two of the men she has fucked are still there, in hopes for a second round. They are stunned and for some reason very jealous when they see her riding the couch like a float at a parade, through the aisles of books. The businessman in the vest holds up a book and after a moment, throws it at her.

You are not Cleopatra! he says, and she ducks and screams, then clamps her hand over her mouth. Her father's funeral is in one day. It is important that there is quiet in a library. The book flies over her head and hits a regular library man who is reading a magazine at a table.

He throws it back, enraged, and they're all over in a second, pages raining down, the dust slapping up into her face. They rustle as they fly and the librarian covers her face because she can't stand to look down at the floor where the books are splayed open on their bindings as if they've been shot.

The muscleman doesn't seem to notice, even though the books are hitting him on his legs, his waist. He lifts her up, on his tiptoes, to the ceiling of the library.

Stand up, he says to her in a low voice, muffled from underneath the couch, stand up and I'll still balance you, I can do it even if you are standing.

She doesn't know what else to do and she can feel his push upward from beneath her. She presses down with her feet to stand, and puts a finger on the huge mural on the ceiling, the mural of the fairies dancing in summer. Right away, she sees the one fairy without the mouth again, and reaches into her bun to remove the pencil that is always kept there. Hair tumbles down. On her tiptoes, she is able to touch the curve of the ceiling where the fairy's mouth should be.

Hold still, she whispers to the muscleman who doesn't hear her, is in his own bliss of strength.

She grips the pencil and with one hand flat on the ceiling steadies herself enough to draw a mouth underneath the nose of the fairy. She tries to draw it as a big wide dancing smile, and darkens the pencil lining a few times. From where she stands, it looks nice, from where she is just inches underneath the painting which is warmed by the sunlight coming into the library.

She doesn't notice until the next day, when she comes to work to clean up the books an hour before her father is put into the ground, that the circle of fairies is altered now. That the laughing ones now pull along one fairy with purple eyes, who is clearly dancing against her will, dragged along with the circle, her mouth wide open and screaming.

Jorge Luis Borges

The stories collected in *Ficciones,* first printed in Buenos Aires in 1956 and
released by the Grove Press in the United States in 1962, established
Jorge Luis Borges (1899–1986) as one of the seminal story writers of the
postmodern period. His stories are an utterly original blend of the mys-
tical, the romantic, and the absurd, stories that laid the groundwork,
along with the fiction of writers like Cortázar, Asturias, and others, for
the magical realism of Gabriel García Márquez and his contemporaries.
Borges was fascinated with the concept of philosophical Idealism, as
elucidated by Berkeley, which posits a spiritual and intellectual way of
perceiving the world rather than a material one. His best-known story,
"Tlön, Uqbar, Orbis Tertius," presents an imagined universe with "its
transparent tigers and towers of blood" that finally, inexplicably, becomes a material presence. The tone of many of Borges's stories is that
of the unhurried scholar dusting off his books or a detective taking his
time in pursuit of some sort of strange and unraveling enlightenment,
and the tone serves to make the incredible seem not only plausible but
matter-of-fact. The author titled the second section of *Ficciones,* "Arti-
fices," and I can think of no better way to characterize Borges's fiction —
the stories are an elaborate tinkering with the inherited concept of what
a story is, and further, what the limits of our perception fail to show us.

   The first of the stories I've chosen here, "Pierre Menard, Author of
Don Quixote," is presented in the form of an article in a scholarly journal, purporting to assess the literary accomplishments of the decidedly
minor writer, Pierre Menard. This is Borges's funniest story. Even as it
revels in a singular feat of the imagination — Pierre Menard's modern
re-creation of portions of Cervantes's seventeenth-century novel — it
makes a satiric mincemeat of a certain school of overblown and pre-
sumptive criticism. The second piece, "Funes, the Memorious," is a
magical take on the notions of perception and memory, which must
necessarily be self-editing and selective — what a horror if they weren't.

Pierre Menard, Author of Don Quixote

To Silvina Ocampo

The *visible* works left by this novelist are easily and briefly enumerated. It is therefore impossible to forgive the omissions and additions perpetrated by Madame Henri Bachelier in a fallacious catalogue that a certain newspaper, whose Protestant tendencies are no secret, was inconsiderate enough to inflict on its wretched readers — even though they are few and Calvinist, if not Masonic and circumcised. Menard's true friends regarded this catalogue with alarm, and even with a certain sadness. It is as if yesterday we were gathered together before the final marble and the fateful cypresses, and already Error is trying to tarnish his Memory. . . . Decidedly, a brief rectification is inevitable.

I am certain that it would be very easy to challenge my meager authority. I hope, nevertheless, that I will not be prevented from mentioning two important testimonials. The Baroness de Bacourt (at whose unforgettable *vendredis* I had the honor of becoming acquainted with the late lamented poet) has seen fit to approve these lines. The Countess de Bagnoregio, one of the most refined minds in the Principality of Monaco (and now of Pittsburgh, Pennsylvania, since her recent marriage to the international philanthropist Simon Kautsch who, alas, has been so slandered by the victims of his disinterested handiwork) has sacrificed to "truth and death" (those are her words) that majestic reserve which distinguishes her, and in an open letter published in the magazine *Luxe* also grants me her consent. These authorizations, I believe, are not insufficient.

I have said that Menard's *visible* lifework is easily enumerated. Having carefully examined his private archives, I have been able to verify that it consists of the following:

a) A symbolist sonnet which appeared twice (with variations) in the magazine *La Conque* (the March and October issues of 1899).

b) A monograph on the possibility of constructing a poetic vocabulary of concepts that would not be synonyms or periphrases of those which make up ordinary language, "but ideal objects created by means of common agreement and destined essentially to fill poetic needs" (Nîmes, 1901).

c) A monograph on "certain connections or affinities" among the ideas of Descartes, Leibnitz and John Wilkins (Nîmes, 1903).

d) A monograph on the *Characteristica Universalis* of Leibnitz (Nîmes, 1904).

e) A technical article on the possibility of enriching the game of chess by means of eliminating one of the rooks' pawns. Menard proposes, recommends, disputes, and ends by rejecting this innovation.

f) A monograph on the *Ars Magna Generalis* of Ramón Lull (Nîmes, 1906).

g) A translation with prologue and notes of the *Libro de la invención y arte del juego del axedrez* by Ruy López de Segura (Paris, 1907).

h) The rough draft of a monograph on the symbolic logic of George Boole.

i) An examination of the metric laws essential to French prose, illustrated with examples from Saint-Simon (*Revue des langues romanes,* Montpellier, October, 1909).

j) An answer to Luc Durtain (who had denied the existence of such laws) illustrated with examples from Luc Durtain (*Revue des langues romanes,* Montpellier, December, 1909).

k) A manuscript translation of the *Aguja de navegar cultos* of Quevedo, entitled *La boussole des précieux.*

1) A preface to the catalogue of the exposition of lithographs by Carolus Hourcade (Nîmes, 1914).

m) His work, *Les problèmes d'un problème* (Paris, 1917), which takes up in chronological order the various solutions of the famous problem of Achilles and the tortoise. Two editions of this book have appeared so far; the second has as an epigraph Leibnitz' advice "Ne craignez point, monsieur, la tortue," and contains revisions of the chapters dedicated to Russell and Descartes.

n) An obstinate analysis of the "syntactic habits" of Toulet (*N.R.F.,* March, 1921). I remember that Menard used to declare that censuring and praising were sentimental operations which had nothing to do with criticism.

o) A transposition into Alexandrines of *Le Cimetière marin* of Paul Valéry (*N.R.F.,* January, 1928).

p) An invective against Paul Valéry in the *Journal for the Suppression of Reality* of Jacques Reboul. (This invective, it should be stated parenthetically, is the exact reverse of his true opinion of Valéry. The latter understood it as such, and the old friendship between the two was never endangered.)

q) A "definition" of the Countess of Bagnoregio in the "victorious volume" — the phrase is that of another collaborator, Gabriele d'Annunzio — which this lady publishes yearly to rectify the inevitable falsifications of journalism and to present "to the world and to Italy" an authentic effigy of her person, which is so exposed (by reason of her beauty and her activities) to erroneous or hasty interpretations.

r) A cycle of admirable sonnets for the Baroness de Bacourt (1934).

s) A manuscript list of verses which owe their effectiveness to punctuation.*

Up to this point (with no other omission than that of some vague, circumstantial sonnets for the hospitable, or greedy, album of Madame Henri Bachelier) we have the *visible* part of Menard's works in chronological order. Now I will pass over to that other part, which is subterranean, interminably heroic, and unequalled, and which is also — oh, the possibilities inherent in the man! — inconclusive. This work, possibly the most significant of our time, consists of the ninth and thirty-eighth chapters of Part One of *Don Quixote* and a fragment of the twenty-second chapter. I realize that such an affirmation seems absurd; but the justification of this "absurdity" is the primary object of this note.**

Two texts of unequal value inspired the undertaking. One was that philological fragment of Novalis — No. 2005 of the Dresden edition — which outlines the theme of *total* identification with a specific author. The other was one of those parasitic books which places Christ on a boulevard, Hamlet on the Cannebière and Don Quixote on Wall Street. Like any man of good taste, Menard detested these useless carnivals, only suitable — he used to say — for evoking plebeian delight in anachronism, or (what is worse) charming us with the primary idea that all epochs are the same, or that they are different. He considered more interesting, even though it had been carried out in a contradictory and superficial way, Daudet's famous plan: to unite in *one* figure, Tartarin, the Ingenious Gentleman and his squire. . . . Any insinuation that Menard dedicated his life to the writing of a contemporary *Don Quixote* is a calumny of his illustrious memory.

He did not want to compose another *Don Quixote* — which would be easy — but *the Don Quixote*. It is unnecessary to add that his aim

---

* Madame Henri Bachelier also lists a literal translation of a literal translation done by Quevedo of the *Introduction à la vie dévote* of Saint Francis of Sales. In Pierre Menard's library there are no traces of such a work. She must have misunderstood a remark of his which he had intended as a joke.

** I also had another, secondary intent — that of sketching a portrait of Pierre Menard. But how would I dare to compete with the golden pages the Baroness de Bacourt tells me she is preparing, or with the delicate and precise pencil of Carolus Hourcade?

was never to produce a mechanical transcription of the original; he did not propose to copy it. His admirable ambition was to produce pages which would coincide word for word and line for line — with those of Miguel de Cervantes.

"My intent is merely astonishing," he wrote me from Bayonne on December 30th, 1934. "The ultimate goal of a theological or metaphysical demonstration — the external world, God, chance, universal forms — are no less anterior or common than this novel which I am now developing. The only difference is that philosophers publish in pleasant volumes the intermediary stages of their work and that I have decided to lose them." And, in fact, not one page of a rough draft remains to bear witness to this work of years.

The initial method he conceived was relatively simple: to know Spanish well, to re-embrace the Catholic faith, to fight against Moors and Turks, to forget European history between 1602 and 1918, and to *be* Miguel de Cervantes. Pierre Menard studied this procedure (I know that he arrived at a rather faithful handling of seventeenth-century Spanish) but rejected it as too easy. Rather because it was impossible, the reader will say! I agree, but the undertaking was impossible from the start, and of all the possible means of carrying it out, this one was the least interesting. To be, in the twentieth century, a popular novelist of the seventeenth seemed to him a diminution. To be, in some way, Cervantes and to arrive at *Don Quixote* seemed to him less arduous — and consequently less interesting — than to continue being Pierre Menard and to arrive at *Don Quixote* through the experiences of Pierre Menard. (This conviction, let it be said in passing, forced him to exclude the autobiographical prologue of the second part of *Don Quixote.* To include this prologue would have meant creating another personage — Cervantes — but it would also have meant presenting *Don Quixote* as the work of this personage and not of Menard. He naturally denied himself such an easy solution.) "My undertaking is not essentially difficult," I read in another part of the same letter. "I would only have to be immortal in order to carry it out." Shall I confess that I often imagine that he finished it and that I am reading *Don Quixote* — the entire work — as if Menard had conceived it? Several nights ago, while leafing through Chapter XXVI — which he had never attempted — I recognized our friend's style and, as it were, his voice in this exceptional phrase: *the nymphs of the rivers, mournful and humid Echo.* This effective combination of two adjectives, one moral and the other physical, reminded me of a line from Shakespeare which we discussed one afternoon:

Where a malignant and turbaned Turk . . .

Why precisely *Don Quixote,* our reader will ask. Such a preference would not have been inexplicable in a Spaniard; but it undoubtedly was in a symbolist from Nîmes, essentially devoted to Poe, who engendered Baudelaire, who engendered Mallarmé, who engendered Valéry, who engendered Edmond Teste. The letter quoted above clarifies this point. "*Don Quixote,*" Menard explains, "interests me profoundly, but it does not seem to me to have been — how shall I say it — inevitable. I cannot imagine the universe without the interjection of Edgar Allan Poe

> *Ah, bear in mind this garden was enchanted!*

or without the *Bateau ivre* or the *Ancient Mariner,* but I know that I am capable of imagining it without *Don Quixote.* (I speak, naturally, of my personal capacity, not of the historical repercussions of these works.) *Don Quixote* is an accidental book, *Don Quixote* is unnecessary. I can premeditate writing, I can write it, without incurring a tautology. When I was twelve or thirteen years old I read it, perhaps in its entirety. Since then I have reread several chapters attentively, but not the ones I am going to undertake. I have likewise studied the *entremeses,* the comedies, the *Galatea,* the exemplary novels, and the undoubtedly laborious efforts of *Pérsiles y Sigismunda* and the *Viaje al Parnaso.* . . . My general memory of *Don Quixote,* simplified by forgetfulness and indifference, is much the same as the imprecise, anterior image of a book not yet written. Once this image (which no one can deny me in good faith) has been postulated, my problems are undeniably considerably more difficult than those which Cervantes faced. My affable precursor did not refuse the collaboration of fate; he went along composing his immortal work a little *à la diable,* swept along by inertias of language and invention. I have contracted the mysterious duty of reconstructing literally his spontaneous work. My solitary game is governed by two polar laws. The first permits me to attempt variants of a formal and psychological nature; the second obliges me to sacrifice them to the 'original' text and irrefutably to rationalize this annihilation. . . . To these artificial obstacles one must add another congenital one. To compose *Don Quixote* at the beginning of the seventeenth century was a reasonable, necessary and perhaps inevitable undertaking; at the beginning of the twentieth century it is almost impossible. It is not in vain that three hundred years have passed, charged with the most complex happenings — among them, to mention only one, that same *Don Quixote.*"

In spite of these three obstacles, the fragmentary *Don Quixote* of Menard is more subtle than that of Cervantes. The latter indulges in a rather coarse opposition between tales of knighthood and the meager, provincial reality of his country; Menard chooses as "reality" the land of Carmen during the century of Lepanto and Lope. What Hispanophile would not have advised Maurice Barrès or Dr. Rodríguez Larreta to make such a choice! Menard, as if it were the most natural thing in the world, eludes them. In his work there are neither bands of gypsies, conquistadors, mystics, Philip the Seconds, nor autos-da-fé. He disregards or proscribes local color. This disdain indicates a new approach to the historical novel. This disdain condemns *Salammbô* without appeal.

It is no less astonishing to consider isolated chapters. Let us examine, for instance, Chapter XXXVIII of Part One "which treats of the curious discourse that Don Quixote delivered on the subject of arms and letters." As is known, Don Quixote (like Quevedo in a later, analogous passage of *La hora de todos*) passes judgment against letters and in favor of arms. Cervantes was an old soldier, which explains such a judgment. But that the *Don Quixote* of Pierre Menard — a contemporary of *La trahison des clercs* and Bertrand Russell — should relapse into these nebulous sophistries! Madame Bachelier has seen in them an admirable and typical subordination of the author to the psychology of the hero; others (by no means perspicaciously) a *transcription* of *Don Quixote;* the Baroness de Bacourt, the influence of Nietzsche. To this third interpretation (which seems to me irrefutable) I do not know if I would dare to add a fourth, which coincides very well with the divine modesty of Pierre Menard: his resigned or ironic habit of propounding ideas which were the strict reverse of those he preferred. (One will remember his diatribe against Paul Valéry in the ephemeral journal of the superrealist Jacques Reboul.) The text of Cervantes and that of Menard are verbally identical, but the second is almost infinitely richer. (More ambiguous, his detractors will say; but ambiguity is a richness.) It is a revelation to compare the *Don Quixote* of Menard with that of Cervantes. The latter, for instance, wrote (*Don Quixote,* Part One, Chapter Nine):

> . . . *la verdad, cuya madre es la historia, émula del tiempo, depósito de las acciones, testigo de lo pasado, ejemplo y aviso de lo presente, advertencia de lo por venir.*
>
> [. . . truth, whose mother is history, who is the rival of time, depository of deeds, witness of the past, example and lesson to the present, and warning to the future.]

Written in the seventeenth century, written by the "ingenious layman" Cervantes, this enumeration is a mere rhetorical eulogy of history. Menard, on the other hand, writes:

> . . . *la verdad, cuya madre es la historia, émula del tiempo, depósito de las acciones, testigo de lo pasado, ejemplo y aviso de lo presente, advertencia de lo por venir.*
>
> [. . . truth, whose mother is history, who is the rival of time, depository of deeds, witness of the past, example and lesson to the present, and warning to the future.]

History, *mother* of truth; the idea is astounding. Menard, a contemporary of William James, does not define history as an investigation of reality, but as its origin. Historical truth, for him, is not what took place; it is what we think took place. The final clauses — *example and lesson to the present, and warning to the future* — are shamelessly pragmatic.

Equally vivid is the contrast in styles. The archaic style of Menard — in the last analysis, a foreigner — suffers from a certain affectation. Not so that of his precursor, who handles easily the ordinary Spanish of his time.

There is no intellectual exercise which is not ultimately useless. A philosophical doctrine is in the beginning a seemingly true description of the universe; as the years pass it becomes a mere chapter — if not a paragraph or a noun — in the history of philosophy. In literature, this ultimate decay is even more notorious. *"Don Quixote,"* Menard once told me, "was above all an agreeable book; now it is an occasion for patriotic toasts, grammatical arrogance and obscene deluxe editions. Glory is an incomprehension, and perhaps the worst."

These nihilist arguments contain nothing new; what is unusual is the decision Pierre Menard derived from them. He resolved to outstrip that vanity which awaits all the woes of mankind; he undertook a task that was complex in the extreme and futile from the outset. He dedicated his conscience and nightly studies to the repetition of a preexisting book in a foreign tongue. The number of rough drafts kept on increasing; he tenaciously made corrections and tore up thousands of manuscript pages.* He did not permit them to be examined, and he took great care that they would not survive him. It is in vain that I have tried to reconstruct them.

I have thought that it is legitimate to consider the "final" *Don Quixote* as a kind of palimpsest, in which should appear traces — tenuous but not undecipherable — of the "previous" handwriting of our friend. Unfortunately, only a second Pierre Menard, inverting the work of the former, could exhume and resuscitate these Troys. . . .

"To think, analyze and invent," he also wrote me, "are not anomalous acts, but the normal respiration of the intelligence. To glorify the occasional fulfillment of this function, to treasure ancient thoughts of others, to remember with incredulous amazement that the *doctor universalis* thought, is to confess our languor or barbarism. Every man should be capable of all ideas, and I believe that in the future he will be."

---

* I remember his square-ruled notebooks, the black streaks where he had crossed out words, his peculiar typographical symbols and his insect-like handwriting. In the late afternoon he liked to go for walks on the outskirts of Nîmes; he would take a notebook with him and make a gay bonfire.

Menard (perhaps without wishing to) has enriched, by means of a new technique, the hesitant and rudimentary art of reading: the technique is one of deliberate anachronism and erroneous attributions. This technique, with its infinite applications, urges us to run through the *Odyssey* as if it were written after the *Aeneid,* and to read *Le jardin du Centaure* by Madame Henri Bachelier as if it were by Madame Henri Bachelier. This technique would fill the dullest books with adventure. Would not the attributing of *The Imitation of Christ* to Louis Ferdinand Céline or James Joyce be a sufficient renovation of its tenuous spiritual counsels?

JORGE LUIS BORGES

Funes, the Memorious

I remember him (I scarcely have the right to use this ghostly verb; only one man on earth deserved the right, and he is dead), I remember him with a dark passionflower in his hand, looking at it as no one has ever looked at such a flower, though they might look from the twilight of day until the twilight of night, for a whole life long. I remember him, his face immobile and Indian-like, and singularly *remote,* behind his cigarette. I remember (I believe) the strong delicate fingers of the plainsman who can braid leather. I remember, near those hands, a vessel in which to make maté tea, bearing the arms of the Banda Oriental;* I remember, in the window of the house, a yellow rush mat, and beyond, a vague marshy landscape. I remember clearly his voice, the deliberate, resentful, nasal voice of the old Eastern Shore man, without the Italianate syllables of today, I did not see him more than three times; the last time, in 1887. . . .

That all those who knew him should write something about him seems to me a very felicitous idea; my testimony may perhaps be the briefest and without doubt the poorest, and it will not be the least impartial. The deplorable fact of my being an Argentinian will hinder me from falling into a dithyramb — an obligatory form in the Uruguay, when the theme is an Uruguayan.

Littérateur, slicker, Buenos Airean: Funes did not use these insulting phrases, but I am sufficiently aware that for him I represented these unfortunate categories. Pedro Leandro Ipuche has written that Funes was a precursor of the superman, "an untamed and vernacular Zarathustra"; I do not doubt it, but one must not forget, either, that he was a countryman from the town of Fray Bentos, with certain incurable limitations.

My first recollection of Funes is quite clear, I see him at dusk, sometime in March or February of the year '84. That year, my father had taken me to spend the summer at Fray Bentos. I was on my way back from the farm at San Francisco with my cousin Bernardo Haedo.

---

* The Eastern Shore (of the Uruguay River); now the Orient Republic of Uruguay. — *Editor's note.*

We came back singing, on horseback; and this last fact was not the only reason for my joy. After a sultry day, an enormous slate-gray storm had obscured the sky. It was driven on by a wind from the south; the trees were already tossing like madmen; and I had the apprehension (the secret hope) that the elemental downpour would catch us out in the open. We were running a kind of race with the tempest. We rode into a narrow lane which wound down between two enormously high brick footpaths. It had grown black of a sudden; I now heard rapid almost secret steps above; I raised my eyes and saw a boy running along the narrow, cracked path as if he were running along a narrow, broken wall. I remember the loose trousers, tight at the bottom, the hemp sandals; I remember the cigarette in the hard visage, standing out against the by now limitless darkness. Bernardo unexpectedly yelled to him: "What's the time, Ireneo?" Without looking up, without stopping, Ireneo replied: "In ten minutes it will be eight o'clock, child Bernardo Juan Francisco." The voice was sharp, mocking.

I am so absentminded that the dialogue which I have just cited would not have penetrated my attention if it had not been repeated by my cousin, who was stimulated, I think, by a certain local pride and by a desire to show himself indifferent to the other's three-sided reply.

He told me that the boy above us in the pass was a certain Ireneo Funes, renowned for a number of eccentricities, such as that of having nothing to do with people and of always knowing the time, like a watch. He added that Ireneo was the son of María Clementina Funes, an ironing woman in the town, and that his father, some people said, was an "Englishman" named O'Connor, a doctor in the salting fields, though some said the father was a horse-breaker, or scout, from the province of El Salto. Ireneo lived with his mother, at the edge of the country house of the Laurels.

In the years '85 and '86 we spent the summer in the city of Montevideo. We returned to Fray Bentos in '87. As was natural, I inquired after all my acquaintances, and finally, about "the chronometer Funes." I was told that he had been thrown by a wild horse at the San Francisco ranch, and that he had been hopelessly crippled. I remember the impression of uneasy magic which the news provoked in me: the only time I had seen him we were on horseback, coming from San Francisco, and he was in a high place; from the lips of my cousin Bernardo the affair sounded like a dream elaborated with elements out of the past. They told me that Ireneo did not move now from his cot, but remained with his eyes fixed on the backyard fig tree, or on a cobweb. At sunset he allowed himself to be brought to the window. He carried pride to the extreme of pretending that the blow which had befallen him was a good thing. . . . Twice I saw him behind the iron grate which sternly delineated his eternal imprisonment: unmoving, once, his eyes closed; unmoving also, another time, absorbed in the contemplation of a sweet-smelling sprig of lavender cotton.

At the time I had begun, not without some ostentation, the methodical study of Latin. My valise contained the *De viris illustribus* of Lhomond, the *Thesaurus* of Quicherat, Caesar's *Commentaries,* and an odd-numbered volume of the *Historia Naturalis* of Pliny, which exceeded (and still exceeds) my modest talents as a Latinist. Everything is noised around in a small town; Ireneo, at his small farm on the outskirts, was not long in learning of the arrival of these anomalous books. He sent me a flowery, ceremonious letter, in which he recalled our encounter, unfortunately brief, "on the seventh day of February of the year '84," and alluded to the glorious services which Don Gregorio Haedo, my uncle, dead the same year, "had rendered to the Two Fatherlands in the glorious campaign of Ituzaingó," and he solicited the loan of any one of the volumes, to be accompanied by a dictionary "for the better intelligence of the original text, for I do not know Latin as yet." He promised to return them in good condition, almost immediately. The letter was perfect, very nicely constructed; the orthography was of the type sponsored by Andrés Bello: *i* for *y, j* for *g.* At first I naturally suspected a jest. My cousins assured me it was not so, that these were the ways of Ireneo. I did not know whether to attribute to impudence, ignorance, or stupidity, the idea that the difficult Latin required no other instrument than a dictionary; in order fully to undeceive him I sent the *Gradus ad Parnassum* of Quicherat, and the Pliny.

On February 14, I received a telegram from Buenos Aires telling me to return immediately, for my father was "in no way well." God forgive me, but the prestige of being the recipient of an urgent telegram, the desire to point out to all of Fray Bentos the contradiction between the negative form of the news and the positive adverb, the temptation to dramatize my sorrow as I feigned a virile stoicism, all no doubt distracted me from the possibility of anguish. As I packed my valise, I noted that I was missing the *Gradus* and the volume of the *Historia Naturalis.* The "Saturn" was to weigh anchor on the morning of the next day; that night, after supper, I made my way to the house of Funes. Outside, I was surprised to find the night no less oppressive than the day.

Ireneo's mother received me at the modest ranch.

She told me that Ireneo was in the back room and that I should not be disturbed to find him in the dark, for he knew how to pass the dead hours without lighting the candle. I crossed the cobblestone patio, the small corridor; I came to the second patio. A great vine covered everything, so that the darkness seemed complete. Of a sudden I heard the high-pitched, mocking voice of Ireneo. The voice spoke in Latin; the voice (which came out of the obscurity) was reading, with obvious delight, a treatise or prayer or incantation. The Roman syllables resounded in the earthen patio; my suspicion made them seem undecipherable, interminable; afterwards, in the enormous dialogue of that night, I learned that they made up the first paragraph of the twenty-fourth chapter of the seventh book of the *Historia Naturalis.* The subject of this chapter is memory; the last words are *ut nihil non iisdem verbis redderetur auditum.*

Without the least change in his voice, Ireneo bade me come in. He was lying on the cot, smoking. It seems to me that I did not see his face until dawn; I seem to recall the momentary glow of the cigarette. The room smelled vaguely of dampness. I sat down, and repeated the story of the telegram and my father's illness.

I come now to the most difficult point in my narrative. For the entire story has no other point (the reader might as well know it by now) than this dialogue of almost a half-century ago. I shall not attempt to reproduce his words, now irrecoverable. I prefer truthfully to make a résumé of the many things Ireneo told me. The indirect style is remote and weak; I know that I sacrifice the effectiveness of my narrative; but let my readers imagine the nebulous sentences which clouded that night.

Ireneo began by enumerating, in Latin and Spanish, the cases of prodigious memory cited in the *Historia Naturalis:* Cyrus, king of the Persians, who could call every soldier in his armies by name; Mithridates Eupator, who administered justice in the twenty-two languages of his empire; Simonides, inventor of mnemotechny; Metrodorus, who practiced the art of repeating faithfully what he heard once. With evident good faith Funes marveled that such things should be considered marvelous. He told me that previous to the rainy afternoon when the blue-tinted horse threw him, he had been — like any Christian — blind, deafmute, somnambulistic, memoryless. (I tried to remind him of his precise perception of time, his memory for proper names; he paid no attention to me). For nineteen years, he said, he had lived like a person in a dream: he looked without seeing, heard without hearing, forgot everything — almost everything. On falling from the horse, he lost consciousness; when he recovered it, the present was almost intolerable it was so rich and bright; the same was true of the most ancient and most trivial memories. A little later he realized that he was crippled. This fact scarcely interested him. He reasoned (or felt) that immobility was a minimum price to pay. And now, his perception and his memory were infallible.

We, in a glance, perceive three wine glasses on the table; Funes saw all the shoots, clusters, and grapes of the vine. He remembered the shapes of the clouds in the south at dawn on the 30th of April of 1882, and he could compare them in his recollection with the marbled grain in the design of a leather-bound book which he had seen only once, and with the lines in the spray which an oar raised in the Rio Negro on the eve of the battle of the Quebracho. These recollections were not simple; each visual image was linked to muscular sensations, thermal sensations, etc. He could reconstruct all his dreams, all his fancies. Two or three times he had reconstructed an entire day. He told me: *I have more memories in myself alone than all men have had since the world was a world.* And again: *My dreams are like your vigils.* And again, toward dawn: *My memory, sir, is like a garbage disposal.*

A circumference on a blackboard, a rectangular triangle, a rhomb, are forms which we can fully intuit; the same held true with Ireneo for the tempestuous mane of a stallion, a herd of cattle in a pass, the ever-changing flame or the innumerable ash, the many faces of a dead man during the course of a protracted wake. He could perceive I do not know how many stars in the sky.

These things he told me; neither then nor at any time later did they seem doubtful. In those days neither the cinema nor the phonograph yet existed; nevertheless, it seems strange, almost incredible, that no one should have experimented on Funes. The truth is that we all live by leaving behind; no doubt we all profoundly know that we are immortal and that sooner or later every man will do all things and know everything.

The voice of Funes, out of the darkness, continued. He told me that toward 1886 he had devised a new system of enumeration and that in a very few days he had gone beyond twenty-four thousand. He had not written it down, for what he once meditated would not be erased. The first stimulus to his work, I believe, had been his discontent with the fact that "thirty-three Uruguayans" required two symbols and three words, rather than a single word and a single symbol. Later he applied his extravagant principle to the other numbers. In place of seven thousand thirteen, he would say (for example) *Máximo Perez;* in place of seven thousand fourteen, *The Train;* other numbers were *Luis Melián Lafinur, Olimar, Brimstone, Clubs, The Whale, Gas, The Cauldron, Napoleon, Agustín de Vedia.* In lieu of five hundred, he would say *nine.* Each word had a particular sign, a species of mark; the last were very complicated. . . . I attempted to explain that this rhapsody of unconnected terms was precisely the contrary of a system of enumeration. I said that to say three hundred and sixty-five was to say three hundreds, six tens, five units: an analysis which does not exist in such numbers as *The Negro Timoteo* or *The Flesh Blanket.* Funes did not understand me, or did not wish to understand me.

Locke, in the seventeenth century, postulated (and rejected) an impossible idiom in which each individual object, each stone, each bird and branch had an individual name; Funes had once projected an analogous idiom, but he had renounced it as being too general, too ambiguous. In effect, Funes not only remembered every leaf on every tree of every wood, but even every one of the times he had perceived or imagined it. He determined to reduce all of his past experience to some seventy thousand recollections, which he would later define numerically. Two considerations dissuaded him: the thought that the task was interminable and the thought that it was useless. He knew that at the hour of his death he would scarcely have finished classifying even all the memories of his childhood.

The two projects I have indicated (an infinite vocabulary for the natural series of numbers, and a usable mental catalogue of all the images of memory) are lacking in sense, but they reveal a certain stammering greatness. They allow us to make out dimly, or to infer, the dizzying world of Funes. He was, let us not forget, almost incapable of general, platonic ideas. It was not only difficult for him to understand that the generic term *dog* embraced so many unlike specimens of differing sizes and different forms; he was disturbed by the fact that a dog at three-fourteen (seen in profile) should have the same name as the dog at three fifteen (seen from the front). His own face in the mirror, his own hands, surprised him on every occasion. Swift writes that the emperor of Lilliput could discern the movement of the minute hand; Funes could continuously make out the tranquil advances of corruption, of caries, of fatigue. He noted the progress of death, of moisture. He was the solitary and lucid spectator of a multiform world which was instantaneously and almost intolerably exact. Babylon, London, and New York have overawed the imagination of men with their ferocious splendor; no one, in those populous towers or upon those surging avenues, has felt the heat and pressure of a reality as indefatigable as that which day and night converged upon the unfortunate Ireneo in his humble South American farmhouse. It was very difficult for him to sleep. To sleep is to be abstracted from the world; Funes, on his back in his cot, in the shadows, imagined every crevice and every molding of the various houses which surrounded him. (I repeat, the least important of his recollections was more minutely precise and more lively than our perception of a physical pleasure or a physical torment.) Toward the east, in a section which was not yet cut into blocks of homes, there were some new unknown houses. Funes imagined them black, compact, made of a single obscurity; he would turn his face in this direction in order to sleep. He would also imagine himself at the bottom of the river, being rocked and annihilated by the current.

Without effort, he had learned English, French, Portuguese, Latin. I suspect, nevertheless, that he was not very capable of thought. To think is to forget a difference, to generalize, to abstract. In the overly replete world of Funes there were nothing but details, almost contiguous details.

The equivocal clarity of dawn penetrated along the earthen patio.

Then it was that I saw the face of the voice which had spoken all through the night. Ireneo was nineteen years old; he had been born in 1868; he seemed as monumental as bronze, more ancient than Egypt, anterior to the prophecies and the pyramids. It occurred to me that each one of my words (each one of my gestures) would live on in his implacable memory; I was benumbed by the fear of multiplying superfluous gestures.

Ireneo Funes died in 1889, of a pulmonary congestion.

T. Coraghessan Boyle

For this anthology I've chosen a story from my latest collection, as well as the single piece that has proven most popular with anthologists over the years, "Greasy Lake." If the earlier stories were in the absurdist mode, often as concerned with language and design as with social issues, these two pieces are realistic and character-oriented. The first, "She Wasn't Soft," from *After the Plague* (2001), deals with the ongoing war between men and women (see Thurber here), and while its final sentence is surprising, perhaps even shocking, it may seem foreordained when one considers the question of point of view. The second, "Greasy Lake," was inspired by the Bruce Springsteen song that provides its epigraph. To my mind, the story resonates because it dramatizes a rite of passage common to American youth in the latter half of the twentieth century and perhaps on into the next: We have all pushed the limits only to discover them, and we have all, every man, woman, and late child of us, been up to Greasy Lake at one time or another.

She Wasn't Soft

She wasn't tender, she wasn't soft, she wasn't sweetly yielding or coquettish, and she was nobody's little woman and never would be. That had been her mother's role, and look at the sad sack of neuroses and alcoholic dysfunction she'd become. And her father. He'd been the pasha of the living room, the sultan of the kitchen, and the emperor of the bedroom, and what had it got him? A stab in the chest, a tender liver, and two feet that might as well have been stumps. Paula Turk wasn't born for that sort of life, with its domestic melodrama and greedy sucking babies — no, she was destined for something richer and more complex, something that would define and elevate her, something great. She wanted to compete and she wanted to win — always, shining before her like some numinous icon was the glittering image of triumph. And whenever she flagged, whenever a sniffle or the flu ate at her reserves and she hit the wall in the numbing waters of the Pacific or the devilish winds at the top of San Marcos Pass, she pushed herself through it, drove herself with an internal whip that accepted no excuses and made no allowances for the limitations of the flesh. She was twenty-eight years old, and she was going to conquer the world.

On the other hand, Jason Barre, the thirty-three-year-old surf-and-dive shop proprietor she'd been seeing pretty steadily over the past nine months, didn't really seem to have the fire of competition in him. Both his parents were doctors (and that, as much as anything, had swayed Paula in his favor when they first met), and they'd set him up in his own business, a business that had continuously lost money since its grand opening three years ago. When the waves were breaking, Jason would be at the beach, and when the surf was flat he'd be stationed behind the counter on his tall swivel stool, selling wax remover to bleached-out adolescents who said things like "gnarly" and "killer" in their penetrating adenoidal tones. Jason liked to surf, and he liked to breathe the cigarette haze in sports bars, a permanent sleepy-eyed, widemouthed California grin on his face, flip-flops on his feet, and his waist encircled by a pair of faded baggy shorts barely held in place by the gentle sag of his belly and the twin anchors of his hipbones.

That was all right with Paula. She told him he should quit smoking, cut down on his drinking, but she didn't harp on it. In truth, she really didn't care all that much — one world-beater in a relationship was enough. When she was in training, which was all the time now, she couldn't help feeling a kind of moral superiority to anyone who wasn't — and Jason most emphatically wasn't. He was no threat, and he didn't want to be — his mind just didn't work that way. He was cute, that was all, and just as she got a little frisson of pleasure from the swell of his paunch beneath the oversized T-shirt and his sleepy eyes and his laid-back ways, he admired her for her drive and the lean, hard triumph of her beauty and her strength. She never took drugs or alcohol — or hardly ever — but he convinced her to try just a puff or two of marijuana before they made love, and it seemed to relax her, open up her pores till she could feel her nerve ends poking through them, and their lovemaking was like nothing she'd ever experienced, except maybe breaking the tape at the end of the twenty-six-mile marathon.

It was a Friday night in August, half past seven, the sun hanging in the window like a piñata, and she'd just stepped out of the shower after a two-hour tuneup for Sunday's triathlon, when the phone rang. Jason's voice came over the wire, low and soft. "Hey, babe," he said, breathing into the phone like a sex maniac (he always called her babe, and she loved it, precisely because she wasn't a babe and never would be — it was their little way of mocking the troglodytes molded into the barstools beside him). "Listen, I was just wondering if you might want to join me down at Clubber's for awhile. Yeah, I know, you need your sleep and the big day's the day after tomorrow and Zinny Bauer's probably already asleep, but how about it. Come on. It's my birthday."

"Your birthday? I thought your birthday was in December?"

There was the ghost of a pause during which she could detect the usual wash of background noise, drunken voices crying out as if from the netherworld, the competing announcers of the six different games unfolding simultaneously on the twelve big-screen TVs, the insistent pulse of the jukebox thumping faintly beneath it all. "No," he said, "my birthday's today, August twenty-sixth — it is. I don't know where you got the idea it was in December . . . but come on, babe, don't you have to load up on carbohydrates?"

She did. She admitted it. "I was going to make pancakes and penne," she said, "with a little cheese sauce and maybe a loaf of that brown-and-serve bread. . . ."

"I'll take you to the Pasta Bowl, all you can eat — and I swear I'll have you back by eleven." He lowered his voice. "And no sex, I know — I wouldn't want to drain you or anything."

She wasn't soft because she ran forty-five miles a week, biked two hundred and fifty, and slashed through fifteen thousand yards of the crawl in the Baños del Mar pool. She was in the best shape of her life, and Sunday's event was nothing, less than half the total distance of the big one — the Hawaii Ironman — in October. She wasn't soft because she'd finished second in the women's division last year in Hawaii and forty-fourth over all, beating out a thousand three hundred and fifty other contestants, twelve hundred of whom, give or take a few, were men. Like Jason. Only fitter. A whole lot fitter.

She swung by Clubber's to pick him up — he wasn't driving, not since his last D.U.I., anyway — and though parking was no problem, she had to endure the stench of cigarettes and the faint sour odor of yesterday's vomit while he finished his cocktail and wrapped up his ongoing analysis of the Dodgers' chances with an abstract point about a blister on somebody or other's middle finger. The guy they called Little Drake, white-haired at thirty-six and with a face that reminded her of one of those naked drooping dogs, leaned out of his Hawaiian shirt and into the radius of Jason's gesticulating hands as if he'd never heard such wisdom in his life. And Paula? She stood there at the bar in her shorts and Lycra halter top, sucking an Evian through a straw while the sports fans furtively admired her pecs and lats and the hard hammered musculature of her legs, for all the world a babe. She didn't mind. In fact, it made her feel luminous and alive, not to mention vastly superior to all those pale lumps of flesh sprouting out of the corners like toadstools and the sagging abrasive girlfriends who hung on their arms and tried to feign interest in whatever sport happened to be on the tube.

But somebody was talking to her, Little Drake, it was Little Drake, leaning across Jason and addressing her as if she were one of them. "So Paula," he was saying. "Paula?"

She swivelled her head toward him, hungry now, impatient. She didn't want to hang around the bar and schmooze about Tommy Lasorda and O.J. and Proposition 187 and how Phil Aguirre had broken both legs and his collarbone in the surf at Rincon; she wanted to go to the Pasta Bowl and carbo-load. "Yes?" she said, trying to be civil, for Jason's sake.

"You going to put them to shame on Sunday, or what?"

Jason was snubbing out his cigarette in the ashtray, collecting his money from the bar. They were on their way out the door — in ten minutes she'd be forking up fettucine or angel hair with black olives and sun-dried tomatoes while Jason regaled her with a satiric portrait of his day and all the crazies who'd passed through his shop. The little man with the white hair didn't require a dissertation, and besides, he couldn't begin to appreciate the difference between what she was doing and the ritualistic farce of the tobacco-spitting, crotch-grabbing "athletes" all tricked out in their pretty unblemished uniforms up on the screen over his head, so she just smiled, like a babe, and said, "Yeah."

Truly, the race was nothing, just a warm-up, and it would have been less than nothing but for the puzzling fact that Zinny Bauer was competing. Zinny was a professional, from Hamburg, and she was the one who'd cranked past Paula like some sort of machine in the final stretch of the Ironman last year. What Paula couldn't fathom was why Zinny was bothering with this small-time event when there were so many other plums out there. On the way out of Clubber's, she mentioned it to Jason. "Not that I'm worried," she said, "just mystified."

It was a fine, soft, glowing night, the air rich with the smell of the surf, the sun squeezing the last light out of the sky as it sank toward Hawaii. Jason was wearing his faded-to-pink 49ers jersey and a pair of shorts so big they made his legs look like sticks. He gave her one of his hooded looks, then got distracted and tapped at his watch twice before lifting it to his ear and frowning. "Damn thing stopped," he said. It wasn't until they were sliding into the car that he came back to the subject of Zinny Bauer. "It's simple, babe," he said, shrugging his shoulders and letting his face go slack. "She's here to psych you out."

He liked to watch her eat. She wasn't shy about it — not like the other girls he'd dated, the ones on a perpetual diet who made you feel like a two-headed hog every time you sat down to a meal, whether it was a Big Mac or the Mexican Plate at La Fondita. No "salad with dressing on the side" for Paula, no butterless bread or child's portions. She attacked her food like a lumberjack, and you'd better keep your hands and fingers clear. Tonight she started with potato gnocchi in a white sauce puddled with butter, and she ate half a loaf of crusty Italian bread with it, sopping up the leftover sauce till the plate gleamed. Next it was the fettucine with Alfredo sauce, and on her third trip to the pasta bar she heaped her plate with mostaccioli marinara and chunks of hot sausage — and more bread, always more bread.

He ordered a beer, lit a cigarette without thinking, and shovelled up some spaghetti carbonara, thick on the fork and sloppy with sauce. The next thing he knew, he was staring up into the hot green gaze of the waitperson, a pencil-necked little fag he could have snapped in two like a breadstick if this weren't California and everything so copacetic and laid back. It was times like this when he wished he lived in Cleveland, even though he'd never been there, but he knew what was coming and he figured people in Cleveland wouldn't put up with this sort of crap.

"You'll have to put that out," the little fag said.

"Sure, man," Jason said, gesturing broadly so that the smoke fanned out around him like the remains of a pissed-over fire. "Just as soon as I" — puff, puff — "take another drag and" — puff, puff — "find me an ashtray somewhere . . . you wouldn't happen" — puff, puff — "to have an ashtray, would you?"

Of course the little fag had been holding one out in front of him all along, as if it were a portable potty or something, but the cigarette was just a glowing stub now, the tiny fag end of a cigarette — fag end, how about that? — and Jason reached out, crushed the thing in the ashtray and said, "Hey, thanks, dude — even though it really wasn't a cigarette but just the *fag* end of one."

And then Paula was there, her fourth plate of the evening mounded high with angel hair, three-bean salad, and wedges of fruit in five different colors. "So what was that all about? Your cigarette?"

Jason ignored her, forking up spaghetti. He took a long swig of his beer and shrugged. "Yeah, whatever," he said finally. "One more fascist doing his job."

"Don't be like that," she said, using the heel of her bread to round up stray morsels on her plate.

"Like what?"

"You know what I mean. I don't have to lecture you."

"Yeah?" He let his eyes droop. "So what do you call this then?"

She sighed and looked away, and that sigh really irritated him, rankled him, made him feel like flipping the table over and sailing a few plates through the window. He was drunk. Or three-quarters drunk anyway. Then her lips were moving again. "Everybody in the world doesn't necessarily enjoy breathing through a tube of incinerated tobacco, you know," she said, "People are into health."

"Who? You maybe. But the rest of them just want to be a pain in the ass. They just want to abrogate my rights in a public place" — abrogate, now where did that come from? — "and then rub my nose in it." The thought soured him even more, and when he caught the waitperson pussyfooting by out of the corner of his eye he snapped his fingers with as much pure malice as he could manage. "Hey, dude, another beer here, huh? I mean, when you get a chance."

It was then that Zinny Bauer made her appearance. She stalked through the door like something crossbred in an experimental laboratory, so rangy and hollow-eyed and fleshless she looked as if she'd been pasted onto her bones. There was a guy with her — her trainer or husband or whatever — and he was right out of an X-Men cartoon, all head and shoulders and great big beefy biceps. Jason recognized them from Houston — he'd flown down to watch Paula compete in the Houston

Ironman, only to see her hit the wall in the run and finish sixth in the women's while Zinny Bauer, the Amazing Bone Woman, took an easy first. And here they were, Zinny and Klaus — or Olaf or whoever — here in the Pasta Bowl, carbo-loading like anybody else. His beer came, cold and dependable, green in the bottle, pale amber in the glass, and he downed it in two gulps. "Hey, Paula," he said, and he couldn't keep the quick sharp stab of joy out of his voice — he was happy suddenly and he didn't know why. "Hey, Paula, you see who's here?"

The thing that upset her was that he'd lied to her, the way her father used to lie to her mother, the same way — casually, almost as a reflex. It wasn't his birthday at all. He'd just said that to get her out because he was drunk and he didn't care if she had to compete the day after to-morrow and needed her rest and peace and quiet and absolutely no stimulation whatever. He was selfish, that was all, selfish and unthink-ing. And then there was the business with the cigarette — he knew as well as anybody in the state that there was an ordinance against smok-ing in public places as of January last, and still he had to push the lim-its like some cocky immature chip-on-the-shoulder surfer. Which is exactly what he was. But all that was forgivable — it was the Zinny Bauer business she just couldn't understand.

Paula wasn't even supposed to be there. She was supposed to be at home, making up a batch of flapjacks and penne with cheese sauce and lying inert on the couch with the remote control. This was the night before the night before the event, a time to fuel up her tanks and veg out. But because of him, because of her silver-tongued hero in the baggy shorts, she was at the Pasta Bowl, carbo-loading in public. And so was Zinny Bauer, the last person on earth she wanted to see.

That was bad enough, but Jason made it worse, far worse — Jason made it into one of the most excruciating moments of her life. What happened was purely crazy, and if she hadn't known Jason better she would have thought he'd planned it. They were squabbling over his cigarette and how unlaid-back and uptight the whole thing had made him — he was drunk, and she didn't appreciate him when he was drunk, not at all — when his face suddenly took on a conspiratorial look and he said, "Hey, Paula, you see who's here?"

"Who?" she said, and she shot a glance over her shoulder and froze: it was Zinny Bauer and her husband Armin. "Oh, shit," she said, and she lowered her head and focussed on her plate as if it were the most fascinating thing she'd ever seen. "She didn't see me, did she? We've got to go. Right now. Right this minute."

Jason was smirking. He looked happy about it, as if he and Zinny Bauer were old friends. "But you've only had four plates, babe," he said. "You sure we got our money's worth? I could go for maybe just a touch more pasta — and I haven't even had any salad yet."

"No joking around, this isn't funny." Her voice withered in her throat. "I don't want to see her. I don't want to talk to her. I just want to get out of here, okay?"

His smile got wider. "Sure, babe, I know how you feel — but you're going to beat her, you are, no sweat. You don't have to let anybody chase you out of your favorite restaurant in your own town — I mean, that's not right, is it? That's not in the spirit of friendly competition."

"Jason," she said, and she reached across the table and took hold of his wrist. "I mean it. Let's get out of here. Now."

Her throat was constricted, as if everything she'd eaten was about to come up. Her legs ached, and her ankle — the one she'd sprained last spring — felt as if someone had driven a nail through it. All she could think of was Zinny Bauer, with her long muscles and the shaved blond stubble of her head and her eyes that never quit. Zinny Bauer was behind her, at her back, right there, and it was too much to bear. "*Jason,*" she hissed.

"Okay, okay," he was saying, and he tipped back the dregs of his beer and reached into his pocket and scattered a couple of rumpled bills across the table by way of a tip. Then he rose from the chair with a slow drunken grandeur and gave her a wink as if to indicate that the coast was clear. She got up, bunching her shoulders as if she could compress herself into invisibility and stared down at her feet as Jason took her arm and led her across the room — if Zinny saw her, Paula wouldn't know about it because she wasn't going to look up, and she wasn't going to make eye contact, she wasn't.

Or so she thought.

She was concentrating on her feet, on the black-and-white checked pattern of the floor tiles and how her running shoes negotiated them as if they were attached to somebody else's legs, when all of a sudden Jason stopped and her eyes flew up and there they were, hovering over Zinny Bauer's table like casual acquaintances, like neighbors on their way to a P.T.A. meeting. "But aren't you Zinny Bauer?" Jason said, his voice gone high and nasal as he shifted into his Valley Girl imitation. "The great triathlete? Oh, God, yes, yes, you are, aren't you? Oh, God, could I have your autograph for my little girl?"

Paula was made of stone. She couldn't move, couldn't speak, couldn't even blink her eyes. And Zinny — she looked as if her plane had just crashed. Jason was playing out the charade, pretending to fumble through his pockets for a pen, when Armin broke the silence. "Why don't you just fock off," he said, and the veins stood out in his neck.

"Oh, she'll be so thrilled," Jason went on, his voice pinched to a squeal. "She's so adorable, only six years old, and, oh, my God, she's not going to believe this —"

Armin rose to his feet. Zinny clutched at the edge of the table with bloodless fingers, her eyes narrow and hard. The waiter — the one Jason had been riding all night — started toward them, crying out, "Is everything all right?" as if the phrase had any meaning.

And then Jason's voice changed, just like that. "Fuck you too, Jack, and your scrawny fucking bald-headed squeeze."

Armin worked out, you could see that, and Paula doubted he'd ever pressed a cigarette to his lips, let alone a joint, but still Jason managed to hold his own — at least until the kitchen staff separated them. There was some breakage, a couple of chairs overturned, a whole lot of noise and cursing and threatening, most of it from Jason. Every face in the restaurant was drained of color by the time the kitchen staff came to the rescue, and somebody went to the phone and called the police, but Jason blustered his way out the door and disappeared before they arrived. And Paula? She just melted away and kept on melting until she found herself behind the wheel of the car, cruising slowly down the darkened streets, looking for Jason.

She never did find him.

When he called the next morning he was all sweetness and apology. He whispered, moaned, sang to her, his voice a continuous soothing current insinuating itself through the line and into her head and right on down through her veins and arteries to the unresisting core of her. "Listen, Paula, I didn't mean for things to get out of hand," he whispered, "you've got to believe me. I just didn't think you had to hide from anybody, that's all."

She listened, her mind gone numb, and let his words saturate her. It was the day before the event, and she wasn't going to let anything distract her. But then, as he went on, pouring himself into the phone with his penitential, self-pitying tones as if he were the one who'd been embarrassed and humiliated, she felt the outrage coming up in her: didn't he understand, didn't he know what it meant to stare into the face of your own defeat? And over a plate of pasta, no less? She cut him off in the middle of a long digression about some surfing legend of the fifties and all the adversity he'd had to face from a host of competitors, a blood-sucking wife and a fearsome backwash off Newport Beach.

"What did you think," she demanded, "that you were protecting me or something? Is that it? Because if that's what you think, let me tell you I don't need you or anybody else to stand up for me —"

"Paula," he said, his voice creeping out at her over the wire, "Paula, I'm on your side, remember? I love what you're doing. I want to help you." He paused. "And yes, I want to protect you too."

"I don't need it."

"Yes, you do. You don't think you do but you do. Don't you see: I was trying to psych her."

"Psych her? At the Pasta Bowl?"

His voice was soft, so soft she could barely hear him: "Yeah." And then, even softer: "I did it for you."

It was Saturday, seventy-eight degrees, sun beaming down unmolested, the tourists out in force. The shop had been buzzing since ten, nothing major — cords, tube socks, T-shirts, a couple of illustrated guides to South Coast hot spots that nobody who knew anything needed a book to find — but Jason had been at the cash register right through lunch and on into the four-thirty breathing spell when the tourist mind tended to fixate on ice-cream cones and those pathetic sidecar bikes they pedalled up and down the street like the true guppies they were. He'd even called Little Drake in to help out for a couple of hours there. Drake didn't mind. He'd grown up rich in Montecito and gone white-haired at twenty-seven, and now he lived with his even whiter-haired old parents and managed their two rental properties downtown — which meant he had nothing much to do except prop up the bar at Clubber's or haunt the shop like the thinnest ghost of a customer. So why not put him to work?

"Nothing to shout about," Jason told him, over the faint hum of the oldies channel. He leaned back against the wall on his high stool and cracked the first beer of the day. "Little stuff, but a lot of it. I almost had that one dude sold on the Al Merrick board — I could taste it — but something scared him off. Maybe mommy took away his Visa card, I don't know."

Drake pulled contemplatively at his beer and looked out the window on the parade of tourists marching up and down State Street. He didn't respond. It was that crucial hour of the day, the hour known as cocktail hour, two for one, the light stuck on the underside of the palms, everything soft and pretty and winding down toward dinner and evening, the whole night held out before them like a promise. "What time's the Dodger game?" Drake said finally.

Jason looked at his watch. It was a reflex. The Dodgers were playing the Mets at five-thirty, Astacio against the Doc, and he knew the time and channel as well as he knew his A.T.M. number. The Angels were on Prime Ticket, seven-thirty, at home against the Orioles. And

Paula — Paula was at home too, focussing (do not disturb, thank you very much) for the big one with the Amazing Bone Woman the next morning. "Five-thirty," he said, after a long pause.

Drake said nothing. His beer was gone, and he shuffled behind the counter to the little reefer for another. When he'd cracked it, sipped, belched, scratched himself thoroughly, and commented on the physique of an overweight Mexican chick in a red bikini making her way up from the beach, he ventured an opinion on the topic under consideration: "Time to close up?"

All things being equal, Jason would have stayed open till six, or near six anyway, on a Saturday in August. The summer months accounted for the lion's share of his business — it was like the Christmas season for everybody else — and he tried to maximize it, he really did, but he knew what Drake was saying. Twenty to five now, and they had to count the receipts, lock up, stop by the night deposit at the B. of A., and then settle in at Clubber's for the game. It would be nice to be there, maybe with a tall tequila tonic and the sports section spread out on the bar, before the game got under way. Just to settle in and enjoy the fruits of their labor. He gave a sigh, for form's sake, and said, "Yeah, why not?"

And then there was cocktail hour and he had a couple of tall tequila tonics before switching to beer, and the Dodgers looked good, real good, red hot, and somebody bought him a shot. Drake was carrying on about something — his girlfriend's cat, the calluses on his mother's feet — and Jason tuned him out, ordered two soft chicken tacos, and watched the sun do all sorts of amazing pink and salmon things to the storefronts across the street before the gray finally settled in. He was thinking he should have gone surfing today, thinking he'd maybe go out in the morning, and then he was thinking of Paula. He should wish her luck or something, give her a phone call at least. But the more he thought about it, the more he pictured her alone in her apartment, power-drinking her fluids, sunk into the shell of her focus like some Chinese Zen master, and the more he wanted to see her.

They hadn't had sex in a week. She was always like that when it was coming down to the wire, and he didn't blame her. Or yes, yes, he did blame her. And he resented it too. What was the big deal? It wasn't like she was playing ball or anything that took any skill, and why lock him out for that? She was like his overachieving, straight-arrow parents, Type A personalities, early risers, joggers, let's go out and beat the world. God, that was anal. But she had some body on her, as firm and flawless as the Illustrated Man's — or Woman's, actually. He thought about that and about the way her face softened when they were in bed together, and he stood at the pay phone seeing her in the hazy soft-focus glow of some made-for-TV movie. Maybe he shouldn't call. Maybe he should just . . . surprise her.

She answered the door in an oversized sweatshirt and shorts, bare-footed, and with the half-full pitcher from the blender in her hand. She looked surprised, all right, but not pleasantly surprised. In fact, she scowled at him and set the pitcher down on the bookcase before pulling back the door and ushering him in. He didn't even get the chance to tell her he loved her or to wish her luck before she started in on him. "What are you doing here?" she demanded. "You know I can't see you tonight, of all nights. What's with you? Are you drunk? Is that it?"

What could he say? He stared at the brown gloop in the pitcher for half a beat and then gave her his best simmering droopy-eyed smile and a shrug that radiated down from his shoulders to his hips. "I just wanted to see you. To wish you luck, you know?" He stepped forward to kiss her, but she dodged away from him, snatching up the pitcher full of gloop like a shield. "A kiss for luck?" he said.

She hesitated. He could see something go in and out of her eyes, the flicker of a worry, competitive anxiety, butterflies, and then she smiled and pecked him a kiss on the lips that tasted of soy and honey and whatever else was in that concoction she drank. "Luck," she said, "but no excitement."

"And no sex," he said, trying to make a joke of it. "I know."

She laughed then, a high girlish tinkle of a laugh that broke the spell. "No sex," she said. "But I was just going to watch a movie if you want to join me —"

He found one of the beers he'd left in the refrigerator for just such an emergency as this and settled in beside her on the couch to watch the movie — some inspirational crap about a demi-cripple who wins the hurdle event in the Swedish Special Olympics — but he was hot, he couldn't help it, and his fingers kept wandering from her shoulder to her breast, from her waist to her inner thigh. At least she kissed him when she pushed him away. "Tomorrow," she promised, but it was only a promise, and they both knew it. She'd been so devastated after the Houston thing she wouldn't sleep with him for a week and a half, strung tight as a bow every time he touched her. The memory of it chewed at him, and he sipped his beer moodily. "Bullshit," he said.

"Bullshit what?"

"Bullshit you'll sleep with me tomorrow. Remember Houston? Remember Zinny Bauer?"

Her face changed suddenly and she flicked the remote angrily at the screen and the picture went blank. "I think you better go," she said.

But he didn't want to go. She was his girlfriend, wasn't she? And what good did it do him if she kicked him out every time some chickenshit race came up? Didn't he matter to her, didn't he matter at all? "I don't want to go," he said.

She stood, put her hands on her hips, and glared at him. "I have to go to bed now."

He didn't budge. Didn't move a muscle. "That's what I mean," he said, and his face was ugly, he couldn't help it. "I want to go to bed too."

Later, he felt bad about the whole thing. Worse than bad. He didn't know how it happened exactly, but there was some resentment there, he guessed, and it just snuck up on him — plus he was drunk, if that was any excuse. Which it wasn't. Anyway, he hadn't meant to get physical, and by the time she'd stopped fighting him and he got her shorts down he hadn't even really wanted to go through with it. This wasn't making love, this wasn't what he wanted. She just lay there beneath him like she was dead, like some sort of zombie, and it made him sick, so sick he couldn't even begin to apologize or excuse himself. He felt her eyes on him as he was zipping up, hard eyes, accusatory eyes, eyes like claws, and he had to stagger into the bathroom and cover himself with the noise of both taps and the toilet to keep from breaking down. He'd gone too far. He knew it. He was ashamed of himself, deeply ashamed, and there really wasn't anything left to say. He just slumped his shoulders and slouched out the door.

And now here he was, contrite and hungover, mooning around on Ledbetter Beach in the cool hush of 7:00 A.M., waiting with all the rest of the guppies for the race to start. Paula wouldn't even look at him. Her mouth was set, clamped shut, a tiny little line of nothing beneath her nose, and her eyes looked no farther than her equipment — her spidery ultra-lightweight bike with the triathlon bars and her little skullcap of a helmet and water bottles and whatnot. She was wearing a two-piece swimsuit, and she'd already had her number — 23 — painted on her upper arms and the long burnished muscles of her thighs. He shook out a cigarette and stared off past her, wondering what they used for the numbers: Magic Marker? Greasepaint? Something that wouldn't come off in the surf, anyway — or with all the sweat. He remembered the way she looked in Houston, pounding through the muggy haze in a sheen of sweat, her face sunk in a mask of suffering, her legs and buttocks taut, her breasts flattened to her chest in the grip of the clinging top. He thought about that, watching her from behind the police line as she bent to fool with her bike, not an ounce of fat on her, nothing, not even a stray hair, and he got hard just looking at her.

But that was short-lived, because he felt bad about last night and knew he'd have to really put himself through the wringer to make it up to her. Plus, just watching the rest of the four hundred and six fleshless masochists parade by with their Gore-Tex T-shirts and Lycra shorts and all the rest of their paraphernalia was enough to make him go cold all over. His stomach felt like a fried egg left out on the counter too long, and his hands shook when he lit the cigarette. He should be in bed, that's where he should be — enough of this seven o'clock in the morning. They were crazy, these people, purely crazy, getting up at dawn to put themselves through something like this — one mile in the water, thirty-four on the bike, and a ten-mile run to wrap it up, and this was a walk compared to the Ironman. They were all bone and long, lean muscle, like whippet dogs or something, the women indistinguishable from the men, stringy and titless. Except for Paula. She was all right in that department, and that was genetic — she referred to her breasts as her fat reserves. He was wondering if they shrank at all during the race, what with all that stress and water loss, when a woman with big hair and too much makeup asked him for a light.

She was milling around with maybe a couple hundred other specta-tors — or sadists, he guessed you'd have to call them — waiting to watch the crazies do their thing. "Thanks," she breathed, after he'd leaned in close to touch the tip of his smoke to hers. Her eyes were big wet pools, and she was no freak, no bone woman. Her lips were wet too, or maybe it was his imagination. "So," she said, the voice caught low in her throat, a real smoker's rasp, "here for the big event?"

He just nodded.

There was a pause. They sucked at their cigarettes. A pair of gulls flailed sharply at the air behind them and then settled down to poke through the sand for anything that looked edible. "My name's Sandra," she offered, but he wasn't listening, not really, because it was then that it came to him, his inspiration, his moment of grace and redemption: suddenly he knew how he was going to make it up to Paula. He cut his eyes away from the woman and through the crowd to where Paula bent over her equipment, the take-no-prisoners look ironed into her face. And what does she want more than anything? he asked himself, his excitement so intense he almost spoke the words aloud. What would make her happy, glad to see him, ready to party, celebrate, dance till dawn and let bygones be bygones?

To win. That was all. To beat Zinny Bauer. And in that moment, even as Paula caught his eye and glowered at him, he had a vision of Zinny Bauer, the Amazing Bone Woman, coming into the final stretch with her legs and arms pumping, in command, no problem, and the bright green cup of Gatorade held out for her by the smiling volunteer in the official volunteer's cap and T-shirt — yes — and Zinny Bauer refreshing herself, drinking it down in mid-stride, running on and on until she hit the wall he was already constructing.

Paula pulled the red bathing cap down over her ears, adjusted her swim goggles, and strode across the beach, her heartbeat as slow and steady as a lizard's. She was focussed, as clearheaded and certain as she'd ever been in her life. Nothing mattered now except leaving all the hotshots and loudmouths and macho types behind in the dust — and Zinny Bauer too. There were a couple of pros competing in the men's division and she had no illusions about beating them, but she was going to teach the rest of them a hard lesson, a lesson about toughness and endurance and will. If anything, what had happened with Jason last night was something she could use, the kind of thing that made her angry, that made her wonder what she'd seen in him in the first place. He didn't care about her. He didn't care about anybody. That was what she was thinking when the gun went off and she hit the water with the great thundering herd of them, the image of his bleary apologetic face burning into her brain — date rape, that's what they called it — and she came out of the surf just behind Zinny Bauer, Jill Eisen, and Tommy Roe, one of the men's pros.

All right. Okay. She was on her bike now, through the gate in a flash and driving down the flat wide concourse of Cabrillo Boulevard in perfect rhythm, effortless, as if the blood were flowing through her legs and into the bike itself. Before she'd gone half a mile she knew she was going to catch Zinny Bauer and pass her to ride with the men's leaders and get off first on the run. It was preordained, she could feel it, feel it pounding in her temples and in the perfect engine of her heart. The anger had settled in her legs now, a bitter, hot-burning fuel. She fed on the air, tucked herself into the handlebars, and flew. If all this time she'd raced for herself, for something uncontainable inside her, now she was racing for Jason, to show him up, to show him what she was, what she really was. There was no excuse for him. None. And she was going to win this event, she was going to beat Zinny Bauer and all those hundreds of soft, winded, undertrained, crowing, chest-thumping jocks too, and she was going to accept her trophy and stride right by him as if he didn't exist, because she wasn't soft, she wasn't, and he was going to find that out once and for all.

By the time he got back to the beach Jason thought he'd run some sort of race himself. He was breathing hard — got to quit smoking — and his tequila headache was heating up to the point where he was seriously considering ducking into Clubber's and slamming a shot or two, though it was only half past nine and all the tourists would be there buttering their French toast and would you pass the syrup please and thank you very much. He'd had to go all the way out to Drake's place and shake him awake to get the Tuinal — one of Drake's mother's six thousand and one prescriptions to fight off the withering aches of her seventy-odd years. Tuinal, Nembutal, Dalmane, Darvocet: Jason didn't care, just so long as there was enough of it. He didn't do barbiturates anymore — probably hadn't swallowed a Tooey in ten years — but he remembered the sweet numb glow they gave him and the way they made his legs feel like tree trunks planted deep in the ground.

The sun had burned off the fog by now, and the day was clear and glittering on the water. They'd started the race at seven-thirty, so that gave him a while yet — the first men would be crossing the finish line in just under three hours, and the women would be coming in at three-ten, three-twelve, something like that. All he needed to do now was finesse himself into the inner sanctum, pick up a stray T-shirt and cap, find the Gatorade and plant himself about two miles from the finish. Of course there was a chance the Amazing Bone Woman wouldn't take the cup from him, especially if she recognized him from the other night, but he was going to pull his cap down low and hide behind his Ray-Bans and show her a face of devotion. One second, that's all it would take. A hand coming out of the crowd, the cup beaded with moisture and moving right along beside her so she didn't even have to break stride — and what was there to think about? She drinks and hits the wall. And if she didn't go for it the first time, he'd hop in the car and catch her a mile farther on.

He'd been watching one of the security volunteers stationed outside the trailer that served as a command center. A kid of eighteen maybe, greasy hair, an oversized cross dangling from one ear, a scurf of residual acne. He was a carbon copy of the kids he sold wetsuits and Killer Beeswax to — maybe he was even one of them. Jason reminded himself to tread carefully. He was a businessman, after all, one of the pillars of the downtown community, and somebody might recognize him. But then so what if they did? He was volunteering his time, that was all, a committed citizen doing his civic best to promote tourism and everything else that was right in the world. He ducked under the rope. "Hey, bro," he said to the kid, extending his hand for the high five — which the kid gave him. "Sorry I'm late. Jeff around?"

The kid's face opened up in a big beaming half-witted grin. "Yeah, sure — I think he went up the beach a ways with Everardo and Linda and some of the press people, but I could maybe look if you want —"

Jeff. It was a safe bet — no crowd of that size, especially one consisting of whippets, bone people and guppies, would be without a Jeff. Jason gave the kid a shrug. "Nah, that's all right. But hey, where's the T-shirts and caps at?"

Then he was in his car, and forget the D.U.I., the big green waxed cup cold between his legs, breaking Tuinal caps and looking for a parking space along the course. He pulled in under a huge Monterey pine that was like its own little city and finished doctoring the Gatorade, stirring the stuff in with his index fingers. What would it take to make her legs go numb and wind up a Did Not Finish without arousing suspicion? Two? Three? He didn't want her to pass out on the spot or take a dive into the bushes or anything, and he didn't want to hurt her, either, not really. But four — four was a nice round number, and that ought to do it. He sucked the finger he'd used as a swizzle stick to see if he could detect the taste, but he couldn't. He took a tentative sip. Nothing. Gatorade tasted like such shit anyway, who could tell the difference?

He found a knot of volunteers in their canary-yellow T-shirts and caps and stationed himself a hundred yards up the street from them, the ice rattling as he swirled his little green time bomb around the lip of the cup. The breeze was soft, the sun caught in the crowns of the trees and reaching out to finger the road here and there in long, slim swatches. He'd never tell Paula, of course, no way, but he'd get giddy with her, pop the champagne cork, and let her fill him with all the ecstasy of victory.

A cheer from the crowd brought him out of his reverie. The first of the men was cranking his way round the long bend in the road, a guy with a beard and wraparound sunglasses — the Finn. He was the one favored to win, or was it the Brit? Jason tucked the cup behind his back and faded into the crowd, which was pretty sparse here, and watched the guy propel himself past, his mouth gaping black, the two holes of his nostrils punched deep into his face, his head bobbing on his neck as if it wasn't attached right. Another guy appeared round the corner just as the Finn passed by, and then two others came slogging along behind him. Somebody cheered, but it was a pretty feeble affair.

Jason checked his watch. It would be five minutes or so, and then he could start watching for the Amazing Bone Woman, tireless freak that she was. And did she fuck Klaus, or Olaf, or whoever he was, the night before the big event, or was she like Paula, all focus and negativity and no, no, no? He fingered the cup lightly, reminding himself not to damage or crease it in any way — it had to look pristine, fresh-dipped from the bucket — and he watched the corner at the end of the street till his eyes began to blur from the sheer concentration of it all.

Two more men passed by, and nobody cheered, not a murmur, but then suddenly a couple of middle-aged women across the street set up a howl, and the crowd chimed in: the first woman, a woman of string and bone with a puffing heaving puppetlike frame, was swinging into the street in distant silhouette. Jason moved forward. He tugged reflexively at the bill of his hat, jammed the rims of the shades back into his eyesockets. And he started to grin, all his teeth on fire, his lips spread wide: Here, take me, drink me, have me!

As the woman closed, loping, sweating, elbows flailing and knees pounding, the crowd getting into it now, cheering her, cheering this first of the women in a man's event, the first Ironwoman of the day, he began to realize that this wasn't Zinny Bauer at all. Her hair was too long, and her legs and chest were too full — and then he saw the number clearly, No. 23, and looked into Paula's face. She was fifty yards from him, but he could see the toughness in her eyes and the tight little frozen smile of triumph and superiority. She was winning. She was beating Zinny Bauer and Jill Eisen and all those pathetic jocks laboring up the hills and down the blacktop streets behind her. This was her moment, this was it.

But then, and he didn't stop to think about it, he stepped forward, right out on the street where she could see him, and held out the cup. He heard her feet beating at the pavement with a hard merciless slap, saw the icy twist of a smile and the cold, triumphant eyes. And he felt the briefest fleeting touch of her flesh as the cup left his hand.

Greasy Lake

It's about a mile down on the dark side of Route 88.
— *Bruce Springsteen*

There was a time when courtesy and winning ways went out of style, when it was good to be bad, when you cultivated decadence like a taste. We were all dangerous characters then. We wore torn-up leather jackets, slouched around with toothpicks in our mouths, sniffed glue and ether and what somebody claimed was cocaine. When we wheeled our parents' whining station wagons out into the street we left a patch of rubber half a block long. We drank gin and grape juice, Tango, Thunderbird, and Bali Hai. We were nineteen. We were bad. We read André Gide and struck elaborate poses to show that we didn't give a shit about anything. At night, we went up to Greasy Lake.

Through the center of town, up the strip, past the housing developments and shopping malls, street lights giving way to the thin streaming illumination of the headlights, trees crowding the asphalt in a black unbroken wall: that was the way out to Greasy Lake. The Indians had called it Wakan, a reference to the clarity of its waters. Now it was fetid and murky, the mud banks glittering with broken glass and strewn with beer cans and the charred remains of bonfires. There was a single ravaged island a hundred yards from shore, so stripped of vegetation it looked as if the air force had strafed it. We went up to the lake because everyone went there, because we wanted to snuff the rich scent of possibility on the breeze, watch a girl take off her clothes and plunge into the festering murk, drink beer, smoke pot, howl at the stars, savor the incongruous full-throated roar of rock and roll against the primeval susurrus of frogs and crickets. This was nature.

I was there one night, late, in the company of two dangerous characters. Digby wore a gold star in his right ear and allowed his father to pay his tuition at Cornell; Jeff was thinking of quitting school to become a painter/musician/head-shop proprietor. They were both expert in the social graces, quick with a sneer, able to manage a Ford with lousy shocks over a rutted and gutted blacktop road at eighty-five while rolling a joint as compact as a Tootsie Roll Pop stick. They could lounge against a bank of booming speakers and trade "man"s with the best of them or roll out across the dance floor as if their joints worked on bearings. They were slick and quick and they wore their mirror shades at breakfast and dinner, in the shower, in closets and caves. In short, they were bad.

I drove. Digby pounded the dashboard and shouted along with Toots & the Maytals while Jeff hung his head out the window and streaked the side of my mother's Bel Air with vomit. It was early June, the air soft as a hand on your cheek, the third night of summer vacation. The first two nights we'd been out till dawn, looking for something we never found. On this, the third night, we'd cruised the strip sixty-seven times, been in and out of every bar and club we could think of in a twenty-mile radius, stopped twice for bucket chicken and forty-cent hamburgers, debated going to a party at the house of a girl Jeff's sister knew, and chucked two dozen raw eggs at mailboxes and hitchhikers. It was 2:00 A.M.; the bars were closing. There was nothing to do but take a bottle of lemon-flavored gin up to Greasy Lake.

The taillights of a single car winked at us as we swung into the dirt lot with its tufts of weed and washboard corrugations; '57 Chevy, mint, metallic blue. On the far side of the lot, like the exoskeleton of some gaunt chrome insect, a chopper leaned against its kickstand. And that was it for excitement: some junkie half-wit biker and a car freak pumping his girlfriend. Whatever it was we were looking for, we weren't about to find it at Greasy Lake. Not that night.

But then all of a sudden Digby was fighting for the wheel. "Hey, that's Tony Lovett's car! Hey!" he shouted, while I stabbed at the brake pedal and the Bel Air nosed up to the gleaming bumper of the parked Chevy. Digby leaned on the horn, laughing, and instructed me to put my brights on. I flicked on the brights. This was hilarious. A joke. Tony would experience premature withdrawal and expect to be confronted by grim-looking state troopers with flashlights. We hit the horn, strobed the lights, and then jumped out of the car to press our witty faces to Tony's windows; for all we knew we might even catch a glimpse of some little fox's tit, and then we could slap backs with red-faced Tony, roughhouse a little, and go on to new heights of adventure and daring.

The first mistake, the one that opened the whole floodgate, was losing my grip on the keys. In the excitement, leaping from the car with the gin in one hand and a roach clip in the other, I spilled them in the grass — in the dark, rank, mysterious nighttime grass of Greasy Lake. This was a tactical error, as damaging and irreversible in its way as Westmoreland's decision to dig in at Khe Sanh. I felt it like a jab of intuition, and I stopped there by the open door, peering vaguely into the night that puddled up round my feet.

The second mistake — and this was inextricably bound up with the first — was identifying the car as Tony Lovett's. Even before the very bad character in greasy jeans and engineer boots ripped out of the driver's door, I began to realize that this chrome blue was much lighter than the robin's-egg of Tony's car, and that Tony's car didn't have rear-mounted speakers. Judging from their expressions, Digby and Jeff were privately groping toward the same inevitable and unsettling conclusion as I was.

In any case, there was no reasoning with this bad greasy character — clearly he was a man of action. The first lusty Rockette kick of his steel-toed boot caught me under the chin, chipped my favorite tooth, and left me sprawled in the dirt. Like a fool, I'd gone down on one knee to comb the stiff hacked grass for the keys, my mind making connections in the most dragged-out, testudineous way, knowing that things had gone wrong, that I was in a lot of trouble, and that the lost ignition key was my grail and my salvation. The three or four succeeding blows were mainly absorbed by my right buttock and the tough piece of bone at the base of my spine.

Meanwhile, Digby vaulted the kissing bumpers and delivered a savage kung-fu blow to the greasy character's collarbone. Digby had just finished a course in martial arts for phys-ed credit and had spent the better part of the past two nights telling us apocryphal tales of Bruce Lee types and of the raw power invested in lightning blows shot from coiled wrists, ankles, and elbows. The greasy character was unimpressed. He merely backed off a step, his face like a Toltec mask, and laid Digby out with a single whistling roundhouse blow . . . but by now Jeff had got into the act, and I was beginning to extricate myself from the dirt, a tinny compound of shock, rage, and impotence wadded in my throat.

Jeff was on the guy's back, biting at his ear. Digby was on the ground, cursing. I went for the tire iron I kept under the driver's seat. I kept it there because bad characters always keep tire irons under the driver's seat, for just such an occasion as this. Never mind that I hadn't been involved in a fight since sixth grade, when a kid with a sleepy eye and two streams of mucus depending from his nostrils hit me in the knee with a Louisville slugger; never mind that I'd touched the tire iron exactly twice before, to change tires: it was there. And I went for it.

I was terrified. Blood was beating in my ears, my hands were shaking, my heart turning over like a dirtbike in the wrong gear. My antagonist was shirtless, and a single cord of muscle flashed across his chest as he bent forward to peel Jeff from his back like a wet overcoat. "Motherfucker," he spat, over and over, and I was aware in that instant that all four of us — Digby, Jeff, and myself included — were chanting "motherfucker, motherfucker," as if it were a battle cry. (What happened next? the detective asks the murderer from beneath the turned-down brim of his porkpie hat. I don't know, the murderer says, something came over me. Exactly.)

Digby poked the flat of his hand in the bad character's face and I came at him like a kamikaze, mindless, raging, stung with humiliation — the whole thing, from the initial boot in the chin to this murderous primal instant involving no more than sixty hyperventilating, gland-flooding seconds — I came at him and brought the tire iron down across his ear. The effect was instantaneous, astonishing. He was a stunt man and this was Hollywood, he was a big grimacing toothy balloon and I was a man with a straight pin. He collapsed. Wet his pants. Went loose in his boots.

A single second, big as a zeppelin, floated by. We were standing over him in a circle, gritting our teeth, jerking our necks, our limbs and hands and feet twitching with glandular discharges. No one said anything. We just stared down at the guy, the car freak, the lover, the bad greasy character laid low. Digby looked at me; so did Jeff. I was still holding the tire iron, a tuft of hair clinging to the crook like dandelion fluff, like down. Rattled, I dropped it in the dirt, already envisioning the headlines, the pitted faces of the police inquisitors, the gleam of handcuffs, clank of bars, the big black shadows rising from the back of the cell . . . when suddenly a raw torn shriek cut through me like all the juice in all the electric chairs in the country.

It was the fox. She was short, barefoot, dressed in panties and a man's shirt. "Animals!" she screamed, running at us with her fists clenched and wisps of blow-dried hair in her face. There was a silver chain round her ankle, and her toenails flashed in the glare of the headlights. I think it was the toenails that did it. Sure, the gin and the cannabis and even the Kentucky Fried may have had a hand in it, but it was the sight of those flaming toes that set us off — the toad emerging from the loaf in *Virgin Spring,* lipstick smeared on a child: she was already tainted. We were on her like Bergman's deranged brothers — see no evil, hear none, speak none — panting, wheezing, tearing at her clothes, grabbing for flesh. We were bad characters, and we were scared and hot and three steps over the line — anything could have happened.

It didn't.

Before we could pin her to the hood of the car, our eyes masked with lust and greed and the purest primal badness, a pair of headlights swung into the lot. There we were, dirty, bloody, guilty, dissociated from humanity and civilization, the first of the Ur-crimes behind us, the second in progress, shreds of nylon panty and spandex brassiere dangling from our fingers, our flies open, lips licked — there we were, caught in the spotlight. Nailed.

We bolted. First for the car, and then, realizing we had no way of starting it, for the woods. I thought nothing. I thought escape. The headlights came at me like accusing fingers. I was gone.

Ram-bam-bam, across the parking lot, past the chopper and into the feculent undergrowth at the lake's edge, insects flying up in my face, weeds whipping, frogs and snakes and red-eyed turtles splashing off into the night: I was already ankle-deep in muck and tepid water and still going strong. Behind me, the girl's screams rose in intensity, disconsolate, incriminating, the screams of the Sabine women, the Christian martyrs, Anne Frank dragged from the garret. I kept going, pursued by those cries, imagining cops and bloodhounds. The water was up to my knees when I realized what I was doing: I was going to swim for it. Swim the breadth of Greasy Lake and hide myself in the thick clot of woods on the far side. They'd never find me there.

I was breathing in sobs, in gasps. The water lapped at my waist as I looked out over the moon-burnished ripples, the mats of algae that clung to the surface like scabs. Digby and Jeff had vanished. I paused. Listened. The girl was quieter now, screams tapering to sobs, but there were male voices, angry, excited, and the high-pitched ticking of the second car's engine. I waded deeper, stealthy, hunted, the ooze sucking at my sneakers. As I was about to take the plunge — at the very instant I dropped my shoulder for the first slashing stroke — I blundered into something. Something unspeakable, obscene, something soft, wet, moss-grown. A patch of weed? A log? When I reached out to touch it, it gave like a rubber duck, it gave like flesh.

In one of those nasty little epiphanies for which we are prepared by films and TV and childhood visits to the funeral home to ponder the shrunken painted forms of dead grandparents, I understood what it was that bobbed there so inadmissibly in the dark. Understood, and stumbled back in horror and revulsion, my mind yanked in six different directions (I was nineteen, a mere child, an infant, and here in the space of five minutes I'd struck down one greasy character and blundered into the waterlogged carcass of a second), thinking, The keys, the keys, why did I have to go and lose the keys? I stumbled back, but the muck took hold of my feet — a sneaker snagged, balance lost — and suddenly I was pitching face forward into the buoyant black mass, throwing out my hands in desperation while simultaneously conjuring the image of reeking frogs and muskrats revolving in slicks of their

own deliquescing juices. AAAAArrrgh! I shot from the water like a
torpedo, the dead man rotating to expose a mossy beard and eyes cold
as the moon. I must have shouted out, thrashing around in the weeds,
because the voices behind me suddenly became animated.

"What was that?"

"It's them, it's them: they tried to, tried to . . . *rape* me!" Sobs.

A man's voice, flat Midwestern accent. "You sons a bitches, we'll
kill you!"

Frogs, crickets.

Then another voice, harsh, *r*-less, Lower East Side: "Motherfucker!"
I recognized the verbal virtuosity of the bad greasy character in the engineer boots. Tooth chipped, sneakers gone, coated in mud and slime
and worse, crouching breathless in the weeds waiting to have my ass
thoroughly and definitively kicked and fresh from the hideous stinking
embrace of a three-days-dead-corpse, I suddenly felt a rush of joy and
vindication: the son of a bitch was alive! Just as quickly, my bowels
turned to ice. "Come on out of there, you pansy motherfuckers!" the
bad greasy character was screaming. He shouted curses till he was out
of breath.

The crickets started up again, then the frogs. I held my breath. All
at once there was a sound in the reeds, a swishing, a splash: thunk-a-
thunk. They were throwing rocks. The frogs fell silent. I cradled my
head. Swish, swish, thunk-a-thunk. A wedge of feldspar the size of a
cue ball glanced off my knee. I bit my finger.

It was then that they turned to the car. I heard a door slam, a curse,
and then the sound of the headlights shattering — almost a good-
natured sound, celebratory, like corks popping from the necks of
bottles. This was succeeded by the dull booming of the fenders, metal
on metal, and then the icy crash of the windshield. I inched forward,
elbows and knees, my belly pressed to the muck, thinking of guerrillas
and commandos and *The Naked and the Dead*. I parted the weeds and
squinted the length of the parking lot.

The second car — it was a Trans-Am — was still running, its high
beams washing the scene in a lurid stagy light. Tire iron flailing, the
greasy bad character was laying into the side of my mother's Bel Air
like an avenging demon, his shadow riding up the trunks of the trees.
Whomp. Whomp. Whomp-whomp. The other two guys — blond types,
in fraternity jackets — were helping out with tree branches and skull-
sized boulders. One of them was gathering up bottles, rocks, muck,
candy wrappers, used condoms, poptops, and other refuse and pitching
it through the window on the driver's side. I could see the fox, a white
bulb behind the windshield of the '57 Chevy. "Bobbie," she whined
over the thumping, "come on." The greasy character paused a moment,

took one good swipe at the left taillight, and then heaved the tire iron halfway across the lake. Then he fired up the '57 and was gone.

Blond head nodded at blond head. One said something to the other, too low for me to catch. They were no doubt thinking that in helping to annihilate my mother's car they'd committed a fairly rash act, and thinking too that there were three bad characters connected with that very car watching them from the woods. Perhaps other possibilities occurred to them as well — police, jail cells, justices of the peace, reparations, lawyers, irate parents, fraternal censure. Whatever they were thinking, they suddenly dropped branches, bottles, and rocks and sprang for their car in unison, as if they'd choreographed it. Five seconds. That's all it took. The engine shrieked, the tires squealed, a cloud of dust rose from the rutted lot and then settled back on darkness.

I don't know how long I lay there, the bad breath of decay all around me, my jacket heavy as a bear, the primordial ooze subtly reconstituting itself to accommodate my upper thighs and testicles. My jaws ached, my knee throbbed, my coccyx was on fire. I contemplated suicide, wondered if I'd need bridgework, scraped the recesses of my brain for some sort of excuse to give my parents — a tree had fallen on the car, I was blindsided by a bread truck, hit and run, vandals had got to it while we were playing chess at Digby's. Then I thought of the dead man. He was probably the only person on the planet worse off than I was. I thought about him, fog on the lake, insects chirring eerily, and felt the tug of fear, felt the darkness opening up inside me like a set of jaws. Who was he, I wondered, this victim of time and circumstance bobbing sorrowfully in the lake at my back. The owner of the chopper, no doubt, a bad older character come to this. Shot during a murky drug deal, drowned while drunkenly frolicking in the lake. Another headline. My car was wrecked; he was dead.

When the eastern half of the sky went from black to cobalt and the trees began to separate themselves from the shadows, I pushed myself up from the mud and stepped out into the open. By now the birds had begun to take over for the crickets, and dew lay slick on the leaves. There was a smell in the air, raw and sweet at the same time, the smell of the sun firing buds and opening blossoms. I contemplated the car. It lay there like a wreck along the highway, like a steel sculpture left over from a vanished civilization. Everything was still. This was nature.

I was circling the car, as dazed and bedraggled as the sole survivor of an air blitz, when Digby and Jeff emerged from the trees behind me. Digby's face was crosshatched with smears of dirt; Jeff's jacket was gone and his shirt was torn across the shoulder. They slouched across the lot, looking sheepish, and silently came up beside me to gape at the ravaged automobile. No one said a word. After a while Jeff swung open the driver's door and began to scoop the broken glass and garbage off the seat. I looked at Digby. He shrugged. "At least they didn't slash the tires," he said.

It was true: the tires were intact. There was no windshield, the headlights were staved in, and the body looked as if it had been sledge-hammered for a quarter a shot at the county fair, but the tires were inflated to regulation pressure. The car was drivable. In silence, all three of us bent to scrape the mud and shattered glass from the interior. I said nothing about the biker. When we were finished, I reached in my pocket for the keys, experienced a nasty stab of recollection, cursed myself, and turned to search the grass. I spotted them almost immediately, no more than five feet from the open door, glinting like jewels in the first tapering shaft of sunlight. There was no reason to get philosophical about it: I eased into the seat and turned the engine over.

It was at that precise moment that the silver Mustang with the flame decals rumbled into the lot. All three of us froze; then Digby and Jeff slid into the car and slammed the door. We watched as the Mustang rocked and bobbed across the ruts and finally jerked to a halt beside the forlorn chopper at the far end of the lot. "Let's go," Digby said. I hesitated, the Bel Air wheezing beneath me.

Two girls emerged from the Mustang. Tight jeans, stiletto heels, hair like frozen fur. They bent over the motorcycle, paced back and forth aimlessly, glanced once or twice at us, and then ambled over to where the reeds sprang up in a green fence round the perimeter of the lake. One of them cupped her hands to her mouth. "Al," she called. "Hey, Al!"

"Come on," Digby hissed. "Let's get out of here."

But it was too late. The second girl was picking her way across the lot, unsteady on her heels, looking up at us and then away. She was older — twenty-five or -six — and as she came closer we could see there was something wrong with her: she was stoned or drunk, lurching now and waving her arms for balance. I gripped the steering wheel as if it were the ejection lever of a flaming jet, and Digby spat out my name, twice, terse and impatient.

"Hi," the girl said.

We looked at her like zombies, like war veterans, like deaf-and-dumb pencil peddlers.

She smiled, her lips cracked and dry. "Listen," she said, bending from the waist to look in the window, "you guys seen Al?" Her pupils were pinpoints, her eyes glass. She jerked her neck. "That's his bike over there — Al's. You seen him?"

Al. I didn't know what to say. I wanted to get out of the car and retch, I wanted to go home to my parents' house and crawl into bed. Digby poked me in the ribs. "We haven't seen anybody," I said.

The girl seemed to consider this, reaching out a slim veiny arm to brace herself against the car. "No matter," she said, slurring the *t*'s, "he'll turn up." And then, as if she'd just taken stock of the whole scene — the ravaged car and our battered faces, the desolation of the place — she said: "Hey, you guys look like some pretty bad characters — been fightin', huh?" We stared straight ahead, rigid as catatonics. She was fumbling in her pocket and muttering something. Finally she held out a handful of tablets in glassine wrappers: "Hey, you want to party, you want to do some of these with me and Sarah?"

I just looked at her. I thought I was going to cry. Digby broke the silence. "No, thanks," he said, leaning over me. "Some other time."

I put the car in gear and it inched forward with a groan, shaking off pellets of glass like an old dog shedding water after a bath, heaving over the ruts on its worn springs, creeping toward the highway. There was a sheen of sun on the lake. I looked back. The girl was still standing there, watching us, her shoulders slumped, hand outstretched.

Italo Calvino

Like Borges, Italo Calvino (1923–1985) was best-known as a fantasist, though his first two postwar works were in the neorealist mode. His comic, absurd novellas, like *The Baron in the Trees* and *The Cloven Viscount,* have the feel of elaborate children's tales. In the first, the Baron of the title decides one day to climb a tree, from which he never descends through a long and active life; the Viscount of the second tale is split in two by a cannonball while at war with the Turks, and the two sides of him live on separately, one for the good and one for evil. Among Calvino's other books is the exquisite *Invisible Cities,* which imagines an array of surreal cities encountered by Marco Polo in his travels, much as Borges catalogued the mythical creatures of literature in his *Book of Imaginary Beings.* In addition to his major works of fiction, Calvino also produced the definitive compilation of Italian folktales, the influence of which can be seen in the imaginative range of his stories.

The stories selected here are from a book of twenty pieces all featuring a single protagonist — *Marcovaldo or The Seasons in the City* — first published in the United States in 1983. I've cheated a bit in that I've chosen the first four stories of the book and considered them as one cycle — spring, summer, autumn, winter — rather than stick strictly to the two-story format. What most attracts me to the Marcovaldo stories is the simple, straightforward charm and lyricism of their telling. They employ the tone of the folktale and present a wonderfully quixotic character in Marcovaldo, a foil for the cosmic forces that seem to blister his every attempt to rise above his environment. He wants above all to live a natural life, in tune with the seasons, but the dehumanizing industrial society of which he is a reluctant part will not allow it. And so, for example, in "Mushrooms in the City," our sad-sack hero (who seems a cousin to both Don Quixote and Buster Keaton) will not enjoy a dish of wild mushrooms without penalty, nor, in "The Municipal Pigeon," will he be feasting on roast woodcock or duck, at least not anytime soon. Poor Marcovaldo. We pity him, we laugh at him, but ultimately, I think, we like and admire him, because he refuses to be the drone society expects him to be.

1. Mushrooms in the City

The wind, coming to the city from far away, brings it unusual gifts, noticed by only a few sensitive souls, such as hay-fever victims, who sneeze at the pollen from flowers of other lands.

One day, to the narrow strip of ground flanking a city avenue came a gust of spores from God knows where; and some mushrooms germinated. Nobody noticed them except Marcovaldo, the worker who caught his tram just there every morning.

This Marcovaldo possessed an eye ill-suited to city life: billboards, traffic-lights, shop-windows, neon signs, posters, no matter how carefully devised to catch the attention, never arrested his gaze, which might have been running over the desert sands. Instead, he would never miss a leaf yellowing on a branch, a feather trapped by a roof-tile; there was no horsefly on a horse's back, no worm-hole in a plank, or fig-peel squashed on the sidewalk that Marcovaldo didn't remark and ponder over, discovering the changes of season, the yearnings of his heart, and the woes of his existence.

Thus, one morning, as he was waiting for the tram that would take him to Sbav and Co., where he was employed as an unskilled laborer, he noticed something unusual near the stop, in the sterile, encrusted strip of earth beneath the avenue's line of trees; at certain points, near the tree trunks, some bumps seemed to rise and, here and there, they had opened, allowing roundish subterranean bodies to peep out.

Bending to tie his shoes, he took a better look: they were mushrooms, real mushrooms, sprouting right in the heart of the city! To Marcovaldo the gray and wretched world surrounding him seemed suddenly generous with hidden riches; something could still be expected of life, beyond the hourly wage of his stipulated salary, with inflation index, family grant, and cost-of-living allowance.

On the job he was more absent-minded than usual; he kept thinking that while he was there unloading cases and boxes, in the darkness of the earth the slow, silent mushrooms, known only to him, were ripening their porous flesh, were assimilating underground humors, breaking the crust of clods. "One night's rain would be enough," he said to himself, "then they would be ready to pick." And he couldn't wait to share his discovery with his wife and his six children.

"I'm telling you!" he announced during their scant supper. "In a week's time we'll be eating mushrooms! A great fry! That's a promise!"

And to the smaller children, who did not know what mushrooms were, he explained ecstatically the beauty of the numerous species, the delicacy of their flavor, the way they should be cooked; and so he also drew into the discussion his wife, Domitilla, who until then had appeared rather incredulous and abstracted.

"Where are these mushrooms?" the children asked. "Tell us where they grow!"

At this question Marcovaldo's enthusiasm was curbed by a suspicious thought: Now if I tell them the place, they'll go and hunt for them with the usual gang of kids, word will spread through the neighborhood, and the mushrooms will end up in somebody else's pan! And so that discovery, which had promptly filled his heart with universal love, now made him wildly possessive, surrounded him with jealous and distrusting fear.

"I know where the mushrooms are, and I'm the only one who knows," he said to his children, "and God help you if you breathe a word to anybody."

The next morning, as he approached the tram stop, Marcovaldo was filled with apprehension. He bent to look at the ground and, to his relief, saw that the mushrooms had grown a little, but not much, and were still almost completely hidden by the earth.

He was bent in this position when he realized there was someone behind him. He straightened up at once and tried to act indifferent. It was the street-cleaner, leaning on his broom and looking at him.

This street-cleaner, whose jurisdiction included the place where the mushrooms grew, was a lanky youth with eyeglasses. His name was Amadigi, and Marcovaldo had long harbored a dislike of him, perhaps because of those eyeglasses that examined the pavement of the streets, seeking any trace of nature, to be eradicated by his broom.

It was Saturday; and Marcovaldo spent his free half-day circling the bed of dirt with an absent air, keeping an eye on the street-cleaner in the distance and on the mushrooms, and calculating how much time they needed to ripen.

That night it rained: like peasants who, after months of drought, wake up and leap with joy at the sound of the first drops, so Marcovaldo, alone in all the city, sat up in bed and called to his family: "It's raining! It's raining!" and breathed in the smell of moistened dust and fresh mold that came from outside.

At dawn — it was Sunday — with the children and a borrowed basket, he ran immediately to the patch. There were the mushrooms, erect on their stems, their caps high over the still-soaked earth. "Hurrah!" — and they fell to gathering them.

"Papà! Look how many that man over there has found," Michelino said, and his father, raising his eyes, saw Amadigi standing beside them, also with a basket full of mushrooms under his arm.

"Ah, you're gathering them, too?" the street-cleaner said. "Then they're edible? I picked a few, but I wasn't sure . . . Farther down the avenue some others have sprouted, even bigger ones . . . Well, now that I know, I'll tell my relatives; they're down there arguing whether it's a good idea to pick them or not . . ." And he walked off in a hurry.

Marcovaldo was speechless: even bigger mushrooms, which he hadn't noticed, an unhoped-for harvest, being taken from him like this, before his very eyes. For a moment he was almost frozen with anger, fury, then — as sometimes happens — the collapse of individual passion led to a generous impulse. At that hour, many people were waiting for the tram, umbrellas over their arms, because the weather was still damp and uncertain. "Hey, you! Do you want to eat fried mushrooms tonight?" Marcovaldo shouted to the crowd of people at the stop. "Mushrooms are growing here by the street! Come along! There's plenty for all!" And he walked off after Amadigi, with a string of people behind him.

They all found plenty of mushrooms, and lacking baskets, they used their open umbrellas. Somebody said: "It would be nice to have a big feast, all of us together!" But, instead, each took his own share and went home.

They saw one another again soon, however; that very evening, in fact, in the same ward of the hospital, after the stomach-pump had saved them all from poisoning. It was not serious, because the number of mushrooms eaten by each person was quite small.

Marcovaldo and Amadigi had adjacent beds; they glared at each other.

SUMMER

2. Park-Bench Vacation

On his way to work each morning, Marcovaldo walked beneath the green foliage of a square with trees, a bit of public garden, isolated in the junction of four streets. He raised his eyes among the boughs of the horse-chestnuts, where they were at their thickest and allowed yellow rays only to glint in the shade transparent with sap; and he listened to the racket of the sparrows, tone-deaf, invisible on the branches. To him they seemed nightingales, and he said to himself: "Oh, if I could wake just once at the twitter of birds and not at the sound of the alarm and the crying of little Paolino and the yelling of my wife, Domitilla!" or else: "Oh, if I could sleep here, alone, in the midst of this cool green shade and not in my cramped, hot room; here amid the silence, not amid the snoring and sleep-talking of my whole family and the racing of trams down below in the street; here in the natural darkness of the night, not in the artificial darkness of closed blinds, streaked by the glare of headlights; oh, if I could see leaves and sky on opening my eyes!" With these thoughts every day Marcovaldo began his eight daily hours — plus overtime — as an unskilled laborer.

In one corner of the square, under a dome of horse-chestnuts, there was a remote, half-hidden bench. And Marcovaldo had picked it as his own. On those summer nights, in the room where five of them slept, when he couldn't get to sleep, he would dream of the bench as a vagabond dreams of a bed in a palace. One night, quietly, while his wife snored and the children kicked in their sleep, he got out of bed, dressed, tucked his pillow under his arm, left the house and went to the square.

There it was cool, peaceful. He was already savoring the contact of those planks, whose wood — he knew — was soft and cozy, preferable in every respect to the flattened mattress of his bed; he would look for a moment at the stars, then close his eyes in a sleep that would compensate him for all the insults of the day.

Cool and peace he found, but not the empty bench. A couple of lovers were sitting there, looking into each other's eyes. Discreetly, Marcovaldo withdrew. "It's late," he thought, "they surely won't spend

93

the whole night outdoors! They'll come to an end of their billing and cooing."

But the two were not billing or cooing: they were quarreling. And when lovers start to quarrel there's no telling how long it will go on.

He was saying: "Why don't you admit that when you said what you said you knew you were going to hurt me and not make me happy the way you were pretending you thought?"

Marcovaldo realized it was going to last quite a while.

"No, I will not admit it," she answered, as Marcovaldo had already expected.

"Why won't you admit it?"

"I'll never admit it."

Damn, Marcovaldo thought. His pillow clutched under his arm, he went for a stroll. He went and looked at the moon, which was full, big above trees and roofs. He came back towards the bench, giving it a fairly wide berth out of fear of disturbing them, but actually hoping to irritate them a little and persuade them to go away. But they were too caught up in the argument to notice him.

"You admit it then?"

"No, no, I don't admit it in the least!"

"But what if you did admit it?"

"Even if I did admit something, I wouldn't admit what you want me to admit!"

Marcovaldo went back to look at the moon, then he went to look at a traffic-light, a bit farther on. The light flashed yellow, yellow, yellow, constantly blinking on and off. Marcovaldo compared the moon with the traffic-light. The moon with her mysterious pallor, also yellow, but also green, in its depths, and even blue; the traffic-light with its common little yellow. And the moon, all calm, casting her light without haste, streaked now and then by fine wisps of clouds, which she majestically allowed to fall around her shoulders; and the traffic-light meanwhile, always there, on and off, on and off, throbbing with a false vitality, but actually weary and enslaved.

He went back to see if the girl had admitted anything. Not on your life: no admission from her. In fact, she wasn't now the one who refused to admit; he was. The situation had changed completely, and it was she who kept saying to him: "Then you admit it?", and he kept saying no. A half hour went by like this. In the end, he admitted, or she did; anyway, Marcovaldo saw them get up and walk off, hand in hand.

He ran to the bench, flung himself on it; but meanwhile, in his waiting, he had lost some of his propensity to feel the sweetness he had been expecting to find there, and his bed at home, as he now remembered it, wasn't as hard as it had been. But these were minor points;

his determination to enjoy the night in the open air remained firm. He stuck his face in the pillow and prepared for sleep, the kind of sleep to which he had long become unaccustomed.

Now he had found the most comfortable position. He wouldn't have shifted a fraction of an inch for anything in the world. Too bad, though, that when he lay like this, his gaze didn't fall on a prospect of trees and sky alone, so that in sleep his eyes would close on a view of absolute natural serenity. Before him, foreshortened, a tree was followed by the sword of a general from the height of his monument, then another tree, a notice-board, a third tree, and then, a bit farther, that false, flashing moon, the traffic-light, still ticking off its yellow, yellow, yellow.

It must be said that Marcovaldo's nervous system had been in such poor shape lately that even when he was dead tired a trifle sufficed to keep him awake; he had only to think something was annoying him, and sleep was out of the question. And now he was annoyed by that traffic-light blinking on and off. It was there in the distance, a yellow eye, winking, alone: it was nothing to bother about. But Marcovaldo must have been suffering from nervous exhaustion: he stared at that blinking and repeated to himself: "How I would sleep if that thing wasn't there! How I would sleep!" He closed his eyes and seemed to feel, under his eyelids, that silly yellow blinking; he screwed his eyes shut and he could see dozens of traffic-lights; he reopened his eyes, it was the same thing all over again.

He got up. He had to put some screen between himself and the traffic-light. He went as far as the general's monument and looked around. At the foot of the monument there was a laurel wreath, nice and thick, but now dry and coming apart, standing on props, with a broad, faded ribbon: *"The 15th Lancers on the Anniversary of The Glorious Victory."* Marcovaldo climbed up on the pedestal, raised the wreath, and hung it on the general's sabre.

Tornaquinci, the night watchman, making his rounds, crossed the square on his bicycle; Marcovaldo hid behind the statue. Tornaquinci saw the shadow of the monument move on the ground: he stopped, filled with suspicion. He studied that wreath on the sabre: he realized something was out of place, but didn't know quite what. He aimed the beam of his flashlight up there; he read: *"The 15th Lancers on the Anniversary of The Glorious Victory."* He nodded approvingly and went away.

To give him time to go off, Marcovaldo made another turn around the square. In a nearby street, a team of workmen was repairing a switch of the tram-track. At night, in the deserted streets, those little groups of men huddling in the glow of the welding torches, their voices ringing, then dying immediately, have a secret look, as of people preparing things the inhabitants of the daytime must never know. Marcovaldo approached, stood looking at the flame, the workmen's movements, with a somewhat embarrassed attention, his eyes growing smaller and smaller with sleepiness. He hunted for a cigarette in his pocket, to keep himself awake; but he had no matches. "Who'll give me a light?" he asked the workmen. "With this?" the man with the torch said, spraying a flurry of sparks.

Another workman stood up, handed him a lighted cigarette. "Do you work nights, too?"

"No, I work days," Marcovaldo said.

"Then what are you doing up at this time of night? We're about to quit."

He went back to the bench. He stretched out. Now the traffic-light was hidden from his eyes; he could fall asleep, at last.

He hadn't noticed the noise, before. Now, that buzz, like a grim, inhaling breath and an endless scraping and also a scratching, filled his ears completely. There is no sound more heart-rending than that of a welding torch, a kind of muffled scream. Without moving, huddled as he was on the bench, his face against the crumpled pillow, Marcovaldo could find no escape, and the noise continued to conjure up the scene illuminated by the gray flame scattering golden sparks all around, the men hunkered on the ground, smoked-glass vizors over their faces, the torch grasped in the hand shaken by a rapid tremor, the halo of shadow around the tool cart, at the tall trellis-like apparatus that reached the wires. He opened his eyes, turned on the bench, looked at the stars among the boughs. The insensitive sparrows continued sleeping up there among the leaves.

To fall asleep like a bird, to have a wing you could stick your head under, a world of branches suspended above the earthly world, barely glimpsed down below, muffled and remote. Once you begin rejecting your present state, there is no knowing where you can arrive. Now Marcovaldo, in order to sleep, needed something; but he himself didn't know quite what; at this point not even a genuine silence would have been enough. He had to have a basis of sound, softer than silence, a faint wind passing through the thick undergrowth of a forest, a murmur of water bubbling up and disappearing in a meadow.

He had an idea and he rose to his feet. It wasn't exactly an idea, because half-dazed by the sleepiness that filled him, he couldn't form any thought properly; but it was like a recollection that somewhere around there was something connected with the idea of water, with its loquacious and subdued flow.

In fact, there was a fountain, nearby, a distinguished work of sculpture and hydraulics, with nymphs, fauns, river gods, who enlaced jets, cascades, a play of water. Only it was dry: at night, in summer, since the aqueduct was functioning less, they turned it off. Marcovaldo wandered around for a little while like a sleep-walker; more by instinct than by reason he knew that a tub must have a tap. A man who has a good eye can find what he is looking for even with his eyes closed. He turned on the tap: from the conch-shells, from the beards, from the nostrils of the horses, great jets rose, the feigned caverns were cloaked in glistening mantles, and all this water resounded like the organ of a choir loft in the great empty square, with all the rustling and turbulence that water can create. The night watchman, Tornaquinci, was coming along again on his coal-black bicycle, thrusting his tickets under doorways, when he suddenly saw the whole fountain explode before his eyes like a liquid firework. He nearly fell off his seat.

Trying to open his eyes as little as possible, to retain that shred of sleep he felt he had grasped, Marcovaldo ran and flung himself again on the bench. There, now it was as if he lay on the bank of a stream, with the woods above him; he slept.

He dreamed of a dinner, the dish was covered as if to keep the pasta warm. He uncovered it and there was a dead mouse, which stank. He looked into his wife's plate: another dead mouse. Before his children, more mice, smaller, but also rotting. He uncovered the tureen and found a cat, belly in the air; and the stink woke him.

Not far away there was the garbage truck that passes at night to empty the garbage cans. He could make out in the dim glow from the headlights, the crane, cackling and jerking, the shadows of men standing on the top of the mountain of refuse, their hands guiding the receptacle attached to the pulley, emptying it into the truck, pounding it with blows of their shovels, their voices grim and jerky like the movement of the crane: "Higher . . . let it go . . . to hell with you . . .," with metallic clashes like opaque gongs, and then the engine picking up, slowly, only to stop a bit farther on, as the maneuver began all over again.

But by now Marcovaldo's sleep had reached a zone where sounds no longer arrived, and these, even so graceless and rasping, came as if muffled in a soft halo, perhaps because of the very consistency of the garbage packed into the trucks. It was the stink that kept him awake, the stink sharpened by an unbearable idea of stink, whereby even the sounds, those dampened and remote sounds, and the image, outlined against the light, of the truck with the crane didn't reach his mind as sound and sight but only as stink. And Marcovaldo was delirious, vainly pursuing with his nostrils' imagination the fragrance of a rose arbor.

The night watchman, Tornaquinci, felt sweat bathe his forehead as he glimpsed a human form running on all fours along a flower-bed, then saw it angrily rip up some buttercups, then disappear. But he thought it must have been either a dog, the responsibility of dog-catchers, or a hallucination, the responsibility of the alienist, or a were-wolf, the responsibility of God knows who but preferably not him; and he turned the corner.

Meanwhile, having gone back to his sleeping place, Marcovaldo pressed the bedraggled clump of buttercups to his nose, trying to fill his sense of smell to the brim with their perfume: but he could press very little from those almost odorless flowers. Still the fragrance of dew, of earth, and of trampled grass was already a great balm. He dis-pelled the obsession of garbage and slept. It was dawn.

His waking was a sudden explosion of sun-filled sky above his head, a sun that virtually obliterated the leaves, then restored them gradually to his half-blinded sight. But Marcovaldo could not stay because a shiver had made him jump up: the spatter of a hydrant, which the city gardeners use for watering the flowerbeds, made cold streams trickle down his clothes. And all around there were trams clamoring, trucks going to market, hand-carts, pickups, workers on motorbikes rushing to factories, and the blinds being rolled up at house windows whose panes were glittering. His mouth and eyes sticky, his back stiff and one hip bruised, bewildered, Marcovaldo rushed to work.

AUTUMN

3. The Municipal Pigeon

The routes birds follow, as they migrate southwards or northwards, in autumn or in spring, rarely cross the city. Their flights cleave the heavens high above the striped humps of fields and along the edge of woods; at one point they seem to follow the curving line of a river or the furrow of a valley; at another, the invisible paths of the wind. But they sheer off as soon as the range of a city's rooftops looms up before them.

And yet, once, a flight of autumn woodcock appeared in a street's slice of sky. And the only person to notice was Marcovaldo, who always walked with his nose in the air. He was on a little tricycle-truck, and seeing the birds he pedaled harder, as if he were chasing them, in the grip of a hunter's fantasy, though the only gun he had ever held was an army rifle.

And as he proceeded, his eyes on the flying birds, he found himself at an intersection, the light red, in the midst of the automobiles; and he came within a hair's breadth of being run over. As a traffic cop, his face purple, wrote name and address in a notebook, Marcovaldo sought again with his eyes those wings in the sky; but they had vanished.

At work, his fine brought him harsh reproaches.

"Can't you even get traffic-lights straight?" his foreman, Signor Viligelmo, shouted at him. "What were you looking at anyway, knuckle-head?"

"I was looking at a flight of woodcock . . ." he said.

"What?" Signor Viligelmo was an old man; his eyes glistened. And Marcovaldo told him the story.

"Saturday I'm going out with dog and gun!" the foreman said, full of vigor, now forgetting his outburst. "The migration's begun, up in the hills. Those birds were certainly scared off by the hunters up there, and they flew over the city . . ."

All that day Marcovaldo's brain ground and ground, like a mill. "Saturday, if the hills are full of hunters, as is quite likely, God knows how many woodcock will fly over the city. If I handle it right, Sunday I'll eat roast woodcock."

❋

The building where Marcovaldo lived had a flat roof, with wires strung for drying laundry. Marcovaldo climbed up there with three of his children, carrying a can of birdlime, a brush, and a sack of corn. While the children scattered kernels of corn everywhere, he spread birdlime on the parapets, the wires, the frames of the chimneypots. He put so much on that Filippetto, while he was playing, almost got stuck fast.

That night Marcovaldo dreamed of the roof dotted with fluttering, trapped woodcock. His wife, Domitilla, more greedy and lazy, dreamed of ducks already roasted, lying on the chimneys. His daughter Isolina, romantic, dreamed of humming-birds to decorate her hat. Michelino dreamed of finding a stork up there.

The next day, every hour one of the children went up to inspect the roof: he would just peek out from the trap-door so, if they were about to alight, they wouldn't be scared; then he would come down and report. The reports were not good. But then, towards noon, Pietruccio came back, shouting: "They're here! Papà! Come and see!"

Marcovaldo went up with a sack. Trapped in the birdlime there was a poor pigeon, one of those gray urban doves, used to the crowds and racket of the squares. Fluttering around, other pigeons contemplated him sadly, as he tried to unstick his wings from the mess on which he had unwisely lighted.

Marcovaldo and his family were sucking the little bones of that thin and stringy pigeon, which had been roasted, when they heard a knocking at the door.

It was the landlady's maid. "The Signora wants you! Come at once!"

Very concerned, because he was six months behind with the rent and feared eviction, Marcovaldo went to the Signora's apartment, on the main floor. As he entered the living room, he saw that there was already a visitor: the purple-faced cop.

"Come in, Marcovaldo," the Signora said. "I am informed that on our roof someone is trapping the city's pigeons. Do you know anything about it?"

Marcovaldo felt himself freeze.

"Signora! Signora!" a woman's voice cried at that moment.

"What is it, Guendalina?"

The laundress came in. "I went up to hang out the laundry, and all the wash is stuck to the lines. I pulled on it, to get it loose, but it tore. Everything's ruined. What can it be?"

Marcovaldo rubbed his hand over his stomach, as if his digestion were giving him trouble.

WINTER

4. The City Lost in the Snow

That morning the silence woke him. Marcovaldo pulled himself out of bed with the sensation there was something strange in the air. He couldn't figure out what time it was, the light between the slats of the blinds was different from all other hours of day and night. He opened the window: the city was gone; it had been replaced by a white sheet of paper. Narrowing his eyes, he could make out, in the whiteness, some almost-erased lines, which corresponded to those of the familiar view: the windows and the roofs and the lamp-posts all around, but they were lost under all the snow that had settled over them during the night.

"Snow!" Marcovaldo cried to his wife; that is, he meant to cry, but his voice came out muffled. As it had fallen on lines and colors and views, the snow had fallen on noises, or rather on the very possibility of making noise; sounds, in a padded space, did not vibrate.

He went to work on foot; the trams were blocked by the snow. Along the street, making his own path, he felt free as he had never felt before. In the city all differences between sidewalk and street had vanished; vehicles could not pass, and Marcovaldo, even if he sank up to his thighs at every step and felt the snow get inside his socks, had become master, free to walk in the middle of the street, to trample on flower-beds, to cross outside the prescribed lines, to proceed in a zig-zag.

Streets and avenues stretched out, endless and deserted, like blanched chasms between mountainous cliffs. There was no telling whether the city hidden under that mantle was still the same or whether, in the night, another had taken its place. Who could say if under those white mounds there were still gasoline pumps, news-stands, tram stops, or if there were only sack upon sack of snow? As he walked along, Marcovaldo dreamed of getting lost in a different city: instead, his footsteps were taking him straight to his everyday place of work, the usual shipping department, and, once he had crossed the threshold, the worker was amazed at finding himself among those walls, the same as ever, as if the change that had cancelled the outside world had spared only his firm.

There, waiting for him, was a shovel, taller than he was. The department foreman, Signor Viligelmo, handing it to him, said: "Shoveling the snow off the sidewalk in front of the building is up to us. To you, that is." Marcovaldo took the shovel and went outside again.

Shoveling snow is no game, especially on an empty stomach; but Marcovaldo felt the snow was a friend, an element that erased the cage of walls which imprisoned his life. And he set to work with a will, sending great shovelfuls of snow flying from the sidewalk to the center of the street.

The jobless Sigismondo was also filled with gratitude for the snow, because having enrolled in the ranks of the municipal snow-shovelers that morning, he now had before him a few days of guaranteed employment. But this feeling, instead of inspiring in him vague fantasies like Marcovaldo's, led him to quite specific calculations, to determine how many cubic feet of snow had to be shoveled to clear so many square feet. In other words, he aimed at impressing the captain of his team; and thus — his secret ambition — at getting ahead in the world.

Now Sigismondo turned, and what did he see? The stretch of road he had just cleared was being covered again with snow, by the helter-skelter shoveling of a character panting there on the sidewalk. Sigismondo almost had a fit. He ran and confronted the other man, thrusting at the stranger's chest his shovel piled high with snow. "Hey, you! Are you the one who's been throwing that snow there?"

"Eh? What?" Marcovaldo started, but admitted, "Ah, maybe I am."

"Well, either you take it right back with your shovel, or I'll make you eat it, down to the last flake."

"But I have to clear the sidewalk."

"And I have to clear the street. So?"

"Where'll I put it?"

"Do you work for the City?"

"No. For Sbav and Co."

Sigismondo taught him how to pile up the snow along the edge of the sidewalk, and Marcovaldo cleared his whole stretch. Content, sticking their shovels into the snow, the two men stood and contemplated their achievement.

"Got a butt?" Sigismondo asked.

They were lighting half a cigarette apiece, when a snowplow came along the street, raising two big white waves that fell at either side. Every sound that morning was a mere rustle: by the time the men raised their heads, the whole section they had shoveled was again covered with snow. "What happened? Has it started snowing again?" And they looked up at the sky. The machine, spinning its huge brushes, was already turning at the corner.

Marcovaldo learned to pile the snow into a compact little wall. If he went on making little walls like that, he could build some streets for himself alone; only he would know where those streets led, and everybody else would be lost there. He could remake the city, pile up mountains high as houses, which no one would be able to tell from real houses. But perhaps by now all the houses had turned to snow, inside and out; a whole city of snow with monuments and spires and trees, a city that could be unmade by shovel and remade in a different way.

On the edge of the sidewalk at a certain point there was a considerable heap of snow. Marcovaldo was about to level it to the height of his little walls when he realized it was an automobile: the de-luxe car of Commendatore Alboino, chairman of the board, all covered with snow. Since the difference between an automobile and a pile of snow was so slight, Marcovaldo began creating the form of an automobile with his shovel. It came out well: you really couldn't tell which of the two was real. To put the final touches on his work Marcovaldo used some rubbish that had turned up in his shovel: a rusted tin served to model the shape of a headlight; an old tap gave the door its handle.

A great bowing and scraping of doormen, attendants and flunkies, and the chairman, Commendatore Alboino, came out of the main entrance. Short-sighted and efficient, he strode straight to his car, grasped the protruding tap, pulled it down, bowed his head, and stepped into the pile of snow up to his neck.

Marcovaldo had already turned the corner and was shoveling in the courtyard.

The boys in the yard had made a snow man. "He needs a nose!" one of them said. "What'll we use? A carrot!" And they ran to their various kitchens to hunt among the vegetables.

Marcovaldo contemplated the snow man. "There, under, the snow you can't tell what is snow and what is only covered. Except in one case: man; because it's obvious I am I and not this man here."

Absorbed in his meditations, he didn't hear two men shouting from the rooftop: "Hey, mister, get out of the way!" They were the men responsible for pushing the snow off the roof-tiles. And all of a sudden, about three hundredweight of snow fell right on top of him.

The children returned with their looted carrots. "Oh, they've made another snow man!" In the courtyard there were two identical dummies, side by side.

"We'll give them each a nose!" And they thrust carrots into the heads of the two snow men.

More dead than alive, Marcovaldo, through the sheath in which he was buried and frozen, felt some nourishment reach him. And he chewed on it.

"Hey, look! The carrot's gone!" The children were very frightened.

The bravest of the boys didn't lose heart. He had a spare nose: a pepper, and he stuck it into the snow man. The snow man ate that, too.

Then they tried giving him a nose made out of coal, a big lump. Marcovaldo spat it out with all his might. "Help! He's alive! He's alive!" The children ran away.

In a corner of the courtyard there was a grille from which a cloud of warmth emerged. With the heavy tread of a snow man, Marcovaldo went and stood there. The snow melted over him, trickled in rivulets down his clothes: a Marcovaldo reappeared, all swollen and stuffed up with a cold.

He took the shovel, mostly to warm himself, and began to work in the courtyard. There was a sneeze blocked at the top of his nose, all ready and waiting, but refusing to make up its mind and burst forth. Marcovaldo shoveled, his eyes half-closed, and the sneeze remained nested in the top of his nose. All of a sudden: the "Aaaaaah . . ." was almost a roar, and the "choo!" was louder than the explosion of a mine. The blast flung Marcovaldo against the wall.

Blast, indeed: that sneeze had caused a genuine tornado. All the snow in the courtyard rose and whirled in a blizzard, drawn upwards, pulverized in the sky.

When Marcovaldo reopened his eyes, after being stunned, the courtyard was completely cleared, with not even one flake of snow. And to his gaze there appeared the familiar courtyard, the gray walls, the boxes from the warehouse, the things of every day, sharp and hostile.

Emily Carter

Glory Goes and Gets Some is Emily Carter's first book of fiction, a collection of twenty-one stories built around the voice and perceptions of her alter ego, Glory B. Like Glory B., Carter is HIV positive, and the drama that fuels these stories is the struggle of the ex-addict to adapt to the new conditions of a life without drugs and alcohol, the controlled life of the detox center and halfway house. Certainly there is a strong autobiographical element in these stories, but it is instructive to see how the author has gone beyond recording the facts of her own life and created a strong and utterly original voice to inform her fiction. "Glory," she has said, "is my megaphone, my mouthpiece, she can utter things that I dare not and she is probably more ruthlessly honest in her declarations than I am. . . . She's like me with Tourette's Syndrome." Glory's voice, the motive force behind these linked stories, which bear comparison with Mary Gaitskill's, is never self-pitying or maudlin. The voice is poetic, imaginative, infused with a dark humor and an edge of danger.

Typical is the first selection here, "East on Houston," the opening story of *Glory Goes and Gets Some*. It begins with a simple statement of fact — "There was this one summer that began in June and ended quite some time later, when I could hear the voices of men in traffic, while I was walking east on Houston" — and becomes increasingly fanciful, so that the voices Glory is hearing are ever darker and more surreal and always accompanied by the refrain, "Excuse me Miss." Carter brilliantly evokes that moment of sexual power and youthful vulnerability when every possibility hangs in the balance. "But I knew what I was walking into," Glory says, "and what I was listening for all along, and how after I heard it I couldn't hear much of anything else for a long time. I don't want to go back there. I only ever think about it when I hear the sound of screeching brakes." The second piece here, "Parachute Silk," employs the same direct conversational tone ("All right then, I'll make a list, one list with two separate headings: Things I Will Never Do, and Things I Would Never Do"), making use of the central, multivalent image of the parachute to explore what it is like to fall free of one life and into another more constrained and cautious one.

East on Houston

There was this one summer that began in June and ended quite some time later, when I could hear the voices of men in traffic, while I was walking east on Houston. They honked and squealed, barked, drawled, groaned, purred, hissed, whispered, and raggedly begged at me as I twitched down the street in a borrowed dress that was as red as the stoplights, the stoplights gleaming in the black air like costume jewelry from a sunken Spanish galleon, gleaming from the bottom of the sea: the night on Houston like a black tropical shipwreck ocean, fathoms deep and full of trinkets for a young girl like yours-ever-true.

Their voices glittered like tossed beer cans on traffic islands and said, Excuse me Miss, excuse me, can I walk you? Excuse me, excuse me Miss, those are some fine young thighs you're sliding along on there, with that creamy swish-swish, sweet, like my wife's when she was still walking. If I call her collect this one last — I'm going to tell her this time that I really mean it, this time, she'll forget about all the hours that piled up like stale blankets until she couldn't get out of bed, and we'll go to that place in Sheepshead, we'll go to that place that serves that crab with the butter sauce you could just about make love to, and you've got those exact same thighs, Miss, just slow them down a little because I'll tell you what, you haven't seen anything yet.

Their voices reflected me in pieces of what they saw, like shattered Christmas ornaments on the sand in July: Excuse me Miss. You can stop can't you, you can spare one second, can't you? Can't you, you little cunt? You little stuck-up cunt? Think it's made of gold or what? All you cunts — don't even care what it was a man used to do for you, it's all what can you do for me right now. From watching too much television, that right-now thing — you've even got it in your walk, you walk like "right-now, right-now" . . . you don't care, do you, what I used . . . I used to . . . I used to know the first four hundred pages of the *Iliad* by heart, memorized, I could quote it from memory, fine, fine, keep walkin', you ugly at any rate.

Do I remember what it was exactly I was walking into when I was walking east on that particular street? Nothing good, but listen, the voices of men lifted me like a murmuring tide and floated me down toward the river, me with my eyeliner making my eyes black and green, smeared, shaped like tears, like black and green chalk-drawing eyes running in the rain.

I was moist, like the sky before a shower, and the voices of men clamored to me like a summer thunderstorm — Excuse me Miss, they cracked, they lit up the sky, Excuse me Miss, but I'm a jazz musician. They blew around me like a light breeze. Excuse me Miss, but do you know how to get to that little place on the end of First and A? What I mean is, I feel a little awkward in this neighborhood, and I'd like to bring something back to show my friends, something I could give a bath and brush its hair, something to lick like a sweet poison plum, something that would climb out my fire escape in the morning and never ask to see my bank statement — I heard them say things like that. Excuse me Miss, but I'm a jazz musician. I heard them clacking their knees together, heard them say, Excuse me Miss, I'm tired and I'm no longer a young stud by any means, but if I could touch the hollow of your ankle, if I could just once see it filled with rainwater, I'd smile like a wolf and bring you something wrestled from the concrete with my bare hands, my hands stained yellow with cigarettes and strength — hell, I'd wrestle the lights off the Chrysler building if you'd just let me look at it, even though I have no teeth.

And that guy, who was always there, with his broken instrument: Excuse me Miss, but I'm a jazz, excuse me, excuse me Miss, but I used to play with Parker, Miss, excuse me, but I'm a jazz musician, and I'm talking to you . . . I heard them say it, their voices twining around, through the pointed scrawny leaves of the plane trees, around the twigs and paper cups at my feet: Excuse me Miss, but my mother was a knife-sharp, slender blue dragon, she spat white hot fire from her eyes, like lasers, and her teeth were shaped like needles, twelve feet long, her scales like sapphires; when she flew overhead she cast a shadow across the face of the sun, her talons were made of black steel, and she would have called you a bitch because you won't talk to me, Miss.

It seems to me now like I had been on roller skates, young enough to slide in and out of traffic, in between taxis and trucks. But I knew what I was walking into, and what I was listening for all along, and how after I heard it I couldn't hear much of anything else for a long time. I don't want to go back there. I only ever think about it when I hear the sound of screeching brakes.

Parachute Silk

All right then, I'll make a list, one list with two separate headings: Things I Will Never Do, and Things I Would Never Do. The Things I Will Never Do preserve my sense of sorrow; the Things I Would Never Do preserve my sense of dignity. My sense of humor preserves itself, like a ghastly, encephalic curio sitting on a dusty shelf in the pitch-black basement of some madman's antique store. I wouldn't give it up, though, and you can put that under the Would Never heading — leaving space above it, naturally, for the more important things, like murder or boinking your best friend's sweetheart.

The Will Never list is much longer than the Would Never; almost anything can give me an idea for an item. The red silk parachute that Matthew left on the porch, for instance, reminds me that I Will Never jump out of an airplane, but that's a doubleheader — I Would Never jump out of an airplane, either. It's a conscious decision, one of the easier ones I've had to make. What kind of person would do that, and what do they get out of it, except a sense of relief when the thing opens correctly?

I'm already relieved, thank you, and — considering what I've done to myself — happy to be alive, if somewhat cranky in the mornings. I'm cranky in the mornings because at night, when I turn out my lights, when, according to my recovery counselor, you're supposed to concentrate on positive, relaxing images, what I get instead is a sort of cavalcade of hits: Gloria's Most Painful and Embarrassing Moments on Parade. It's especially bad if I remember all the times I made a fool of myself when I was drunk. Once that starts, I can be up for hours, snapping to my memories, "Go away." Just imagine some woman you saw in a bar once, hair tumbled and greasy, eye makeup hopeful the day before yesterday, loudly tossing inappropriate remarks into the closed circles of other people's conversations. Her charming and incisive bons mots land on the floor with an unpleasant splat, as if someone had just hurled a dead frog to the ground at your feet; you turn around, and there she is, smiling like the belle of the ball. If you wish she'd just go away, believe me, so do I. Here in Minnesota, Land of Ten Thousand Treatment Centers, they've got a program for any addiction you might care to name, but memories are something they can't do all that much about.

I didn't last that long as a rowdy drunkard, and when I switched to opiates at least I quieted down. In fact, I should quiet down right now and look over this list, which has gotten a little bit out of control. As a list, however, it's typical of me — Glory at her most self-centered, self-involved, self-pitying, and a list of other terms that start with my favorite word, "self."

My counselor had told me to write down a list of things that had to do with Matthew, who left the red parachute on my porch — what I felt good about, what I felt bad about. I've been out of the halfway house for over a year, but I still take my counselor's advice. If this list isn't quite what she had in mind, it's because I've always had a creative approach to advice-taking.

But for the moment I'll reject creativity; I'll just do what they say — Get Honest, Talk About My Feelings. What I feel most strongly at this moment is a desire not to think or talk about Matthew. His name said aloud embarrasses me. It's like something that happened when I was six or seven, when I was playing with puppets in the office of one of the innumerable kiddies' shrinks my baffled and worried parents were sending me to. Because the puppets were birds, I was putting them into a nest. The shrink looked at me and said, "You know, Gloria, why you're doing that? Because you want a nest, too. You want someplace where you can feel safe and warm." I was overcome with revulsion — I felt as if he'd just stuck his hand up my dress — and I decided I hadn't heard his comment. I'm bringing up that little childhood idyll to illustrate how the name Matthew makes me feel at this very moment. But I'm too big a girl now to go on playing with puppets, pretending not to hear something.

To make myself really uncomfortable, I could make a list of the things I valued about Matthew. The first was his lack of glamour. When we began to spend time together in the occupational-therapy room of Sunrise House, I remember thinking that if I had not been an addict I would never have been there, hanging out with some dark, overweight guy who wore sandals and socks like a tourist from the Netherlands. Never even mind the sweaters his mother sent him.

In the program, we had to make lists of our own character defects. There were certainly some things I despised about myself. Two of these were a desire to be liked and a desire to be glamorous. Matthew told me that my desire to be glamorous was only the made-for-TV version of my desire to be liked, but he didn't quite get what I was saying; I had trouble explaining to him how much I loathed my own idea of what constituted glamour. That idea was by no means an unusual one: Like so many other kids gone wrong from my time, place, and class, I thought it glamorous to be self-destructive. Unfortunately, I had also always known that this was a stupid and callow way to think. I knew that self-destruction was a vile method of slumming; I knew that there were people who got destroyed whether or not they wanted to. Here was Glory, beloved baby girl of professional parents, going into neighborhoods her great-grandfather had worked all his life to get his family out of, sniffing around for heroin, the opiate of the people. Marie Antoinette in her little peasant dress, Glory in her leather jacket. I knew all this, and yet I couldn't stop. Matthew had other reasons for being unable to stop, but eventually we both couldn't stop simply because we could not stop, and we wound up in the OT room pouring out molds of ceramic owls — lucky for us. I say "lucky" because I'm not so far gone that I don't know there are many, many worse places to end up and worse things to have to do than Occupational Therapy.

Matthew looked, to me, like the kind of kid nobody would socialize with in school, like I'd been. As a penance for having wanted to hang out with the cool kids, I attached myself to him. We stayed up as late as we could, drinking decaf out of Styrofoam cups and listening to Matthew's mix tapes on the tape recorder we snuck out of the office. The white fluorescent lamps overhead would hum, and eventually a night staffer would tell us to get to our rooms.

The staff told me to try to make friends with more women. I was a little insulted that they thought I hung out with Matthew because I couldn't get anybody better-looking to have an exclusive relationship with. Matthew would make me a tape every week, of songs from other tapes. From his selection of songs I would know, or think I knew, how he was feeling. How much did I really know, I wonder, about anything? I was thirty pounds overweight from the methadone I'd been on before and the antidepressants they had me on then. Between those and my AZT, I could hardly find my butt with both hands, as the old-timers like to say.

Eventually I became more lucid and ready for the outside world. Matthew did, too; armed with the Twelve Steps and our newly acquired Tools for Living, we graduated from the residence within days of each other. Matthew had asked me to come back to the House for his ceremony and be the one to give him his graduation medallion. But I was too busy: I'd dropped that thirty pounds by then and met a boy. At that point a boy wasn't much use to me, because of what I liked to call "my health status," but I was as excited as if every night were my first boy-girl movie date. If I kept things at that first-night level, I would not have to talk seriously with any boy about the risk of transmission; no one has to talk about condoms on a first date when she's sober.

Anyway, I sent Matthew a note instead. It was a charming note, of course, but so what? Put that on a list of things I would like to have among my memories but don't: giving Matthew his graduation medallion.

Matthew was back at work two weeks after he got out. He had that going for him: He might not have been the guy to get into the VIP lounge at some glitter-trash night club, but he was fit for the aspects of life that I feared the most. While I bounced around among different service jobs, learning how to complete tasks and show up on time, Matthew was working at InfoSystem as a computer-repair trouble-shooter. He'd worked for the head office in Detroit, and when he went into treatment his boss had gotten his insurance to pay for the cushiest among the many chemical-dependency centers that dot the Minnesota landscape. They'd held his position for him, then found him a transfer slot in the Cities. That was the kind of addict Matthew was: He'd used for five years before anybody was wise to him, and he was so good at his job that they overlooked the funds he'd fiddled. I admired him for his control, never having had any to speak of myself.

He said to me, "There's a lot of things about you that I admire, too, but they're probably not the things you would admire about yourself."

Some people don't like to be praised; apparently it makes them un-comfortable. I am not one of them. I like praise, and I like my praise specific, so I asked him, "What? What things?"

"I admire your ability to be someone I know well. That's not some-thing I can do that easily — be someone anybody knows well."

Matthew's job was to drive around the Cities to various InfoSystem offices and help them fix their computers when they went down, which they did on a daily basis. Around lunchtime he was usually parked in his blue office-issue van near the capitol. I was doing phone-survey work in a place right there on Rice and Marion, so I'd step into his van and we'd eat sandwiches together in the front seat.

Usually our conversations were interrupted when Matthew's car phone buzzed and he had to talk some panicked office employee through the steps needed to get the system back up. "Do you have your system disk?" he would ask, his voice like sleep. Then, never altering the com-forting lack of expression in his tone, he'd take them through all the logical procedures. "If anything else comes up, call me right back," he'd say, then he'd hang up the phone, looking away at the clumpy little skyline of downtown St. Paul.

"Do you have to do that on your lunch hour?" I asked him once, feeling foolish because I'd been in the middle of an animated bout of storytelling when the call came in.

"They're so scared when the system goes down," he said. "They're afraid they'll lose their jobs. I'm supposed to report all the calls, but I don't."

One evening in late March, Matthew showed up at my door with his latest mix tape and a bundle of things that he'd found in the closet of his new apartment. One of the things was the red silk parachute. "I thought you might want to use it for a bedspread, or a curtain," he said. "It reminds me of you."

In an uncharacteristic spasm of self-restraint, I didn't ask why. Instead, I suggested we take it outside on the porch.

It was windy that night, and not too cold — a miracle in Minnesota, where spring doesn't come until the very last minute. The next-door kids were still outside, clanking around on their one bike for the half-dozen of them. Looking down Dayton Avenue, Matthew and I could see the cathedral, with its oxidized-green dome looking like jade in the moon-white floodlights. The real moon floated above it, courteous and pale and distant, as a Minnesota moon would be. We held the chute over the side of the porch and the wind took it up with a definite, firm thunk. The red silk flew out, and we could feel it straining at our hands; it leaped and danced, like a flag. I had the feeling for a moment that we were sailing, Matthew and I, up over the cathedral. We weren't of course, and it wasn't really warm, so we went back inside. That's on the list for my counselor, that evening.

Another reason I valued Matthew was his honesty. Every single member of his family was in what is ominously referred to as "the program." They were in different branches of it, all over the country — branches that seemed to be growing and multiplying at a dazzling rate of speed: Overeaters Anonymous, Spenders Anonymous, Parents or Adult Children of Alcoholics Anonymous, Clutterers Anonymous, Love Addicts Anonymous, and, my personal favorite, Emotions Anonymous.

Matthew said to me, "Sometimes I get so sick of all this health."

I asked him if he wasn't grateful to be alive, didn't he want to live and be well. Standard party line, but sometimes it's all there is to work with.

"I am sometimes," he said. "But sometimes I'm not. Sometimes I have no gratitude at all."

I liked hearing that. That first six months, there were an awful lot of people I met who talked the talk, all the time. Their faces seemed to glow, and they'd go on about so-and-so "getting it," "getting" the program, having that much-touted aura of serenity about them. It was my experience that such persons usually relapsed and stole their roommate's stereo equipment, or charged five thousand dollars' worth of lingerie at Dayton's. Nobody gives up an addiction that easily, or it wouldn't be an addiction, just a problem. But it was easy to talk the talk. Everyone praised you and loved you to pieces if you could talk the talk. So Matthew's bleak words did not make me, as they say, "concerned." I just thought that in his own way he was braver than a lot of us and saying what we all were thinking. Besides, if there was anybody who tried to work those Twelve Simple Steps for Complicated People it was him.

That might have been one of the reasons I didn't get too concerned about his sex-addiction thing — pornography and prostitutes. I just didn't think the boy needed another Twelve-Step Program, and, to be honest, I refused to see what was so terrible about it. I just thought it was sad and creepy, but my frame of reference, when it came to men, told me that most men were, at heart, sad and creepy. He didn't beat the women up, he didn't harm them, so what was the need for yet another Anonymous group? Anyway, some men were just born to be customers: that's what a friend of mine, a former working girl, told me when I mentioned it. She is very tough, that woman is, the way I've always wanted to be.

The truth is, I thought it was funny when I found the stack of magazines in his bathroom. They were a little on the severe side, with piston shots and all the rest of it, but not the worst I'd ever seen. When I first got out of the House, I'd worked in a bookstore that had an adult section. At first, when I was sorting the magazines for stacking, I had looked at the glossy pictures, but they quickly grew boring; not a lot interested me in those early days except thinking about drugs. Certainly not sex, except as a possible means for procuring drugs, in case I decided to relapse. Matthew, though, when he realized he'd forgotten to remove the magazines from the bathroom, acted as if I'd found some kind of forensic evidence. The color went right out of his face, and I could see what he looked like when he was thinking up a lie. "They're my roommate's," he said.

It didn't seem like a big deal to me. But I went back in there before I left, and surreptitiously checked the dates: the magazines were all new, the very latest. There was about five hundred dollars' worth of pornography stacked up in his pink-tiled bathroom. Just one month's supply. When I mentioned it to his roommate, he said, "You should get a load of his video collection."

Matthew went to Sex Addicts Anonymous on Tuesday nights, but, as I recall, he never managed more than a month of abstinence. I tried to talk Twelve-Step with him. I tried it while we were laughing about something else, so I wouldn't sound fatuous: "Look, every time you pay some little hooker on University Avenue you're enabling an addict. I mean maybe there are some prostitutes who aren't chemically dependent, but no street-level tootsie — which, let's face it, is all you can afford — is out there for any other reason. You should be taking those girls to meetings."

I was not exactly on the mark with that one. Matthew didn't see them as addicts in need of recovery; he didn't see them at all. He told me it was just a thing he couldn't stop doing. "It seems like I get something out of making myself disgusting to myself. I mean, while I'm doing it, it feels good." I knew all about that, most certainly. "But you know me," he said. "You know that in real life I respect people." I knew about that, too — the loathsome thing about yourself that you refuse to let into your real life, because it isn't you, it isn't you at all.

I decided I didn't need to know about it. He didn't need to know everything about me, either. Your friends do not need to know everything about you. For instance, when my office pals would pick me up outside the Ramsey Medical Center on certain mornings to take me to work and save me an hour on the bus, I felt fine about just telling them I was seeing a dentist. Sometimes I was afraid that my prescription would fall out of my pocket and they'd recognize the name. That little drug is one medicine that gets a lot of press. It is the star, the celebrity, the Marilyn of medicines, so I made sure to keep its label tucked safely down in the lint-lined caverns of my old tweed coat.

Matthew, especially, I didn't feel like telling. When he asked me why I'd stopped seeing this or that boy, I gave him sardonic Twelve-Step jargon. "I didn't want to defocus off my own issues?" I said, lilting upward at the end of my sentence, imitating the passive-aggressive vocal patterns of a Minnesota treatment person. By inflecting your sentence as though it were a question you force the other person, rather than yourself, to take some kind of a stand. They can agree or disagree; you're merely asking questions. It's a somewhat manipulative manner of dialogue?

And that should go on my list — that I wish I'd told Matthew I was not at the dentist's.

Telling Matthew might not have made a difference to what he eventually did, but it would have made a difference to me. I like to see myself as someone who is honest and loyal to her friends, even if she sometimes lies to them. Matthew thought I was, which is why he didn't mind saying what he said that day in his van.

"What woman," he asked, "would go with me if I didn't pay her?"

We were listening to Matthew's latest tape. It was a collection of new folk-music bands. The vocalists were all women with gentle, quavering voices.

"That's ridiculous," I told him. "You're kind, you're decent, you've got a job, and you're very smart. Any woman would be proud to call you sweetie."

But that evening he came around to see if I could walk the walk as well as talk the talk. He'd bought a new sweater, and although it looked a bit like the sweaters his mother used to send him, it was a sweater that showed some daring. His mother's taste ran to pastels, with corporate-looking patterns worked into the textiles. This sweater was only one color, red, and it was made of some kind of yarn that did not look entirely synthetic.

I gave his shoulder a punch and said, "Come *on*. What *is* this?" Oh, I was getting good at Minnesota hide-and-seek. I knew exactly what he was doing.

"I want to take you out," he said, and his eyes rested on me, so pale-blue that they seemed gray. I felt that I was looking pale myself. I felt my old revulsion start up, the desire to keep on playing with the puppets and not hear what was being said.

"Matthew, I'm not sure that's a good idea? We have a very valuable friendship?"

"That's why it's a good idea. We've both been sober a year, and neither of us has been in what you could call a 'relationship.' So we could just, you know, just try it . . . Unless — " He didn't finish the unless, but I could have finished it for him: "Unless you were lying. Unless I really am disgusting to your eyes and the eyes of women."

I was having trouble — I *am* having trouble — thinking of myself as a "woman." Anyhow, I had plenty of reasons not to step out in a serious manner, with him or with anyone. The problem was that I didn't want to think about any of these particular reasons. I didn't want to think about the fact that I wasn't in tip-top relationship shape. I didn't want to tell him about my health status. There are some things that I Would Never tell anyone, and I didn't want to tell my friend Matthew anything at all. He was holding the flowers, and I could see them trembling gently, as if touched by a small draft.

"Matthew," I said, "it's probably not real sober behavior for me to start dating perverts."

Not that we never spoke to each other again, or anything so efficient, so tidy, as all that. I passed it off as a joke; he passed it off as passing insanity. But we didn't meet at lunchtime anymore, and if we talked on the phone one of us always had to hang up and do something pressing. Usually he was going to some kind of Meeting. He was starting to go to more and more different kinds. He was excited about one called No More Shame. I'd gone back to school, and I was making a lot of noise about how when you start living an actual life you don't have time to just endlessly hang out with people anymore.

It was the next spring when I last talked to Matthew on the telephone. He told me he was leaving to go set up a new line for InfoSystem in a city in Indonesia. I reminded him that Southeast Asia was where they manufactured his drug of choice, but he didn't seem concerned. I didn't press it; I hate to sound like some AA Aunt Nellie. Besides, I could tell from his hushed, gravelly-sounding voice that he had already slipped out of our little recovery community. Which is just something that happens: people come, they go, they leave town. Sometimes they come back, sometimes not. If I were a lounge singer, I'd name it "A Little Process Called Life."

Matthew's parents came to Minnesota from Sault Ste. Marie a few months after he'd left. They said they needed to straighten out some business, but I think they just wanted to see the place that he had told them about, back when he was telling them things. For three months, he hadn't told them, or anyone else, anything; he had asked them to take out some of his savings and send him a Western Union money order in June — and then nothing. They sat across from me at the coffee shop with their backs straight and their hands under the table. His father was wearing a sweater that had clearly been purchased by his wife. On his father it did not look at all out of place. He was a man with huge, bony hands — knuckles and sinew, planklike wrists. He said, "Matthew told us you and he liked to listen to music together. He loves music. I always thought he had interesting taste. Very sophisticated."

"Jim and I have been praying," his mother said. "Not for any results, but just for acceptance."

"And for Matthew to get well," his father added. "For Matthew to find some peace." I didn't point out the contradiction between this and his wife's "acceptance" remark. Instead, I tried to smile, as if we all knew the same prayers, and I kept looking at Matthew's father, who had put his arm behind his wife's shoulders. If Matthew ever came back, he would fit into his father's sweaters in about twenty years. Every time the shop door opened I shivered a little; the breeze went right through the chiffon blouse I was wearing. It was see-through, so I wore a tank top under it, insouciant and very fashionable. I'd seen it on all sorts of beautiful young girls, in restaurants and coffee shops all over town.

I seem to have trouble sticking to the list idea; my counselor would probably tell me to get some distance from it, go take a walk in the sun. Well, the sun is good for you only in small doses, but I'm making my peace with it. I no longer plot my walk to work exclusively along streets I know will be in the shade. I even sit on my porch in the daytime; it's a good porch, because it gets just a little sun, about twenty minutes in the late afternoon. Which is when the kids from next door come over to swing on my hammock and ask me questions. There are six of them, I think, but they seem like more because I can't keep their names straight. Their names are Cambodian, and I can't pronounce them. They're from the same region as Matthew's drug of choice, and mine, and yet they have come here; that should tell me something. I wish I were better at saying their names, but it's pretty clear at this point that I don't have much of an ear for language, and I can put that on the list: I Will Never learn to speak another language. It's not important, in this case, since these kids speak English, which is sometimes a bad thing, depending on what they have to tell me. For instance, when the oldest girl told me that she used to have a baby brother but a soldier swung him into a tree and cracked his head, I would have been perfectly happy if she hadn't known how to tell me this. All I could find to say was, "Are you sure?" She might have been making it up to get me to give her more crackers and jelly.

"Sure," she says. "That day, it was rain." But she's only thirteen years old, so maybe she won't have to keep seeing that picture at night, when her eyes are shut and she's trying to focus on positive, relaxing images, the way she'll surely learn to do — this being America, after all.

Her ten-year-old sister is too young to remember anything like that, but she enjoys punching people in the arm. A painful and annoying habit, but at least it usually distracts her from snooping around inside my house. Last week, she and the two boys came running out of my kitchen brandishing a half-empty container of AZT.

"Why you take medicine?" they shouted. "Are you sick?"

"Stay out of my kitchen!" I shouted back, making a grab for my tablets. "No. They're like vitamins. I take them so I won't get sick."

The girl, obviously the ringleader of the kitchen-snooping expedition, punched me in the arm. "You won't get sick," she said. "You're strong. You just have to let me punch you in the arm every day, and you won't get sick." I wish that were true. I'd still rather get punched in the arm every day than take drugs that don't get me high. It's unnatural as a concept, and frightening in its implication. And what if I have to put that, finally, on my list: I Will Never get high again.

Matthew probably had something like that on his list — something with the word "never" in it. It's no good to think like that, in such grandiose and sweeping language. I could have told him. It may be jargon, but it's true. It's better not to think in these agonized, religious extremes. Better to just break it down into smaller, more manageable units of time. The nice thing about small units of time is how they add up. I've added them up, so far, into two years, three months, four days, and right up into this minute, right now, on my porch, where I am watching these children play the parachute game, which is their favorite game because it involves an unlimited amount of shrieking, yelling, kicking, and bossing each other around.

It's a simple game. One by one, the kids crawl under the parachute, and I twist them up inside it. I roll them around and drape the fabric over them in labyrinthine folds until all that can be seen is a big pile of red silk, full of squealing lumps, and then I say, "Go!" The game is to get out while accidentally clocking as many of your brothers and sisters on the jaw as you possibly can. The silk never rips: it's designed to take on the wind in the sky; there's no chance a little kid is going to put a sneaker through it. When one emerges, he or she stands there yelling instructions to the ones still inside. "The other way, kick with your legs." As they begin to tumble out, they start to count: "That's two of us . . . That's four . . ." But the sixth and last, a tiny girl of three, can't find her way out. We can hear a thin, terrified wail coming from deep inside the red silk folds. The oldest girl, with a slight, hissing breath, goes to the parachute and unfolds it with quick, flinging motions, as if she were making a bed. In three seconds, the sixth and littlest is out, standing upright, silent, an embarrassed smile on her face, sparkling quietly like a candied plum.

Raymond Carver

The stories of Raymond Carver (1938–1988) fomented a revolution in American letters similar to the effect the work of certain seminal punk bands had on the epicene rock music of the late seventies. His stories took the postmodern epics of writers like Barth, Pynchon, Gardner, and Grass back down to ground zero, and his deceptively simple style, working-class characters, and economical approach gave rise to the realist/minimalist movement of the late seventies and early eighties. The twenty-two stories of *Will You Please Be Quiet, Please?* appeared in 1977 and were followed by 1981's *What We Talk About When We Talk About Love,* his most radical experiment with the stripped-down, minimalist story, and his masterwork, *Cathedral,* in 1983.

I haven't exactly held to the two-story format here. "The Bath," from *What We Talk About When We Talk About Love,* is an early version of the magisterial "A Small, Good Thing" from *Cathedral.* This is one of the few examples I can think of in which a writer has taken a finished, twice-published story (it appeared first in a periodical) and allowed it to blossom into something far more beautiful, richer, and deeper, and it is a telling exercise to compare the two versions. While "The Bath" and "A Small, Good Thing" are, at base, the same story, the evolution — one to the next — makes them different enough to include here as two.

In addition to his four major collections of short fiction — *Will You Please Be Quiet, Please?; What We Talk About When We Talk About Love; Cathedral;* and *Where I'm Calling From* — Carver published four books of poetry and a collection of fiction, poetry, and essays, *Fires.*

The Bath

Saturday afternoon the mother drove to the bakery in the shopping center. After looking through a loose-leaf binder with photographs of cakes taped onto the pages, she ordered chocolate, the child's favorite. The cake she chose was decorated with a spaceship and a launching pad under a sprinkling of white stars. The name SCOTTY would be iced on in green as if it were the name of the spaceship.

The baker listened thoughtfully when the mother told him Scotty would be eight years old. He was an older man, this baker, and he wore a curious apron, a heavy thing with loops that went under his arms and around his back and then crossed in front again where they were tied in a very thick knot. He kept wiping his hands on the front of the apron as he listened to the woman, his wet eyes examining her lips as she studied the samples and talked.

He let her take her time. He was in no hurry.

The mother decided on the spaceship cake, and then she gave the baker her name and her telephone number. The cake would be ready Monday morning, in plenty of time for the party Monday afternoon. This was all the baker was willing to say. No pleasantries, just this small exchange, the barest information, nothing that was not necessary.

Monday morning, the boy was walking to school. He was in the company of another boy, the two boys passing a bag of potato chips back and forth between them. The birthday boy was trying to trick the other boy into telling what he was going to give in the way of a present.

At an intersection, without looking, the birthday boy stepped off the curb, and was promptly knocked down by a car. He fell on his side, his head in the gutter, his legs in the road moving as if he were climbing a wall.

The other boy stood holding the potato chips. He was wondering if he should finish the rest or continue on to school.

The birthday boy did not cry. But neither did he wish to talk anymore. He would not answer when the other boy asked what it felt like to be hit by a car. The birthday boy got up and turned back for home, at which time the other boy waved good-bye and headed off for school.

The birthday boy told his mother what had happened. They sat to-gether on the sofa. She held his hands in her lap. This is what she was doing when the boy pulled his hands away and lay down on his back.

Of course, the birthday party never happened. The birthday boy was in the hospital instead. The mother sat by the bed. She was waiting for the boy to wake up. The father hurried over from his office. He sat next to the mother. So now the both of them waited for the boy to wake up. They waited for hours, and then the father went home to take a bath.

The man drove home from the hospital. He drove the streets faster than he should. It had been a good life till now. There had been work, fatherhood, family. The man had been lucky and happy. But fear made him want a bath.

He pulled into the driveway. He sat in the car trying to make his legs work. The child had been hit by a car and he was in the hospital, but he was going to be all right. The man got out of the car and went up to the door. The dog was barking and the telephone was ringing. It kept ringing while the man unlocked the door and felt the wall for the light switch.

He picked up the receiver. He said, "I just got in the door!"

"There's a cake that wasn't picked up."

This is what the voice on the other end said.

"What are you saying?" the father said.

"The cake," the voice said. "Sixteen dollars."

The husband held the receiver against his ear, trying to understand. He said, "I don't know anything about it."

"Don't hand me that," the voice said.

The husband hung up the telephone. He went into the kitchen and poured himself some whiskey. He called the hospital.

The child's condition remained the same.

While the water ran into the tub, the man lathered his face and shaved. He was in the tub when he heard the telephone again. He got himself out and hurried through the house, saying, "Stupid, stupid," because he wouldn't be doing this if he'd stayed where he was in the hospital. He picked up the receiver and shouted, "Hello!"

The voice said, "It's ready."

The father got back to the hospital after midnight. The wife was sit-ting in the chair by the bed. She looked up at the husband and then she looked back at the child. From an apparatus over the bed hung a bottle with a tube running from the bottle to the child.

"What's this?" the father said.

"Glucose," the mother said.

The husband put his hand to the back of the woman's head.

"He's going to wake up," the man said.

"I know," the woman said.

In a little while the man said, "Go home and let me take over."

She shook her head. "No," she said.

"Really," he said. "Go home for a while. You don't have to worry. He's sleeping, is all."

A nurse pushed open the door. She nodded to them as she went to the bed. She took the left arm out from under the covers and put her fingers on the wrist. She put the arm back under the covers and wrote on the clipboard attached to the bed.

"How is he?" the mother said.

"Stable," the nurse said. Then she said, "Doctor will be in again shortly."

"I was saying maybe she'd want to go home and get a little rest," the man said. "After the doctor comes."

"She could do that," the nurse said.

The woman said, "We'll see what the doctor says." She brought her hand up to her eyes and leaned her head forward.

The nurse said, "Of course."

The father gazed at his son, the small chest inflating and deflating under the covers. He felt more fear now. He began shaking his head. He talked to himself like this. The child is fine. Instead of sleeping at home, he's doing it here. Sleep is the same wherever you do it.

The doctor came in. He shook hands with the man. The woman got up from the chair.

"Ann," the doctor said and nodded. The doctor said, "Let's just see how he's doing." He moved to the bed and touched the boy's wrist. He peeled back an eyelid and then the other. He turned back the covers and listened to the heart. He pressed his fingers here and there on the body. He went to the end of the bed and studied the chart. He noted the time, scribbled on the chart, and then he considered the mother and the father.

This doctor was a handsome man. His skin was moist and tan. He wore a three-piece suit, a vivid tie, and on his shirt were cufflinks.

The mother was talking to herself like this. He has just come from somewhere with an audience. They gave him a special medal.

The doctor said, "Nothing to shout about, but nothing to worry about. He should wake up pretty soon." The doctor looked at the boy again. "We'll know more after the tests are in."

"Oh, no," the mother said.

The doctor said, "Sometimes you see this."

The father said, "You wouldn't call this a coma, then?"

The father waited and looked at the doctor.

"No, I don't want to call it that," the doctor said. "He's sleeping. It's restorative. The body is doing what it has to do."

"It's a coma," the mother said. "A kind of coma."

The doctor said, "I wouldn't call it that."

He took the woman's hands and patted them. He shook hands with the husband.

The woman put her fingers on the child's forehead and kept them there for a while. "At least he doesn't have a fever," she said. Then she said, "I don't know. Feel his head."

The man put his fingers on the boy's forehead. The man said, "I think he's supposed to feel this way."

The woman stood there awhile longer, working her lip with her teeth. Then she moved to her chair and sat down.

The husband sat in the chair beside her. He wanted to say something else. But there was no saying what it should be. He took her hand and put it in his lap. This made him feel better. It made him feel he was saying something. They sat like that for a while, watching the boy, not talking. From time to time he squeezed her hand until she took it away.

"I've been praying," she said.

"Me too," the father said. "I've been praying too."

A nurse came back in and checked the flow from the bottle.

A doctor came in and said what his name was. This doctor was wearing loafers.

"We're going to take him downstairs for more pictures," he said. "And we want to do a scan."

"A scan?" the mother said. She stood between this new doctor and the bed.

"It's nothing," he said.

"My God," she said.

Two orderlies came in. They wheeled a thing like a bed. They unhooked the boy from the tube and slid him over onto the thing with wheels.

It was after sunup when they brought the birthday boy back out. The mother and father followed the orderlies into the elevator and up to the room. Once more the parents took up their places next to the bed.

They waited all day. The boy did not wake up. The doctor came again and examined the boy again and left after saying the same things again. Nurses came in. Doctors came in. A technician came in and took blood.

"I don't understand this," the mother said to the technician.

"Doctor's orders," the technician said.

The mother went to the window and looked out at the parking lot. Cars with their lights on were driving in and out. She stood at the window with her hands on the sill. She was talking to herself like this. We're into something now, something hard.

She was afraid.

She saw a car stop and a woman in a long coat get into it. She made believe she was that woman. She made believe she was driving away from here to someplace else.

The doctor came in. He looked tanned and healthier than ever. He went to the bed and examined the boy. He said, "His signs are fine. Everything's good."

The mother said, "But he's sleeping."

"Yes," the doctor said.

The husband said, "She's tired. She's starved."

The doctor said, "She should rest. She should eat. Ann," the doctor said.

"Thank you," the husband said.

He shook hands with the doctor and the doctor patted their shoulders and left.

"I suppose one of us should go home and check on things," the man said. "The dog needs to be fed."

"Call the neighbors," the wife said. "Someone will feed him if you ask them to."

She tried to think who. She closed her eyes and tried to think anything at all. After a time she said, "Maybe I'll do it. Maybe if I'm not here watching, he'll wake up. Maybe it's because I'm watching that he won't."

"That could be it," the husband said.

"I'll go home and take a bath and put on something clean," the woman said.

"I think you should do that," the man said.

She picked up her purse. He helped her into her coat. She moved to the door, and looked back. She looked at the child, and then she looked at the father. The husband nodded and smiled.

She went past the nurses' station and down to the end of the corridor, where she turned and saw a little waiting room, a family in there, all sitting in wicker chairs, a man in a khaki shirt, a baseball cap pushed back on his head, a large woman wearing a housedress, slippers, a girl in jeans, hair in dozens of kinky braids, the table littered with flimsy wrappers and styrofoam and coffee sticks and packets of salt and pepper.

"Nelson," the woman said. "Is it about Nelson?"

The woman's eyes widened.

"Tell me now, lady," the woman said. "Is it about Nelson?"

The woman was trying to get up from her chair. But the man had his hand closed over her arm.

"Here, here," the man said.

"I'm sorry," the mother said. "I'm looking for the elevator. My son is in the hospital. I can't find the elevator."

"Elevator is down that way," the man said, and he aimed a finger in the right direction.

"My son was hit by a car," the mother said. "But he's going to be all right. He's in shock now, but it might be some kind of coma too. That's what worries us, the coma part. I'm going out for a little while. Maybe I'll take a bath. But my husband is with him. He's watching. There's a chance everything will change when I'm gone. My name is Ann Weiss."

The man shifted in his chair. He shook his head.

He said, "Our Nelson."

She pulled into the driveway. The dog ran out from behind the house. He ran in circles on the grass. She closed her eyes and leaned her head against the wheel. She listened to the ticking of the engine.

She got out of the car and went to the door. She turned on lights and put on water for tea. She opened a can and fed the dog. She sat down on the sofa with her tea.

The telephone rang.

"Yes!" she said. "Hello!" she said.

"Mrs. Weiss," a man's voice said.

"Yes," she said. "This is Mrs. Weiss. Is it about Scotty?" she said.

"Scotty," the voice said. "It is about Scotty," the voice said. "It has to do with Scotty, yes."

A Small, Good Thing

Saturday afternoon she drove to the bakery in the shopping center. After looking through a loose-leaf binder with photographs of cakes taped onto the pages, she ordered chocolate, the child's favorite. The cake she chose was decorated with a space ship and launching pad under a sprinkling of white stars, and a planet made of red frosting at the other end. His name, SCOTTY, would be in green letters beneath the planet. The baker, who was an older man with a thick neck, listened without saying anything when she told him the child would be eight years old next Monday. The baker wore a white apron that looked like a smock. Straps cut under his arms, went around in back and then to the front again, where they were secured under his heavy waist. He wiped his hands on his apron as he listened to her. He kept his eyes down on the photographs and let her talk. He let her take her time. He'd just come to work and he'd be there all night, baking, and he was in no real hurry.

She gave the baker her name, Ann Weiss, and her telephone number. The cake would be ready on Monday morning, just out of the oven, in plenty of time for the child's party that afternoon. The baker was not jolly. There were no pleasantries between them, just the minimum exchange of words, the necessary information. He made her feel uncomfortable, and she didn't like that. While he was bent over the counter with the pencil in his hand, she studied his coarse features and wondered if he'd ever done anything else with his life besides be a baker. She was a mother and thirty-three years old, and it seemed to her that everyone, especially someone the baker's age — a man old enough to be her father — must have children who'd gone through this special time of cakes and birthday parties. There must be that between them, she thought. But he was abrupt with her — not rude, just abrupt. She gave up trying to make friends with him. She looked into the back of the bakery and could see a long, heavy wooden table with aluminum pie pans stacked at one end, and beside the table a metal container filled with empty racks. There was an enormous oven. A radio was playing country-Western music.

The baker finished printing the information on the special order card and closed up the binder. He looked at her and said, "Monday morning." She thanked him and drove home.

On Monday morning, the birthday boy was walking to school with another boy. They were passing a bag of potato chips back and forth and the birthday boy was trying to find out what his friend intended to give him for his birthday that afternoon. Without looking, the birthday boy stepped off the curb at an intersection and was immediately knocked down by a car. He fell on his side with his head in the gutter and his legs out in the road. His eyes were closed, but his legs moved back and forth as if he were trying to climb over something. His friend dropped the potato chips and started to cry. The car had gone a hundred feet or so and stopped in the middle of the road. The man in the driver's seat looked back over his shoulder. He waited until the boy got unsteadily to his feet. The boy wobbled a little. He looked dazed, but okay. The driver put the car into gear and drove away.

The birthday boy didn't cry, but he didn't have anything to say about anything either. He wouldn't answer when his friend asked him what it felt like to be hit by a car. He walked home, and his friend went on to school. But after the birthday boy was inside his house and was telling his mother about it — she sitting beside him on the sofa, holding his hands in her lap, saying, "Scotty, honey, are you sure you feel all right, baby?" thinking she would call the doctor anyway — he suddenly lay back on the sofa, closed his eyes, and went limp. When she couldn't wake him up, she hurried to the telephone and called her husband at work. Howard told her to remain calm, remain calm, and then he called an ambulance for the child and left for the hospital himself.

Of course, the birthday party was canceled. The child was in the hospital with a mild concussion and suffering from shock. There'd been vomiting, and his lungs had taken in fluid which needed pumping out that afternoon. Now he simply seemed to be in a very deep sleep — but no coma, Dr. Francis had emphasized, no coma, when he saw the alarm in the parents' eyes. At eleven o'clock that night, when the boy seemed to be resting comfortably enough after the many X-rays and the lab work, and it was just a matter of his waking up and coming around, Howard left the hospital. He and Ann had been at the hospital with the child since that afternoon, and he was going home for a short while to bathe and change clothes. "I'll be back in an hour," he said. She nodded. "It's fine," she said. "I'll be right here." He kissed her on the forehead, and they touched hands. She sat in the chair beside the bed and looked at the child. She was waiting for him to wake up and be all right. Then she could begin to relax.

Howard drove home from the hospital. He took the wet, dark streets very fast, then caught himself and slowed down. Until now, his life had gone smoothly and to his satisfaction — college, marriage, another year of college for the advanced degree in business, a junior partnership in an investment firm. Fatherhood. He was happy and, so far, lucky — he knew that. His parents were still living, his brothers and his sister were established, his friends from college had gone out to take their places in the world. So far, he had kept away from any real harm, from those forces he knew existed and that could cripple or bring down a man if the luck went bad, if things suddenly turned. He pulled into the driveway and parked. His left leg began to tremble. He sat in the car for a minute and tried to deal with the present situation in a rational manner. Scotty had been hit by a car and was in the hospital, but he was going to be all right. Howard closed his eyes and ran his hand over his face. He got out of the car and went up to the front door. The dog was barking inside the house. The telephone rang and rang while he unlocked the door and fumbled for the light switch. He shouldn't have left the hospital, he shouldn't have. "Goddamn it!" he said. He picked up the receiver and said, "I just walked in the door!"

"There's a cake here that wasn't picked up," the voice on the other end of the line said.

"What are you saying?" Howard asked.

"A cake," the voice said. "A sixteen-dollar cake."

Howard held the receiver against his ear, trying to understand. "I don't know anything about a cake," he said. "Jesus, what are you talking about?"

"Don't hand me that," the voice said.

Howard hung up the telephone. He went into the kitchen and poured himself some whiskey. He called the hospital. But the child's condition remained the same; he was still sleeping and nothing had changed there. While water poured into the tub, Howard lathered his face and shaved. He'd just stretched out in the tub and closed his eyes when the telephone rang again. He hauled himself out, grabbed a towel, and hurried through the house, saying, "Stupid, stupid," for having left the hospital. But when he picked up the receiver and shouted, "Hello!" there was no sound at the other end of the line. Then the caller hung up.

He arrived back at the hospital a little after midnight. Ann still sat in the chair beside the bed. She looked up at Howard, and then she looked back at the child. The child's eyes stayed closed, the head was still wrapped in bandages. His breathing was quiet and regular. From an apparatus over the bed hung a bottle of glucose with a tube running from the bottle to the boy's arm.

"How is he?" Howard said. "What's all this?" waving at the glucose and the tube.

"Dr. Francis's orders," she said. "He needs nourishment. He needs to keep up his strength. Why doesn't he wake up, Howard? I don't understand, if he's all right."

Howard put his hand against the back of her head. He ran his fingers through her hair. "He's going to be all right. He'll wake up in a little while. Dr. Francis knows what's what."

After a time, he said, "Maybe you should go home and get some rest. I'll stay here. Just don't put up with this creep who keeps calling. Hang up right away."

"Who's calling?" she asked.

"I don't know who, just somebody with nothing better to do than call up people. You go on now."

She shook her head. "No," she said, "I'm fine."

"Really," he said. "Go home for a while, and then come back and spell me in the morning. It'll be all right. What did Dr. Francis say? He said Scotty's going to be all right. We don't have to worry. He's just sleeping now, that's all."

A nurse pushed the door open. She nodded at them as she went to the bedside. She took the left arm out from under the covers and put her fingers on the wrist, found the pulse, then consulted her watch. In a little while, she put the arm back under the covers and moved to the foot of the bed, where she wrote something on a clipboard attached to the bed.

"How is he?" Ann said. Howard's hand was a weight on her shoulder. She was aware of the pressure from his fingers.

"He's stable," the nurse said. Then she said, "Doctor will be in again shortly. Doctor's back in the hospital. He's making rounds right now."

"I was saying maybe she'd want to go home and get a little rest," Howard said. "After the doctor comes," he said.

"She could do that," the nurse said. "I think you should both feel free to do that, if you wish." The nurse was a big Scandinavian woman with blond hair. There was the trace of an accent in her speech.

"We'll see what the doctor says," Ann said. "I want to talk to the doctor. I don't think he should keep sleeping like this. I don't think that's a good sign." She brought her hand up to her eyes and let her head come forward a little. Howard's grip tightened on her shoulder, and then his hand moved up to her neck, where his fingers began to knead the muscles there.

"Dr. Francis will be here in a few minutes," the nurse said. Then she left the room.

Howard gazed at his son for a time, the small chest quietly rising and falling under the covers. For the first time since the terrible minutes after Ann's telephone call to him at his office, he felt a genuine fear starting in his limbs. He began shaking his head. Scotty was fine, but instead of sleeping at home in his own bed, he was in a hospital bed with bandages around his head and a tube in his arm. But this help was what he needed right now.

Dr. Francis came in and shook hands with Howard, though they'd just seen each other a few hours before. Ann got up from the chair. "Doctor?"

"Ann," he said and nodded. "Let's just first see how he's doing," the doctor said. He moved to the side of the bed and took the boy's pulse. He peeled back one eyelid and then the other. Howard and Ann stood beside the doctor and watched. Then the doctor turned back the covers and listened to the boy's heart and lungs with his stethoscope. He pressed his fingers here and there on the abdomen. When he was finished, he went to the end of the bed and studied the chart. He noted the time, scribbled something on the chart, and then looked at Howard and Ann.

"Doctor, how is he?" Howard said. "What's the matter with him exactly?"

"Why doesn't he wake up?" Ann said.

The doctor was a handsome, big-shouldered man with a tanned face. He wore a three-piece blue suit, a striped tie, and ivory cufflinks. His gray hair was combed along the sides of his head, and he looked as if he had just come from a concert. "He's all right," the doctor said. "Nothing to shout about, he could be better, I think. But he's all right. Still, I wish he'd wake up. He should wake up pretty soon." The doctor looked at the boy again. "We'll know some more in a couple of hours, after the results of a few more tests are in. But he's all right, believe me, except for the hairline fracture of the skull. He does have that."

"Oh, no," Ann said.

"And a bit of a concussion, as I said before. Of course, you know he's in shock," the doctor said. "Sometimes you see this in shock cases. This sleeping."

"But he's out of any real danger?" Howard said. "You said before he's not in a coma. You wouldn't call this a coma, then — would you, doctor?" Howard waited. He looked at the doctor.

"No, I don't want to call it a coma," the doctor said and glanced over at the boy once more. "He's just in a very deep sleep. It's a restorative measure the body is taking on its own. He's out of any real danger, I'd say that for certain, yes. But we'll know more when he wakes up and the other tests are in," the doctor said.

"It's a coma," Ann said. "Of sorts."

"It's not a coma yet, not exactly," the doctor said. "I wouldn't want to call it coma. Not yet, anyway. He's suffered shock. In shock cases, this kind of reaction is common enough; it's a temporary reaction to bodily trauma. Coma. Well, coma is a deep, prolonged unconsciousness, something that could go on for days, or weeks even. Scotty's not in that area, not as far as we can tell. I'm certain his condition will show improvement by morning. I'm betting that it will. We'll know more when he wakes up, which shouldn't be long now. Of course, you may do as you like, stay here or go home for a time. But by all means feel free to leave the hospital for a while if you want. This is not easy, I know." The doctor gazed at the boy again, watching him, and then he turned to Ann and said, "You try not to worry, little mother. Believe me, we're doing all that can be done. It's just a question of a little more time now." He nodded at her, shook hands with Howard again, and then he left the room.

Ann put her hand over the child's forehead. "At least he doesn't have a fever," she said. Then she said, "My God, he feels so cold, though. Howard? Is he supposed to feel like this? Feel his head."

Howard touched the child's temples. His own breathing had slowed. "I think he's supposed to feel this way right now," he said. "He's in shock, remember? That's what the doctor said. The doctor was just in here. He would have said something if Scotty wasn't okay."

Ann stood there a while longer, working her lip with her teeth. Then she moved over to her chair and sat down.

Howard sat in the chair next to her chair. They looked at each other. He wanted to say something else and reassure her, but he was afraid, too. He took her hand and put it in his lap, and this made him feel better, her hand being there. He picked up her hand and squeezed it. Then he just held her hand. They sat like that for a while, watching the boy and not talking. From time to time, he squeezed her hand. Finally, she took her hand away.

"I've been praying," she said.

He nodded.

She said, "I almost thought I'd forgotten how, but it came back to me. All I had to do was close my eyes and say, 'Please God, help us — help Scotty,' and then the rest was easy. The words were right there. Maybe if you prayed, too," she said to him.

"I've already prayed," he said. "I prayed this afternoon, yesterday afternoon, I mean — after you called, while I was driving to the hospital. I've been praying," he said.

"That's good," she said. For the first time, she felt they were together in it, this trouble. She realized with a start that, until now, it had only been happening to her and to Scotty. She hadn't let Howard into it, though he was there and needed all along. She felt glad to be his wife.

The same nurse came in and took the boy's pulse again and checked the flow from the bottle hanging above the bed.

In an hour, another doctor came in. He said his name was Parsons, from Radiology. He had a bushy mustache. He was wearing loafers, a Western shirt, and a pair of jeans.

"We're going to take him downstairs for more pictures," he told them. "We need to do some more pictures, and we want to do a scan."

"What's that?" Ann said. "A scan?" She stood between this new doctor and the bed. "I thought you'd already taken all your X-rays."

"I'm afraid we need some more," he said. "Nothing to be alarmed about. We just need some more pictures, and we want to do a brain scan on him."

"My God," Ann said.

"It's perfectly normal procedure in cases like this," this new doctor said. "We just need to find out for sure why he isn't back awake yet. It's normal medical procedure, and nothing to be alarmed about. We'll be taking him down in a few minutes," this doctor said.

In a little while, two orderlies came into the room with a gurney. They were black-haired, dark-complexioned men in white uniforms, and they said a few words to each other in a foreign tongue as they un-hooked the boy from the tube and moved him from his bed to the gur-ney. Then they wheeled him from the room. Howard and Ann got on the same elevator. Ann gazed at the child. She closed her eyes as the el-evator began its descent. The orderlies stood at either end of the gur-ney without saying anything, though once one of the men made a comment to the other in their own language, and the other man nod-ded slowly in response.

Later that morning, just as the sun was beginning to lighten the windows in the waiting room outside the X-ray department, they brought the boy out and moved him back up to his room. Howard and Ann rode up on the elevator with him once more, and once more they took up their places beside the bed.

They waited all day, but still the boy did not wake up. Occasionally, one of them would leave the room to go downstairs to the cafeteria to drink coffee and then, as if suddenly remembering and feeling guilty, get up from the table and hurry back to the room. Dr. Francis came again that afternoon and examined the boy once more and then left after telling them he was coming along and could wake up at any minute now. Nurses, different nurses from the night before, came in from time to time. Then a young woman from the lab knocked and entered the room. She wore white slacks and a white blouse and carried a little tray of things which she put on the stand beside the bed. Without a word to them, she took blood from the boy's arm. Howard closed his eyes as the woman found the right place on the boy's arm and pushed the needle in.

"I don't understand this," Ann said to the woman.

"Doctor's orders," the young woman said. "I do what I'm told. They say draw that one, I draw. What's wrong with him, anyway?" she said. "He's a sweetie."

"He was hit by a car," Howard said. "A hit-and-run."

The young woman shook her head and looked again at the boy. Then she took her tray and left the room.

"Why won't he wake up?" Ann said. "Howard? I want some answers from these people."

Howard didn't say anything. He sat down again in the chair and crossed one leg over the other. He rubbed his face. He looked at his son and then he settled back in the chair, closed his eyes, and went to sleep.

Ann walked to the window and looked out at the parking lot. It was night, and cars were driving into and out of the parking lot with their lights on. She stood at the window with her hands gripping the sill, and knew in her heart that they were into something now, something hard. She was afraid, and her teeth began to chatter until she tightened her jaws. She saw a big car stop in front of the hospital and someone, a woman in a long coat, get into the car. She wished she were that woman and somebody, anybody, was driving her away from here to somewhere else, a place where she would find Scotty waiting for her when she stepped out of the car, ready to say *Mom* and let her gather him in her arms.

In a little while, Howard woke up. He looked at the boy again. Then he got up from the chair, stretched, and went over to stand beside her at the window. They both stared out at the parking lot. They didn't say anything. But they seemed to feel each other's insides now, as though the worry had made them transparent in a perfectly natural way.

The door opened and Dr. Francis came in. He was wearing a different suit and tie this time. His gray hair was combed along the sides of his head, and he looked as if he had just shaved. He went straight to the bed and examined the boy. "He ought to have come around by now. There's just no good reason for this," he said. "But I can tell you we're all convinced he's out of any danger. We'll just feel better when he wakes up. There's no reason, absolutely none, why he shouldn't come around. Very soon. Oh, he'll have himself a dilly of a headache when he does, you can count on that. But all of his signs are fine. They're as normal as can be."

"It is a coma, then?" Ann said.

The doctor rubbed his smooth cheek. "We'll call it that for the time being, until he wakes up. But you must be worn out. This is hard. I know this is hard. Feel free to go out for a bite," he said. "It would do you good. I'll put a nurse in here while you're gone if you'll feel better about going. Go and have yourselves something to eat."

"I couldn't eat anything," Ann said.

"Do what you need to do, of course," the doctor said. "Anyway, I wanted to tell you that all the signs are good, the tests are negative, nothing showed up at all, and just as soon as he wakes up he'll be over the hill."

"Thank you, doctor," Howard said. He shook hands with the doctor again. The doctor patted Howard's shoulder and went out.

"I suppose one of us should go home and check on things," Howard said. "Slug needs to be fed, for one thing."

"Call one of the neighbors," Ann said. "Call the Morgans. Anyone will feed a dog if you ask them to."

"All right," Howard said. After a while, he said, "Honey, why don't *you* do it? Why don't you go home and check on things, and then come back? It'll do you good. I'll be right here with him. Seriously," he said. "We need to keep up our strength on this. We'll want to be here for a while even after he wakes up."

"Why don't *you* go?" she said. "Feed Slug. Feed yourself."

"I already went," he said. "I was gone for exactly an hour and fifteen minutes. You go home for an hour and freshen up. Then come back."

She tried to think about it, but she was too tired. She closed her eyes and tried to think about it again. After a time, she said, "Maybe I *will* go home for a few minutes. Maybe if I'm not just sitting right here watching him every second, he'll wake up and be all right. You know? Maybe he'll wake up if I'm not here. I'll go home and take a bath and put on clean clothes. I'll feed Slug. Then I'll come back."

"I'll be right here," he said. "You go on home, honey. I'll keep an eye on things here." His eyes were bloodshot and small, as if he'd been drinking for a long time. His clothes were rumpled. His beard had come out again. She touched his face, and then she took her hand back. She understood he wanted to be by himself for a while, not have to talk or share his worry for a time. She picked her purse up from the nightstand, and he helped her into her coat.

"I won't be gone long," she said.

"Just sit and rest for a little while when you get home," he said. "Eat something. Take a bath. After you get out of the bath, just sit for a while and rest. It'll do you a world of good, you'll see. Then come back," he said. "Let's try not to worry. You heard what Dr. Francis said."

She stood in her coat for a minute trying to recall the doctor's exact words, looking for any nuances, any hint of something behind his words other than what he had said. She tried to remember if his expression had changed any when he bent over to examine the child. She remembered the way his features had composed themselves as he rolled back the child's eyelids and then listened to his breathing.

She went to the door, where she turned and looked back. She looked at the child, and then she looked at the father. Howard nodded. She stepped out of the room and pulled the door closed behind her.

She went past the nurses' station and down to the end of the corridor, looking for the elevator. At the end of the corridor, she turned to her right and entered a little waiting room where a Negro family sat in wicker chairs. There was a middle-aged man in a khaki shirt and pants, a baseball cap pushed back on his head. A large woman wearing a housedress and slippers was slumped in one of the chairs. A teenaged girl in jeans, hair done in dozens of little braids, lay stretched out in one of the chairs smoking a cigarette, her legs crossed at the ankles. The family swung their eyes to Ann as she entered the room. The little table was littered with hamburger wrappers and Styrofoam cups.

"Franklin," the large woman said as she roused herself. "Is it about Franklin?" Her eyes widened. "Tell me now, lady," the woman said. "Is it about Franklin?" She was trying to rise from her chair, but the man had closed his hand over her arm.

"Here, here," he said. "Evelyn."

"I'm sorry," Ann said. "I'm looking for the elevator. My son is in the hospital, and now I can't find the elevator."

"Elevator is down that way, turn left," the man said as he aimed a finger.

The girl drew on her cigarette and stared at Ann. Her eyes were narrowed to slits, and her broad lips parted slowly as she let the smoke escape. The Negro woman let her head fall on her shoulder and looked away from Ann, no longer interested.

"My son was hit by a car," Ann said to the man. She seemed to need to explain herself. "He has a concussion and a little skull fracture, but he's going to be all right. He's in shock now, but it might be some kind of coma, too. That's what really worries us, the coma part. I'm going out for a little while, but my husband is with him. Maybe he'll wake up while I'm gone."

"That's too bad," the man said and shifted in the chair. He shook his head. He looked down at the table, and then he looked back at Ann. She was still standing there. He said, "Our Franklin, he's on the operating table. Somebody cut him. Tried to kill him. There was a fight where he was at. At this party. They say he was just standing and watching. Not bothering nobody. But that don't mean nothing these days. Now he's on the operating table. We're just hoping and praying, that's all we can do now." He gazed at her steadily.

Ann looked at the girl again, who was still watching her, and at the older woman, who kept her head down, but whose eyes were now closed. Ann saw the lips moving silently, making words. She had an urge to ask what those words were. She wanted to talk more with these people who were in the same kind of waiting she was in. She was afraid, and they were afraid. They had that in common. She would have liked to have said something else about the accident, told them more about Scotty, that it had happened on the day of his birthday, Monday, and that he was still unconscious. Yet she didn't know how to begin. She stood looking at them without saying anything more.

She went down the corridor the man had indicated and found the elevator. She waited a minute in front of the closed doors, still wondering if she was doing the right thing. Then she put out her finger and touched the button.

She pulled into the driveway and cut the engine. She closed her eyes and leaned her head against the wheel for a minute. She listened to the ticking sounds the engine made as it began to cool. Then she got out of the car. She could hear the dog barking inside the house. She went to the front door, which was unlocked. She went inside and turned on lights and put on a kettle of water for tea. She opened some dogfood and fed Slug on the back porch. The dog ate in hungry little smacks. It kept running into the kitchen to see that she was going to stay. As she sat down on the sofa with her tea, the telephone rang.

"Yes!" she said as she answered. "Hello!"

"Mrs. Weiss," a man's voice said. It was five o'clock in the morning, and she thought she could hear machinery or equipment of some kind in the background.

"Yes, yes! What is it?" she said. "This is Mrs. Weiss. This is she. What is it, please?" She listened to whatever it was in the background. "Is it Scotty, for Christ's sake?"

"Scotty," the man's voice said. "It's about Scotty, yes. It has to do with Scotty, that problem. Have you forgotten about Scotty?" the man said. Then he hung up.

She dialed the hospital's number and asked for the third floor. She demanded information about her son from the nurse who answered the telephone. Then she asked to speak to her husband. It was, she said, an emergency.

She waited, turning the telephone cord in her fingers. She closed her eyes and felt sick at her stomach. She would have to make herself eat. Slug came in from the back porch and lay down near her feet. He wagged his tail. She pulled at his ear while he licked her fingers. Howard was on the line.

"Somebody just called here," she said. She twisted the telephone cord. "He said it was about Scotty," she cried.

"Scotty's fine," Howard told her. "I mean, he's still sleeping. There's been no change. The nurse has been in twice since you've been gone. A nurse or else a doctor. He's all right."

"This man called. He said it was about Scotty," she told him.

"Honey, you rest for a little while, you need the rest. It must be that same caller I had. Just forget it. Come back down here after you've rested. Then we'll have breakfast or something."

"Breakfast," she said. "I don't want any breakfast."

"You know what I mean," he said. "Juice, something. I don't know. I don't know anything, Ann. Jesus, I'm not hungry, either. Ann, it's hard to talk now. I'm standing here at the desk. Dr. Francis is coming again at eight o'clock this morning. He's going to have something to tell us then, something more definite. That's what one of the nurses said. She didn't know any more than that. Ann? Honey, maybe we'll know something more then. At eight o'clock. Come back here before eight. Meanwhile, I'm right here and Scotty's all right. He's still the same," he added.

"I was drinking a cup of tea," she said, "when the telephone rang. They said it was about Scotty. There was a noise in the background. Was there a noise in the background on that call you had, Howard?"

"I don't remember," he said. "Maybe the driver of the car, maybe he's a psychopath and found out about Scotty somehow. But I'm here with him. Just rest like you were going to do. Take a bath and come back by seven or so, and we'll talk to the doctor together when he gets here. It's going to be all right, honey. I'm here, and there are doctors and nurses around. They say his condition is stable."

"I'm scared to death," she said.

She ran water, undressed, and got into the tub. She washed and dried quickly, not taking the time to wash her hair. She put on clean underwear, wool slacks, and a sweater. She went into the living room, where the dog looked up at her and let its tail thump once against the floor. It was just starting to get light outside when she went out to the car.

She drove into the parking lot of the hospital and found a space close to the front door. She felt she was in some obscure way responsible for what had happened to the child. She let her thoughts move to the Negro family. She remembered the name Franklin and the table that was covered with hamburger papers, and the teenaged girl staring at her as she drew on her cigarette. "Don't have children," she told the girl's image as she entered the front door of the hospital. "For God's sake, don't."

She took the elevator up to the third floor with two nurses who were just going on duty. It was Wednesday morning, a few minutes before seven. There was a page for a Dr. Madison as the elevator doors slid open on the third floor. She got off behind the nurses, who turned in the other direction and continued the conversation she had interrupted when she'd gotten into the elevator. She walked down the corridor to the little alcove where the Negro family had been waiting. They were gone now, but the chairs were scattered in such a way that it looked as if people had just jumped up from them the minute before. The tabletop was cluttered with the same cups and papers, the ashtray was filled with cigarette butts.

She stopped at the nurses' station. A nurse was standing behind the counter, brushing her hair and yawning.

"There was a Negro boy in surgery last night," Ann said. "Franklin was his name. His family was in the waiting room. I'd like to inquire about his condition."

A nurse who was sitting at a desk behind the counter looked up from a chart in front of her. The telephone buzzed and she picked up the receiver, but she kept her eyes on Ann.

"He passed away," said the nurse at the counter. The nurse held the hairbrush and kept looking at her. "Are you a friend of the family or what?"

"I met the family last night," Ann said. "My own son is in the hospital. I guess he's in shock. We don't know for sure what's wrong. I just wondered about Franklin, that's all. Thank you." She moved down the corridor. Elevator doors the same color as the walls slid open and a gaunt, bald man in white pants and white canvas shoes pulled a heavy cart off the elevator. She hadn't noticed these doors last night. The man wheeled the cart out into the corridor and stopped in front of the room nearest the elevator and consulted a clipboard. Then he reached down and slid a tray out of the cart. He rapped lightly on the door and entered the room. She could smell the unpleasant odors of warm food as she passed the cart. She hurried on without looking at any of the nurses and pushed open the door to the child's room.

Howard was standing at the window with his hands behind his back. He turned around as she came in.

"How is he?" she said. She went over to the bed. She dropped her purse on the floor beside the nightstand. It seemed to her she had been gone a long time. She touched the child's face. "Howard?"

"Dr. Francis was here a little while ago," Howard said. She looked at him closely and thought his shoulders were bunched a little.

"I thought he wasn't coming until eight o'clock this morning," she said quickly.

"There was another doctor with him. A neurologist."

"A neurologist," she said.

Howard nodded. His shoulders were bunching, she could see that. "What'd they say, Howard? For Christ's sake, what'd they say? What is it?"

"They said they're going to take him down and run more tests on him, Ann. They think they're going to operate, honey. Honey, they *are* going to operate. They can't figure out why he won't wake up. It's more than just shock or concussion, they know that much now. It's in his skull, the fracture, it has something, something to do with that, they think. So they're going to operate. I tried to call you, but I guess you'd already left the house."

"Oh, God," she said. "Oh, please, Howard, please," she said, taking his arms.

"Look!" Howard said. "Scotty! Look, Ann!" He turned her toward the bed.

The boy had opened his eyes, then closed them. He opened them again now. The eyes stared straight ahead for a minute, then moved slowly in his head until they rested on Howard and Ann, then traveled away again.

"Scotty," his mother said, moving to the bed.

"Hey, Scott," his father said. "Hey, son."

They leaned over the bed. Howard took the child's hand in his hands and began to pat and squeeze the hand. Ann bent over the boy and kissed his forehead again and again. She put her hands on either side of his face. "Scotty, honey, it's Mommy and Daddy," she said. "Scotty?"

The boy looked at them, but without any sign of recognition. Then his mouth opened, his eyes scrunched closed, and he howled until he had no more air in his lungs. His face seemed to relax and soften then. His lips parted as his last breath was puffed through his throat and exhaled gently through the clenched teeth.

☀

The doctors called it a hidden occlusion and said it was a one-in-a-million circumstance. Maybe if it could have been detected somehow and surgery undertaken immediately, they could have saved him. But more than likely not. In any case, what would they have been looking for? Nothing had shown up in the tests or in the X-rays.

Dr. Francis was shaken. "I can't tell you how badly I feel. I'm so very sorry, I can't tell you," he said as he led them into the doctors' lounge. There was a doctor sitting in a chair with his legs hooked over the back of another chair, watching an early-morning TV show. He was wearing a green delivery room outfit, loose green pants and green blouse, and a green cap that covered his hair. He looked at Howard and Ann and then looked at Dr. Francis. He got to his feet and turned off the set and went out of the room. Dr. Francis guided Ann to the sofa, sat down beside her, and began to talk in a low, consoling voice. At one point, he leaned over and embraced her. She could feel his chest rising and falling evenly against her shoulder. She kept her eyes open and let him hold her. Howard went into the bathroom, but he left the door open. After a violent fit of weeping, he ran water and washed his face. Then he came out and sat down at the little table that held a telephone. He looked at the telephone as though deciding what to do first. He made some calls. After a time, Dr. Francis used the telephone.

"Is there anything else I can do for the moment?" he asked them.

Howard shook his head. Ann stared at Dr. Francis as if unable to comprehend his words.

The doctor walked them to the hospital's front door. People were entering and leaving the hospital. It was eleven o'clock in the morning. Ann was aware of how slowly, almost reluctantly, she moved her feet. It seemed to her that Dr. Francis was making them leave when she felt they should stay, when it would be more the right thing to do to stay. She gazed out into the parking lot and then turned around and looked back at the front of the hospital. She began shaking her head. "No, no," she said. "I can't leave him here, no." She heard herself say that and thought how unfair it was that the only words that came out were the sort of words used on TV shows where people were stunned by violent or sudden deaths. She wanted her words to be her own. "No," she said, and for some reason the memory of the Negro woman's head lolling on the woman's shoulder came to her. "No," she said again.

"I'll be talking to you later in the day," the doctor was saying to Howard. "There are still some things that have to be done, things that have to be cleared up to our satisfaction. Some things that need explaining."

"An autopsy," Howard said.

Dr. Francis nodded.

"I understand," Howard said. Then he said, "Oh, Jesus. No, I don't understand, doctor. I can't, I can't. I just can't."

Dr. Francis put his arm around Howard's shoulders. "I'm sorry. God, how I'm sorry." He let go of Howard's shoulders and held out his hand. Howard looked at the hand, and then he took it. Dr. Francis put his arms around Ann once more. He seemed full of some goodness she didn't understand. She let her head rest on his shoulder, but her eyes stayed open. She kept looking at the hospital. As they drove out of the parking lot, she looked back at the hospital.

At home, she sat on the sofa with her hands in her coat pockets. Howard closed the door to the child's room. He got the coffee-maker going and then he found an empty box. He had thought to pick up some of the child's things that were scattered around the living room. But instead he sat down beside her on the sofa, pushed the box to one side, and leaned forward, arms between his knees. He began to weep. She pulled his head over into her lap and patted his shoulder. "He's gone," she said. She kept patting his shoulder. Over his sobs, she could hear the coffee-maker hissing in the kitchen. "There, there," she said tenderly. "Howard, he's gone. He's gone and now we'll have to get used to that. To being alone."

In a little while, Howard got up and began moving aimlessly around the room with the box, not putting anything into it, but collecting some things together on the floor at one end of the sofa. She continued to sit with her hands in her coat pockets. Howard put the box down and brought coffee into the living room. Later, Ann made calls to relatives. After each call had been placed and the party had answered, Ann would blurt out a few words and cry for a minute. Then she would quietly explain, in a measured voice, what had happened and tell them about arrangements. Howard took the box out to the garage, where he saw the child's bicycle. He dropped the box and sat down on the pavement beside the bicycle. He took hold of the bicycle awkwardly so that it leaned against his chest. He held it, the rubber pedal sticking into his chest. He gave the wheel a turn.

Ann hung up the telephone after talking to her sister. She was looking up another number when the telephone rang. She picked it up on the first ring.

"Hello," she said, and she heard something in the background, a humming noise. "Hello!" she said. "For God's sake," she said. "Who is this? What is it you want?"

"Your Scotty, I got him ready for you," the man's voice said. "Did you forget him?"

"You evil bastard!" she shouted into the receiver. "How can you do this, you evil son of a bitch?"

"Scotty," the man said. "Have you forgotten about Scotty?" Then the man hung up on her.

Howard heard the shouting and came in to find her with her head on her arms over the table, weeping. He picked up the receiver and listened to the dial tone.

Much later, just before midnight, after they had dealt with many things, the telephone rang again.

"You answer it," she said. "Howard, it's him, I know." They were sitting at the kitchen table with coffee in front of them. Howard had a small glass of whiskey beside his cup. He answered on the third ring.

"Hello," he said. "Who is this? Hello! Hello!" The line went dead. "He hung up," Howard said. "Whoever it was."

"It was him," she said. "That bastard, I'd like to kill him," she said. "I'd like to shoot him and watch him kick," she said.

"Ann, my God," he said.

"Could you hear anything?" she said. "In the background? A noise, machinery, something humming?"

"Nothing, really. Nothing like that," he said. "There wasn't much time. I think there was some radio music. Yes, there was a radio going, that's all I could tell. I don't know what in God's name is going on," he said.

She shook her head. "If I could, could get my hands on him." It came to her then. She knew who it was. Scotty, the cake, the telephone number. She pushed the chair away from the table and got up. "Drive me down to the shopping center," she said. "Howard."

"What are you saying?"

"The shopping center. I know who it is who's calling. I know who it is. It's the baker, the son-of-a-bitching baker, Howard. I had him bake a cake for Scotty's birthday. That's who's calling. That's who has the number and keeps calling us. To harass us about that cake. The baker, that bastard."

They drove down to the shopping center. The sky was clear and stars were out. It was cold, and they ran the heater in the car. They parked in front of the bakery. All of the shops and stores were closed, but there were cars at the far end of the lot in front of the movie theater. The bakery windows were dark, but when they looked through the glass they could see a light in the back room and, now and then, a big man in an apron moving in and out of the white, even light. Through the glass, she could see the display cases and some little tables with chairs. She tried the door. She rapped on the glass. But if the baker heard them, he gave no sign. He didn't look in their direction.

They drove around behind the bakery and parked. They got out of the car. There was a lighted window too high up for them to see inside. A sign near the back door said THE PANTRY BAKERY, SPECIAL ORDERS. She could hear faintly a radio playing inside and something creak — an oven door as it was pulled down? She knocked on the door and waited. Then she knocked again, louder. The radio was turned down and there was a scraping sound now, the distinct sound of something, a drawer, being pulled open and then closed.

Someone unlocked the door and opened it. The baker stood in the light and peered out at them. "I'm closed for business," he said. "What do you want at this hour? It's midnight. Are you drunk or something?"

She stepped into the light that fell through the open door. He blinked his heavy eyelids as he recognized her. "It's you," he said.

"It's me," she said. "Scotty's mother. This is Scotty's father. We'd like to come in."

The baker said, "I'm busy now. I have work to do."

She had stepped inside the doorway anyway. Howard came in behind her. The baker moved back. "It smells like a bakery in here. Doesn't it smell like a bakery in here, Howard?"

"What do you want?" the baker said. "Maybe you want your cake? That's it, you decided you want your cake. You ordered a cake, didn't you?"

"You're pretty smart for a baker," she said. "Howard, this is the man who's been calling us." She clenched her fists. She stared at him fiercely. There was a deep burning inside her, an anger that made her feel larger than herself, larger than either of these men.

"Just a minute here," the baker said. "You want to pick up your three-day-old cake? That it? I don't want to argue with you, lady. There it sits over there, getting stale. I'll give it to you for half of what I quoted you. No. You want it? You can have it. It's no good to me, no good to anyone now. It cost me time and money to make that cake. If you want it, okay, if you don't, that's okay, too. I have to get back to work." He looked at them and rolled his tongue behind his teeth.

"More cakes," she said. She knew she was in control of it, of what was increasing in her. She was calm.

"Lady, I work sixteen hours a day in this place to earn a living," the baker said. He wiped his hands on his apron. "I work night and day in here, trying to make ends meet." A look crossed Ann's face that made the baker move back and say, "No trouble, now." He reached to the counter and picked up a rolling pin with his right hand and began to tap it against the palm of his other hand. "You want the cake or not? I have to get back to work. Bakers work at night," he said again. His eyes were small, mean-looking, she thought, nearly lost in the bristly flesh around his cheeks. His neck was thick with fat.

"I know bakers work at night," Ann said. "They make phone calls at night, too. You bastard," she said.

The baker continued to tap the rolling pin against his hand. He glanced at Howard. "Careful, careful," he said to Howard.

"My son's dead," she said with a cold, even finality. "He was hit by a car Monday morning. We've been waiting with him until he died. But, of course, you couldn't be expected to know that, could you? Bakers can't know everything — can they, Mr. Baker? But he's dead. He's dead, you bastard!" Just as suddenly as it had welled in her, the anger dwindled, gave way to something else, a dizzy feeling of nausea. She leaned against the wooden table that was sprinkled with flour, put her hands over her face, and began to cry, her shoulders rocking back and forth. "It isn't fair," she said. "It isn't, isn't fair."

Howard put his hand at the small of her back and looked at the baker. "Shame on you," Howard said to him. "Shame."

The baker put the rolling pin back on the counter. He undid his apron and threw it on the counter. He looked at them, and then he shook his head slowly. He pulled a chair out from under the card table that held papers and receipts, an adding machine, and a telephone directory. "Please sit down," he said. "Let me get you a chair," he said to Howard. "Sit down now, please." The baker went into the front of the shop and returned with two little wrought-iron chairs. "Please sit down, you people."

Ann wiped her eyes and looked at the baker. "I wanted to kill you," she said. "I wanted you dead."

The baker had cleared a space for them at the table. He shoved the adding machine to one side, along with the stacks of notepaper and receipts. He pushed the telephone directory onto the floor, where it landed with a thud. Howard and Ann sat down and pulled their chairs up to the table. The baker sat down, too.

"Let me say how sorry I am," the baker said, putting his elbows on the table. "God alone knows how sorry. Listen to me. I'm just a baker. I don't claim to be anything else. Maybe once, maybe years ago, I was a different kind of human being. I've forgotten, I don't know for sure. But I'm not any longer, if I ever was. Now I'm just a baker. That don't excuse my doing what I did, I know. But I'm deeply sorry. I'm sorry for your son, and sorry for my part in this," the baker said. He spread his hands out on the table and turned them over to reveal his palms. "I don't have any children myself, so I can only imagine what you must be feeling. All I can say to you now is that I'm sorry. Forgive me, if you can," the baker said. "I'm not an evil man, I don't think. Not evil, like you said on the phone. You got to understand what it comes down to is I don't know how to act anymore, it would seem. Please," the man said, "let me ask you if you can find it in your hearts to forgive me?"

It was warm inside the bakery. Howard stood up from the table and took off his coat. He helped Ann from her coat. The baker looked at them for a minute and then nodded and got up from the table. He went to the oven and turned off some switches. He found cups and poured coffee from an electric coffee-maker. He put a carton of cream on the table, and a bowl of sugar.

"You probably need to eat something," the baker said. "I hope you'll eat some of my hot rolls. You have to eat and keep going. Eating is a small, good thing in a time like this," he said.

He served them warm cinnamon rolls just out of the oven, the icing still runny. He put butter on the table and knives to spread the butter. Then the baker sat down at the table with them. He waited. He waited until they each took a roll from the platter and began to eat. "It's good to eat something," he said, watching them. "There's more. Eat up. Eat all you want. There's all the rolls in the world in here."

They ate rolls and drank coffee. Ann was suddenly hungry, and the rolls were warm and sweet. She ate three of them, which pleased the baker. Then he began to talk. They listened carefully. Although they were tired and in anguish, they listened to what the baker had to say. They nodded when the baker began to speak of loneliness, and of the sense of doubt and limitation that had come to him in his middle years. He told them what it was like to be childless all these years. To repeat the days with the ovens endlessly full and endlessly empty. The party food, the celebrations he'd worked over. Icing knuckle-deep. The tiny wedding couples stuck into cakes. Hundreds of them, no, thousands by now. Birthdays. Just imagine all those candles burning. He had a necessary trade. He was a baker. He was glad he wasn't a florist. It was better to be feeding people. This was a better smell anytime than flowers.

"Smell this," the baker said, breaking open a dark loaf. "It's a heavy bread, but rich." They smelled it, then he had them taste it. It had the taste of molasses and coarse grains. They listened to him. They ate what they could. They swallowed the dark bread. It was like daylight under the fluorescent trays of light. They talked on into the early morning, the high, pale cast of light in the windows, and they did not think of leaving.

John Cheever

John Cheever's formal education ended when he was expelled from the Thayer Academy as a teenager, and yet he was among our most formal and elegant writers. His prose is resonant with the diction and cadences of the classics of English and American literature, of Shakespeare, Dickens, and the King James Version of the Bible. More than any American writer since Wharton and James, Cheever (1912–1982) was concerned with the question of ethical behavior in a morally ambiguous society, with the struggle to behave decorously in a world shaded between good intentions and expediency. Throughout his work, from early pieces like "The Housebreaker of Shady Hill," in which the protagonist loses his job and begins pilfering from his upper-middle-class neighbors, to the late story, "A World of Apples," which deals humorously and poignantly with an old man's struggle to suppress his unseemly erotic urges, we encounter characters engaged not so much with the world but with their own moral conflicts.

Best known for his cutting stories of the joys and sorrows — mainly sorrows — of life in New York's suburbs, Cheever published his first story in *The New Republic* at the age of nineteen and went on from there to become a mainstay of *The New Yorker* for more than thirty years. Though he was principally a realist, his stories often take lyrical and imaginative flights that make his work more difficult to categorize than it might at first seem. "Experimental" was the catchword of the day when I was Cheever's student in the seventies, and he once told me that all good writing was experimental in some sense, and adduced his own fluent and mysterious dream of a story, "The Death of Justina," as an example.

The first of the stories here is the earliest piece from his volume of collected short fiction, *The Stories of John Cheever*. "Goodbye, My Brother" features a prejudicial narrator; a graceful, unhurried, formal introduction; and an ending celebrated for its lyrical expostulation to the reader ("Oh, what can you do with a man like that? What can you do?"). One wonders how the story would read if written from the brother's — Lawrence's — point of view, and this can open up the entire piece to reevaluation. The second story, "The Five-Forty-Eight," is one of the few Cheever fictions to feature a gun and the threat of overt violence. It is remarkable for its revelation of character and the moral certainty of its denouement, and its straightforward telling serves to enhance the tension that builds from the first line to the prosaic release of the last.

Goodbye, My Brother

We are a family that has always been very close in spirit. Our father was drowned in a sailing accident when we were young, and our mother had always stressed the fact that our familial relationships have a kind of permanence that we will never meet with again. I don't think about the family much, but when I remember its members and the coast where they lived and the sea salt that I think is in our blood, I am happy to recall that I am a Pommeroy — that I have the nose, the coloring, and the promise of longevity — and that while we are not a distinguished family, we enjoy the illusion, when we are together, that the Pommeroys are unique. I don't say any of this because I'm interested in family history or because this sense of uniqueness is deep or important to me but in order to advance the point that we are loyal to one another in spite of our differences, and that any rupture in this loyalty is a source of confusion and pain.

We are four children; there is my sister Diana and the three men — Chaddy, Lawrence, and myself. Like most families in which the children are out of their twenties, we have been separated by business, marriage, and war. Helen and I live on Long Island now, with our four children. I teach in a secondary school, and I am past the age where I expect to be made headmaster — or principal, as we say — but I respect the work. Chaddy, who has done better than the rest of us, lives in Manhattan, with Odette and their children. Mother lives in Philadelphia, and Diana, since her divorce, has been living in France, but she comes back to the States in the summer to spend a month at Laud's Head. Laud's Head is a summer place on the shore of one of the Massachusetts islands. We used to have a cottage there, and in the twenties our father built the big house. It stands on a cliff above the sea and, excepting St. Tropez and some of the Apennine villages, it is my favorite place in the world. We each have an equity in the place and we contribute some money to help keep it going.

Our youngest brother, Lawrence, who is a lawyer, got a job with a Cleveland firm after the war, and none of us saw him for four years. When he decided to leave Cleveland and go to work for a firm in Albany, he wrote Mother that he would, between jobs, spend ten days at Laud's Head, with his wife and their two children. This was when I had planned to take my vacation — I had been teaching summer school — and Helen and Chaddy and Odette and Diana were all going to be there, so the family would be together. Lawrence is the member of the family with whom the rest of us have least in common. We have never seen a great deal of him, and I suppose that's why we still call him Tifty — a nickname he was given when he was a child, because when he came down the hall toward the dining room for breakfast, his slippers made a noise that sounded like "Tifty, tifty, tifty." That's what Father called him, and so did everyone else. When he grew older, Diana sometimes used to call him Little Jesus, and Mother often called him the Croaker. We had disliked Lawrence, but we looked forward to his return with a mixture of apprehension and loyalty, and with some of the joy and delight of reclaiming a brother.

Lawrence crossed over from the mainland on the four-o'clock boat one afternoon late in the summer, and Chaddy and I went down to meet him. The arrivals and departures of the summer ferry have all the outward signs that suggest a voyage — whistles, bells, hand trucks, reunions, and the smell of brine — but it is a voyage of no import, and when I watched the boat come into the blue harbor that afternoon and thought that it was completing a voyage of no import, I realized that I had hit on exactly the kind of observation that Lawrence would have made. We looked for his face behind the windshields as the cars drove off the boat, and we had no trouble in recognizing him. And we ran over and shook his hand and clumsily kissed his wife and the children. "Tifty!" Chaddy shouted. "Tifty!" It is difficult to judge changes in the appearance of a brother, but both Chaddy and I agreed, as we drove back to Laud's Head, that Lawrence still looked very young. He got to the house first, and we took the suitcases out of his car. When I came in, he was standing in the living room, talking with Mother and Diana. They were in their best clothes and all their jewelry, and they were welcoming him extravagantly, but even then, when everyone was endeavoring to seem most affectionate and at a time when these endeavors come easiest, I was aware of a faint tension in the room. Thinking about this as I carried Lawrence's heavy suitcases up the stairs, I realized that our dislikes are as deeply ingrained as our better passions, and I remembered that once, twenty-five years ago, when I had hit Lawrence on the head with a rock, he had picked himself up and gone directly to our father to complain.

I carried the suitcases up to the third floor, where Ruth, Lawrence's wife, had begun to settle her family. She is a thin girl, and she seemed very tired from the journey, but when I asked her if she didn't want me to bring a drink upstairs to her, she said she didn't think she did.

When I got downstairs, Lawrence wasn't around, but the others were all ready for cocktails, and we decided to go ahead. Lawrence is the only member of the family who has never enjoyed drinking. We took our cocktails onto the terrace, so that we could see the bluffs and the sea and the islands in the east, and the return of Lawrence and his wife, their presence in the house, seemed to refresh our responses to the familiar view; it was as if the pleasure they would take in the sweep and the color of that coast, after such a long absence, had been imparted to us. While we were there, Lawrence came up the path from the beach.

"Isn't the beach fabulous, Tifty?" Mother asked. "Isn't it fabulous to be back? Will you have a Martini?"

"I don't care," Lawrence said. "Whiskey, gin — I don't care what I drink. Give me a little rum."

"We don't have any *rum*," Mother said. It was the first note of asperity. She had taught us never to be indecisive, never to reply as Lawrence had. Beyond this, she is deeply concerned with the propriety of her house, and anything irregular by her standards, like drinking straight rum or bringing a beer can to the dinner table, excites in her a conflict that she cannot, even with her capacious sense of humor, surmount. She sensed the asperity and worked to repair it. "Would you like some Irish, Tifty dear?" she said. "Isn't Irish what you've always liked? There's some Irish on the sideboard. Why don't you get yourself some Irish?" Lawrence said that he didn't care. He poured himself a Martini, and then Ruth came down and we went in to dinner.

In spite of the fact that we had, through waiting for Lawrence, drunk too much before dinner, we were all anxious to put our best foot forward and to enjoy a peaceful time. Mother is a small woman whose face is still a striking reminder of how pretty she must have been, and whose conversation is unusually light, but she talked that evening about a soil-reclamation project that is going on up-island. Diana is as pretty as Mother must have been; she is an animated and lovely woman who likes to talk about the dissolute friends that she had made in France, but she talked that night about the school in Switzerland where she had left her two children. I could see that the dinner had been planned to please Lawrence. It was not too rich, and there was nothing to make him worry about extravagance.

After supper, when we went back onto the terrace, the clouds held that kind of light that looks like blood, and I was glad that Lawrence had such a lurid sunset for his homecoming. When we had been out there a few minutes, a man named Edward Chester came to get Diana. She had met him in France, or on the boat home, and he was staying for ten days at the inn in the village. He was introduced to Lawrence and Ruth, and then he and Diana left.

"Is that the one she's sleeping with now?" Lawrence asked.

"What a horrid thing to say!" Helen said.

"You ought to apologize for that, Tifty," Chaddy said.

"I don't know," Mother said tiredly. "I don't know, Tifty. Diana is in a position to do whatever she wants, and I don't ask sordid questions. She's my only daughter. I don't see her often."

"Is she going back to France?"

"She's going back the week after next."

Lawrence and Ruth were sitting at the edge of the terrace, not in the chairs, not in the circle of chairs. With his mouth set, my brother looked to me then like a Puritan cleric. Sometimes, when I try to understand his frame of mind, I think of the beginnings of our family in this country, and his disapproval of Diana and her lover reminded me of this. The branch of the Pommeroys to which we belong was founded by a minister who was eulogized by Cotton Mather for his untiring abjuration of the Devil. The Pommeroys were ministers until the middle of the nineteenth century, and the harshness of their thought — man is full of misery, and all earthly beauty is lustful and corrupt — has been preserved in books and sermons. The temper of our family changed somewhat and became more lighthearted, but when I was of school age, I can remember a cousinage of old men and women who seemed to hark back to the dark days of the ministry and to be animated by perpetual guilt and the deification of the scourge. If you are raised in this atmosphere — and in a sense we were — I think it is a trial of the spirit to reject its habits of guilt, self-denial, taciturnity, and penitence, and it seemed to me to have been a trial of the spirit in which Lawrence had succumbed.

"Is that Cassiopeia?" Odette asked.

"No, dear," Chaddy said. "That isn't Cassiopeia."

"Who was Cassiopeia?" Odette said.

"She was the wife of Cepheus and the mother of Andromeda," I said.

"The cook is a Giants fan," Chaddy said. "She'll give you even money that they win the pennant."

It had grown so dark that we could see the passage of light through the sky from the lighthouse at Cape Heron. In the dark below the cliff, the continual detonations of the surf sounded. And then, as she often does when it is getting dark and she has drunk too much before dinner, Mother began to talk about the improvements and additions that would someday be made on the house, the wings and bathrooms and gardens.

"This house will be in the sea in five years," Lawrence said.

"Tifty the Croaker," Chaddy said.

"Don't call me Tifty," Lawrence said.

"Little Jesus." Chaddy said.

"The sea wall is badly cracked," Lawrence said. "I looked at it this afternoon. You had it repaired four years ago, and it cost eight thousand dollars. You can't do that every four years."

"Please, Tifty," Mother said.

"Facts are facts," Lawrence said, "and it's a damned-fool idea to build a house at the edge of the cliff on a sinking coastline. In my lifetime, half the garden has washed away and there's four feet of water where we used to have a bathhouse."

"Let's have a very *general* conversation," Mother said bitterly. "Let's talk about politics or the boat-club dance."

"As a matter of fact," Lawrence said, "the house is probably in some danger now. If you had an unusually high sea, a hurricane sea, the wall would crumble and the house would go. We could all be drowned."

"I can't *bear* it," Mother said. She went into the pantry and came back with a full glass of gin.

I have grown too old now to think that I can judge the sentiments of others, but I was conscious of the tension between Lawrence and Mother, and I knew some of the history of it. Lawrence couldn't have been more than sixteen years old when he decided that Mother was frivolous, mischievous, destructive, and overly strong. When he had determined this, he decided to separate himself from her. He was at boarding school then, and I remember that he did not come home for Christmas. He spent Christmas with a friend. He came home very seldom after he had made his unfavorable judgment on Mother, and when he did come home, he always tried, in his conversation, to remind her of his estrangement. When he married Ruth, he did not tell Mother. He did not tell her when his children were born. But in spite of these principled and lengthy exertions he seemed, unlike the rest of us, never to have enjoyed any separation, and when they are together, you feel at once a tension, an unclearness.

And it was unfortunate, in a way, that Mother should have picked that night to get drunk. It's her privilege, and she doesn't get drunk often, and fortunately she wasn't bellicose, but we were all conscious of what was happening. As she quietly drank her gin, she seemed sadly to be parting from us; she seemed to be in the throes of travel. Then her mood changed from travel to injury, and the few remarks she made were petulant and irrelevant. When her glass was nearly empty, she stared angrily at the dark air in front of her nose, moving her head a little, like a fighter. I knew that there was not room in her mind then for all the injuries that were crowding into it. Her children were stupid, her husband was drowned, her servants were thieves, and the chair she sat in was uncomfortable. Suddenly she put down her empty glass and interrupted Chaddy, who was talking about baseball. "I know one *thing,*" she said hoarsely. "I know that if there is an afterlife, I'm going to have a very different kind of family. I'm going to have nothing but fabulously rich, witty, and enchanting children." She got up and, starting for the door, nearly fell. Chaddy caught her and helped her up the stairs. I could hear their tender good-nights, and then Chaddy came back. I thought that Lawrence by now would be tired from his journey and his return, but he remained on the terrace, as if he were waiting to see the final malfeasance, and the rest of us left him there and went swimming in the dark.

When I woke the next morning, or half woke, I could hear the sound of someone rolling the tennis court. It is a fainter and deeper sound than the iron buoy bells off the point — an unrhythmic iron chiming — that belongs in my mind to the beginnings of a summer day, a good portent. When I went downstairs, Lawrence's two kids were in the living room, dressed in ornate cowboy suits. They are frightened and skinny children. They told me their father was rolling the tennis court but that they did not want to go out because they had seen a snake under the doorstep. I explained to them that their cousins — all the other children — ate breakfast in the kitchen and that they'd better run along in there. At this announcement, the boy began to cry. Then his sister joined him. They cried as if to go in the kitchen and eat would destroy their most precious rights. I told them to sit down with me. Lawrence came in, and I asked him if he wanted to play some tennis. He said no, thanks, although he thought he might play some singles with Chaddy. He was in the right here, because both he and Chaddy play better tennis than I, and he did play some singles with Chaddy after breakfast, but later on, when the others came down to play family doubles, Lawrence disappeared. This made me cross — unreasonably so, I suppose — but we play darned interesting family doubles and he could have played in a set for the sake of courtesy.

Late in the morning, when I came up from the court alone, I saw Tifty on the terrace, prying up a shingle from the wall with his jackknife. "What's the matter, Lawrence?" I said. "Termites?" There are termites in the wood and they've given us a lot of trouble.

He pointed out to me, at the base of each row of shingles, a faint blue line of carpenter's chalk. "This house is about twenty-two years old," he said. "These shingles are about two hundred years old. Dad must have bought shingles from all the farms around here when he built the place, to make it look venerable. You can still see the carpenter's chalk put down where these antiques were nailed into place."

It was true about the shingles, although I had forgotten it. When the house was built, our father, or his architect, had ordered it covered with lichened and weather-beaten shingles. I didn't follow Lawrence's reasons for thinking that this was scandalous.

"And look at these doors," Lawrence said. "Look at these doors and window frames." I followed him over to a big Dutch door that opens onto the terrace and looked at it. It was a relatively new door, but someone had worked hard to conceal its newness. The surface had been deeply scored with some metal implement, and white paint had been rubbed into the incisions to imitate brine, lichen, and weather rot. "Imagine spending thousands of dollars to make a sound house look like a wreck," Lawrence said. "Imagine the frame of mind this implies. Imagine wanting to live so much in the past that you'll pay men carpenters' wages to disfigure your front door." Then I remembered Lawrence's sensitivity to time and his sentiments and opinions about our feelings for the past. I had heard him say, years ago, that we and our friends and our part of the nation, finding ourselves unable to cope with the problems of the present, had, like a wretched adult, turned back to what we supposed was a happier and a simpler time, and that our taste for reconstruction and candlelight was a measure of this irremediable failure. The faint blue line of chalk had reminded him of these ideas, the scarified door had reinforced them, and now clue after clue presented itself to him — the stern light at the door, the bulk of the chimney, the width of the floorboards and the pieces set into them to resemble pegs. While Lawrence was lecturing me on these frailties, the others came up from the court. As soon as Mother saw Lawrence, she responded, and I saw that there was little hope of any rapport between the matriarch and the changeling. She took Chaddy's arm. "Let's go swimming and have Martinis on the beach," she said. "Let's have a *fabulous* morning."

The sea that morning was a solid color, like verd stone. Everyone went to the beach but Tifty and Ruth. "I don't mind *him,*" Mother said. She was excited, and she tipped her glass and spilled some gin into the sand. "I don't mind *him.* It doesn't matter to me how *rude* and *horrid* and *gloomy* he is, but what I can't bear are the faces of his wretched little children, those fabulously unhappy little children." With the height of the cliff between us, everyone talked wrathfully about Lawrence; about how he had grown worse instead of better, how unlike the rest of us he was, how he endeavored to spoil every pleasure. We drank our gin; the abuse seemed to reach a crescendo, and then, one by one, we went swimming in the solid green water. But when we came out no one mentioned Lawrence unkindly; the line of abusive conversation had been cut, as if swimming had the cleansing force claimed for baptism. We dried our hands and lighted cigarettes, and if Lawrence was mentioned, it was only to suggest, kindly, something that might please him. Wouldn't he like to sail to Barin's cove, or go fishing?

And now I remember that while Lawrence was visiting us, we went swimming oftener than we usually do, and I think there was a reason for this. When the irritability that accumulated as a result of his company began to lessen our patience, not only with Lawrence but with one another, we would all go swimming and shed our animus in the cold water. I can see the family now, smarting from Lawrence's rebukes as they sat on the sand, and I can see them wading and diving and surface-diving and hear in their voices the restoration of patience and the rediscovery of inexhaustible good will. If Lawrence noticed this change — this illusion of purification — I suppose that he would have found in the vocabulary of psychiatry, or the mythology of the Atlantic, some circumspect name for it, but I don't think he noticed the change. He neglected to name the curative powers of the open sea, but it was one of the few chances for diminution that he missed.

The cook we had that year was a Polish woman named Anna Ostrovick, a summer cook. She was first-rate — a big, fat, hearty, industrious woman who took her work seriously. She liked to cook and to have the food she cooked appreciated and eaten, and whenever we saw her, she always urged us to eat. She cooked hot bread — crescents and brioches — for breakfast two or three times a week, and she would bring these into the dining room herself and say, "Eat, eat, eat!" When the maid took the serving dishes back into the pantry, we could sometimes hear Anna, who was standing there, say, "Good! They eat." She fed the garbage man, the milkman, and the gardener. "Eat!" she told them. "Eat, eat!" On Thursday afternoons, she went to the movies with the maid, but she didn't enjoy the movies, because the actors were all so thin. She would sit in the dark theatre for an hour and a half watching the screen anxiously for the appearance of someone who had enjoyed his food. Bette Davis merely left with Anna the impression of a woman who has not eaten well. "They are all so skinny," she would say when she left the movies. In the evenings, after she had gorged all of us, and washed the pots and pans, she would collect the table scraps and go out to feed the creation. We had a few chickens that year, and although they would have roosted by then, she would dump food into their troughs and urge the sleeping fowl to eat. She fed the songbirds in the orchard and the chipmunks in the yard. Her appearance at the edge of the garden and her urgent voice — we could hear her calling

"Eat, eat, eat" — had become, like the sunset gun at the boat club and the passage of light from Cape Heron, attached to that hour. "Eat, eat, eat," we could hear Anna say. "Eat, eat . . ." Then it would be dark.

When Lawrence had been there three days, Anna called me into the kitchen. "You tell your mother," she said, "that *he* doesn't come into my kitchen. If *he* comes into my kitchen all the time, I go. *He* is always coming into my kitchen to tell me what a sad woman I am. He is always telling me that I work too hard and that I don't get paid enough and that I should belong to a union with vacations. Ha! He is so skinny but he is always coming into my kitchen when I am busy to pity me, but I am as good as him, I am as good as *anybody,* and I do not have to have people like that getting into my way all the time and feeling sorry for me. I am a famous and a wonderful cook and I have jobs everywhere and the only reason I come here to work this summer is because I was never before on an island, but I can have other jobs tomorrow, and if he is always coming into my kitchen to pity me, you tell your mother I am going. I am as good as *anybody* and I do not have to have that skinny all the time telling how poor I am."

I was pleased to find that the cook was on our side, but I felt that the situation was delicate. If Mother asked Lawrence to stay out of the kitchen, he would make a grievance out of the request. He could make a grievance out of anything, and it sometimes seemed that as he sat darkly at the dinner table, every word of disparagement, wherever it was aimed, came home to him. I didn't mention the cook's complaint to anyone, but somehow there wasn't any more trouble from that quarter.

The next cause for contention that I had from Lawrence came over our backgammon games.

When we are at Laud's Head, we play a lot of backgammon. At eight o'clock, after we have drunk our coffee, we usually get out the board. In a way, it is one of our pleasantest hours. The lamps in the room are still unlighted, Anna can be seen in the dark garden, and in the sky above her head there are continents of shadow and fire. Mother turns on the light and rattles the dice as a signal. We usually play three games apiece, each with the others. We play for money, and you can win or lose a hundred dollars on a game, but the stakes are usually much lower. I think that Lawrence used to play — I can't remember — but he doesn't play any more. He doesn't gamble. This is not because he is poor or because he has any principles about gambling but because he thinks the game is foolish and a waste of time. He was ready enough, however, to waste his time watching the rest of us play. Night after night, when the game began, he pulled a chair up beside the board, and watched the checkers and the dice. His expression was scornful, and yet he watched carefully. I wondered why he watched us night after night, and, through watching his face, I think that I may have found out.

Lawrence doesn't gamble, so he can't understand the excitement of winning and losing money. He has forgotten how to play the game, I think, so that its complex odds can't interest him. His observations were bound to include the facts that backgammon is an idle game and a game of chance, and that the board, marked with points, was a symbol of our worthlessness. And since he doesn't understand gambling or the odds of the game, I thought that what interested him must be the members of his family. One night when I was playing with Odette — I had won thirty-seven dollars from Mother and Chaddy — I think I saw what was going on in his mind.

Odette has black hair and black eyes. She is careful never to expose her white skin to the sun for long, so the striking contrast of blackness and pallor is not changed in the summer. She needs and deserves admiration — it is the element that contents her — and she will flirt, unseriously, with any man. Her shoulders were bare that night, her dress was cut to show the division of her breasts and to show her breasts when she leaned over the board to play. She kept losing and flirting and making her losses seem like a part of the flirtation. Chaddy was in the other room. She lost three games, and when the third game ended, she fell back on the sofa and, looking at me squarely, said something about going out on the dunes to settle the score. Lawrence heard her. I looked at Lawrence. He seemed shocked and gratified at the same time, as if he had suspected all along that we were not playing for anything so insubstantial as money. I may be wrong, of course, but I think that Lawrence felt that in watching our backgammon he was observing the progress of a mordant tragedy in which the money we won and lost served as a symbol for more vital forfeits. It is like Lawrence to try to read significance and finality into every gesture that we make, and it is certain of Lawrence that when he finds the inner logic to our conduct, it will be sordid.

Chaddy came in to play with me. Chaddy and I have never liked to lose to each other. When we were younger, we used to be forbidden to play games together, because they always ended in a fight. We think we know each other's mettle intimately. I think he is prudent; he thinks I am foolish. There is always bad blood when we play anything — tennis or backgammon or softball or bridge — and it does seem at times as if we were playing for the possession of each other's liberties. When I lose to Chaddy, I can't sleep. All this is only half the truth of our competitive relationship, but it was the half-truth that would be discernible to Lawrence, and his presence at the table made me so self-conscious that I lost two games. I tried not to seem angry when I got up from the board. Lawrence was watching me. I went out onto the terrace to suffer there in the dark the anger I always feel when I lose to Chaddy.

When I came back into the room, Chaddy and Mother were playing. Lawrence was still watching. By his lights, Odette had lost her virtue to me, I had lost my self-esteem to Chaddy, and now I wondered what he saw in the present match. He watched raptly, as if the opaque checkers and the marked board served for an exchange of critical power. How dramatic the board, in its ring of light, and the quiet players and the crash of the sea outside must have seemed to him! Here was spiritual cannibalism made visible; here, under his nose, were the symbols of the rapacious use human beings make of one another.

Mother plays a shrewd, an ardent, and an interfering game. She always has her hands in her opponent's board. When she plays with Chaddy, who is her favorite, she plays intently. Lawrence would have noticed this. Mother is a sentimental woman. Her heart is good and easily moved by tears and frailty, a characteristic that, like her handsome nose, has not been changed at all by age. Grief in another provokes her deeply, and she seems at times to be trying to divine in Chaddy some grief, some loss, that she can succor and redress, and so re-establish the relationship that she enjoyed with him when he was sickly and young. She loves defending the weak and the childlike, and now that we are old, she misses it. The world of debts and business, men and war, hunting and fishing has on her an exacerbating effect. (When Father drowned, she threw away his fly rods and his guns.) She has lectured us all endlessly on self-reliance, but when we come back to her for comfort and for help — particularly Chaddy — she seems to feel most like herself. I suppose Lawrence thought that the old woman and her son were playing for each other's soul.

She lost. "Oh *dear,*" she said. She looked stricken and bereaved, as she always does when she loses. "Get me my glasses, get me my checkbook, get me something to drink." Lawrence got up at last and stretched his legs. He looked at us all bleakly. The wind and the sea had risen, and I thought that if he heard the waves, he must hear them only as a dark answer to all his dark questions; that he would think that the tide had expunged the embers of our picnic fires. The company of a lie is unbearable, and he seemed like the embodiment of a lie. I couldn't explain to him the simple and intense pleasures of playing for money, and it seemed to me hideously wrong that he should have sat at the edge of the board and concluded that we were playing for one another's soul. He walked restlessly around the room two or three times and then, as usual, gave us a parting shot. "I should think you'd go crazy," he said, "cooped up with one another like this, night after night. Come on, Ruth. I'm going to bed."

That night, I dreamed about Lawrence. I saw his plain face magnified into ugliness, and when I woke in the morning, I felt sick, as if I had suffered a great spiritual loss while I slept, like the loss of courage and heart. It was foolish to let myself be troubled by my brother. I needed a vacation. I needed to relax. At school, we live in one of the dormitories, we eat at the house table, and we never get away. I not only teach English winter and summer but I work in the principal's office and fire the pistol at track meets. I needed to get away from this and from every other form of anxiety, and I decided to avoid my brother. Early that day, I took Helen and the children sailing, and we stayed out until suppertime. The next day, we went on a picnic. Then I had to go to New York for a day, and when I got back, there was the costume dance at the boat club. Lawrence wasn't going to this, and it's a party where I always have a wonderful time.

The invitations that year said to come as you wish you were. After several conversations, Helen and I had decided what to wear. The thing she most wanted to be again, she said, was a bride, and so she decided to wear her wedding dress. I thought this was a good choice — sincere, lighthearted, and inexpensive. Her choice influenced mine, and I decided to wear an old football uniform. Mother decided to go as Jenny Lind, because there was an old Jenny Lind costume in the attic. The others decided to rent costumes, and when I went to New York, I got the clothes. Lawrence and Ruth didn't enter into any of this.

Helen was on the dance committee, and she spent most of Friday decorating the club. Diana and Chaddy and I went sailing. Most of the sailing that I do these days is in Manhasset, and I am used to setting a homeward course by the gasoline barge and the tin roofs of the boat shed, and it was a pleasure that afternoon, as we returned, to keep the bow on a white church spire in the village and to find even the inshore water green and clear. At the end of our sail, we stopped at the club to get Helen. The committee had been trying to give a submarine appearance to the ballroom, and the fact that they had nearly succeeded in accomplishing this illusion made Helen very happy. We drove back to Laud's Head. It had been a brilliant afternoon, but on the way home we could smell the east wind — the dark wind, as Lawrence would have said — coming in from the sea.

My wife, Helen, is thirty-eight, and her hair would be gray, I guess, if it were not dyed, but it is dyed an unobtrusive yellow — a faded color — and I think it becomes her. I mixed cocktails that night while she was dressing, and when I took a glass upstairs to her, I saw her for the first time since our marriage in her wedding dress. There would be no point in saying that she looked to me more beautiful than she did on our wedding day, but because I have grown older and have, I think, a greater depth of feeling, and because I could see in her face that night both youth and age, both her devotion to the young woman that she had been and the positions that she had yielded graciously to time, I think I have never been so deeply moved. I had already put on the football uniform, and the weight of it, the heaviness of the pants and the shoulder guards, had worked a change in me, as if in putting on these old clothes I had put off the reasonable anxieties and troubles of my life. It felt as if we had both returned to the years before our marriage, the years before the war.

The Collards had a big dinner party before the dance, and our family — excepting Lawrence and Ruth — went to this. We drove over to the club, through the fog, at about half past nine. The orchestra was playing a waltz. While I was checking my raincoat, someone hit me on the back. It was Chucky Ewing, and the funny thing was that Chucky had on a football uniform. This seemed comical as hell to both of us. We were laughing when we went down the hall to the dance floor. I stopped at the door to look at the party, and it was beautiful. The committee had hung fish nets around the sides and over the high ceiling. The nets on the ceiling were filled with colored balloons. The light was soft and uneven, and the people — our friends and neighbors — dancing in the soft light to "Three O'Clock in the Morning" made a pretty picture. Then I noticed the number of women dressed in white, and I realized that they, like Helen, were wearing wedding dresses. Patsy Hewitt and Mrs. Gear and the Lackland girl waltzed by, dressed as brides. Then Pep Talcott came over to where Chucky and I were standing. He was dressed to be Henry VIII, but he told us that the Auerbach twins and Henry Barrett and Dwight MacGregor were all wearing football uniforms, and that by the last count there were ten brides on the floor.

This coincidence, this funny coincidence, kept everybody laughing, and made this one of the most lighthearted parties we've ever had at the club. At first I thought that the women had planned with one another to wear wedding dresses, but the ones that I danced with said it was a coincidence and I'm sure that Helen had made her decision alone. Everything went smoothly for me until a little before midnight. I saw Ruth standing at the edge of the floor. She was wearing a long red dress. It was all wrong. It wasn't the spirit of the party at all. I danced with her, but no one cut in, and I was darned if I'd spend the rest of the night dancing with her and I asked her where Lawrence was. She said he was out on the dock, and I took her over to the bar and left her and went out to get Lawrence.

The east fog was thick and wet, and he was alone on the dock. He was not in costume. He had not even bothered to get himself up as a fisherman or a sailor. He looked particularly saturnine. The fog blew around us like a cold smoke. I wished that it had been a clear night, because the easterly fog seemed to play into my misanthropic brother's hands. And I knew that the buoys — the groaners and bells that we could hear then — would sound to him like half-human, half-drowned cries, although every sailor knows that buoys are necessary and reliable fixtures, and I knew that the foghorn at the lighthouse would mean wanderings and losses to him and that he could misconstrue the vivacity of the dance music. "Come on in, Tifty," I said, "and dance with your wife or get her some partners."

"Why should I?" he said. "Why should I?" And he walked to the window and looked in at the party. "Look at it," he said. "Look at that . . ."

Chucky Ewing had got hold of a balloon and was trying to organize a scrimmage line in the middle of the floor. The others were dancing a samba. And I knew that Lawrence was looking bleakly at the party as he had looked at the weather-beaten shingles on our house, as if he saw here an abuse and a distortion of time; as if in wanting to be brides and football players we exposed the fact that, the lights of youth having been put out in us, we had been unable to find other lights to go by and, destitute of faith and principle, had become foolish and sad. And that he was thinking this about so many kind and happy and generous people made me angry, made me feel for him such an unnatural abhorrence that I was ashamed, for he is my brother and a Pommeroy. I put my arm around his shoulders and tried to force him to come in, but he wouldn't.

I got back in time for the Grand March, and after the prizes had been given out for the best costumes, they let the balloons down. The room was hot, and someone opened the big doors onto the dock, and the easterly wind circled the room and went out, carrying across the dock and out onto the water most of the balloons. Chucky Ewing went running out after the balloons, and when he saw them pass the dock and settle on the water, he took off his football uniform and dove in. Then Eric Auerbach dove in and Lew Phillips dove in and I dove in, and you know how it is at a party after midnight when people start jumping into the water. We recovered most of the balloons and dried off and went on dancing, and we didn't get home until morning.

The next day was the day of the flower show. Mother and Helen and Odette all had entries. We had a pickup lunch, and Chaddy drove the women and children over to the show. I took a nap, and in the middle of the afternoon I got some trunks and a towel and, on leaving the house, passed Ruth in the laundry. She was washing clothes. I don't know why she should seem to have so much more work to do than anyone else, but she is always washing or ironing or mending clothes. She may have been taught, when she was young, to spend her time like this, or she may be at the mercy of an expiatory passion. She seems to scrub and iron with a penitential fervor, although I can't imagine what it is that she thinks she's done wrong. Her children were with her in the laundry. I offered to take them to the beach, but they didn't want to go.

It was late in August, and the wild grapes that grow profusely all over the island made the land wind smell of wine. There is a little grove of holly at the end of the path, and then you climb the dunes, where nothing grows but that coarse grass. I could hear the sea, and I remember thinking how Chaddy and I used to talk mystically about the sea. When we were young, we had decided that we could never live in the West because we would miss the sea. "It is very nice here," we used to say politely when we visited people in the mountains, "but we miss the Atlantic." We used to look down our noses at people from Iowa and Colorado who had been denied this revelation, and we scorned the Pacific. Now I could hear the waves, whose heaviness sounded like a reverberation, like a tumult, and it pleased me as it had pleased me when I was young, and it seemed to have a purgative force, as if it had cleared my memory of, among other things, the penitential image of Ruth in the laundry.

But Lawrence was on the beach. There he sat. I went in without speaking. The water was cold, and when I came out, I put on a shirt. I told him that I was going to walk up to Tanners Point, and he said that he would come with me. I tried to walk beside him. His legs are no longer than mine, but he always likes to stay a little ahead of his companion. Walking along behind him, looking at his bent head and his shoulders, I wondered what he could make of that landscape.

There were the dunes and cliffs, and then, where they declined, there were some fields that had begun to turn from green to brown and yellow. The fields were used for pasturing sheep, and I guess Lawrence would have noticed that the soil was eroded and that the sheep would accelerate this decay. Beyond the fields there are a few coastal farms, with square and pleasant buildings, but Lawrence could have pointed out the hard lot of an island farmer. The sea, at our other side, was the open sea. We always tell guests that there, to the east, lies the coast of Portugal, and for Lawrence it would be an easy step from the coast of Portugal to the tyranny of Spain. The waves broke with a noise like a "hurrah, hurrah, hurrah," but to Lawrence they would say *"Vale, vale."* I suppose it would have occurred to his baleful and incisive mind that the coast was terminal moraine, the edge of the prehistoric world, and it must have occurred to him that we walked along the edge of the known world in spirit as much as in fact. If he should otherwise have overlooked this, there were some Navy planes bombing an uninhabited island to remind him.

That beach is a vast and preternaturally clean and simple landscape. It is like a piece of the moon. The surf had pounded the floor solid, so it was easy walking, and everything left on the sand had been twice changed by the waves. There was the spine of a shell, a broomstick, part of a bottle and part of a brick, both of them milled and broken until they were nearly unrecognizable, and I suppose Lawrence's sad frame of mind — for he kept his head down — went from one broken thing to another. The company of his pessimism began to infuriate me, and I caught up with him and put a hand on his shoulder. "It's only a summer day, Tifty," I said. "It's only a summer day. What's the matter? Don't you like it here?"

"I don't like it here," he said blandly, without raising his eyes. "I'm going to sell my equity in the house to Chaddy. I didn't expect to have a good time. The only reason I came back was to say goodbye."

I let him get ahead again and I walked behind him, looking at his shoulders and thinking of all the goodbyes he had made. When Father drowned, he went to church and said goodbye to Father. It was only three years later that he concluded that Mother was frivolous and said goodbye to her. In his freshman year at college, he had been very good friends with his roommate, but the man drank too much, and at the beginning of the spring term Lawrence changed roommates and said goodbye to his friend. When he had been in college for two years, he concluded that the atmosphere was too sequestered and he said goodbye to Yale. He enrolled at Columbia and got his law degree there, but he found his first employer dishonest, and at the end of six months he said goodbye to a good job. He married Ruth in City Hall and said goodbye to the Protestant Episcopal Church; they went to live on a back street in Tuckahoe and said goodbye to the middle class. In 1938, he went to Washington to work as a government lawyer, saying goodbye to private enterprise, but after eight months in Washington he concluded that the Roosevelt administration was sentimental and he said goodbye to it. They left Washington for a suburb of Chicago, where he said goodbye to his neighbors, one by one, on counts of drunkenness, boorishness, and stupidity. He said goodbye to Chicago and went to Kansas; he said goodbye to Kansas and went to Cleveland. Now he had said goodbye to Cleveland and come East again, stopping at Laud's Head long enough to say goodbye to the sea.

It was elegiac and it was bigoted and narrow, it mistook circum-
spection for character, and I wanted to help him. "Come out of it," I
said. "Come out of it, Tifty."

"Come out of what?"

"Come out of this gloominess. Come out of it. It's only a summer
day. You're spoiling your own good time and you're spoiling everyone
else's. We need a vacation, Tifty. I need one. I need to rest. We all do.
And you've made everything tense and unpleasant. I only have two
weeks in the year. Two weeks. I need to have a good time and so do all
the others. We need to rest. You think that your pessimism is an advantage, but it's nothing but an unwillingness to grasp realities."

"What are the realities?" he said. "Diana is a foolish promiscuous
woman. So is Odette. Mother is an alcoholic. If she doesn't discipline
herself, she'll be in a hospital in a year or two. Chaddy is dishonest. He
always has been. The house is going to fall into the sea." He looked at
me and added, as an afterthought, "You're a fool."

"You're a gloomy son of a bitch," I said. "You're a gloomy son of a
bitch."

"Get your fat face out of mine," he said. He walked along.

Then I picked up a root and, coming at his back — although I have
never hit a man from the back before — I swung the root, heavy with
sea water, behind me, and the momentum sped my arm and I gave
him, my brother, a blow on the head that forced him to his knees on
the sand, and I saw the blood come out and begin to darken his hair.
Then I wished that he was dead, dead and about to be buried, not buried
but about to be buried, because I did not want to be denied ceremony
and decorum in putting him away, in putting him out of my consciousness, and I saw the rest of us — Chaddy and Mother and Diana and
Helen — in mourning in the house on Belvedere Street that was torn
down twenty years ago, greeting our guests and our relatives at the
door and answering their mannerly condolences with mannerly grief.
Nothing decorous was lacking so that even if he had been murdered on
a beach, one would feel before the tiresome ceremony ended that he
had come into the winter of his life and that it was a law of nature, and
a beautiful one, that Tifty should be buried in the cold, cold ground.

He was still on his knees. I looked up and down. No one had seen
us. The naked beach, like a piece of the moon, reached to invisibility.
The spill of a wave, in a glancing run, shot up to where he knelt. I
would still have liked to end him, but now I had begun to act like two
men, the murderer and the Samaritan. With a swift roar, like hollow-
ness made sound, a white wave reached him and encircled him, boiling
over his shoulders, and I held him against the undertow. Then I led
him to a higher place. The blood had spread all through his hair, so

that it looked black. I took off my shirt and tore it to bind up his head. He was conscious, and I didn't think he was badly hurt. He didn't speak. Neither did I. Then I left him there.

I walked a little way down the beach and turned to watch him, and I was thinking of my own skin then. He had got to his feet and he seemed steady. The daylight was still clear, but on the sea wind fumes of brine were blowing in like a light fog, and when I had walked a little way from him, I could hardly see his dark figure in this obscurity. All down the beach I could see the heavy salt air blowing in. Then I turned my back on him, and as I got near the house, I went swimming again, as I seem to have done after every encounter with Lawrence that summer.

When I got to the house, I lay down on the terrace. The others came back. I could hear Mother defaming the flower arrangements that had won prizes. None of ours had won anything. Then the house quieted, as it always does at that hour. The children went into the kitchen to get supper and the others went upstairs to bathe. Then I heard Chaddy making cocktails, and the conversation about the flower show judges was resumed. Then Mother cried, "Tifty! Tifty! Oh, Tifty!"

He stood in the door, looking half dead. He had taken off the bloody bandage and he held it in his hand. "My brother did his," he said. "My brother did it. He hit me with a stone — something — on the beach." His voice broke with self-pity. I thought he was going to cry. No one else spoke. "Where's Ruth?" he cried. "Where's Ruth? Where in hell is Ruth? I want her to start packing. I don't have any more time to waste here. I have important things to do. I have *important* things to do." And he went up the stairs.

They left for the mainland the next morning, taking the six-o'clock boat. Mother got up to say goodbye, but she was the only one, and it is a harsh and an easy scene to imagine — the matriarch and the changeling, looking at each other with a dismay that would seem like the powers of love reversed. I heard the children's voices and the car go down the drive, and I got up and went to the window, and what a morning that was! Jesus, what a morning! The wind was northerly. The air was clear. In the early heat, the roses in the garden smelled like strawberry jam. While I was dressing, I heard the boat whistle, first the warning signal and then the double blast, and I could see the good people on the top deck drinking coffee out of fragile paper cups, and Lawrence at the bow, saying to the sea, "*Thalassa, thalassa,*" while his timid and unhappy children watched the creation from the encirclement of their mother's arms. The buoys would toll mournfully for Lawrence, and while the grace of the light would make it an exertion not to throw out your arms and swear exultantly, Lawrence's eyes would trace the black sea as it fell astern; he would think of the bottom, dark and strange, where full fathom five our father lies.

Oh, what can you do with a man like that? What can you do? How can you dissuade his eye in a crowd from seeking out the cheek with acne, the infirm hand; how can you teach him to respond to the inestimable greatness of the race, the harsh surface beauty of life; how can you put his finger for him on the obdurate truths before which fear and horror are powerless? The sea that morning was iridescent and dark. My wife and my sister were swimming — Diana and Helen — and I saw their uncovered heads, black and gold in the dark water. I saw them come out and I saw that they were naked, unshy, beautiful, and full of grace, and I watched the naked women walk out of the sea.

The Five-Forty-Eight

When Blake stepped out of the elevator, he saw her. A few people, mostly men waiting for girls, stood in the lobby watching the elevator doors. She was among them. As he saw her, her face took on a look of such loathing and purpose that he realized she had been waiting for him. He did not approach her. She had no legitimate business with him. They had nothing to say. He turned and walked toward the glass doors at the end of the lobby, feeling that faint guilt and bewilderment we experience when we bypass some old friend or classmate who seems threadbare, or sick, or miserable in some other way. It was five-eighteen by the clock in the Western Union office. He could catch the express. As he waited his turn at the revolving doors, he saw that it was still raining. It had been raining all day, and he noticed now how much louder the rain made the noises of the street. Outside, he started walking briskly east toward Madison Avenue. Traffic was tied up, and horns were blowing urgently on a crosstown street in the distance. The sidewalk was crowded. He wondered what she had hoped to gain by a glimpse of him coming out of the office building at the end of the day. Then he wondered if she was following him.

Walking in the city, we seldom turn and look back. The habit restrained Blake. He listened for a minute — foolishly — as he walked, as if he could distinguish her footsteps from the worlds of sound in the city at the end of a rainy day. Then he noticed, ahead of him on the other side of the street, a break in the wall of buildings. Something had been torn down; something was being put up, but the steel structure had only just risen above the sidewalk fence and daylight poured through the gap. Blake stopped opposite here and looked into the store window. It was a decorator's or an auctioneer's. The window was arranged like a room in which people live and entertain their friends. There were cups on the coffee table, magazines to read, and flowers in the vases, but the flowers were dead and the cups were empty and the guests had not come. In the plate glass, Blake saw a clear reflection of himself and the crowds that were passing, like shadows, at his back. Then he saw her image — so close to him that it shocked him. She was standing only a foot or two behind him. He could have turned then and asked her what she wanted, but instead of recognizing her, he

167

shied away abruptly from the reflection of her contorted face and went along the street. She might be meaning to do him harm — she might be meaning to kill him.

The suddenness with which he moved when he saw the reflection of her face tipped the water out of his hat brim in such a way that some of it ran down his neck. It felt unpleasantly like the sweat of fear. Then the cold water falling into his face and onto his bare hands, the rancid smell of the wet gutters and paving, the knowledge that his feet were beginning to get wet and that he might catch cold — all the common discomforts of walking in the rain — seemed to heighten the menace of his pursuer and to give him a morbid consciousness of his own physicalness and of the ease with which he could be hurt. He could see ahead of him the corner of Madison Avenue, where the lights were brighter. He felt that if he could get to Madison Avenue he would be all right. At the corner, there was a bakery shop with two entrances, and he went in by the door on the crosstown street, bought a coffee ring, like any other commuter, and went out the Madison Avenue door. As he started down Madison Avenue, he saw her waiting for him by a hut where newspapers were sold.

She was not clever. She would be easy to shake. He could get into a taxi by one door and leave by the other. He could speak to a policeman. He could run — although he was afraid that if he did run, it might precipitate the violence he now felt sure she had planned. He was approaching a part of the city that he knew well and where the maze of street-level and underground passages, elevator banks, and crowded lobbies made it easy for a man to lose a pursuer. The thought of this, and a whiff of sugary warmth from the coffee ring, cheered him. It was absurd to imagine being harmed on a crowded street. She was foolish, misled, lonely perhaps — that was all it could amount to. He was an insignificant man, and there was no point in anyone's following him from his office to the station. He knew no secrets of any consequence. The reports in his briefcase had no bearing on war, peace, the dope traffic, the hydrogen bomb, or any of the other international skulduggeries that he associated with pursuers, men in trench coats, and wet sidewalks. Then he saw ahead of him the door of a men's bar. Oh, it was so simple!

He ordered a Gibson and shouldered his way in between two other men at the bar, so that if she should be watching from the window she would lose sight of him. The place was crowded with commuters putting down a drink before the ride home. They had brought in on their clothes — on their shoes and umbrellas — the rancid smell of the wet dusk outside, but Blake began to relax as soon as he tasted his Gibson and looked around at the common, mostly not-young faces that surrounded him and that were worried, if they were worried at all, about tax rates and who would be put in charge of merchandising. He tried to remember her name — Miss Dent, Miss Bent, Miss Lent — and he was surprised to find that he could not remember it, although he was proud of the retentiveness and reach of his memory and it had only been six months ago.

Personnel had sent her up one afternoon — he was looking for a secretary. He saw a dark woman — in her twenties, perhaps — who was slender and shy. Her dress was simple, her figure was not much, one of her stockings was crooked, but her voice was soft and he had been willing to try her out. After she had been working for him a few days, she told him that she had been in the hospital for eight months and that it had been hard after this for her to find work, and she wanted to thank him for giving her a chance. Her hair was dark, her eyes were dark; she left with him a pleasant impression of darkness. As he got to know her better, he felt that she was oversensitive and, as a consequence, lonely. Once, when she was speaking to him of what she imagined his life to be — full of friendships, money, and a large and loving family — he had thought he recognized a peculiar feeling of deprivation. She seemed to imagine the lives of the rest of the world to be more brilliant than they were. Once, she had put a rose on his desk, and he had dropped it into the wastebasket. "I don't like roses," he told her.

She had been competent, punctual, and a good typist, and he had found only one thing in her that he could object to — her handwriting. He could not associate the crudeness of her handwriting with her appearance. He would have expected her to write a rounded backhand, and in her writing there were intermittent traces of this, mixed with clumsy printing. Her writing gave him the feeling that she had been the victim of some inner — some emotional — conflict that had in its violence broken the continuity of the lines she was able to make on paper. When she had been working for him three weeks — no longer — they stayed late one night and he offered, after work, to buy her a drink. "If you really want a drink," she said, "I have some whiskey at my place."

She lived in a room that seemed to him like a closet. There were suit boxes and hatboxes piled in a corner, and although the room seemed hardly big enough to hold the bed, the dresser, and the chair he sat in, there was an upright piano against one wall, with a book of Beethoven sonatas on the rack. She gave him a drink and said that she was going to put on something more comfortable. He urged her to; that was, after all, what he had come for. If he had any qualms, they would have been practical. Her diffidence, the feeling of deprivation in her point of view, promised to protect him from any consequences.

Most of the many women he had known had been picked for their lack of self-esteem.

When he put on his clothes again, an hour or so later, she was weeping. He felt too contented and warm and sleepy to worry much about her tears. As he was dressing, he noticed on the dresser a note she had written to a cleaning woman. The only light came from the bathroom — the door was ajar — and in this half light the hideously scrawled letters again seemed entirely wrong for her, and as if they must be the handwriting of some other and very gross woman. The next day, he did what he felt was the only sensible thing. When she was out for lunch, he called personnel and asked them to fire her. Then he took the afternoon off. A few days later, she came to the office, asking to see him. He told the switchboard girl not to let her in. He had not seen her again until this evening.

Blake drank a second Gibson and saw by the clock that he had missed the express. He would get the local — the five-forty-eight. When he left the bar the sky was still light; it was still raining. He looked carefully up and down the street and saw that the poor woman had gone. Once or twice, he looked over his shoulder, walking to the station, but he seemed to be safe. He was still not quite himself, he realized, because he had left his coffee ring at the bar, and he was not a man who forgot things. This lapse of memory pained him.

He bought a paper. The local was only half full when he boarded it, and he got a seat on the river side and took off his raincoat. He was a slender man with brown hair — undistinguished in every way, unless you could have divined in his pallor or his gray eyes his unpleasant tastes. He dressed — like the rest of us — as if he admitted the existence of sumptuary laws. His raincoat was the pale buff color of a mushroom. His hat was dark brown; so was his suit. Except for the few bright threads in his necktie, there was scrupulous lack of color in his clothing that seemed protective.

He looked around the car for neighbors. Mrs. Compton was several seats in front of him, to the right. She smiled, but her smile was fleeting. It died swiftly and horribly. Mr. Watkins was directly in front of Blake. Mr. Watkins needed a haircut, and he had broken the sumptuary laws; he was wearing a corduroy jacket. He and Blake had quarreled, so they did not speak.

The swift death of Mrs. Compton's smile did not affect Blake at all. The Comptons lived in the house next to the Blakes, and Mrs. Compton had never understood the importance of minding her own business. Louise Blake took her troubles to Mrs. Compton, Blake knew, and instead of discouraging her crying jags, Mrs. Compton had come to imagine herself a sort of confessor and had developed a lively curiosity about the Blakes' intimate affairs. She had probably been given an account of their most recent quarrel. Blake had come home one night, overworked and tired, and had found that Louise had done nothing about getting supper. He had gone into the kitchen, followed by Louise, and had pointed out to her that the date was the fifth. He had drawn a circle around the date on the kitchen calendar. "One week is the twelfth," he had said. "Two weeks will be the nineteenth." He drew a circle around the nineteenth. "I'm not going to speak to you for two weeks," he had said. "That will be the nineteenth." She had wept, she had protested, but it had been eight or ten years since she had been able to touch him with her entreaties. Louise had got old. Now the lines in her face were ineradicable, and when she clapped her glasses onto her nose to read the evening paper, she looked to him like an unpleasant stranger. The physical charms that had been her only attraction were gone. It had been nine years since Blake had built a bookshelf in the doorway that connected their rooms and had fitted into the bookshelf wooden doors that could be locked, since he did not want the children to see his books. But their prolonged estrangement didn't seem remarkable to Blake. He had quarreled with his wife, but so did every other man born of woman. It was human nature. In any place where you can hear their voices — a hotel courtyard, an air shaft, a street on a summer evening — you will hear harsh words.

The hard feeling between Blake and Mr. Watkins also had to do with Blake's family, but it was not as serious or as troublesome as what lay behind Mrs. Compton's fleeting smile. The Watkinses rented. Mr. Watkins broke the sumptuary laws day after day — he once went to the eight-fourteen in a pair of sandals — and he made his living as a commercial artist. Blake's oldest son — Charlie was fourteen — had made friends with the Watkins boy. He had spent a lot of time in the sloppy rented house where the Watkinses lived. The friendship had affected his manners and his neatness. Then he had begun to take some meals with the Watkinses, and to spend Saturday nights there. When he had moved most of his possessions over to the Watkinses' and had begun to spend more than half his nights there, Blake had been forced to act. He had spoken not to Charlie but to Mr. Watkins, and had, of necessity, said a number of things that must have sounded critical. Mr. Watkins' long and dirty hair and his corduroy jacket reassured Blake that he had been in the right.

But Mrs. Compton's dying smile and Mr. Watkins' dirty hair did not lessen the pleasure Blake took in setting himself in an uncomfortable seat on the five-forty-eight deep underground. The coach was old and smelled oddly like a bomb shelter in which whole families had spent the night. The light that spread from the ceiling down onto their heads and shoulders was dim. The filth on the window glass was streaked with rain from some other journey, and clouds of rank pipe and cigarette smoke had begun to rise from behind each newspaper, but it was a scene that meant to Blake that he was on a safe path, and after his brush with danger he even felt a little warmth toward Mrs. Compton and Mr. Watkins.

The train traveled up from underground into the weak daylight, and the slums and the city reminded Blake vaguely of the woman who had followed him. To avoid speculation or remorse about her, he turned his attention to the evening paper. Out of the corner of his eye he could see the landscape. It was industrial and, at that hour, sad. There were machine sheds and warehouses, and above these he saw a break in the clouds — a piece of yellow light. "Mr. Blake," someone said. He looked up. It was she. She was standing there holding one hand on the back of the seat to steady herself in the swaying coach. He remembered her name then — Miss Dent. "Hello, Miss Dent," he said.

"Do you mind if I sit here?"

"I guess not."

"Thank you. It's very kind of you. I don't like to inconvenience you like this. I don't want to . . ." He had been frightened when he looked up and saw her, but her timid voice rapidly reassured him. He shifted his hams — that futile and reflexive gesture of hospitality — and she sat down. She sighed. He smelled her wet clothing. She wore a formless black hat with a cheap crest stitched onto it. Her coat was thin cloth, he saw, and she wore gloves and carried a large pocketbook.

"Are you living out in this direction now, Miss Dent?"

"No."

She opened her purse and reached for her handkerchief. She had begun to cry. He turned his head to see if anyone in the car was looking, but no one was. He had sat beside a thousand passengers on the evening train. He had noticed their clothes, the holes in their gloves; and if they fell asleep and mumbled he had wondered what their worries were. He had classified almost all of them briefly before he buried his nose in the paper. He had marked them as rich, poor, brilliant or dull, neighbors or strangers, but no one of the thousand had ever wept. When she opened her purse, he remembered her perfume. It had clung to his skin the night he went to her place for a drink.

"I've been very sick," she said. "This is the first time I've been out of bed in two weeks. I've been terribly sick."

"I'm sorry that you've been sick, Miss Dent," he said in a voice loud enough to be heard by Mr. Watkins and Mrs. Compton. "Where are you working now?"

"What?"

"Where are you working now?"

"Oh, don't make me laugh," she said softly.

"I don't understand."

"You poisoned their minds."

He straightened his neck and braced his shoulders. These wrenching movements expressed a brief — and hopeless — longing to be in some other place. She meant trouble. He took a breath. He looked with deep feeling at the half-filled, half-lighted coach to affirm his sense of actuality, of a world in which there was not very much bad trouble after all. He was conscious of her heavy breathing and the smell of her rain-soaked coat. The train stopped. A nun and a man in overalls got off. When it started again, Blake put on his hat and reached for his raincoat.

"Where are you going?" she said.

"I'm going to the next car."

"Oh, no," she said. "No, no, no." She put her white face so close to his ear that he could feel her warm breath on his cheek. "Don't do that," she whispered. "Don't try and escape me. I have a pistol and I'll have to kill you and I don't want to. All I want to do is to talk with you. Don't move or I'll kill you. Don't, don't, don't!"

Blake sat back abruptly in his seat. If he had wanted to stand and shout for help, he would not have been able to. His tongue had swelled to twice its size, and when he tried to move it, it stuck horribly to the roof of his mouth. His legs were limp. All he could think of to do then was to wait for his heart to stop its hysterical beating, so that he could judge the extent of his danger. She was sitting a little sidewise, and in her pocketbook was the pistol, aimed at his belly.

"You understand me now, don't you?" she said. "You understand that I'm serious?" He tried to speak but he was still mute. He nodded his head. "Now we'll sit quietly for a little while," she said. "I got so excited that my thoughts are all confused. We'll sit quietly for a little while, until I can get my thoughts in order again."

Help would come, Blake thought. It was only a question of minutes. Someone, noticing the look on his face or her peculiar posture, would stop and interfere, and it would all be over. All he had to do was to wait until someone noticed his predicament. Out of the window he saw the river and the sky. The rain clouds were rolling down like a shutter, and while he watched, a streak of orange light on the horizon became brilliant. Its brilliance spread — he could see it move — across the waves until it raked the banks of the river with a dim firelight. Then it was put out. Help would come in a minute, he thought. Help would come before they stopped again; but the train stopped, there were some comings and goings, and Blake still lived on, at the mercy of the woman beside him. The possibility that help might not come was one that he could not face. The possibility that his predicament was not noticeable, that Mrs. Compton would guess that he was taking a poor relation out to dinner at Shady Hill, was something he would think about later. Then the saliva came back into his mouth and he was able to speak.

"Miss Dent?"

"Yes."

"What do you want?"

"I want to talk to you."

"You can come to my office."

"Oh, no. I went there every day for two weeks."

"You could make an appointment."

"No," she said. "I think we can talk here. I wrote you a letter but I've been too sick to go out and mail it. I've put down all my thoughts. I like to travel. I like trains. One of my troubles has always been that I could never afford to travel. I suppose you see this scenery every night and don't notice it any more, but it's nice for someone who's been in bed a long time. They say that He's not in the river and the hills but I think He is. 'Where shall wisdom be found?' it says. 'Where is the place of understanding? The depth saith it is not in me; the sea saith it is not with me. Destruction and death say we have heard the force with our ears.'

"Oh, I know what you're thinking," she said. "You're thinking that I'm crazy, and I have been very sick again but I'm going to be better. It's going to make me better to talk with you. I was in the hospital all the time before I came to work for you but they never tried to cure me, they only wanted to take away my self-respect. I haven't had any work now for three months. Even if I did have to kill you, they wouldn't be able to do anything to me except put me back in the hospital, so you see I'm not afraid. But let's sit quietly for a little while longer. I have to be calm."

The train continued its halting progress up the bank of the river, and Blake tried to force himself to make some plans for escape, but the immediate threat to his life made this difficult, and instead of planning sensibly, he thought of the many ways in which he could have avoided her in the first place. As soon as he had felt these regrets, he realized their futility. It was like regretting his lack of suspicion when she first mentioned her months in the hospital. It was like regretting his failure to have been warned by her shyness, her diffidence, and the handwriting that looked like the marks of a claw. There was no way of rectifying his mistakes, and he felt — for perhaps the first time in his mature life — the full force of regret. Out of the window, he saw some men fishing on the nearly dark river, and then a ramshackle boat club that seemed to have been nailed together out of scraps of wood that had been washed up on the shore.

Mr. Watkins had fallen asleep. He was snoring. Mrs. Compton read her paper. The train creaked, slowed, and halted infirmly at another station. Blake could see the southbound platform, where a few passengers were waiting to go into the city. There was a workman with a lunch pail, a dressed-up woman, and a woman with a suitcase. They stood apart from one another. Some advertisements were posted on the wall behind them. There was a picture of a couple drinking a toast in wine, a picture of a Cat's Paw rubber heel, and a picture of a Hawaiian dancer. Their cheerful intent seemed to go no farther than the puddles of water on the platform and to expire there. The platform and the people on it looked lonely. The train drew away from the station into the scattered lights of a slum and then into the darkness of the country and the river.

"I want you to read my letter before we get to Shady Hill," she said. "It's on the seat. Pick it up. I would have mailed it to you, but I've been too sick to go out. I haven't gone out for two weeks. I haven't had any work for three months. I haven't spoken to anybody but the landlady. Please read my letter."

He picked up the letter from the seat where she had put it. The cheap paper felt abhorrent and filthy to his fingers. It was folded and refolded. "Dear Husband," she had written, in that crazy, wandering hand, "they say that human love leads us to divine love, but is this true? I dream about you every night. I have such terrible desires. I have always had a gift for dreams. I dreamed on Tuesday of a volcano erupting with blood. When I was in the hospital they said they wanted to cure me but they only wanted to take away my self-respect. They only wanted me to dream about sewing and basketwork but I protected my gift for dreams. I'm clairvoyant. I can tell when the telephone is going to ring. I've never had a true friend in my whole life. . . ."

The train stopped again. There was another platform, another picture of the couple drinking a toast, the rubber heel, and the Hawaiian dancer. Suddenly she pressed her face close to Blake's again and whispered in his ear. "I know what you're thinking. I can see it in your face. You're thinking you can get away from me in Shady Hill, aren't you? Oh, I've been planning this for weeks. It's all I've had to think about. I won't harm you if you'll let me talk. I've been thinking about devils. I mean, if there are devils in the world, if there are people in the world who represent evil, is it our duty to exterminate them? I know that you always prey on weak people. I can tell. Oh, sometimes I think

I ought to kill you. Sometimes I think you're the only obstacle between me and my happiness. Sometimes . . ."

She touched Blake with the pistol. He felt the muzzle against his belly. The bullet, at that distance, would make a small hole where it entered, but it would rip out of his back a place as big as a soccer ball. He remembered the unburied dead he had seen in the war. The memory came in a rush; entrails, eyes, shattered bone, ordure, and other filth.

"All I've ever wanted in life is a little love," she said. She lightened the pressure of the gun. Mr. Watkins still slept. Mrs. Compton was sitting calmly with her hands folded in her lap. The coach rocked gently, and the coats and mushroom-colored raincoats that hung between the windows swayed a little as the car moved. Blake's elbow was on the window sill and his left shoe was on the guard above the steampipe. The car smelled like some dismal classroom. The passengers seemed asleep and apart, and Blake felt that he might never escape the smell of heat and wet clothing and the dimness of the light. He tried to summon the calculated self-deceptions with which he sometimes cheered himself, but he was left without any energy for hope of self-deception.

The conductor put his head in the door and said, "Shady Hill, next, Shady Hill."

"Now," she said. "Now you get out ahead of me."

Mr. Watkins waked suddenly, put on his coat and hat, and smiled at Mrs. Compton, who was gathering her parcels to her in a series of maternal gestures. They went to the door. Blake joined them, but neither of them spoke to him or seemed to notice the woman at his back. The conductor threw open the door, and Blake saw on the platform of the next car a few other neighbors who had missed the express, waiting patiently and tiredly in the wan light for their trip to end. He raised his head to see through the open door the abandoned mansion out of town, a NO TRESPASSING sign nailed to a tree, and then the oil tanks. The concrete abutments of the bridge passed, so close to the open door that he could have touched them. Then he saw the first of the lampposts on the northbound platform, the sign SHADY HILL in black and gold, and the little lawn and flower bed kept up by the Improvement Association, and then the cab stand and a corner of the old-fashioned depot. It was raining again; it was pouring. He could hear the splash of water and see the lights reflected in puddles and in the shining pavement, and the idle sound of splashing and dripping formed in his mind a conception of shelter, so light and strange that it seemed to belong to a time of his life that he could not remember.

He went down the steps with her at his back. A dozen or so cars were waiting by the station with their motors running. A few people got off from each of the other coaches; he recognized most of them, but none of them offered to give him a ride. They walked separately or in pairs — purposefully out of the rain to the shelter of the platform, where the car horns called to them. It was time to go home, time for a drink, time for love, time for supper, and he could see the lights on the hill — lights by which children were being bathed, meat cooked, dishes washed — shining in the rain. One by one, the cars picked up the heads of families, until there were only four left. Two of the stranded passengers drove off in the only taxi the village had. "I'm sorry, darling," a woman said tenderly to her husband when she drove up a few minutes later. "All our clocks are slow." The last man looked at his watch, looked at the rain, and then walked off into it, and Blake saw him go as if they had some reason to say goodbye — not as we say goodbye to friends after a party but as we say goodbye when we are faced with an inexorable and unwanted parting of the spirit and the heart. The man's footsteps sounded as he crossed the parking lot to the sidewalk, and then they were lost. In the station, a telephone began to ring. The ringing was loud, evenly spaced, and unanswered. Someone wanted to know about the next train to Albany, but Mr. Flanagan, the stationmaster, had gone home an hour ago. He had turned on all his lights before he went away. They burned in the empty waiting room. They burned, tin-shaded, at intervals up and down the platform and with the peculiar sadness of dim and purposeless lights. They lighted the Hawaiian dancer, the couple drinking a toast, the rubber heel.

"I've never been here before," she said. "I thought it would look different. I didn't think it would look so shabby. Let's get out of the light. Go over there."

His legs felt sore. All his strength was gone. "Go on," she said.

North of the station there were a freight house and a coal yard and an inlet where the butcher and the baker and the man who ran the service station moored the dinghies, from which they fished on Sundays, sunk now to the gunwales with the rain. As he walked toward the freight house, he saw a movement on the ground and heard a scraping sound, and then he saw a rat take its head out of a paper bag and regard him. The rat seized the bag in its teeth and dragged it into a culvert.

"Stop," she said. "Turn around. Oh, I ought to feel sorry for you. Look at your poor face. But you don't know what I've been through. I'm afraid to go out in the daylight. I'm afraid the blue sky will fall down on me. I'm like poor Chicken-Licken. I only feel like myself when it begins to get dark. But still and all I'm better than you. I still have good dreams sometimes. I dream about picnics and heaven and the brotherhood of man, and about castles in the moonlight and a river with willow trees all along the edge of it and foreign cities, and after all I know more about love than you."

He heard from off the dark river the drone of an outboard motor, a sound that drew slowly behind it across the dark water such a burden of clear, sweet memories of gone summers and gone pleasures that it made his flesh crawl, and he thought of dark in the mountains and the children singing. "They never wanted to cure me," she said. "They . . ." The noise of a train coming down from the north drowned out her voice, but she went on talking. The noise filled his ears, and the windows where people ate, drank, slept, and read flew past. When the train had passed beyond the bridge, the noise grew distant, and he heard her screaming at him, "*Kneel down!* Kneel down! Do what I say. *Kneel down!*"

He got to his knees. He bent his head. "There," she said. "You see, if you do what I say, I won't harm you, because I really don't want to harm you, I want to help you, but when I see your face it sometimes seems to me that I can't help you. Sometimes it seems to me that if I were good and loving and sane — oh, much better than I am — sometimes it seems to me that if I were all these things and young and beautiful, too, and if I called to show you the right way, you wouldn't heed me. Oh, I'm better than you, I'm better than you, and I shouldn't waste my time or spoil my life like this. Put your face in the dirt. *Put your face in the dirt!* Do what I say. Put your face in the dirt."

He fell forward in the filth. The coal skinned his face. He stretched out on the ground, weeping. "Now I feel better," she said. "Now I can wash my hands of you, I can wash my hands of all this, because you see there is some kindness, some saneness in me that I can find and use. I can wash my hands." Then he heard her footsteps go away from him, over the rubble. He heard the clearer and more distant sound they made on the hard surface of the platform. He heard them diminish. He raised his head. He saw her climb the stairs of the wooden footbridge and cross it and go down to the other platform, where her figure in the dim light looked small, common, and harmless. He raised himself out of the dust — warily at first, until he saw by her attitude, her looks, that she had forgotten him; that she had completed what she had wanted to do, and that he was safe. He got to his feet and picked up his hat from the ground where it had fallen and walked home.

Robert Coover

Throughout his career, Robert Coover has been reexamining the myths our culture is founded upon, from the Biblical accounts of Noah and the virgin birth in *Pricksongs & Descants* to Aesop's fables ("Aesop's Forest"), the western (*Ghost Town*), the fairy tale (*Briar Rose*), and the mythos of American politics ("The Cat in the Hat for President"). His stories are complex and allusive, formally inventive, absurd, subversive, and very, very funny. Best-known among his short stories — or at least the most anthologized — is "The Babysitter," an experiment in deconstructing a narrative and reassembling it from multiple and often conflicting points of view. Coover also practices what I call a fiction of interruption, in which the ordered and selected world of the writer's creation is undermined by the sort of chaos that intrudes on the life we all live beyond the page. His 1996 novel, *John's Wife,* is an example on a larger scale of what he achieves in the first piece selected here, "the convention," from *In Bed One Night & Other Brief Encounters.*

"the convention" is set in enjambed lines, as if it were a poem, and the form strengthens the breathless feeling of the headlong pace of the story and the comedy that derives from it. The second piece, "The Brother," one of the "Seven Exemplary Fictions" from Coover's first collection, *Pricksongs & Descants* (1969), achieves the same breathless effect in the opposite way: It consists in its entirety of a single long run-on sentence that never gives the reader a chance to pull back from it. Not only does the story reimagine the Biblical tale of Noah's Ark, but it also serves, like Cheever's "Goodbye, My Brother," as a lesson in point of view.

Coover is the author of *The Origin of the Brunists, The Universal Baseball Association, J. Henry Waugh, Prop., Spanking the Maid, Gerald's Party,* and *Pinocchio in Venice,* among other books, as well as his much-litigated masterwork, *The Public Burning* (1977), in which the fictional creations of Dick and Pat Nixon dance to the tune of the greatest mythological beast of all, Uncle Sam.

the convention

now Tom's in an elevator in a great hotel
there's a convention the elevator is full of men
there's comradeship a hunger for women important things going on ci-
    gars good jokes
on every floor men rush noisily from room to room dark suits clean
    chins Tom goes among them
the doors are all open hey look who's here big slaps it's great
Tom's at a window in someone's room looking down on the lights of
    the city men press in and out wearing nametags Wally Duncan
    Duane Williams don't mind if I do
in another room Tom switches to whiskey finds somebody's key on the
    floor and takes a piss
in another room they are singing the night is young and I am so beau-
    tiful Tom laughs with them after
someone's on his knees looking for a quarter Tom eats an olive hey
    where are all the women toilets flush addresses are taken down cards
    exchanged he helps himself to a cold turkey sandwich hears there's a
    game up in room 1420
glasses are emptied down lavatories and refilled oh shit someone says
    there are fluffy white towels mirrors porters with bottles thick car-
    pets light glittering in the icecubes
it's a great hotel
the flash of cufflinks in the elevator collars white and crisp a man with
    gray hair speaks of Suzie and laughs Tom laughs they all laugh
then in the lobby Tom runs into an old friend not a friend exactly but
    a guy he used to drink with a guy he probably drank with once the
    lobby is noisy and all lit up with chandeliers men standing by the
    elevators
hey fella whaddaya say hey howzit goin man they shake hands say
    things like that glancing around it's happening can't miss it they go
    to the bar for a drink how's yer ole tomata
well Tom's sorry now he's run into this guy wants to be back in the
    rooms and elevators right just a quick one he says the bar is dark
    and full of men

they push through the dark suits hunched shoulders the men of the
convention cigarsmoke important talk his friend wears a nametag
I. M. Horney

Sally someone says

some guy's secretary

so whaddaya been doin been gettin any you know me pal Tom is laughing doesn't know why ef you see Kay tell her I want her they listen to
the others laugh Tom does knock knock eighteenth floor someone says

Shirley

or Shelley

how's business can't complain hey Eddie howaya

did the contract come through how'd it go

they're squeezed in among the elbows Tom's friend is putting people
on with a pocketfull of nametags Willie Phukker E. Z. Laye R. U.
Pistoff the barman's down at the other end rushed in a bad mood his
friend snaps his fingers nothing happens Ivan E. Reckshin Tom's
back up in the rooms once more

there are beds and desks again icecubes suddenly damp towels recogni-
tions flashing mirrors horselaughs telephones

sandwich debris

sure like candy from a baby

in one room a glass breaks they kick it under the chest of drawers

in another room a guy is talking about Copenhagen he's an old guy
with soft dewlaps nametag Pete Peterson we fucked all night he
says and her mother brought us breakfast after

what's your poison

gin and tonic he says the barman's scowling at them his friend asks for
something complicated starts putting the barman on the bar is dark
and jammed up

that's how it is

he's there in the bar with his friend who's now calling himself Kenny
Nokkerup where there's a lot of shoving going on bad feeling building up and at the same time he's up in Pete's room with his shoes
up on a wrinkled chenille spread hearing about Copenhagen where
they all do it

it's part of their fucking religion boys

Jesus this is some convention Tom says to his friend Horace S. Sass and
Pete winks she taught me the Danish twist he says

and meanwhile he's also in the elevator where men grin light up talk
shop kid around didja hear the one about the guy who takes a broad
with a wooden leg up to his hotel room and hey here's where we get
out wait this'll kill ya

he takes the leg apart see the wooden leg but then

I. Ben Scrood Annie Cockledoo there's something about limes or lemons the barman's pissed off and slams the drinks down what made him ask for a gin and tonic anyway Tom wonders holding his glass out for Pete to pour whiskey in it

Edna or Emma

tell her you know Walt

everybody laughs Pete blows out his pink cheeks pats his soft belly what are we out of ice people are getting angry shouting taking sides Mike Oxonphire Les Gitlade Chuck S. Assout

the elevator doors open three guys holding each other up you goin up or down one of them asks wait a minute he takes the goddamn thing apart see but he can't get it back together again so he runs out into the hall

we're goin up someone says and his friend says go fuck yourself shitface and Pete says hello is this room service and the guy in the elevator who's telling the joke says so anyhow he goes running out in the hall see with the pieces and he bumps into this drunk who

Walt who the woman asks blearily but she lets him in anyway he's surprised how easy it is even how he got up here

thick smoke music some woman is doing a strip the men are laughing drinking one of them hits his friend he goes crashing scuse me boys says Pete farting

wait a minute Tom says

but the woman who let him in has already dragged him over to a bed and opened his pants up someone relights his cigar there's a porter with ice the phone rings stains on the carpet cards being dealt the stripper is twirling tassels attached to her nipples one guy steps out of the elevator and falls flat on his face

what the fuck stop shoving someone thumps him in the stomach he doubles over we're voting for Pete some guy whispers

she pulls his cock out booze is spilled a table tips the elevator stops shit says the drunk you think you got problems I got a woman in my room with BOTH legs apart there's laughter singing fists flying and hell he says

hell he says

the stripper has invited a guy to pull her panties down with his teeth Pete is snoring his friend's nose is bloodied and his suit torn the woman is tonguing the tip of Tom's cock the bartender swings a bottle it's your bet you staying in? and hell he says

hell *I can't even find the goddamn room!*

the men are laughing Tom is throwing up all over the bartender who slugs Pete just waking up whereupon his friend nametag Isaac

Cummin is sent flying into a table scattering chips cards coins the tray's pushed in the porter's face and the woman sucking Tom off falls out of the elevator on her face leaving her wooden leg behind

friend of yours asks a guy holding up the leg and grinning

Christ says another I heard about third legs but that one takes the prize it's even got hinges

just don't take it apart says the first guy laughing and handing the leg back to Tom as the elevator doors open and they all step out you know what they say

Tom knows

in fact hell he thinks as he walks through the bright chandeliered lobby holding the leg in front of him to hide his gaping fly stared at solemnly by the men of the convention in their dark suits nametags Russ Edwards Jim McInerny white cuffs bruised faces

tough about old Pete he hears one of them say

yeah well you only live once

so they tell me

and on into the bar where his friend is staggering to his feet with a pair of bloody silk panties on his head like a baby bonnet nametag Harry Bawls and wrapping his arms around Tom telling him it's the best goddamn convention he's ever been to whaddaya say we have another round and go find some women in fact hell

sure laughs Tom why not

hell

it's what conventions are all about

The Brother

right there right there in the middle of the damn field he says he wants to put that thing together him and his buggy ideas and so me I says "how the hell you gonna get it down to the water?" but he just focuses me out sweepin the blue his eyes rollin like they do when he gets het on some new lunatic notion and he says not to worry none about that just would I help him for God's sake and because he don't know how he can get it done in time otherwise and though you'd have to be loonier than him to say yes I says I will of course I always would crazy as my brother is I've done little else since I was born and my wife she says "I can't figure it out I can't see why you always have to be babyin that old fool he ain't never done nothin for you God knows and you got enough to do here fields need plowin it's a bad enough year already my God and now that red-eyed brother of yours wingin around like a damn cloud and not knowin what in the world he's doin buildin a damn boat in the country my God what next? you're a damn fool I tell you" but packs me some sandwiches just the same and some sandwiches for my brother Lord knows *his* wife don't have no truck with him no more says he can go starve for all she cares she's fed up ever since the time he made her sit out on a hillside for three whole days rain and everything because he said she'd see God and she didn't see nothin and in fact she like to die from hunger nothin but berries and his boys too they ain't so bright neither but at least they come to help him out with his damn boat so it ain't just the two of us thank God for *that* and it ain't no goddamn fishin boat he wants to put up neither in fact it's the biggest damn thing I ever heard of and for weeks *weeks* I'm tellin you we ain't doin nothin but cuttin down pine trees and haulin them out to his field which is really pretty high up a hill and my God *that's* work lemme tell you and my wife she sighs and says I am really crazy r-e-a-l-l-y crazy and her four months with a child and tryin to do my work and hers too and still when I come home from haulin timbers around all day she's got enough left to rub my shoulders and the small of my back and fix a hot meal her long black hair pulled to a knot behind her head and hangin marvelously down her back her eyes gentle but very tired my God and I says to my brother I says "look I got a lotta work to do buddy you'll have to finish this

idiot thing yourself I wanna help you all I can you know that but" and
he looks off and he says "it don't matter none your work" and I says
"the hell it don't how you think me and my wife we're gonna eat I
mean where do you think this food comes from you been puttin away
man? you can't eat this goddamn boat out here ready to rot in that
bastard sun" and he just sighs long and says "no it just don't matter"
and he sits him down on a rock kinda tired like and stares off and
looks like he might even for God's sake cry and so I go back to bringin
wood up to him and he's already started on the keel and frame God
knows how *he* ever found out to build a damn boat lost in *his* fog
where he is Lord he was twenty when I was born and the first thing I
remember was havin to lead him around so he didn't get kicked by a
damn mule him who couldn't never do nothin in a normal way just a
huge oversize fuzzyface boy so anyway I take to gettin up a few hours
earlier ever day to do my farmin my wife apt to lose the baby if she
should keep pullin around like she was doin then I go to work on the
boat until sundown and on and on the days hot and dry and my wife
keepin good food in me or else I'd of dropped sure and no matter what
I say to try and get out of it my brother he says "you come and help
now the rest don't matter" and we just keep hammerin away and my
God the damn thing is big enough for a hundred people and at least I
think at *least* it's a place to live and not too bad at that at least it's
good for somethin but my wife she just sighs and says no good will
come of it and runs her hands through my hair but she don't ask me to
stop helpin no more because she knows it won't do no good and she's
kinda turned into herself now these days and gettin herself all ready
and still we keep workin on that damn thing that damn boat and the
days pass and my brother he says we gotta work harder we ain't got
much time and from time to time he gets a coupla neighbors to come
over and give a hand them sucked in by the size and the novelty of the
thing makin jokes some but they don't stay around more than a day or
two and they go away shakin their heads and swearin under their
breath and disgusted they got weaseled into the thing in the first place
and me I only get about half my place planted and see to my stock as
much as I can my wife she takes more care of them than I can but at
least we won't starve we say if we just get some rain and finally we get
the damn thing done all finished by God and we cover it in and out
with pitch and put a kinda fancy roof on it and I come home on that
last day and I ain't never goin back ain't *never* gonna let him talk me
into nothin again and I'm all smellin of tar and my wife she cries and
cries and I says to her not to worry no more I'll be home all the time
and me I'm cryin a little too though she don't notice just thinkin how
she's had it so lonely and hard and all and for one whole day I just

sleep the whole damn day and the rest of the week I work around the farm and one day I get an idea and I go over to my brother's place and get some pieces of wood left over and whaddaya know? they are all livin on that damn boat there in the middle of nowhere him and his boys and some women and my brother's wife she's there too but she's madder than hell and carpin at him to get outa that damn boat and come home and he says she's got just one more day and then he's gonna drug her on the boat but he don't say it like a threat or nothin more like a fact a plain fact tomorrow he's gonna drug her on the boat well I ain't one to get mixed up in domestic quarrels God knows so I grab up the wood and beat it back to my farm and that evenin I make a little cradle a kinda fancy one with little animal figures cut in it and polished down and after supper I give it to my wife as a surprise and she cries and cries and holds me tight and says don't never go away again and stay close by her and all and I feel so damn good and warm about it all and glad the boat thing is over and we get out a little wine and we decide the baby's name is gonna be either Nathaniel or Anna and so we drink an extra cup to Nathaniel's health and we laugh and we sigh and drink one to Anna and my wife she gently fingers the lit-tle animal figures and says they're beautiful and really they ain't I ain't much good at that sorta thing but I know what she means and then she says "where did you get the wood?" and I says "it's left over from the boat" and she don't say nothin for a moment and then she says "you been over there again today?" and I says "yes just to get the wood" and she says "what's he doin now he's got the boat done?" and I says "funny thing they're all living in the damn thing all except the old lady she's over there hollerin at him how he's gettin senile and where does he think he's sailin to and how if he ain't afraid of runnin into a octypuss on the way he oughta get back home and him sayin she's a nut there ain't no water and her sayin that's what *she's* been tellin him for six months" and my wife she laughs and it's the happiest laugh I've heard from her in half a year and I laugh and we both have another cup of wine and my wife she says "so he's just livin on that big thing all by hisself?" and I says "no he's got his boys on there and some young women who are maybe wives of the boys or somethin I don't know I ain't never seen them before and all kindsa damn animals and birds and things I ain't never seen the likes" and my wife she says "an-imals? what animals?" and I says "oh all kinds I don't know a whole damn menagerie all clutterin and stinkin up the boat *God* what a mess" and my wife laughs again and she's a little silly with the wine and she says "I bet he ain't got no pigs" and "oh yes I seen them" I says and we laugh thinkin about pigs rootin around in that big tub and she says "I bet he ain't got no jackdaws" and I says "yes I seen a couple of

them too or mostly I heard them you couldn't hardly hear nothin else"
and we laugh again thinkin about them crows and his old lady and the
pigs and all and my wife she says "*I* know what he ain't got I bet he
ain't got no lice" and we both laugh like crazy and when I can I says
"oh yes he does less he's took a bath" and we both laugh till we're cryin
and we finish off the wine and my wife says "look now I *know* what he
ain't got he ain't got no termites" and I says "you're right I don't recollect no termites maybe we oughta make him a present" and my wife
she holds me close quiet all of a sudden and says "he's really movin
Nathaniel's really movin" and she puts my hand down on her round
belly and the little fella is kickin up a terrific storm and I says kinda
anxious "does it hurt? do you think that — ?" and "no" she says "it's
good" she says and so I says with my hand on her belly "here's to you
Nathaniel" and we drain what's left in the bottom of our cups and the
next day we wake up in each other's arms and it's rainin and *thank God*
we say and since it's rainin real good we stay inside and do things
around the place and we're happy because the rain has come just in
time and in the evenin things smell green and fresh and delicious and
it's still rainin a little but not too hard so I decide to take a walk and I
wander over by my brother's place thinkin I'll ask him if he'd like to
take on some pet termites to go with his collection and there by God is
his wife on the boat and I don't know if he drug her on or if she just
finally come by herself but she ain't sayin nothin which is damn unusual and the boys they ain't sayin nothin neither and my brother he
ain't sayin nothin they're just all standin up there on top and gazin off
and I holler up at them "nice rain ain't it?" and my brother he looks
down at me standin there in the rain and still he don't say nothin but
he raises his hand kinda funny like and then puts it back on the rail
and I decide not to say nothin about the termites and it's startin to rain
a little harder again so I turn away and go back home and I tell my
wife about what happened and my wife she just laughs and says
"they're *all* crazy he's finally got them *all* crazy" and she's cooked me
up a special pastry with fresh meat and so we forget about them but by
God the next day the rain's still comin down harder than ever and
water's beginnin to stand around in places and after a week of rain I
can see the crops is pretty well ruined and I'm havin trouble keepin my
stock fed and my wife she's cryin and talkin about our bad luck that
we might as well of built a damn boat as plant all them crops and still
we don't figure things out I mean it just don't come to our minds not
even when the rain keeps spillin down like a ocean dumped upside-
down and now water is beginnin to stand around in big pools really
big ones and water up to the ankles around the house and leakin in
and pretty soon the whole damn house is gettin fulla water and I keep

sayin maybe we oughta go use my brother's boat till this blows over
but my wife she says "never" and then she starts in cryin again so finally I says to her I says "we can't be so proud I'll go ask him" and so I
set out in the storm and I can hardly see where I'm goin and I slip up
to my neck in places and finally I get to where the boat is and I holler
up and my brother he comes out and he looks down at where I am and
he don't say nothin that bastard he just looks at me and I shout up at
him I says "hey is it all right for me and my wife to come over until
this thing blows over?" and still he don't say a damn word he just
raises his hand in that same sillyass way and I holler "hey you stupid
sonuvabitch I'm soakin wet goddamn it and my house is fulla water
and my wife she's about to have a kid and she's apt to get sick all wet
and cold to the bone and all I'm askin you — " and right then right
while I'm still talkin he turns around and he goes back in the boat and
I can't hardly believe it me his brother but he don't come back out and
I push up under the boat and I beat on it with my fists and scream at
him and call him ever name I can think up and I shout for his boys
and for his wife and for anybody inside and nobody comes out "GOD-
damn YOU" I cry out at the top of my lungs and half sobbin and sick
and then feelin too beat out to do anythin more I turn around and head
back for home but the rain is thunderin down like mad now and in
places I gotta swim and I can't make it no further and I recollect a hill
nearby and I head for it and when I get to it I climb up on top of it
and it feels good to be on land again even if it is soggy and greasy and
I vomit and retch there awhile and move further up and the next thing
I know I'm wakin up the rain still in my face and the water halfway up
the hill toward me and I look out and I can see my brother's boat is
floatin and I wave at it but I don't see nobody wave back and then I
quick look out towards my own place and all I can see is the top of it
and of a sudden I'm scared scared about my wife and I go tearin for the
house swimmin most all the way and cryin and shoutin and the rain
still comin down like crazy and so now well now I'm back here on the
hill again what little there is left of it and I'm figurin maybe I got a
day left if the rain keeps comin and it don't show no signs of stoppin
and I can't see my brother's boat no more gone just water how *how* did
he know? that bastard and yet I gotta hand it to him it's not hard to
see who's crazy around here I can't see my house no more I just left my
wife inside where I found her I couldn't hardly stand to look at her the
way she was

Roald Dahl

Though most readers know Roald Dahl (1916–1990) for his revolutionary children's books like *Matilda, The BFG, James and the Giant Peach,* and *Charlie and the Chocolate Factory,* his short fiction also gained a wide currency, particularly in the fifties and sixties. The stories from his 1954 and 1959 collections, *Someone Like You* and *Kiss Kiss,* were serialized for television, and a number of them were later dramatized for *Alfred Hitchcock Presents* and *Tales of the Unexpected*. His stories rarely appear in anthologies these days because they represent a kind of fiction that seems to have gone out of fashion — the story that relies for its effect on strong plotting and the twist ending. Raymond Carver said famously that he hated tricks in fiction ("At the first sign of a trick or gimmick . . ., a cheap trick or even an elaborate trick, I tend to look for cover"), and one could argue that Dahl's short stories fall into this category. Several of his most familiar pieces, like "Man from the South" or "The Visitor," depend on startling revelations in the final paragraphs, but there is a long and satisfying tradition of such stories in our literature, running from Kipling to Saki to O. Henry, and Dahl is the master here. There is a real pleasure in examining the faultless construction of his stories, the precise line-to-line writing, the inevitability — and rightness — of the denouement.

The first piece, "Taste," begins with a placid statement of fact ("There were six of us to dinner that night at Mike Schofield's house in London: Mike and his wife and daughter, my wife and I, and a man called Richard Pratt. Richard Pratt was a famous gourmet.") and plunges into a story of hand-wringing tension, betrayal, and comeuppance. It also involves a bet, as does the second piece, "Dip in the Pool." The author is at his satiric best here, and Mr. Botibol's fate could stand as a textbook example of the reclamatory use of irony.

Taste

There were six of us to dinner that night at Mike Schofield's house in London: Mike and his wife and daughter, my wife and I, and a man called Richard Pratt.

Richard Pratt was a famous gourmet. He was president of a small society known as the Epicures, and each month he circulated privately to its members a pamphlet on food and wines. He organized dinners where sumptuous dishes and rare wines were served. He refused to smoke for fear of harming his palate, and when discussing a wine, he had a curious, rather droll habit of referring to it as though it were a living being. "A prudent wine," he would say, "rather diffident and evasive, but quite prudent." Or, "a good-humoured wine, benevolent and cheerful — slightly obscene, perhaps, but nonetheless good-humoured."

I had been to dinner at Mike's twice before when Richard Pratt was there, and on each occasion Mike and his wife had gone out of their way to produce a special meal for the famous gourmet. And this one, clearly, was to be no exception. The moment we entered the dining room, I could see that the table was laid for a feast. The tall candles, the yellow roses, the quantity of shining silver, the three wineglasses to each person, and above all, the faint scent of roasting meat from the kitchen brought the first warm oozings of saliva to my mouth.

As we sat down, I remembered that on both Richard Pratt's previous visits Mike had played a little betting game with him over the claret, challenging him to name its breed and its vintage. Pratt had replied that that should not be too difficult provided it was one of the great years. Mike had then bet him a case of the wine in question that he could not do it. Pratt had accepted, and had won both times. Tonight I felt sure that the little game would be played over again, for Mike was quite willing to lose the bet in order to prove that his wine was good enough to be recognized, and Pratt, for his part, seemed to take a grave, restrained pleasure in displaying his knowledge.

The meal began with a plate of whitebait, fried very crisp in butter, and to go with it there was a Moselle. Mike got up and poured the wine himself, and when he sat down again, I could see that he was watching Richard Pratt. He had set the bottle in front of me so that I could read the label. It said, "Geierslay Ohligsberg, 1945." He leaned over and whispered to me that Geierslay was a tiny village in the Moselle, almost unknown outside Germany. He said that this wine we were drinking was something unusual, that the output of the vineyard was so small that it was almost impossible for a stranger to get any of it. He had visited Geierslay personally the previous summer in order to obtain the few dozen bottles that they had finally allowed him to have.

"I doubt anyone else in the country has any of it at the moment," he said. I saw him glance again at Richard Pratt. "Great thing about Moselle," he continued, raising his voice, "it's the perfect wine to serve before a claret. A lot of people serve a Rhine wine instead, but that's because they don't know any better. A Rhine wine will kill a delicate claret, you know that? It's barbaric to serve a Rhine before a claret. But a Moselle — ah! — a Moselle is exactly right."

Mike Schofield was an amiable, middle-aged man. But he was a stock-broker. To be precise, he was a jobber in the stock market, and like a number of his kind, he seemed to be somewhat embarrassed, almost ashamed to find that he had made so much money with so slight a talent. In his heart he knew that he was not really much more than a bookmaker — an unctuous, infinitely respectable, secretly unscrupulous bookmaker — and he knew that his friends knew it, too. So he was seeking now to become a man of culture, to cultivate a literary and aesthetic taste, to collect paintings, music, books, and all the rest of it. His little sermon about Rhine wine and Moselle was a part of this thing, this culture that he sought.

"A charming little wine, don't you think?" he said. He was still watching Richard Pratt. I could see him give a rapid furtive glance down the table each time he dropped his head to take a mouthful of whitebait. I could almost *feel* him waiting for the moment when Pratt would take his first sip, and look up from his glass with a smile of pleasure, of astonishment, perhaps even of wonder, and then there would be a discussion and Mike would tell him about the village of Geierslay.

But Richard Pratt did not taste his wine. He was completely engrossed in conversation with Mike's eighteen-year-old daughter, Louise. He was half turned toward her, smiling at her, telling her, so far as I could gather, some story about a chef in a Paris restaurant. As he spoke, he leaned closer and closer to her, seeming in his eagerness almost to impinge upon her, and the poor girl leaned as far as she could away from him, nodding politely, rather desperately, and looking not at his face but at the topmost button of his dinner jacket.

We finished our fish, and the maid came around removing the plates. When she came to Pratt, she saw that he had not yet touched his food, so she hesitated, and Pratt noticed her. Her waved her away, broke off his conversation, and quickly began to eat, popping the little crisp brown fish quickly into his mouth with rapid jabbing movements of his fork. Then, when he had finished, he reached for his glass, and in two short swallows he tipped the wine down his throat and turned immediately to resume his conversation with Louise Schofield.

Mike saw it all. I was conscious of him sitting there, very still, containing himself, looking at his guest. His round jovial face seemed to loosen slightly and to sag, but he contained himself and was still and said nothing.

Soon the maid came forward with the second course. This was a large roast of beef. She placed it on the table in front of Mike who stood up and carved it, cutting the slices very thin, laying them gently on the plates for the maid to take around. When he had served everyone, including himself, he put down the carving knife and leaned forward with both hands on the edge of the table.

"Now," he said, speaking to all of us but looking at Richard Pratt. "Now for the claret. I must go and fetch the claret, if you'll excuse me."

"You go and fetch it, Mike?" I said. "Where is it?"

"In my study, with the cork out — breathing."

"Why the study?"

"Acquiring room temperature, of course. It's been there twenty-four hours."

"But why the study?"

"It's the best place in the house. Richard helped me choose it last time he was here."

At the sound of his name, Pratt looked around.

"That's right, isn't it?" Mike said.

"Yes," Pratt answered, nodding gravely. "That's right."

"On top of the green filing cabinet in my study," Mike said. "That's the place we chose. A good draft-free spot in a room with an even temperature. Excuse me now, will you, while I fetch it."

The thought of another wine to play with had restored his humor, and he hurried out the door, to return a minute later more slowly, walking softly, holding in both hands a wine basket in which a dark bottle lay. The label was out of sight, facing downward. "Now!" he cried as he came toward the table. "What about this one, Richard? You'll never name this one!"

Richard Pratt turned slowly and looked up at Mike; then his eyes travelled down to the bottle nestling in its small wicker basket, and he raised his eyebrows, a slight, supercilious arching of the brows, and with it a pushing outward of the wet lower lip, suddenly imperious and ugly.

"You'll never get it," Mike said. "Not in a hundred years."

"A claret?" Richard Pratt asked, condescending.

"Of course."

"I assume, then, that it's from one of the smaller vineyards?"

"Maybe it is, Richard. And then again, maybe it isn't."

"But it's a good year? One of the great years?"

"Yes, I guarantee that."

"Then it shouldn't be too difficult," Richard Pratt said, drawling his words, looking exceedingly bored. Except that, to me, there was something strange about his drawling and his boredom: between the eyes a shadow of something evil, and in his bearing an intentness that gave me a faint sense of uneasiness as I watched him.

"This one is really rather difficult," Mike said, "I won't force you to bet on this one."

"Indeed. And why not?" Again the slow arching of the brows, the cool, intent look.

"Because it's difficult."

"That's not very complimentary to me, you know."

"My dear man," Mike said, "I'll bet you with pleasure, if that's what you wish."

"It shouldn't be too hard to name it."

"You mean you want to bet?"

"I'm perfectly willing to bet," Richard Pratt said.

"All right, then, we'll have the usual. A case of the wine itself."

"You don't think I'll be able to name it, do you?"

"As a matter of fact, and with all due respect, I don't," Mike said. He was making some effort to remain polite, but Pratt was not bothering overmuch to conceal his contempt for the whole proceeding. And yet, curiously, his next question seemed to betray a certain interest.

"You like to increase the bet?"

"No, Richard. A case is plenty."

"Would you like to bet fifty cases?"

"That would be silly."

Mike stood very still behind his chair at the head of the table, carefully holding the bottle in its ridiculous wicker basket. There was a trace of whiteness around his nostrils now, and his mouth was shut very tight.

Pratt was lolling back in his chair, looking up at him, the eyebrows raised, the eyes half closed, a little smile touching the corners of his lips. And again I saw, or thought I saw, something distinctly disturbing about the man's face, that shadow of intentness between the eyes, and in the eyes themselves, right in their centers where it was black, a small slow spark of shrewdness, hiding.

"So you don't want to increase the bet?"

"As far as I'm concerned, old man, I don't give a damn," Mike said. "I'll bet you anything you like."

The three women and I sat quietly, watching the two men. Mike's wife was becoming annoyed; her mouth had gone sour and I felt that at any moment she was going to interrupt. Our roast beef lay before us on our plates, slowly steaming.

"So you'll bet me anything I like?"

"That's what I told you. I'll bet you anything you damn well please, if you want to make an issue out of it."

"Even ten thousand pounds?"

"Certainly I will, if that's the way you want it." Mike was more confident now. He knew quite well that he could call any sum Pratt cared to mention.

"So you say I can name the bet?" Pratt asked again.

"That's what I said."

There was a pause while Pratt looked slowly around the table, first at me, then at the three women, each in turn. He appeared to be reminding us that we were witness to the offer.

"Mike!" Mrs. Schofield said. "Mike, why don't we stop this nonsense and eat our food. It's getting cold."

"But it isn't nonsense," Pratt told her evenly. "We're making a little bet."

I noticed the maid standing in the background holding a dish of vegetables, wondering whether to come forward with them or not.

"All right, then," Pratt said. "I'll tell you what I want you to bet."

"Come on, then," Mike said, rather reckless. "I don't give a damn what it is — you're on."

Pratt nodded, and again the little smile moved the corners of his lips, and then, quite slowly, looking at Mike all the time, he said, "I want you to bet me the hand of your daughter in marriage."

Louise Schofield gave a jump. "Hey!" she cried. "No! That's not funny! Look here, Daddy, that's not funny at all."

"No, dear," her mother said. "They're only joking."

"I'm not joking," Richard Pratt said.

"It's ridiculous," Mike said. He was off balance again now.

"You said you'd bet anything I liked."

"I meant money."

"You didn't *say* money."

"That's what I meant."

"Then it's a pity you didn't say it. But anyway, if you wish to go back on your offer, that's quite all right with me."

"It's not a question of going back on my offer, old man. It's a no-bet anyway, because you can't match the stake. You yourself don't happen to have a daughter to put up against mine in case you lose. And if you had, I wouldn't want to marry her."

"I'm glad of that, dear," his wife said.

"I'll put up anything you like," Pratt announced. "My house, for example. How about my house?"

"Which one?" Mike asked, joking now.

"The country one."

"Why not the other one as well?"

"All right then, if you wish it. Both my houses."

At that point I saw Mike pause. He took a step forward and placed the bottle in its basket gently down on the table. He moved the salt-cellar to one side, then the pepper, and then he picked up his knife, studied the blade thoughtfully for a moment, and put it down again. His daughter, too, had seen him pause.

"Now, Daddy!" she cried. "Don't be *absurd!* It's *too* silly for words. I refuse to be betted on like this."

"Quite right, dear," her mother said. "Stop it at once, Mike, and sit down and eat your food."

Mike ignored her. He looked over at his daughter and he smiled, a slow, fatherly, protective smile. But in his eyes, suddenly, there glimmered a little triumph. "You know," he said, smiling as he spoke. "You know, Louise, we ought to think about this a bit."

"Now, stop it, Daddy! I refuse even to listen to you! Why, I've never heard anything so ridiculous in my life!"

"No, seriously, my dear. Just wait a moment and hear what I have to say."

"But I don't *want* to hear it."

"Louise! Please! It's like this. Richard here, has offered us a serious bet. He is the one who wants to make it, not me. And if he loses, he will have to hand over a considerable amount of property. Now, wait a minute, my dear, don't interrupt. The point is this. *He cannot possibly win.*"

"He seems to think he can."

"Now listen to me, because I know what I'm talking about. The expert, when tasting a claret — so long as it is not one of the famous great wines like Lafite or Latour — can only get a certain way toward naming the vineyard. He can, of course, tell you the Bordeaux district from which the wine comes, whether it is from St. Emilion, Pomerol, Graves, or Médoc. But then each district has several communes, little counties, and each county has many, many small vineyards. It is impossible for a man to differentiate between them all by taste and smell alone. I don't mind telling you that this one I've got here is a wine from a small vineyard that is surrounded by many other small vineyards, and he'll never get it. It's impossible."

"You can't be sure of that," his daughter said.

"I'm telling you I can. Though I say it myself, I understand quite a bit about this wine business, you know. And anyway, heavens alive, girl, I'm your father and you don't think I'd let you in for — for something you didn't want, do you? I'm trying to make you some money."

"Mike!" his wife said sharply. "Stop it now, Mike, please!"

Again he ignored her. "If you will take this bet," he said to his daughter, "in ten minutes you will be the owner of two large houses."

"But I don't want two large houses, Daddy."

"Then sell them. Sell them back to him on the spot. I'll arrange all that for you. And then, just think of it, my dear, you'll be rich! You'll be independent for the rest of your life!"

"Oh, Daddy, I don't like it. I think it's silly."

"So do I," the mother said. She jerked her head briskly up and down as she spoke, like a hen. "You ought to be ashamed of yourself, Michael, ever suggesting such a thing! Your own daughter, too!"

Mike didn't even look at her. "Take it!" he said eagerly, staring hard at the girl. "Take it, quick! I'll guarantee you won't lose."

"But I don't like it, Daddy."

"Come on, girl. Take it!"

Mike was pushing her hard. He was leaning toward her, fixing her with two hard bright eyes, and it was not easy for the daughter to resist him.

"But what if I lose?"

"I keep telling you, you can't lose. I'll guarantee it."

"Oh, Daddy, must I?"

"I'm making you a fortune. So come on now. What do you say, Louise? All right?"

For the last time, she hesitated. Then she gave a helpless little shrug of the shoulders and said, "Oh, all right, then. Just so long as you swear there's no danger of losing."

"Good!" Mike cried. "That's fine! Then it's a bet!"

"Yes," Richard Pratt said, looking at the girl. "It's a bet."

Immediately, Mike picked up the wine, tipped the first thimbleful into his own glass, then skipped excitedly around the table filling up the others. Now everyone was watching Richard Pratt, watching his face as he reached slowly for his glass with his right hand and lifted it to his nose. The man was about fifty years old and he did not have a pleasant face. Somehow, it was all mouth — mouth and lips — the full, wet lips of the professional gourmet, the lower lip hanging downward in the center, a pendulous, permanently open taster's lip, shaped open to receive the rim of a glass or a morsel of food. Like a keyhole, I thought, watching it; his mouth is like a large wet keyhole.

Slowly he lifted the glass to his nose. The point of the nose entered the glass and moved over the surface of the wine, delicately sniffing. He swirled the wine gently around in the glass to receive the bouquet. His concentration was intense. He had closed his eyes, and now the whole top half of his body, the head and neck and chest, seemed to become a kind of huge sensitive smelling-machine, receiving, filtering, analysing the message from the sniffing nose.

Mike, I noticed, was lounging in his chair, apparently unconcerned, but he was watching every move. Mrs. Schofield, the wife, sat prim and upright at the other end of the table, looking straight ahead, her face tight with disapproval. The daughter, Louise, had shifted her chair away a little, and sidewise, facing the gourmet, and she, like her father, was watching closely.

For at least a minute, the smelling process continued; then, without opening his eyes or moving his head, Pratt lowered the glass to his mouth and tipped in almost half the contents. He paused, his mouth full of wine, getting the first taste; then he permitted some of it to trickle down his throat and I saw his Adam's apple move as it passed by. But most of it he retained in his mouth. And now, without swallowing again, he drew in through his lips a thin breath of air which mingled with the fumes of the wine in the mouth and passed on down into his lungs. He held the breath, blew it out through his nose, and finally began to roll the wine around under the tongue, and chewed it, actually chewed it with his teeth as though it were bread.

It was a solemn, impressive performance, and I must say he did it well.

"Um," he said, putting down the glass, running a pink tongue over his lips. "Um — yes. A very interesting little wine — gentle and gracious, almost feminine in the aftertaste."

There was an excess of saliva in his mouth, and as he spoke he spat an occasional bright speck of it onto the table.

"Now we can start to eliminate," he said. "You will pardon me for doing this carefully, but there is much at stake. Normally I would perhaps take a bit of a chance, leaping forward quickly and landing right in the middle of the vineyard of my choice. But this time — I must move cautiously this time, must I not?" He looked up at Mike and he smiled, a thick-lipped, wet-lipped smile. Mike did not smile back.

"First, then, which district in Bordeaux does this wine come from? That is not too difficult to guess. It is far too light in the body to be from either St. Emilion or Graves. It is obviously a Médoc. There's no doubt about *that.*

"Now — from which commune in Médoc does it come? That also, by elimination, should not be too difficult to decide. Margaux? No. It cannot be Margaux. It has not the violent bouquet of a Margaux. Pauillac? It cannot be Pauillac, either. It is too tender, too gentle and wistful for a Pauillac. The wine of Pauillac has a character that is almost imperious in its taste. And also, to me, a Pauillac contains just a little pith, a curious, dusty, pithy flavor that the grape acquires from the soil of the district. No, no. This — this is a very gentle wine, demure and bashful in the first taste, emerging shyly but quite graciously in the second. A little arch, perhaps, in the second taste, and a little naughty also, teasing the tongue with a trace, just a trace, of tannin. Then, in the aftertaste, delightful — consoling and feminine, with a certain blithely generous quality that one associates only with the wines of the commune of St. Julien. Unmistakably this is a St. Julien."

He leaned back in his chair, held his hands up level with his chest, and placed the fingertips carefully together. He was becoming ridiculously pompous, but I thought that some of it was deliberate, simply to mock his host. I found myself waiting rather tensely for him to go on. The girl Louise was lighting a cigarette. Pratt heard the match strike and he turned on her, flaring suddenly with real anger. "Please!" he said. "Please don't do that! It's a disgusting habit, to smoke at table!"

She looked up at him, still holding the burning match in one hand, the big slow eyes settling on his face, resting there a moment, moving away again, slow and contemptuous. She bent her head and blew out the match, but continued to hold the unlighted cigarette in her fingers.

"I'm sorry, my dear," Pratt said, "but I simply cannot have smoking at table."

She didn't look at him again.

"Now, let me see — where were we?" he said. "Ah, yes. This wine is from Bordeaux, from the commune of St. Julien, in the district of Médoc. So far, so good. But now we come to the more difficult part — the name of the vineyard itself. For in St. Julien there are many vineyards, and as our host so rightly remarked earlier on, there is often not much difference between the wine of one and the wine of another. But we shall see."

He paused again, closing his eyes. "I am trying to establish the 'growth,'" he said. "If I can do that, it will be half the battle. Now, let me see. This wine is obviously not from a first-growth vineyard — nor even a second. It is not a great wine. The quality, the — the — what do you call it? — the radiance, the power, is lacking. But a third growth — that it could be. And yet I doubt it. We know it is a good year — our host has said so — and this is probably flattering it a little bit. I must be careful. I must be very careful here."

He picked up his glass and took another small sip.

"Yes," he said, sucking his lips, "I was right. It is a fourth growth. Now I am sure of it. A fourth growth from a very good year — from a great year, in fact. And that's what made it taste for a moment like a third — or even a second-growth wine. Good! That's better! Now we are closing in! What are the fourth-growth vineyards in the commune of St. Julien?"

Again he paused, took up his glass, and held the rim against that sagging, pendulous lower lip of his. Then I saw the tongue shoot out, pink and narrow, the tip of it dipping into the wine, withdrawing swiftly again — a repulsive sight. When he lowered the glass, his eyes remained closed, the face concentrated, only the lips moving, sliding over each other like two pieces of wet, spongy rubber.

"There it is again!" he cried. "Tannin in the middle taste, and the quick astringent squeeze upon the tongue. Yes, yes, of course! Now I have it! This wine comes from one of those small vineyards around Beychevelle. I remember now. The Beychevelle district, and the river and the little harbor that has silted up so the wine ships can no longer use it. Beychevelle . . . could it actually be a Beychevelle itself? No, I don't think so. Not quite. But it is somewhere very close. Château Talbot? Could it be Talbot? Yes, it could. Wait one moment."

He sipped the wine again, and out of the side of my eye I noticed Mike Schofield and how he was leaning farther and farther forward over the table, his mouth slightly open, his small eyes fixed upon Richard Pratt.

"No. I was wrong. It was not a Talbot. A Talbot comes forward to you just a little quicker than this one; the fruit is nearer to the surface. If it is a '34, which I believe it is, then it couldn't be Talbot. Well, well. Let me think. It is not a Beychevelle and it is not a Talbot, and yet — yet it is so close to both of them, so close, that the vineyard must be almost in between. Now, which could that be?"

He hesitated, and we waited, watching his face. Everyone, even Mike's wife, was watching him now. I heard the maid put down the dish of vegetables on the sideboard behind me, gently, so as not to disturb the silence.

"Ah!" he cried. "I have it! Yes, I think I have it!"

For the last time, he sipped the wine. Then, still holding the glass up near his mouth, he turned to Mike and he smiled, a slow, silky smile, and he said, "You know what this is? This is the little Château Branaire-Ducru."

Mike sat tight, not moving.

"And the year, 1934."

We all looked at Mike, waiting for him to turn the bottle around in its basket and show the label.

"Is that your final answer?" Mike said.

"Yes, I think so."

"Well, is it or isn't it?"

"Yes, it is."

"What was the name again?"

"Château Branaire-Ducru. Pretty little vineyard. Lovely old château. Know it quite well. Can't think why I didn't recognize it at once."

"Come on, Daddy," the girl said. "Turn it round and let's have a peek. I want my two houses."

"Just a minute," Mike said. "Wait just a minute." He was sitting very quiet, bewildered-looking, and his face was becoming puffy and pale, as though all the force was draining slowly out of him.

"Michael!" his wife called sharply from the other end of the table. "What's the matter?"

"Keep out of this, Margaret, will you please."

Richard Pratt was looking at Mike, smiling with his mouth, his eyes small and bright. Mike was not looking at anyone.

"Daddy!" the daughter cried, agonized. "But, Daddy, you don't mean to say he's guessed it right!"

"Now, stop worrying, my dear," Mike said. "There's nothing to worry about."

I think it was more to get away from his family than anything else that Mike then turned to Richard Pratt and said, "I'll tell you what, Richard. I think you and I better slip off into the next room and have a little chat?"

"I don't want a little chat," Pratt said. "All I want is to see the label on that bottle." He knew he was a winner now; he had the bearing, the quiet arrogance of a winner, and I could see that he was prepared to become thoroughly nasty if there was any trouble. "What are you waiting for?" he said to Mike. "Go on and turn it round."

Then this happened: The maid, the tiny, erect figure of the maid in her white-and-black uniform, was standing beside Richard Pratt, holding something out in her hand. "I believe these are yours, sir," she said.

Pratt glanced around, saw the pair of thin horn-rimmed spectacles that she held out to him, and for a moment he hesitated. "Are they? Perhaps they are. I don't know."

"Yes sir, they're yours." The maid was an elderly woman — nearer seventy than sixty — a faithful family retainer of many years' standing. She put the spectacles down on the table beside him.

Without thanking her, Pratt took them up and slipped them into his top pocket, behind the white handkerchief.

But the maid didn't go away. She remained standing beside and slightly behind Richard Pratt, and there was something so unusual in her manner and in the way she stood there, small, motionless, and erect, that I for one found myself watching her with a sudden apprehension.

Her old gray face had a frosty, determined look, the lips were compressed, the little chin was out, and the hands were clasped together tight before her. The curious cap on her head and the flash of white down the front of her uniform made her seem like some tiny, ruffled, white-breasted bird.

"You left them in Mr. Scofield's study," she said. Her voice was unnaturally, deliberately polite. "On top of the green filing cabinet in his study, sir, when you happened to go in there by yourself before dinner."

It took a few moments for the full meaning of her words to penetrate, and in the silence that followed I became aware of Mike and how he was slowly drawing himself up in his chair, and the color coming to his face, and the eyes opening wide, and the curl of the mouth, and the dangerous little patch of whiteness beginning to spread around the area of the nostrils.

"Now, Michael!" his wife said. "Keep calm now, Michael, dear! Keep calm!"

Dip in the Pool

On the morning of the third day, the sea calmed. Even the most delicate passengers — those who had not been seen around the ship since sailing time — emerged from their cabins and crept up onto the sun deck where the deck steward gave them chairs and tucked rugs around their legs and left them lying in rows, their faces upturned to the pale, almost heatless January sun.

It had been moderately rough the first two days, and this sudden calm and the sense of comfort that it brought created a more genial atmosphere over the whole ship. By the time evening came, the passengers, with twelve hours of good weather behind them, were beginning to feel confident, and at eight o'clock that night the main dining room was filled with people eating and drinking with the assured, complacent air of seasoned sailors.

The meal was not half over when the passengers became aware, by a slight friction between their bodies and the seats of their chairs, that the big ship had actually started rolling again. It was very gentle at first, just a slow, lazy leaning to one side, then to the other, but it was enough to cause a subtle, immediate change of mood over the whole room. A few of the passengers glanced up from their food, hesitating, waiting, almost listening for the next roll, smiling nervously, little secret glimmers of apprehension in their eyes. Some were completely unruffled, some were openly smug, a number of the smug ones making jokes about food and weather in order to torture the few who were beginning to suffer. The movement of the ship then became rapidly more and more violent, and only five or six minutes after the first roll had been noticed, she was swinging heavily from side to side, the passengers bracing themselves in their chairs, leaning against the pull as in a car cornering.

At last the really bad roll came, and Mr. William Botibol, sitting at the purser's table, saw his plate of poached turbot with hollandaise sauce sliding suddenly away from under his fork. There was a flutter of excitement, everybody reaching for plates and wineglasses. Mrs. Renshaw, seated at the purser's right, gave a little scream and clutched that gentleman's arm.

"Going to be a dirty night," the purser said, looking at Mrs. Renshaw. "I think it's blowing up for a very dirty night." There was just the faintest suggestion of relish in the way he said it.

A steward came hurrying up and sprinkled water on the tablecloth between the plates. The excitement subsided. Most of the passengers continued with their meal. A small number, including Mrs. Renshaw, got carefully to their feet and threaded their ways with a kind of concealed haste between the tables and through the doorway.

"Well," the purser said, "there she goes." He glanced around with approval at the remainder of his flock who were sitting quiet, looking complacent, their faces reflecting openly that extraordinary pride that travellers seem to take in being recognized as "good sailors."

When the eating was finished and the coffee had been served, Mr. Botibol, who had been unusually grave and thoughtful since the rolling started, suddenly stood up and carried his cup of coffee around to Mrs. Renshaw's vacant place, next to the purser. He seated himself in her chair, then immediately leaned over and began to whisper urgently in the purser's ear. "Excuse me," he said, "but could you tell me something please?"

The purser, small and fat and red, bent forward to listen.

"What's the trouble, Mr. Botibol?"

"What I want to know is this." The man's face was anxious and the purser was watching it. "What I want to know is will the captain already have made his estimate on the day's run — you know, for the auction pool? I mean before it began to get rough like this?"

The purser, who had prepared himself to receive a personal confidence, smiled and leaned back in his seat to relax his full belly. "I should say so — yes," he answered. He didn't bother to whisper his reply, although automatically he lowered his voice, as one does when answering a whisperer.

"About how long ago do you think he did it?"

"Some time this afternoon. He usually does it in the afternoon."

"About what time?"

"Oh, I don't know. Around four o'clock I should guess."

"Now tell me another thing. How does the captain decide which number it shall be? Does he take a lot of trouble over that?"

The purser looked at the anxious frowning face of Mr. Botibol and he smiled, knowing quite well what the man was driving at. "Well, you see, the captain has a little conference with the navigating officer, and they study the weather and a lot of other things, and then they make their estimate."

Mr. Botibol nodded, pondering this answer for a moment. Then he said, "Do you think the captain knew there was bad weather coming today?"

"I couldn't tell you," the purser replied. He was looking into the small black eyes of the other man, seeing the two single little sparks of excitement dancing in their centers. "I really couldn't tell you, Mr. Botibol. I wouldn't know."

"If this gets any worse it might be worth buying some of the low numbers. What do you think?" The whispering was more urgent, more anxious now.

"Perhaps it will," the purser said. "I doubt the old man allowed for a really rough night. It was pretty calm this afternoon when he made his estimate."

The others at the table had become silent and were trying to hear, watching the purser with that intent, half-cocked, listening look that you can see also at the race track when they are trying to overhear a trainer talking about his chance: the slightly open lips, the upstretched eyebrows, the head forward and cocked a little to one side — that desperately straining, half-hypnotized, listening look that comes to all of them when they are hearing something straight from the horse's mouth.

"Now suppose *you* were allowed to buy a number, which one would *you* choose today?" Mr. Botibol whispered.

"I don't know what the range is yet," the purser patiently answered. "They don't announce the range till the auction starts after dinner. And I'm really not very good at it anyway. I'm only the purser, you know."

At that point Mr. Botibol stood up. "Excuse me, all," he said, and he walked carefully away over the swaying floor between the other tables, and twice he had to catch hold of the back of a chair to steady himself against the ship's roll.

"The sun deck, please," he said to the elevator man.

The wind caught him full in the face as he stepped out onto the open deck. He staggered and grabbed hold of the rail and held on tight with both hands, and he stood there looking out over the darkening sea where the great waves were welling up high and white horses were riding against the wind with plumes of spray behind them as they went.

"Pretty bad out there, wasn't it, sir?" the elevator man said on the way down.

Mr. Botibol was combing his hair back into place with a small red comb. "Do you think we've slackened speed at all on account of the weather?" he asked.

"Oh my word yes, sir. We slacked off considerable since this started. You got to slacken off speed in weather like this or you'll be throwing the passengers all over the ship."

Down in the smoking room people were already gathering for the auction. They were grouping themselves politely around the various tables, the men a little stiff in their dinner jackets, a little pink and over-shaved and stiff beside their cool, white-armed women. Mr. Botibol took a chair close to the auctioneer's table. He crossed his legs, folded his arms, and settled himself in his seat with the rather desperate air of a man who has made a tremendous decision and refuses to be frightened.

The pool, he was telling himself, would probably be around seven thousand dollars. That was almost exactly what it had been the last two days with the numbers selling for between three and four hundred apiece. Being a British ship they did it in pounds, but he liked to do his thinking in his own currency. Seven thousand dollars was plenty of money. My goodness yes! And what he would do he would get them to pay him in hundred-dollar bills and he would take it ashore in the inside pocket of his jacket. No problem there. And right away, yes right away, he would buy a Lincoln convertible. He would pick it up on the way from the ship and drive it home just for the pleasure of seeing Ethel's face when she came out the front door and looked at it. Wouldn't that be something, to see Ethel's face when he glided up to the door in a brand-new pale-green Lincoln convertible! Hello Ethel honey, he would say, speaking very casual. I just thought I'd get you a little present. I saw it in the window as I went by, so I thought of you and how you were always wanting one. You like it, honey? he would say. You like the colour? And then he would watch her face.

The auctioneer was standing up behind his table now. "Ladies and gentlemen!" he shouted. "The captain has estimated the day's run, ending midday tomorrow, at five hundred and fifteen miles. As usual we will take the ten numbers on either side of it to make up the range. That makes it five hundred and five to five hundred and twenty-five. And of course for those who think the true figure will be still farther away, there'll be 'low field' and 'high field' sold separately as well. Now, we'll draw the first number out of the hat ... here we are ... five hundred and twelve?"

The room became quiet. The people sat still in their chairs, all eyes watching the auctioneer. There was a certain tension in the air, and as the bids got higher, the tension grew. This wasn't a game or a joke; you could be sure of that by the way one man would look across at another who had raised his bid — smiling perhaps, but only the lips smiling, the eyes bright and absolutely cold.

Number five hundred and twelve was knocked down for one hundred and ten pounds. The next three or four numbers fetched roughly the same amount.

The ship was rolling heavily, and each time she went over, the wooden panelling on the walls creaked as if it were going to split. The passengers held on to the arms of their chairs, concentrating upon the auction.

"Low field!" the auctioneer called out. "The next number is low field."

Mr. Botibol sat up very straight and tense. He would wait, he had decided, until the others had finished bidding, then he would jump in and make the last bid. He had figured that there must be at least five hundred dollars in his account at the bank at home, probably nearer six. That was about two hundred pounds — over two hundred. This ticket wouldn't fetch more than that.

"As you all know," the auctioneer was saying, "low field covers every number *below* the smallest number in the range, in this case every number below five hundred and five. So, if you think this ship is going to cover less than five hundred and five miles in the twenty-four hours ending at noon tomorrow, you better get in and buy this number. So what am I bid?"

It went clear up to one hundred and thirty pounds. Others besides Mr. Botibol seemed to have noticed that the weather was rough. One hundred and forty . . . fifty . . . There it stopped. The auctioneer raised his hammer.

"Going at one hundred and fifty . . ."

"Sixty!" Mr. Botibol called, and every face in the room turned and looked at him.

"Seventy!"

"Eighty!" Mr. Botibol called.

"Ninety!"

"Two hundred!" Mr. Botibol called. He wasn't stopping now — for anyone.

There was a pause.

"Any advance on two hundred pounds?"

Sit still, he told himself. Sit absolutely still and don't look up. Hold your breath. No one's going to bid you up so long as you hold your breath.

"Going for two hundred pounds . . ." The auctioneer had a pink bald head and there were little beads of sweat sparkling on top of it. "Going . . ." Mr. Botibol held his breath. "Going . . . Gone!" The man banged the hammer on the table. Mr. Botibol wrote out a check and handed it to the auctioneer's assistant, then he settled back in his chair to wait for the finish. He did not want to go to bed before he knew how much there was in the pool.

They added it up after the last number had been sold and it came to twenty-one hundred-odd pounds. That was around six thousand dollars. Ninety per cent to go to the winner, ten per cent to seamen's charities. Ninety per cent of six thousand was five thousand four hundred. Well — that was enough. He could buy the Lincoln convertible and there would be something left over, too. With this gratifying thought he went off, happy and excited, to his cabin.

When Mr. Botibol awoke the next morning he lay quite still for several minutes with his eyes shut, listening for the sound of the gale, waiting for the roll of the ship. There was no sound of any gale and the ship was not rolling. He jumped up and peered out of the porthole. The sea — Oh Jesus God — was smooth as glass, the great ship was moving through it fast, obviously making up for time lost during the night. Mr. Botibol turned away and sat slowly down on the edge of his bunk. A fine electricity of fear was beginning to prickle under the skin of his stomach. He hadn't a hope now. One of the higher numbers was certain to win it after this.

"Oh my God," he said aloud. "What shall I do?"

What, for example, would Ethel say? It was simply not possible to tell her that he had spent almost all of their two years' savings on a ticket in the ship's pool. Nor was it possible to keep the matter secret. To do that he would have to tell her to stop drawing checks. And what about the monthly installments on the television set and the Encyclopaedia Britannica? Already he could see the anger and contempt in the woman's eyes, the blue becoming gray and the eyes themselves narrowing as they always did when there was anger in them.

"Oh my God. What *shall* I do?"

There was no point in pretending that he had the slightest chance now — not unless the goddam ship started to go backward. They'd have to put her in reverse and go full speed astern and keep right on going if he was to have any chance of winning it now. Well, maybe he should ask the captain to do just that. Offer him ten per cent of the profits. Offer him more if he wanted it. Mr. Botibol started to giggle. Then very suddenly he stopped, his eyes and mouth both opening wide in a kind of shocked surprise. For it was at this moment that the idea came. It hit him hard and quick, and he jumped up from his bed, terribly excited, ran over to the porthole and looked out again. Well, he thought, why not? Why ever not? The sea was calm and he wouldn't have any trouble keeping afloat until they picked him up. He had a vague feeling that someone had done this thing before, but that didn't prevent him from doing it again. The ship would have to stop and lower a boat, and the boat would have to go back maybe half a mile to get him, and then it would have to return to the ship and be hoisted back on board. It would take at least an hour, the whole thing. An hour was about thirty miles. It would knock thirty miles off the day's run. That would do it. "Low field" would be sure to win it then. Just so long as he made certain someone saw him falling over; but that would be simple to arrange. And he'd better wear light clothes, something easy to swim in. Sports clothes, that was it. He would dress as though he were going up to play some deck tennis — just a shirt and a pair of shorts and tennis shoes. And leave his watch behind. What was the time? Nine-fifteen. The sooner the better, then. Do it now and get it over with. Have to do it soon, because the time limit was midday.

Mr. Botibol was both frightened and excited when he stepped out onto the sundeck in his sports clothes. His small body was wide at the hips, tapering upward to extremely narrow sloping shoulders, so that it resembled, in shape at any rate, a bollard. His white skinny legs were covered with black hairs, and he came cautiously out on deck, treading softly in his tennis shoes. Nervously he looked around him. There was only one other person in sight, an elderly woman with very thick ankles and immense buttocks who was leaning over the rail staring at the sea. She was wearing a coat of Persian lamb and the collar was turned up so Mr. Botibol couldn't see her face.

He stood still, examining her carefully from a distance. Yes, he told himself, she would probably do. She would probably give the alarm just as quickly as anyone else. But wait one minute, take your time, William Botibol, take your time. Remember what you told yourself a few minutes ago in the cabin when you were changing? You remember that?

The thought of leaping off a ship into the ocean a thousand miles from the nearest land had made Mr. Botibol — a cautious man at the best of times — unusually advertent. He was by no means satisfied yet that this woman he saw before him was *absolutely certain* to give the alarm when he made his jump. In his opinion there were two possible reasons why she might fail him. Firstly, she might be deaf and blind. It was not very probable, but on the other hand it *might* be so, and why take a chance? All he had to do was check it by talking to her for a moment beforehand. Secondly — and this will demonstrate how suspicious the mind of a man can become when it is working through self-preservation and fear — secondly, it had occurred to him that the woman might herself be the owner of one of the high numbers in the pool and as such would have a sound financial reason for not wishing to stop the ship. Mr. Botibol recalled that people had killed their fellows for far less than six thousand dollars. It was happening every day in the newspapers. So why take a chance on that either? Check on it first. Be sure of your facts. Find out about it by a little polite conversation. Then, provided that the woman appeared also to be a pleasant, kindly human being, the thing was a cinch and he could leap overboard with a light heart.

Mr. Botibol advanced casually toward the woman and took up a position beside her, leaning on the rail. "Hullo," he said pleasantly.

She turned and smiled at him, a surprisingly lovely, almost a beautiful smile, although the face itself was very plain. "Hullo," she answered him.

Check, Mr. Botibol told himself, on the first question. She is neither blind nor deaf. "Tell me," he said, coming straight to the point, "what did you think of the auction last night?"

"Auction?" she asked, frowning. "Auction? What auction?"

"You know, that silly old thing they have in the lounge after dinner, selling numbers on the ship's daily run. I just wondered what you thought about it."

She shook her head, and again she smiled, a sweet and pleasant smile that had in it perhaps the trace of an apology. "I'm very lazy," she said. "I always go to bed early. I have my dinner in bed. It's so restful to have dinner in bed."

Mr. Botibol smiled back at her and began to edge away. "Got to go and get my exercise now," he said. "Never miss my exercise in the morning. It was nice seeing you. Very nice seeing you . . ." He retreated about ten paces, and the woman let him go without looking around.

Everything was now in order. The sea was calm, he was lightly dressed for swimming, there were almost certainly no man-eating sharks in this part of the Atlantic, and there was this pleasant kindly old woman to give the alarm. It was a question now only of whether the ship would be delayed long enough to swing the balance in his favor. Almost certainly it would. In any event, he could do a little to help in that direction himself. He could make a few difficulties about getting hauled up into the lifeboat. Swim around a bit, back away from them surreptitiously as they tried to come up close to fish him out. Every minute, every second gained would help him win. He began to move forward again to the rail, but now a new fear assailed him. Would he get caught in the propeller? He had heard about that happening to persons falling off the sides of big ships. But then, he wasn't going to fall, he was going to jump, and that was a very different thing. Provided he jumped out far enough he would be sure to clear the propeller.

Mr. Botibol advanced slowly to a position at the rail about twenty yards away from the woman. She wasn't looking at him now. So much the better. He didn't want her watching him as he jumped off. So long as no one was watching he would be able to say afterward that he had slipped and fallen by accident. He peered over the side of the ship. It was a long, long drop. Come to think of it now, he might easily hurt himself badly if he hit the water flat. Wasn't there someone who once split his stomach open that way, doing a belly flop from the high dive? He must jump straight and land feet first. Go in like a knife. Yes sir. The water seemed cold and deep and gray and it made him shiver to look at it. But it was now or never. Be a man, William Botibol, be a man. All right then . . . now . . . here goes . . .

He climbed up onto the wide wooden toprail, stood there poised, balancing for three terrifying seconds, then he leaped — he leaped up and out as far as he could go and at the same time he shouted *"Help!"*

 "Help! Help!" he shouted as he fell. Then he hit the water and went under.

When the first shout for help sounded, the woman who was leaning on the rail started up and gave a little jump of surprise. She looked around quickly and saw sailing past her through the air this small man dressed in white shorts and tennis shoes, spread-eagled and shouting as he went. For a moment she looked as though she weren't quite sure what she ought to do: throw a life belt, run away and give the alarm, or simply turn and yell. She drew back a pace from the rail and swung half around facing up to the bridge, and for this brief moment she re- mained motionless, tense, undecided. Then almost at once she seemed to relax, and she leaned forward far over the rail, staring at the water where it was turbulent in the ship's wake. Soon a tiny round black head appeared in the foam, an arm was raised about it, once, twice, vigorously waving, and a small faraway voice was heard calling some- thing that was difficult to understand. The woman leaned still farther over the rail, trying to keep the little bobbing black speck in sight, but soon, so very soon, it was such a long way away that she couldn't even be sure it was there at all.

After a while another woman came out on deck. This one was bony and angular, and she wore horn-rimmed spectacles. She spotted the first woman and walked over to her, treading the deck in the deliber- ate, military fashion of all spinsters.

"So *there* you are," she said.

The woman with the fat ankles turned and looked at her, but said nothing.

"I've been searching for you," the bony one continued. "Searching all over."

"It's very odd," the woman with the fat ankles said. "A man dived overboard just now, with his clothes on."

"Nonsense!"

"Oh yes. He said he wanted to get some exercise and he dived in and didn't even bother to take his clothes off."

"You better come down now," the bony woman said. Her mouth had suddenly become firm, her whole face sharp and alert, and she spoke less kindly than before. "And don't you ever go wandering about on deck alone like this again. You know quite well you're meant to wait for me."

"Yes, Maggie," the woman with the fat ankles answered, and again she smiled, a tender, trusting smile, and she took the hand of the other one and allowed herself to be led away across the deck.

"Such a nice man," she said. "He waved to me."

Lydia Davis

The fifty-one pieces that compose Lydia Davis's fifth story collection, *Almost No Memory,* range from single-paragraph excursions into the emotional territory of a marriage to a mock eighteenth-century travelogue and brief, abstract stories that bring to mind the comic ontological disquisitions of Samuel Beckett. Here is one of the marriage pieces, called "Odd Behavior," in its entirety: "You see how circumstances are to blame. I am not really an odd person if I put more and more small pieces of shredded Kleenex in my ears and tie a scarf around my head: when I lived alone I had all the silence I needed." What draws me to the work of Davis is her experimentation with both form and language — she eschews plot in favor of reportage and psychological investigation, and she is concerned with the way in which remembered events are altered through the act of writing. In addition, she has adopted an idiosyncratic style based on a root vocabulary: "I love the Anglo-Saxon words as opposed to the Latinate," she has said. "Bread, milk, love, war, peace, cow, dog. . . . Maybe it has to do with those early Dick and Jane books." This style — cold, clear, without frills — defines her unique voice.

Both the selections here have to do with memory. The first, the title story of the collection, is a fable about the convoluted link between writing and recollection. The second, "St. Martin," lists and reorders the events of a year the narrator and her husband spent in a house in a foreign country. There is an ordinariness to the daily rituals, to the progression (or nonprogression) of events, to the unadorned prose, that challenges the idea of what a story is. There is no plot and little drama here — excepting the disappearance of a dog — and yet the character of the narrator begins to take shape through the quality of her recollections and the simple beauty of the writing ("Now and then a stranger came to the house by mistake. Once it was a young girl who entered the kitchen suddenly in a gust of wind, pale, thin, and strange, like a stray thought."). It is intriguing to compare this piece with the stories of writers like Dahl, Richter, or Cheever, who rely on the conventions of plot, ascending action, climax, and denouement.

Lydia Davis is the author of a novel, *The End of the Story,* in addition to five collections of short fiction. She is also well-known as the translator of a number of French authors, including Sartre, Simenon, Foucault, and Blanchot.

Almost No Memory

A certain woman had a very sharp consciousness but almost no memory. She remembered enough to get by from day to day. She remembered enough to work, and she worked hard. She did good work, and was paid for it, and earned enough to get by, but she did not remember her work, so that she could not answer questions about it, when people asked, as they did ask, since the work she did was interesting.

She remembered enough to get by, and to do her work, but she did not learn from what she did, or heard, or read. For she did read, she loved to read, and she took good notes on what she read, on the ideas that came to her from what she read, since she did have some ideas of her own, and even on her ideas about these ideas. Some of her ideas were even very good ideas, since she had a very sharp consciousness. And so she kept good notebooks and added to them year by year, and because many years passed this way, she had a long shelf of these notebooks, in which her handwriting became smaller and smaller.

Sometimes, when she was tired of reading a book, or when she was moved by a sudden curiosity she did not altogether understand, she would take an earlier notebook from the shelf and read a little of it, and she would be interested in what she read. She would be interested in the notes she had once taken on a book she was reading or on her own ideas. It would seem all new to her, and indeed most of it would be new to her. Sometimes she would only read and think, and sometimes she would make a note in her current notebook of what she was reading in a notebook from an earlier time, or she would make a note of an idea that came to her from what she was reading. Other times she would want to make a note but choose not to, since she did not think it quite right to make a note of what was already a note, though she did not fully understand what was not right about it. She wanted to make a note of a note she was reading, because this was her way of understanding what she read, though she was not assimilating what she read into her mind, or not for long, but only into another notebook. Or she wanted to make a note because to make a note was her way of thinking this thought.

Although most of what she read was new to her, sometimes she immediately recognized what she read and had no doubt that she herself had written it, and thought it. It seemed perfectly familiar to her, as though she had just thought it that very day, though in fact she had not thought it for some years, unless reading it again was the same as thinking it again, or the same as thinking it for the first time, and though she might never have thought it again, if she had not happened to read it in her notebook. And so she knew by this that these note-books truly had a great deal to do with her, though it was hard for her to understand, and troubled her to try to understand, just how they had to do with her, how much they were of her and how much they were outside her and not of her, as they sat there on the shelf, being what she knew but did not know, being what she had read but did not remember reading, being what she had thought but did not now think, or remember thinking, or if she remembered, then did not know whether she was thinking it now or whether she had only once thought it, or understand why she had had a thought once and then years later the same thought, or a thought once and then never that same thought again.

St. Martin

We were caretakers for most of that year, from early fall until summer. There was a house and grounds to look after, two dogs, and two cats. We fed the cats, one white and one calico, who lived outside and ate their meals on the kitchen windowsill, sparring in the sunlight as they waited for their food, but we did not keep the house very clean, or the weeds cut in the yard, and our employers, kind people though they were, probably never quite forgave us for what happened to one of the dogs.

We hardly knew what a clean house should look like. We would begin to think we were quite tidy, and then we would see the dust and clutter of the rooms, and the two hearths covered with ash. Sometimes we argued about it, sometimes we cleaned it. The oil stove became badly blocked and we did nothing for days because the telephone was out of order. When we needed help, we went to see the former caretakers, an old couple who lived with their cages of breeding canaries in the nearest village. The old man came by sometimes, and when he saw how the grass had grown so tall around the house, he scythed it without comment.

What our employers needed most from us was simply that we stay in the house. We were not supposed to leave it for more than a few hours, because it had been robbed so often. We left it overnight only once, to celebrate New Year's Eve with a friend many miles away. We took the dogs with us on a mattress in the back of the car. We stopped at village fountains along the way and sprinkled water on their backs. We had too little money, anyway, to go anywhere. Our employers sent us a small amount each month, most of which we spent immediately on postage, cigarettes, and groceries. We brought home whole mackerels, which we cleaned, and whole chickens, which we beheaded and cleaned and prepared to roast, tying their legs together. The kitchen often smelled of garlic. We were told many times that year that garlic would give us strength. Sometimes we wrote letters home asking for money, and sometimes a check was sent for a small sum, but the bank took weeks to cash it.

We could not go much farther than the closest town to shop for food and to a village half an hour away over a small mountain covered with scrub oaks. There we left our sheets, towels, table linen, and other laundry to be washed, as our employers had instructed us to do, and when we picked it up a week later, we sometimes stayed to see a movie. Our mail was delivered to the house by a woman on a motorcycle.

But even if we had had the money, we would not have gone far, since we had chosen to live there in that house, in that isolation, in order to do work of our own, and we often sat inside the house trying to work, not always succeeding. We spent a great deal of time sitting inside one room or another looking down at our work and then up and out the window, though there was not much to see, one bit of landscape or another depending on which room we were in — trees, fields, clouds in the sky, a distant road, distant cars on the road, a village that lay on the horizon to the west of us, piled around its square church tower like a mirage, another village on a hilltop to the north of us across the valley, a person walking or working in a field, a bird or a pair of birds walking or flying, the ruined outbuilding not far from the house.

The dogs stayed near us almost all the time, sleeping in tight curls. If we spoke to them, they looked up with the worried eyes of old people. They were pure-bred yellow Labradors, brother and sister. The male was large, muscular, perfectly formed, of a blond color so light he was nearly white, with a fine head and a lovely broad face. His nature was simple and good. He ran, sniffed, came when we called, ate, and slept. Strong, adept, and willing, he retrieved as long as we asked him to, running down a cliff of sand no matter how steep or how long, plunging into a body of water in pursuit of a stick. Only in villages and towns did he turn shy and fearful, trembling and diving toward the shelter of a café table or a car.

His sister was very different, and as we admired her brother for his simple goodness and beauty, we admired her for her peculiar sense of humor, her reluctance, her cunning, her bad moods, her deviousness. She was calm in villages and cities and would not retrieve at all. She was small, with a rusty-brown coat, and not well formed, a barrel of a body on thin legs and a face like a weasel.

Because of the dogs, we went outside the house often in the course of the day. Sometimes one of us would have to leave the warm bed at five in the morning and hurry down the cold stone steps to let them out, and they were so eager that they leaked and left a pattern of drops on the red tiles of the kitchen and the patio. As we waited for them, we would look up at the stars, bright and distinct, the whole sky having shifted from where it was when we last saw it.

In the early fall, as grape-pickers came into the neighboring fields to harvest, snails crept up the outside of the windowpanes, their undersides greenish-gold. Flies infested the rooms. We swatted them in the wide bands of sunlight that came through the glass doors of the music room. They tormented us while alive, then died in piles on the windowsills, covering our notebooks and papers. They were one of our seven plagues, the others being the fighter jets that thundered suddenly over our roof, the army helicopters that batted their more leisurely way over the treetops, the hunters who roamed close to the house, the thunderstorms, the two thieving cats, and, after a time, the cold.

The guns of the hunters boomed from beyond the hills or under our windows, waking us early in the morning. Men walked alone or in pairs, sometimes a woman trailed by a small child, spaniels loping out of sight and smoke rising from the mouths of the rifles. When we were in the woods, we would find a hunter's mess by the ruins of a stone house where he had settled for lunch — a plastic wine bottle, a glass wine bottle, scraps of paper, a crumpled paper bag, and an empty cartridge box. Or we would come upon a hunter squatting so motionless in the bushes, his gun resting in his arms, that we did not see him until we were on top of him, and even then he did not move, his eyes fixed on us.

In the village café, at the end of the day, the owner's young son, in olive-green pants, would slip around the counter and up the stairs with his two aged, slinking, tangerine-colored dogs, at the same time that women would come in with the mushrooms they had gathered just before dusk. Cartridge cases peppered the ground across a flat field near the house, one of the odd waste patches that lay in this valley of cultivated fields. Its dry autumn grass was strewn with boulders, among them two abandoned cars. Here from one direction came the smell of wild thyme, from the other the smell of sewage from a sewage bed.

We visited almost no one, only a farmer, a butcher, and a rather pompous retired businessman from the city. The farmer lived alone with his dog and his two cats in a large stone house a field or two away. The businessman, whose hyphenated name in fact contained the word "pomp," lived in a new house in the closest village, to the west of us across the fields. The young butcher lived with his childless wife in town, and we would sometimes encounter him there moving meat across the street from his van to his shop. Cradling a beef carcass or a lamb in his arms, he would stop to talk to us in the sunlight, a wary smile on his face. When he was finished working for the day, he often went out to take photographs. He had studied photography through a correspondence course and received a degree. He photographed town festivals and processions, fairs and shooting matches. Sometimes he took us with him. Now and then a stranger came to the house by mistake. Once it was a young girl who entered the kitchen suddenly in a gust of wind, pale, thin, and strange, like a stray thought.

Because we had so little money, our amusements were simple. We would go out into the sun that beat down on the white gravel and shone off the leaves of the olive tree and toss pebbles one by one, overhand, from a distance of ten feet or so into a large clay urn that stood among the rosemary plants. We did this as a contest with each other, but also alone when we were finished working or couldn't work. One would be working and hear the dull click, over and over, of a pebble striking the urn and falling back onto the gravel, and the more resonant pock of the pebble landing inside the urn, and would know the other was outside.

When the weather grew too cold, we stayed inside and played gin rummy. By the middle of winter, when only a few rooms in the house were heated, we were playing so much, day and night, that we organized our games into tournaments. Then, for a few weeks, we stopped playing and studied German in the evenings by the fire. In the spring, we went back to our pebble game.

Nearly every afternoon, we took the dogs for a walk. On the coldest days of winter, we went out only long enough to gather kindling wood and pine cones for the fire. On warmer days, we went out for an hour or more at a time, most often into the government forest that spread for miles on a plateau above and behind the house, sometimes into the fields of vines or lavender in the valley, or into the meadows, or across to the far side of the valley, into old groves of olive trees. We were surrounded for so long by scrub brush, rocks, pine trees, oaks, red earth, fields, that we felt enclosed by them even once we were back inside the house.

We would walk, and return with burrs in our socks and scratches on our legs and arms where we had pushed through the brambles to get up into the forest, and go out again the next day and walk, and the dogs always trusted that we were setting out in a certain direction for a reason, and then returning home for a reason, but in the forest, which seemed so endless, there was hardly a distinguishing feature that could be taken as a destination for a walk, and we were simply walking, watching the sameness pass on both sides, the thorny, scrubby oaks growing densely together along the dusty track that ran quite straight until it came to a gentle bend and perhaps a slight rise and then ran straight again.

If we came home by an unfamiliar route, skirting the forest, avoiding a deeply furrowed, overgrown field and then stepping into the edge of a reedy marsh, veering close to a farmyard, where a farmer in blue and his wife in red were doing chores trailed by their dog, we felt so changed ourselves that we were surprised nothing about home had changed: for a moment the placidity of the house and yard nearly persuaded us we had not even left.

Between the forest and the fields, in the thickets of underbrush, we would sometimes come upon a farmhouse in ruins, with a curving flight of deep stone steps, worn at the edges, leading to an upper story that was now empty air, brambles and nettles and mint growing up inside and around it, and sometimes, nearby, an ancient, awkward and shaggy fruit tree, half its branches dead. In the form of this farmhouse, we recognized our own house. We went up the same curving flight of stone steps to bed at night. The animals had lived downstairs in our house, too — our vaulted dining room had once been a sheepfold.

Sometimes, in our walks, we came upon inexplicable things, once, in the cinders of an abandoned fire, two dead jackrabbits. Sometimes we lost our way, and were still lost after the sun had set, when we would start to run, and run without tiring, afraid of the dark, until we saw where we were again.

We had visitors who came from far away to stay with us for several days and sometimes several weeks, sometimes welcome, sometimes less so, as they stayed on and on. One was a young photographer who had worked with our employer and was in the habit of stopping at the house. He would travel through the region on assignments for his magazine, always taking his pictures at dawn or at sunset when the shadows were long. For every night he stayed with us, he paid us the amount he would have paid for a room at a good hotel, since he traveled on a company expense account. He was a small, neat man with a quick, toothy smile. He came alone, or he came with his girlfriend.

He played with the dogs, fondling them, wrestling with them overhead as we sat in the room below trying to work, while we spoke against him angrily, to ourselves. Or he and his girlfriend ironed their clothes above us, with noises we did not at first understand, the stiff cord knocking and sliding against the floorboards. It was hard enough for us to work, sometimes.

They were curiously disorganized, and when they went out on an errand left water coming to a boil on the stove or the sink full of warm soapy water as though they were still at home. Or when they returned from an errand, they left the doors wide open so that the cold air and the cats came in. They were still at breakfast close to noon, and left crumbs on the table. Late in the evening, sometimes, we would find the girlfriend asleep on the sofa.

But we were lonely, and the photographer and his girlfriend were friendly, and they would sometimes cook dinner for us, or take us out to a restaurant. A visit from them meant money in our pockets again.

At the beginning of December, when we began to have the oil stove going full blast in the kitchen all day, the dogs slept next to it while we worked at the dining-room table. We watched through the window as two men returned to work in a cultivated field, one on a tractor and one behind a plow that had been sitting for weeks growing rusty, after opening perhaps ten furrows. Violent high winds sometimes rose during the night and then continued blowing all day so that the birds had trouble flying and dust sifted down through the floorboards. Sometimes one of us would get up in the night, hearing a shutter bang, and go out in pajamas onto the tiles of the garage roof to tie it back again or remove it from its hinge.

A rainstorm would last hours, soaking the ruined outbuilding nearby, darkening its stones. The air in the morning would be soft and limp. After the constant dripping of the rain or wuthering of the wind, there was sometimes complete silence, minute after minute, and then abruptly the rocky echoes of a plane far away in the sky. The light on the wet gravel outside the house was so white, after a storm, it looked like snow.

By the middle of the month, the trees and bushes had begun to lose their leaves and in a nearby field a stone shed, its black doorway overgrown by brambles, gradually came into view.

A flock of sheep gathered around the ruined outbuilding, fat, long-tailed, a dirty brown color, with pale scrawny lambs. Jostling one another, they poured up out of the ruin, climbing the tumble-down walls, the little ones crying in high human voices over the dull clamor of the bells. The shepherd, dressed all in brown with a cap pulled low over his eyes, sat eating on the grass by the woodpile, his face glowing and his chin unshaven. When the sheep became too active, he grunted and his small black dog raced once around the side of the flock and the sheep cantered away in a forest of stick-like legs. When they came near again, streaming out between the walls, the dog sent them flying again. When they disappeared into the next field, the shepherd continued to sit for a while, then moved off slowly, in his baggy brown pants, a leather pouch hanging on long straps down his back, a light stick in one hand, his coat flung over his shoulder, the little black dog charging and veering when he whistled.

One afternoon we had almost no money left, and almost no food. Our spirits were low. Hoping to be invited to dinner, we dropped in on the businessman and his wife. They had been upstairs reading, and came down one after the other holding their reading glasses in their hands, looking tired and old. We saw that when they were not expecting company, they had in their living room a blanket and a sleeping bag arranged over the two armchairs in front of the television. They invited us to have dinner with them the next night.

When we went to their house the next night, we were offered rum cocktails by Monsieur Assiez-de-Pompignan before dinner and afterward we watched a movie with them. When it ended, we left, hurrying to our car against the wind, through the narrow, shuttered streets, dust flying in our teeth.

The following day, for dinner, we had one sausage. The only money left now was a pile of coins on the living-room table collected from saucers around the house and amounting to 2.97 francs, less than fifty cents, but enough to buy something for dinner the next day.

Then we had no money at all anywhere in the house, and almost nothing left to eat. What we found, when we searched the kitchen carefully, was some onions, an old but unopened box of pastry crust mix, a little fat, and a little dried milk. Out of this, we realized, we could make an onion pie. We made it, baked it, cut ourselves two pieces, and put the rest back in the hot oven to cook a little more while we ate. It was surprisingly good. Our spirits lifting, we talked as we ate and forgot all about the pie as it went on baking. By the time we smelled it, it had burned too badly to be saved.

In the afternoon of that day, we went out onto the gravel, not knowing what to do now. We tossed pebbles for a while, there in the boiling sun and the cool air, saying very little because we had no answer to our problem. Then we heard the sound of an approaching car. Along the bumpy dirt road that led to our house from the main road, past the house of the weekend people, of pink stucco with black ironwork, and then past a vineyard on one side and a field on the other, came the photographer in his neat rented car. By pure chance, or like an angel, he was arriving to rescue us at the very moment we had used up our last resource.

We were not embarrassed to say we had no money, and no food either, and he was pleased to invite us out to dinner. He took us into town to a very good restaurant on the main square where the rows of plantain trees stood. A television crew were also dining there, twelve at the table, including a hunchback. By the large, bright fire on one wall, three old women sat knitting: one with liver spots covering her face and hands, the second pinched and bony, the third younger and merrier but slow-witted. The photographer fed us well on his expense account. He stayed with us that night and a few nights after, leaving us with several fifty-franc notes, so we were all right for a while, since a bottle of local wine, for instance, cost no more than one franc fifty.

When winter set in, we closed one by one the other rooms in the house and confined ourselves to the kitchen with its fat oil-burning stove, the vaulted dining room with its massive oak table where we played cards in the thick heat from the kitchen, the music room with its expensive electric heater burning our legs, and at the top of the stone stairway the unheated bedroom with its floor of red tiles so vast there was ample time for it to dip down in the center and rise again on its way to the single small casement window that looked out onto the almond tree and the olive tree below. The house had a different feeling to it when the wind was blowing and parts of it were darkened because we had closed the shutters.

Larks fluttered over the fields in the afternoons, showing silver. The long, straight, deeply rutted road to the village turned to soft mud. In certain lights, the inner walls of the ruined outbuilding were as rosy as a seashell. The dogs sighed heavily as they lay down on the cold tiles, closing their almond-shaped eyes. When they were let out into the sunlight, they fought, panting and scattering gravel. The shadow of the almond tree in the bright, hard sunlight flowed over the gravel like a dark river and lapped up against the wall of the house.

One night, during a heavy rainstorm, we went to the farmer's house for dinner. Nothing grew around his house, not even grass; there was only the massive stone house in a yard of deep mud. The front door was heavy to push open. The entryway was filled with a damp, musty smell from the truffles hanging in a leather pouch from a peg. Sacks full of seed and grain lined the wall.

With the farmer, we went out to the side of the house to collect eggs for dinner. Under the house, in the pens where he had once kept sheep, hens roosted now, their faces sharp in the beam of his flashlight. He gathered the eggs, holding the flashlight in one hand, and gave them to us to carry. The umbrella, as we started back around to the front of the house, turned inside out in the wind.

The kitchen was warm from the heat of a large oil stove. The oven door was open and a cat sat inside looking out. When he was in the house, the farmer spent most of his time in the kitchen. When he had something to throw away, he threw it out the window, burying it later. The table was crowded with bottles — vinegar, oil, his own wine in whiskey bottles which he had brought up from the cellar — and among them cloth napkins and large lumps of sea salt. Behind the table was a couch piled with coats. Two rifles hung in racks against the wall. Taped to the refrigerator was a photograph of the farmer and the truck he used to drive from Paris to Marseille.

For dinner he gave us leeks with oil and vinegar, bits of hard sausage and bread, black olives like cardboard, and scrambled eggs with truffles. He dried lettuce leaves by shaking them in a dishtowel and gave us a salad full of garlic, and then some Roquefort. He told us that his first breakfast, before he went out to work in the fields, was a piece of bread and garlic. He called himself a Communist and talked about the Resistance, telling us that the people of the area knew just who the collaborators were. The collaborators stayed at home out of sight, did not go to the cafés much, and in fact would be killed immediately if there was trouble, though he did not say what he meant by trouble. He had opinions about many things, even the Koran, in which, he said, lying and stealing were not considered sins, and he had questions for us: he wondered if it was the same year over there, in our country.

To get to his new, clean bathroom, we took the flashlight and lit our way past the head of the stairs and through an empty, high-ceilinged room of which we could see nothing but a great stone fireplace. After dinner, we listened in silence to a record of revolutionary songs which he took from a pile on the floor, while he grew sleepy, yawning and twiddling his thumbs.

When we returned home, we let the dogs out, as we always did, to run around before they were shut in for the night. The hunting season had begun again. We should not have let the dogs out loose, but we did not know that. More than an hour passed and the female came back but her brother did not. We were afraid right away, because he never stayed out more than an hour or so. We called and called, near the house, and then the next morning, when he had still not returned, we walked through the woods in all directions, calling and searching among the trees.

We knew he would not have stayed away so long unless he had somehow been stopped from coming back. He could have wandered into the nearest village, lured by the scent of a female in heat. He could have been spotted near the road and taken by a passing motorist. He could have been stolen by a hunter, someone avid for a good-natured, handsome hunting dog, proud to show it off in a smoke-filled café. But we believed first, and longest, that he lay in the underbrush poisoned, or caught in a trap, or wounded by a bullet.

Day after day passed and he did not come home and we had no news of him. We drove from village to village asking questions, and put up notices with his photograph attached, but we also knew that the people we talked to might lie to us, and that such a beautiful dog would probably not be returned.

People called us who had a yellow dog, or had found a stray, but each time we went to see it, it was not much like our dog. Because we did not know what had happened to him, because it was always possible that he might return, it was hard for us to accept the fact that he was gone. That he was not our dog only made it worse.

After a month, we still hoped the dog would return, though signs of spring began to appear and other things came along to distract us. The almond tree blossomed with flowers so white that against the soft plowed field beyond them they were almost blue. A pair of magpies came to the scrub oak beside the woodpile, fluttering, squawking, diving obliquely down.

The weekend people returned, and every Sunday they called out to each other as they worked the long strip of earth in the field below us. The dog went to the border of our land and barked at them, tense on her stiff legs.

Once we stopped to talk to a woman at the edge of the village and she showed us her hand covered with dirt from digging in the ground. Behind her we could see a man leading another man back into his garden to give him some herbs.

Drifts of daffodils and narcissus bloomed in the fields. We gathered a vase full of them and slept with them in the room, waking up drugged and sluggish. Irises bloomed and then the first roses opened, yellow. The flies became numerous again, and noisy.

We took long walks again, with one dog now. There were bugs in the wiry, stiff grass near the house, small cracks in the dirt, ants. In the field, purple clover grew around our ankles, and large white and yellow daisies at our knees. Blood-red bumblebees landed on buttercups as high as our hands. The long, lush grass in the field rose and fell in waves before the wind, and near us in a thick grove of trees dead branches clacked together. Whenever the wind died, we could hear the trickle of a swollen stream as though it were falling into a stone basin.

In May, we heard the first nightingale. Just as the night fully darkened, it began to sing. Its song was not really unlike the song of a mockingbird, with warbles, and twitters, and trills, warbles, chirps, and warbles again, but it issued in the midst of the silence of the night, in the dark, or in the moonlight, from a spot mysteriously hidden among the black branches.

Junot Díaz

Junot Díaz's first book, a collection of ten stories called *Drown,* was published in 1996 to an outpouring of praise from writers as diverse as Walter Mosley, Ana Castillo, and Francine Prose, and periodicals ranging from *The New York Times Book Review* to *Newsweek* and *Elle.* These stories are spare and powerful, and they incorporate the argot of the barrio, combining the Spanish of Díaz's native Dominican Republic with the English of the New Jersey neighborhood in which he was raised. In the best of them, the melding of the two languages makes for something new, a street lyricism that pushes the boundaries of the form. The epigraph Díaz chose for *Drown,* from Gustavo Pérez Firmat, stands as a sort of manifesto for many of his characters, caught between two worlds: "The fact that I/am writing to you/in English/already falsifies what I/wanted to tell you./My subject:/how to explain to you that I/don't belong to English/though I belong nowhere else." What results is a new way of viewing things, with a new set of referents.

"The Brief Wondrous Life of Oscar Wao," which appeared in *The New Yorker*'s December 25, 2000, & January 1, 2001, issue, is a compressed novella that showcases the author's ongoing experiment with language. The story's narrator mixes the colloquial and the formal; street grammar, tense changes, and Spanglish with standard English; and allusions drawn from a constricted barrio world and its culture. Its opening ("Oscar de Leon was not one of those Dominican cats everybody's always going on about. He wasn't no player.") seems to be from a third-person point of view, which makes the language all the more surprising; it isn't until we get deep into the story that a first-person narrator appears, a macho foil for the soft and ridiculous Oscar. The second story, "How to Date a Browngirl, Blackgirl, Whitegirl, or Halfie," is from *Drown.* It borrows its form from Lorrie Moore's *Self-Help* collection, and while its mode is comic, it achieves a real poignancy in its narrator's obsession with self-image and the final telling line that brings him back down to earth.

The Brief Wondrous Life
of Oscar Wao

The Golden Age

Oscar de León was not one of those Dominican cats everybody's always going on about. He wasn't no player. Except for one time, he'd never had much luck with women.

He'd been seven then.

It's true: Oscar was a carajito who was into girls mad young. Always trying to kiss them, always coming up behind them during a merengue, the first nigger to learn the perrito and the one who danced it every chance he got. Because he was a Dominican boy raised in a relatively "normal" Dominican family, his nascent pimp-liness was encouraged by family and friends alike. During the parties — and there were many, many parties in those long-ago seventies days, before Washington Heights was Washington Heights, before the Bergenline became a straight shot of Spanish for almost a hundred blocks — some drunk relative inevitably pushed Oscar onto some little girl, and then everyone would howl as boy and girl approximated the hipmotism of the adults.

You should have seen him, his mother sighed. He was our little Porfirio Rubirosa.

He had "girlfriends" early. (Oscar was a stout kid, heading straight to fat, but his mother kept him nice in haircuts, and before the proportions of his head changed he'd had these lovely flashing eyes and these cute-ass cheeks.) The girls — his older sister's friends, his mother's friends, even his neighbor, a twenty-something postal employee who wore red on her lips and walked like she had a brass bell for an ass — all fell for him. Ese muchacho está bueno! Once, he'd even had two girlfriends at the same time, his only ménage à trois ever. With Maritza Chacón and Olga Polanca, two girls from his school.

The relationship amounted to Oscar's standing close to both girls at the bus stop, some undercover hand holding, and some very serious kissing on the lips, first Maritza, then Olga, while the three of them hid behind some bushes. (Look at that little macho, his mother's friends said. Qué hombre.)

The threesome lasted only a week. One day after school, Maritza cornered Oscar behind the swing set and laid down the law. It's either her or me! Oscar held Maritza's hand and talked seriously and at great length about his love for her and suggested that maybe they could all share, but Maritza wasn't having any of it. Maritza, with her chocolate skin and gray eyes, already expressing the Ogún energy that would chop down obstacles for her the rest of her life. Didn't take him long to decide: after all, Maritza was beautiful, and Olga was not. His logic as close to the yes/no math of insects as a nigger could get. He broke up with Olga the next day on the playground, Maritza at his side, and how Olga cried! Snots pouring out of her nose and everything! In later years, when he and Olga had both turned into overweight freaks, Oscar could not resist feeling the occasional flash of guilt when he saw Olga loping across a street or staring blankly out near the New York bus stop, wondering how much his cold-as-balls breakup had contributed to her present fuckedupness. (Breaking up with her, he would remember, hadn't felt like anything; even when she started crying, he hadn't been moved. He'd said, Don't be a baby.)

What *had* hurt, however, was when Maritza dumped *him*. The Monday after he'd shed Olga, he arrived at the bus stop only to discover beautiful Maritza holding hands with butt-ugly Nelson Pardo. At first Oscar thought it a mistake; the sun was in his eyes, he'd not slept enough the night before. But Maritza wouldn't even smile at him! Pretended he wasn't there. We should get married, she was saying to Nelson, and Nelson grinned moronically, turning up the street to look for the bus. Oscar was too hurt to speak; he sat down on the curb and felt something overwhelming surge up from his chest, and before he knew it he was crying, and when his sister Lola walked over and asked him what was the matter he shook his head. Look at the mariconcito, somebody snickered. Somebody else kicked his beloved lunchbox. When he got on the bus, still crying, the driver, a famously reformed PCP addict, said, Christ, what a fucking *baby*.

Maybe coincidence, maybe self-serving Dominican hyperbole, but it seemed to Oscar that from the moment Maritza dumped him his life shot straight down the tubes. Over the next couple of years he grew fatter and fatter, and early adolescence scrambled his face into nothing you could call cute; he got uncomfortable with himself and no longer went anywhere near the girls, because they always shrieked and called him gordo asqueroso. He forgot the perrito, forgot the pride he felt when the women in the family had called him hombre. He did not kiss another girl for a long, long time. As though everything he had in the girl department had burned up that one fucking week. Olga caught the same bad, no-love karma. She got huge and scary — a troll gene in her somewhere — and started drinking 151 straight out of the bottle and was taken out of school because she had a habit of screaming NATAS! in the middle of homeroom. Sorry, loca, home instruction for you. Even her breasts, when they finally emerged, were huge and scary.

And the lovely Maritza Chacón? Well, as luck would have it, Maritza blew up into the flyest girl in Paterson, New Jersey, one of the queens of New Peru, and, since she and Oscar were neighbors, he saw her plenty, hair as black and lush as a thunderhead, probably the only Peruvian girl on the planet with curly hair (he hadn't heard of Afro Peruvians yet or of a town called Chincha), body fine enough to make old men forget their infirmities, and from age thirteen steady getting in or out of some roughneck's ride. (Maritza might not have been good at much — not sports, not school, not work — but she was good at boys.) Oscar would watch Maritza's getting in and out all through his cheerless, sexless adolescence. The only things that changed in those years were the models of the cars, the size of Maritza's ass, and the music volting out of the car's speakers. First freestyle, then Special Ed-era hip-hop, and right at the very end, for just a little while, Hector Lavoe and the boys.

Oscar didn't imagine that she remembered their kisses but of course he remembered.

The Moronic Inferno

High school was Don Bosco Tech and since Don Bosco Tech was an all-boys Catholic school run by the Salesian Fathers and Brothers and packed with a couple of hundred insecure, hyperactive adolescents it was, for a fat, girl-crazy nigger like Oscar, a source of endless anguish.

Sophomore year Oscar's weight stabilized at about two-ten (two-twenty when he was depressed, which was often), and it had become clear to everybody, especially his family, that he'd become the neighborhood pariguayo. He wore his semikink hair in a Puerto Rican Afro, had enormous Section-8 glasses (his anti-pussy devices, his boys Al and Miggs called them), sported an unappealing trace of mustache, and possessed a pair of close-set eyes that made him look somewhat retarded. The Eyes of Mingus (a comparison he made himself one day, going through his mother's record collection; she was the only old-school Dominicana he knew who loved jazz; she'd arrived in the States in the early sixties and shacked up with morenos for years until she met Oscar's father, who put an end to that particular chapter of the All-African World Party). Throughout high school he did the usual ghettonerd things: he collected comic books, he played role-playing games, he worked at a hardware store to save money for an outdated Apple IIe. He was an introvert who trembled with fear every time gym class rolled around. He watched nerd shows like "Doctor Who" and "Blake's 7," could tell you the difference between a Veritech fighter and a Zentraedi battle pod, and he used a lot of huge-sounding nerd words like "indefatigable" and "ubiquitous" when talking to niggers who would barely graduate from high school. He read Margaret Weis and Tracy Hickman novels (his favorite character was, of course, Raistlin) and became an early devotee of the End of the World. He devoured every book he could find that dealt with the End Times, from John Christopher's "Empty World" to Hal Lindsey's "The Late Great Planet Earth." He didn't date no one. Didn't even come close. Inside, he was a passionate person who fell in love easily and deeply. His affection — that gravitational mass of love, fear, longing, desire, and lust that he directed at any and every girl in the vicinity — roamed across all Paterson, affixed itself everywhere without regard to looks, age, or availability. Despite the fact that he considered his affection this tremendous, sputtering force, it was actually more like a ghost because no girl ever seemed to notice it.

Anywhere else, his triple-zero batting average with the girls might have passed unremarked, but this is a Dominican kid, in a Dominican family. Everybody noticed his lack of game and everybody offered him advice. His tío Rodolfo (only recently released from Rahway State) was especially generous in his tutelage. We wouldn't want you to turn into one of those Greenwich Village maricones, Tío Rodolfo muttered ominously. You have to grab a muchacha, broder, y méteselo. That will take care of everything. Start with a fea. Coge that fea y méteselo! Rodolfo had four kids with three different women, so the nigger was without doubt the family's resident metiéndolo expert.

Oscar's sister Lola (who I'd start dating in college) was a lot more practical. She was one of those tough Jersey Latinas, a girl soccer star who drove her own car, had her own checkbook, called men bitches, and would eat a fat cat in front of you without a speck of vergüenza. When she was in sixth grade, she was raped by an older acquaintance, and surviving that urikán of pain, judgment, and bochinche had stripped her of cowardice. She'd say anything to anybody and she cut her hair short (anathema to late-eighties Jersey Dominicans) partially, I think, because when she'd been little her family had let it grow down past her ass — a source of pride, something I'm sure her rapist noticed and admired.

Oscar, Lola warned repeatedly, you're going to die a virgin.

Don't you think I know that? Another five years of this and I'll bet you somebody tries to name a church after me.

Cut the hair, lose the glasses, exercise. And get rid of those porn magazines. They're disgusting, they bother Mami, and they'll never get you a date.

Sound counsel, which he did not adopt. He was one of those niggers who didn't have any kind of hope. It wouldn't have been half bad if Paterson and its surrounding precincts had been, like Don Bosco, all male. Paterson, however, was girls the way N.Y.C. was girls. And if that wasn't guapas enough for you, well, then, head south, and there'd be Newark, Elizabeth, Jersey City, the Oranges, Union City, West New York, Weehawken — an urban swath known to niggers everywhere as Negrapolis One. He wasn't even safe in his own house; his sister's girlfriends were always hanging out, and when they were around he didn't need no *Penthouses.* Her girls were the sort of hot-as-balls Latinas who dated only weight-lifting morenos or Latino cats with guns in their cribs. (His sister was the anomaly — she dated the same dude all four years of high school, a failed Golden Gloves welterweight who was excruciatingly courteous and fucked her like he was playing connect the dots, a pretty boy she'd eventually dump after he dirty-dicked her with some Pompton Lakes Irish bitch.) His sister's friends were the Bergen County All-Stars, New Jersey's very own Ciguapas: primera was Gladys, who complained constantly about her chest being too big; Marisol, who'd end up in M.I.T. and could out-salsa even the Goya dancers; Leticia, just off the boat, half Haitian, half Dominican, that special blend the Dominican government swears no existe, who spoke with the deepest accent, a girl so good she refused to sleep with three consecutive boyfriends! It wouldn't have been so bad if these girls hadn't treated Oscar like some deaf-mute harem guard; they blithely went on about the particulars of their sex lives while he sat in the kitchen clutching the latest issue of *Dragon.* Hey, he would yell, in case you're wondering, there's a male unit in here. Where? Marisol would say blandly. I don't see one.

Oscar Is Brave

Senior year found him bloated, dyspeptic, and, most cruelly, alone in his lack of a girlfriend. His two nerd boys, Al and Miggs, had, in the craziest twist of fortune, both succeeded in landing themselves girls that summer. Nothing special, skanks really, but girls nonetheless. Al had met his at Menlo Park Mall, near the arcade; she'd come on to him, he bragged, and when she informed him, after she sucked his dick, that she had a girlfriend *desperate* to meet somebody, Al had dragged Miggs away from his Atari and out to a movie, and the rest was, as they say, history. By the end of the week, Miggs had his, too, and only then did Oscar find out about any of it, while they were in his room setting up for another "hair-raising" Champions adventure against the Death-Dealing Destroyers. At first, he didn't say much. He just rolled his dice over and over. Said, You guys sure got lucky. Guess

I'm next. It killed him that they hadn't thought to include him in their girl heists; he hated Al for inviting Miggs instead of him, and he hated Miggs for getting a girl, period. Al's getting a girl Oscar could comprehend; Al looked completely normal, and he had a nice gold necklace he wore everywhere. It was Miggs's girl-getting that astounded him. Miggs was an even bigger freak than Oscar. Acne galore and a retard's laugh and gray fucking teeth from having been given some medicine too young. What little faith Oscar had in the world took an SS-N-17 Snipe to the head. When, finally, he couldn't take it no more, he asked pathetically, What, these girls don't have any other friends?

Al and Miggs traded glances over their character sheets. I don't think so, dude.

And right there he realized something he'd never known: his fucked-up, comic-book-reading, role-playing, game-loving, no-sports-playing friends were embarrassed by *him.*

Knocked the architecture right out of his legs. He closed the game early — the Exterminators found the Destroyers' hideout right away; that was bogus, Al groused as Oscar showed them the door. Locked himself in his room, lay in bed for a couple of stunned hours, then got up, undressed in the bathroom he no longer had to share because his sister was at Rutgers, and examined himself in the mirror. The fat! The miles of stretch marks! The tumescent horribleness of his proportions! He looked straight out of a Daniel Clowes comic book. Like the fat, blackish kid in Beto Hernández's Palomar.

Jesus Christ, he whispered. I'm a Morlock.

Spent a week looking at himself in the mirror, turned himself every which way, took stock, didn't flinch, and then he went to Chucho's and had the barber shave his Puerto Rican 'fro off, lost the mustache, then the glasses, bought contacts, was already trying to stop eating, starving himself dizzy, and the next time Al and Miggs saw him Miggs said, Dude, what's the matter with you?

Changes, Oscar said pseudo-cryptically.

He, Miggs, and Al were never quite the same friends again. He hung out, saw movies, talked Los Brothers Hernández, Frank Miller, and Alan Moore with them but, over all, he kept his distance. Listened to their messages on the machine and resisted the urge to run over to their places. Didn't see them but once, twice a week. I've been finishing up my first novel, he told them when they asked about his absences.

Oscar Comes Close

In December, after all his college applications were in (Fairleigh Dickinson, Montclair, Rutgers, Drew, Glassboro State, William Paterson; he also sent an application to N.Y.U., a one-in-a-million shot, and they rejected him so fast he was amazed the shit hadn't come back Pony Express) and winter was settling its pale, miserable ass across northern New Jersey, Oscar fell in love with a girl in his S.A.T.-prep class. Ana Acuña was a pretty, loud-mouthed gordita who read Henry Miller books while she should have been learning to defeat problem sets. Their fifth class, he noticed her reading "Sexus," and she noticed him noticing and, leaning over, she showed him a passage and he got an erection like a motherfucker.

You must think I'm weird, right? she said, during the break.

You ain't weird, he said. Believe me — I'm the top expert in the state.

Ana was a talker, had beautiful Caribbean-girl eyes, pure anthracite, and was the sort of heavy that almost every Island nigger dug (and wasn't shy about her weight, either), and, like every other girl in the neighborhood, wore tight black stirrup pants and the sexiest underwear she could afford. She was a peculiar combination of badmash and little girl — even before he visited her house, he knew there'd be an avalanche of stuffed animals on the bed — and there was something in the ease with which she switched between these two Anas that convinced him that there existed a third Ana, who was otherwise obscure and impossible to know. She'd got into Miller because her ex-boyfriend Manny had given her the books before he joined the Army. She'd been thirteen when they started dating, he'd been twenty-four, a recovering coke addict — Ana talking about these things like they weren't nothing at all.

You were thirteen and your mother *let* you date some old-ass nigger?

My parents *loved* Manny, she said. My mom used to cook dinner for him.

He said, That's crazy. (And later, at home, he asked his sister, back on winter break, Would you let your thirteen-year-old daughter date some twenty-four-year-old guy? Sure, she snorted, right after they killed me. But they better cut my fucking head off because, believe me, I'd come back from the dead and get them both.)

Oscar and Ana in S.A.T. class, Oscar and Ana in the parking lot afterward, Oscar and Ana at the McDonald's, Oscar and Ana become friends. Each day, Oscar expected her to be adiós, each day she was still there. They got into the habit of talking on the phone a couple times a week, about nothing, really, spinning words out of their everyday; the first time *she* called *him,* offering him a ride to the S.A.T. class; a week later, he called her, just to try it. His heart beating so hard he thought he would die, but all she did was say, Oscar, listen to the *bullshit* my sister pulled, and off they'd go, building another one of their word-scrapers. By the fifth time he called, he no longer expected the Big Blowoff. She was the first girl outside his family who admitted to having a period, who actually said to him, I'm bleeding like a hog, an astounding confidence that he kept turning over and over in his head. Because her appearance in his life was sudden, because she'd come in under his radar, he didn't have time to raise his usual wall of nonsense or throw some wild-ass expectations her way. Maybe, after four years of not getting ass, he'd finally found his zone, because amazingly enough, instead of making an idiot of himself as one might have expected, given the hard fact that this was the first girl he'd ever had a conversation with, he actually took it a day at a time. He spoke to her plainly and without effort, and discovered that his sharp, self-deprecating world view pleased her immensely. He would say something obvious and uninspired, and she'd say, Oscar, you're really fucking smart. When she said, I *love* men's hands, he spread both of his across his face and said faux-casual-like, Oh, *really?* It cracked her up.

Man, she said, I'm glad I got to know you.

And he said, I'm glad I'm me knowing you.

One night while he was listening to New Order and trying to chug through "Clay's Ark," his sister knocked on his door. At Rutgers, she'd shaved her head down to the bone, Sinéad style, and now everybody, including their mother, was convinced she was a jota.

You got a visitor, she said.

I do?

Yup. But you might want to clean up some, she warned.

It was Ana. Standing in his foyer, in full-length leather, her trigueña skin blood-charged from the cold, her face gorgeous with eyeliner, mascara, base, lipstick, and blush.

Freezing out, she said. She had her gloves in one hand like a crumpled bouquet.

Hey, was all he managed to say. He knew his sister was upstairs, listening.

What you doing? Ana asked.

Nothing.

Like let's go to a movie then.

Like O.K., he said.

When he went upstairs to change, his sister was jumping up and down on his bed, low screaming, It's a date, it's a date, and she jumped onto his back and nearly toppled him clean through the bedroom window.

So is this some kind of date? he said as he slipped into her car.

She smiled wanly. You could call it that.

Ana drove a Cressida, and instead of taking them to the local theatre she headed down to the Amboy Multiplex. It was so hard for Oscar to believe what was happening that he couldn't take it seriously. The whole time the movie was on, Oscar kept expecting niggers to jump out with cameras and scream, Surprise! Boy, he said, trying to remain on her map, this is some movie. Ana nodded; she smelled of a perfume, and when she pressed close the heat of her body was *vertiginous.*

On the ride home, Ana complained about having a headache and they didn't speak for a long time. He tried to turn on the radio but she said, No, my head's really killing me. So he sat back and watched the Hess Building and the rest of Woodbridge slide past through a snarl of overpasses. The longer they went without speaking, the more morose he became. It's just a movie, he told himself. It's not like it's a date.

Ana seemed unaccountably sad and she chewed her bottom lip, a real bembe, until most of her lipstick was on her teeth and he was going to make a comment about it, but he decided not to.

I'm reading "Dune," he said, finally.

She nodded. I *hate* that book.

They reached the Elizabeth exit, which is what New Jersey is really known for, industrial wastes on both sides of the turnpike, when Ana let loose a scream that threw him against the door.

Elizabeth! she shrieked. Close your fucking legs! Then she looked over at him, threw back her head, and laughed.

When he returned to the house, his sister said, Well?

Well, what?

Did you *fuck* her?

Jesus, Lola.

Don't lie to me. I know you Dominican men. She held up her hands and flexed the fingers in playful menace. Son pulpos.

The next day he woke up feeling like he'd been unshackled from his fat, like he'd been washed clean of his misery, and for a long time he couldn't remember why he felt this way and then finally he said her name. Little did he know that he'd entered into the bane of nerds everywhere: a let's-be-friends relationship.

In April, Oscar learned he was heading to Rutgers-New Brunswick. You'll love it, his sister promised him. I know I will, he said. I was meant for college. Ana was on her way to Penn State, honors program, full ride. It was also in April that her ex-boyfriend Manny returned from the Army — Ana told Oscar during one of their trips to Yaohan, the Japanese mall in Edgewater. Manny's sudden reappearance and Ana's joy over it shattered the hopes Oscar had cultivated. He's back, Oscar asked, like forever? Ana nodded, Apparently, Manny had got into trouble again, drugs, but this time, Ana insisted, he'd been set up by these three cocolos, a word he'd never heard her use, so he figured she'd got it from Manny. Poor Manny, she said.

Yeah, poor Manny, Oscar muttered.

Poor Manny, poor Ana, poor Oscar. Things changed quickly. First, Ana stopped being home all the time, and Oscar found himself stacking messages on her machine: This is Oscar, a bear is chewing my legs off, please call me. This is Oscar, they want a million dollars or it's over, please call me. She always got back to him after a couple of days and was pleasant about it, but still. Then she cancelled three Fridays in a row, and he had to settle for the clearly reduced berth of Sunday after church. She picked him up, and they drove out to Boulevard East and parked the car, and together they stared out at the Manhattan skyline. It wasn't an ocean, or a mountain range; it was, at least to Oscar, better.

On one of these little trips, she let slip, God, I'd forgotten how big Manny's cock is.

Like I really need to hear that, Oscar snapped.

I'm sorry, she said hesitantly. I thought we could talk about everything.

Well, it actually wouldn't be bad if you kept Manny's anatomical enormity to yourself.

With Manny and his *big cock* around, Oscar began dreaming about nuclear annihilation, how through some miracle he was first to hear about a planned attack, and without pausing to think he stole his tío's car, drove it to the store, stocked it full of supplies (shooting a couple of looters on the way), and then fetched Ana. What about Manny? she wailed. There's no time! he'd insisted, peeling out. When he was in a better mood, he let Ana discover Manny, who would be hanging from a light fixture in his apartment, his tongue bulbous in his mouth. The news of the imminent attack on the TV, a note pinned to his chest. *I koona taek it.* And then Oscar would comfort Ana and say something like, He was too weak for this hard new world.

Oscar even got — joy of joys! — the opportunity to meet the famous Manny, which was about as much fun as being called a fag during a school assembly (which had happened). Met him outside Ana's house. He was this intense emaciated guy with voracious eyes.

When they shook hands, Oscar was sure the nigger was going to smack him; he acted so surly. Manny was muy bald and completely shaved his head to hide it, had a hoop in each ear, and this leathery out-in-the-sun look of an old cat straining for youth.

So you're Ana's little friend, Manny said derisively.

That's me, Oscar said in a voice so full of cheerful innocuousness that he could have shot himself for it.

He snorted. I hope you ain't trying to chisel in on my girl.

Oscar said, Ha-ha. Ana flushed red, looked at the ground.

With Manny around, Oscar was exposed to an entirely new side of Ana. All they talked about on the few times they saw each other, was Manny and the terrible things he did to her. Manny smacked her, Manny kicked her, Manny called her a fat twat, Manny cheated on her, she was sure, with this Cuban chickie from the middle school. They couldn't talk ten minutes without Manny beeping her and her having to call him back and assure him she wasn't with anybody else.

What am I going to do? she asked over and over, and Oscar always found himself holding her awkwardly and telling her, Well, I think if he's this bad you should break up with him, but she shook her head and said, I know I should, but I can't. I love him.

Oscar liked to kid himself that it was only cold, anthropological interest that kept him around to see how it would all end, but the truth was he couldn't extricate himself. He was totally and irrevocably in love with Ana. What he used to feel for those girls he'd never really known was nothing compared with the amor he was carrying in his heart for Ana. It had the density of a dwarf motherfucking star and at times he was a hundred per cent sure it would drive him mad. Every Dominican family has stories about niggers who take love too far, and Oscar was beginning to suspect that they'd be telling one of these stories about him real soon.

Miraculous things started happening. Once, he blacked out while crossing an intersection. Another time, Miggs was goofing on him, talking smack, and for the first time ever Oscar lost his temper and swung on the nigger, connected so hard that homeboy's mouth spouted blood. Jesus Christ, Al said. Calm down! I didn't mean to do it, Oscar said unconvincingly. It was an accident. Mudafuffer, Miggs said. Mudafuffer! Oscar got so bad that one desperate night, after listening to Ana sobbing to him on the phone about Manny's latest bullshit, he said, I have to go to church now, and put down the phone, went to his tío's room and stole his antique Dragoon pistol, that oh-so-famous First Nation exterminating Colt .44, stuck its impressive snout down the front of his pants, and proceeded to stand in front of Manny's apartment. Come on, motherfucker, he said calmly. I got a nice eleven-year-old girl for you. He didn't care that he would more than likely be put away forever and that niggers like him got ass- and mouth-raped in jail, or that if the cops picked him up and found the gun they'd send his tío's ass up the river for parole violation. He didn't care about jack. His head contained nothing, it felt like it had been excavated, a perfect vacuum.

Folks started noticing that he was losing it. His mother, his tío, even Al and Miggs, not known for their solicitude, were like, Dude, what the fuck's the matter with you?

After he went on his third Manny hunt, he broke down and confessed to his sister, and she got them both on their knees in front of the altar she'd built to their dead abuela and had him swear on their mother's soul that he'd never pull anything like that again as long as he lived. She even cried, she was so worried about him.

You need to stop this, Mister.

I know I do, he said. But it's hard.

That night, he and his sister both fell asleep on the couch, she first. Her shins were covered in bruises. Before he joined her, he decided that this would be the end of it. He would tell Ana how he felt, and if she didn't come away with him then he wouldn't speak to her ever again.

They met at the Yaohan mall. Ordered two chicken-katsu curries and then sat in the large cafeteria with the view of Manhattan, the only *gaijin* in the whole joint.

He could tell by Ana's clothes that she had other plans that night. She was in a pair of black leather pants and had on one of those fuzzy light-pink sweaters that girls with nice chests can rock forever. Her face was so swollen from recent crying it looked like she was on cortisone.

You have beautiful breasts, he said as an opener.

Confusion, alarm. Oscar! What's the matter with you?

He looked out through the glass at Manhattan's western flank, looked out like he was some deep nigger. Then he told her.

There were no surprises. Her eyes went soft, she put a hand on his hand, her chair scraped closer, there was a strand of yellow in her teeth. Oscar, she said gently, I have a boyfriend.

So you don't love me?

Oscar. She breathed deep. I love you as a *friend*.

She drove him home; at the house, he thanked her for her time, walked inside, lay in bed. They didn't speak again.

In June, he graduated from Don Bosco. He heard in passing that, of everybody in their section of P-town, only he and Olga, poor, fucked-up Olga, had not attended even one prom. Dude, Miggs joked, maybe you should have asked her out.

He spent the summer working at the hardware store. Had so much time on his hands he started writing a novel for real. In September, he headed to Rutgers, and quickly buried himself in what amounted to the college version of what he'd majored in throughout high school: getting no ass. Despite swearing to be different, he went back to his nerdy ways, eating, not exercising, using flash words, and after a couple consecutive Fridays alone he joined the university's resident geek organization, R.U. Gamers.

Sentimental Education

The first time I met Oscar was at Rutgers. We were roommates our sophomore year, cramped up in Demarest, the university's official homo dorm, because Oscar wanted to be a writer and because I'd pulled the last number in the housing lottery. You never met more opposite niggers in your life. He was a dork, totally into Dungeons & Dragons and comic books; he had like a billion science-fiction paperbacks, all in his closet; and me, I was into girls, weight lifting, and Danocrine. (What is it with us niggers and our bodies? Not even Fanon can explain it to me.) I had this beautiful Irish–Puerto Rican girlfriend, a Plainfield girl I couldn't get enough of, a firefighter's daughter who didn't speak a word of Spanish, and I was into clubs like a motherfucker — Illusions, Foxes, Mercedes and Mink (on Springfield Ave. in Newark, the only club on the planet with a Ghettogirl Appreciation Night). Those were the Boricua Posse days, and I never got home before six in the morning, so mostly what I saw of Oscar was a big, dormant hump crashed out under a sheet. When we were in the dorm together, he was either working on his novel or talking on the phone to his sister, who I'd seen a few times at Douglass. (I'd tried to put a couple of words on her because she was no joke in the body department, but she cold-crumbed me.) Those first months, me and my boys ragged on Oscar a lot — I mean, he was a nerd, wasn't he? — and right before Halloween I told him he looked like that fat homo Oscar Wilde, which was bad news for him, because then all of us started calling him Oscar Wao. The sad part? After a couple of weeks, he started *answering* to it.

Besides me fucking with him, we never had no problems; he never got mad at me when I said shit, just sat there with a hurt stupid smile on his face. Made a brother feel kinda bad, and after the others left I would say, You know I was just kidding, right? By second semester, I even started to like the kid a little. Wasn't it Turgenev who said, Whom you laugh at you forgive and come near to loving? I didn't invite him out to no clubs, but we did start going to Brower Commons to eat, even checked out an occasional movie. We talked a little, mostly about girls, comic books, and our corny white-boy neighbors who were pussy asshole cocksuckers. Girls, though, were point zero; they were the world to Oscar. I mean, they were the world to me, too, but with him it was on some next shit. He got around a cute one and the nigger would almost start shaking. Easy to understand; our first month as roommates, he'd told me he'd never kissed one! Never! Jesus fucking Christ! The horror! It wasn't like I couldn't sympathize, but I didn't think acting like a nut around the mamacitas was going to help his case. I tried to give him advice — first off, cristiano, you have to stop gunning on the superbabes — but he wouldn't listen. He said, Nothing else works, I might as well make a fool out of myself.

It wasn't until the middle of spring semester that I ever saw Oscar really in love. Catalyn Sangre de Toro Luperón. Catalyn was this Puerto

Rican Goth girl — in 1990, niggers were having trouble wrapping their heads around Goths, period, but a Puerto Rican Goth, that was as strange to us as a black Nazi. Anyway, Catalyn was her real name, but her around-the-cauldron name was La Jablesse. You think I'm kidding? Every standard a brother like me had, this girl short-circuited. Her hair she wore in this black Egypto cut, her eyes caked with eyeliner and mascara, her lips painted black, a Navajo tattoo across her whole back, and none of it mattered, because homegirl was *luminous.* She had no waist, big perfect tits, wore black spiderweb clothes, and her accent in Spanish and English was puro Guayama. Even I had been hot for Catalyn, but the one time I'd tried to mack her at the Douglass Library she picked up her books and moved to another table, and when I tried to come over to apologize she did it again.

Ice.

So: one day I caught Oscar talking to La Jablesse in Brower, and I had to watch, because I figured if I got roasted she was going to vaporize his ass. Of course, he was full on, and homegirl was holding her tray and looking at him askance, like, What the fuck does this freak want? She started walking away, and Oscar yelled out, We'll talk later, O.K.? And she shot back a Sure, all larded with sarcasm.

You have to give it to Oscar. He didn't let up. He just kept hitting on her with absolutely no regard for self or dignity, and eventually she must have decided he was harmless, because she started treating him civil. Soon enough, I saw them walking together down College Avenue. One day, I came home from classes and found La Jablesse sitting on my bed, Oscar sitting on his. I was speechless. She remembered me. You can always tell. She said, You want me to get off your bed? I said, Nah, picked up my gym bag, and ran out of there like a pussy. When I got back from the weight room, Oscar was on his computer. On page one billion of his novel.

I said, What's up with you and Miss Scarypants?

Nothing much. Then he smiled and I knew he'd heard about my lame-ass pickup attempt.

I was one sore loser; I said, Well, good luck, Wao. I just hope she doesn't sacrifice you to Beelzebub or anything.

Later, the two of them started going to movies together. Some narratives never die. She was the first person to get him to try mushrooms, and once, right at the end, when he was starting to talk about her like she was the Queen of Everything, she took him to her room, turned off the lights, lit some witchy candles, and danced for him.

What the hell was this girl thinking?

In less than a week, Oscar was in bed crying, and La Jablesse had a restraining order on his ass. Turns out Oscar walked in on Catalyn while she was "entertaining" some Goth kid, caught them both naked, probably covered with blood or something, and he berserked. Started tearing her place up, and Gothdude jumped butt-naked out the window. Same night, I found Oscar on his top bunk, bare-chested, the night he said, I fucked up real bad, Yunior.

He had to attend counselling, to keep from losing his housing, but now everybody in the dorm thought he was some kind of major psycho. This is how our year together ended. Him at his computer, typing, me being asked in the hall how I liked dorming with Mr. Crazyman.

Would probably never have chilled with him again, but then, a year later, I started speaking to his sister, Lola de León. Femme-matador. The sort of girlfriend God gives you young, so you'll know loss the rest of your life. The head of every black and brown women's progressive organization at Douglass, beloved Phi Chi hermana, blah, blah, blah. She didn't have no kind of tact and talked too much for my taste, but, man, could she move, and her smile was enough to pull you across a room. I began noticing every time she was around, it was like she was on a high wire; I couldn't keep my eyes off her. I asked my boys what they thought about her and they laughed, said, Yo, she looks like a slave. Never forgave any of them for that.

Our first night together was at her place on Commercial Ave., and before I put my face between her legs she dragged me up by my ears. Why is this the face I cannot forget? Tired from finals, swollen from kissing. She said, Don't ever cheat on me.

I won't, I promised her. Don't laugh. My intentions were good.

We were still together at graduation, and we took pictures with each other's families — there's even a couple of me and Oscar. We look like a couple of circus freaks: I'm muscle-bound, hands as big as hams, and Oscar's heavy, squinting into the camera like we just pulled him out of a trunk and he doesn't know where the fuck he is.

The Dark Age

After college, Oscar moved back home. Left a virgin, returned one. Took down his childhood posters (Star Blazers, Captain Harlock) and tacked up his college ones (Akira and Terminator II). These were the early Bush years, the economy still sucked, and he kicked around doing nada for almost seven months until he started substituting at Don Bosco. A year later, the substituting turned into a full-time job. He could have refused, could have made a "saving throw" versus Death Magic, but instead he went with the flow. Watched his horizon collapse, told himself it didn't matter.

Had Don Bosco, since last we visited, been miraculously transformed by the spirit of Christian brotherhood? Had the eternal benevolence of the Lord cleansed the students of their bile? Negro, please. The only change that Oscar saw was in the older brothers, who all seemed to have acquired the inbred Innsmouth "look"; everything else (like white arrogance and the self-hate of people of color) was the same, and a familiar gleeful sadism still electrified the halls. Oscar wasn't great at teaching, his heart wasn't in it, and boys of all grades and dispositions shitted on him effusively. Students laughed when they spotted him in the halls. Pretended to hide their sandwiches. Asked in the middle of lectures if he ever got laid, and no matter how he responded they guffawed mercilessly. How demoralizing was that? And every day he found himself watching the "cool" kids torture the crap out of the fat, the ugly, the smart, the poor, the dark, the black, the unpopular, the African, the Indian, the Arab, the immigrant, the strange, the femenino, the gay — and in every one of these clashes he must have been seeing himself. Sometimes he tried to reach out to the school's whipping boys — You ain't alone, you know? — but the last thing a freak wants is a helping hand from another freak. In a burst of enthusiasm, he attempted to start a science-fiction club, and for two Thursdays in a row he sat in his classroom after school, his favorite books laid out in an attractive pattern, listened to the roar of receding footsteps in the halls, the occasional shout outside his door of Beam me up! and Nanoo-Nanoo! Then, after thirty minutes, he collected his books, locked the room, and walked down those same halls, alone, his footsteps sounding strangely dainty.

Social life? He didn't have one. Once a week he drove out to Woodbridge Mall and stared at the toothpick-thin black girl who worked at the Friendly's, who he was in love with but to whom he would never speak.

At least at Rutgers there'd been multitudes and an institutional pretense that allowed a mutant like him to approach without causing a panic. In the real world, girls turned away in disgust when he walked past. Changed seats at the cinema, and one woman on the crosstown bus even told him to stop thinking about her. I know what you're up to, she hissed. So stop it.

I'm a permanent bachelor, he told his sister.

There's nothing permanent in the world, his sister said tersely.

He pushed his fist into his eye. There is in me.

The home life? Didn't kill him, but didn't sustain him, either. His moms, smaller, rounder, less afflicted by the suffering of her youth, still the work golem, still sold second-rate clothes out of the back of her house, still allowed her Peruvian boarders to pack as many relatives as they wanted into the first floors. And Tío Rodolfo, Fofo to his friends, had reverted back to some of his hard pre-prison habits. He was on the caballo again, broke into lightning sweats at dinner, had moved into Lola's room, and now Oscar got to listen to him chicken-boning his stripper girlfriends almost every single night. Hey, Tío, he yelled out, try to use the headboard a little less.

Oscar knew what he was turning into, the worst kind of human on the planet: an old, bitter dork. He was depressed for long periods of time. The Darkness. Some mornings, he would wake up and not be able to get out of bed. Had dreams that he was wandering around the evil planet Gordo, searching for parts for his crashed rocket ship, but all he encountered were burned-out ruins. I don't know what's wrong with me, he said to his sister over the phone. He threw students out of class for breathing, told his mother to fuck off, went into his tío's closet and put the Colt up between his eyes, then lay in bed and thought about his mother fixing him his plate for the rest of his life. (He heard her say into the phone when she thought he wasn't around, I don't care, I'm happy he's here.)

Afterward — when he no longer felt like a whipped dog inside, when he could go to work without wanting to cry — he suffered from overwhelming feelings of guilt. He would apologize to his mother.

He would take the car and visit Lola. She lived in the city now, was letting her hair grow, had been pregnant once, a real moment of excitement, but she aborted it because I was cheating on her with a neighbor. (Our only baby.) He went on long rides. He drove as far as Amish country, would eat alone at a roadside diner, eye the Amish girls, imagine himself in a preacher suit, sleep in the back of the car, and then drive home.

Oscar Takes a Vacation

When Oscar had been at Don Bosco nearly three years, his moms asked him what plans he had for the summer. Every year, the family spent the better part of June, July, and August in Santo Domingo; Oscar hadn't accompanied them since Abuela had screamed out *Haitians!* once and died.

It's strange. If he'd said no, nigger would probably still be alive. But this ain't no Marvel Comics "What if?" — this ain't about stupid speculation, and time, as they say, is growing short. That May, Oscar was, for once, in better spirits. A couple of months earlier, after a particularly nasty bout with the Darkness, he'd started another one of his diets and combined it with long, lumbering walks around the neighborhood, and guess what? The nigger stuck with it and lost close on twenty pounds! A milagro! He'd finally repaired his ion drive; the evil planet Gordo was pulling him back but his fifties-style rocket, the Hijo de Sacrificio, wouldn't quit. Behold our cosmic explorer: eyes wide, lashed to his acceleration couch, his hand over his mutant heart.

He wasn't svelte by any stretch of the imagination, but he wasn't Joseph Conrad's wife no more, either. Earlier in the month, he'd even spoken to a bespectacled black girl on a bus, said, So, you're into photosynthesis, and she'd actually lowered her issue of *Cell* and said, Yes, I am. So what if he hadn't ever got past Earth Sciences and hadn't been able to convert that slight communication into a phone number or a date? Homeboy was, for the first time in ten years, feeling resurgent; nothing seemed to bother him, not his students, not the fact that "Doctor Who" had gone off the air, not his loneliness; he felt *insuperable,* and summer in Santo Domingo . . . Well, Santo Domingo summers have their own particular allure. For two months, Santo Domingo slaps the diaspora engine into reverse, yanks back as many of its expelled children as it can; airports choke with the overdressed; necks and luggage carrousels groan under the accumulated weight of that year's cadenas and paquetes; restaurants, bars, clubs, theatres, malecones, beaches, resorts, hotels, moteles, extra rooms, barrios, colonias, campos, ingenios swarm with quisqueyanos from the world over: from Washington Heights to Roma, from Perth Amboy to Tokyo, from Brijeporr to Amsterdam, from Anchorage to San Juan; it's one big party; one big party for everybody but the poor, the dark, the jobless, the sick, the Haitian, their children, the bateyes, the kids whom certain Canadian, American, German, and Italian tourists love to rape — yes, sir, nothing like a Santo Domingo summer, and so for the first time in years Oscar said, My elder spirits have been talking to me, Ma. I think I might go. He was imagining himself in the middle of all that ass-getting, imagining himself in love with an Island girl. (A brother can't be wrong forever, can he?)

So curious a change in policy was this that even Lola quizzed him about it. You never go to Santo Domingo.

He shrugged. I guess I want to try something new.

Return to a Native Land

Family de León flew down to the capital on the fourteenth of June. (Oscar told his bosses, My aunt got eaten by a shark, it's horrible, so he could bail out of work early. His mother couldn't believe it. You lied to a *priest?*)

In the pictures Lola brought home — she had to leave early; her job gave her only two weeks and she'd already killed off all her aunts — there are shots of Oscar in the back of the house reading Octavia Butler, shots of Oscar on the Malecón with a bottle of Presidente in his hand, shots of Oscar at the Columbus lighthouse, where half of Villa Duarte used to stand, shots of Oscar in Villa Juana buying spark plugs, shots of Oscar trying on a hat on the Conde, shots of Oscar standing next to a burro. You can tell he's trying. He's smiling a lot, despite the bafflement in his eyes.

He's also, you might notice, not wearing his fat-guy coat.

Oscar Meets a Babe

After his initial two weeks on the Island, after he'd got somewhat used to the scorching weather and the surprise of waking up in another country, after he refused to succumb to that whisper that all long-term immigrants carry inside themselves, the whisper that says You Do Not Belong, after he'd gone to about ten clubs and, because he couldn't dance salsa or merengue or bachata, had sat and drunk his Presidentes while Lola and his cousins burned holes in the floor, after he'd explained to people a hundred times that he'd been separated from his sister at birth, after he spent a couple of quiet mornings on his own on the Malecón, after he'd given out all his taxi money to beggars and had to call his cousin to get home, after he'd watched shirtless, shoeless seven-year-olds fighting each other for the scraps he'd left on his plate at an outdoor café, after the family visited the shack in Baitoa where his moms had been born, after he had taken a dump in a latrine and wiped his ass with a corncob, after he'd got somewhat used to the surreal whirligig that was life in the capital — the guaguas, the cops, the mind-boggling poverty, the Dunkin' Donuts, the beggars, the Pizza Huts, the tígueres selling newspapers at the intersections, the snarl of streets and shacks that were the barrios, the masses of niggers he waded through every day and who ran him over if he stood still, the mind-boggling poverty, the skinny watchmen standing in front of stores with their shotguns, the music, the raunchy jokes heard on the streets, the Friday-night strolls down the Avenida, the mind-boggling poverty — after he'd gone to Boca Chica and Villa Mella, after the relatives berated him for having stayed away so long, after he heard the stories about his father and his mother, after he stopped marvelling at the amount of political propaganda plastered up on every spare wall, after the touched-in-the-head tío who'd been tortured during Balaguer's reign came over and cried, after he'd swum in the Caribbean, after Tío Rodolfo had got the clap from a puta (Man, his tío cracked, what a pisser! Har-har!), after he'd seen his first Haitians kicked off a guagua because niggers claimed they "smelled," after he'd nearly gone nuts over all the bellezas he saw, after the gifts they'd brought had been properly distributed, after he'd brought flowers to his abuela's grave, after he had diarrhea so bad his mouth watered before each detonation, after he'd visited all the rinky-dink museums in the capital, after he stopped being dismayed that everybody called him gordo, after he'd been overcharged for almost everything he wanted to buy, after the terror and joy of his return subsided, after he settled down in his abuela's house, the house that the diaspora had built, and resigned himself to a long, dull, quiet summer, after his fantasy of an Island girlfriend caught a quick dicko (who the fuck had he been kidding? he couldn't dance, he didn't have loot, he didn't dress, he wasn't confident, he wasn't handsome, he wasn't from Europe, he wasn't fucking no Island girl), after Lola flew back to the States, Oscar fell in love with a semiretired puta.

Her name was Yvón Pimentel. Oscar considered her the start of his *real* life. (She was the end of it, too.)

She lived two houses over and was a newcomer to Mirador Norte. She was one of those golden mulatas that French-speaking Caribbeans call "chabines," that my boys call chicas de oro; she had snarled apocalyptic hair, amber eyes, and was one white-skinned relative away from jabao.

At first Oscar thought she was only a visitor, this tiny, slightly paunchy babe who was always high-heeling it out to her Pathfinder. (She didn't have the Mirador Norte wanna-be American look.) The two times Oscar bumped into her at the local café she smiled at him and he smiled at her. The second time — here, folks, is where the miracles begin — she sat at his table and chatted him up. At first he didn't know what was happening and then he realized, *Holy shit!* A girl was rapping to *him*. Turned out Yvón had known his abuela, even attended her funeral. You I don't remember. I was little, he said defensively. And, besides, that was before the war changed me.

She didn't laugh. That's probably what it is. You were a boy. On went the shades, up went the ass, out went the girl, Oscar's erection following her like a dowser's wand.

Yvón had attended the U.A.S.D. a long time ago, but she was no college girl. She had lines around her eyes and seemed, to Oscar at least, mad open, mad worldly, and had the sort of intense zipper gravity that hot middle-aged women exude effortlessly. The next time he ran into her, in front of her house (he had watched for her), she screamed, Oscar, querido! Invited him into her near-empty casa — Haven't had the time to move in yet, she said offhandedly — and because there wasn't any furniture besides a kitchen table, a chair, a bureau, a bed, and a TV, they had to sit on the bed. (Oscar peeped at the astrology books under the bed and the complete collection of Paulo Coelho's novels. She followed his gaze and said with a smile, Paulo Coelho saved my life.) She gave him a beer, had a double Scotch, then for the next six hours regaled him with tales from her life. It wasn't until midway through their chat that it hit Oscar that the job she talked so profusely about was prostitution. It was *Holy shit!* the Sequel.

Even though putas were one of Santo Domingo's premier exports, Oscar had never been near one in his entire life.

Yvón was an odd, odd bird. She was talkative, the sort of easygoing woman a brother can relax around, but there was also something slightly detached about her, as though (Oscar's words now) she were some marooned alien princess who existed partially in another dimension. She was the sort of woman who, cool as she was, slipped out of your head a little too quickly, a quality she recognized and was thankful for, as though she relished the short bursts of attention she provoked from niggers, but didn't want anything sustained. She didn't seem to mind being the girl you called every couple of months at eleven at night, just to see what she was up to. As much relationship as she could handle.

Her Jedi mind tricks did not, however, work on Oscar. When it came to girls, the brother had a mind like a four-hundred-year-old yogi. He latched on and stayed latched. By the time he left her house that night and walked home through the Island's million attack mosquitoes, he was lost. He was head over heels. (Did it matter that Yvón started mixing Italian in with her Spanish after her fourth drink or that she almost fell flat on her face when she showed him out? Of course not!) He was in love.

His mother met him at the door and couldn't believe his sinvergüencería. Do you know that woman's a PUTA? Do you know she bought that house CULEANDO?

He shot back, Do you know her mother was a DOCTOR? Do you know her father was a JUDGE?

The next day at one, Oscar pulled on a clean chacabana and strolled over to her house. (Well, he sort of trotted.) A red Jeep was parked outside, nose to nose with her Pathfinder. A Policía Nacional plate. And felt like a stooge. Of course she had boyfriends. His optimism, that swollen red giant, collapsed down to a bone-crushing point of gloom. Didn't stop him coming back the next day, but no one was home, and by the time he saw her again three days later he was convinced that she had warped back to whatever Forerunner world had spawned her. Where were you? he said, trying not to sound as miserable as he felt. I thought maybe you fell in the tub or something. I thought maybe you'd got amnesia.

She smiled and gave her ass a little shiver. I was making the patria strong, mi amor.

He had caught her in front of the TV, doing aerobics in a pair of sweatpants and what might have been described as a halter top. It was hard for him not to stare at her body. When she first let him in she'd screamed, Oscar, querido! Come in! Come in!

∗

I know what niggers are going to say. Look, he's writing Suburban Tropical now. A puta and she's not an underage, snort-addicted mess? Not believable. Should I go down to the Feria and pick me up a more representative model? Would it be better if I turned Yvón into Jahyra, a friend and a neighbor in Villa Juana, who still lives in one of those old-style pink wooden houses with a tin roof? Jahyra — your quintessential Caribbean puta, half cute, half not — who'd left home at the age of fifteen and lived in Curaçao, Madrid, Amsterdam, and Rome, has two kids and a breast job bigger than Luba's in "Love and Rockets," and who claimed, proudly, that her aparato had paved half the streets in her mother's home town. Or would it be better if I had Oscar meet Yvón at the World Famous Lavacaro, the carwash where a brother can get his head and his fenders polished (talk about convenience!). Would this be better?

But then I'd be lying. This is a true account of the Brief Wondrous Life of Oscar Wao. Can't we believe that an Yvón can exist and that a brother like Oscar might be due a little luck after twenty-three years?

This is your chance. If yes, continue. If no, return to the Matrix.

The Girl from Sabana Iglesia

In their photos, Yvón looks young. It's her smile and the way she perks up her body for every shot as if she's presenting herself to the world, as if she's saying, ta-da, here I am, take it or leave it. It doesn't hurt that she's barely five feet tall or that she doesn't weigh nothing. She dressed young, too, but she was a solid thirty-six, a perfect age for anybody but a puta. In the closeups, you can see the crow's-feet, and the little belly she complains all the time about, and the way her breasts and her ass are starting to lose their swell, which was why, she said, she had to be in the gym five days a week. When you're sixteen, a body like this is free; when you're forty — pffft! — it's a full-time occupation. The third time Oscar came over, Yvón doubled up on the Scotches again and then took down her photo albums from the closet and showed him all the pictures of herself when she was sixteen, seventeen, eighteen, always on a beach, always in an eighties bikini, always smiling, always with her arms around some middle-aged eighties yakub. Looking at those old hairy blancos, Oscar couldn't help but feel hopeful. Each photo had a date and a place at the bottom, and this was how he was able to follow Yvón's puta's progress through Italy, Portugal, and Spain. I was so beautiful in those days, she said wistfully. It was true — her smile could have put out a sun, but Oscar didn't think she was any less fine now, the slight declensions in her appearance only seemed to add to her lustre and he told her so.

You're so sweet, mi amor. She knocked back another double and rasped, What's your sign?

How lovesick he became! He began to go over to her house nearly every day, even when he knew she was working, just in case she was sick or decided to quit the profession so she could marry him. The gates of his heart had swung open and he felt light on his feet, he felt weightless, he felt lithe. His moms steady gave him shit, told him that not even God loves a puta. Yeah, his tío laughed, but everybody knows that God loves a puto. His tío seemed thrilled that he no longer had a pájaro for a nephew. I can't believe it, he said proudly. The palomo is finally a man. He put Oscar's neck in the New Jersey State Police patented niggerkiller lock. When did it happen? What was the date? I want to play that número as soon I get home.

Here we go again: Oscar and Yvón at her house, Oscar and Yvón at the movies, Oscar and Yvón at the beach, Oscar and Yvón talking, voluminously. She told him about her two sons, Sterling and Perfecto, who lived with their grandparents in Puerto Rico, who she saw only on holidays. She told him about the two abortions she had, which she called Marisol and Pepita, and about the time she'd been jailed in Madrid and how hard it was to sell your ass, and asked, Can something be impossible and not impossible at once? She told him about her Dominican boyfriend, the Capitán, and her foreign boyfriends, the Italian, the German, and the Canadian, the three benditos, how they each visited her on different months. You're lucky they all have families, she said, or I'd have been working this whole summer. (He wanted to ask her not to talk about any of these dudes, but she would only have laughed.)

Maybe we should get married, he said once, not joking, and she said, I make a terrible wife. He was around so often that he even got to see her in a couple of her notorious "moods," when her alien princess took over and she became very cold and uncommunicative and called him an idiot americano for spilling his beer. On these days, she threw herself into bed and didn't want to do anything. Hard to be around her, but he would convince her to see a movie and afterward she'd be a little easier. She'd take him to an Italian restaurant, and no matter how much her mood had improved she'd insist on drinking herself ridiculous — so bad he'd have to put her in the truck and drive her home through a city he did not know. (Early on, he hit on a great scheme: he called Clives, the evangelical taxista his family always used, who would swing by — no sweat — and lead him home.) When he drove, she always put her head in his lap and talked to him, sometimes in Italian, sometimes in Spanish, sometimes sweet, sometimes not, and having her mouth so close to his nuts was finer than your best yesterday.

Oh, they got close, all right, but we have to ask the hard questions: Did they ever kiss in her Pathfinder? Did he ever put his hands up her super-short skirt? Did she ever push up against him and say his name in a throaty whisper? Did they ever fuck?

Of course not. Miracles go only so far. He watched her for the signs that would tell him she loved him. He began to suspect that it might not happen this summer, but already he had plans to come back for Thanksgiving and then for Christmas. When he told her, she looked at him strangely and said only his name, Oscar, a little sadly.

She liked him, it was obvious. It seemed to Oscar that he was one of her few real friends. Outside the boyfriends, foreign and domestic, outside her psychiatrist sister in San Cristóbal and her ailing mother in Sabana Iglesia, her life seemed as spare as, say, her house.

Travel light, was all she ever said about the house when he suggested buying her a lamp or something, and he suspected that she would have said the same thing about having more friends. He knew, of course, that he wasn't her only visitor. One day, he found three discarded condom foils on the floor and asked, Are you having trouble with incubuses? She smiled. This is one man who doesn't know the word quit.

Poor Oscar. At night he dreamed that his rocket ship, the Hijo de Sacrificio, was up and off but that it was heading for the Ana Acuña Barrier at the speed of light.

Oscar at the Rubicon

At the beginning of August, Yvón started mentioning her ex-boyfriend the Capitán a lot more. Seems he'd heard about Oscar and wanted to meet him. He's really jealous, Yvón said, rather weakly. Just have him meet me, Oscar said. I make all boyfriends feel better about themselves. I don't know, Yvón said. Maybe we shouldn't spend so much time together. Shouldn't you be looking for a girlfriend?

I got one, he said.

A jealous Third World cop ex-boyfriend? Maybe we shouldn't spend so much time together? Any other nigger would have pulled a Scooby-Doo double take — Eeuoooorr? — would have thought twice about staying in Santo Domingo another day, but not Oscar.

Two days later, Oscar found his tío examining the front door. What's the matter? His tío showed him the door and pointed at the concrete-block wall on the other side of the foyer. I think somebody shot our house last night. He shook his head. Fucking Dominicans. Probably hosed the whole neighborhood down.

For a second, Oscar felt this strange tugging in the back of his head, what someone else might have called Instinct, but instead of hunkering down and sifting through it he said, We probably didn't hear it because of all our air-conditioners. Then he walked over to Yvón's. They were going to the Duarte that day.

Oscar Gets Beat

In the middle of August, Oscar finally met the Capitán. Yvón had passed out again. It was super-late and he'd been following Clives in the Pathfinder, the usual routine, when a crowd of cops up ahead let Clives pass and then asked Oscar to please step out of the vehicle. These were the D.R.'s new highway police, brand-new uniforms and esprit de corps up to here. It's not my truck, he explained, it's hers. He pointed to sleeping Yvón. We understand. If you could please step out of the truck. It wasn't until these two plainclothes — who we'll call Solomon Grundy and Gorilla Grodd, for simplicity's sake — tossed him into the back of a black Volkswagen bug that he realized something was up. Wait a minute, he said as they pulled out, where the hell are you taking me? Wait! Gorilla Grodd gave him one cold glance and that was all it took to quiet his ass down. This is fucked up, he said under his breath. I didn't *do* nothing.

The Capitán was waiting for him on a noticeably unelectrified stretch of road. A skinny fortysomething-year-old jabao standing near his spotless red Jeep, dressed nice in slacks and a crisply pressed white button-down, his shoes bright as scarabs. The Capitán was one of those tall, arrogant, handsome niggers that most of the planet feels inferior to. (The Capitán was also one of those very bad men who not even postmodernism can explain away.)

So you're the New Yorker, he said with great cheer. When Oscar saw the Capitán's close-set eyes he knew he was fucked. (He had the Eyes of Lee Van Cleef!) If it hadn't been for the courage of his sphincter, Oscar's lunch and his dinner and his breakfast would have whooshed straight out of him.

I didn't do anything, Oscar quailed. Then he blurted out, I'm an American citizen.

The Capitán waved away a mosquito. I'm an American citizen, too. I was sworn in in the city of Buffalo, in the State of New York.

I bought mine in Miami, Gorilla Grodd said.

Not me, Solomon Grundy lamented. I only got my damn residency.

Please, you have to believe me, I didn't do anything.

The Capitán smiled. Motherfucker even had First World teeth. Oscar was lucky; if he had looked like my pana Pedro, the Dominican Superman, he probably would have got shot right there. But because he was a young homely slob the Capitán punched him only a couple of times, warned him away from Yvón in no uncertain terms, and then remanded him to Messrs. Grundy and Grodd, who squeezed him back into the bug and drove out to the cane fields between Santo Domingo and Villa Mella.

Oscar was too scared to speak. He was a shook daddy. He couldn't believe it. He was going to die. He tried to imagine Yvón at the funeral in her nearly see-through black sheath and couldn't. Watched Santo Domingo race past and felt impossibly alone. Thought about his mother and his sister and started crying.

You need to keep it down, Grundy said, but Oscar couldn't stop, even when he put his hands in his mouth.

At the cane fields, Messrs. Grodd and Grundy pulled Oscar out of the car, walked him into the cane, and then with their pistol butts proceeded to give him the beating to end all beatings. It was the Götterdämmerung of beatdowns, a beatdown so cruel and relentless that even Camden, the City of the Ultimate Beatdown, would have been impressed. (Yessir, nothing like getting smashed in the face with those patented Pachmayr Presentation Grips.) He shrieked, but that didn't stop the beating; he begged, but that didn't stop it, either; he blacked out, but that was no relief; the niggers kicked him in the nuts and perked him right up! It was like one of those nightmare 8 A.M. M.L.A. panels that you think will never, ever end. Man, Gorilla Grodd said, this kid is making me *sweat.* Toward the end, Oscar found himself thinking about his old dead abuela, who used to scratch his back and fry him yaniqueques; she was sitting in her rocking chair and when she saw him she snarled, What did I tell you about those putas?

The only reason he didn't lie out in that rustling endless cane for the rest of his life was because Clives the evangelical taxista had had the guts to follow the cops on the sly, and when they broke out he turned on his headlights and pulled up to where they'd last been and found poor Oscar. Are you alive? Clives whispered. Oscar said, Blub, blub. Clives couldn't hoist Oscar into the car alone so he drove to a nearby batey and recruited a couple of Haitian braceros to help him. This is a big one, one of the braceros joked. The only thing Oscar said the whole ride back was her name. *Yvón.* Broken nose, broken zygomatic arch, crushed seventh cranial nerve, three of his front teeth snapped off at the gum, concussion, alive.

※

That was the end of it. When Moms de León heard it was the police, she called first a doctor and then the airlines. She wasn't no fool; she'd lived through Trujillo and the Devil Balaguer; knew that the cops hadn't forgotten shit from those days. She put it in the simplest of terms. You stupid, worthless, no-good son of a whore are going home. No, he said, through demolished lips. He wasn't fooling, either. When he first woke up and realized that he was still alive, he insisted on seeing Yvón. I love her, he whispered, and his mother said, Shut up, you! Just shut up!

The doctor ruled out epidural hematoma but couldn't guarantee that Oscar didn't have brain damage. (She was a cop's girlfriend? Tío Rodolfo whistled. I'll vouch for the brain damage.) Send him home right now, homegirl said, but for four whole days Oscar resisted any attempt to be packed up in a plane, which says a lot about this fat kid's fortitude; he was eating morphine by the handful and his grill was in agony, he had an around-the-clock quadruple migraine and couldn't see squat out of his right eye; motherfucker's head was so swollen he looked like John Merrick, Jr., and anytime he attempted to stand, the ground whisked right out from under him. My God! he thought. So this is what it feels like to get your ass *kicked*. It wasn't all bad, though; the beating granted him strange insights: he heard his tío, three rooms over, stealing money from his mother's purse; and he realized that had he and Yvón not been serious the Capitán would probably never have fucked with him. Proof positive that he and Yvón had a relationship.

Yvón didn't answer her cell, and the few times Oscar managed to limp to the window he saw that her Pathfinder wasn't there. I love you, he shouted into the street. I love you! Once, he made it to her door and buzzed before his tío realized that he was gone and dragged him back inside.

And, then, on Day Three, she came. While she sat on the edge of his bed, his mother banged pots in the kitchen and said "puta" loudly enough for them to hear.

Forgive me if I don't get up, Oscar whispered. I'm having a little trouble with my face.

She was dressed in white, like an angel, and her hair was still wet from the shower, a tumult of brownish curls. Of course the Capitán had beaten the shit out of her, too; of course she had two black eyes. (He'd also put his .44 Magnum in her vagina and asked her who she really loved.) There was nothing about her that Oscar wouldn't have gladly kissed. She put her fingers on his hand and told him that she could never be with him again. For some reason, Oscar couldn't see her face; it was a blur, she had retreated completely into that other plane of hers. Heard only the sorrow of her breathing. He tried to focus but all he saw was his love for her. Yvón? he croaked, but she was already gone.

Se acabó. Oscar refused to look at the ocean as they drove to the airport. It's beautiful today, Clives remarked. On the flight over, Oscar sat between his tío and his moms. Jesus, Oscar, Rodolfo said nervously. You look like they put a shirt on a turd.

P-Town Blues

Oscar returned to Paterson. He lay in bed, he stared at his games, he read Andre Norton books, he healed. He talked to the school, and they told him not to worry about the job; it was his when he was ready. You're lucky you're alive, his mother told him. Maybe you could save up your money and get an operation for your face, his tío suggested. Oscar, his sister sighed, Oscar. On the darkest days, he sat in his tío's closet, the Dragoon on his lap, looked back over the past two decades of his life, saw nothing but cowardice and fear. So why was there still a fortress in his heart? Why did he feel like he could be Minas Tirith if he wanted to? He really tried to forget, but he couldn't. He dreamed that he was adrift, alone in his spacesuit, and that she was calling to him.

Me and Lola were living up in the Heights — this was before the white kids started their invasion, when you could walk the entire length of Harlem and see not a single "homesteader." September, October? I was home for the week, curling ninety, when Oscar buzzed me from the street. Hadn't seen him in weeks. Jesus, Oscar, I said. Come up, come up. I waited for him in the hall and when he stepped out of the elevator I put the mitts on him. How are you, bro?

I'm fine, he said, smiling sheepishly.

We sat down and I broke up a dutch, asked him how it was going.

I'm going back to Don Bosco soon.

Word? I said.

Word, he said. His face was still fucked up, the left side was paralyzed and wouldn't get better anytime soon, but he wasn't hiding it anymore. I still got the Two-Face going on bad, he said, laughing.

You gonna smoke?

Just a little. I don't want to cloud my faculties.

That last day on our couch, he looked like a man at peace with himself. You should have seen him. He was so thin, had lost all the weight, and was still, still.

I want to know, Yunior, if you can do me a favor.

Anything, bro. Just ask it.

He needed money for a security deposit, was finally moving into his own apartment, and of course I gave it to him. All I had, but if anybody was going to pay me back it was Oscar.

We smoked the dutch and talked about the problems me and Lola were having.

You should never have had carnal relations with that Paraguayan girl, he pointed out.

I know, I said, I know. He seemed confident that it would work itself out, though, and there was something in his tone that made me hopeful. You ain't going to wait for Lola?

Have to get back to Paterson. I got a date.

You're shitting me?

He shook his head, the tricky fuck.

On Saturday, he was gone.

The Last Days

As soon as he hit the airport exit, Oscar called Clives and homeboy picked him up an hour later. Cristiano, Clives said, eyes tearing, what are you doing here?

It's the Ancient Powers, Oscar said. They won't leave me alone.

They parked in front of her house and waited almost seven hours before she returned. Pulled up in the Pathfinder. She looked thinner. For a moment, he thought about letting the whole thing go, returning to Bosco and getting on with his life, but then she stooped over to pick up her gym bag, as if the whole world were watching, and that settled it. He winched down the window and called her name. She stopped, shaded her eyes, and then recognized him. She said his name, terrified. *Oscar.* He popped the door and walked over to where she was standing and embraced her and she said, Mi amor, you have to leave right now.

In the middle of the street, he told her how it was. He was in love with her. He'd been hurt, but now he was all right, and if he could just have a week alone with her, one short week, then everything would be fine, and he would be able to go on with his life, and he said it again, that he loved her more than the universe, and it wasn't something that he could shake, so, please, come away with him for a little while, and then it would be over if she wanted.

Maybe she did love him a little bit. Maybe in her heart of hearts she left the gym bag on the concrete and got in the taxi with him. But she'd known men like the Capitán all her life. Knew, also, that in the D.R. they called a bullet a cop's divorce. The gym bag was not left on the street.

I'm going to call him, Oscar, she said, misting up a little. So, please, go, before he gets here.

I'm not going anywhere, he said.

For twenty-seven days he chased her. He sat in front of her house, he called her on her cell, he went to the World Famous Riverside, a casa de putas where she worked. The neighbors, when they saw him on the curb, shook their heads and said, Look at that loco.

She was miserable when she saw him and miserable, she would tell him later, when she didn't, convinced that he'd been killed. He slipped long passionate letters under her gate, written in English, and the only response he got was when the Capitán and his friends called and threatened to chop him in pieces. After each threat, he recorded the time and then phoned the Embassy and told them that the Capitán had threatened to kill him, and asked, Could you please help?

She started scribbling back notes and passed them to him at the club or had them mailed to his house. Please, Oscar, I haven't slept in a week. I don't want you to end up hurt or dead. Go home.

But, beautiful girl above all beautiful girls, he wrote back. This *is* my home.

Your real home, mi amor.

A person can't have two?

Night Nineteen, she honked her horn, and he opened his eyes and knew it was her. She leaned over and unlocked the truck door, and when he got in he tried to kiss her, but she said, Please stop it. They drove out toward La Romana, where the Capitán didn't have no friends. Nothing new was discussed, but he said, I like your new haircut, and she started laughing and crying and said, Really? You don't think it makes me look cheap?

You and cheap do not compute, Yvón.

What could we do? Lola flew down to see him, begged him to come home, told him that he was only going to get Yvón and himself killed; he listened and then said angrily that she didn't understand how he felt, never had. How incredibly short are twenty-seven days.

One night, the Capitán and his friends came into the Riverside, and Oscar stared at the man for a good ten seconds and then, whole body shaking, he left. Didn't bother to call Clives, jumped in the first taxi he could find. The next night Oscar was back and, in the parking lot of the Riverside, he tried again to kiss Yvón; she turned her head away (but not her body). Please don't, she said. He'll kill us.

Twenty-seven days, and then the expected happened. One night, he and Clives were driving back from the World Famous Riverside and at a light two men got into the cab with them. It was, of course, Gorilla Grodd and Solomon Grundy. Good to see you again, Grodd said, and then they beat him as best they could, given the limited space inside the cab.

This time, Oscar didn't cry when they drove him back to the cane fields. Zafra would be here soon, and the cane had grown well and thick and in places you could hear the stalks clack-clack-clacking against each other like triffids, and you could hear the kriyol voices lost in the night. There was a moon, and Clives begged the men to spare Oscar, but they laughed. You should be worrying, Grodd said, about yourself. Oscar sent telepathic messages to his moms (I love you, Señora), to Rodolfo (Quit, Tío, and live), to Lola (I'm so sorry it happened; I always loved you), and the longest to Yvón.

They walked him into the cane and then turned him around. (Clives they left tied up in the cab.) They looked at him and he looked at them, and then he started to speak. He told them that what they were doing was wrong, that they were going to take a great love out of the world. Love was a rare thing, he told them, easily confused with a million other things, and if anybody knew this to be true it was him. He told them about Yvón and the way he loved her and how much they had risked and that they'd started to dream the same dreams and say the same words, and he told them that if they killed him they would probably feel nothing and their children would probably feel nothing, either, not until they were old and weak or about to be struck by a car, and then they would sense his waiting for them on the other side, and over there he wouldn't be no fat boy or dork or kid no girl had ever loved, over there he'd be a hero, an avenger. Because anything you can dream (he put his hand up) you can be.

They waited for him to finish, and then they shot him to pieces.

Oscar —

The End of the Story

Lola and I flew down to claim the body. We went to the funeral. A year later, we broke up.

Four times, the family hired lawyers, but no charges were ever filed. The Embassy didn't help and neither did the government. Yvón, I hear, is still living in Mirador Norte, still dancing at the Riverside. The de Leóns sold their house a year later.

Lola swore she would never return to that terrible country, and I don't think she ever has. On one of our last nights, she said, Eight million Trujillos is all we are.

(Of course things like this don't happen in Santo Domingo no more. We have enlightened, uncorrupt politicians and a kind benevolent President and a people who are clearheaded and loving. The country is kind, no Haitian or dark-skinned person is hated, the élites fuck nobody, and the police measure their probity by the mile.)

Almost eight weeks after Oscar died, a package arrived at the house in Paterson. Two manuscripts enclosed. One was chapters of his never-to-be-completed opus, an E. E. (Doc) Smithesque space opera called "Starscourge." The other was a long letter to Lola. Turns out that to-ward the end the palomo *did* get Yvón away from the capital. For two whole days, they hid out on some beach in Barahona while the Capitán was away on "business," and guess what? Yvón actually kissed him! Guess what else? Yvón actually fucked him. Yahoo! He reported that he'd liked it and that Yvón's you-know-what hadn't tasted the way he had expected. She tastes like Heineken, he said. He wrote that at night Yvón had nightmares that the Capitán had found them; once, she'd woken up and said in the voice of true fear, Oscar, he's here, really be-lieving he was, and Oscar woke up and threw himself at the Capitán but it turned out to be only a turtle shell the hotel had hung on the wall for decoration. Almost busted my nose! He wrote that Yvón had little hairs coming up almost to her bellybutton and that she crossed her eyes when she fucked but what really got him were the little inti-macies that he'd never in his whole life anticipated, like combing her hair or getting her underwear off a line or watching her walk naked to the bathroom or the way she would suddenly sit on his lap and put her face into his neck. The intimacies like listening to her tell him about being a little girl and him telling her that he'd been a virgin all his life. He wrote that he couldn't believe he'd had to wait for this so god-dam long. (Yvón was the one who suggested calling the wait some-thing else. Yeah, like what? Maybe, she said, you could call it life.) He wrote: So this is what everybody's always talking about! Diablo! If only I'd known. The beauty! The beauty!

JUNOT DÍAZ

How to Date a Browngirl, Blackgirl, Whitegirl, or Halfie

Wait for your brother and your mother to leave the apartment. You've already told them that you're feeling too sick to go to Union City to visit that tía who likes to squeeze your nuts. (He's gotten big, she'll say.) And even though your moms knows you ain't sick you stuck to your story until finally she said, Go ahead and stay, malcriado.

Clear the government cheese from the refrigerator. If the girl's from the Terrace stack the boxes behind the milk. If she's from the Park or Society Hill hide the cheese in the cabinet above the oven, way up where she'll never see. Leave yourself a reminder to get it out before morning or your moms will kick your ass. Take down any embarrassing photos of your family in the campo, especially the one with the half-naked kids dragging a goat on a rope leash. The kids are your cousins and by now they're old enough to understand why you're doing what you're doing. Hide the pictures of yourself with an Afro. Make sure the bathroom is presentable. Put the basket with all the crapped-on toilet paper under the sink. Spray the bucket with Lysol, then close the cabinet.

Shower, comb, dress. Sit on the couch and watch TV. If she's an outsider her father will be bringing her, maybe her mother. Neither of them want her seeing any boys from the Terrace — people get stabbed in the Terrace — but she's strong-headed and this time will get her way. If she's a whitegirl you know you'll at least get a hand job.

The directions were in your best handwriting, so her parents won't think you're an idiot. Get up from the couch and check the parking lot. Nothing. If the girl's local, don't sweat it. She'll flow over when she's good and ready. Sometimes she'll run into her other friends and a whole crowd will show up at your apartment and even though that means you ain't getting shit it will be fun anyway and you'll wish these people would come over more often. Sometimes the girl won't flow over at all and the next day in school she'll say sorry, smile and you'll be stupid enough to believe her and ask her out again.

Wait and after an hour go out to your corner. The neighborhood is full of traffic. Give one of your boys a shout and when he says, Are you still waiting on that bitch? say, Hell yeah.

Get back inside. Call her house and when her father picks up ask if she's there. He'll ask, Who is this? Hang up. He sounds like a principal or a police chief, the sort of dude with a big neck, who never has to watch his back. Sit and wait. By the time your stomach's ready to give out on you, a Honda or maybe a Jeep pulls in and out she comes.

Hey, you'll say.

Look, she'll say. My mom wants to meet you. She's got herself all worried about nothing.

Don't panic. Say, Hey, no problem. Run a hand through your hair like the whiteboys do even though the only thing that runs easily through your hair is Africa. She will look good. The white ones are the ones you want the most, aren't they, but usually the out-of-towners are black, blackgirls who grew up with ballet and Girl Scouts, who have three cars in their driveways. If she's a halfie don't be surprised that her mother is white. Say, Hi. Her moms will say hi and you'll see that you don't scare her, not really. She will say that she needs easier directions to get out and even though she has the best directions in her lap give her new ones. Make her happy.

You have choices. If the girl's from around the way, take her to El Cibao for dinner. Order everything in your busted-up Spanish. Let her correct you if she's Latina and amaze her if she's black. If she's not from around the way, Wendy's will do. As you walk to the restaurant talk about school. A local girl won't need stories about the neighborhood but the other ones might. Supply the story about the loco who'd been storing canisters of tear gas in his basement for years, how one day the canisters cracked and the whole neighborhood got a dose of the military strength stuff. Don't tell her that your moms knew right away what it was, that she recognized its smell from the year the United States invaded your island.

Hope that you don't run into your nemesis, Howie, the Puerto Rican kid with the two killer mutts. He walks them all over the neighborhood and every now and then the mutts corner themselves a cat and tear it to shreds, Howie laughing as the cat flips up in the air, its neck twisted around like an owl, red meat showing through the soft fur. If his dogs haven't cornered a cat, he will walk behind you and ask, Hey, Yunior, is that your new fuckbuddy?

Let him talk. Howie weighs about two hundred pounds and could eat you if he wanted. At the field he will turn away. He has new sneakers, and doesn't want them muddy. If the girl's an outsider she will hiss now and say, What a fucking asshole. A homegirl would have been yelling back at him the whole time, unless she was shy. Either way don't feel bad that you didn't do anything. Never lose a fight on a first date or that will be the end of it.

Dinner will be tense. You are not good at talking to people you don't know. A halfie will tell you that her parents met in the Movement, will say, Back then people thought it a radical thing to do. It will sound like something her parents made her memorize. Your brother once heard that one and said, Man, that sounds like a whole lot of Uncle Tomming to me. Don't repeat this.

Put down your hamburger and say, It must have been hard.

She will appreciate your interest. She will tell you more. Black people, she will say, treat me real bad. That's why I don't like them. You'll wonder how she feels about Dominicans. Don't ask. Let her speak on it and when you're both finished eating walk back into the neighborhood. The skies will be magnificent. Pollutants have made Jersey sunsets one of the wonders of the world. Point it out. Touch her shoulder and say, That's nice, right?

Get serious. Watch TV but stay alert. Sip some of the Bermúdez your father left in the cabinet, which nobody touches. A local girl may have hips and a thick ass but she won't be quick about letting you touch. She has to live in the same neighborhood you do, has to deal with you being all up in her business. She might just chill with you and then go home. She might kiss you and then go, or she might, if she's reckless, give it up, but that's rare. Kissing will suffice. A white-girl might just give it up right then. Don't stop her. She'll take her gum out of her mouth, stick it to the plastic sofa covers and then will move close to you. You have nice eyes, she might say.

Tell her that you love her hair, that you love her skin, her lips, because, in truth, you love them more than you love your own.

She'll say, I like Spanish guys, and even though you've never been to Spain, say, I like you. You'll sound smooth.

You'll be with her until about eight-thirty and then she will want to wash up. In the bathroom she will hum a song from the radio and her waist will keep the beat against the lip of the sink. Imagine her old lady coming to get her, what she would say if she knew her daughter had just lain under you and blown your name, pronounced with her eighth-grade Spanish, into your ear. While she's in the bathroom call one of your boys and say, Lo hice, loco. Or just sit back on the couch and smile.

But usually it won't work this way. Be prepared. She will not want to kiss you. Just cool it, she'll say. The halfie might lean back, breaking away from you. She will cross her arms, say, I hate my tits. Stroke her hair but she will pull away. I don't like anybody touching my hair, she will say. She will act like somebody you don't know. In school she is known for her attention-grabbing laugh, as high and far-ranging as a gull, but here she will worry you. You will not know what to say.

You're the only kind of guy who asks me out, she will say. Your neighbors will start their hyena calls, now that the alcohol is in them. You and the blackboys.

Say nothing. Let her button her shirt, let her comb her hair, the sound of it stretching like a sheet of fire between you. When her father pulls in and beeps, let her go without too much of a good-bye. She won't want it. During the next hour the phone will ring. You will be tempted to pick it up. Don't. Watch the shows you want to watch, without a family around to debate you. Don't go downstairs. Don't fall asleep. It won't help. Put the government cheese back in its place before your moms kills you.

Richard Ford

Rock Springs, Richard Ford's first collection, appeared in 1987, after he'd already established his reputation with three novels, *A Piece of My Heart, The Ultimate Good Luck,* and *The Sportswriter.* Understated, beautifully crafted, the stories often feature an untutored first-person narrator giving a formal account of an emotional storm that passed through his life at some point. The effect is a kind of authenticity and beauty that has no artifice in it, as if the reader is privy to a stranger's diary or is overhearing him testify in private. Ford dispenses with the contractions of the conversational style — these characters want to get it right — and allows his speakers to directly express what they are feeling or have felt, as in this, from the last piece in the book, "Communist": "And what I felt was only that I had somehow been pushed out into the world, into the real life then, the one I hadn't lived yet." Or this, from the ending of "Great Falls": "Though possibly it — the answer — is simple: it is just low-life, some coldness in us all, some helplessness that causes us to misunderstand life when it is pure and plain, makes our existence seem like a border between two nothings, and makes us no more or less than animals who meet on the road — watchful, unforgiving, without patience or desire." There is an elegiac tone here, the sadness of Ford's puzzled characters meditating on what has happened to them, giving their honest assessments of the trouble in their lives, lives which always come cloaked in shadow and ambiguity. Ford's later books include the collection *Women with Men* and *Independence Day,* the sequel to *The Sportswriter.*

The first of the two pieces here, "Rock Springs," is a story about appearances and how deceptive they can be. The narrator, Earl, is a small-time criminal and con man who has a hard time differentiating between himself and the doctor whose Mercedes he's stolen, a man who tries on roles in the way others might try on clothes. A series of questions he poses to himself closes out the piece in a troubling way as he gropes toward self-awareness while at the same time throwing the onus on the reader. "Great Falls" begins, famously, with the lines, "This is not a happy story. I warn you." The admonition is well-taken. The narrator is looking back on a time when his life changed radically, when his parents split up and he was set adrift, unable to read exactly what went wrong, and still, in sorrow, musing on it all these many years later.

Richard Ford

Rock Springs

Edna and I had started down from Kalispell, heading for Tampa-St. Pete where I still had some friends from the old glory days who wouldn't turn me in to the police. I had managed to scrape with the law in Kalispell over several bad checks — which is a prison crime in Montana. And I knew Edna was already looking at her cards and thinking about a move, since it wasn't the first time I'd been in law scrapes in my life. She herself had already had her own troubles, losing her kids and keeping her ex-husband, Danny, from breaking in her house and stealing her things while she was at work, which was really why I had moved in in the first place, that and needing to give my little daughter, Cheryl, a better shake in things.

I don't know what was between Edna and me, just beached by the same tides when you got down to it. Though love has been built on frailer ground than that, as I well know. And when I came in the house that afternoon, I just asked her if she wanted to go to Florida with me, leave things where they sat, and she said, "Why not? My datebook's not that full."

Edna and I had been a pair eight months, more or less man and wife, some of which time I had been out of work, and some when I'd worked at the dog track as a lead-out and could help with the rent and talk sense to Danny when he came around. Danny was afraid of me because Edna had told him I'd been in prison in Florida for killing a man, though that wasn't true. I had once been in jail in Tallahassee for stealing tires and had gotten into a fight on the county farm where a man had lost his eye. But I hadn't done the hurting, and Edna just wanted the story worse than it was so Danny wouldn't act crazy and make her have to take her kids back, since she had made a good adjustment to not having them, and I already had Cheryl with me. I'm not a violent person and would never put a man's eye out, much less kill someone. My former wife, Helen, would come all the way from Waikiki Beach to testify to that. We never had violence, and I believe in crossing the street to stay out of trouble's way. Though Danny didn't know that.

But we were half down through Wyoming, going toward I-80 and feeling good about things, when the oil light flashed on in the car I'd stolen, a sign I knew to be a bad one.

I'd gotten us a good car, a cranberry Mercedes I'd stolen out of an ophthalmologist's lot in Whitefish, Montana. I stole it because I thought it would be comfortable over a long haul, because I thought it got good mileage, which it didn't, and because I'd never had a good car in my life, just old Chevy junkers and used trucks back from when I was a kid swamping citrus with Cubans.

The car made us all high that day. I ran the windows up and down, and Edna told us some jokes and made faces. She could be lively. Her features would light up like a beacon and you could see her beauty, which wasn't ordinary. It all made me giddy, and I drove clear down to Bozeman, then straight on through the park to Jackson Hole. I rented us the bridal suite in the Quality Court in Jackson and left Cheryl and her little dog, Duke, sleeping while Edna and I drove to a rib barn and drank beer and laughed till after midnight.

It felt like a whole new beginning for us, bad memories left behind and a new horizon to build on. I got so worked up, I had a tattoo done on my arm that said FAMOUS TIMES, and Edna bought a Bailey hat with an Indian feather band and a little turquoise-and-silver bracelet for Cheryl, and we made love on the seat of the car in the Quality Court parking lot just as the sun was burning up on the Snake River, and everything seemed then like the end of the rainbow.

It was that very enthusiasm, in fact, that made me keep the car one day longer instead of driving it into the river and stealing another one, like I should've done and *had* done before.

Where the car went bad there wasn't a town in sight or even a house, just some low mountains maybe fifty miles away or maybe a hundred, a barbed-wire fence in both directions, hardpan prairie, and some hawks riding the evening air seizing insects.

I got out to look at the motor, and Edna got out with Cheryl and the dog to let them have a pee by the car. I checked the water and checked the oil stick, and both of them said perfect.

"What's that light mean, Earl?" Edna said. She had come and stood by the car with her hat on. She was just sizing things up for herself.

"We shouldn't run it," I said. "Something's not right in the oil."

She looked around at Cheryl and Little Duke, who were peeing on the hardtop side-by-side like two little dolls, then out at the mountains, which were becoming black and lost in the distance. "What're we doing?" she said. She wasn't worried yet, but she wanted to know what I was thinking about.

"Let me try it again."

"That's a good idea," she said, and we all got back in the car.

When I turned the motor over, it started right away and the red light stayed off and there weren't any noises to make you think something was wrong. I let it idle a minute, then pushed the accelerator down and watched the red bulb. But there wasn't any light on, and I started wondering if maybe I hadn't dreamed I saw it, or that it had been the sun catching an angle off the window chrome, or maybe I was scared of something and didn't know it.

"What's the matter with it, Daddy?" Cheryl said from the backseat. I looked back at her, and she had on her turquoise bracelet and Edna's hat set back on the back of her head and that little black-and-white Heinz dog on her lap. She looked like a little cowgirl in the movies.

"Nothing, honey, everything's fine now," I said.

"Little Duke tinkled where I tinkled," Cheryl said, and laughed.

"You're two of a kind," Edna said, not looking back. Edna was usually good with Cheryl, but I knew she was tired now. We hadn't had much sleep, and she had a tendency to get cranky when she didn't sleep. "We oughta ditch this damn car first chance we get," she said.

"What's the first chance we got?" I asked, because I knew she'd been at the map.

"Rock Springs, Wyoming," Edna said with conviction. "Thirty miles down this road." She pointed out ahead.

I had wanted all along to drive the car into Florida like a big success story. But I knew Edna was right about it, that we shouldn't take crazy chances. I had kept thinking of it as my car and not the ophthalmologist's, and that was how you got caught in these things.

"Then my belief is we ought to go to Rock Springs and negotiate ourselves a new car," I said. I wanted to stay upbeat, like everything was panning out right.

"That's a great idea," Edna said, and she leaned over and kissed me hard on the mouth.

"That's a great idea," Cheryl said. "Let's pull on out of here right now."

The sunset that day I remember as being the prettiest I'd ever seen. Just as it touched the rim of the horizon, it all at once fired the air into jewels and red sequins the precise likes of which I had never seen before and haven't seen since. The West has it all over everywhere for sunsets, even Florida, where it's supposedly flat but where half the time trees block your view.

"It's cocktail hour," Edna said after we'd driven awhile. "We ought to have a drink and celebrate something." She felt better thinking we were going to get rid of the car. It certainly had dark troubles and was something you'd want to put behind you.

Edna had out a whiskey bottle and some plastic cups and was measuring levels on the glove-box lid. She liked drinking, and she liked drinking in the car, which was something you got used to in Montana, where it wasn't against the law, but where, strangely enough, a bad check would land you in Deer Lodge Prison for a year.

"Did I ever tell you I once had a monkey?" Edna said, setting my drink on the dashboard where I could reach it when I was ready. Her spirits were already picked up. She was like that, up one minute and down the next.

"I don't think you ever did tell me that," I said. "Where were you then?"

"Missoula," she said. She put her bare feet on the dash and rested the cup on her breasts. "I was waitressing at the AmVets. This was before I met you. Some guy came in one day with a monkey. A spider monkey. And I said, just to be joking, 'I'll roll you for that monkey.' And the guy said, 'Just one roll?' And I said, 'Sure.' He put the monkey down on the bar, picked up the cup, and rolled out boxcars. I picked it up and rolled out three fives. And I just stood there looking at the guy. He was just some guy passing through, I guess a vet. He got a strange look on his face — I'm sure not as strange as the one I had — but he looked kind of sad and surprised and satisfied all at once. I said, 'We can roll again.' But he said, 'No, I never roll twice for anything.' And he sat and drank a beer and talked about one thing and another for a while, about nuclear war and building a stronghold somewhere up in the Bitterroot, whatever it was, while I just watched the monkey, wondering what I was going to do with it when the guy left. And pretty soon he got up and said, 'Well, good-bye, Chipper' — that was this monkey's name, of course. And then he left before I could say anything. And the monkey just sat on the bar all that night. I don't know what made me think of that, Earl. Just something weird. I'm letting my mind wander."

"That's perfectly fine," I said. I took a drink of my drink. "I'd never own a monkey," I said after a minute. "They're too nasty. I'm sure Cheryl would like a monkey, though, wouldn't you, honey?" Cheryl was down on the seat playing with Little Duke. She used to talk about monkeys all the time then. "What'd you ever do with that monkey?" I said, watching the speedometer. We were having to go slower now because the red light kept fluttering on. And all I could do to keep it off was go slower. We were going maybe thirty-five and it was an hour before dark, and I was hoping Rock Springs wasn't far away.

"You really want to know?" Edna said. She gave me a quick glance, then looked back at the empty desert as if she was brooding over it.

"Sure," I said. I was still upbeat. I figured I could worry about breaking down and let other people be happy for a change.

"I kept it a week." And she seemed gloomy all of a sudden, as if she saw some aspect of the story she had never seen before. "I took it home and back and forth to the AmVets on my shifts. And it didn't cause any trouble. I fixed a chair up for it to sit on, back of the bar, and people liked it. It made a nice little clicking noise. We changed its name to Mary because the bartender figured out it was a girl. Though I was never really comfortable with it at home. I felt like it watched me too much. Then one day a guy came in, some guy who'd been in Vietnam, still wore a fatigue coat. And he said to me, 'Don't you know that a monkey'll kill you? It's got more strength in its fingers than you got in your whole body.' He said people had been killed in Vietnam by monkeys, bunches of them marauding while you were asleep, killing you and covering you with leaves. I didn't believe a word of it, except that when I got home and got undressed I started looking over across the room at Mary on her chair in the dark watching me. And I got the creeps. And after a while I got up and went out to the car, got a length of clothesline wire, and came back in and wired her to the doorknob through her little silver collar, then went back and tried to sleep. And I guess I must've slept the sleep of the dead — though I don't remember it — because when I got up I found Mary had tipped off her chairback and hanged herself on the wire line. I'd made it too short."

Edna seemed badly affected by that story and slid low in the seat so she couldn't see out over the dash. "Isn't that a shameful story, Earl, what happened to that poor little monkey?"

"I see a town! I see a town!" Cheryl started yelling from the back seat, and right up Little Duke started yapping and the whole car fell into a racket. And sure enough she had seen something I hadn't, which was Rock Springs, Wyoming, at the bottom of a long hill, a little glowing jewel in the desert with I-80 running on the north side and the black desert spread out behind.

"That's it, honey," I said. "That's where we're going. You saw it first."

"We're hungry," Cheryl said. "Little Duke wants some fish, and I want spaghetti." She put her arms around my neck and hugged me.

"Then you'll just get it," I said. "You can have anything you want. And so can Edna and so can Little Duke." I looked over at Edna, smiling, but she was staring at me with eyes that were fierce with anger. "What's wrong?" I said.

"Don't you care anything about that awful thing that happened to me?" Her mouth was drawn tight, and her eyes kept cutting back at Cheryl and Little Duke, as if they had been tormenting her.

"Of course I do," I said. "I thought that was an awful thing." I didn't want her to be unhappy. We were almost there, and pretty soon we could sit down and have a real meal without thinking somebody might be hurting us.

"You want to know what I did with that monkey?" Edna said.

"Sure I do," I said.

"I put her in a green garbage bag, put it in the trunk of my car, drove to the dump, and threw her in the trash." She was staring at me darkly, as if the story meant something to her that was real important but that only she could see and that the rest of the world was a fool for.

"Well, that's horrible," I said. "But I don't see what else you could do. You didn't mean to kill it. You'd have done it differently if you had. And then you had to get rid of it, and I don't know what else you could have done. Throwing it away might seem unsympathetic to somebody, probably, but not to me. Sometimes that's all you can do, and you can't worry about what somebody else thinks." I tried to smile at her, but the red light was staying on if I pushed the accelerator at all, and I was trying to gauge if we could coast to Rock Springs before the car gave out completely. I looked at Edna again. "What else can I say?" I said.

"Nothing," she said, and stared back at the dark highway. "I should've known that's what you'd think. You've got a character that leaves something out, Earl. I've known that a long time."

"And yet here you are," I said. "And you're not doing so bad. Things could be a lot worse. At least we're all together here."

"Things could always be worse," Edna said. "You could go to the electric chair tomorrow."

"That's right," I said. "And somewhere somebody probably will. Only it won't be you."

"I'm hungry," said Cheryl. "When're we gonna eat? Let's find a motel. I'm tired of this. Little Duke's tired of it too."

Where the car stopped rolling was some distance from the town, though you could see the clear outline of the interstate in the dark with Rock Springs lighting up the sky behind. You could hear the big tractors hitting the spacers in the overpass, revving up for the climb to the mountains.

I shut off the lights.

"What're we going to do now?" Edna said irritably, giving me a bitter look.

"I'm figuring it," I said. "It won't be hard, whatever it is. You won't have to do anything."

"I'd hope not," she said and looked the other way.

Across the road and across a dry wash a hundred yards was what looked like a huge mobile-home town, with a factory or a refinery of some kind lit up behind it and in full swing. There were lights on in a lot of the mobile homes, and there were cars moving along an access road that ended near the freeway overpass a mile the other way. The lights in the mobile homes seemed friendly to me, and I knew right then what I should do.

"Get out," I said, opening my door.

"Are we walking?" Edna said.

"We're pushing."

"I'm not pushing." Edna reached up and locked her door.

"All right," I said. "Then you just steer."

"You're pushing us to Rock Springs, are you, Earl? It doesn't look like it's more than about three miles."

"I'll push," Cheryl said from the back.

"No, hon. Daddy'll push. You just get out with Little Duke and move out of the way."

Edna gave me a threatening look, just as if I'd tried to hit her. But when I got out she slid into my seat and took the wheel, staring angrily ahead straight into the cottonwood scrub.

"Edna can't drive that car," Cheryl said from out in the dark. "She'll run it in the ditch."

"Yes, she can, hon. Edna can drive it as good as I can. Probably better."

"No she can't," Cheryl said. "No she can't either." And I thought she was about to cry, but she didn't.

I told Edna to keep the ignition on so it wouldn't lock up and to steer into the cottonwoods with the parking lights on so she could see. And when I started, she steered it straight off into the trees, and I kept pushing until we were twenty yards into the cover and the tires sank in the soft sand and nothing at all could be seen from the road.

"Now where are we?" she said, sitting at the wheel. Her voice was tired and hard, and I knew she could have put a good meal to use. She had a sweet nature, and I recognized that this wasn't her fault but mine. Only I wished she could be more hopeful.

"You stay right here, and I'll go over to that trailer park and call us a cab," I said.

"What cab?" Edna said, her mouth wrinkled as if she'd never heard anything like that in her life.

"There'll be cabs," I said, and tried to smile at her. "There's cabs everywhere."

"What're you going to tell him when he gets here? Our stolen car broke down and we need a ride to where we can steal another one? That'll be a big hit, Earl."

"I'll talk," I said. "You just listen to the radio for ten minutes and then walk on out to the shoulder like nothing was suspicious. And you and Cheryl act nice. She doesn't need to know about this car."

"Like we're not suspicious enough already, right?" Edna looked up at me out of the lighted car. "You don't think right, did you know that, Earl? You think the world's stupid and you're smart. But that's not how it is. I feel sorry for you. You might've *been* something, but things just went crazy someplace."

I had a thought about poor Danny. He was a vet and crazy as a shit-house mouse, and I was glad he wasn't in for all this. "Just get the baby in the car," I said, trying to be patient. "I'm hungry like you are."

"I'm tired of this," Edna said. "I wish I'd stayed in Montana."

"Then you can go back in the morning," I said. "I'll buy the ticket and put you on the bus. But not till then."

"Just get on with it, Earl." She slumped down in the seat, turning off the parking lights with one foot and the radio on with the other.

The mobile-home community was as big as any I'd ever seen. It was attached in some way to the plant that was lighted up behind it, because I could see a car once in a while leave one of the trailer streets, turn in the direction of the plant, then go slowly into it. Everything in the plant was white, and you could see that all the trailers were painted white and looked exactly alike. A deep hum came out of the plant, and I thought as I got closer that it wouldn't be a location I'd ever want to work in.

I went right to the first trailer where there was a light, and knocked on the metal door. Kids' toys were lying in the gravel around the little wood steps, and I could hear talking on TV that suddenly went off. I heard a woman's voice talking, and then the door opened wide.

A large Negro woman with a wide, friendly face stood in the door-way. She smiled at me and moved forward as if she was going to come out, but she stopped at the top step. There was a little Negro boy behind her peeping out from behind her legs, watching me with his eyes half closed. The trailer had that feeling that no one else was inside, which was a feeling I knew something about.

"I'm sorry to intrude," I said. "But I've run up on a little bad luck tonight. My name's Earl Middleton."

The woman looked at me, then out into the night toward the free-way as if what I had said was something she was going to be able to see. "What kind of bad luck?" she said, looking down at me again.

"My car broke down out on the highway," I said. "I can't fix it my-self, and I wondered if I could use your phone to call for help."

The woman smiled down at me knowingly. "We can't live without cars, can we?"

"That's the honest truth," I said.

"They're like our hearts," she said, her face shining in the little bulb light that burned beside the door. "Where's your car situated?"

I turned and looked over into the dark, but I couldn't see anything because of where we'd put it. "It's over there," I said. "You can't see it in the dark."

"Who all's with you now?" the woman said. "Have you got your wife with you?"

"She's with my little girl and our dog in the car," I said. "My daughter's asleep or I would have brought them."

"They shouldn't be left in the dark by themselves," the woman said and frowned. "There's too much unsavoriness out there."

"The best I can do is hurry back." I tried to look sincere, since everything except Cheryl being asleep and Edna being my wife was the truth. The truth is meant to serve you if you'll let it, and I wanted it to serve me. "I'll pay for the phone call," I said. "If you'll bring the phone to the door I'll call from right here."

The woman looked at me again as if she was searching for a truth of her own, then back out into the night. She was maybe in her sixties, but I couldn't say for sure. "You're not going to rob me, are you, Mr. Middleton?" She smiled like it was a joke between us.

"Not tonight," I said, and smiled a genuine smile. "I'm not up to it tonight. Maybe another time."

"Then I guess Terrel and I can let you use our phone with Daddy not here, can't we, Terrel? This is my grandson, Terrel Junior, Mr. Middleton." She put her hand on the boy's head and looked down at him. "Terrel won't talk. Though if he did he'd tell you to use our phone. He's a sweet boy." She opened the screen for me to come in.

The trailer was a big one with a new rug and a new couch and a living room that expanded to give the space of a real house. Something good and sweet was cooking in the kitchen, and the trailer felt like it was somebody's comfortable new home instead of just temporary. I've lived in trailers, but they were just snailbacks with one room and no toilet, and they always felt cramped and unhappy — though I've thought maybe it might've been me that was unhappy in them.

There was a big Sony TV and a lot of kids' toys scattered on the floor. I recognized a Greyhound bus I'd gotten for Cheryl. The phone was beside a new leather recliner, and the Negro woman pointed for me to sit down and call and gave me the phone book. Terrel began fingering his toys and the woman sat on the couch while I called, watching me and smiling.

There were three listings for cab companies, all with one number different. I called the numbers in order and didn't get an answer until the last one, which answered with the name of the second company. I said I was on the highway beyond the interstate and that my wife and family needed to be taken to town and I would arrange for a tow later. While I was giving the location, I looked up the name of a tow service to tell the driver in case he asked.

When I hung up, the Negro woman was sitting looking at me with the same look she had been staring with into the dark, a look that seemed to want truth. She was smiling, though. Something pleased her and I reminded her of it.

"This is a very nice home," I said, resting in the recliner, which felt like the driver's seat of the Mercedes, and where I'd have been happy to stay.

"This isn't *our* house, Mr. Middleton," the Negro woman said. "The company owns these. They give them to us for nothing. We have our own home in Rockford, Illinois."

"That's wonderful," I said.

"It's never wonderful when you have to be away from home, Mr. Middleton, though we're only here three months, and it'll be easier when Terrel Junior begins his special school. You see, our son was killed in the war, and his wife ran off without Terrel Junior. Though you shouldn't worry. He can't understand us. His little feelings can't be hurt." The woman folded her hands in her lap and smiled in a satisfied way. She was an attractive woman, and had on a blue-and-pink floral dress that made her seem bigger than she could've been, just the right woman to sit on the couch she was sitting on. She was good nature's picture, and I was glad she could be, with her little brain-damaged boy, living in a place where no one in his right mind would want to live a minute. "Where do *you* live, Mr. Middleton?" she said politely, smiling in the same sympathetic way.

"My family and I are in transit," I said. "I'm an ophthalmologist, and we're moving back to Florida, where I'm from. I'm setting up practice in some little town where it's warm year-round. I haven't decided where."

"Florida's a wonderful place," the woman said. "I think Terrel would like it there."

"Could I ask you something?" I said.

"You certainly may," the woman said. Terrel had begun pushing his Greyhound across the front of the TV screen, making a scratch that no one watching the set could miss. "Stop that, Terrel Junior," the woman said quietly. But Terrel kept pushing his bus on the glass, and she smiled at me again as if we both understood something sad. Except I knew Cheryl would never damage a television set. She had respect for nice things, and I was sorry for the lady that Terrel didn't. "What did you want to ask?" the woman said.

"What goes on in that plant or whatever it is back there beyond these trailers, where all the lights are on?"

"Gold," the woman said and smiled.

"It's what?" I said.

"Gold," the Negro woman said, smiling as she had for almost all the time I'd been there. "It's a gold mine."

"They're mining gold back there?" I said, pointing.

"Every night and every day." She smiled in a pleased way.

"Does your husband work there?" I said.

"He's the assayer," she said. "He controls the quality. He works three months a year, and we live the rest of the time at home in Rockford. We've waited a long time for this. We've been happy to have our grandson, but I won't say I'll be sorry to have him go. We're ready to start our lives over." She smiled broadly at me and then at Terrel, who was giving her a spiteful look from the floor. "You said you had a daughter," the Negro woman said. "And what's her name?"

"Irma Cheryl," I said. "She's named for my mother."

"That's nice. And she's healthy, too. I can see it in your face." She looked at Terrel Junior with pity.

"I guess I'm lucky," I said.

"So far you are. But children bring you grief, the same way they bring you joy. We were unhappy for a long time before my husband got his job in the gold mine. Now, when Terrel starts to school, we'll be kids again." She stood up. "You might miss your cab, Mr. Middleton," she said, walking toward the door, though not to be forcing me out. She was too polite. "If *we* can't see your car, the cab surely won't be able to."

"That's true." I got up off the recliner, where I'd been so comfortable. "None of us have eaten yet, and your food makes me know how hungry we probably all are."

"There are fine restaurants in town, and you'll find them," the Negro woman said. "I'm sorry you didn't meet my husband. He's a wonderful man. He's everything to me."

"Tell him I appreciate the phone," I said. "You saved me."

"You weren't hard to save," the woman said. "Saving people is what we were all put on earth to do. I just passed you on to whatever's coming to you."

"Let's hope it's good," I said, stepping back into the dark.

"I'll be hoping, Mr. Middleton. Terrel and I will both be hoping."

I waved to her as I walked out into the darkness toward the car where it was hidden in the night.

The cab had already arrived when I got there. I could see its little red-and-green roof lights all the way across the dry wash, and it made me worry that Edna was already saying something to get us in trouble, something about the car or where we'd come from, something that would cast suspicion on us. I thought, then, how I never planned things well enough. There was always a gap between my plan and what happened, and I only responded to things as they came along and hoped I wouldn't get in trouble. I was an offender in the law's eyes. But I always *thought* differently, as if I weren't an offender and had no intention of being one, which was the truth. But as I read on a napkin

once, between the idea and the act a whole kingdom lies. And I had a
hard time with my acts, which were oftentimes offender's acts, and my
ideas, which were as good as the gold they mined there where the
bright lights were blazing.

"We're waiting for you, Daddy," Cheryl said when I crossed the
road. "The taxicab's already here."

"I see, hon," I said, and gave Cheryl a big hug. The cabdriver was
sitting in the driver's seat having a smoke with the lights on inside.
Edna was leaning against the back of the cab between the taillights,
wearing her Bailey hat. "What'd you tell him?" I said when I got close.

"Nothing," she said. "What's there to tell?"

"Did he see the car?"

She glanced over in the direction of the trees where we had hid the
Mercedes. Nothing was visible in the darkness, though I could hear
Little Duke combing around in the underbrush tracking something,
his little collar tinkling. "Where're we going?" she said. "I'm so hungry I could pass out."

"Edna's in a terrible mood," Cheryl said. "She already snapped at me."

"We're tired, honey," I said. "So try to be nicer."

"She's never nice," Cheryl said.

"Run go get Little Duke," I said. "And hurry back."

"I guess *my* questions come last here, right?" Edna said.

I put my arm around her. "That's not true."

"Did you find somebody over there in the trailers you'd rather stay
with? You were gone long enough."

"That's not a thing to say," I said. "I was just trying to make things
look right, so we don't get put in jail."

"So *you* don't, you mean." Edna laughed a little laugh I didn't like
hearing.

"That's right. So I don't," I said. "I'd be the one in Dutch." I stared
out at the big, lighted assemblage of white buildings and white lights
beyond the trailer community, plumes of white smoke escaping up
into the heartless Wyoming sky, the whole company of buildings looking like some unbelievable castle, humming away in a distorted dream.
"You know what all those buildings are there?" I said to Edna, who
hadn't moved and who didn't really seem to care if she ever moved
anymore ever.

"No. But I can't say it matters, because it isn't a motel and it isn't a
restaurant."

"It's a gold mine," I said, staring at the gold mine, which, I knew
now, was a greater distance from us than it seemed, though it seemed
huge and near, up against the cold sky. I thought there should've been
a wall around it with guards instead of just the lights and no fence. It

seemed as if anyone could go in and take what they wanted, just the way I had gone up to that woman's trailer and used the telephone, though that obviously wasn't true.

Edna began to laugh then. Not the mean laugh I didn't like, but a laugh that had something caring behind it, a full laugh that enjoyed a joke, a laugh she was laughing the first time I laid eyes on her, in Missoula in the East Gate Bar in 1979, a laugh we used to laugh together when Cheryl was still with her mother and I was working steady at the track and not stealing cars or passing bogus checks to merchants. A better time all around. And for some reason it made me laugh just hearing her, and we both stood there behind the cab in the dark, laughing at the gold mine in the desert, me with my arm around her and Cheryl out rustling up Little Duke and the cabdriver smoking in the cab and our stolen Mercedes-Benz, which I'd had such hopes for in Florida, stuck up to its axle in sand, where I'd never get to see it again.

"I always wondered what a gold mine would look like when I saw it," Edna said, still laughing, wiping a tear from her eye.

"Me too," I said. "I was always curious about it."

"We're a couple of fools, aren't we, Earl?" she said, unable to quit laughing completely. "We're two of a kind."

"It might be a good sign, though," I said.

"How could it be? It's not our gold mine. There aren't any drive-up windows." She was still laughing.

"We've seen it," I said, pointing. "That's it right there. It may mean we're getting closer. Some people never see it at all."

"In a pig's eye, Earl," she said. "You and me see it in a pig's eye."

And she turned and got in the cab to go.

The cabdriver didn't ask anything about our car or where it was, to mean he'd noticed something queer. All of which made me feel like we had made a clean break from the car and couldn't be connected with it until it was too late, if ever. The driver told us a lot about Rock Springs while he drove, that because of the gold mine a lot of people had moved there in just six months, people from all over, including New York, and that most of them lived out in the trailers. Prostitutes from New York City, who he called "B-girls," had come into town, he said, on the prosperity tide, and Cadillacs with New York plates cruised the little streets every night, full of Negroes with big hats who ran the women. He told us that everybody who got in his cab now wanted to know where the women were, and when he got our call he almost didn't come because some of the trailers were brothels operated by the mine for engineers and computer people away from home. He said he got tired of running back and forth out there just for vile business. He said that *60 Minutes* had even done a program about Rock Springs and that a blow-up had resulted in Cheyenne, though nothing could be done unless the boom left town. "It's prosperity's fruit," the driver said. "I'd rather be poor, which is lucky for me."

He said all the motels were sky-high, but since we were a family he could show us a nice one that was affordable. But I told him we wanted a first-rate place where they took animals, and the money didn't matter because we had had a hard day and wanted to finish on a high note. I also knew that it was in the little nowhere places that the police look for you and find you. People I'd known were always being arrested in cheap hotels and tourist courts with names you'd never heard of before. Never in Holiday Inns or TraveLodges.

I asked him to drive us to the middle of town and back out again so Cheryl could see the train station, and while we were there I saw a pink Cadillac with New York plates and a TV aerial being driven slowly by a Negro in a big hat down a narrow street where there were just bars and a Chinese restaurant. It was an odd sight, nothing you could ever expect.

"There's your pure criminal element," the cabdriver said and seemed sad. "I'm sorry for people like you to see a thing like that. We've got a nice town here, but there're some that want to ruin it for everybody. There used to be a way to deal with trash and criminals, but those days are gone forever."

"You said it," Edna said.

"You shouldn't let it get *you* down," I said to him. "There's more of you than them. And there always will be. You're the best advertisement this town has. I know Cheryl will remember you and not *that* man, won't you, honey?" But Cheryl was asleep by then, holding Little Duke in her arms on the taxi seat.

The driver took us to the Ramada Inn on the interstate, not far from where we'd broken down. I had a small pain of regret as we drove under the Ramada awning that we hadn't driven up in a cranberry-colored Mercedes but instead in a beat-up old Chrysler taxi driven by an old man full of complaints. Though I knew it was for the best. We were better off without that car; better, really, in any other car but that one, where the signs had turned bad.

I registered under another name and paid for the room in cash so there wouldn't be any questions. On the line where it said "Representing" I wrote "Ophthalmologist" and put "M.D." after the name. It had a nice look to it, even though it wasn't my name.

When we got to the room, which was in the back where I'd asked for it, I put Cheryl on one of the beds and Little Duke beside her so they'd sleep. She'd missed dinner, but it only meant she'd be hungry in the morning, when she could have anything she wanted. A few missed meals don't make a kid bad. I'd missed a lot of them myself and haven't turned out completely bad.

"Let's have some fried chicken," I said to Edna when she came out of the bathroom. "They have good fried chicken at Ramadas, and I noticed the buffet was still up. Cheryl can stay right here, where it's safe, till we're back."

"I guess I'm not hungry anymore," Edna said. She stood at the window staring out into the dark. I could see out the window past her some yellowish foggy glow in the sky. For a moment I thought it was the gold mine out in the distance lighting the night, though it was only the interstate.

"We could order up," I said. "Whatever you want. There's a menu on the phone book. You could just have a salad."

"You go ahead," she said. "I've lost my hungry spirit." She sat on the bed beside Cheryl and Little Duke and looked at them in a sweet way and put her hand on Cheryl's cheek just as if she'd had a fever. "Sweet little girl," she said. "Everybody loves you."

"What do you want to do?" I said. "I'd like to eat. Maybe *I'll* order up some chicken."

"Why don't you do that?" she said. "It's your favorite." And she smiled at me from the bed.

I sat on the other bed and dialed room service. I asked for chicken, garden salad, potato and a roll, plus a piece of hot apple pie and iced tea. I realized I hadn't eaten all day. When I put down the phone I saw that Edna was watching me, not in a hateful way or a loving way, just in a way that seemed to say she didn't understand something and was going to ask me about it.

"When did watching me get so entertaining?" I said and smiled at her. I was trying to be friendly. I knew how tired she must be. It was after nine o'clock.

"I was just thinking how much I hated being in a motel without a car that was mine to drive. Isn't that funny? I started feeling like that last night when that purple car wasn't mine. That purple car just gave me the willies, I guess, Earl."

"One of those cars *outside* is yours," I said. "Just stand right there and pick it out."

"I know," she said. "But that's different, isn't it?" She reached and got her blue Bailey hat, put it on her head, and set it way back like Dale Evans. She looked sweet. "I used to like to go to motels, you know," she said. "There's something secret about them and free — I was never paying, of course. But you felt safe from everything and free to do what you wanted because you'd made the decision to be there and paid that price, and all the rest was the good part. Fucking and everything, you know." She smiled at me in a good-natured way.

"Isn't that the way this is?" I was sitting on the bed, watching her, not knowing what to expect her to say next.

"I don't guess it is, Earl," she said and stared out the window. "I'm thirty-two and I'm going to have to give up on motels. I can't keep that fantasy going anymore."

"Don't you like this place?" I said and looked around at the room. I appreciated the modern paintings and the lowboy bureau and the big TV. It seemed like a plenty nice enough place to me, considering where we'd been.

"No, I don't," Edna said with real conviction. "There's no use in my getting mad at you about it. It isn't your fault. You do the best you can for everybody. But every trip teaches you something. And I've learned I need to give up on motels before some bad thing happens to me. I'm sorry."

"What does that mean?" I said, because I really didn't know what she had in mind to do, though I should've guessed.

"I guess I'll take that ticket you mentioned," she said, and got up and faced the window. "Tomorrow's soon enough. We haven't got a car to take me anyhow."

"Well, that's a fine thing," I said, sitting on the bed, feeling like I was in shock. I wanted to say something to her, to argue with her, but I couldn't think what to say that seemed right. I didn't want to be mad at her, but it made me mad.

"You've got a right to be mad at me, Earl," she said, "but I don't think you can really blame me." She turned around and faced me and sat on the windowsill, her hands on her knees. Someone knocked on the door, and I just yelled for them to set the tray down and put it on the bill.

"I guess I *do* blame you," I said, and I was angry. I thought about how I could've disappeared into that trailer community and hadn't, had come back to keep things going, had tried to take control of things for everybody when they looked bad.

"Don't. I wish you wouldn't," Edna said and smiled at me like she wanted me to hug her. "Anybody ought to have their choice in things if they can. Don't you believe that, Earl? Here I am out here in the desert where I don't know anything, in a stolen car, in a motel room under an assumed name, with no money of my own, a kid that's not mine, and the law after me. And I have a choice to get out of all of it by getting on a bus. What would you do? I know exactly what you'd do."

"You think you do," I said. But I didn't want to get into an argument about it and tell her all I could've done and didn't do. Because it wouldn't have done any good. When you get to the point of arguing, you're past the point of changing anybody's mind, even though it's supposed to be the other way, and maybe for some classes of people it is, just never mine.

Edna smiled at me and came across the room and put her arms around me where I was sitting on the bed. Cheryl rolled over and looked at us and smiled, then closed her eyes, and the room was quiet. I was beginning to think of Rock Springs in a way I knew I would always think of it, a lowdown city full of crimes and whores and disappointments, a place where a woman left me, instead of a place where I got things on the straight track once and for all, a place I saw a gold mine.

"Eat your chicken, Earl," Edna said. "Then we can go to bed. I'm tired, but I'd like to make love to you anyway. None of this is a matter of not loving you, you know that."

Sometime late in the night, after Edna was asleep, I got up and walked outside into the parking lot. It could've been anytime because there was still the light from the interstate frosting the low sky and the big red Ramada sign humming motionlessly in the night and no light at all in the east to indicate it might be morning. The lot was full of cars all nosed in, a couple of them with suitcases strapped to their roofs and their trunks weighed down with belongings the people were taking someplace, to a new home or a vacation resort in the mountains. I had laid in bed a long time after Edna was asleep, watching the Atlanta Braves on television, trying to get my mind off how I'd feel when I saw that bus pull away the next day, and how I'd feel when I turned around and there stood Cheryl and Little Duke and no one to see about them but me alone, and that the first thing I had to do was get hold of some automobile and get the plates switched, then get them some breakfast and get us all on the road to Florida, all in the space of probably two hours, since that Mercedes would certainly look less hid in the daytime than the night, and word travels fast. I've always taken care of Cheryl myself as long as I've had her with me. None of the women ever did. Most of them didn't even seem to like her, though they took care of me in a way so that I could take care of her. And I knew that once Edna left, all that was going to get harder. Though what I wanted most to do was not think about it just for a little while, try to let my mind go limp so it could be strong for the rest of what there was. I thought that the difference between a successful life and an unsuccessful one, between me at that moment and all the people who owned the cars that were nosed into their proper places in the lot, maybe between me and that woman out in the trailers by the gold mine, was how well you were able to put things like this out of your mind and not be bothered by them, and maybe, too, by how many troubles like this one you had to face in a lifetime. Through luck or design they had all faced fewer troubles, and by their own characters, they forgot them faster. And that's what I wanted for me. Fewer troubles, fewer memories of trouble.

I walked over to a car, a Pontiac with Ohio tags, one of the ones with bundles and suitcases strapped to the top and a lot more in the trunk, by the way it was riding. I looked inside the driver's window. There were maps and paperback books and sunglasses and the little plastic holders for cans that hang on the window wells. And in the back there were kids' toys and some pillows and a cat box with a cat sitting in it staring up at me like I was the face of the moon. It all looked familiar to me, the very same things I would have in my car if I had a car. Nothing seemed surprising, nothing different. Though I had a funny sensation at that moment and turned and looked up at the windows along the back of the motel. All were dark except two. Mine and another one. And I wondered, because it seemed funny, what would you think a man was doing if you saw him in the middle of the night looking in the windows of cars in the parking lot of the Ramada Inn? Would you think he was trying to get his head cleared? Would you think he was trying to get ready for a day when trouble would come down on him? Would you think his girlfriend was leaving him? Would you think he had a daughter? Would you think he was anybody like you?

Great Falls

This is not a happy story. I warn you.

My father was a man named Jack Russell, and when I was a young boy in my early teens, we lived with my mother in a house to the east of Great Falls, Montana, near the small town of Highwood and the Highwood Mountains and the Missouri River. It is a flat, treeless benchland there, all of it used for wheat farming, though my father was never a farmer, but was brought up near Tacoma, Washington, in a family that worked for Boeing.

He — my father — had been an Air Force sergeant and had taken his discharge in Great Falls. And instead of going home to Tacoma, where my mother wanted to go, he had taken a civilian's job with the Air Force, working on planes, which was what he liked to do. And he had rented the house out of town from a farmer who did not want it left standing empty.

The house itself is gone now — I have been to the spot. But the double row of Russian olive trees and two of the outbuildings are still standing in the milkweeds. It was a plain, two-story house with a porch on the front and no place for the cars. At the time, I rode the school bus to Great Falls every morning, and my father drove in while my mother stayed home.

My mother was a tall pretty woman, thin, with black hair and slightly sharp features that made her seem to smile when she wasn't smiling. She had grown up in Wallace, Idaho, and gone to college a year in Spokane, then moved out to the coast, which is where she met Jack Russell. She was two years older than he was, and married him, she said to me, because he was young and wonderful looking, and because she thought they could leave the sticks and see the world to-gether — which I suppose they did for a while. That was the life she wanted, even before she knew much about wanting anything else or about the future.

When my father wasn't working on airplanes, he was going hunt-ing or fishing, two things he could do as well as anyone. He had learned to fish, he said, in Iceland, and to hunt ducks up on the DEW line — stations he had visited in the Air Force. And during the time of this — it was 1960 — he began to take me with him on what he called his "expeditions." I thought even then, with as little as I knew, that these were opportunities other boys would dream of having but probably never would. And I don't think that I was wrong in that.

It is a true thing that my father did not know limits. In the spring, when we would go east to the Judith River Basin and camp up on the banks, he would catch a hundred fish in a weekend, and sometimes more than that. It was all he did from morning until night, and it was never hard for him. He used yellow corn kernels stacked onto a #4 snelled hook, and he would rattle this rig-up along the bottom of a deep pool below a split-shot sinker, and catch fish. And most of the time, because he knew the Judith River and knew how to feel his bait down deep, he could catch fish of good size.

It was the same with ducks, the other thing he liked. When the northern birds were down, usually by mid-October, he would take me and we would build a cattail and wheatstraw blind on one of the tule ponds or sloughs he knew about down the Missouri, where the water was shallow enough to wade. We would set out his decoys to the leeward side of our blind, and he would sprinkle corn on a hunger-line from the decoys to where we were. In the evenings when he came home from the base, we would go and sit out in the blind until the roosting flights came and put down among the decoys — there was never calling involved. And after a while, sometimes it would be an hour and full dark, the ducks would find the corn, and the whole raft of them — sixty, sometimes — would swim in to us. At the moment he judged they were close enough, my father would say to me, "Shine, Jackie," and I would stand and shine a seal-beam car light out onto the pond, and he would stand up beside me and shoot all the ducks that were there, on the water if he could, but flying and getting up as well. He owned a Model 11 Remington with a long-tube magazine that would hold ten shells, and with that many, and shooting straight over the surface rather than down onto it, he could kill or wound thirty ducks in twenty seconds' time. I remember distinctly the report of that gun and the flash of it over the water into the dark air, one shot after another, not even so fast, but measured in a way to hit as many as he could.

What my father did with the ducks he killed, and the fish, too, was sell them. It was against the law then to sell wild game, and it is against the law now. And though he kept some for us, most he would take — his fish laid on ice, or his ducks still wet and bagged in the burlap corn sacks — down to the Great Northern Hotel, which was still open then on Second Street in Great Falls, and sell them to the Negro caterer who bought them for his wealthy customers and for the dining car passengers who came through. We would drive in my father's

Plymouth to the back of the hotel — always this was after dark — to a concrete loading ramp and lighted door that were close enough to the yards that I could sometimes see passenger trains waiting at the station, their car lights yellow and warm inside, the passengers dressed in suits, all bound for someplace far away from Montana — Milwaukee or Chicago or New York City, unimaginable places to me, a boy fourteen years old, with my father in the cold dark selling illegal game.

The caterer was a tall, stooped-back man in a white jacket, who my father called "Professor Ducks" or "Professor Fish," and the Professor referred to my father as "Sarge." He paid a quarter per pound for trout, a dime for whitefish, a dollar for a mallard duck, two for a speckle or a blue goose, and four dollars for a Canada. I have been with my father when he took away a hundred dollars for fish he'd caught and, in the fall, more than that for ducks and geese. When he had sold game in that way, we would drive out 10th Avenue and stop at a bar called The Mermaid which was by the air base, and he would drink with some friends he knew there, and they would laugh about hunting and fishing while I played pinball and wasted money in the jukebox.

It was on such a night as this that the unhappy things came about. It was in late October. I remember the time because Halloween had not been yet, and in the windows of the houses that I passed every day on the bus to Great Falls, people had put pumpkin lanterns, and set scarecrows in their yards in chairs.

My father and I had been shooting ducks in a slough on the Smith River, upstream from where it enters on the Missouri. He had killed thirty ducks, and we'd driven them down to the Great Northern and sold them there, though my father had kept two back in his corn sack. And when we had driven away, he suddenly said, "Jackie, let's us go back home tonight. Who cares about those hard-dicks at The Mermaid. I'll cook these ducks on the grill. We'll do something different tonight." He smiled at me in an odd way. This was not a thing he usually said, or the way he usually talked. He liked The Mermaid, and my mother — as far as I knew — didn't mind it if he went there.

"That sounds good," I said.

"We'll surprise your mother," he said. "We'll make her happy."

We drove out past the air base on Highway 87, past where there were planes taking off into the night. The darkness was dotted by the green and red beacons, and the tower light swept the sky and trapped planes as they disappeared over the flat landscape toward Canada or Alaska and the Pacific.

"Boy-oh-boy," my father said — just out of the dark. I looked at him and his eyes were narrow, and he seemed to be thinking about something. "You know, Jackie," he said, "your mother said something to me once I've never forgotten. She said, 'Nobody dies of a broken heart.' This was somewhat before you were born. We were living down in Texas and we'd had some big blow-up, and that was the idea she had. I don't know why." He shook his head.

He ran his hand under the seat, found a half-pint bottle of whiskey, and held it up to the lights of the car behind us to see what there was left of it. He unscrewed the cap and took a drink, then held the bottle out to me. "Have a drink, son," he said. "Something oughta be good in life." And I felt that something was wrong. Not because of the whiskey, which I had drunk before and he had reason to know about, but because of some sound in his voice, something I didn't recognize and did not know the importance of, though I was certain it was important.

I took a drink and gave the bottle back to him, holding the whiskey in my mouth until it stopped burning and I could swallow it a little at a time. When we turned out the road to Highwood, the lights of Great Falls sank below the horizon, and I could see the small white lights of farms, burning at wide distances in the dark.

"What do you worry about, Jackie," my father said. "Do you worry about girls? Do you worry about your future sex life? Is that some of it?" He glanced at me, then back at the road.

"I don't worry about that," I said.

"Well, what then?" my father said. "What else is there?"

"I worry if you're going to die before I do," I said, though I hated saying that, "or if Mother is. That worries me."

"It'd be a miracle if we didn't," my father said, with the half-pint held in the same hand he held the steering wheel. I had seen him drive that way before. "Things pass too fast in your life, Jackie. Don't worry about that. If I were you, I'd worry we might not." He smiled at me, and it was not the worried, nervous smile from before, but a smile that meant he was pleased. And I don't remember him ever smiling at me that way again.

We drove on out behind the town of Highwood and onto the flat field roads toward our house. I could see, out on the prairie, a moving light where the farmer who rented our house to us was disking his field for winter wheat. "He's waited too late with that business," my father said and took a drink, then threw the bottle right out the window. "He'll lose that," he said, "the cold'll kill it." I did not answer him, but what I thought was that my father knew nothing about farming, and if he was right it would be an accident. He knew about planes and hunting game, and that seemed all to me.

"I want to respect your privacy," he said then, for no reason at all that I understood. I am not even certain he said it, only that it is in my memory that way. I don't know what he was thinking of. Just words. But I said to him, I remember well, "It's all right. Thank you."

We did not go straight out the Geraldine Road to our house. Instead my father went down another mile and turned, went a mile and turned back again so that we came home from the other direction. "I want to stop and listen now," he said. "The geese should be in the stubble." We stopped and he cut the lights and engine, and we opened the car windows and listened. It was eight o'clock at night and it was getting colder, though it was dry. But I could hear nothing, just the sound of air moving lightly through the cut field, and not a goose sound. Though I could smell the whiskey on my father's breath and on mine, could hear the motor ticking, could hear him breathe, hear the sound we made sitting side by side on the car seat, our clothes, our feet, almost our hearts beating. And I could see out in the night the yellow lights of our house, shining through the olive trees south of us like a ship on the sea. "I hear them, by God," my father said, his head stuck out the window. "But they're high up. They won't stop here now, Jackie. They're high flyers, those boys. Long gone geese."

There was a car parked off the road, down the line of wind-break trees, beside a steel thresher the farmer had left there to rust. You could see moonlight off the taillight chrome. It was a Pontiac, a two-door hardtop. My father said nothing about it and I didn't either, though I think now for different reasons.

The floodlight was on over the side door of our house and lights were on inside, upstairs and down. My mother had a pumpkin on the front porch, and the wind chime she had hung by the door was tinkling. My dog, Major, came out of the quonset shed and stood in the car lights when we drove up.

"Let's see what's happening here," my father said, opening the door and stepping out quickly. He looked at me inside the car, and his eyes were wide and his mouth drawn tight.

We walked in the side door and up the basement steps into the kitchen, and a man was standing there — a man I had never seen before, a young man with blond hair, who might've been twenty or twenty-five. He was tall and was wearing a short-sleeved shirt and beige slacks with pleats. He was on the other side of the breakfast table, his fingertips just touching the wooden tabletop. His blue eyes were on my father, who was dressed in hunting clothes.

"Hello," my father said.

"Hello," the young man said, and nothing else. And for some reason I looked at his arms, which were long and pale. They looked like a young man's arms, like my arms. His short sleeves had each been neatly rolled up, and I could see the bottom of a small green tattoo edging out from underneath. There was a glass of whiskey on the table, but no bottle.

"What's your name?" my father said, standing in the kitchen under the bright ceiling light. He sounded like he might be going to laugh.

"Woody," the young man said and cleared his throat. He looked at me, then he touched the glass of whiskey, just the rim of the glass. He wasn't nervous, I could tell that. He did not seem to be afraid of anything.

"Woody," my father said and looked at the glass of whiskey. He looked at me, then sighed and shook his head. "Where's Mrs. Russell, Woody? I guess you aren't robbing my house, are you?"

Woody smiled. "No," he said. "Upstairs. I think she went upstairs."

"Good," my father said, "that's a good place." And he walked straight out of the room, but came back and stood in the doorway. "Jackie, you and Woody step outside and wait on me. Just stay there and I'll come out." He looked at Woody then in a way I would not have liked him to look at me, a look that meant he was studying Woody. "I guess that's your car," he said.

"That Pontiac." Woody nodded.

"Okay. Right," my father said. Then he went out again and up the stairs. At that moment the phone started to ring in the living room, and I heard my mother say, "Who's that?" And my father say, "It's me. It's Jack." And I decided I wouldn't go answer the phone. Woody looked at me, and I understood he wasn't sure what to do. Run, maybe. But he didn't have run in him. Though I thought he would probably do what I said if I would say it.

"Let's just go outside," I said.

And he said, "All right."

Woody and I walked outside and stood in the light of the flood-lamp above the side door. I had on my wool jacket, but Woody was cold and stood with his hands in his pockets, and his arms bare, moving from foot to foot. Inside, the phone was ringing again. Once I looked up and saw my mother come to the window and look down at Woody and me. Woody didn't look up or see her, but I did. I waved at her, and she waved back at me and smiled. She was wearing a powder-blue dress. In another minute the phone stopped ringing.

Woody took a cigarette out of his shirt pocket and lit it. Smoke shot through his nose into the cold air, and he sniffed, looked around the ground and threw his match on the gravel. His blond hair was combed backwards and neat on the sides, and I could smell his after-shave on him, a sweet, lemon smell. And for the first time I noticed his shoes. They were two-tones, black with white tops and black laces. They stuck out below his baggy pants and were long and polished and shiny, as if he had been planning on a big occasion. They looked like shoes some country singer would wear, or a salesman. He was handsome, but only like someone you would see beside you in a dime store and not notice again.

"I like it out here," Woody said, his head down, looking at his shoes. "Nothing to bother you. I bet you'd see Chicago if the world was flat. The Great Plains commence here."

"I don't know," I said.

Woody looked up at me, cupping his smoke with one hand. "Do you play football?"

"No," I said. I thought about asking him something about my mother. But I had no idea what it would be.

"I *have* been drinking," Woody said, "but I'm not drunk now."

The wind rose then, and from behind the house I could hear Major bark once from far away, and I could smell the irrigation ditch, hear it hiss in the field. It ran down from Highwood Creek to the Missouri, twenty miles away. It was nothing Woody knew about, nothing he could hear or smell. He knew nothing about anything that was here. I heard my father say the words, "That's a real joke," from inside the house, then the sound of a drawer being opened and shut, and a door closing. Then nothing else.

Woody turned and looked into the dark toward where the glow of Great Falls rose on the horizon, and we both could see the flashing lights of a plane lowering to land there. "I once passed my brother in the Los Angeles airport and didn't even recognize him," Woody said, staring into the night. "He recognized *me*, though. He said, 'Hey, bro, are you mad at me, or what?' I wasn't mad at him. We both had to laugh."

Woody turned and looked at the house. His hands were still in his pockets, his cigarette clenched between his teeth, his arms taut. They were, I saw, bigger, stronger arms than I had thought. A vein went down the front of each of them. I wondered what Woody knew that I didn't. Not about my mother — I didn't know anything about that and didn't want to — but about a lot of things, about the life out in the dark, about coming out here, about airports, even about me. He and I were not so far apart in age, I knew that. But Woody was one thing, and I was another. And I wondered how I would ever get to be like him, since it didn't necessarily seem so bad a thing to be.

"Did you know your mother was married before?" Woody said.

"Yes," I said. "I knew that."

"It happens to all of them, now," he said. "They can't wait to get divorced."

"I guess so," I said.

Woody dropped his cigarette into the gravel and toed it out with his black-and-white shoe. He looked up at me and smiled the way he had inside the house, a smile that said he knew something he wouldn't tell, a smile to make you feel bad because you weren't Woody and never could be.

It was then that my father came out of the house. He still had on his plaid hunting coat and his wool cap, but his face was as white as snow, as white as I have ever seen a human being's face to be. It was odd. I had the feeling that he might've fallen inside, because he looked roughed up, as though he had hurt himself somehow.

My mother came out the door behind him and stood in the flood-light at the top of the steps. She was wearing the powder-blue dress I'd seen through the window, a dress I had never seen her wear before, though she was also wearing a car coat and carrying a suitcase. She looked at me and shook her head in a way that only I was supposed to notice, as if it was not a good idea to talk now.

My father had his hands in his pockets, and he walked right up to Woody. He did not even look at me. "What do you do for a living?" he said, and he was very close to Woody. His coat was close enough to touch Woody's shirt.

"I'm in the Air Force," Woody said. He looked at me and then at my father. He could tell my father was excited.

"Is this your day off, then?" my father said. He moved even closer to Woody, his hands still in his pockets. He pushed Woody with his chest, and Woody seemed willing to let my father push him.

"No," he said, shaking his head.

I looked at my mother. She was just standing, watching. It was as if someone had given her an order, and she was obeying it. She did not smile at me, though I thought she was thinking about me, which made me feel strange.

"What's the matter with you?" my father said into Woody's face, right into his face — his voice tight, as if it had gotten hard for him to talk. "Whatever in the world is the matter with you? Don't you under-stand something?" My father took a revolver pistol out of his coat and put it up under Woody's chin, into the soft pocket behind the bone, so that Woody's whole face rose, but his arms stayed at his sides, his hands open. "I don't know what to do with you," my father said. "I don't have any idea what to do with you. I just don't." Though I thought that what he wanted to do was hold Woody there just like that until something important took place, or until he could simply forget about all this.

My father pulled the hammer back on the pistol and raised it tighter under Woody's chin, breathing into Woody's face — my mother in the light with her suitcase, watching them, and me watching them. A half a minute must've gone by.

And then my mother said, "Jack, let's stop now. Let's just stop."

My father stared into Woody's face as if he wanted Woody to consider doing something — moving or turning around or anything on his own to stop this — that my father would then put a stop to. My father's eyes grew narrowed, and his teeth were gritted together, his lips snarling up to resemble a smile. "You're crazy, aren't you?" he said. "You're a goddamned crazy man. Are you in love with her, too? Are you, crazy man? Are you? Do you say you love her? Say you love her! Say you love her so I can blow your fucking brains in the sky."

"All right," Woody said. "No. It's all right."

"He doesn't love me, Jack. For God's sake," my mother said. She seemed so calm. She shook her head at me again. I do not think she thought my father would shoot Woody. And I don't think Woody thought so. Nobody did, I think, except my father himself. But I think he did, and was trying to find out how to.

My father turned suddenly and glared at my mother, his eyes shiny and moving, but with the gun still on Woody's skin. I think he was afraid, afraid he was doing this wrong and could mess all of it up and make matters worse without accomplishing anything.

"You're leaving," he yelled at her. "That's why you're packed. Get out. Go on."

"Jackie has to be at school in the morning," my mother said in just her normal voice. And without another word to any one of us, she walked out of the floodlamp light carrying her bag, turned the corner at the front porch steps and disappeared toward the olive trees that ran in rows back into the wheat.

My father looked back at me where I was standing in the gravel, as if he expected to see me go with my mother toward Woody's car. But I hadn't thought about that — though later I would. Later I would think I should have gone with her, and that things between them might've been different. But that isn't how it happened.

"You're sure you're going to get away now, aren't you, mister?" my father said into Woody's face. He was crazy himself, then. Anyone would've been. Everything must have seemed out of hand to him.

"I'd like to," Woody said. "I'd like to get away from here."

"And I'd like to think of some way to hurt you," my father said and blinked his eyes. "I feel helpless about it." We all heard the door to

Woody's car close in the dark. "Do you think that I'm a fool?" my father said.

"No," Woody said. "I don't think that."

"Do you think you're important?"

"No," Woody said. "I'm not."

My father blinked again. He seemed to be becoming someone else at that moment, someone I didn't know. "Where are you from?"

And Woody closed his eyes. He breathed in, then out, a long sigh. It was as if this was somehow the hardest part, something he hadn't expected to be asked to say.

"Chicago," Woody said. "A suburb of there."

"Are your parents alive?" my father said, all the time with his blue magnum pistol pushed under Woody's chin.

"Yes," Woody said. "Yessir."

"That's too bad," my father said. "Too bad they have to know what you are. I'm sure you stopped meaning anything to them a long time ago. I'm sure they both wish you were dead. You didn't know that. But I know it. I can't help them out, though. Somebody else'll have to kill you. I don't want to have to think about you anymore. I guess that's it."

My father brought the gun down to his side and stood looking at Woody. He did not back away, just stood, waiting for what I don't know to happen. Woody stood a moment, then he cut his eyes at me uncomfortably. And I know that I looked down. That's all I could do. Though I remember wondering if Woody's heart was broken and what any of this meant to him. Not to me, or my mother, or my father. But to him, since he seemed to be the one left out somehow, the one who would be lonely soon, the one who had done something he would someday wish he hadn't and would have no one to tell him that it was all right, that they forgave him, that these things happen in the world.

Woody took a step back, looked at my father and at me again as if he intended to speak, then stepped aside and walked away toward the front of our house, where the wind chime made a noise in the new cold air.

My father looked at me, his big pistol in his hand. "Does this seem stupid to you?" he said. "All this? Yelling and threatening and going nuts? I wouldn't blame you if it did. You shouldn't even see this. I'm sorry. I don't know what to do now."

"It'll be all right," I said. And I walked out to the road. Woody's car started up behind the olive trees. I stood and watched it back out, its red taillights clouded by exhaust. I could see their two heads inside, with the headlights shining behind them. When they got into the road,

Woody touched his brakes, and for a moment I could see that they
were talking, their heads turned toward each other, nodding. Woody's
head and my mother's. They sat that way for a few seconds, then drove
slowly off. And I wondered what they had to say to each other, something important enough that they had to stop right at that moment
and say it. Did she say, *I love you?* Did she say, *This is not what I expected
to happen?* Did she say, *This is what I've wanted all along?* And did he
say, *I'm sorry for all this,* or *I'm glad,* or *None of this matters to me?* These
are not the kinds of things you can know if you were not there. And I
was not there and did not want to be. It did not seem like I should
be there. I heard the door slam when my father went inside, and I
turned back from the road where I could still see their taillights disappearing, and went back into the house where I was to be alone with
my father.

Things seldom end in one event. In the morning I went to school on
the bus as usual, and my father drove in to the air base in his car. We
had not said very much about all that had happened. Harsh words, in a
sense, are all alike. You can make them up yourself and be right. I
think we both believed that we were in a fog we couldn't see through
yet, though in a while, maybe not even a long while, we would see
lights and know something.

In my third-period class that day a messenger brought a note for
me that said I was excused from school at noon, and I should meet my
mother at a motel down 10th Avenue South — a place not so far from
my school — and we would eat lunch together.

It was a gray day in Great Falls that day. The leaves were off the
trees and the mountains to the east of town were obscured by a low
sky. The night before had been cold and clear, but today it seemed as if
it would rain. It was the beginning of winter in earnest. In a few days
there would be snow everywhere.

The motel where my mother was staying was called the Tropicana,
and was beside the city golf course. There was a neon parrot on the
sign out front, and the cabins made a U shape behind a little white office building. Only a couple of cars were parked in front of cabins, and
no car was in front of my mother's cabin. I wondered if Woody would
be here, or if he was at the air base. I wondered if my father would see
him there, and what they would say.

I walked back to cabin 9. The door was open, though a DO NOT
DISTURB sign was hung on the knob outside. I looked through the
screen and saw my mother sitting on the bed alone. The television was
on, but she was looking at me. She was wearing the powder-blue dress
she had had on the night before. She was smiling at me, and I liked

the way she looked at that moment, through the screen, in shadows. Her features did not seem as sharp as they had before. She looked comfortable where she was, and I felt like we were going to get along, no matter what had happened, and that I wasn't mad at her — that I had never been mad at her.

She sat forward and turned the television off. "Come in, Jackie," she said, and I opened the screen door and came inside. "It's the height of grandeur in here, isn't it?" My mother looked around the room. Her suitcase was open on the floor by the bathroom door, which I could see through and out the window onto the golf course, where three men were playing under the milky sky. "Privacy can be a burden, sometimes," she said, and reached down and put on her high-heeled shoes. "I didn't sleep very well last night, did you?"

"No," I said, though I had slept all right. I wanted to ask her where Woody was, but it occurred to me at that moment that he was gone now and wouldn't be back, that she wasn't thinking in terms of him and didn't care where he was or ever would be.

"I'd like a nice compliment from you," she said. "Do you have one of those to spend?"

"Yes," I said. "I'm glad to see you."

"That's a nice one," she said and nodded. She had both her shoes on now. "Would you like to go have lunch? We can walk across the street to the cafeteria. You can get hot food."

"No," I said. "I'm not really hungry now."

"That's okay," she said and smiled at me again. And, as I said before, I liked the way she looked. She looked pretty in a way I didn't remember seeing her, as if something that had had a hold on her had let her go, and she could be different about things. Even about me.

"Sometimes, you know," she said, "I'll think about something I did. Just anything. Years ago in Idaho, or last week, even. And it's as if I'd read it. Like a story. Isn't that strange?"

"Yes," I said. And it did seem strange to me because I was certain then what the difference was between what had happened and what hadn't, and knew I always would be.

"Sometimes," she said, and she folded her hands in her lap and stared out the little side window of her cabin at the parking lot and the curving row of other cabins. "Sometimes I even have a moment when I completely forget what life's like. Just altogether." She smiled. "That's not so bad, finally. Maybe it's a disease I have. Do you think I'm just sick and I'll get well?"

"No. I don't know," I said. "Maybe. I hope so." I looked out the bathroom window and saw the three men walking down the golf course fairway carrying golf clubs.

"I'm not very good at sharing things right now," my mother said. "I'm sorry." She cleared her throat, and then she didn't say anything for almost a minute while I stood there. "I *will* answer anything you'd like me to answer, though. Just ask me anything, and I'll answer it the truth, whether I want to or not. Okay? I will. You don't even have to trust me. That's not a big issue with us. We're both grown-ups now."

And I said, "Were you ever married before?"

My mother looked at me strangely. Her eyes got small, and for a moment she looked the way I was used to seeing her — sharp-faced, her mouth set and taut. "No," she said. "Who told you that? That isn't true. I never was. Did Jack say that to you? Did your father say that? That's an awful thing to say. I haven't been that bad."

"He didn't say that," I said.

"Oh, of course he did," my mother said. "He doesn't know just to let things go when they're bad enough."

"I wanted to know that," I said. "I just thought about it. It doesn't matter."

"No, it doesn't," my mother said. "I could've been married eight times. I'm just sorry he said that to you. He's not generous sometimes."

"He didn't say that," I said. But I'd said it enough, and I didn't care if she believed me or didn't. It was true that trust was not a big issue between us then. And in any event, I know now that the whole truth of anything is an idea that stops existing finally.

"Is that all you want to know, then?" my mother said. She seemed mad, but not at me, I didn't think. Just at things in general. And I sympathized with her. "Your life's your own business, Jackie," she said. "Sometimes it scares you to death it's so much your own business. You just want to run."

"I guess so," I said.

"I'd like a less domestic life, is all." She looked at me, but I didn't say anything. I didn't see what she meant by that, though I knew there was nothing I could say to change the way her life would be from then on. And I kept quiet.

In a while we walked across 10th Avenue and ate lunch in the cafeteria. When she paid for the meal I saw that she had my father's silver-dollar money clip in her purse and that there was money in it. And I understood that he had been to see her already that day, and no one cared if I knew it. We were all of us on our own in this.

When we walked out onto the street, it was colder and the wind was blowing. Car exhausts were visible and some drivers had their lights on, though it was only two o'clock in the afternoon. My mother had called a taxi, and we stood and waited for it. I didn't know where she was going, but I wasn't going with her.

"Your father won't let me come back," she said, standing on the curb. It was just a fact to her, not that she hoped I would talk to him or stand up for her or take her part. But I did wish then that I had never let her go the night before. Things can be fixed by staying; but to go out into the night and not come back hazards life, and everything can get out of hand.

My mother's taxi came. She kissed me and hugged me very hard, then got inside the cab in her powder-blue dress and high heels and her car coat. I smelled her perfume on my cheeks as I stood watching her. "I used to be afraid of more things than I am now," she said, looking up at me, and smiled. "I've got a knot in my stomach, of all things." And she closed the cab door, waved at me, and rode away.

I walked back toward my school. I thought I could take the bus home if I got there by three. I walked a long way down 10th Avenue to Second Street, beside the Missouri River, then over to town. I walked by the Great Northern Hotel, where my father had sold ducks and geese and fish of all kinds. There were no passenger trains in the yard and the loading dock looked small. Garbage cans were lined along the edge of it, and the door was closed and locked.

As I walked toward school I thought to myself that my life had turned suddenly, and that I might not know exactly how or which way for possibly a long time. Maybe, in fact, I might never know. It was a thing that happened to you — I knew that — and it had happened to me in this way now. And as I walked on up the cold street that afternoon in Great Falls, the questions I asked myself were these: why wouldn't my father let my mother come back? Why would Woody stand in the cold with me outside my house and risk being killed? Why would he say my mother had been married before, if she hadn't been? And my mother herself — why would she do what she did? In five years my father had gone off to Ely, Nevada, to ride out the oil strike there, and been killed by accident. And in the years since then I have seen my mother from time to time — in one place or another, with one man or other — and I can say, at least, that we know each other. But I have never known the answer to these questions, have never asked anyone their answers. Though possibly it — the answer — is simple: it is just low-life, some coldness in us all, some helplessness that causes us to misunderstand life when it is pure and plain, makes our existence seem like a border between two nothings, and makes us no more or less than animals who meet on the road — watchful, unforgiving, without patience or desire.

Mary Gaitskill

The epigraph from *Because They Wanted To,* Mary Gaitskill's second volume of stories, provides some insight into the thematic territory of both her collections. The quote is from Carson McCullers's novella of perverse and tortured love, *The Ballad of the Sad Café,* and reads, in part, ". . . most of us would rather love than be loved. Almost everyone wants to be the lover. And the curt truth is, in a deep secret way, the state of being beloved is intolerable to many." Gaitskill's stories often deal with sex in its multifarious varieties and with lovers who are jaded or frightened or filled with unrealistic expectations. There is a decided antiromantic bent here — that is, Gaitskill's stories serve to subvert the conventional romantic scenario and all the sentimentality associated with it. Her stories are savage, shocking, and written with a precision and lyricism few can match, and her characters — straights, gays, sadists, and masochists — achieve an immediacy and poignancy often absent from their portrayals in the works of lesser writers.

Both the stories I've chosen are from Gaitskill's first book, *Bad Behavior.* The first, "Secretary," is a beautifully detailed evocation of a working-class life, of a girl entering on her first job with few prospects and little to hope for. Debby has a lot in common with some of the heroines of Ann Beattie's early stories — she is passive, acted upon, born a victim, and unable to escape her fate. Her family is both a comfort and a morass, and one of the triumphs of Gaitskill's writing is how deftly she portrays the family dynamics here, from the mother's forced cheeriness to the father's animal presence to the elder sister's despair. The second piece, the ironically titled "A Romantic Weekend," is a grimly funny examination of lovers' expectations, of how it is preferable to "love than be loved," if only to escape the mold in which our partners so implacably seek to fit us. It is notable too, I think, for its dual point of view — the irony and tension, and a good deal of the humor, derive from the fact that the reader is privy to the thoughts of both the would-be lovers: "He was enjoying himself now. He was beginning to see her as a locked garden that he could sneak into and sit in for days, tearing the heads off the flowers." / "On one hand, she was beside herself with bliss. On the other, she was scrutinizing him carefully from behind an opaque facade as he entered her pasteboard scene of flora and fauna. Could he function as a character in this landscape?"

Secretary

The typing and secretarial class was held in a little basement room in the Business Building of the local community college. The teacher was an old lady with hair that floated in vague clouds around her temples and Kleenex stuck up the sleeve of her dress for some future, probably nasal purpose. She held a stopwatch in one old hand and tilted her hip as she watched us all with severe, imperial eyes, not caring that her stomach hung out. The girl in front of me had short, clenched blond curls sitting on her thin shoulders. Lone strands would stick straight out from her head in cold, dry weather.

It was a two-hour class with a ten-minute break. Everybody would go out into the hall during the break to get coffee or candy from the machines. The girls would stand in groups and talk, and the two male typists would walk slowly up and down the corridor with round shoulders, holding their Styrofoam cups and looking into the bright slits of light in the business class doors as they passed by.

I would go to the big picture window that looked out onto the parking lot and stare at the streetlights shining on the hoods of the cars.

After class, I'd come home and put my books on the dining room table among the leftover dinner things: balled-up napkins, glasses of water, a dish of green beans sitting on a pot holder. My father's plate would always be there, with gnawed bones and hot pepper on it. He would be in the living room in his pajama top with a dish of ice cream in his lap and his hair on end. "How many words a minute did you type tonight?" he'd ask.

It wasn't an unreasonable question, but the predictable and agitated delivery of it was annoying. It reflected his way of hoarding silly details and his obsessive fear that I would meet my sister's fate. She'd had a job at a home for retarded people for the past eight years. She wore jeans and a long army coat to work every day. When she came home, she went up to her room and lay in bed. Every now and then she would come down and joke around or watch TV, but not much.

Mother would drive me around to look for jobs. First we would go through ads in the paper, drawing black circles, marking X's. The defaced newspaper sat on the dining room table in a gray fold and we argued.

"I'm not friendly and I'm not personable. I'm not going to answer an ad for somebody like that. It would be stupid."

"You can be friendly. And you are personable when you aren't busy putting yourself down."

"I'm not putting myself down. You just want to think that I am so you can have something to talk about."

"You're backing yourself into a corner, Debby."

"Oh, shit." I picked up a candy wrapper and began pinching it together in an ugly way. My hands were red and rough. It didn't matter how much lotion I used.

"Come on, we're getting started on the wrong foot."

"Shut up."

My mother crossed her legs. "Well," she said. She picked up the "Living" section of the paper and cracked it into position. She tilted her head back and dropped her eyelids. Her upper lip became hostile as she read. She picked up her green teacup and drank.

"I'm dependable. I could answer an ad for somebody dependable."

"You are that."

We wound up in the car. My toes swelled in my high heels. My mother and I both used the flowered box of Kleenex on the dashboard and stuck the used tissue in a brown bag that sat near the hump in the middle of the car. There was a lot of traffic in both lanes. We drove past the Amy Joy doughnut shop. They still hadn't put the letter Y back on the Amy sign.

Our first stop was Wonderland. There was a job in the clerical department of Sears. The man there had a long disapproving nose, and he held his hands stiffly curled in the middle of his desk. He mainly looked at his hands. He said he would call me, but I knew he wouldn't.

On the way back to the parking lot, we passed a pet store. There were only hamsters, fish and exhausted yellow birds. We stopped and looked at slivers of fish swarming in their tank of thick green water. I had come to this pet store when I was ten years old. The mall had just opened up and we had all come out to walk through it. My sister, Donna, had wanted to go into the pet store. It was very warm and damp in the store, and smelled like fur and hamster. When we walked out, it seemed cold. I said I was cold and Donna took off her white leatherette jacket and put it around my shoulders, letting one hand sit on my left shoulder for a minute. She had never touched me like that before and she hasn't since.

The next place was a tax information office in a slab of building with green trim. They gave me an intelligence test that was mostly spelling and "What's wrong with this sentence?" The woman came out of her office holding my test and smiling. "You scored higher than anyone else I've interviewed," she said. "You're really overqualified for this job. There's no challenge. You'd be bored to death."

"I want to be bored," I said.

She laughed. "Oh, I don't think that's true."

We had a nice talk about what people want out of their jobs and then I left.

"Well, I hope you weren't surprised that you had the highest score," said my mother.

We went to the French bakery on Eight-Mile Road and got cookies called elephant ears. We ate them out of a bag as we drove. I felt so comfortable, I could have driven around in the car all day.

Then we went to a lawyer's office on Telegraph Road. It was a receding building made of orange brick. There were no other houses or stores around it, just a parking lot and some taut fir trees that looked like they had been brushed. My mother waited for me in the car. She smiled, took out a crossword puzzle and focused her eyes on it, the smile still gripping her face.

The lawyer was a short man with dark, shiny eyes and dense immobile shoulders. He took my hand with an indifferent aggressive snatch. It felt like he could have put his hand through my rib cage, grabbed my heart, squeezed it a little to see how it felt, then let go. "Come into my office," he said.

We sat down and he fixed his eyes on me. "It's not much of a job," he said. "I have a paralegal who does research and legwork, and the proofreading gets done at an agency. All I need is a presentable typist who can get to work on time and answer the phone."

"I can do that," I said.

"It's very dull work," he said.

"I like dull work."

He stared at me, his eyes becoming hooded in thought. "There's something about you," he said. "You're closed up, you're tight. You're like a wall."

"I know."

My answer surprised him and his eyes lost their hoods. He tilted his head back and looked at me, his shiny eyes bared again. "Do you ever loosen up?"

The corners of my mouth jerked, smilelike. "I don't know." My palms sweated.

His secretary, who was leaving, called me the next day and said that he wanted to hire me. Her voice was serene, flat and utterly devoid of inflection.

"That typing course really paid off," said my father. "You made a good investment." He wandered in and out of the dining room in pleased agitation, holding his glass of beer. "A law office could be a fascinating place." He arched his chin and scratched his throat.

Donna even came downstairs and made popcorn and put it in a big yellow bowl on the table for everybody to eat. She ate lazily, her large hand dawdling in the bowl. "It could be okay. Interesting people could come in. Even though that lawyer's probably an asshole."

My mother sat quietly, pleased with her role in the job-finding project, pinching clusters of popcorn in her fingers and popping them into her mouth.

That night I put my new work clothes on a chair and looked at them. A brown skirt, a beige blouse. I was attracted to the bland ugliness, but I didn't know how long that would last. I looked at their gray shapes in the night-light and then rolled over toward the dark corner of my bed.

My family's enthusiasm made me feel sarcastic about the job — about any effort to do anything, in fact. In light of their enthusiasm, the only intelligent course of action seemed to be immobility and rudeness. But in the morning, as I ate my poached eggs and toast, I couldn't help but feel curious and excited. The feeling grew as I rode in the car with my mother to the receding orange building. I felt like I was accomplishing something. I wanted to do well. When we drove past the Amy Joy doughnut shop, I saw, through a wall of glass, expectant construction workers in heavy boots and jackets sitting on vinyl swivel seats, waiting for coffee and bags of doughnuts. I had sentimental thoughts about workers and the decency of unthinking toil. I was pleased to be like them, insofar as I was. I returned my mother's smile when I got out of the car and said "thanks" when she said "good luck."

"Well, here you are," said the lawyer. He clapped his short, hard-packed little hands together and made a loud noise. "On time. Good morning!"

He began training me then and continued to do so all week. No interesting people came into the office. Very few people came into the office at all. The first week there were three. One was a nervous middle-aged woman who had an uneven haircut and was wearing lavender rubber children's boots. She sat on the edge of the waiting room chair with her rubber boots together, rearranging the things in her purse. Another was a fat woman in a bright, baglike dress who had yellow in the whites of her wild little eyes, and who carried her purse like a weapon. The last was a man who sat desperately turning his head as if he wanted to disconnect it from his body. I could hear him raising his voice inside the lawyer's office. When he left, the lawyer came out and said, "He is completely crazy," and told me to type him a bill for five hundred dollars.

Everyone who sat in the waiting room looked random and unwelcome. They all fidgeted. The elegant old armchairs and puffy upholstered couch were themselves disoriented in the stiff modernity of the waiting room. My heavy oak desk was an idiot standing against a wall covered with beige plaster. The brooding plants before me gave the appearance of weighing a lot for plants, even though one of them was a slight, frondy thing.

I was surprised that a person like the lawyer, who seemed to be mentally organized and evenly distributed, would have such an office. But I was comfortable in it. Its jumbled nature was like a nest of available rags gathered tightly together for warmth. My first two weeks were serene. I enjoyed the dullness of days, the repetition of motions, the terse, polite interactions between the lawyer and me. I enjoyed feeling him impose his brainlessly confident sense of existence on me. He would say, "Type this letter," and my sensibility would contract until the abstractions of achievement and production found expression in the typing of the letter. I was useful.

My mother picked me up every day. We would usually stop at the A&P before we went home to get a loaf of white French bread, beer and kielbasa sausage for my father. When we got home I would go upstairs to my room, take off my shirt and blouse, and throw them on the floor. I would get into my bed of jumbled blankets in my underwear and panty hose and listen to my father yelling at my mother until I fell asleep. I woke up when Donna pounded on my door and yelled, "Dinner!"

I would go down with her then and sit at the table. We would all watch the news on TV as we ate. My mother would have a shrunken, abstracted look on her face. My father would hunch over his plate like an animal at its dish.

After dinner, I would go upstairs and listen to records and write in my diary or play Parcheesi with Donna until it was time to get ready for bed. I'd go to sleep at night looking at the skirt and blouse I would wear the next day. I'd wake up looking at my ceramic weather poodle, which was supposed to turn pink, blue or green, depending on the weather, but had only turned gray and stayed gray. I would hear my father in the bathroom, the tumble of radio patter, the water, the clink of a glass being set down, the creak and click as he closed the medicine cabinet. Donna would be standing outside my door, waiting for him to finish, muttering "shit" or something.

Looking back on it, I don't know why that time was such a contented one, but it was.

The first day of the third week, the lawyer came out of his office, stiffer than usual, his eyes lit up in a peculiar, stalking way. He was carrying one of my letters. He put it on my desk, right in front of me. "Look at it," he said. I did.

"Do you see that?"

"What?" I asked.

"This letter has three typing errors in it, one of which is, I think, a spelling error."

"I'm sorry."

"This isn't the first time, either. There have been others that I let go because it was your first few weeks. But this can't go on. Do you know what this makes me look like to the people who receive these letters?"

I looked at him, mortified. There had been a catastrophe hidden in the folds of my contentment for two weeks and he hadn't even told me. It seemed unfair, although when I thought about it I could understand his reluctance, maybe even embarrassment, to draw my attention to something so stupidly unpleasant.

"Type it again."

I did, but I was so badly shaken that I made even more mistakes. "You are wasting my time," he said, and handed it to me once again. I typed it correctly the third time, but he sulked in his office for the rest of the day.

This kind of thing kept occurring all week. Each time, the lawyer's irritation and disbelief mounted. In addition, I sensed something else growing in him, an intimate tendril creeping from one of his darker areas, nursed on the feeling that he had discovered something about me.

I was very depressed about the situation. When I went home in the evening I couldn't take a nap. I lay there looking at the gray weather poodle and fantasized about having a conversation with the lawyer that would clear up everything, explain to him that I was really trying to do my best. He seemed to think that I was making the mistakes on purpose.

At the end of the week he began complaining about the way I answered the phone. "You're like a machine," he said. "You sound like you're in the Twilight Zone. You don't think when you respond to people."

When he asked me to come into his office at the end of the day, I thought he was going to fire me. The idea was a relief, but a numbing one. I sat down and he fixed me with a look that was speculative but benign, for him. He leaned back in his chair in a comfortable way, one hand dangling sideways from his wrist. To my surprise, he began talking to me about my problems, as he saw them.

"I sense that you are a very nice but complex person, with wild mood swings that you keep hidden. You just shut up the house and act like there's nobody home."

"That's true," I said. "I do that."

"Well, why? Why don't you open up a little bit? It would probably help your typing."

It was really not any of his business, I thought.

"You should try to talk more. I know I'm your employer and we have a prescribed relationship, but you should feel free to discuss your problems with me."

The idea of discussing my problems with him was preposterous. "It's hard to think of having that kind of discussion with you," I said. I hesitated. "You have a strong personality and . . . when I encounter a personality like that, I tend to step back because I don't know how to deal with it."

He was clearly pleased with this response, but he said, "You shouldn't be so shy."

When I thought about this conversation later, it seemed, on the one hand, that this lawyer was just an asshole. On the other, his comments were weirdly moving, and had the effect of making me feel horribly sensitive. No one had ever made such personal comments to me before.

The next day I made another mistake. The intimacy of the previous day seemed to make the mistake even more repulsive to him because he got madder than usual. I wanted him to fire me. I would have suggested it, but I was struck silent. I sat and stared at the letter while he yelled. "What's wrong with you!"

"I'm sorry," I said.

He stood quietly for a moment. Then he said, "Come into my office. And bring that letter."

I followed him into his office.

"Put that letter on my desk," he said.

I did.

"Now bend over so that you are looking directly at it. Put your elbows on the desk and your face very close to the letter."

Shaken and puzzled, I did what he said.

"Now read the letter to yourself. Keep reading it over and over again."

I read: "Dear Mr. Garvy: I am very grateful to you for referring . . ." He began spanking me as I said "referring." The funny thing was, I wasn't even surprised. I actually kept reading the letter, although my understanding of it was not very clear. I began crying on it, which blurred the ink. The word "humiliation" came into my mind with such force that it effectively blocked out all other words. Further, I felt that the concept it stood for had actually been a major force in my life for quite a while.

He spanked me for about ten minutes, I think. I read the letter only about five times, partly because it rapidly became too wet to be legible. When he stopped he said, "Now straighten up and go type it again."

I went to my desk. He closed the office door behind him. I sat down, blew my nose and wiped my face. I stared into space for several minutes, every now and then dwelling on the tingling sensation in my buttocks. I typed the letter again and took it into his office. He didn't look up as I put it on his desk.

I went back out and sat, planning to sink into a stupor of some sort. But a client came in, so I couldn't. I had to buzz the lawyer and tell him the client had arrived. "Tell him to wait," he said curtly.

When I told the client to wait, he came up to my desk and began to talk to me. "I've been here twice before," he said. "Do you recognize me?"

"Yes," I said. "Of course." He was a small, tight-looking middle-aged man with agitated little hands and a pale scar running over his lip and down his chin. The scar didn't make him look tough; he was too anxious to look tough.

"I never thought anything like this would ever happen to me," he said. "I never thought I'd be in a lawyer's office even once, and I've been here three times now. And absolutely nothing's been accomplished. I've always hated lawyers." He looked as though he expected me to take offense.

"A lot of people do," I said.

"It was either that or I would've shot those miserable blankety-blanks next door and I'd have to get a lawyer to defend me anyway. You know the story?"

I did. He was suing his neighbors because they had a dog that "barked all goddamn day." I listened to him talk. It surprised me how this short conversation quickly restored my sensibility. Everything seemed perfectly normal by the time the lawyer came out of his office to greet the client. I noticed he had my letter in one hand. Just before he turned to lead the client away, he handed it to me, smiling. "Good letter," he said.

When I went home that night, everything was the same. My life had not been disarranged by the event except for a slight increase in the distance between me and my family. My behind was not even red when I looked at it in the bathroom mirror.

But when I got into bed and thought about the thing, I got excited. I was more excited, in fact, than I had ever been in my life. That didn't surprise me, either. I felt a numbness; I felt that I could never have a normal conversation with anyone again. I masturbated slowly, to put off the climax as long as I could. But there was no climax, even though I tried for a long time. Then I couldn't sleep.

It happened twice more in the next week and a half. The following week, when I made a typing mistake, he didn't spank me. Instead, he told me to bend over his desk, look at the typing mistake and repeat "I am stupid" for several minutes.

Our relationship didn't change otherwise. He was still brisk and friendly in the morning. And, because he seemed so sure of himself, I could not help but react to him as if he were still the same domineering but affable boss. He did not, however, ever invite me to discuss my problems with him again.

I began to have recurring dreams about him. In one, the most frequent, I walked with him in a field of big bright red poppies. The day was brilliant and warm. We were smiling at each other, and there was a tremendous sense of release and goodwill between us. He looked at me and said, "I understand you now, Debby." Then we held hands.

There was one time I felt disturbed about what was happening at the office. It was just before dinner, and my father was upset about something that had happened to him at work. I could hear him yelling in the living room while my mother tried to comfort him. He yelled, "I'd rather work in a circus! In one of those things where you put your head through a hole and people pay to throw garbage at you!"

"No circus has that anymore," said my mother, "Stop it, Shep."

By the time I went down to eat dinner, everything was as usual. I looked at my father and felt a sickening sensation of love nailed to contempt and panic.

The last time I made a typing error and the lawyer summoned me to his office, two unusual things occurred. The first was that after he finished spanking me he told me to pull up my skirt. Fear hooked my stomach and pulled it toward my chest. I turned my head and tried to look at him.

"You're not worried that I'm going to rape you, are you?" he said. "Don't. I'm not interested in that, not in the least. Pull up your skirt."

I turned my head away from him. I thought, I don't have to do this. I can stop right now. I can straighten up and walk out. But I didn't. I pulled up my skirt.

"Pull down your panty hose and underwear."

A finger of nausea poked my stomach.

"I told you I'm not going to fuck you. Do what I say."

The skin on my face and throat was hot, but my fingertips were cold on my legs as I pulled down my underwear and panty hose. The letter before me became distorted beyond recognition. I thought I might faint or vomit, but I didn't. I was held up by a feeling of dizzying suspension, like the one I have in dreams where I can fly, but only if I get into some weird position.

At first he didn't seem to be doing anything. Then I became aware of a small frenzy of expended energy behind me. I had an impression of a vicious little animal frantically burrowing dirt with its tiny claws and teeth. My hips were sprayed with hot sticky muck.

"Go clean yourself off," he said. "And do that letter again."

I stood slowly, and felt my skirt fall over the sticky gunk. He briskly swung open the door and I left the room, not even pulling up my panty hose and underwear, since I was going to use the bathroom anyway. He closed the door behind me, and the second unusual thing occurred. Susan, the paralegal, was standing in the waiting room with a funny look on her face. She was a blonde who wore short, fuzzy sweaters and fake gold jewelry around her neck. At her friendliest, she had a whining, abrasive quality that clung to her voice. Now, she could barely say hello. Her stupidly full lips were parted speculatively.

"Hi," I said. "Just a minute." She noted the awkwardness of my walk, because of the lowered panty hose.

I got to the bathroom and wiped myself off. I didn't feel embarrassed. I felt mechanical. I wanted to get that dumb paralegal out of the office so I could come back to the bathroom and masturbate.

Susan completed her errand and left. I masturbated. I retyped the letter. The lawyer sat in his office all day.

When my mother picked me up that afternoon, she asked me if I was all right.

"Why do you ask?"

"I don't know. You look a little strange."

"I'm as all right as I ever am."

"That doesn't sound good, honey."

I didn't answer. My mother moved her hands up and down the steering wheel, squeezing it anxiously.

"Maybe you'd like to stop by the French bakery and get some elephant ears," she said.

"I don't want any elephant ears." My voice was unexpectedly nasty. It almost made me cry.

"All right," said my mother.

When I lay on my bed to take my nap, my body felt dense and heavy, as though it would be very hard to move again, which was just as well, since I didn't feel like moving. When Donna banged on my door and yelled "Dinner!" I didn't answer. She put her head in and asked if I was asleep, and I told her I didn't feel like eating. I felt so inert, I thought I'd go to sleep, but I couldn't. I lay awake through the sounds of argument and TV and everybody going to the bathroom. Bedtime came, drawers rasped open and shut, doors slammed, my father eased into sleep with radio mumble. The orange digits on my clock said 1:30. I thought: I should get out of this panty hose and slip. I sat up and looked out into the gray, cold street. The shrubbery on the lawn across the street looked frozen and miserable. I thought about the period of time a year before when I couldn't sleep because I kept thinking that someone was going to break into the house and kill everybody. Eventually that fear went away and I went back to sleeping again. I lay back down without taking off my clothes, and pulled a light blanket tightly around me. Sooner or later, I thought, I would sleep. I would just have to wait.

But I didn't sleep, although I became mentally incoherent for long, ugly stretches of time. Hours went by; the room turned gray. I heard the morning noises: the toilet, the coughing, Donna's hostile muttering. Often, in the past, I had woken early and lain in bed listening to my family clumsily trying to organize itself for the day. Often as not, their sounds made me feel irrational loathing. This morning, I felt despair and a longing for them, and a sureness that we would never be close as long as I lived. My nasal passages became active with tears that didn't reach my eyes.

My mother knocked on the door. "Honey, aren't you going to be late?"

"I'm not going to work. I feel sick. I'll call in."

"I'll do it for you, just stay in bed."

"No, I'm going to call. It has to be me."

I didn't call in. The lawyer didn't call the house. I didn't go in or call the next day or the day after that. The lawyer still didn't call. I was slightly hurt by his absent phone call, but my relief was far greater than my hurt.

After I'd stayed home for four days, my father asked if I wasn't worried about taking so much time off. I told him I'd quit, in front of Donna and my mother. He was dumbfounded.

"That wasn't very smart," he said. "What are you going to do now?"

"I don't care," I said. "That lawyer was an asshole." To everyone's discomfort, I began to cry. I left the room, and they all watched me stomp up the stairs.

The next day at dinner my father said, "Don't get discouraged because your first job didn't work out. There're plenty of other places out there."

"I don't want to think about another job right now."

There was disgruntlement all around the table. "Come on now Debby, you don't want to throw away everything you worked for in that typing course," said my father.

"I don't blame her," said Donna. "I'm sick of working for assholes."

"Oh, shit," said my father. "If I had quit every job I've had on those grounds, you would've all starved. Maybe that's what I should've done."

"What happened, Debby?" said my mother.

I said, "I don't want to talk about it," and I left the room again.

After that they may have sensed, with their intuition for the miserable, that something hideous had happened. Because they left the subject alone.

I received my last paycheck from the lawyer in the mail. It came with a letter folded around it. It said, "I am so sorry for what happened between us. I have realized what a terrible mistake I made with you. I can only hope that you will understand, and that you will not worsen an already unfortunate situation by discussing it with others. All the best." As a P.S. he assured me that I could count on him for excellent references. He enclosed a check for three hundred and eighty dollars, a little over two hundred dollars more than he owed me.

It occurred to me to tear up the check, or mail it back to the lawyer. But I didn't do that. Two hundred dollars was worth more then than it is now. Together with the money I had in the bank, it was enough to put a down payment on an apartment and still have some left over. I went upstairs and wrote "380" on the deposit side of my checking account. I didn't feel like a whore or anything. I felt I was doing the right thing. I looked at the total figure of my balance with satisfaction. Then I went downstairs and asked my mother if she wanted to go get some elephant ears.

For the next two weeks, I forgot about the idea of a job and moving out of my parents' house. I slept through all the morning noise until noon. I got up and ate cold cereal and ran the dishwasher. I watched the gray march of old sitcoms on TV. I worked on crossword puzzles. I lay on my bed in a tangle of quilt and fuzzy blanket and masturbated two, three, four times in a row, always thinking about the thing.

I was still in this phase when my father stuck the newspaper under my nose and said, "Did you see what your old boss is doing?" There was a small article on the upcoming mayoral elections in Westland. He was running for mayor. I took the paper from my father's offering hands. For the first time, I felt an uncomplicated disgust for the lawyer. Westland was nothing but malls and doughnut stands and a big ugly theater with an artificial volcano in the front of it. What kind of idiot would want to be mayor of Westland? Again, I left the room.

I got the phone call the next week. It was a man's voice, a soft, probing, condoling voice. "Miss Roe?" he said. "I hope you'll forgive this unexpected call. I'm Mark Charming of *Detroit Magazine.*"

I didn't say anything. The voice continued more uncertainly. "Are you free to talk, Miss Roe?"

There was no one in the kitchen, and my mother was running the vacuum in the next room. "Talk about what?" I said.

"Your previous employer." The voice became slightly harsh as he said these words, and then hurriedly rushed back to condolence. "Please don't be startled or upset. I know this could be a disturbing phone call for you, and it must certainly seem intrusive." He paused so I could laugh or something. I didn't, and his voice became more cautious. "The thing is, we're doing a story on your ex-employer in the context of his running for mayor. To put it mildly, we think he has no business running for public office. We think he would be very bad for the whole Detroit area. He has an awful reputation, Miss Roe — which may not surprise you." There was another careful pause that I did not fill.

"Miss Roe, are you still with me?"

"Yes."

"What all this is leading up to is that we have reason to believe that you could reveal information about your ex-employer that would be damaging to him. This information would never be connected to your name. We would use a pseudonym. Your privacy would be protected completely."

The vacuum cleaner shut off, and silence encircled me. My throat constricted.

"Do you want time to think about it, Miss Roe?"

"I can't talk now," I said, and hung up.

I couldn't go through the living room without my mother asking me who had been on the phone, so I went downstairs to the basement. I sat on the mildewed couch and curled up, unmindful of centipedes. I rested my chin on my knee and stared at the boxes of my father's old paperbacks and the jumble of plastic Barbie-doll cases full of Barbie equipment that Donna and I used to play with on the front porch. A stiff white foot and calf stuck out of a sky-blue case, helpless and pitifully rigid.

For some reason, I remembered the time, a few years before, when my mother had taken me to see a psychiatrist. One of the more obvious questions he had asked me was, "Debby, do you ever have the sensation of being outside yourself, almost as if you can actually watch yourself from another place?" I hadn't at the time, but I did now. And it wasn't such a bad feeling at all.

A Romantic Weekend

She was meeting a man she had recently and abruptly fallen in love with. She was in a state of ghastly anxiety. He was married, for one thing, to a Korean woman whom he described as the embodiment of all that was feminine and elegant. Not only that, but a psychic had told her that a relationship with him could cripple her emotionally for the rest of her life. On top of this, she was tormented by the feeling that she looked inadequate. Perhaps her body tilted too far forward as she walked, per-haps her jacket made her torso look bulky in contrast to her calves and ankles, which were probably skinny. She felt like an object unraveling in every direction. In anticipation of their meeting, she had not been able to sleep the night before; she had therefore eaten some ampheta-mines and these had heightened her feeling of disintegration.

When she arrived at the corner he wasn't there. She stood against a building, trying to arrange her body in the least repulsive configura-tion possible. Her discomfort mounted. She crossed the street and stood on the other corner. It seemed as though everyone who walked by was eating. A large, distracted businessman went by holding a half-eaten hot dog. Two girls passed, sharing cashews from a white bag. The eating added to her sense that the world was disorderly and un-beautiful. She became acutely aware of the garbage on the street. The wind stirred it; a candy wrapper waved forlornly from its trapped posi-tion in the mesh of a jammed public wastebasket. This was all wrong, all horrible. Her meeting with him should be perfect and scrap-free. She couldn't bear the thought of flapping trash. Why wasn't he there to meet her? Minutes passed. Her shoulders drew together.

She stepped into a flower store. The store was clean and white, ex-cept for a few smudges on the linoleum floor. Homosexuals with low voices stood behind the counter. Arranged stalks bearing absurd blos-soms protruded from sedate round vases and bristled in the aisles. She had a paroxysm of fantasy. He held her, helpless and swooning, in his arms. They were supported by a soft ball of puffy blue stuff. Thornless roses surrounded their heads. His gaze penetrated her so thoroughly, it was as though he had thrust his hand into her chest and begun feel-ing her ribs one by one. This was all right with her. "I have never met anyone I felt this way about," he said. "I love you." He made her do things she'd never done before, and then they went for a walk and looked at the new tulips that were bound to have grown up somewhere. None of this felt stupid or corny, but she knew that it was. Miserably, she tried to gain a sense of proportion. She stared at the flowers. They were an agony of bright, organized beauty. She couldn't help it. She wanted to give him flowers. She wanted to be with him in a room full of flowers. She visualized herself standing in front of him, bearing a handful of blameless flowers trapped in the ugly pastel paper the florist would staple around them. The vision was brutally embarrassing, too much so to stay in her mind for more than seconds.

She stepped out of the flower store. He was not there. Her anxiety approached despair. They were supposed to spend the weekend together.

He stood in a cheap pizza stand across the street, eating a greasy slice and watching her as she stood on the corner. Her anxiety was visible to him. It was at once disconcerting and weirdly attractive. Her appearance otherwise was not pleasing. He couldn't quite put his finger on why this was. Perhaps it was the suggestion of meekness in her dress, of a desire to be inconspicuous, or worse, of plain thoughtlessness about how clothes looked on her.

He had met her at a party during the previous week. She immediately reminded him of a girl he had known years before, Sharon, a painfully serious girl with a pale, gentle face whom he had tormented off and on for two years before leaving for his wife. Although it had gratified him enormously to leave her, he had missed hurting her for years, and had been half-consciously looking for another woman with a similarly fatal combination of pride, weakness and a foolish lust for something resembling passion. On meeting Beth, he was astonished at how much she looked, talked and moved like his former victim. She was delicately morbid in all her gestures, sensitive, arrogant, vulnerable to flattery. She veered between extravagant outbursts of opinion and sudden, uncertain halts, during which she seemed to look to him for approval. She was in love with the idea of intelligence, and she overestimated her own. Her sense of the world, though she presented it aggressively, could be, he sensed, snatched out from under her with little or no trouble. She said, "I hope you are a savage."

He went home with her that night. He lay with her on her sagging, lumpy single mattress, tipping his head to blow smoke into the room. She butted her forehead against his chest. The mattress squeaked with every movement. He told her about Sharon. "I had a relationship like that when I was in college," she said. "Somebody opened me up in a way that I had no control over. He hurt me. He changed me completely. Now I can't have sex normally."

The room was pathetically decorated with postcards, pictures of huge-eyed Japanese cartoon characters, and tiny, maddening toys that she had obviously gone out of her way to find, displayed in a tightly arranged tumble on her dresser. A frail model airplane dangled from the light above her dresser. Next to it was a pasted-up cartoon of a pink-haired girl cringing open-mouthed before a spike-haired boy-villain in shorts and glasses. Her short skirt was blown up by the force of his threatening expression, and her panties showed. What kind of person would put crap like this up on her wall?

"I'm afraid of you," she murmured.

"Why?"

"Because I just am."

"Don't worry. I won't give you any more pain than you can handle."

She curled against him and squeezed her feet together like a stretching cat. Her socks were thick and ugly, and her feet were large for her size. Details like this could repel him, but he felt tenderly toward the long, grubby, squeezed-together feet. He said, "I want a slave."

She said, "I don't know. We'll see."

He asked her to spend the weekend with him three days later.

It had seemed like a good idea at the time, but now he felt an irritating combination of guilt and anxiety. He thought of his wife, making breakfast with her delicate, methodical movements, or in the bathroom, painstakingly applying kohl under her huge eyes, flicking away the excess with pretty, birdlike finger gestures, her thin elbows raised, her eyes blank with concentration. He thought of Beth, naked and bound, blind-folded and spread-eagled on the floor of her cluttered apartment. Her cartoon characters grinned as he beat her with a whip. Welts rose on her breasts, thighs, stomach and arms. She screamed and twisted, wrenching her neck from side to side. She was going to be scarred for life. He had another picture of her sitting across from him at a restaurant, very erect, one arm on the table, her face serious and intent. Her large glasses drew her face down, made it look somber and elegant. She was smoking a cigarette with slow, mournful intakes of breath. These images lay on top of one another, forming a hideously confusing grid. How was he going to sort them out? He managed to separate the picture of his wife and the original picture of blindfolded Beth and hold them apart. He imagined himself traveling happily between the two. Perhaps, as time went on, he could bring Beth home and have his wife beat her too. She would do the dishes and serve them dinner. The grid closed up again and his stomach went into a moil. The thing was complicated and potentially exhausting. He looked at the anxious girl on the corner. She had said that she wanted to be hurt, but he suspected that she didn't understand what that meant.

He should probably just stay in the pizza place and watch her until she went away. It might be entertaining to see how long she waited. He felt a certain pity for her. He also felt, from his glassed-in vantage point, as though he were torturing an insect. He gloated as he ate his pizza.

At the height of her anxiety she saw him through the glass wall of the pizza stand. She immediately noticed his gloating countenance. She recognized the coldly scornful element in his watching and waiting as opposed to greeting her. She suffered, but only for an instant; she was then smitten by love. She smiled and crossed the street with a senseless confidence in the power of her smile.

"I was about to come over," he said. "I had to eat first. I was starving." He folded the last of his pizza in half and stuck it in his mouth.

She noticed a piece of bright orange pizza stuck between his teeth, and it endeared him to her.

They left the pizza stand. He walked with wide steps, and his heavy black overcoat swung rakishly, she thought, above his boots. He was a slight, slender boy with a pale, narrow face and blond hair that wisped across one brow. In the big coat he looked like the young pet of a budding secret police force. She thought he was beautiful.

He hailed a cab and directed the driver to the airport. He looked at her sitting beside him. "This is going to be a disaster," he said. "I'll probably wind up leaving you there and coming back alone."

"I hope not," she said. "I don't have any money. If you left me there, I wouldn't be able to get back by myself."

"That's too bad. Because I might." He watched her face for a reaction. It showed discomfort and excitement and something that he could only qualify as foolishness, as if she had just dropped a tray full of glasses in public. "Don't worry, I wouldn't do that," he said. "But I like the idea that I could."

"So do I." She was terribly distressed. She wanted to throw her arms around him.

He thought: There is something wrong. Her passivity was pleasing, as was her silence and her willingness to place herself in his hands. But he sensed another element present in her that he could not define and did not like. Her tightly folded hands were nervous and repulsive. Her public posture was brittle, not pliant. There was a rigidity that if cracked would yield nothing. He was disconcerted to realize that he didn't know if he could crack it anyway. He began to feel uncomfortable. Perhaps the weekend would be a disaster.

They arrived at the airport an hour early. They went to a bar and drank. The bar was an open-ended cube with a red neon sign that said "Cocktails." There was no sense of shelter in it. The furniture was spindly and exposed, and there were no doors to protect you from the sight of dazed, unattractive passengers wandering through the airport with their luggage. She ordered a Bloody Mary.

"I can't believe you ordered that," he said.

"Why not?"

"Because I want a bloody Beth." He gave her a look that made her think of a neurotic dog with its tongue hanging out, waiting to bite someone.

"Oh," she said.

He offered her a cigarette.

"I don't smoke," she said. "I told you twice."

"Well, you should start."

They sat quietly and drank for several minutes.

"Do you like to look at people?" she asked.

She was clearly struggling to talk to him. He saw that her face had become very tense. He could've increased her discomfort, but for the moment he had lost the energy to do so. "Yes," he said. "I do."

They spent some moments regarding the people around them. They were short on material. There were only a few customers in the bar; most of them were men in suits who sat there seemingly enmeshed in a web of habit and accumulated rancor that they called their personalities, so utterly unaware of their entanglement that they clearly considered themselves men of the world, even though they had long ago stopped noticing it. Then a couple walked through the door, carrying luggage. The woman's bright skirt flashed with each step. The man walked ahead of her. He walked too fast for her to keep up. She looked harried. Her eyes were wide and dark and clotted with makeup; there was a mole on her chin. He paused, as though considering whether he would stop for a drink. He decided not to and strode again. Her earrings jiggled as she followed. They left a faint trail of sex and disappointment behind them.

Beth watched the woman's hips move under her skirt. "There was something unpleasant about them," she said.

"Yes, there was."

It cheered her to find this point of contact. "I'm sorry I'm not more talkative," she said.

"That's all right." His narrow eyes became feral once again. "Women should be quiet." It suddenly struck her that it would seem completely natural if he lunged forward and bit her face.

"I agree," she said sharply. "There aren't many men around worth talking to."

He was nonplussed by her peevish tone. Perhaps, he thought, he'd imagined it.

He hadn't.

They had more drinks on the plane. They were served a hunk of white-frosted raisin pastry in a red paper bag. He wasn't hungry, but the vulgar cake appealed to him so he stuck it in his baggage.

They had a brief discussion about shoes, from the point of view of expense and aesthetics. They talked about intelligence and art. There were large gaps of silence that were disheartening to both of them. She began talking about old people, and how nice they could be. He had a picture of her kneeling on the floor in black stockings and handcuffs. This picture became blurred, static-ridden, and then obscured by their conversation. He felt a ghastly sense of longing. He called back the picture, which no longer gave him any pleasure. He superimposed it upon a picture of himself standing in a nightclub the week before, holding a drink and talking to a rather combative girl who wanted his number.

"Some old people are beautiful in an unearthly way," she continued. "I saw this old lady in the drugstore the other day who must've been in her nineties. She was so fragile and pretty, she was like a little elf."

He looked at her and said, "Are you going to start being fun to be around or are you going to be a big drag?"

She didn't answer right away. She didn't see how this followed her comment about the old lady. "I don't know."

"I don't think you're very sexual," he said. "You're not the way I thought you were when I first met you."

She was so hurt by this that she had difficulty answering. Finally, she said, "I can be very sexual or very unsexual depending on who I'm with and in what situation. It has to be the right kind of thing. I'm sort of a cerebral person. I think I respond to things in a cerebral way, mostly."

"That's what I mean."

She was struck dumb with frustration. She had obviously disappointed him in some fundamental way, which she felt was completely due to misunderstanding. If only she could think of the correct thing to say, she was sure she could clear it up. The blue puffball thing unfurled itself before her with sickening power. It was the same image of him holding her and gazing into her eyes with bone-dislodging intent, thinly veiling the many shattering events that she anticipated between them. The prospect made her disoriented with pleasure. The only problem was, this image seemed to have no connection with what was happening now. She tried to think back to the time they had spent in her apartment, when he had held her and said, "You're cute." What had happened between then and now to so disappoint him?

She hadn't yet noticed how much he had disappointed her.

He couldn't tell if he was disappointing her or not. She completely mystified him, especially after her abrupt speech on cerebralism. It was now impossible to even have a clear picture of what he wanted to do to this unglamorous creature, who looked as though she bit her nails and read books at night. Dim, half-formed pictures of his wife, Sharon, Beth and a sixteen-year-old Chinese hooker he'd seen a month before crawled aimlessly over each other. He sat and brooded in a bad-natured and slightly drunken way.

She sat next to him, diminished and fretful, with idiot radio songs about sex in her head.

They were staying in his grandmother's deserted apartment in Washington, D.C. The complex was a series of building blocks seemingly arranged at random, stuck together and painted the least attractive colors available. It was surrounded by bright green grass and a circular driveway, and placed on a quiet highway that led into the city. There was a drive-in bank and an insurance office next to it. It was enveloped in the steady, continuous noise of cars driving by at roughly the same speed.

"This is a horrible building," she said as they traveled up in the elevator.

The door slid open and they walked down a hall carpeted with dense brown nylon. The grandmother's apartment opened before them. Beth found the refrigerator and opened it. There was a crumpled package of French bread, a jar of hot peppers, several lumps covered with aluminum foil, two bottles of wine and a six-pack. "Is your grandmother an alcoholic?" she asked.

"I don't know." He dropped his heavy leather bag and her white canvas one in the living room, took off his coat and threw it on the bags. She watched him standing there, pale and gaunt in a black leather shirt tied at his waist with a leather belt. That image of him would stay with her for years for no good reason and with no emotional significance. He dropped into a chair, his thin arms flopping lightly on its arms. He nodded at the tray of whiskey, Scotch and liqueurs on the coffee table before him. "Why don't you make yourself a drink?"

She dropped to her knees beside the table and nervously played with the bottles. He was watching her quietly, his expression hooded. She plucked a bottle of thick chocolate liqueur from the cluster, poured herself a glass and sat in the chair across from his with both hands around it. She could no longer ignore the character of the apartment. It was brutally ridiculous, almost sadistic in its absurdity. The couch and chairs were covered with a floral print. A thin maize carpet zipped across the floor. There were throw rugs. There were artificial flowers. There was an abundance of small tables and shelves housing a legion of figures; grinning glass maidens in sumptuous gowns bore baskets of glass roses, ceramic birds warbled from the ceramic stumps they clung to, glass horses galloped across teakwood pastures. A ceramic weather poodle and his diamond-eyed kitty-cat companions silently watched the silent scene in the room.

"Are you all right?" he asked.

"I hate this apartment. It's really awful."

"What were you expecting? Jesus Christ. It's a lot like yours, you know."

"Yes. That's true, I have to admit." She drank her liqueur.

"Do you think you could improve your attitude about this whole thing? You might try being a little more positive."

Coming from him, this question was preposterous. He must be so pathologically insecure that his perception of his own behavior was thoroughly distorted. He saw rejection everywhere, she decided; she must reassure him. "But I do feel positive about being here," she said. She paused, searching for the best way to express the extremity of her positive feelings. She invisibly implored him to see and mount their blue puffball bed. "It would be impossible for you to disappoint me. The whole idea of you makes me happy. Anything you do will be all right."

Her generosity unnerved him. He wondered if she realized what she was saying. "Does anybody know you're here?" he asked. "Did you tell anyone where you were going?"

"No." She had in fact told several people.

"That wasn't very smart."

"Why not?"

"You don't know me at all. Anything could happen to you." She put her glass on the coffee table, crossed the floor and dropped to her knees between his legs. She threw her arms around his thighs. She nuzzled his groin with her nose. He tightened. She unzipped his pants. "Stop," he said. "Wait." She took his shoulders — she had a surprisingly strong grip — and pulled him to the carpet. His hovering brood of images and plans was suddenly upended, as though it had been sitting on a table that a rampaging crazy person had flipped over. He felt assaulted and invaded. This was not what he had in mind, but to refuse would make him seem somehow less virile than she. Queasily, he stripped off her clothes and put their bodies in a viable position. He fastened his teeth on her breast and bit her. She made a surprised noise and her body stiffened. He bit her again, harder. She screamed. He wanted to draw blood. Her screams were short and stifled. He could tell that she was trying to like being bitten, but that she did not. He gnawed her breast. She screamed sharply. They screwed. They broke apart and regarded each other warily. She put her hand on his tentatively. He realized what had been disturbing him about her. With other women whom he had been with in similar situations, he had experienced a relaxing sense of emptiness within them that had made it easy for him to get inside them and, once there, smear himself all over their innermost territory until it was no longer theirs but his. His wife did not have this empty quality, yet the gracious way in which she emptied herself for him made her submission, as far as it went, all the more poignant. This exasperating girl, on the other hand, contained a tangible somethingness that she not only refused to expunge, but that seemed to willfully expand itself so that he banged into it with every attempt to invade her. He didn't mind the somethingness; he rather liked it, in fact, and had looked forward to seeing it demolished. But she refused to let him do it. Why had she told him she was a masochist? He looked at her body. Her limbs were muscular and alert. He considered taking her by the neck and bashing her head against the floor.

He stood abruptly. "I want to get something to eat. I'm starving."

She put her hand on his ankle. Her desire to abase herself had been completely frustrated. She had pulled him to the rug certain that if only they could fuck, he would enter her with overwhelming force and take complete control of her. Instead she had barely felt him, and what she had felt was remote and cold. Somewhere on her exterior he'd been doing some biting thing that meant nothing to her and was quite unpleasant. Despairing, she held his ankle tighter and put her forehead on the carpet. At least she could stay at his feet, worshiping. He twisted free and walked away. "Come on," he said.

The car was in the parking lot. It was because of the car that this weekend had come about. It was his wife's car, an expensive thing that her ex-husband had given her. It had been in Washington for over a year; he was here to retrieve it and drive it back to New York.

Beth was appalled by the car. It was a loud yellow monster with a narrow, vicious shape and absurd doors that snapped up from the roof and out like wings. In another setting it might have seemed glamorous, but here, behind this equally monstrous building, in her unsatisfactory clothing, the idea of sitting in it with him struck her as comparable to putting on a clown nose and wearing it to dinner.

They drove down a suburban highway lined with small businesses, malls and restaurants. It was twilight; several neon signs blinked consolingly.

"Do you think you could make some effort to change your mood?" he said.

"I'm not in a bad mood," she said wearily. "I just feel blank."

Not blank enough, he thought.

He pulled into a Roy Rogers fast food cafeteria. She thought: He is not even going to take me to a nice place. She was insulted. It seemed as though he was insulting her on purpose. The idea was incredible to her.

She walked through the line with him, but did not take any of the shiny dishes of food displayed on the fluorescent-lit aluminum shelves. He felt a pang of worry. He was no longer angry, and her drawn white face disturbed him.

"Why aren't you eating?"

"I'm not hungry."

They sat down. He picked at his food, eyeing her with veiled alarm. It occurred to her that it might embarrass him to eat in front of her while she ate nothing. She asked if she could have some of his salad. He eagerly passed her the entire bowl of pale leaves strewn with orange dressing. "Have it all."

He huddled his shoulders orphanlike as he ate; his blond hair stood tangled like pensive weeds. "I don't know why you're not eating," he said fretfully. "You're going to be hungry later on."

Her predisposition to adore him was provoked. She smiled.

"Why are you staring at me like that?" he asked.

"I'm just enjoying the way you look. You're very airy."

Again, his eyes showed alarm.

"Sometimes when I look at you, I feel like I'm seeing a tank of small, quick fish, the bright darting kind that go every which way."

He paused, stunned and dangle-forked over his pinched, curled-up steak. "I'm beginning to think you're out of your fucking mind."

Her happy expression collapsed.

"Why can't you talk to me in a half-normal fucking way?" he continued. "Like the way we talked on the plane. I liked that. That was a conversation." In fact, he hadn't liked the conversation on the plane either, but compared to this one, it seemed quite all right.

When they got back to the apartment, they sat on the floor and drank more alcohol. "I want you to drink a lot," he said. "I want to make you do things you don't want to do."

"But I won't do anything I don't want to do. You have to make me want it."

He lay on his back in silent frustration.

"What are your parents like?" she asked.

"What?"

"Your parents. What are they like?"

"I don't know. I don't have that much to do with them. My mother is nice. My father's a prick. That's what they're like." He put one hand over his face; a square-shaped album-style view of his family presented itself. They were all at the breakfast table, talking and reaching for things. His mother moved in the background, a slim, worried shadow in her pink robe. His sister sat next to him, tall, blond and arrogant, talking and flicking at toast crumbs in the corners of her mouth. His father sat at the head of the table, his big arms spread over everything, leaning over his plate as if he had to defend it, gnawing his breakfast. He felt unhappy and then angry. He thought of a little Italian girl he had met in a go-go bar a while back, and comforted himself with the memory of her slim haunches and pretty high-heeled feet on either side of his head as she squatted over him.

"It seems that way with my parents when you first look at them. But in fact my mother is much more aggressive and, I would say, more cruel than my father, even though she's more passive and soft on the surface."

She began a lengthy and, in his view, incredible and unnecessary history of her family life, including descriptions of her brother and sister. Her entire family seemed to have a collectively disturbed personality characterized by long brooding silences, unpleasing compulsive sloppiness (unflushed toilets, used Kleenex abandoned everywhere, dirty underwear on the floor) and outbursts of irrational, violent anger. It was horrible. He wanted to go home.

He poked himself up on his elbows. "Are you a liar?" he asked. "Do you lie often?"

She stopped in midsentence and looked at him. She seemed to consider the question earnestly. "No," she said. "Not really. I mean, I can be, but I usually don't about important things. Why do you ask?"

"Why did you tell me you were a masochist?"

"What makes you think I'm not?"

"You don't act like one."

"Well, I don't know how you can say that. You hardly know me. We've hardly done anything yet."

"What do you want to do?"

"I can't just come out and tell you. It would ruin it."

He picked up his cigarette lighter and flicked it, picked up her shirt and stuck the lighter underneath. She didn't move fast enough. She screamed and leapt to her feet.

"Don't do that! That's awful!"

He rolled over on his stomach. "See. I told you. You're not a masochist."

"Shit! That wasn't erotic in the least. I don't come when I stub my toe either."

In the ensuing silence it occurred to her that she was angry, and had been for some time.

"I'm tired," she said. "I want to go to bed." She walked out of the room.

He sat up. "Well, we're making decisions, aren't we?"

She reentered the room. "Where are we supposed to sleep, anyway?"

He showed her the guest room and the fold-out couch. She immediately began dismantling the couch with stiff, angry movements. Her body seemed full of unnatural energy and purpose. She had, he decided, ruined the weekend, not only for him but for herself. Her willful, masculine, stupid somethingness had obstructed their mutual pleasure and satisfaction. The only course of action left was hostility. He opened his grandmother's writing desk and took out a piece of paper and a Magic Marker. He wrote the word "stupid" in thick black letters. He held it first near her chest, like a placard, and then above her crotch. She ignored him.

"Where are the sheets?" she asked.

"How'd you get so tough all of a sudden?" He threw the paper on the desk and took a sheet from a dresser drawer.

"We'll need a blanket too, if we open the window. And I want to open the window."

He regarded her sarcastically. "You're just keeping yourself from getting what you want by acting like this."

"You obviously don't know what I want."

They got undressed. He contemptuously took in the muscular, energetic look of her body. She looked more like a boy than a girl, in spite of her pronounced hips and round breasts. Her short, spiky red hair was more than enough to render her masculine. Even the dark bruise he had inflicted on her breast and the slight burn from his lighter failed to lend her a more feminine quality.

She opened the window. They got under the blanket on the fold-out couch and lay there, not touching, as though they really were about to sleep. Of course, neither one of them could.

"Why is this happening?" she asked.

"You tell me."

"I don't know. I really don't know." Her voice was small and pathetic.

"Part of it is that you don't talk when you should, and then you talk too much when you shouldn't be saying anything at all."

In confusion, she reviewed the various moments they had spent together, trying to classify them in terms of whether or not it had been appropriate to speak, and to rate her performance accordingly. Her confusion increased. Tears floated on her eyes. She curled her body against his.

"You're hurting my feelings," she said, "but I don't think you're doing it on purpose."

He was briefly touched. "Accidental pain," he said musingly. He took her head in both hands and pushed it between his legs. She opened her mouth compliantly. He had hurt her after all, he reflected. She was confused and exhausted, and at this instant, anyway, she was doing what he wanted her to do. Still, it wasn't enough. He released her and she moved upward to lie on top of him, resting her head on his shoulder. She spoke dreamily. "I would do anything with you."

"You would not. You would be disgusted."

"Disgusted by what?"

"You would be disgusted if I even told you."

She rolled away from him. "It's probably nothing."

"Have you ever been pissed on?"

He gloated as he felt her body tighten.

"No."

"Well, that's what I want to do to you."

"On your grandmother's rug?"

"I want you to drink it. If any got on the rug, you'd clean it up."

"Oh."

"I knew you'd be shocked."

"I'm not. I just never wanted to do it."

"So? That isn't any good to me."

In fact, she was shocked. Then she was humiliated, and not in the way she had planned. Her seductive puffball cloud deflated with a flaccid hiss, leaving two drunken, bad-tempered, incompetent, malodorous people blinking and uncomfortable on its remains. She stared at the ugly roses with their heads collapsed in a dead wilt and slowly saw what a jerk she'd been. Then she got mad.

"Do you like people to piss on you?" she asked.

"Yeah. Last month I met this great girl at Billy's Topless. She pissed in my face for only twenty bucks."

His voice was high-pitched and stupidly aggressive, like some weird kid who would walk up to you on the street and offer to take care of your sexual needs. How, she thought miserably, could she have mistaken this hostile moron for the dark, brooding hero who would crush her like an insect and then talk about life and art?

"There's a lot of other things I'd like to do too," he said with odd self-righteousness. "But I don't think you could handle it."

"It's not a question of handling it." She said these last two words very sarcastically. "So far everything you've said to me has been incredibly banal. You haven't presented anything in a way that's even remotely attractive." She sounded like a prim, prematurely adult child complaining to her teacher about someone putting a worm down her back.

He felt like an idiot. How had he gotten stuck with this prissy, reedy-voiced thing with a huge forehead who poked and picked over everything that came out of his mouth? He longed for a dim-eyed little slut with a big, bright mouth and black vinyl underwear. What had he had in mind when he brought this girl here, anyway? Her serious, desperate face, panicked and tear-stained. Her ridiculous air of sacrifice and abandonment as he spread-eagled and bound her. White skin that marked easily. Frightened eyes. An exposed personality that could be yanked from her and held out of reach like . . . oh, he could see it only in scraps; his imagination fumbled and lost its grip. He looked at her hatefully self-possessed, compact little form. He pushed her roughly. "Oh, I'd do anything with you," he mimicked. "You would not."

She rolled away on her side, her body curled tightly. He felt her trembling. She sniffed.

"Don't tell me I've broken your heart."

She continued crying.

"This isn't bothering me at all," he said. "In fact, I'm rather enjoying it."

The trembling stopped. She sniffed once, turned on her back and looked at him with puzzled eyes. She blinked. He suddenly felt tired. I shouldn't be doing this, he thought. She is actually a nice person. For a moment he had an impulse to embrace her. He had a stronger impulse to beat her. He looked around the room until he saw a light wood stick that his grandmother had for some reason left standing in the corner. He pointed at it.

"Get me that stick. I want to beat you with it."

"I don't want to."

"Get it. I want to humiliate you even more."

She shook her head, her eyes wide with alarm. She held the blanket up to her chin.

"Come on," he coaxed. "Let me beat you. I'd be much nicer after I beat you."

"I don't think you're capable of being as nice as you'd have to be to interest me at this point."

"All right. I'll get it myself." He got the stick and snatched the blanket from her body.

She sat, her legs curled in a kneeling position. "Don't," she said. "I'm scared."

"You should be scared," he said. "I'm going to torture you." He brandished the stick, which actually felt as though it would break on the second or third blow. They froze in their positions, staring at each other.

She was the first to drop her eyes. She regarded the torn-off blanket meditatively. "You have really disappointed me," she said. "This whole thing has been a complete waste of time."

He sat on the bed, stick in lap. "You don't care about my feelings."

"I think I want to sleep in the next room."

They couldn't sleep separately any better than they could sleep together. She lay curled up on the couch pondering what seemed to be the ugly nature of her life. He lay wound in a blanket, blinking in the dark, as a dislocated, manic and unpleasing revue of his sexual experiences stumbled through his memory in a queasy scramble.

In the morning they agreed that they would return to Manhattan immediately. Despite their mutual ill humor, they fornicated again, mostly because they could more easily ignore each other while doing so.

They packed quickly and silently.

"It's going to be a long drive back," he said. "Try not to make me feel like too much of a prick, okay?"

"I don't care what you feel like."

He would have liked to dump her at the side of the road somewhere, but he wasn't indifferent enough to societal rules to do that. Besides, he felt vaguely sorry that he had made her cry, and while this made him view her grudgingly, he felt obliged not to worsen the situation. Ideally she would disappear, taking her stupid canvas bag with her. In reality, she sat beside him in the car with more solidity and presence than she had displayed since they met on the corner in Manhattan. She seemed fully prepared to sit in silence for the entire six-hour drive. He turned on the radio.

"Would you mind turning that down a little?"

"Anything for you."

She rolled her eyes.

Without much hope, he employed a tactic he used to pacify his wife when they argued. He would give her a choice and let her make it. "Would you like something to eat?" he asked. "You must be starving."

She was. They spent almost an hour driving up and down the available streets trying to find a restaurant she wanted to be in. She finally chose a small, clean egg-and-toast place. Her humor visibly improved as they sat before their breakfast. "I like eggs," she said. "They are so comforting."

He began to talk to her out of sheer curiosity. They talked about music, college, people they knew in common and drugs they used to take as teenagers. She said that when she had taken LSD, she had often lost her sense of identity so completely that she didn't recognize herself in the mirror. This pathetic statement brought back her attractiveness in a terrific rush. She noted the quick dark gleam in his eyes.

"You should've let me beat you," he said. "I wouldn't have hurt you too much."

"That's not the point. The moment was wrong. It wouldn't have meant anything."

"It would've meant something to me." He paused. "But you probably would've spoiled it. You would've started screaming right away and made me stop."

The construction workers at the next table stared at them quizzically. She smiled pleasantly at them and returned her gaze to him. "You don't know that."

He was so relieved at the ease between them that he put his arm around her as they left the restaurant. She stretched up and kissed his neck.

"We just had the wrong idea about each other," she said. "It's nobody's fault that we're incompatible."

"Well, soon we'll be in Manhattan, and it'll be all over. You'll never have to see me again." He hoped she would dispute this, but she didn't.

They continued to talk in the car, about the nature of time, their parents and the injustice of racism.

She was too exhausted to extract much from the pedestrian conversation, but the sound of his voice, the position of his body and his sudden receptivity were intoxicating. Time took on a grainy, dreamy aspect that made impossible conversations and unlikely gestures feasible, like a space capsule that enables its inhabitants to happily walk up the wall. The peculiar little car became a warm, humming cocoon, like a miniature house she had, as a little girl, assembled out of odds and ends for invented characters. She felt as if she were a very young child, when every notion that appeared in her head was new and naked of association and thus needed to be expressed carefully so it didn't become malformed. She wanted to set every one of them before him in a row, as she had once presented crayon drawings to her father in a neat many-colored sequence. Then he would shift his posture slightly or make a gesture that suddenly made him seem so helpless and frail that she longed to protect him and cosset him away, like a delicate pet in a matchbox filled with cotton. She rested her head on his shoulder and lovingly regarded the legs that bent at the knee and tapered to the booted feet resting on the brakes or the accelerator. This was as good as her original fantasy, possibly even better.

"Can I abuse you some more now?" he asked sweetly. "In the car?"

"What do you want to do?"

"Gag you. That's all, I'd just like to gag you."

"But I want to talk to you."

He sighed. "You're really not a masochist, you know."

She shrugged. "Maybe not. It always seemed like I was."

"You might have fantasies, but I don't think you have any concept of a real slave mentality. You have too much ego to be part of another person."

"I don't know, I've never had the chance to try it. I've never met anyone I wanted to do that with."

"If you were a slave, you wouldn't make the choice."

"All right, I'm not a slave. With me it's more a matter of love." She was just barely aware that she was pitching her voice higher and softer than it was naturally, so that she sounded like a cartoon girl. "It's like the highest form of love."

He thought this was really cute. Sure it was nauseating, but it was feminine in a radio-song kind of way.

"You don't seem interested in love. It's not about that for you."

"That's not true. That's not true at all. Why do you think I was so rough back there? Deep down, I'm afraid I'll fall in love with you, that I'll need to be with you and fuck you . . . forever." He was enjoying himself now. He was beginning to see her as a locked garden that he could sneak into and sit in for days, tearing the heads off the flowers.

On one hand, she was beside herself with bliss. On the other, she was scrutinizing him carefully from behind an opaque facade as he entered her pasteboard scene of flora and fauna. Could he function as a character in this landscape? She imagined sitting across from him in a Japanese restaurant, talking about anything. He would look intently into her eyes. . . .

He saw her apartment and then his. He saw them existing a nice distance apart, each of them blocked off by cleanly cut boundaries. Her apartment bloomed with scenes that spiraled toward him in colorful circular motions and then froze suddenly and clearly in place. She was crawling blindfolded across the floor. She was bound and naked in an S&M bar. She was sitting next to him in a taxi, her skirt pulled up, his fingers in her vagina.

. . . and then they would go back to her apartment. He would beat her and fuck her mouth.

Then he would go home to his wife, and she would make dinner for him. It was so well balanced, the mere contemplation of it gave him pleasure.

The next day he would send her flowers.

He let go of the wheel with one hand and patted her head. She gripped his shirt frantically.

He thought: This could work out fine.

Gabriel García Márquez

When Gabriel García Márquez's novel *One Hundred Years of Solitude* (*Cien Años de Soledad*) was published in translation in 1970, it was universally praised and ignited a firestorm of interest in contemporaneous Latin American writers like Carlos Fuentes, Miguel Angel Asturias, Julio Cortázar, and Borges. García Márquez is often associated with magical realism, a technique that invokes the enchantment of the folktale to transform realistic depictions into something unexpected, a hybrid that is both airy and gritty at the same time. In *One Hundred Years of Solitude,* for example, flowers drop from the sky, Remedios the Beauty ascends to heaven, and it rains for four years, eleven months, and two days, and yet the endless wars of the revolution and counter-revolution go on all the same. García Márquez has said that he was influenced by the tales his grandmother used to tell him in his native Colombia, tales that freely mixed the observable and the hidden realities, and which drew on Indian myths for their substance. His other books include *The Autumn of the Patriarch, Love in the Time of Cholera,* and the extraordinary *Chronicle of a Death Foretold*, a novel that moves backward and forward to inevitability through a series of interweaving incidents.

In the early editions of *Leaf Storm and Other Stories,* in which the two pieces here were first collected, García Márquez identified each of them with the subtitle, "A Tale for Children." Clearly, though, while the stories do display both the tone and psychic ambience of the fairy tale, they are far too complex to be meant for children, and it is interesting to attempt to define the limits of the conventional children's tale in contrast to García Márquez's take on it. Perhaps "folktales" would better describe these stories — or perhaps they need no subtitles at all. The first of them, "A Very Old Man with Enormous Wings," takes a few pokes at organized religion and its claim to have the answers to the miracles that confront us every day, presenting us with the image of an angel with "huge buzzard wings, dirty and half-plucked, [that] were forever entangled in the mud." The second piece, "The Handsomest Drowned Man in the World," works on an allegorical level to explore the effect on an isolated village of a radiant and magnificent corpse, and it ends with one of the most beautiful, breathless, seventeen-line sentences you will ever find.

A Very Old Man with Enormous Wings

A TALE FOR CHILDREN

On the third day of rain they had killed so many crabs inside the house that Pelayo had to cross his drenched courtyard and throw them into the sea, because the newborn child had a temperature all night and they thought it was due to the stench. The world had been sad since Tuesday. Sea and sky were a single ash-gray thing and the sands of the beach, which on March nights glimmered like powdered light, had become a stew of mud and rotten shellfish. The light was so weak at noon that when Pelayo was coming back to the house after throwing away the crabs, it was hard for him to see what it was that was moving and groaning in the rear of the courtyard. He had to go very close to see that it was an old man, a very old man, lying face down in the mud, who, in spite of his tremendous efforts, couldn't get up, impeded by his enormous wings.

Frightened by that nightmare, Pelayo ran to get Elisenda, his wife, who was putting compresses on the sick child, and he took her to the rear of the courtyard. They both looked at the fallen body with mute stupor. He was dressed like a ragpicker. There were only a few faded hairs left on his bald skull and very few teeth in his mouth, and his pitiful condition of a drenched great-grandfather had taken away any sense of grandeur he might have had. His huge buzzard wings, dirty and half-plucked, were forever entangled in the mud. They looked at him so long and so closely that Pelayo and Elisenda very soon overcame their surprise and in the end found him familiar. Then they dared speak to him, and he answered in an incomprehensible dialect with a strong sailor's voice. That was how they skipped over the inconvenience of the wings and quite intelligently concluded that he was a lonely castaway from some foreign ship wrecked by the storm. And yet, they called in a neighbor woman who knew everything about life and death to see him, and all she needed was one look to show them their mistake.

"He's an angel," she told them. "He must have been coming for the child, but the poor fellow is so old that the rain knocked him down."

On the following day everyone knew that a flesh-and-blood angel was held captive in Pelayo's house. Against the judgment of the wise neighbor woman, for whom angels in those times were the fugitive survivors of a celestial conspiracy, they did not have the heart to club him to death. Pelayo watched over him all afternoon from the kitchen, armed with his bailiff's club, and before going to bed he dragged him out of the mud and locked him up with the hens in the wire chicken coop. In the middle of the night, when the rain stopped, Pelayo and Elisenda were still killing crabs. A short time afterward the child woke up without a fever and with a desire to eat. Then they felt magnanimous and decided to put the angel on a raft with fresh water and provisions for three days and leave him to his fate on the high seas. But when they went out into the courtyard with the first light of dawn, they found the whole neighborhood in front of the chicken coop having fun with the angel, without the slightest reverence, tossing him things to eat through the openings in the wire as if he weren't a supernatural creature but a circus animal.

Father Gonzaga arrived before seven o'clock, alarmed at the strange news. By that time onlookers less frivolous than those at dawn had already arrived and they were making all kinds of conjectures concerning the captive's future. The simplest among them thought that he should be named mayor of the world. Others of sterner mind felt that he should be promoted to the rank of five-star general in order to win all wars. Some visionaries hoped that he could be put to stud in order to implant on earth a race of winged wise men who could take charge of the universe. But Father Gonzaga, before becoming a priest, had been a robust woodcutter. Standing by the wire, he reviewed his catechism in an instant and asked them to open the door so that he could take a close look at that pitiful man who looked more like a huge decrepit hen among the fascinated chickens. He was lying in a corner drying his open wings in the sunlight among the fruit peels and breakfast leftovers that the early risers had thrown him. Alien to the impertinences of the world, he only lifted his antiquarian eyes and murmured something in his dialect when Father Gonzaga went into the chicken coop and said good morning to him in Latin. The parish priest had his first suspicion of an imposter when he saw that he did not understand the language of God or know how to greet His ministers. Then he noticed that seen close up he was much too human: he had an unbearable smell of the outdoors, the back side of his wings was strewn with parasites and his main feathers had been mistreated by terrestrial winds, and nothing about him measured up to the proud dignity of angels. Then he came out of the chicken coop and in a brief sermon warned the curious against the risks of being ingenuous. He reminded them that the devil had the bad habit of making use of carnival tricks in order to confuse the unwary. He argued that if wings were not the essential element in determining the difference between a hawk and an airplane, they were even less so in the recognition of angels. Nevertheless, he promised to write a letter to his bishop so that the latter would write to his primate so that the latter would write to the Supreme Pontiff in order to get the final verdict from the highest courts.

His prudence fell on sterile hearts. The news of the captive angel spread with such rapidity that after a few hours the courtyard had the bustle of a marketplace and they had to call in troops with fixed bayonets to disperse the mob that was about to knock the house down. Elisenda, her spine all twisted from sweeping up so much marketplace trash, then got the idea of fencing in the yard and charging five cents admission to see the angel.

The curious came from far away. A traveling carnival arrived with a flying acrobat who buzzed over the crowd several times, but no one paid any attention to him because his wings were not those of an angel but, rather, those of a sidereal bat. The most unfortunate invalids on earth came in search of health: a poor woman who since childhood had been counting her heartbeats and had run out of numbers; a Portuguese man who couldn't sleep because the noise of the stars disturbed him; a sleepwalker who got up at night to undo the things he had done while awake; and many others with less serious ailments. In the midst of that shipwreck disorder that made the earth tremble, Pelayo and Elisenda were happy with fatigue, for in less than a week they had crammed their rooms with money and the line of pilgrims waiting their turn to enter still reached beyond the horizon.

The angel was the only one who took no part in his own act. He spent his time trying to get comfortable in his borrowed nest, befuddled by the hellish heat of the oil lamps and sacramental candles that had been placed along the wire. At first they tried to make him eat some mothballs, which, according to the wisdom of the wise neighbor woman, were the food prescribed for angels. But he turned them down, just as he turned down the papal lunches that the penitents brought him, and they never found out whether it was because he was an angel or because he was an old man that in the end he ate nothing but eggplant mush. His only supernatural virtue seemed to be patience. Especially during the first days, when the hens pecked at him, searching for the stellar parasites that proliferated in his wings, and the cripples pulled out feathers to touch their defective parts with, and even the most merciful threw stones at him, trying to get him to rise so they could see him standing. The only time they succeeded in arousing him was when they burned his side with an iron for branding steers, for he had been motionless for so many hours that they thought he was dead. He awoke with a start, ranting in his hermetic language and with tears in his eyes, and he flapped his wings a couple of times, which brought on a whirlwind of chicken dung and lunar dust and a gale of panic that did not seem to be of this world. Although many thought that his reaction had been one not of rage but of pain, from then on they were careful not to annoy him, because the majority understood that his passivity was not that of a hero taking his ease but that of a cataclysm in repose.

Father Gonzaga held back the crowd's frivolity with formulas of maidservant inspiration while awaiting the arrival of a final judgment on the nature of the captive. But the mail from Rome showed no sense of urgency. They spent their time finding out if the prisoner had a navel, if his dialect had any connection with Aramaic, how many times he could fit on the head of a pin, or whether he wasn't just a Norwegian with wings. Those meager letters might have come and gone until the end of time if a providential event had not put an end to the priest's tribulations.

It so happened that during those days, among so many other carnival attractions, there arrived in town the traveling show of the woman who had been changed into a spider for having disobeyed her parents. The admission to see her was not only less than the admission to see the angel, but people were permitted to ask her all manner of questions about her absurd state and to examine her up and down so that no one would ever doubt the truth of her horror. She was a frightful tarantula the size of a ram and with the head of a sad maiden. What was most heart-rending, however, was not her outlandish shape but the sincere affliction with which she recounted the details of her misfortune. While still practically a child she had sneaked out of her parents' house to go to a dance, and while she was coming back through the woods after having danced all night without permission, a fearful thunderclap rent the sky in two and through the crack came the lightning bolt of brimstone that changed her into a spider. Her only nourishment came from the meatballs that charitable souls chose to toss into her mouth. A spectacle like that, full of so much human truth and with such a fearful lesson, was bound to defeat without even trying that of a haughty angel who scarcely deigned to look at mortals. Besides, the few miracles attributed to the angel showed a certain mental disorder, like the blind man who didn't recover his sight but grew three new teeth, or the paralytic who didn't get to walk but almost won the lottery, and the leper whose sores sprouted sunflowers. Those consolation miracles, which were more like mocking fun, had already ruined the angel's reputation when the woman who had been changed into a spider finally crushed him completely. That was how Father Gonzaga was cured forever of his insomnia and Pelayo's courtyard went back to being as empty as during the time it had rained for three days and crabs walked through the bedrooms.

The owners of the house had no reason to lament. With the money they saved they built a two-story mansion with balconies and gardens and high netting so that crabs wouldn't get in during the winter, and with iron bars on the windows so that angels wouldn't get in. Pelayo also set up a rabbit warren close to town and gave up his job as bailiff for good, and Elisenda bought some satin pumps with high heels and many dresses of iridescent silk, the kind worn on Sunday by the most desirable women in those times. The chicken coop was the only thing that didn't receive any attention. If they washed it down with creolin and burned tears of myrrh inside it every so often, it was not in homage to the angel but to drive away the dungheap stench that still hung everywhere like a ghost and was turning the new house into an old one. At first, when the child learned to walk, they were careful that he not get too close to the chicken coop. But then they began to lose their fears and got used to the smell, and before the child got his second teeth he'd gone inside the chicken coop to play, where the wires were falling apart. The angel was no less standoffish with him than with other mortals, but he tolerated the most ingenious infamies with the patience of a dog who had no illusions. They both came down with chicken pox at the same time. The doctor who took care of the child couldn't resist the temptation to listen to the angel's heart, and he found so much whistling in the heart and so many sounds in his kidneys that it seemed impossible for him to be alive. What surprised him most, however, was the logic of his wings. They seemed so natural on that completely human organism that he couldn't understand why other men didn't have them too.

When the child began school it had been some time since the sun and rain had caused the collapse of the chicken coop. The angel went dragging himself about here and there like a stray dying man. They would drive him out of the bedroom with a broom and a moment later find him in the kitchen. He seemed to be in so many places at the same time that they grew to think that he'd been duplicated, that he was reproducing himself all through the house, and the exasperated and unhinged Elisenda shouted that it was awful living in that hell full of angels. He could scarcely eat and his antiquarian eyes had also become so foggy that he went about bumping into posts. All he had left were the bare cannulae of his last feathers. Pelayo threw a blanket over him and extended him the charity of letting him sleep in the shed, and only then did they notice that he had a temperature at night, and was delirious with the tongue twisters of an old Norwegian. That was one of the few times they became alarmed, for they thought he was going to die and not even the wise neighbor woman had been able to tell them what to do with dead angels.

And yet he not only survived his worst winter, but seemed improved with the first sunny days. He remained motionless for several days in the farthest corner of the courtyard, where no one would see him, and at the beginning of December some large, stiff feathers began to grow on his wings, the feathers of a scarecrow, which looked more like another misfortune of decrepitude. But he must have known the reason for those changes, for he was quite careful that no one should notice them, that no one should hear the sea chanteys that he sometimes sang under the stars. One morning Elisenda was cutting some bunches of onions for lunch when a wind that seemed to come from the high seas blew into the kitchen. Then she went to the window and caught the angel in his first attempts at flight. They were so clumsy that his fingernails opened a furrow in the vegetable patch and he was on the point of knocking the shed down with the ungainly flapping that slipped on the light and couldn't get a grip on the air. But he did manage to gain altitude. Elisenda let out a sigh of relief, for herself and for him, when she saw him pass over the last houses, holding himself up in some way with the risky flapping of a senile vulture. She kept watching him even when she was through cutting the onions and she kept on watching until it was no longer possible for her to see him, because then he was no longer an annoyance in her life but an imaginary dot on the horizon of the sea.

The Handsomest Drowned Man in the World

A TALE FOR CHILDREN

The first children who saw the dark and slinky bulge approaching through the sea let themselves think it was an enemy ship. Then they saw it had no flags or masts and they thought it was a whale. But when it washed up on the beach, they removed the clumps of seaweed, the jellyfish tentacles, and the remains of fish and flotsam, and only then did they see that it was a drowned man.

They had been playing with him all afternoon, burying him in the sand and digging him up again, when someone chanced to see them and spread the alarm in the village. The men who carried him to the nearest house noticed that he weighed more than any dead man they had ever known, almost as much as a horse, and they said to each other that maybe he'd been floating too long and the water had got into his bones. When they laid him on the floor they said he'd been taller than all other men because there was barely enough room for him in the house, but they thought that maybe the ability to keep on growing after death was part of the nature of certain drowned men. He had the smell of the sea about him and only his shape gave one to suppose that it was the corpse of a human being, because the skin was covered with a crust of mud and scales.

They did not even have to clean off his face to know that the dead man was a stranger. The village was made up of only twenty-odd wooden houses that had stone courtyards with no flowers and which were spread about on the end of a desertlike cape. There was so little land that mothers always went about with the fear that the wind would carry off their children and the few dead that the years had caused among them had to be thrown off the cliffs. But the sea was calm and bountiful and all the men fit into seven boats. So when they found the drowned man they simply had to look at one another to see that they were all there.

That night they did not go out to work at sea. While the men went to find out if anyone was missing in neighboring villages, the women stayed behind to care for the drowned man. They took the mud off with grass swabs, they removed the underwater stones entangled in his hair, and they scraped the crust off with tools used for scaling fish. As they were doing that they noticed that the vegetation on him came from faraway oceans and deep water and that his clothes were in tatters, as if he had sailed through labyrinths of coral. They noticed too that he bore his death with pride, for he did not have the lonely look of other drowned men who came out of the sea or that haggard, needy look of men who drowned in rivers. But only when they finished cleaning him off did they become aware of the kind of man he was and it left them breathless. Not only was he the tallest, strongest, most virile, and best built man they had ever seen, but even though they were looking at him there was no room for him in their imagination.

They could not find a bed in the village large enough to lay him on nor was there a table solid enough to use for his wake. The tallest men's holiday pants would not fit him, nor the fattest ones' Sunday shirts, nor the shoes of the one with the biggest feet. Fascinated by his huge size and his beauty, the women then decided to make him some pants from a large piece of sail and a shirt from some bridal brabant linen so that he could continue through his death with dignity. As they sewed, sitting in a circle and gazing at the corpse between stitches, it seemed to them that the wind had never been so steady nor the sea so restless as on that night and they supposed that the change had something to do with the dead man. They thought that if that magnificent man had lived in the village, his house would have had the widest doors, the highest ceiling, and the strongest floor, his bedstead would have been made from a midship frame held together by iron bolts, and his wife would have been the happiest woman. They thought that he would have had so much authority that he could have drawn fish out of the sea simply by calling their names and that he would have put so much work into his land that springs would have burst forth from among the rocks so that he would have been able to plant flowers on the cliffs. They secretly compared him to their own men, thinking that for all their lives theirs were incapable of doing what he could do in one night, and they ended up dismissing them deep in their hearts as the weakest, meanest, and most useless creatures on earth. They were wandering through that maze of fantasy when the oldest woman, who as the oldest had looked upon the drowned man with more compassion than passion, sighed:

"He has the face of someone called Esteban."

It was true. Most of them had only to take another look at him to see that he could not have any other name. The more stubborn among them, who were the youngest, still lived for a few hours with the illusion that

340 Gabriel García Márquez

when they put his clothes on and he lay among the flowers in patent leather shoes his name might be Lautaro. But it was a vain illusion. There had not been enough canvas, the poorly cut and worse sewn pants were too tight, and the hidden strength of his heart popped the buttons on his shirt. After midnight the whistling of the wind died down and the sea fell into its Wednesday drowsiness. The silence put an end to any last doubts: he was Esteban. The women who had dressed him, who had combed his hair, had cut his nails and shaved him were unable to hold back a shudder of pity when they had to resign themselves to his being dragged along the ground. It was then that they understood how unhappy he must have been with that huge body since it bothered him even after death. They could see him in life, condemned to going through doors sideways, cracking his head on crossbeams, remaining on his feet during visits, not knowing what to do with his soft, pink, sea lion hands while the lady of the house looked for her most resistant chair and begged him, frightened to death, sit here, Esteban, please, and he, leaning against the wall, smiling, don't bother, ma'am, I'm fine where I am, his heels raw and his back roasted from having done the same thing so many times whenever he paid a visit, don't bother, ma'am, I'm fine where I am, just to avoid the embarrassment of breaking up the chair, and never knowing perhaps that the ones who said don't go, Esteban, at least wait till the coffee's ready, were the ones who later on would whisper the big boob finally left, how nice, the handsome fool has gone. That was what the women were thinking beside the body a little before dawn. Later, when they covered his face with a handkerchief so that the light would not bother him, he looked so forever dead, so defenseless, so much like their men that the first furrows of tears opened in their hearts. It was one of the younger ones who began the weeping. The others, coming to, went from sighs to wails, and the more they sobbed the more they felt like weeping, because the drowned man was becoming all the more Esteban for them, and so they wept so much, for he was the most destitute, most peaceful, and most obliging man on earth, poor Esteban. So when the men returned with the news that the drowned man was not from the neighboring villages either, the women felt an opening of jubilation in the midst of their tears.

"Praise the Lord," they sighed, "he's ours!"

The men thought the fuss was only womanish frivolity. Fatigued because of the difficult nighttime inquiries, all they wanted was to get rid of the bother of the newcomer once and for all before the sun grew strong on that arid, windless day. They improvised a litter with the remains of foremasts and gaffs, tying it together with rigging so that it would bear the weight of the body until they reached the cliffs. They wanted to tie the anchor from a cargo ship to him so that he would sink easily into the deepest waves, where fish are blind and divers die of nostalgia, and bad currents would not bring him back to shore, as had happened with other bodies. But the more they hurried, the more the women thought of ways to waste time. They walked about like startled hens, pecking with the sea charms on their breasts, some interfering on one side to put a scapular of the good wind on the drowned man, some on the other side to put a wrist compass on him, and after a great deal of *get away from there, woman, stay out of the way, look, you almost made me fall on top of the dead man,* the men began to feel mistrust in their livers and started grumbling about why so many main-altar decorations for a stranger, because no matter how many nails and holy-water jars he had on him, the sharks would chew him all the same, but the women kept piling on their junk relics, running back and forth, stumbling, while they released in sighs what they did not in tears, so that the men finally exploded with *since when has there ever been such a fuss over a drifting corpse, a drowned nobody, a piece of cold Wednesday meat.* One of the women, mortified by so much lack of care, then removed the handkerchief from the dead man's face and the men were left breathless too.

He was Esteban. It was not necessary to repeat it for them to recognize him. If they had been told Sir Walter Raleigh, even they might have been impressed with his gringo accent, the macaw on his shoulder, his cannibal-killing blunderbuss, but there could be only one Esteban in the world and there he was, stretched out like a sperm whale, shoeless, wearing the pants of an undersized child, and with those stony nails that had to be cut with a knife. They only had to take the handkerchief off his face to see that he was ashamed, that it was not his fault that he was so big or so heavy or so handsome, and if he had known that this was going to happen, he would have looked for a more discreet place to drown in, seriously, I even would have tied the anchor off a galleon around my neck and staggered off a cliff like someone who doesn't like things in order not to be upsetting people now with this Wednesday dead body, as you people say, in order not to be bothering anyone with this filthy piece of cold meat that doesn't have anything to do with me. There was so much truth in his manner that even the most mistrustful men, the ones who felt the bitterness of endless nights at sea fearing that their women would tire of dreaming about them and begin to dream of drowned men, even they and others who were harder still shuddered in the marrow of their bones at Esteban's sincerity.

That was how they came to hold the most splendid funeral they could conceive of for an abandoned drowned man. Some women who had gone to get flowers in the neighboring villages returned with other women who could not believe what they had been told, and those women went back for more flowers when they saw the dead man, and they brought more and more until there were so many flowers and so many people that it was hard to walk about. At the final moment it pained them to return him to the waters as an orphan and they chose a father and mother from among the best people, and aunts and uncles and cousins, so that through him all the inhabitants of the village became kinsmen. Some sailors who heard the weeping from a distance went off course and people heard of one who had himself tied to the mainmast, remembering ancient fables about sirens. While they fought for the privilege of carrying him on their shoulders along the steep escarpment by the cliffs, men and women became aware for the first time of the desolation of their streets, the dryness of their courtyards, the narrowness of their dreams as they faced the splendor and beauty of their drowned man. They let him go without an anchor so that he could come back if he wished and whenever he wished, and they all held their breath for the fraction of centuries the body took to fall into the abyss. They did not need to look at one another to realize that they were no longer all present, that they would never be. But they also knew that everything would be different from then on, that their houses would have wider doors, higher ceilings, and stronger floors so that Esteban's memory could go everywhere without bumping into beams and so that no one in the future would dare whisper the big boob finally died, too bad, the handsome fool has finally died, because they were going to paint their house fronts gay colors to make Esteban's memory eternal and they were going to break their backs digging for springs among the stones and planting flowers on the cliffs so that in future years at dawn the passengers on great liners would awaken, suffocated by the smell of gardens on the high seas, and the captain would have to come down from the bridge in his dress uniform, with his astrolabe, his pole star, and his row of war medals and, pointing to the promontory of roses on the horizon, he would say in fourteen languages, look there, where the wind is so peaceful now that it's gone to sleep beneath the beds, over there, where the sun's so bright that the sunflowers don't know which way to turn, yes, over there, that's Esteban's village.

Ellen Gilchrist

Best-known for her blackly funny and subversive take on southern society, Ellen Gilchrist has, over the years, created a series of willful, wild, and disaffected heroines whose lives are interwoven through her separate story collections until the collections read like a novel in several volumes. Rhoda Manning, introduced in Gilchrist's first collection, *In the Land of Dreamy Dreams,* is typical. She's rich, bored, materialistic, a daddy's girl who always gets what she wants, and yet for all that, there is something real and compelling in her selfish obliviousness — and that something allows Gilchrist, an accomplished satirist, to expose the hypocrisy of a society built on manners and mores that are jettisoned the moment they become inconvenient. Gilchrist's story collections include *Victory over Japan, Drunk with Love, Flights of Angels,* and a volume of collected stories, and she is the author of the novels *The Annunciation, Sarah Conley,* and *Starcarbon* as well.

The stories selected here are both from *In the Land of Dreamy Dreams.* The first, "Rich," begins with the line, "Tom and Letty Wilson were rich in everything," and proceeds from there, in the way of a fable, to examine just what the value of riches is. Moving forward from Tom and Letty's courtship through their marriage and the growth of their family and burgeoning prosperity, making use of flashbacks and three distinct points of view, the story reads like a compressed novel. Its power derives from the tone — detached, reportorial, and yet acidic too — and the final cataclysm, which takes us back into the story to reassess the controlling metaphor. The title story introduces LaGrande McGruder, a savagely competitive and utterly pampered Southern Belle, whose violation of the unwritten code of honor — her cheating at tennis — demonstrates the shallowness of the rationale of moral and ethnic superiority on which her society is built. Brand names — things — are the final consolation of the rich, and LaGrande comes to understand that and to wield her knowledge like a weapon. The final line, with its thumping use of the vernacular, is both dismissive and triumphant at the same time — the rules define her whether she sees through them or not, but she isn't about to change for the sake of a mere epiphany.

Rich

Tom and Letty Wilson were rich in everything. They were rich in friends because Tom was a vice-president of the Whitney Bank of New Orleans and liked doing business with his friends, and because Letty was vice-president of the junior League of New Orleans and had her picture in *Town and Country* every year at the Symphony Ball.

The Wilsons were rich in knowing exactly who they were because every year from Epiphany to Fat Tuesday they flew the beautiful green and gold and purple flag outside their house that meant that Letty had been queen of the Mardi Gras the year she was a debutante. Not that Letty was foolish enough to take the flag seriously.

Sometimes she was even embarrassed to call the yardman and ask him to come over and bring his high ladder.

"Preacher, can you come around on Tuesday and put up my flag?" she would ask.

"You know I can," the giant black man would answer. "I been saving time to put up your flag. I won't forget what a beautiful queen you made that year."

"Oh, hush, Preacher. I was a skinny little scared girl. It's a wonder I didn't fall off the balcony I was so scared. I'll see you on Monday." And Letty would think to herself what a big phony Preacher was and wonder when he was going to try to borrow some more money from them.

Tom Wilson considered himself a natural as a banker because he loved to gamble and wheel and deal. From the time he was a boy in a small Baptist town in Tennessee he had loved to play cards and match nickels and lay bets.

In high school he read *The Nashville Banner* avidly and kept an eye out for useful situations such as the lingering and suspenseful illnesses of Pope Pius.

"Let's get up a pool on the day the Pope will die," he would say to the football team, "I'll hold the bank." And because the Pope took a very long time to die with many close calls there were times when Tom was the richest left tackle in Franklin, Tennessee.

Tom had a favorite saying about money. He had read it in the *Reader's Digest* and attributed it to Andrew Carnegie. "Money," Tom would say, "is what you keep score with. Andrew Carnegie."

Another way Tom made money in high school was performing as an amateur magician at local birthday parties and civic events. He could pull a silver dollar or a Lucky Strike cigarette from an astonished six-year-old's ear or from his own left palm extract a seemingly endless stream of multicolored silk chiffon or cause an ordinary piece of clothesline to behave like an Indian cobra.

He got interested in magic during a convalescence from German measles in the sixth grade. He sent off for books of magic tricks and practiced for hours before his bedroom mirror, his quick clever smile flashing and his long fingers curling and uncurling from the sleeves of a black dinner jacket his mother had bought at a church bazaar and remade to fit him.

Tom's personality was too flamboyant for the conservative Whitney Bank, but he was cheerful and cooperative and when he made a mistake he had the ability to turn it into an anecdote.

"Hey, Fred," he would call to one of his bosses. "Come have lunch on me and I'll tell you a good one."

They would walk down St. Charles Avenue to where it crosses Canal and turns into Royal Street as it enters the French Quarter. They would walk into the crowded, humid excitement of the quarter, admiring the girls and watching the Yankee tourists sweat in their absurd spun-glass leisure suits, and turn into the side door of Antoine's or breeze past the maitre d' at Galatoire's or Brennan's.

When a red-faced waiter in funereal black had seated them at a choice table, Tom would loosen his Brooks Brothers' tie, turn his handsome brown eyes on his guest, and begin.

"That bunch of promoters from Dallas talked me into backing an idea to videotape all the historic sights in the quarter and rent the tapes to hotels to show on closed-circuit television. Goddamnit, Fred, I could just see those fucking tourists sitting around their hotel rooms on rainy days ordering from room service and taking in the Cabildo and the Presbytere on T.V." Tom laughed delightedly and waved his glass of vermouth at an elegantly dressed couple walking by the table.

"Well, they're barely breaking even on that one, and now they want to buy up a lot of soft porn movies and sell them to motels in Jefferson Parish. What do you think? Can we stay with them for a few more months?"

Then the waiter would bring them cold oysters on the half shell and steaming pompano *en papillote* and a wine steward would serve them a fine Meursault or a Piesporter, and Tom would listen to whatever advice he was given as though it were the most intelligent thing he had ever heard in his life.

Of course he would be thinking, "You stupid, impotent son of a bitch. You scrawny little frog bastard, I'll buy and sell you before it's over. I've got more brains in my balls than the whole snotty bunch of you."

"Tom, you always throw me off my diet," his friend would say, "damned if you don't."

"I told Letty the other day," Tom replied, "that she could just go right ahead and spend her life worrying about being buried in her wedding dress, but I didn't hustle my way to New Orleans all the way from north Tennessee to eat salads and melba toast. Pass me the French bread."

Letty fell in love with Tom the first time she laid eyes on him. He came to Tulane on a football scholarship and charmed his way into a fraternity of wealthy New Orleans boys famed for its drunkenness and its wild practical jokes. It was the same old story. Even the second, third, and fourth generation blue bloods of New Orleans need an infusion of new genes now and then.

The afternoon after Tom was initiated he arrived at the fraternity house with two Negro painters and sat in the low-hanging branches of a live oak tree overlooking Henry Clay Avenue directing them in painting an official-looking yellow-and-white-striped pattern on the street in front of the property. "D-R-U-N-K," he yelled to his painters, holding on to the enormous limb with one hand and pushing his black hair out of his eyes with the other. "Paint it to say D-R-U-N-K Z-O-N-E."

Letty stood near the tree with a group of friends watching him. He was wearing a blue shirt with the sleeves rolled up above his elbows, and a freshman beanie several sizes too small was perched on his head like a tipsy sparrow.

"I'm wearing this goddamn beanie forever," Tom yelled. "I'm wearing this beanie until someone brings me a beer," and Letty took the one she was holding and walked over to the tree and handed it to him.

One day a few weeks later, he commandeered a Bunny Bread truck while it was parked outside the fraternity house making a delivery. He picked up two friends and drove the truck madly around the Irish Channel, throwing fresh loaves of white and whole-wheat and rye bread to the astonished housewives.

"Steal from the rich, give to the poor," Tom yelled, and his companions gave up trying to reason with him and helped him yell.

"Free bread, free cake," they yelled, handing out powdered doughnuts and sweet rolls to a gang of kids playing baseball on a weed-covered vacant lot.

They stopped off at Darby's, an Irish bar where Tom made bets on races and football games, and took on some beer and left off some cinnamon rolls.

"Tom, you better go turn that truck in before they catch you," Darby advised, and Tom's friends agreed, so they drove the truck to the second-precinct police headquarters and turned themselves in. Tom used up half a year's allowance paying the damages, but it made his reputation.

In Tom's last year at Tulane a freshman drowned during a hazing accident at the Southern Yacht Club, and the event frightened Tom. He had never liked the boy and had suspected him of being involved with the queers and nigger lovers who hung around the philosophy department and the school newspaper. The boy had gone to prep school in the East and brought weird-looking girls to rush parties. Tom had resisted the temptation to blackball him as he was well connected in uptown society.

After the accident, Tom spent less time at the fraternity house and more time with Letty, whose plain sweet looks and expensive clothes excited him.

"I can't go in the house without thinking about it," he said to Letty. "All we were doing was making them swim from pier to pier carrying martinis. I did it fifteen times the year I pledged."

"He should have told someone he couldn't swim very well," Letty answered. "It was an accident. Everyone knows it was an accident. It wasn't your fault." And Letty cuddled up close to him on the couch, breathing as softly as a cat.

Tom had long serious talks with Letty's mild, alcoholic father, who held a seat on the New York Stock Exchange, and in the spring of the year Tom and Letty were married in the Cathedral of Saint Paul with twelve bridesmaids, four flower girls, and seven hundred guests. It was pronounced a marriage made in heaven, and Letty's mother ordered masses said in Rome for their happiness.

They flew to New York on the way to Bermuda and spent their wedding night at the Sherry Netherland Hotel on Fifth Avenue. At least half a dozen of Letty's friends had lost their virginity at the same address, but the trip didn't seem prosaic to Letty.

She stayed in the bathroom a long time gazing at her plain face in the oval mirror and tugging at the white lace nightgown from the Lylian Shop, arranging it now to cover, now to reveal her small breasts. She crossed herself in the mirror, suddenly giggled, then walked out into the blue and gold bedroom as though she had been going to bed with men every night of her life. She had been up until three the night before reading a book on sexual intercourse. She offered her small unpainted mouth to Tom. Her pale hair smelled of Shalimar and carnations and candles. Now she was safe. Now life would begin.

"Oh, I love you, I love, I love, I love you," she whispered over and over. Tom's hands touching her seemed a strange and exciting passage that would carry her simple dreamy existence to a reality she had never encountered. She had never dreamed anyone so interesting would marry her.

Letty's enthusiasm and her frail body excited him, and he made love to her several times before he asked her to remove her gown.

The next day they breakfasted late and walked for a while along the avenue. In the afternoon Tom explained to his wife what her clitoris was and showed her some of the interesting things it was capable of generating, and before the day was out Letty became the first girl in her crowd to break the laws of God and the Napoleonic Code by indulging in oral intercourse.

Fourteen years went by and the Wilsons' luck held. Fourteen years is a long time to stay lucky even for rich people who don't cause trouble for anyone.

Of course, even among the rich there are endless challenges, unyielding limits, rivalry, envy, quirks of fortune. Letty's father grew increasingly incompetent and sold his seat on the exchange, and Letty's irresponsible brothers went to work throwing away the money in Las Vegas and L.A. and Zurich and Johannesburg and Paris and anywhere they could think of to fly to with their interminable strings of mistresses.

Tom envied them their careless, thoughtless lives and he was annoyed that they controlled their own money while Letty's was tied up in some mysterious trust, but he kept his thoughts to himself as he did his obsessive irritation over his growing obesity.

"Looks like you're putting on a little weight there," a friend would observe.

"Good, good," Tom would say, "makes me look like a man. I got a wife to look at if I want to see someone who's skinny."

He stayed busy gambling and hunting and fishing and being the life of the party at the endless round of dinners and cocktail parties and benefits and Mardi Gras functions that consume the lives of the Roman Catholic hierarchy that dominates the life of the city that care forgot.

Letty was preoccupied with the details of their domestic life and her work in the community. She took her committees seriously and actually believed that the work she did made a difference in the lives of other people.

The Wilsons grew rich in houses. They lived in a large Victorian house in the Garden District, and across Lake Pontchartrain they had another Victorian house to stay in on the weekends, with a private beach surrounded by old moss-hung oak trees. Tom bought a duck camp in Plaquemines Parish and kept an apartment in the French Quarter in case one of his business friends fell in love with his secretary and needed someplace to be alone with her. Tom almost never used the apartment himself. He was rich in being satisfied to sleep with his own wife.

The Wilsons were rich in common sense. When five years of a good Catholic marriage went by and Letty inexplicably never became pregnant, they threw away their thermometers and ovulation charts and litmus paper and went down to the Catholic adoption agency and adopted a baby girl with curly black hair and hazel eyes. Everyone declared she looked exactly like Tom. The Wilsons named the little girl Helen and, as the months went by, everyone swore she even walked and talked like Tom.

At about the same time Helen came to be the Wilsons' little girl, Tom grew interested in raising Labrador retrievers. He had large wire runs with concrete floors built in the side yard for the dogs to stay in when he wasn't training them on the levee or at the park lagoon. He used all the latest methods for training Labs, including an electric cattle prod given to him by Chalin Perez himself and live ducks supplied by a friend on the Audubon Park Zoo Association Committee.

"Watch this, Helen," he would call to the little girl in the stroller, "watch this." And he would throw a duck into the lagoon with its secondary feathers neatly clipped on the left side and its feet tied loosely together, and one of the Labs would swim out into the water and carry it safely back and lay it at his feet.

As so often happens when childless couples are rich in common sense, before long Letty gave birth to a little boy, and then to twin boys, and finally to another little Wilson girl. The Wilsons became so rich in children the neighbors all lost count.

"Tom," Letty said, curling up close to him in the big walnut bed, "Tom, I want to talk to you about something important." The new baby girl was three months old. "Tom I want to talk to Father Delahoussaye and ask him if we can use some birth control. I think we have all the children we need for now."

Tom put his arms around her and squeezed her until he wrinkled her new green linen B. H. Wragge, and she screamed for mercy.

"Stop it," she said, "be serious. Do you think it's all right to do that?"

Then Tom agreed with her that they had had all the luck with children they needed for the present, and Letty made up her mind to call the cathedral and make an appointment. All her friends were getting dispensations so they would have time to do their work at the Symphony League and the Thrift Shop and the New Orleans Museum Association and the PTAs of the private schools.

All the Wilson children were in good health except Helen. The pediatricians and psychiatrists weren't certain what was wrong with Helen.

Helen couldn't concentrate on anything. She didn't like to share and she went through stages of biting other children at the Academy of the Sacred Heart of Jesus.

The doctors decided it was a combination of prenatal brain damage and dyslexia, a complicated learning disability that is a fashionable problem with children in New Orleans.

Letty felt like she spent half her life sitting in offices talking to people about Helen. The office she sat in most often belonged to Dr. Zander. She sat there twisting her rings and avoiding looking at the box of Kleenex on Dr. Zander's desk. It made her feel like she was sleeping in a dirty bed even to think of plucking a Kleenex from Dr. Zander's container and crying in a place where strangers cried. She imagined his chair was filled all day with women weeping over terrible and sordid things like their husbands running off with their secretaries or their children not getting into the right clubs and colleges.

"I don't know what we're going to do with her next," Letty said. "If we let them hold her back a grade it's just going to make her more self-conscious than ever."

"I wish we knew about her genetic background. You people have pull with the sisters. Can't you find out?"

"Tom doesn't want to find out. He says we'll just be opening a can of worms. He gets embarrassed even talking about Helen's problem."

"Well," said Dr. Zander, crossing his short legs and setting his steel-rimmed glasses on his nose like a tiny bicycle stuck on a hill, "let's start her on Dexedrine."

So Letty and Dr. Zander and Dr. Mullins and Dr. Pickett and Dr. Smith decided to try an experiment. They decided to give Helen five milligrams of Dexedrine every day for twenty days each month, taking her off the drug for ten days in between.

"Children with dyslexia react to drugs strangely," Dr. Zander said. "If you give them tranquilizers it peps them up, but if you give them Ritalin or Dexedrine it calms them down and makes them able to think straight."

"You may have to keep her home and have her tutored on the days she is off the drug," he continued, "but the rest of the time she should be easier to live with." And he reached over and patted Letty on the leg and for a moment she thought it might all turn out all right after all.

Helen stood by herself on the playground of the beautiful old pink-brick convent with its drooping wrought-iron balconies covered with ficus. She was watching the girl she liked talking with some other girls who were playing jacks. All the little girls wore blue-and-red-plaid skirts and navy blazers or sweaters. They looked like a disorderly marching band. Helen was waiting for the girl, whose name was Lisa, to decide if she wanted to go home with her after school and spend the afternoon. Lisa's mother was divorced and worked downtown in a department store, so Lisa rode the streetcar back and forth from school and could go anywhere she liked until 5:30 in the afternoon. Sometimes she went home with Helen so she wouldn't have to ride the streetcar. Then Helen would be so excited the hours until school let out would seem to last forever.

Sometimes Lisa liked her and wanted to go home with her and other times she didn't, but she was always nice to Helen and let her stand next to her in lines.

Helen watched Lisa walking toward her. Lisa's skirt was two inches shorter than those of any of the other girls, and she wore high white socks that made her look like a skater. She wore a silver identification bracelet and Revlon nail polish.

"I'll go home with you if you get your mother to take us to get an Icee," Lisa said. "I was going last night but my mother's boyfriend didn't show up until after the place closed so I was going to walk to Manny's after school. Is that O.K.?"

"I think she will," Helen said, her eyes shining. "I'll go call her up and see."

"Naw, let's just go swing. We can ask her when she comes." Then Helen walked with her friend over to the swings and tried to be patient waiting for her turn.

The Dexedrine helped Helen concentrate and it helped her get along better with other people, but it seemed to have an unusual side effect. Helen was chubby and Dr. Zander had led the Wilsons to believe the drug would help her lose weight, but instead she grew even fatter. The Wilsons were afraid to force her to stop eating for fear they would make her nervous, so they tried to reason with her.

"Why can't I have any ice cream?" she would say. "Daddy is fat and he eats all the ice cream he wants." She was leaning up against Letty, stroking her arm and petting the baby with her other hand. They were in an upstairs sitting room with the afternoon sun streaming in through the French windows. Everything in the room was decorated with different shades of blue, and the curtains were white with old-fashioned blue-and-white-checked ruffles.

"You can have ice cream this evening after dinner," Letty said. "I just want you to wait a few hours before you have it. Won't you do that for me?"

"Can I hold the baby for a while?" Helen asked, and Letty allowed her to sit in the rocker and hold the baby and rock it furiously back and forth crooning to it.

"Is Jennifer beautiful, Mother?" Helen asked.

"She's O.K., but she doesn't have curly black hair like you. She just has plain brown hair. Don't you see, Helen, that's why we want you to stop eating between meals, because you're so pretty and we don't want you to get too fat. Why don't you go outside and play with Tim and not try to think about ice cream so much?"

"I don't care," Helen said, "I'm only nine years old and I'm hungry. I want you to tell the maids to give me some ice cream now," and she handed the baby to her mother and ran out of the room.

The Wilsons were rich in maids, and that was a good thing because there were all those children to be taken care of and cooked for and cleaned up after. The maids didn't mind taking care of the Wilson children all day. The Wilsons' house was much more comfortable than the ones they lived in, and no one cared whether they worked very hard or not as long as they showed up on time so Letty could get to her meetings. The maids left their own children with relatives or at home watching television, and when they went home at night they liked them much better than if they had spent the whole day with them.

The Wilson house had a wide white porch across the front and down both sides. It was shaded by enormous oak trees and furnished with swings and wicker rockers. In the afternoons the maids would sit on the porch and other maids from around the neighborhood would come up pushing prams and strollers and the children would all play together on the porch and in the yard. Sometimes the maids fixed lemonade and the children would sell it to passersby from a little stand.

The maids hated Helen. They didn't care whether she had dyslexia or not. All they knew was that she was a lot of trouble to take care of. One minute she would be as sweet as pie and cuddle up to them and say she loved them and the next minute she wouldn't do anything they told her.

"You're a nigger, nigger, nigger, and my mother said I could cross St. Charles Avenue if I wanted to," Helen would say, and the maids would hold their lips together and look into each other's eyes.

One afternoon the Wilson children and their maids were sitting on the porch after school with some of the neighbors' children and maids. The baby was on the porch in a bassinet on wheels and a new maid was looking out for her. Helen was in the biggest swing and was swinging as high as she could go so that none of the other children could get in the swing with her.

"Helen," the new maid said, "it's Tim's turn in the swing. You been swinging for fifteen minutes while Tim's been waiting. You be a good girl now and let Tim have a turn. You too big to act like that."

"You're just a high yeller nigger," Helen called, "and you can't make me do anything." And she swung up higher and higher.

This maid had never had Helen call her names before and she had a quick temper and didn't put up with children calling her a nigger. She walked over to the swing and grabbed the chain and stopped it from moving.

"You say you're sorry for that, little fat honky white girl," she said, and made as if to grab Helen by the arms, but Helen got away and started running, calling over her shoulder, "Nigger, can't make me do anything."

She was running and looking over her shoulder and she hit the bassinet and it went rolling down the brick stairs so fast none of the maids or children could stop it. It rolled down the stairs and threw the baby onto the sidewalk and the blood from the baby's head began to move all over the concrete like a little ruby lake.

The Wilsons' house was on Philip Street, a street so rich it even had its own drugstore. Not some tacky chain drugstore with everything on special all the time, but a cute drugstore made out of a frame bungalow with gingerbread trim. Everything inside cost twice as much as it did in a regular drugstore, and the grown people could order any kind of drugs they needed and a green Mazda pickup would bring them right over. The children had to get their drugs from a fourteen-year-old pusher in Audubon Park named Leroi, but they could get all the ice cream and candy and chewing gum they wanted from the drugstore and charge it to their parents.

No white adults were at home in the houses where the maids worked so they sent the children running to the drugstore to bring the druggist to help with the baby. They called the hospital and ordered an ambulance and they called several doctors and they called Tom's bank. All the children who were old enough ran to the drugstore except Helen. Helen sat on the porch steps staring down at the baby with the maids hovering over it like swans, and she was crying and screaming and beating her hands against her head. She was in one of the periods when she couldn't have Dexedrine. She screamed and screamed, but none of the maids had time to help her. They were too busy with the baby.

"Shut up, Helen," one of the maids called. "Shut up that goddamn screaming. This baby is about to die."

A police car and the local patrol service drove up. An ambulance arrived and the yard filled with people. The druggist and one of the maids rode off in the ambulance with the baby. The crowd in the yard swarmed and milled and swam before Helen's eyes like a parade.

Finally they stopped looking like people and just looked like spots of color on the yard. Helen ran up the stairs and climbed under her cherry four-poster bed and pulled her pillows and her eiderdown comforter under it with her. There were cereal boxes and an empty ice cream carton and half a tin of English cookies under the headboard. Helen was soaked with sweat and her little Lily playsuit was tight under the arms and cut into her flesh. Helen rolled up in the comforter and began to dream the dream of the heavy clouds. She dreamed she was praying, but the beads of the rosary slipped through her fingers so quickly she couldn't catch them and it was cold in the church and beautiful and fragrant, then dark, then light, and Helen was rolling in the heavy clouds that rolled her like biscuit dough. Just as she was about to suffocate they rolled her face up to the blue air above the clouds. Then Helen was a pink kite floating above the houses at evening. In the yards children were playing and fathers were driving up and baseball games were beginning and the sky turned gray and closed upon the city like a lid.

And now the baby is alone with Helen in her room and the door is locked and Helen ties the baby to the table so it won't fall off.

"Hold still, Baby, this will just be a little shot. This won't hurt much. This won't take a minute." And the baby is still and Helen begins to work on it.

Letty knelt down beside the bed. "Helen, please come out from under there. No one is mad at you. Please come out and help me, Helen. I need you to help me."

Helen held on tighter to the slats of the bed and squeezed her eyes shut and refused to look at Letty.

Letty climbed under the bed to touch the child. Letty was crying and her heart had an anchor in it that kept digging in and sinking deeper and deeper.

Dr. Zander came into the bedroom and knelt beside the bed and began to talk to Helen. Finally he gave up being reasonable and wiggled his small gray-suited body under the bed and Helen was lost in the area of arms that tried to hold her.

Tom was sitting in the bank president's office trying not to let Mr. Saunders know how much he despised him or how much it hurt and mattered to him to be listening to a lecture. Tom thought he was too old to have listen to lectures. He was tired and he wanted a drink and he wanted to punch the bastard in the face.

"I know, I know," he answered, "I can take care of it. Just give me a month or two. You're right. I'll take care of it."

And he smoothed the pants of his cord suit and waited for the rest of the lecture.

A man came into the room without knocking. Tom's secretary was behind him.

"Tom, I think your baby has had an accident. I don't know any details. Look, I've called for a car. Let me go with you."

Tom ran up the steps of his house and into the hallway full of neighbors and relatives. A girl in a tennis dress touched him on the arm, someone handed him a drink. He ran up the winding stairs to Helen's room. He stood in the doorway. He could see Letty's shoes sticking out from under the bed. He could hear Dr. Zander talking. He couldn't go near them.

"Letty," he called, "Letty, come here, my god, come out from there."

No one came to the funeral but the family. Letty wore a plain dress she would wear any day and the children all wore their school clothes.

The funeral was terrible for the Wilsons, but afterward they went home and all the people from the Garden District and from all over town started coming over to cheer them up. It looked like the biggest cocktail party ever held in New Orleans. It took four rented butlers just to serve the drinks. Everyone wanted to get in on the Wilsons' tragedy.

In the months that followed the funeral Tom began to have sinus headaches for the first time in years. He was drinking a lot and smoking again. He was allergic to whiskey, and when he woke up in the morning his nose and head were so full of phlegm he had to vomit before he could think straight.

He began to have trouble with his vision.

One November day the high yellow windows of the Shell Oil Building all turned their eyes upon him as he stopped at the corner of Poydras and Carondelet to wait for a streetlight, and he had to pull the car over to a curb and talk to himself for several minutes before he could drive on.

He got back all the keys to his apartment so he could go there and be alone and think. One afternoon he left work at two o'clock and drove around Jefferson Parish all afternoon drinking Scotch and eating potato chips.

Not as many people at the bank wanted to go out to lunch with him anymore. They were sick and tired of pretending his expensive mistakes were jokes.

One night Tom was gambling at the Pickwick Club with a poker group and a man jokingly accused him of cheating. Tom jumped up from the table, grabbed the man and began hitting him with his fists. He hit the man in the mouth and knocked out his new gold inlays.

"You dirty little goddamn bond peddler, you son of a bitch! I'll kill you for that," Tom yelled, and it took four waiters to hold him while the terrified man made his escape. The next morning Tom resigned from the club.

He started riding the streetcar downtown to work so he wouldn't have to worry about driving his car home if he got drunk. He was worrying about money and he was worrying about his gambling debts, but most of the time he was thinking about Helen. She looked so much like him that he believed people would think she was his illegitimate child. The more he tried to talk himself into believing the baby's death was an accident, the more obstinate his mind became.

The Wilson children were forbidden to take the Labs out of the kennels without permission. One afternoon Tom came home earlier than usual and found Helen sitting in the open door of one of the kennels playing with a half-grown litter of puppies. She was holding one of the puppies and the others were climbing all around her and spilling out onto the grass. She held the puppy by its forelegs, making it dance in the air, then letting it drop. Then she would gather it in her arms and hold it tight and sing to it.

Tom walked over to the kennel and grabbed her by an arm and began to paddle her as hard as he could.

"Goddamn you, what are you trying to do? You know you aren't supposed to touch those dogs. What in the hell do you think you're doing?"

Helen was too terrified to scream. The Wilsons never spanked their children for anything.

"I didn't do anything to it. I was playing with it," she sobbed.

Letty and the twins came running out of the house and when Tom saw Letty he stopped hitting Helen and walked in through the kitchen door and up the stairs to the bedroom. Letty gave the children to the cook and followed him.

Tom stood by the bedroom window trying to think of something to say to Letty. He kept his back turned to her and he was making a nickel disappear with his left hand. He thought of himself at Tommie Keenen's birthday party wearing his black coat and hat and doing his famous rope trick. Mr. Keenen had given him fifteen dollars. He remembered sticking the money in his billfold.

"My god, Letty, I'm sorry. I don't know what the shit's going on. I thought she was hurting the dog. I know I shouldn't have hit her and there's something I need to tell you about the bank. Kennington is getting sacked. I may be part of the housecleaning."

"Why didn't you tell me before? Can't Daddy do anything?"

"I don't want him to do anything. Even if it happens it doesn't have anything to do with me. It's just bank politics. We'll say I quit. I want to get out of there anyway. That fucking place is driving me crazy."

Tom put the nickel in his pocket and closed the bedroom door. He could hear the maid down the hall comforting Helen. He didn't give a fuck if she cried all night. He walked over to Letty and put his arms around her. He smelled like he'd been drinking for a week. He reached under her dress and pulled down her pantyhose and her underpants and began kissing her face and hair while she stood awkwardly with the pants and hose around her feet like a halter. She was trying to cooperate.

She forgot that Tom smelled like sweat and whiskey. She was thinking about the night they were married. Every time they made love Letty pretended it was that night. She had spent thousands of nights in a bridal suite at the Sherry Netherland Hotel in New York City.

Letty lay on the walnut bed leaning into a pile of satin pillows and twisting a gold bracelet around her wrist. She could hear the children playing outside. She had a headache and her stomach was queasy, but she was afraid to take a Valium or an aspirin. She was waiting for the doctor to call her back and tell her if she was pregnant. She already knew what he was going to say.

Tom came into the room and sat by her on the bed.

"What's wrong?"

"Nothing's wrong. Please don't do that. I'm tired."

"Something's wrong."

"Nothing's wrong. Tom, please leave me alone."

Tom walked out through the French windows and onto a little balcony that overlooked the play yard and the dog runs. Sunshine flooded Philip Street, covering the houses and trees and dogs and children with a million volts a minute. It flowed down to hide in the roots of trees, glistening on the cars, baking the street, and lighting Helen's rumpled hair where she stooped over the puppy. She was singing a little song. She had made up the song she was singing.

"The baby's dead. The baby's dead. The baby's gone to heaven."

"Jesus God," Tom muttered. All up and down Philip Street fathers were returning home from work. A jeep filled with teenagers came tearing past and threw a beer can against the curb.

Six or seven pieces of Tom's mind sailed out across the street and stationed themselves along the power line that zigzagged back and forth along Philip Street between the live oak trees.

The pieces of his mind sat upon the power line like a row of black starlings. They looked him over.

Helen took the dog out of the buggy and dragged it over to the kennel.

"Jesus Christ," Tom said, and the pieces of his mind flew back to him as swiftly as they had flown away and entered his eyes and ears and nostrils and arranged themselves in their proper places like parts of a phrenological head.

Tom looked at his watch. It said 6:15. He stepped back into the bedroom and closed the French windows. A vase of huge roses from the garden hid Letty's reflection in the mirror.

"I'm going to the camp for the night. I need to get away. Besides, the season's almost over."

"All right," Letty answered. "Who are you going with?"

"I think I'll take Helen with me. I haven't paid any attention to her for weeks."

"That's good," Letty said, "I really think I'm getting a cold. I'll have a tray up for supper and try to get some sleep."

Tom moved around the room, opening drawers and closets and throwing some gear into a canvas duffel bag. He changed into his hunting clothes.

He removed the guns he needed from a shelf in the upstairs den and cleaned them neatly and thoroughly and zipped them into their carriers.

"Helen," he called from the downstairs porch. "Bring the dog in the house and come get on some play clothes. I'm going to take you to the duck camp with me. You can take the dog."

"Can we stop and get beignets?" Helen called back, coming running at the invitation.

"Sure we can, honey. Whatever you like. Go get packed. We'll leave as soon as dinner is over."

It was past 9:00 at night. They crossed the Mississippi River from the New Orleans side on the last ferry going to Algier's Point. There was an offshore breeze and a light rain fell on the old brown river. The Mississippi River smelled like the inside of a nigger cabin, powerful and fecund. The smell came in Tom's mouth until he felt he could chew it.

He leaned over the railing and vomited. He felt better and walked back to the red Chevrolet pickup he had given himself for a birthday present. He thought it was chic for a banker to own a pickup.

Helen was playing with the dog, pushing him off the seat and laughing when he climbed back on her lap. She had a paper bag of doughnuts from the French Market and was eating them and licking the powdered sugar from her fingers and knocking the dog off the seat.

She wasn't the least bit sleepy.

"I'm glad Tim didn't get to go. Tim was bad at school, that's why he had to stay home, isn't it? The sisters called Momma. I don't like Tim. I'm glad I got to go by myself." She stuck her fat arms out the window and rubbed Tom's canvas hunting jacket. "This coat feels hard. It's all dirty. Can we go up in the cabin and talk to the pilot?"

"Sit still, Helen."

"Put the dog in the back, he's bothering me." She bounced up and down on the seat. "We're going to the duck camp. We're going to the duck camp."

The ferry docked. Tom drove the pickup onto the blacktop road past the city dump and on into Plaquemines Parish.

They drove into the brackish marshes that fringe the Gulf of Mexico where it extends in ragged fingers along the coast below and to the east of New Orleans. As they drove closer to the sea the hardwoods turned to palmetto and water oak and willow.

The marshes were silent. Tom could smell the glasswort and black mangrove, the oyster and shrimp boats.

He wondered if it were true that children and dogs could penetrate a man's concealment, could know him utterly.

Helen leaned against his coat and prattled on.

In the Wilson house on Philip Street Tim and the twins were cuddled up by Letty, hearing one last story before they went to bed.

A blue wicker tray held the remains of the children's hot chocolate. The china cups were a confirmation present sent to Letty from Limoges, France.

Now she was finishing reading a wonderful story by Ludwig Bemelmans about a little convent girl in Paris named Madeline who reforms the son of the Spanish ambassador, putting an end to his terrible habit of beheading chickens on a miniature guillotine.

Letty was feeling better. She had decided God was just trying to make up to her for Jennifer.

The camp was a three-room wooden shack built on pilings out over Bayou Lafouche, which runs through the middle of the parish.

The inside of the camp was casually furnished with old leather office furniture, hand-me-down tables and lamps, and a walnut poker table from Neiman-Marcus. Photographs of hunts and parties were tacked around the walls. Over the poker table were pictures of racehorses and their owners and an assortment of ribbons won in races.

Tom laid the guns down on the bar and opened a cabinet over the sink in the part of the room that served as a kitchen. The nigger hadn't come to clean up after the last party and the sink was piled with half-washed dishes. He found a clean glass and a bottle of Tanqueray gin and sat down behind the bar.

Helen was across the room on the floor finishing the beignets and trying to coax the dog to come closer. He was considering it. No one had remembered to feed him.

Tom pulled a new deck of cards out of a drawer, broke the seal, and began to shuffle them.

Helen came and stood by the bar. "Show me a trick, Daddy. Make the queen disappear. Show me how to do it."

"Do you promise not to tell anyone the secret? A magician never tells his secrets."

"I won't tell. Daddy, please show me, show me now."

Tom spread out the cards. He began to explain the trick.

"All right, you go here and here, then here. Then pick up these in just the right order, but look at the people while you do it, not at the cards."

"I'm going to do it for Lisa."

"She's going to beg you to tell the secret. What will you do then?"

"I'll tell her a magician never tells his secrets."

Tom drank the gin and poured some more.

"Now let me do it to you, Daddy."

"Not yet, Helen. Go sit over there with the dog and practice it where I can't see what you're doing. I'll pretend I'm Lisa and don't know what's going on."

Tom picked up the Kliengunther 7 mm. magnum rifle and shot the dog first, splattering its brains all over the door and walls. Without pausing, without giving her time to raise her eyes from the red and gray and black rainbow of the dog, he shot the little girl.

The bullet entered her head from the back. Her thick body rolled across the hardwood floor and lodged against a hat rack from Jody Mellon's old office in the Hibernia Bank Building. One of her arms landed on a pile of old *Penthouse* magazines and her disordered brain flung its roses north and east and south and west and rejoined the order from which it casually arose.

Tom put down the rifle, took a drink of the thick gin, and, carrying the pistol, walked out onto the pier through the kitchen door. Without removing his glasses or his hunting cap he stuck the .38 Smith and Wesson revolver against his palate and splattered his own head all over the new pier and the canvas covering of the Boston Whaler. His body struck the boat going down and landed in eight feet of water beside a broken crab trap left over from the summer.

A pair of deputies from the Plaquemines Parish sheriff's office found the bodies.

Everyone believed it was some terrible inexplicable mistake or accident.

No one believed that much bad luck could happen to a nice lady like Letty Dufrechou Wilson, who never hurt a flea or gave anyone a minute's trouble in her life.

No one believed that much bad luck could get together between the fifteenth week after Pentecost and the third week in Advent.

No one believed a man would kill his own little illegitimate dyslexic daughter just because she was crazy.

And no one, not even the district attorney of New Orleans, wanted to believe a man would shoot a $3,000 Labrador retriever sired by Super Chief out of Prestidigitation.

In the Land of Dreamy Dreams

On the third of May, 1977, LaGrande McGruder drove out onto the Huey P. Long Bridge, dropped two Davis Classics and a gut-strung PDP tournament racket into the Mississippi River, and quit playing tennis forever.

"That was it," she said. "That was the last goddamn straw." She heaved a sigh, thinking this must be what it feels like to die, to be through with something that was more trouble than it was worth.

As long as she could remember LaGrande had been playing tennis four or five hours a day whenever it wasn't raining or she didn't have a funeral to attend. In her father's law office was a whole cabinet full of her trophies.

After the rackets sank LaGrande dumped a can of brand new Slazenger tennis balls into the river and stood for a long time watching the cheerful, little, yellow constellation form and re-form in the muddy current.

"Jesus Fucking A Christ," she said to herself. "Oh, well," she added, "maybe now I can get my arms to be the same size for the first time in my life."

LaGrande leaned into the bridge railing, staring past the white circles on her wrists, souvenirs of twenty years of wearing sweatbands in the fierce New Orleans sunlight, and on down to the river where the little yellow constellation was overtaking a barge.

"That goddamn little new-rich Yankee bitch," she said, kicking the bridge with her leather Tretorns.

There was no denying it. There was no undoing it. At ten o'clock that morning LaGrande McGruder, whose grandfather had been president of the United States Lawn Tennis Association, had cheated a crippled girl out of a tennis match, had deliberately and without hesitation made a bad call in the last point of a crucial game, had defended the call against loud protests, taken a big drink of her Gatorade, and proceeded to win the next twelve games while her opponent reeled with disbelief at being done out of her victory.

At exactly three minutes after ten that morning she had looked across the net at the impassive face of the interloper who was about to humiliate her at her own tennis club and she had changed her mind about honor quicker than the speed of light. "Out," she had said, not giving a damn whether the serve was in or out. "Nice try."

"It couldn't be out," the crippled girl said. "Are you sure?"

"Of course I'm sure," LaGrande said. "I wouldn't have called it unless I was sure."

"Are you positive?" the crippled girl said.

"For God's sake," LaGrande said, "look, if you don't mind, let's hurry up and get this over with. I have to be at the country club for lunch." That ought to get her, LaGrande thought. At least they don't let Jews into the country club yet. At least that's still sacred.

"Serving," the crippled girl said, trying to control her rage.

LaGrande took her position at the back of the court, reached up to adjust her visor, and caught the eye of old Claiborne Redding, who was sitting on the second-floor balcony watching the match. He smiled and waved. How long has he been standing there, LaGrande wondered. How long has that old fart been watching me? But she was too busy to worry about Claiborne now. She had a tennis match to save, and she was going to save it if it was the last thing she ever did in her life.

The crippled girl set her mouth into a tight line and prepared to serve into the forehand court. Her name was Roxanne Miller, and she had traveled a long way to this morning's fury. She had spent thousands of dollars on private tennis lessons, hundreds of dollars on equipment, and untold time and energy giving cocktail parties and dinner parties for the entrenched players who one by one she had courted and blackmailed and finagled into giving her matches and return matches until finally one day she would catch them at a weak moment and defeat them. She kept a mental list of such victories. Sometimes when she went to bed at night she would pull the pillows over her head and lie there imagining herself as a sort of Greek figure of justice, sitting on a marble chair in the clouds, holding a scroll, a little parable of conquest and revenge.

It had taken Roxanne five years to fight and claw and worm her way into the ranks of respected Lawn Tennis Club Ladies. For five years she had dragged her bad foot around the carefully manicured courts of the oldest and snottiest tennis club in the United States of America.

For months now her ambitions had centered around LaGrande. A victory over LaGrande would mean she had arrived in the top echelons of the Lawn Tennis Club Ladies.

A victory over LaGrande would surely be followed by invitations to play in the top doubles games, perhaps even in the famous Thursday foursome that played on Rena Clark's private tennis court. Who knows, Roxanne dreamed, LaGrande might even ask her to be her doubles partner. LaGrande's old doubles partners were always retiring to have babies.

At any moment she might need a new one. Roxanne would be there waiting, the indefatigable handicapped wonder of the New Orleans tennis world.

She had envisioned this morning's victory a thousand times, had seen herself walking up to the net to shake LaGrande's hand, had planned her little speech of condolence, after which the two of them would go into the snack bar for lunch and have a heart-to-heart talk about rackets and balls and backhands and forehands and volleys and lobs.

Roxanne basked in her dreams. It did not bother her that LaGrande never returned her phone calls, avoided her at the club, made vacant replies to her requests for matches. Roxanne had plenty of time. She could wait. Sooner or later she would catch LaGrande in a weak moment.

That moment came at the club's 100th Anniversary Celebration. Everyone was drunk and full of camaraderie. The old members were all on their best behavior, trying to be extra nice to the new members and pretend like the new members were just as good as they were even if they didn't belong to the Boston Club or the Southern Yacht Club or Comus or Momus or Proteus.

Roxanne cornered LaGrande while she was talking to a famous psychiatrist-player from Washington, a bachelor who was much adored in tennis circles for his wit and political connections.

LaGrande was trying to impress him with how sane she was and hated to let him see her irritation when Roxanne moved in on them.

"When are you going to give me that match you promised me?" Roxanne asked, looking wistful, as if this were something the two of them had been discussing for years.

"I don't know," LaGrande said. "I guess I just stay so busy. This is Semmes Talbot, from Washington. This is Roxanne, Semmes. I'm sorry. I can't remember your last name. You'll have to help me."

"Miller," Roxanne said. "My name is Miller. Really now, when will you play with me?"

"Well, how about Monday?" LaGrande heard herself saying. "I guess I could do it Monday. My doubles game was canceled." She looked up at the doctor to see if he appreciated how charming she was to everyone, no matter who they were.

"Fine," Roxanne said. "Monday's fine. I'll be here at nine. I'll be counting on it so don't let me down." She laughed. "I thought you'd never say yes. I was beginning to think you were afraid I'd beat you."

"Oh, my goodness," LaGrande said, "anyone can beat me, I don't take tennis very seriously anymore, you know. I just play enough to keep my hand in."

"Who was that?" Semmes asked when Roxanne left them. "She certainly has her nerve!"

"She's one of the new members," LaGrande said. "I really try so hard not to be snotty about them. I really do believe that every human being is just as valuable as everyone else, don't you? And it doesn't matter a bit to me what anyone's background is, but some of the new people are sort of hard to take. They're so, oh, well, so *eager.*"

Semmes looked down the front of her silk blouse and laughed happily into her aristocratic eyes. "Well, watch out for that one," he said. "There's no reason for anyone as pretty as you to let people make you uncomfortable."

Across the room Roxanne collected Willie and got ready to leave the party. She was on her way home to begin training for the match.

Willie was glad to leave. He didn't like hanging around places where he wasn't wanted. He couldn't imagine why Roxanne wanted to spend all her time playing tennis with a bunch of snotty people.

Roxanne and Willie were new members. Willie's brand-new 15 million dollars and the New Orleans Lawn Tennis Club's brand new $700,000 dollar mortgage had met at a point in history, and Willie's application for membership had been approved by the board and railroaded past the watchful noses of old Claiborne Redding and his buddies. Until then the only Jewish member of the club had been a globe-trotting Jewish bachelor who knew his wines, entertained lavishly at Antoine's, and had the courtesy to stay in Europe most of the time.

Willie and Roxanne were something else again. "What in the hell are we going to do with a guy who sells ties and a crippled woman who runs around Audubon Park all day in a pair of tennis shorts," Claiborne said, pulling on a pair of the thick white Australian wool socks he wore to play in. The committee had cornered him in the locker room.

"The membership's not for him," they said. "He doesn't even play. You'll never see him. And she really isn't a cripple. One leg is a little bit shorter than the other one, that's all."

"I don't know," Claiborne said. "Not just Jews, for God's sake, but Yankee Jews to boot."

"The company's listed on the American Stock Exchange, Claiborne. It was selling at 16½ this morning, up from 5. And he buys his insurance from me. Come on, you'll never see them. All she's going to do is play a little tennis with the ladies."

Old Claiborne rued the day he had let himself be talked into Roxanne and Willie. The club had been forced to take in thirty new families to pay for its new building and some of them were Jews, but, as Claiborne was fond of saying, at least the rest of them tried to act like white people.

Roxanne was something else. It seemed to him that she lived at the club. The only person who hung around the club more than Roxanne was old Claiborne himself. Pretty soon she was running the place. She wrote *The Lawn Tennis Newsletter.* She circulated petitions to change the all-white dress rule. She campaigned for more court privileges for women. She dashed in and out of the bar and the dining room making plans with the waiters and chefs for Mixed Doubles Nights, Round Robin Galas, Benefit Children's Jamborees, Saturday Night Luaus.

Claiborne felt like his club was being turned into a cruise ship.

On top of everything else Roxanne was always trying to get in good with Claiborne. Every time he settled down on the balcony to watch a match she came around trying to talk to him, talking while the match was going on, remembering the names of his grandchildren, complimenting him on their serves and backhands and footwork, taking every conceivable liberty, as if at any moment she might start showing up at their weddings and debuts.

Claiborne thought about Roxanne a lot. He was thinking about her this morning when he arrived at the club and saw her cream-colored Rolls-Royce blocking his view of the Garth Humphries Memorial Plaque. He was thinking about her as he got a cup of coffee from a stand the ladies had taken to setting up by the sign-in board. This was some more of her meddling, he thought, percolated coffee in Styrofoam cups with plastic spoons and some kind of powder instead of cream.

At the old clubhouse waiters had brought steaming cups of thick chicory-flavored café au lait out onto the balcony with cream and sugar in silver servers.

Claiborne heaved a sigh, pulled his pants out of his crotch, and went up to the balcony to see what the morning would bring.

He had hardly reached the top of the stairs when he saw Roxanne leading LaGrande to a deserted court at the end of the property. My God in Heaven, he thought, how did she pull that off? How in the name of God did she get hold of Leland's daughter.

Leland McGruder had been Claiborne's doubles partner in their youth. Together they had known victory and defeat in New Orleans and Jackson and Monroe and Shreveport and Mobile and Atlanta and as far away as Forest Hills during one never to be forgotten year when they had thrown their rackets into a red Ford and gone off together on the tour.

Down on the court LaGrande was so aggravated she could barely be civil. How did I end up here, she thought, playing second-class tennis against anyone who corners me at a party.

LaGrande was in a bad mood all around. The psychiatrist had squired her around all weekend, fucked her dispassionately in someone's *garçon-*

nière, and gone back to Washington without making further plans to see her.

She bounced a ball up and down a few times with her racket, thinking about a line of poetry that kept occurring to her lately whenever she played tennis. "Their only monument the asphalt road, and a thousand lost golf balls."

"Are you coming to Ladies Day on Wednesday?" Roxanne was saying, "we're going to have a great time. You really ought to come. We've got a real clown coming to give out helium balloons, and we're going to photograph the winners sitting on his lap for the newsletter. Isn't that a cute idea?"

"I'm afraid I'm busy Wednesday," LaGrande said, imagining balloons flying all over the courts when the serious players arrived for their noon games. "Look," she said, "let's go on and get started. I can't stay too long."

They set down their pitchers of Gatorade, put on their visors and sweatbands, sprayed a little powdered resin on their hands, and walked out to their respective sides of the court.

Before they hit the ball four times LaGrande knew something was wrong. The woman wasn't going to warm her up! LaGrande had hit her three nice long smooth balls and each time Roxanne moved up to the net and put the ball away on the sidelines.

"How about hitting me some forehands," LaGrande said. "I haven't played in a week. I need to warm up."

"I'll try," Roxanne said, "I have to play most of my game at the net, you know, because of my leg."

"Well, stay back there and hit me some to warm up with," LaGrande said, but Roxanne went right on putting her shots away with an assortment of tricks that looked more like a circus act than a tennis game.

"Are you ready to play yet?" she asked. "I'd like to get started before I get too tired."

"Sure," LaGrande said. "Go ahead, you serve first. There's no reason to spin a racket over a fun match." Oh, well, she thought, I'll just go ahead and slaughter her. Of course, I won't lob over her head, I don't suppose anyone does that to her.

Roxanne pulled the first ball out of her pants. She had a disconcerting habit of sticking the extra ball up the leg of her tights instead of keeping it in a pocket. She pulled the ball out of her pants, tossed it expertly up into the air, and served an ace to LaGrande's extreme backhand service corner.

"Nice serve," LaGrande said. Oh, well, she thought, everyone gets one off occasionally. Let her go on and get overconfident. Then I can get this over in a hurry.

They changed courts for the second serve. Roxanne hit short into the backhand court. LaGrande raced up and hit a forehand right into Roxanne's waiting racket. The ball dropped neatly into a corner and the score was 30-love.

How in the shit did she get to the net so fast, LaGrande thought. Well, I'll have to watch out for that. I thought she was supposed to be crippled.

Roxanne served again, winning the point with a short spinning forehand. Before LaGrande could gather her wits about her she had lost the first game.

Things went badly with her serve and she lost the second game. While she was still recovering from that she lost the third game. Calm down, she told herself. Get hold of yourself. Keep your eye on the ball. Anticipate her moves. It's only because I didn't have a chance to warm up. I'll get going in a minute.

Old Claiborne stood watching the match from a secluded spot near the door to the dining room, watching it with his heart in his throat, not daring to move any farther out onto the balcony for fear he might distract LaGrande and make things worse.

Why doesn't she lob, Claiborne thought. Why in the name of God doesn't she lob? Maybe she thinks she shouldn't do it just because one of that woman's legs is a little bit shorter than the other.

He stood squeezing the Styrofoam cup in his hand. A small hole had developed in the side, and drops of coffee were making a little track down the side of his Fred Perry flannels, but he was oblivious to everything but the action on the court.

He didn't even notice when Nailor came up behind him. Nailor was a haughty old black man who had been with the club since he was a young boy and now was the chief groundskeeper and arbiter of manners among the hired help.

Nailor had spent his life tending Rubico tennis courts without once having the desire to pick up a racket. But he had watched thousands of tennis matches and he knew more about tennis than most players did.

He knew how the little fields of energy that surround men and women move and coalesce and strike and fend off and retreat and attack and conquer. That was what he looked for when he watched tennis. He wasn't interested in the details.

If it was up to Nailor no one but a few select players would ever be allowed to set foot on his Rubico courts. The only time of day when he was really at peace was the half hour from when he finished the courts around 7:15 each morning until they opened the iron gates at 7:45 and the members started arriving.

Nailor had known LaGrande since she came to her father's matches in a perambulator. He had lusted after her ass ever since she got her first white tennis skirt and her first Wilson autograph racket. He had been the first black man to wax her first baby-blue convertible, and he had been taking care of her cars ever since.

Nailor moonlighted at the club polishing cars with a special wax he had invented.

Nailor hated the new members worse than Claiborne did. Ever since the club had moved to its new quarters and they had come crowding in bringing their children and leaving their paper cups all over the courts he had been thinking of retiring.

Now he was watching one of them taking his favorite little missy to the cleaners. She's getting her little booty whipped for sure this morning, he thought. She can't find a place to turn and make a stand. She don't know where to start to stop it. She's got hind teat today whether she likes it or not and I'm glad her daddy's not here to watch it.

Claiborne was oblivious to Nailor. He was trying to decide who would benefit most if he made a show of walking out to the balcony and taking a seat.

He took a chance. He waited until LaGrande's back was to him, then walked out just as Roxanne was receiving serve.

LaGrande made a small rally and won her service, but Roxanne took the next three games for the set. "I don't need to rest between sets unless you do," she said, walking up to the net. "We really haven't been playing that long. I really don't know why I'm playing so well. I guess I'm just lucky today."

"I just guess you are," LaGrande said. "Sure, let's go right on. I've got a date for lunch." Now I'll take her, she thought. Now I'm tired of being polite. Now I'm going to beat the shit out of her.

Roxanne picked up a ball, tossed it into the air, and served another ace into the backhand corner of the forehand court.

Jesus Fucking A Christ, LaGrande thought. She did it again. Where in the name of God did that little Jewish housewife learn that shot.

LaGrande returned the next serve with a lob. Roxanne ran back, caught it on the edge of her racket and dribbled it over the net.

Now LaGrande lost all powers of reason. She began trying to kill the ball on every shot. Before she could get hold of herself she had lost three games, then four, then five, then she was only one game away from losing the match, then only one point.

This is it, LaGrande thought. Armageddon.

Roxanne picked up the balls and served the first one out. She slowed herself down, took a deep breath, tossed up the second ball and shot a clean forehand into the service box.

"Out," LaGrande said. "Nice try."

"It couldn't be out," Roxanne said, "are you sure?"

"Of course I'm sure," LaGrande said. "*I wouldn't have called it unless I was sure.*"

Up on the balcony Old Claiborne's heart was opening and closing like a geisha's fan. He caught LaGrande's eye, smiled and waved, and, turning around, realized that Nailor was standing behind him.

"Morning, Mr. Claiborne," Nailor said, leaning politely across him to pick up the cup. "Looks like Mr. Leland's baby's having herself a hard time this morning. Let me bring you something nice to drink while you watch."

Claiborne sent him for coffee and settled back in the chair to watch LaGrande finish her off, thinking, as he often did lately, that he had outlived his time and his place. "I'm not suited for a holding action," he told himself, imagining the entire culture of the white Christian world to be stretched out on some sort of endless Maginot Line besieged by the children of the poor carrying portable radios and boxes of fried chicken.

Here Claiborne sat, on a beautiful spring morning, in good spirits, still breathing normally, his blood coursing through his veins on its admirable and accustomed journeys, and only a few minutes before he had been party to a violation of a code he had lived by all his life.

He sat there, sipping his tasteless coffee, listening to the Saturday lawn mowers starting upon the lawn of the Poydras Retirement Home, which took up the other half of the square block of prime New Orleans real estate on which the new clubhouse was built. It was a very exclusive old folks' home, with real antiques and Persian rugs and a board of directors made up of members of the New Orleans Junior League. Some of the nicest old people in New Orleans went there to die.

Claiborne had suffered through a series of terrible luncheons at the Poydras Home in an effort to get them to allow the tennis club to unlock one of the gates that separated the two properties. But no matter how the board of directors of the Lawn Tennis Club pleaded and bargained and implored, the board of directors of the Poydras Home stoutly refused to allow the tennis-club members to set foot on their lawn to retrieve the balls that flew over the fence. A ball lost to the Poydras Home was a ball gone forever.

The old-fashioned steel girders of the Huey P. Long Bridge hung languidly in the moist air. The sun beat down on the river. The low-hanging clouds pushed against each other in fat cosmic orgasms.

LaGrande stood on the bridge until the constellation of yellow balls was out of sight around a bend in the river. Then she drove to her house on Philip Street, changed clothes, got in the car, and began to drive aimlessly up and down Saint Charles Avenue, thinking of things to do with the rest of her life.

She decided to cheer herself up. She turned onto Carrollton Avenue and drove down to Gus Mayer.

She went in, found a saleslady, took up a large dressing room, and bought some cocktail dresses and some sun dresses and some summer skirts and blouses and some pink linen pants and a beige silk Calvin Klein evening jacket.

Then she went downstairs and bought some hose and some makeup and some perfume and some brassieres and some panties and a blue satin Christian Dior gown and robe.

She went into the shoe department and bought some Capezio sandals and some Bass loafers and some handmade espadrilles. She bought a red umbrella and a navy blue canvas handbag.

When she had bought one each of every single thing she could possibly imagine needing she felt better and went on out to the Country Club to see if anyone she liked to fuck was hanging around the pool.

Amy Hempel

Amy Hempel has said that she wrote the stories that comprise her first collection, *Reasons to Live,* in response to a period of loss in her own life. The epigraph she chose, from the work of William Matthews, reflects the thematic concerns of many of these stories: "Because grief unites us,/like the locked antlers of moose/who die on their knees in pairs." To genuinely move the reader, to make him or her feel the deep sorrow of a character's loss, is no small task. Too often a writer will rely on polemic, histrionics, or sentimentality, but Hempel is able to achieve her effects through economy and indirection. Her minimalist style, which allows for the reader to make the connections another writer might impose on a story, serves her well, and her best work is haunting, beautiful, and emotionally devastating. She is the author of two other collections, *At the Gates of the Animal Kingdom* and *Tumble Home.*

The first of the stories I've chosen here, "In the Cemetery Where Al Jolson Is Buried," is Hempel's best-known and most frequently reprinted work. It bears comparison to Raymond Carver's "A Small, Good Thing" in its success in dramatizing the death of an intimate. Whereas Carver's story relies on plot and its transcendent ending, Hempel's consists of a series of snapshots of the narrator and her dying friend, which bring their relationship into intense focus. Best of all, she uses trivia — the inane facts that stick in our heads though they tell us nothing about the world and the forces that control it — as a means of distracting both her characters and the reader from the underlying and wrenching horror of the situation. Her final image of the ape and its dead baby — mere trivia — is heartbreaking. Similarly, "Beg, Sl Tog, Inc, Cont, Rep" employs indirection ("'Kill him!' the girl had shrieked" when a dead frog comes to life at the funeral she has prepared for it) as a way of getting at the emotional core of grief and irremediable loss. The central image of knitting, both as distraction and obsessive-compulsive activity, gives the story its resonance and power.

AMY HEMPEL

In the Cemetery Where
Al Jolson Is Buried

"Tell me things I won't mind forgetting," she said. "Make it useless stuff or skip it."

I began. I told her insects fly through rain, missing every drop, never getting wet. I told her no one in America owned a tape recorder before Bing Crosby did. I told her the shape of the moon is like a banana — you see it looking full, you're seeing it end-on.

The camera made me self-conscious and I stopped. It was trained on us from a ceiling mount — the kind of camera banks use to photograph robbers. It played us to the nurses down the hall in Intensive Care.

"Go on, girl," she said. "You get used to it."

I had my audience. I went on. Did she know that Tammy Wynette had changed her tune? Really. That now she sings "Stand by Your *Friends*"? That Paul Anka did it too, I said. Does "You're Having *Our* Baby." That he got sick of all that feminist bitching.

"What else?" she said. "Have you got something else?"

Oh, yes.

For her I would always have something else.

"Did you know that when they taught the first chimp to talk, it lied? That when they asked her who did it on the desk, she signed back the name of the janitor. And that when they pressed her, she said she was sorry, that it was really the project director. But she was a mother, so I guess she had her reasons."

"Oh, that's good," she said. "A parable."

"There's more about the chimp," I said. "But it will break your heart."

"No, thanks," she says, and scratches at her mask.

We look like good-guy outlaws. Good or bad, I am not used to the mask yet. I keep touching the warm spot where my breath, thank God, comes out. She is used to hers. She only ties the strings on top. The other ones — a pro by now — she lets hang loose.

We call this place the Marcus Welby Hospital. It's the white one with the palm trees under the opening credits of all those shows. A Hollywood hospital, though in fact it is several miles west. Off camera, there is a beach across the street.

She introduces me to a nurse as the Best Friend. The impersonal article is more intimate. It tells me that *they* are intimate, the nurse and my friend.

"I was telling her we used to drink Canada Dry ginger ale and pretend we were in Canada."

"That's how dumb we were," I say.

"You could be sisters," the nurse says.

So how come, I'll bet they are wondering, it took me so long to get to such a glamorous place? But do they ask?

They do not ask.

Two months, and how long is the drive?

The best I can explain it is this — I have a friend who worked one summer in a mortuary. He used to tell me stories. The one that really got to me was not the grisliest, but it's the one that did. A man wrecked his car on 101 going south. He did not lose consciousness. But his arm was taken down to the wet bone — and when he looked at it — it scared him to death.

I mean, he died.

So I hadn't dared to look any closer. But now I'm doing it — and hoping that I will live through it.

She shakes out a summer-weight blanket, showing a leg you did not want to see. Except for that, you look at her and understand the law that requires *two* people to be with the body at all times.

"I thought of something," she says. "I thought of it last night. I think there is a real and present need here. You know," she says, "like for someone to do it for you when you can't do it yourself. You call them up whenever you want — like when push comes to shove."

She grabs the bedside phone and loops the cord around her neck.

"Hey," she says, "the end o' the line."

She keeps on, giddy with something. But I don't know with what.

"I can't remember," she says. "What does Kübler-Ross say comes after Denial?"

It seems to me Anger must be next. Then Bargaining, Depression, and so on and so forth. But I keep my guesses to myself.

"The only thing is," she says, "is where's Resurrection? God knows, I want to do it by the book. But she left out Resurrection."

✺

She laughs, and I cling to the sound the way someone dangling above a ravine holds fast to the thrown rope.

"Tell me," she says, "about that chimp with the talking hands. What do they do when the thing ends and the chimp says, 'I don't want to go back to the zoo'?"

When I don't say anything, she says, "Okay — then tell me another animal story. I like animal stories. But not a sick one — I don't want to know about all the seeing-eye dogs going blind."

No, I would not tell her a sick one.

"How about the hearing-ear dogs?" I say. "They're not going deaf, but they are getting very judgmental. For instance, there's this golden retriever in New Jersey, he wakes up the deaf mother and drags her into the daughter's room because the kid has got a flashlight and is reading under the covers."

"Oh, you're killing me," she says. "Yes, you're definitely killing me."

"They say the smart dog obeys, but the smarter dog knows when to disobey."

"Yes," she says, "the smarter anything knows when to disobey. Now, for example."

She is flirting with the Good Doctor, who has just appeared. Unlike the Bad Doctor, who checks the IV drip before saying good morning, the Good Doctor says things like "God didn't give epileptics a fair shake." The Good Doctor awards himself points for the cripples he could have hit in the parking lot. Because the Good Doctor is a little in love with her, he says maybe a year. He pulls a chair up to her bed and suggests I might like to spend an hour on the beach.

"Bring me something back," she says. "Anything from the beach. Or the gift shop. Taste is no object."

He draws the curtain around her bed.

"Wait!" she cries.

I look in at her.

"Anything," she says, "except a magazine subscription!"

The doctor turns away.

I watch her mouth laugh.

What seems dangerous often is not — black snakes, for example, or clear-air turbulence. While things that just lie there, like this beach, are loaded with jeopardy. A yellow dust rising from the ground, the heat that ripens melons overnight — this is earthquake weather. You can sit here braiding the fringe on your towel and the sand will all of a sudden suck down like an hourglass. The air roars. In the cheap apartments on-shore, bathtubs fill themselves and gardens roll up and over like green waves. If nothing happens, the dust will drift and the heat deepen till fear turns to desire. Nerves like that are only bought off by catastrophe.

"It never happens when you're thinking about it," she once observed. "Earthquake, earthquake, earthquake," she said.

"Earthquake, earthquake, earthquake," I said.

Like the aviaphobe who keeps the plane aloft with prayer, we kept it up until an aftershock cracked the ceiling.

That was after the big one in seventy-two. We were in college; our dormitory was five miles from the epicenter. When the ride was over and my jabbering pulse began to slow, she served five parts champagne to one part orange juice, and joked about living in Ocean View, Kansas. I offered to drive her to Hawaii on the new world psychics predicted would surface the next time, or the next.

I could not say that now — next.

Whose next? she could ask.

Was I the only one who noticed that the experts had stopped saying *if* and now spoke of *when*? Of course not; the fearful ran to thousands. We watched the traffic of Japanese beetles for deviation. Deviation might mean more natural violence.

I wanted her to be afraid with me. But she said, "I don't know. I'm just not."

She was afraid of nothing, not even of flying.

I have this dream before a flight where we buckle in and the plane moves down the runway. It takes off at thirty-five miles an hour, and then we're airborne, skimming the tree tops. Still, we arrive in New York on time.

It is so pleasant.

One night I flew to Moscow this way.

She flew with me once. That time she flew with me she ate macadamia nuts while the wings bounced. She knows the wing tips can bend thirty feet up and thirty feet down without coming off. She believes it. She trusts the laws of aerodynamics. My mind stampedes. I can almost accept that a battleship floats when everybody knows steel sinks.

I see fear in her now, and am not going to try to talk her out of it. She is right to be afraid.

After a quake, the six o'clock news airs a film clip of first-graders yelling at the broken playground per their teacher's instructions.

"*Bad* earth!" they shout, because anger is stronger than fear.

But the beach is standing still today. Everyone on it is tranquilized, numb, or asleep. Teenaged girls rub coconut oil on each other's hard-to-reach places. They smell like macaroons. They pry open compacts like clamshells; mirrors catch the sun and throw a spray of white rays across glazed shoulders. The girls arrange their wet hair with silk flowers the way they learned in *Seventeen.* They pose.

A formation of low-riders pulls over to watch with a six-pack. They get vocal when the girls check their tan lines. When the beer is gone, so are they — flexing their cars on up the boulevard.

Above this aggressive health are the twin wrought-iron terraces, painted flamingo pink, of the Palm Royale. Someone dies there every time the sheets are changed. There's an ambulance in the driveway, so the remaining residents line the balconies, rocking and not talking, one-upped.

The ocean they stare at is dangerous, and not just the undertow. You can almost see the slapping tails of sand sharks keeping cruising bodies alive.

If she looked, she could see this, some of it, from her window. She would be the first to say how little it takes to make a thing all wrong.

There was a second bed in the room when I got back to it!

For two beats I didn't get it. Then it hit me like an open coffin.

She wants every minute, I thought. She wants my life.

"You missed Gussie," she said.

Gussie is her parents' three-hundred-pound narcoleptic maid. Her attacks often come at the ironing board. The pillowcases in that family are all bordered with scorch.

"It's a hard trip for her," I said. "How is she?"

"Well, she didn't fall asleep, if that's what you mean. Gussie's great — you know what she said? She said, 'Darlin', stop this worriation. Just keep prayin', down on your knees' — me, who can't even get out of bed."

She shrugged. "What am I missing?"

"It's earthquake weather," I told her.

"The best thing to do about earthquakes," she said, "is not to live in California."

"That's useful," I said. "You sound like Reverend Ike — 'The best thing to do for the poor is not to be one of them.'"

We're crazy about Reverend Ike.

I noticed her face was bloated.

"You know," she said, "I feel like hell. I'm about to stop having fun."

"The ancients have a saying," I said. "'There are times when the wolves are silent; there are times when the moon howls.'"

"What's that, Navaho?"

"Palm Royale lobby graffiti," I said. "I bought a paper there. I'll read you something."

"Even though I care about nothing?"

I turned to the page with the trivia column. I said, "Did you know the more shrimp flamingo birds eat, the pinker their feathers get?" I said, "Did you know that Eskimos need refrigerators? Do you know *why* Eskimos need refrigerators? Did you know that Eskimos need refrigerators because how else would they keep their food from freezing?"

I turned to page three, to a UPI filler datelined Mexico City. I read her Man Robs Bank with Chicken, about a man who bought a barbecued chicken at a stand down the block from a bank. Passing the bank, he got the idea. He walked in and approached a teller. He pointed the brown paper bag at her and she handed over the day's receipts. It was the smell of barbecue sauce that eventually led to his capture.

The story had made her hungry, she said — so I took the elevator down six floors to the cafeteria, and brought back all the ice cream she wanted. We lay side by side, adjustable beds cranked up for optimal TV-viewing, littering the sheets with Good Humor wrappers, picking toasted almonds out of the gauze. We were Lucy and Ethel, Mary and Rhoda in extremis. The blinds were closed to keep light off the screen.

We watched a movie starring men we used to think we wanted to sleep with. Hers was a tough cop out to stop mine, a vicious rapist who went after cocktail waitresses.

"This is a good movie," she said when snipers felled them both.

I missed her already.

A Filipino nurse tiptoed in and gave her an injection. The nurse removed the pile of popsicle sticks from the nightstand — enough to splint a small animal.

The injection made us both sleepy. We slept.

I dreamed she was a decorator, come to furnish my house. She worked in secret, singing to herself. When she finished, she guided me proudly to the door. "How do you like it?" she asked, easing me inside.

Every beam and sill and shelf and knob was draped in gay bunting, with streamers of pastel crepe looped around bright mirrors.

☀

"I have to go home," I said when she woke up.

She thought I meant home to her house in the Canyon, and I had to say No, *home* home. I twisted my hands in the time-honored fashion of people in pain. I was supposed to offer something. The Best Friend. I could not even offer to come back.

I felt weak and small and failed.

Also exhilarated.

I had a convertible in the parking lot. Once out of that room, I would drive it too fast down the Coast highway through the crab-smelling air. A stop in Malibu for sangria. The music in the place would be sexy and loud. They'd serve papaya and shrimp and water-melon ice. After dinner I would shimmer with lust, buzz with heat, vibrate with life, and stay up all night.

Without a word, she yanked off her mask and threw it on the floor. She kicked at the blankets and moved to the door. She must have hated having to pause for breath and balance before slamming out of Isola-tion, and out of the second room, the one where you scrub and tie on the white masks.

A voice shouted her name in alarm, and people ran down the corridor. The Good Doctor was paged over the intercom. I opened the door and the nurses at the station stared hard, as if this flight had been my idea.

"Where is she?" I asked, and they nodded to the supply closet.

I looked in. Two nurses were kneeling beside her on the floor, talking to her in low voices. One held a mask over her nose and mouth, the other rubbed her back in slow circles. The nurses glanced up to see if I was the doctor — and when I wasn't, they went back to what they were doing.

"There, there, honey," they cooed.

On the morning she was moved to the cemetery, the one where Al Jol-son is buried, I enrolled in a "Fear of Flying" class. "What is your worst fear?" the instructor asked, and I answered, "That I will finish this course and still be afraid."

I sleep with a glass of water on the nightstand so I can see by its level if the coastal earth is trembling or if the shaking is still me.

What do I remember?

I remember only the useless things I hear — that Bob Dylan's mother invented Wite-Out, that twenty-three people must be in a room before there is a fifty-fifty chance two will have the same birthday. Who cares whether or not it's true? In my head there are bath towels swaddling this stuff. Nothing else seeps through.

I review those things that will figure in the retelling: a kiss through surgical gauze, the pale hand correcting the position of the wig. I noted these gestures as they happened, not in any retrospect, though I don't know why looking back should show us more than looking *at*.

It is just possible I will say I stayed the night.

And who is there that can say that I did not?

I think of the chimp, the one with the talking hands.

In the course of the experiment, that chimp had a baby. Imagine how her trainers must have thrilled when the mother, without prompting, began to sign to her newborn.

Baby, drink milk.

Baby, play ball.

And when the baby died, the mother stood over the body, her wrinkled hands moving with animal grace, forming again and again the words: Baby, come hug, Baby, come hug, fluent now in the language of grief.

Beg, Sl Tog, Inc, Cont, Rep

The mohair was scratchy, the stria too bulky, but the homespun tweed was right for a small frame. I bought slate-blue skeins softened with flecks of pink, and size-10 needles for a sweater that was warm but light. The pattern I chose was a two-tone V-neck with an optional six-stitch cable up the front. Pullovers mess the hair, but I did not want to buttonhole the first time out.

From a needlework book, I learned to cast on. In the test piece, I got the gauge and correct tension. Knit and purl came naturally, as though my fingers had been rubbed in spiderwebs at birth. The sliding of the needles was as rhythmic as water.

Learning to knit was the obvious thing. The separation of tangled threads, the working-together of raveled ends into something tangible and whole — this *mending* was as confounding as the groom who drives into a stop sign on the way to his wedding. Because symptoms mean just what they are. What about the woman whose empty hand won't close because she cannot grasp that her child is gone?

"Would you get me a Dr Pep, gal, and would you turn up the a-c?"

I put down my knitting. In the kitchen I found some sugar-free, and took it, with ice, to Dale Anne. It was August. Air-conditioning lifted her hair as she pressed the button on the Niagara bed. Dr. Diamond insisted she have it the last month. She was also renting a swivel TV table and a vibrating chaise — the Niagara adjustable home.

When the angle was right, she popped a Vitamin E and rubbed the oil where the stretch marks would be.

I could be doing this, too. But I had had the procedure instead. That was after the father had asked me, Was I sure? To his credit, he meant — sure that I *was,* not sure was it he. He said he had never made a girl pregnant before. He said that he had never even made a girl late.

I moved in with Dale Anne to help her near the end. Her husband is often away — in a clinic or in a lab. He studies the mind. He is not a doctor yet, but we call him one by way of encouragement.

I had picked up a hank of yarn and was winding it into a ball when the air-conditioner choked to a stop.

Dale Anne sighed. "I will *cook* in this robe. Would you get me that flowered top in the second drawer?"

While I looked for the top, Dale Anne twisted her hair and held it tight against her head. She took one of my double-pointed six-inch needles and wove it in and out of her hair, securing the twist against her scalp. With the hair off her face, she looked wholesome and very young — "the person you would most like to go camping with if you couldn't have sex," is how she put it.

I turned my back while Dale Anne changed. She was as modest as I was. If the house caught fire one night, we would both die struggling to hook brassieres beneath our gowns.

I went back to my chair, and as I did, a sensational cramp snapped me over until I was nearly on the floor.

"Easy, gal — what's the trouble?" Dale Anne started out of bed to come see.

I said it sometimes happens since the procedure, and Dale Anne said, "Let's not talk about that for at *least* ten years."

I could not think of what to say to that. But I didn't have to. The front door opened, earlier than it usually did. It was Dr. Diamond, home from the world of spooks and ghosts and loony bins and Ouija boards. I knew that a lack of concern for others was a hallmark of mental illness, so I straightened up and said, after he'd kissed his pregnant wife, "You look hot, Dr. Diamond. Can I get you a drink?"

I buy my materials at a place in the residential section. The owner's name is Ingrid. She is a large Norwegian woman who spells needles "kneedles." She wears sample knits she makes up for the class demonstrations. The vest she wore the day before will be hanging in the window.

There are always four or five women at Ingrid's round oak table, knitting through a stretch they would not risk alone.

Often I go there when I don't need a thing. In the small back room that is stacked high with pattern books, I can sift for hours. I scan the instructions abbreviated like musical notation: *K10, sl 1, K2 tog, psso, sl 1, K10 to end.* I feel I could *sing* these instructions. It is compression of language into code; your ability to decipher it makes you privy to the secrets shared by Ingrid and the women at the round oak table.

In the other room, Ingrid tells a customer she used to knit two hundred stitches a minute.

I scan the French and English catalogues, noting the longer length of coat. There is so much to absorb on each visit.

Mary had a little lamb, I am humming when I leave the shop. *Its feet were — its fleece was white as wool.*

꙳

Dale Anne wanted a nap, so Dr. Diamond and I went out for margaritas. At La Rondalla, the colored lights on the Virgin tell you every day is Christmas. The food arrives on manhole covers and mariachis fill the bar. Dr. Diamond said that in Guadalajara there is a mariachi college that turns out mariachis by the classful. But I could tell that these were not graduates of even mariachi high school.

I shooed the serenaders away, but Dr. Diamond said they meant well.

Dr. Diamond likes for people to mean well. He could be president of the Well-Meaning Club. He has had a buoyant feeling of fate since he learned Freud died the day he was born.

He was the person to talk to, all right, so I brought up the stomach pains I was having for no bodily reason that I could think of.

"You know how I think," he said. "What is it you can't stomach?"

I knew what he was asking.

"Have you thought about how you will feel when Dale Anne has the baby?" he asked.

With my eyes, I wove strands of tinsel over the Blessed Virgin. That was the great thing about knitting, I thought — everything was fiber, the world a world of natural resource.

"I thought I would burn that bridge when I come to it," I said, and when he didn't say anything to that, I said, "I guess I will think that there is a mother who *kept* hers."

"*One* of hers might be more accurate," Dr. Diamond said.

I arrived at the yarn shop as Ingrid turned over the *Closed* sign to *Open.* I had come to buy Shetland wool for a Fair Isle sweater. I felt nothing would engage my full attention more than a pattern of ancient Scottish symbols and alternate bands of delicate design. Every stitch in every color is related to the one above, below, and to either side.

I chose the natural colors of Shetland sheep — the chalky brown of the Moorit, the blackish brown of the black sheep, fawn, gray, and pinky beige from a mixture of Moorit and white. I held the wool to my nose, but Ingrid said it was fifty years since the women of Fair Isle dressed the yarn with fish oil.

She said the yarn came from Sheep Rock, the best pasture on Fair Isle. It is a ten-acre plot that is four hundred feet up a cliff, Ingrid said. "Think what a man has to go through to harvest the wool."

I was willing to feel an obligation to the yarn, and to the hardy Scots who supplied it. There was heritage there, and I could keep it alive with my hands.

Dale Anne patted capers into a mound of raw beef, and spread some onto toast. It was not a pretty sight. She offered some to me, and I said not a chance. I told her Johnny Carson is someone else who won't go near that. I said, "Johnny says he won't eat steak tartare because he has seen things hurt worse than that get better."

"Johnny was never pregnant," Dale Anne said.

When the contractions began, I left a message with the hospital and with Dr. Diamond's lab. I turned off the air-conditioner and called for a cab.

"Look at you," Dale Anne said.

I told her I couldn't help it. I get rational when I panic.

The taxi came in minutes.

"Hold on," the driver said. "I know every bump in these roads, and I've never been able to miss one of them."

Dale Anne tried to squeeze my wrist, but her touch was weightless, as porous as wet silk.

"When this is over . . ." Dale Anne said.

When the baby was born, I did not go far. I sublet a place on the other side of town. I filled it with patterns and needles and yarn. It was what I did in the day. On a good day, I made a front and two sleeves. On a bad day, I ripped out stitches from neck to hem. For variety, I made socks. The best ones I made had beer steins on the sides, and the tops spilled over with white angora foam.

I did not like to work with sound in the room, not even the sound of a fan. Music slowed me down, and there was a great deal to do. I planned to knit myself a mailbox and a car, perhaps even a dog and a lead to walk him.

I blocked the finished pieces and folded them in drawers.

Dr. Diamond urged me to exercise. He called from time to time, looking in. He said exercise would set me straight, and why not have some fun with it? Why not, for example, tap-dancing lessons?

I told him it would be embarrassing because the rest of the class would be doing it right. And with all the knitting, there wasn't time to dance.

Dale Anne did not look in. She had a pretty good reason not to.

The day I went to see her in the hospital, I stopped at the nursery first. I saw the baby lying face down. He wore yellow duck-print flannels. I saw that he was there — and then I went straight home.

That night the dreams began. A giant lizard ate people from the feet upwards, swallowing the argyles on the first bite, then drifting into obscurity like a ranger of forgotten death. I woke up remembering and, like a chameleon, assumed every shade of blame.

Asleep at night, I went to an elegant ball. In the center of the dance floor was a giant aquarium. Hundreds of goldfish swam inside. At a sign from the bandleader, the tank was overturned. Until someone tried to dance on the fish, the floor was aswirl with gold glory.

Dr. Diamond told a story about the young daughter of a friend. The little girl had found a frog in the yard. The frog appeared to be dead, so her parents let her prepare a burial site — a little hole surrounded by pebbles. But at the moment of the lowering, the frog, which had only been stunned, kicked its legs and came to.

"Kill him!" the girl had shrieked.

I began to take walks in the park. In the park, I saw a dog try to eat his own shadow, and another dog — I am sure of it — was herding a stand of elms. I stopped telling people how handsome their dogs were; too many times what they said was, "You want him?"

When the weather got nicer, I stayed home to sit for hours.

I had accidents. Then I had bigger ones. But the part that hurt was never the part that got hurt.

The dreams came back and back until they were just — again. I wished that things would stay out of sight the way they did in mountain lakes. In one that I know, the water is so cold, gas can't form or bring a corpse to the surface. Although you would not want to think about the bottom of the lake, what you can say about it is — the dead stay down.

Around that time I talked to Dr. Diamond.

The point that he wanted to make was this: that conception was not like walking in front of traffic. No matter how badly timed, it was, he said, an affirmation of life.

"You have to believe me here," he said. "Do you see that this is true? Do you know this about yourself?"

"I do and I don't," I said.

"You do and you *do*," he said.

I remembered when another doctor made the news. A young retarded boy had found his father's gun, and while the family slept, he shot them all in bed. The police asked the boy what he had done. But the boy went mute. He told them nothing. Then they called in the doctor.

"We know *you* didn't do it," the doctor said to the boy, "but tell me, did the *gun* do it?"

And yes, the boy was eager to tell him just what that gun had done.

I wanted the same out, and Dr. Diamond wouldn't let me have it.

"Dr. Diamond," I said, "I am giving up."

"Now you are ready to begin," he said.

I thought of Andean alpaca because that was what I planned to work up next. The feel of that yarn was not the only wonder — there was also the name of it: Alpaquita Superfina.

Dr. Diamond was right.

I was ready to begin.

Beg, sl tog, inc, cont, rep.

Begin, slip together, increase, continue, repeat.

Dr. Diamond answered the door. He said Dale Anne had run to the store. He was leaving, too, flying to a conference back East. The baby was asleep, he said, I should make myself at home.

I left my bag of knitting in the hall and went into Dale Anne's kitchen. It had been a year. I could have looked in on the baby. Instead, I washed the dishes that were soaking in the sink. The scouring pad was steel wool waiting for knitting needles.

The kitchen was filled with specialized utensils. When Dale Anne couldn't sleep she watched TV, and that's where the stuff was advertised. She had a thing to core tomatoes — it was called a Tomato Shark — and a metal spaghetti wheel for measuring out spaghetti. She had plastic melon-ballers and a push-in device that turned ordinary cake into ladyfingers.

I found pasta primavera in the refrigerator. My fingers wanted to knit the cold linguini, laying precisely cabled strands across the oily red peppers and beans.

Dale Anne opened the door.

"*Look* out, gal," she said, and dropped a shopping bag on the counter.

I watched her unload ice cream, potato chips, carbonated drinks, and cake.

"It's been a long time since I walked into a market and expressed myself," she said.

She turned to toss me a carton of cigarettes.

"Wait for me in the bedroom," she said. "*West Side Story* is on."

I went in and looked at the color set. I heard the blender crushing ice in the kitchen. I adjusted the contrast, then Dale Anne handed me an enormous peach daiquiri. The goddamn thing had a tide factor.

Dale Anne left the room long enough to bring in the take-out chicken. She upended the bag on a plate and picked out a leg and a wing.

"I like my dinner in a bag and my life in a box," she said, nodding toward the TV.

We watched the end of the movie, then part of a lame detective program. Dale Anne said the show *owed* Nielsen four points, and reached for the *TV Guide.*

"Eleven-thirty," she read. *"The Texas Whiplash Massacre:* Unexpected stop signs were their weapon."

"Give me that," I said.

Dale Anne said there was supposed to be a comet. She said we could probably see it if we watched from the living room. Just to be sure, we pushed the couch up close to the window. With the lights off, we could see everything without it seeing us. Although both of us had quit, we smoked at either end of the couch.

"Save my place," Dale Anne said.

She had the baby in her arms when she came back in. I looked at the sleeping child and thought, Mercy, Land Sakes, Lordy Me. As though I had aged fifty years. For just a moment then I wanted nothing that I had and everything I did not.

"He told his first joke today," Dale Anne said.

"What do you mean he told a joke?" I said. "I didn't think they could talk."

"Well, he didn't really *tell* a joke — he poured his orange juice over his head, and when I started after him, he said, 'Raining?'"

"'Raining?' That's what he said? The kid is a genius," I told Dale Anne. "What Art Linkletter could do with this kid."

Dale Anne laid him down in the middle of the couch, and we watched him or watched the sky.

"What a gyp," Dale Anne said at dawn.

There had not been a comet. But I did not feel cheated, or even tired. She walked me to the door.

The knitting bag was still in the hall.

"Open it later," I said. "It's a sweater for him."

But Dale Anne had to see it then.

She said the blue one matched his eyes and the camel one matched his hair. The red would make him glow, she said, and then she said, "Help me out."

Cables had become too easy; three more sweaters had pictures knitted in. They buttoned up the front. Dale Anne held up a parade of yellow ducks.

There were the Fair Isles, too — one in the pattern called Tree of Life, another in the pattern called Hearts.

It was an excess of sweaters — a kind of precaution, a rehearsal against disaster.

Dale Anne looked at the two sweaters still in the bag. "Are you really okay?" she said.

The worst of it is over now, and I can't say that I am glad. Lose that sense of loss — you have gone and lost something else. But the body moves toward health. The mind, too, in steps. One step at a time. Ask a mother who has just lost a child, How many children do you have? "Four," she will say, " — three," and years later, "Three," she will say, "— four."

It's the little steps that help. Weather, breakfast, crossing with the light — sometimes it is all the pleasure I can bear to sleep, and know that on a rack in the bath, damp wool is pinned to dry.

Dale Anne thinks she would like to learn to knit. She measures the baby's crib and I take her over to Ingrid's. Ingrid steers her away from the baby pastels, even though they are machine-washable. Use a pure wool, Ingrid says. Use wool in a grown-up shade. And don't boast of your achievements or you'll be making things for the neighborhood.

On Fair Isle there are only five women left who knit. There is not enough lichen left growing on the island for them to dye their yarn. But knitting machines can't produce their designs, and they keep on, these women, working the undyed colors of the sheep.

I wait for Dale Anne in the room with the patterns. The songs in these books are like lullabies to me.

K tog rem st. Knit together remaining stitches.

Cast off loosely.

Isabel Huggan

Isabel Huggan is a master of the excruciating moment dredged up from the memory banks of childhood. Her first collection, *The Elizabeth Stories* (1987), traces the development of the title character from elementary school through high school graduation and spares us none of the humiliations encountered along the way. In the course of these stories, Elizabeth suffers the rigidity of her conformist parents; is forced, as a chubby adolescent, to play the male role in the local ballet; has her first groping sexual encounter interrupted by her inamorato's enraged father; and falls in love with an angelic high school teacher who turns out to be a wife abuser. If it is hard growing up, Huggan reminds us of just how and why, with a sense of humor and perfect recall of childhood and adolescence that bring to mind the work of Roddy Doyle. And the character of Elizabeth is a triumph — never idealized and always clearheaded and honest as she schemes to get out from under her parents' dominion.

Both selections here are from *The Elizabeth Stories*. "Celia Behind Me" is notable for its unsentimental look at the Darwinian world of elementary school and its divided loyalties: "My mother always said, 'You must be nice to Celia, she won't live forever,' and even as early as seven I could see the unfairness of that position. Everybody died sooner or later, I'd die too, but that didn't mean everybody was nice to me . . ." The second piece, "Sorrows of the Flesh," deals in a complex way with the teenage crush: "I was fourteen, three inches under six feet and going into Grade 10 when Jerry Wheeling, teacher of junior biology and senior chemistry, came to Garten District High School. He was 24, at least 6'5", with long bony wrists that hung from his shirtcuffs so poignantly it made me want to cry . . ." What I like about this story is the way in which Elizabeth reevaluates not only her impression of Jerry Wheeling, but her parents' bond — and their sexuality — as well.

Celia Behind Me

There was a little girl with large smooth cheeks and very thick glasses who lived up the street when I was in public school. Her name was Celia. It was far too rare and grown-up a name, so we always laughed at it. And we laughed at her because she was a chubby, diabetic child, made peevish by our teasing.

My mother always said, "You must be nice to Celia, she won't live forever," and even as early as seven I could see the unfairness of that position. Everybody died sooner or later, I'd die too, but that didn't mean everybody was nice to me or to each other. I already knew about mortality and was prepared to go to heaven with my two aunts who had died together in a car crash with their heads smashed like overripe melons. I overheard the bit about the melons when my mother was on the telephone, repeating that phrase and sobbing. I used to think about it often, repeating the words to myself as I did other things so that I got a nice rhythm: "Their heads smashed like melons, like melons, like melons." I imagined the pulpy insides of muskmelons and watermelons all over the road.

I often thought about the melons when I saw Celia because her head was so round and she seemed so bland and stupid and fruitlike. All rosy and vulnerable at the same time as being the most *awful* pain. She'd follow us home from school, whining if we walked faster than she did. Everybody always walked faster than Celia because her short little legs wouldn't keep up. And she was bundled in long stockings and heavy underwear, summer and winter, so that even her clothes held her back from our sturdy, leaping pace over and under hedges and across backyards and, when it was dry, or when it was frozen, down the stream bed and through the drainage pipe beneath the bridge on Church Street.

Celia, by the year I turned nine in December, had failed once and was behind us in school, which was a relief because at least in class there wasn't someone telling you to be nice to Celia. But she'd always be in the playground at recess, her pleading eyes magnified behind those ugly lenses so that you couldn't look at her when you told her she couldn't play skipping unless she was an ender. "Because you can't skip worth a fart," we'd whisper in her ear. "Fart, fart, fart," and watch her round pink face crumple as she stood there, turning, turning, turning the rope over and over.

As the fall turned to winter, the five of us who lived on Brubacher Street and went back and forth to school together got meaner and meaner to Celia. And, after the brief diversions of Christmas, we returned with a vengeance to our running and hiding and scaring games that kept Celia in a state of terror all the way home.

My mother said, one day when I'd come into the kitchen and she'd just turned away from the window so I could see she'd been watching us coming down the street, "You'll be sorry, Elizabeth. I see how you're treating that poor child, and it makes me sick. You wait, young lady. Some day you'll see how it feels yourself. Now you be nice to her, d'you hear?"

"But it's not just me," I protested. "I'm nicer to her than anybody else, and I don't see why I have to be. She's nobody special, she's just a pain. She's really dumb and she can't do anything. Why can't I just play with the other kids like everybody else?"

"You just remember I'm watching," she said, ignoring every word I'd said. "And if I see one more snowball thrown in her direction, by you or by anybody else, I'm coming right out there and spanking you in front of them all. Now you remember that!"

I knew my mother, and knew this was no idle threat. The awesome responsibility of now making sure the other kids stopped snowballing Celia made me weep with rage and despair, and I was locked in my room after supper to "think things over."

I thought things over. I hated Celia with a dreadful and absolute passion. Her round guileless face floated in the air above me as I finally fell asleep, taunting me: "You have to be nice to me because I'm going to die."

I did as my mother bid me, out of fear and the thought of the shame that a public spanking would bring. I imagined my mother could see much farther up the street than she really could, and it prevented me from throwing snowballs or teasing Celia for the last four blocks of our homeward journey. And then came the stomach-wrenching task of making the others quit.

"You'd better stop," I'd say. "If my mother sees you she's going to thrash us all."

Terror of terrors that they wouldn't be sufficiently scared of her strap-wielding hand; gut-knotting fear that they'd find out or guess what she'd really said and throw millions of snowballs just for the joy of seeing me whipped, pants down in the snowbank, screaming. I visualized that scene all winter, and felt a shock of relief when March brought such a cold spell that the snow was too crisp for packing. It meant a temporary safety for Celia, and respite for me. For I knew, deep in my wretched heart, that were it not for Celia I was next in line for humiliation. I was kind of chunky and wore glasses too, and had sucked my thumb so openly in kindergarten that "Sucky" had stuck with me all the way to Grade 3 where I now balanced at a hazardous point, nearly accepted by the amorphous Other Kids and always at the brink of being laughed at, ignored or teased. I cried very easily, and prayed during those years — not to become pretty or smart or popular, all aims too far out of my or God's reach, but simply to be strong enough not to cry when I got called Sucky.

During that cold snap, we were all bundled up by our mothers as much as poor Celia ever was. Our comings and goings were hampered by layers of flannel bloomers and undershirts and ribbed stockings and itchy wool against us no matter which way we turned; mitts, sweaters, scarves and hats, heavy and wet-smelling when the snot from our dripping noses mixed with the melting snow on our collars and we wiped, in frigid resignation, our sore red faces with rough sleeves knobbed over with icy pellets.

Trudging, turgid little beasts we were, making our way along slippery streets, breaking the crusts on those few front yards we'd not yet stepped all over in glee to hear the glorious snapping sound of boot through hard snow. Celia, her glasses steamed up even worse than mine, would scuffle and trip a few yards behind us, and I walked along wishing that some time I'd look back and she wouldn't be there. But she always was, and I was always conscious of the abiding hatred that had built up during the winter, in conflict with other emotions that gave me no peace at all. I felt pity, and a rising urge within me to cry as hard as I could so that Celia would cry too, and somehow realize how bad she made me feel, and ask my forgiveness.

It was the last day before the thaw when the tension broke, like northern lights exploding in the frozen air. We were all a little wingy after days of switching between the extremes of bitter cold outdoors and the heat of our homes and school. Thermostats had been turned up in a desperate attempt to combat the arctic air, so that we children suffered scratchy, tingly torment in our faces, hands and feet as the blood in our bodies roared in confusion, first freezing, then boiling. At school we had to go outside at recess — only an act of God would have ever prevented recess, the teachers had to have their cigarettes and tea — and in bad weather we huddled in a shed where the bicycles and the janitor's outdoor equipment were stored.

During the afternoon recess of the day I'm remembering, at the end of the shed where the girls stood, a sudden commotion broke out when Sandra, a rich big girl from Grade 4, brought forth a huge milk-chocolate bar from her pocket. It was brittle in the icy air, and snapped into little bits in its foil wrapper, to be divided among the chosen. I made my way cautiously to the fringe of her group, where many of my classmates were receiving their smidgens of sweet chocolate, letting it melt on their tongues like dark communion wafers. Behind me hung Celia, who had mistaken my earlier cries of "Stop throwing snowballs at Celia!" for kindness. She'd been mooning behind me for days, it seemed to me, as I stepped a little farther forward to see that there were only a few pieces left. Happily, though, most mouths were full and the air hummed with the murmuring sound of chocolate being pressed between tongue and palate.

Made bold by cold and desire, I spoke up. "Could I have a bit, Sandra?" She turned to where Celia and I stood, holding the precious foil in her mittened hand. Wrapping it in a ball, she pushed it over at Celia. Act of kindness, act of spite, vicious bitch or richness seeking expiation? She gave the chocolate to Celia and smiled at her. "This last bit is for Celia," she said to me.

"But I can't eat it," whispered Celia, her round red face aflame with the sensation of being singled out for a gift. "I've got di-a-beet-is." The word. Said so carefully. As if it were a talisman, a charm to protect her against our rough healthiness.

I knew it was a trick. I knew she was watching me out of the corner of her eye, that Sandra, but I was driven. "Then could I have it, eh?" The duress under which I acted prompted my chin to quiver and a tear to start down my cheek before I could wipe it away.

"No, no, no!" jeered Sandra then. "Suckybabies can't have sweets either. Di-a-beet-ics and Suck-y-ba-bies can't eat chocolate. Give it back, you little fart, Celia! That's the last time I ever give you anything!"

Wild, appreciative laughter from the chocolate-tongued mob, and they turned their backs on us, Celia and me, and waited while Sandra crushed the remaining bits into minuscule slivers. They had to take off their mitts and lick their fingers to pick up the last fragments from the foil. I stood there and prayed: "Dear God and Jesus, I would please like very much not to cry. Please help me. Amen." And with that the clanging recess bell clanked through the playground noise, and we all lined up, girls and boys in straight, straight rows, to go inside.

After school there was the usual bunch of us walking home and, of course, Celia trailing behind us. The cold of the past few days had been making us hurry, taking the shortest routes on our way to steaming cups of Ovaltine and cocoa. But this day we were all full of that peculiar energy that swells up before a turn in the weather and, as one body, we turned down the street that meant the long way home. Past the feed store where the Mennonites tied their horses, out the back of the town hall parking-lot and then down a ridge to the ice-covered stream and through the Church Street culvert to come out in the unused field behind the Front Street stores; the forbidden adventure we indulged in as a gesture of defiance against the parental "come right home."

We slid down the snowy slope at the mouth of the pipe that seemed immense then but was really only five feet in diameter. Part of its attraction was the tremendous racket you could make by scraping a stick along the corrugated sides as you went through. It was also long enough to echo very nicely if you made good booming noises, and we occasionally titillated each other by saying bad words at one end that grew as they bounced along the pipe and became wonderfully shocking in their magnitude . . . poopy, Poopy, POOpy, POOOOPy, POOOOOPPYYY!

I was last because I had dropped my schoolbag in the snow and stopped to brush it off. And when I looked up, down at the far end, where the white plate of daylight lay stark in the darkness, the figures of my four friends were silhouetted as they emerged into the brightness. As I started making great sliding steps to catch up, I heard Celia behind me, and her plaintive, high voice: "Elizabeth! Wait for me, okay? I'm scared to go through alone. Elizabeth?"

And of course I slid faster and faster, unable to stand the thought of being the only one in the culvert with Celia. Then we would come out together and we'd really be paired up. What if they always ran on ahead and left us to walk together? What would I ever do? And behind me I heard the rising call of Celia, who had ventured as far as a few yards into the pipe, calling my name to come back and walk with her. I got right to the end, when I heard another noise and looked up. There they all were, on the bridge looking down, and as soon as they saw my face began to chant, "Better wait for Celia, Sucky. Better get Celia, Sucky."

The sky was very pale and lifeless, and I looked up in the air at my breath curling in spirals and felt, I remember this very well, an exhilarating, clear-headed instant of understanding. And with that, raced back into the tunnel where Celia stood whimpering half-way along.

"You little fart!" I screamed at her, my voice breaking and tearing at the words. "You little diabetic fart! I hate you! I hate you! Stop it, stop crying, I hate you! I could bash your head in I hate you so much, you fart, you fart! I'll smash your head like a melon! And it'll go in pieces all over and you'll die. You'll die, you diabetic. You're going to die!" Shaking her, shaking her and banging her against the cold, ribbed metal, crying and sobbing for grief and gasping with the exertion of pure hatred. And then there were the others, pulling at me, yanking me away, and in the moral tones of those who don't actually take part, warning me that they were going to tell, that Celia probably was going to die now, that I was really evil, they would tell what I said.

And there, slumped in a little heap, was Celia, her round head in its furry bonnet all dirty at the back where it had hit against the pipe, and she was hiccupping with fear. And for a wild, terrible moment I thought I had killed her, that the movements and noises her body made were part of dying.

I ran.

I ran as fast as I could back out the way we had come, and all the way back to the schoolyard. I didn't think about where I was going, it simply seemed the only bulwark to turn to when I knew I couldn't go home. There were a few kids still in the yard but they were older and ignored me as I tried the handle of the side door and found it open. I'd never been in the school after hours, and was stricken with another kind of terror that it might be a strappable offense. But no-one saw me, even the janitor was blessedly in another part of the building, so I was able to creep down to the girls' washroom and quickly hide in one of the cubicles. Furtive, criminal, condemned.

I was so filled with horror I couldn't even cry. I just sat on the toilet seat, reading all the things that were written in pencil on the green, wooden walls. *G.R. loves M.H.* and *Y.F. hates W.S. for double double sure. Mr. Becker wears ladies pants.* Thinking that I might die myself, die right here, and then it wouldn't matter if they told on me that I had killed Celia.

But the inevitable footsteps of retribution came down the stone steps before I had been there very long. I heard the janitor's voice explaining he hadn't seen any children come in and then my father's voice saying that the others were sure this is where Elizabeth would be. And they called my name, and then came in, and I guess saw my boots beneath the door because I suddenly thought it was too late to scrunch them up on the seat and my father was looking down at me and grabbed my arm, hurting it, pulling me, saying "Get in the car, Elizabeth."

Both my mother and my father spanked me that night. At first I tried not to cry, and tried to defend myself against their diatribe, tried to tell them when they asked, "But whatever possessed you to do such a terrible thing?" But whatever I said seemed to make them more angry and they became so soured by their own shame that they slapped my stinging buttocks for personal revenge as much as for any rehabilitative purposes.

"I'll never be able to lift my head on this street again!" my mother cried, and it struck me then, as it still does now, as a marvellous turn of phrase. I thought about her head on the street as she hit me, and wondered what Celia's head looked like, and if I had dented it at all.

Celia hadn't died, of course. She'd been half-carried, half-dragged home by the heroic others, and given pills and attention and love, and the doctor had come to look at her head but she didn't have so much as a bruise. She had a dirty hat, and a bad case of hiccups all night, but she survived.

Celia forgave me, all too soon. Within weeks her mother allowed her to walk back and forth to school with me again. But, in all the years before she finally died at seventeen, I was never able to forgive her. She made me discover a darkness far more frightening than the echoing culvert, far more enduring than her smooth, pink face.

Sorrows of the Flesh

Because my father was a banker, I was never allowed to have any pets while I was growing up. It wasn't, as you might think, because of the expense that he objected, although he usually brought that up as an additional factor. No, it was because he couldn't tolerate animal hair on his clothes. He wasn't allergic, just neat. He wore navy three-piece suits winter and summer, and the notion of meeting the public with dog hair or cat fluff clinging to his trousers was unthinkable, as unlikely to happen as his neglecting to visit his barber once a week to have his own hair trimmed close to his head.

"Now see here, Elizabeth," he would begin on those occasions when I was wheedling for whatever newborn kitten or hand-licking stray had taken my fancy. His voice would be patient, but sternly turned to the problem at hand, as if we were doing arithmetic questions together and I needed extra explanation. "We've been over this before. I cannot afford to turn up at the bank looking as if I had slept in a nest of monkeys. People need to have absolute trust in their bank manager, they have to look up to him as someone who knows what he's doing. Now what impression would I give with hair sticking to my suit?"

"But Daddy . . ." I would be allowed to break in, but only as a matter of form, to give the appearance of rational dialogue between father and daughter.

"And I've never known a man yet who came from a house where there were pets who didn't look like it!"

"We could keep it outside all the time, Daddy," I'd say, getting specific on the idea of a big dog on a rope by the back door.

"Fine in the summer, too cold in the winter," he'd reply. "Not fair to the animal, anyway. Now think about *that,* Elizabeth. Think about that!"

I would offer to brush his suits every morning, to vacuum the house every night, to never let so much as a hair go ungroomed on the body of the longed-for pet, but always the answer was the same. "It simply isn't worth the fuss, Elizabeth. No."

Once, reading about cats, I came across a variety called "Russian Blue." The Prussian blue in my paintbox was a lovely dark greeny blue, and hope sprang up as an idea took me — maybe this kind of cat had dark blue fur and then, oh maybe, if the hair didn't show on his navy suit. . . . I went to the Carnegie Library the following Saturday and looked up cats until I found a colour photograph and two descriptive references: a distinctive grey coat with a bluish cast, nothing like navy at all. I gave up on cats.

When I was in Grade 4, I became friends with a boy named Billy who lived on the edge of town. He and his sister Beatrice were known as "the poor kids" because their house looked more like a shack than anything else, and because the clothes they wore seemed always to be faded, patched and the wrong size. They were as mysterious as foreigners and I would not likely have made any attempt to know them except that one day during composition, Billy read aloud his paragraph about raising rabbits. After school that day I asked if I could come and see them, and he said yes, I could even help him feed the rabbits and clean their cages.

There was a whole wall of rabbits along the back of his father's chicken coop and Billy pointed to it with pride, beaming. Cage after cage of breathing fur, silent and unblinking. Not until he opened a cage door and gave me a big black female to hold did I understand what there was to like about rabbits: the heavy warmth against my body was so comforting I knew I had to have one or die. I began then to save from my weekly allowance and by early June had the dollar to pay him for a black-and-white baby rabbit. Billy said I could borrow a cage until I could buy or make another, and I set off for home with the rabbit in its cage balanced on the handlebars of my bicycle, full of plans, a little worried, but confident. I set the cage behind the garage in the shade of a lilac bush and went inside to ask my mother for some lettuce and old newspaper.

Although I had tried to sound offhand it was such a peculiar request, and I was so flushed with excitement, that she followed me outside. "Your father will never allow it," was the first thing she said. I argued with her a little, and knew when I said, "I just want something of my own to take care of and love," that I had scored a telling point. It worried her, I knew, that I was an only child and she felt guilty that she might have deprived me of a normal childhood. Sure enough, it had been exactly the right thing to say, for I heard her through the kitchen door when my father came home.

"Listen to me, Frank, this is important. That child has gone out and bought a rabbit because she wants a pet so badly. She can keep it out in the garage, it'll never be in the house. Really, by the end of the summer she'll be bored with it and the whole thing will be over."

Such insight and compassion on my mother's part was nearly unheard of, but for her own reasons she had decided to take on my father and he gave in, grudgingly. He came out once to look at the animal and grunted something about "stew," warned me to keep it outside, and that was all.

I sold the rabbit back to Billy before school was finished for 50¢, which I spent on butterscotch wafers. My mother smiled knowingly at my father, but she was wrong, I had *not* become bored. I had begun to hate the rabbit with such passion I was frightened to death I was going to kill it. The damp newspaper and pellets of poo gave off a sickening smell, and the pulpy bits of nibbled lettuce on the bottom of the cage were disgusting — but it was the animal itself that I loathed. The very thing that made it lovable to begin with, its idiotic passivity and furry heartbeat, grew to offend me so much I wanted to wring its neck. It was stupid, stupid, stupid, and my hands would clench around its little neck tighter and tighter. "Stupid goddamn rabbit," I would whisper. "You are too stupid to live."

The foolish creature would twitch its ears and whiskers and nose, and look blankly at me with its glassy eyes, and my heart turned to stone. I discovered that no matter how much love I lavished on it, or how much hate, it stayed exactly the same. I wanted something, *anything* to happen. I would have been charmed at that point if it had bitten me. But it didn't, and I had nightmare after nightmare about squeezing the soft fur around its neck until the head lolled to one side, finished with rabbity thoughts forever. Full of guilt and fear, I made the deal with Billy, and told my mother I couldn't bear to see the poor thing caged. She was touched, and we had a little talk about freedom, and how awful it must be to be my grandmother's canary. And that was the end of it.

By the time my father was no longer a banker, I was well over the need for a pet, had even completed the brief but obligatory fling with horseflesh that all my friends went through. By that time I was in ove, and whether my father wore navy suits or hairy suits or none at all didn't matter to me. All I cared about was Mr. Wheeling, and staying in Garten the rest of my life.

I was fourteen, three inches under six feet and going into Grade 10 when Jerry Wheeling, teacher of junior biology and senior chemistry, came to Garten District High School. He was 24, at least 6'5", with long bony wrists that hung from his shirt-cuffs so poignantly it made me want to cry until I watched him on the basketball court, coaching the boys' team, and I saw those same wrists fluid and flexible as rubber. It was like visible music. "It is wonderful to be in love," I wrote in the diary I began that year, "because it means you notice all the little things about a person."

There were far more obvious things than his wrists to notice about Jerry Wheeling. He was good-looking in a Hollywood way, with a thatch of cornsilk hair and a square but not jutting jaw. He was the first honest-to-goodness American many of us had ever met, and he had come up out of Ohio like a live advertisement for the great United States. He talked with a slight twang that soon all the basketball players were copying, used American slang like "cool" and "neat," and wore "sneakers" instead of running-shoes.

The reason he had come to Garten was that his bride of a year had become homesick for her family who lived about 40 miles away. He had applied for teaching jobs in a 100-mile radius of her home, he said, and Garten was the first town to reply. Her name was Mayruth, and when he spoke of her it was not with the professional detachment that other teachers used if it was necessary to speak of their spouses in the classroom. He called her his sweet Mayruth, and long before we met her, when he brought her with him to chaperone a dance that autumn, we knew all about her. We knew, for example, that they had met while she was down at Oberlin studying music, that she could play the piano with her eyes closed, that she was just a little bit of a thing, and that she was going to have a baby soon after Christmas.

He was, besides being our science teacher that year, homeroom adviser for 10A, and he changed my life. I rose an hour earlier so that I could practise my piano scales before breakfast (a discipline I had resisted for years), and then I would rush to school to get to the room, to be the first one there. He'd be sitting at his desk, marking assignments or reading, yet he always seemed accessible, open to conversation, even eager. I had never known an adult to be so casual, so ready to talk. Sometimes we would talk about sports, a favourite subject of his, and the boys would cluster around his desk too, showing off and butting in. One of these mornings he singled me out and said, "Now you, Elizabeth, have a natural advantage with your height. You'll be on the junior team, right?"

Said as an assumption, as if no-one had told him how awkward I was, as if he couldn't see it with his own two eyes. The boys all hooted, derisive as always, and said, "Oh, Mr. Wheeling, she's no good!" And he smiled right at me, so that it felt as if my chest was opening and my heart fluttering and flaming up into the air the way it does in Roman Catholic holy pictures, and he said, "Well, she *will* be good. Won't you, Elizabeth?"

So of course I tried out and got on the team for exactly the reason he had mentioned — I was big enough to be of some use. Sometimes he would drop into our practice sessions and chat with Mrs. Ridley, who'd been leading girls' teams to early defeats for years and years. Eventually he had her warmed up enough so that she didn't object when he came on the courts with us, showing us all kinds of neat plays we could do even within the rigid confines of Girls' Rules that prevented us from taking more than three steps with the ball and kept us on certain sections of the floor according to our positions, forwards and guards. Oh, how I longed to dribble down the floor, ball bouncing tenderly beneath my palm, the way Mr. Wheeling did. And then up, in a smooth, effortless muscular curve, the arm arching up and up and in, the ball would flip itself over the red rim and plop through the net and he would catch it, casual as fate, in his outstretched cupping hand.

I wanted to *be* him, and to be the ball at the same time. It was as near as I ever came to understanding the Holy Trinity.

In some ways Jerry Wheeling did become a kind of religion for me, supplanting all the old ways of seeing the world, bringing my life into a new focus. I had always been naturally inclined toward maths and sciences, high marks in these subjects balancing my lower grades in languages. I had an aptitude for the logic of the scientific method, loved the slow, peeling process of discovery in the labs, learning the names and functions of parts. Grasshopper, petunia, amoeba, everything had its place. Somehow, learning the names, you got power over the universe. It was Mr. Wheeling who first put that idea into my head. And then more. "The more you find out about the world," he said, "the more you find out there is to know. In science, every answer brings another question. You must never stop asking. Never." Then he would hand out the day's assignment, something so utterly removed from our normal school routine we would be baffled. Something like: *On the front desk you will find a (dead) frog. What are ten questions you might ask about it? Arrange these questions in a logical sequence of investigation.* And after our initial nervous laughter we would begin, and I would think of twenty questions, 30, more than enough to share with the girls around me. In Mr. Wheeling's class, I was popular.

Almost overnight I also became a good basketball player. My body suddenly slimming found within itself a core of energy, an intuitive knowledge of where the ball would arrive in the air, of when to jump and where to turn, when to block and where to run. I had never even dreamed of such success for myself and so quite naturally attributed everything to Mr. Wheeling. "If it weren't for him . . ." I would think, and then shudder. He, in his turn, must have found me equally necessary for his own view of himself. I was scientific proof of his growing skill as a teacher; and my devoted enthusiasm encouraged him in the face of a groundswell of opposition in the school and in the town.

At first, it was only a vague and predictable resentment of anyone new, especially one with that abrasive American openness so foreign in Garten. But worse than his manner was his confidence in new "educational methodology" and his disdain for old ways. We heard what the teachers said about him in the staff-room from Wendy, whose mother taught us Home Economics. She said they didn't much like him because he really thought he was somebody, didn't he? *And* because he refused to use the prescribed biology text that had been in service in Garten District High School for seventeen years and done us all very well, thank you. But that was just normal griping and would have eventually faded away, had he not made mistakes that kept him in the foreground of public attention.

The initial error was his usurping of Mrs. Ridley's authority with the junior girls' team. He didn't mean to, but if he was there, as he was more and more often, we turned to him for advice or praise and left her watching us from the side of the floor, swinging her whistle on its yellow rope in smaller and smaller circles. Possibly it came from her, the spinning threads of ugly speculation about why a young man would want to be hanging around girls' basketball practice. It had never been done before in Garten — women coached girls and men coached boys and any variation of that was "unnatural." Or maybe it came from one of the mothers — but it soon reached Mavis and she would ask peculiar, obvious questions like, "He doesn't touch you at all, does he dear?" I would lie and say no, of course not, all the while my body still thrilling to the memory of his hand on my shoulder-blade, his twangy voice urging me, "Up, up, Elizabeth!"

However, Mrs. Ridley and the mothers were soon silenced by the fact that our team, like the boys' teams, was suddenly winning every game they played with neighbouring towns and villages, and had a good chance to bring back to Garten trophies and cups at the end of the season. The male teachers, who had now begun to think of Wheeling as "a real asset to the school," and the principal, who saw the possibility of a little glory rubbing off on his shoulders, helped to quash the unsavoury rumours. In no time, tongues were stilled.

Then, in December, he made his second, more serious error. In our science class the conversation turned from the earthworm's procreation to more conventional methods, and Mr. Wheeling was asking us questions, I guess to see how much we knew. Half the class was bused in from the country and knew the facts of life from the barnyard on up, certainly knew what they had and what it was for. But Mr. Wheeling asked Amy, who was bright-looking but not very smart. She had taken, that year, to sitting hunched over with her arms folded against her chest, hoping to hide the truth we all knew; her breasts had not arrived. Nor had her period, according to Trudy who was the class informant on such matters. "What is the female organ of procreation in the mammal?" he asked her, as he leaned against the board, a yardstick held between his two flat open palms. Hesitant, hunching down with embarrassment, Amy asked back, "The belly-button?"

One of the boys at the back guffawed, but before it could roll and gather more laughter across the room Mr. Wheeling silenced us all with the tapping yardstick. "No, Amy," he said gently. "Not at all. That's where the umbilical cord connects while the baby still lives in the womb."

The room went as still as church as the image of sweet Mayruth rose up before our eyes, the way we had seen her two weeks ago at the dance — short, dark-haired, with a flat, freckled face, sitting pale and un-smiling with the chaperone teachers. She had clearly been uncomfort-able, her enormous belly jutting up and out so that she seemed nearly deformed, a less than human thing. She had stayed sitting most of the night, her hands folded over the giant puffball of her body, watching wistfully as her husband roamed the floor among the dancers, now and again giving his basketball players approving pats on their shoulders. He introduced some of us — "my homeroom girls," he said — but of course none of us knew what to say. She seemed hurt by our open, curi-ous stares and lowered her eyes after a few moments as if giving us a sig-nal to leave. We did. In the girls' washroom there was a sudden flurry of supposition about what it must feel like, how heavy and awful it must be, and how Mr. Wheeling had stuck his thing in her to get her that way and he was so tall and she was so little, how did they ever . . . ?

Now, in the classroom, we waited for his next words. "Let me show you, Amy," he said. He turned to the board and drew the stylized bull's head of uterus and fallopian tubes, the double squiggle of ova-ries, and the long narrow channel of the vagina, like a stem. "These are the female organs, Amy," he said. "With some minor variations, they are present in the abdomens of all female mammals." Throughout the room girls put hands on their stomachs involuntarily, aware of them-selves as mammals whose hidden organs procreate the race. Faces flam-ing, hearts pounding, praying inside ourselves, don't stop, don't stop.

He didn't. He went on to trace the egg from the ovary down the tube where it met a quick, chalky sperm he drew to look like a tad-pole. Then the cell division, and the embryo, his blackboard brush working in jerky sweeps as the drawings grew and changed, the uterus enlarging to accommodate the next curling foetus, and then, as he was finishing the final stage, where the bulging baby lay connected to its placental home but ready to emerge, the end-of-class buzzer rang. The room jolted, as if out of a dream. We had all, Mr. Wheeling and each of us, been growing and growing inside the white outlines of sweet May-ruth's womb. It had been magic and peaceful, hardly a word spoken, the secret of life unfolding before our eyes, flesh conquered in his dia-grams. Beautiful, sad and frightening: because the narrow stem below the baby hadn't changed at all. How could the baby get through that? How? We left the room quietly but as soon as we were in the hall the talk began. Maybe tomorrow he would draw *that*.

Of course, there was no tomorrow. Phones were ringing around Garten that very night and by nine o'clock a white-faced Mavis was standing at the door of my bedroom. Inquisitor, guardian of virtue.

"No, Mommy, no, he didn't," I said. "It was just the place where the baby is."

"But didn't he show you how it got there?" she asked, her mouth nervous around such details.

"Only the little sperm thing that meets the egg, just like in that book you showed me *years* ago," I said.

"Mrs. Tabor says that she heard he drew (here, a grimace of disgust) the male organ inserting itself." Horror and shame manifest in my mother's wrinkled nose.

"Oh honestly, no, that's a lie! That's just kids making up a big story, honestly, believe me. Really, no," I said.

(In fact, Josh, one of the big farm kids who sat at the back, spread the even better lie that Mr. Wheeling had taken out his own penis, laid it out on the desk and said, "That there's the male organ what done it!" Probably nobody believed it, but the story was titillating enough to make the rounds for some weeks after.)

I barely slept, so frightened of what might happen. I knew what could happen if men like my father decided someone was a bad influ-ence in Garten — he'd be fired, banished tomorrow. But luck played fair with truth for this one time, and Mr. Wheeling was able to con-vince the principal that what he had done was not conducive to impro-priety. In return for his promise never to take sex education into his own hands again, the principal backed him against the irate parents — after all, there were the basketball trophies in February still to be won. All that Mr. Wheeling had to do was to apologize to our class the next day, and ask any of us who had made notes from his blackboard sketches to turn them in. And we returned, relieved and chastened, to the lowly divisions of the earthworm.

Then it was Christmas and we all forgot about the excitement of scandal in the swollen anticipations of the season. What would we get this year? What my father got at Christmas was a letter he had long been expecting from the Toronto office, telling where his next appoint-ment would be. To have stayed ten years in one town was either a rare privilege the bank gave to those managers considered a credit and an influence, or else a punishment for those who were better left in the backwaters. Until he learned where they would be sending him next, my father wouldn't really know how he was regarded, whether he was on his way up or down.

"North Bay!" my mother said. "Oh Frank, we can't, we can't!" She'd waited so long, praying for so many years that we would be sent back to Toronto, that he would be given a nice bank in Weston or even Willowdale. She had dreamed and dreamed of getting out of Garten, of getting back into what she called "the mainstream of life." The blow was severe; she said she felt shattered. She and I united immediately in an odd sort of partnership against my father, neither of us willing to move to a place we'd never been. I would not leave Mr. Wheeling, I promised myself in the dark, listening to the urgent whispers from their bedroom across the hall. Somehow, somehow life had to stay as it was, there had to be some way of halting the awful flux threatening to sweep me and Mavis along.

"The north is opening up," my father said, trying to calm my mother. "This is a great promotion, Mavis, I'll be manager of a bank doing very big business. Mining, forestry, it's all happening up there. North Bay is the heart of the province, the heart, Mavis."

My mother would not be comforted. I think she would have preferred Sudbury, ugly as it was, where she had an uncle and there would be the wealthy Inco wives to play bridge with, to have to tea. Some kind of establishment, some kind of connection with Bay Street in Toronto, the real world of finance and culture. But North Bay? Who in the world had ever heard of North Bay? A town for tourists, she sniffed, but not a place of consequence, not suitable for giving the child a proper education. The bush, it was really just glorified bush!

Frank Kessler looked at his life, his wife and his daughter united against him, and for what was (as far as I know) the only time in his life, he gambled. "If you had a choice, Mavis, would you really rather stay here forever?"

"At least I know Garten," she said. "At least I have a *place* in the community."

It wasn't an unequivocal yes, but it was enough for him to pursue an offer that had been made to him months before. Three men had come to his office in the summer, saying they wanted a loan to begin a wholesale hardware business in the town. "Say, Frank," one of them had said, "if you ever get tired of the bank here, we'd take you on as an accountant, make you a partner, even. What do you say?"

At that point, still waiting for the Imperial to steer his life onto some more rewarding course, he had demurred, given them a good loan, and ushered them out of his office. Good men, all of them, with good sound business sense. Two were Mennonite, a blacksmith and a buggymaker, and the other of German stock, like himself. Men who saw a need and a way to fill it, opportunists in the classical mould. Able to take a chance, which he, by his very nature, was not. But here, now, the odds had changed — if he followed the bank's orders, he would have a living hell with his wife and child. And if he defied the bank, asked for an extension or showed any hesitancy, they'd see him as dead-wood, a man of 50 not able to handle new fields. And he'd be passed on down to far worse, far smaller places than Garten. No, he thought, there was no point in refusing the post unless he had somewhere else to go. I heard him telling my mother all this late one night in the living-room as I lay at the top of the stairs, my heart thudding dangerously loud in my ears.

So he phoned Elisha Martin the blacksmith, and they talked, and in a matter of days a deal was made and he agreed to take out his pension as a lump sum on leaving the bank and invest it in the new company. They would supply hardware stores in the area and let owners of stores buy shares in their company so that all profits would be shared and it would be in their interest to invest. It would be called Honesty Distributing and they would run the company along the most Christian of guidelines. And they would have all those Mennonite farmers, all the small hardware store owners in all those small towns in the county falling over themselves investing. It *would* work, he told my mother. Everything he knew about business from all those years in the bank told him it would work. And now, here was a chance for him to be part of the action, not just the man behind a desk doling out loans. "Oh Mavis," he said, "trust me. I love you."

Lying on the carpet, my body froze as if his words were needles of ice injected in all my limbs. Frank loved her. I'd never heard him say it before — oh, it had been written on birthday cards and on anniversary and Christmas presents and was of course assumed. But this had been the voice of someone other than my father, doing his husbandly duty. It had been the voice of a young man, pleading; for everything was out there to gain if only his true love would trust him.

She did. She really had no choice, and she was not particularly giv-ing or gracious about it; in fact, she went through six or seven months of the worst tension headaches she had ever had. Coinciding as they did with the hot flushes and depressions that were the bane of her exis-tence those days, life was not easy for any of us. But the Imperial Bank accepted my father's resignation with regrets — 27 years he had given them, and for that he got a plaque on his marble desk set. His pension, as he had requested, was immediately transferred to his savings account from where it went as part of his investment in Honesty Distributing.

All I cared about during these events was that the outcome meant we could stay in Garten, and I could see Jerry Wheeling five days a week, and he could smile at me and say, in his twangy American way, "You are one neat kid, Elizabeth."

The trials of my father's life were overlaid in my mind by a tapestry of a far more tragic, vivid design. During the Christmas holidays, we learned when we got back to school, the Wheelings' baby had been born while they were visiting Mayruth's parents. A girl, named Nancy. Born three weeks early, with spina bifida. None of us had ever heard of spina bifida before, and relying on Wendy as we were for all our news, we were in a froth of horror and excitement by the time Mr. Wheeling returned, a week late, his face white and drawn.

"I'm sure you have all heard, from one source or another, that I am now a father," he said to our homeroom that morning. The winter sun shone mercilessly through the windows as if this was an occasion when we should all be smiling. "Her name is Nancy, and she is a beautiful baby with reddish-blond hair. But she has an impairment of the spine that I will describe to you in science class later today."

And he did, with clinical detachment and great care not to frighten us, tell us then how the vertebrae had not connected at the base of the baby's spine, and how there was no likelihood that she would ever walk. "She's still in the hospital now so they can keep observing the spinal fluid for a few more weeks," he said. "But when she comes home, you may all come visit and see what a pretty little girl she is."

This is what I choose to remember about Jerry Wheeling: his courage, his compassion, his concern for our ignorant fears of what might lie ahead for us when we grew up, had babies. Explaining and explaining, as if scientific language could dispel our misgivings and his disappointment.

The tragedy softened the mothers' hearts in Garten and took the starch out of their opposition to his brash, foreign ways. "Poor thing," they all said. And he was invited to homes for supper all the time Mayruth was away, given encouragement and support and sympathy. Not by the Kesslers, though. Mavis was having so many nervous headaches that our house was perpetually draped in twilight as she lay in various rooms with curtains pulled, blinds down. My father and I walked softly, whispering whenever we spoke, which was not often. We barely communicated, each of us in our own egg of pain. I know now that he was going through a very difficult time then, wondering if indeed he had done the right thing, wondering if these fool Mennonites knew what they were doing with his money. But there was no-one for him to talk to, no-one to give him comfort. Mavis lay in the dark with a cool cloth on her forehead, seeing before her a nightmare, the wrong choice made, the rest of her life as the wife of a merchant, a hardware wholesaler. And I? How could *I* suddenly give Frank Kessler *comfort?* I knew only to avoid him and study my own grief.

My sadness took on the gaudy colours of guilt as it became apparent to me that there was something wrong with the baby because of my feelings for my teacher. God worked in strange ways; that had been drummed into us all since earliest Sunday school. Maybe this punishment had been sent down on Jerry Wheeling for invoking my love. "Oh punish me, Lord," I would weep into my pillow. "Punish me, but heal poor Nancy's spine."

Poor Nancy and sweet Mayruth came back to Garten in March, after our team had won the junior girls' basketball trophy for the southwest end of the province. Mr. Wheeling had been able to devote hours and hours to our improvement on the courts, and we repaid his efforts with absolute determination. The junior and senior boys' teams won as well, and only the senior girls, still coached solely by Mrs. Ridley, failed to place. The school honoured us all with a Celebration Dance at which Mr. Wheeling was the star. He was wearing a pale-blue shirt and his fair hair was longer than usual so that it curled a little around his ears and fell forward on his forehead. He seemed feverish from the adulation being heaped upon him; he was flushed and his eyes were skimmed over, unfocused. He must have had a flask of vodka in his jacket; it is a boozy kind of looseness I recall in his jaw. But of course, I didn't think that then, only that he seemed so relaxed.

"Will one of the stars dance with her coach?" he said as I passed him, coming back from the girls' washroom where I spent most of my time at dances.

"Sure, sir," I said, and let myself be taken by the hand and led out into the protective dark of the gymnasium floor. It was crowded and noisy and Jo Stafford's voice flowed like warm honeybutter from the loudspeakers. It was the first of many times we danced together and for that the most memorable. My height suddenly became the same advantage it was on the basketball court, for with my high-heeled shoes on my face came nearly even with his, and as we danced sometimes his cheek would brush against my hair. I was a good dancer — so light on my feet for a girl my size, Mrs. Ridley had often said when we were learning polkas and horas and foxtrots in Grade 9 — and now I was like a shadow, following his lean body around the room.

At the end of the first dance we stood for a moment, self-conscious, until he said, "May I have the next, Miss Kessler?" and I said, "Of course, Mr. Wheeling," and then before the third we didn't say anything, we just looked at each other. My legs felt as if they might splay away from my body at any moment and then *Stars Fell on Alabama* came on and he took me in his arms and we moved like fish in a darkened aquarium through the seaweed of music and bodies. Like fish in the deep, like stars in the dark, we clung and glided. He was making me happier than I'd ever been — in every cell of myself I felt expanded, filled with an entirely new sense of purpose.

At the end of that song one of the other chaperones cut in and said, "Hey now, Jer, just because you're the coach doesn't mean you get to dance with the pretty girls all the time, eh?" and before I knew it I was in the arms of Nels Ferguson, the math teacher, who was, by common consent, a real turd, and smelled under the arms.

It didn't matter. Nothing mattered except this: I knew now I wasn't just fantasizing the way I used to do with movie stars. He liked me too; I knew it, it was all true.

Then, when Mayruth came home, he suddenly became a distant, remote figure on the edge of our lives. Once basketball was over there was no reason for him to stay around the school after classes, he went right home at four. And in the mornings, even if we were in the room early he had so many papers to mark he never had time for talking. "Sorry," he'd say, if one of us tried to open a conversation with him. "I'm up to my neck."

No-one ever saw either of the Wheelings out and about, and he never invited us to see Nancy as he had promised. Mayruth seemed more reclusive than ever, and we speculated endlessly on why they were never seen on the streets like everyone else in Garten — shame, or grief, or shyness? Finally, in May, I could stand it no longer. "Look, Mr. Wheeling, if you ever need a babysitter so you and Mrs. Wheeling can go out, I take care of kids in the neighbourhood all the time. I'm sure I could sit Nancy for you. Just ask if you ever need me." He looked at me with the most startled expression and I blushed because I knew my motives were not pure. I simply wanted greater access to his life. But he said, "Why, Elizabeth, what a good idea. Terrific."

Mayruth called me the next week and I went over after supper on a Friday night and they went out shopping and then to a restaurant. She was so nervous and grateful I felt as if I were doing something truly good, letting her out of a cage. They lived in one of the wartime houses, right across town from Brubacher Street, and I was struck by the temporariness of the place in contrast to the solid brick walls I knew. Everything there was clapboard and peeling paint, small wooden porches and bare lightbulbs over the front doors. Inside, the Wheelings' house had the same unsettled quality, as if they had never meant to be there. On the turquoise plaster walls they had hung several family photographs in an attempt to personalize the rooms; but for some reason that only heightened the sense of transience.

The baby's room was painted a violent pink colour, and all the furniture was white. Nancy slept in a large wooden crib, covered by pink and white blankets. She was asleep when I arrived, and as soon as they left I went into her room to look at her. Her little face was puckered and her fist clenched by her cheek, as if she were worrying. Gingerly, I lifted the covers from her small body and turned her over so that I could look at her back. But all there was, under the loosened diaper, was a raised dome of flesh, about the size of a small half-orange. Only that, and her legs would never work. I stood in a kind of sickened fascination for a long time, watching her sleep, wondering what it was that I felt. And then I returned to the living-room and read through all their back issues of *Time*.

I took care of Nancy several times before they left in July to spend the summer with Mayruth's parents in Muskoka, and came to know the house and their lives in a peculiar, vicarious way. Girls like Trudy were openly jealous when I flaunted my knowledge ("They have a book called *The Sexual Side of Marriage* on the bedside table") and called me a teacher's pet. But I felt my prestige as spy was above such pettiness, and I made the Wheelings my primary topic of conversation. I kept secret, however, the feelings I had about being walked home by Jerry Wheeling through the tree-lined streets of Garten — they had no car, and he was compelled by custom to see the sitter home once it was dark. The pale night sky of late spring and early summer, the heavy fragrance of lilacs and false orange, the sounds of the last late tag-players on Faber Street calling out "Home free!" . . . and the slow, earnest conversation we would have about stars, or birds, or God. It was, even at the time, very nearly like dancing.

By the time school began again in the fall, I was an inch taller than I'd been in June, but mercifully that was the end of it. The extra height seemed to finish me off, so that I appeared as graceful as I ever would, and I used to stand alone in my bedroom, underpants and brassière simulating cheesecake bathing-suit, posing in front of my mirror so that I could admire my shape. But after I was dressed, in layers of crinolines and full cotton skirt clinched in by a wide elastic belt, I looked badly put together, drawn too large for the page. And once I got to school, I felt myself looming over the smaller, more appropriately sized girls.

We didn't have Mr. Wheeling for homeroom teacher that year, nor did we have him for any classes. This was the year we had to take physics, and his courses, chemistry and biology, would come in our final two years. Happily for me there was still basketball, and there I was able to see him, be touched by him. My mother's health had improved over the summer, as had the chances of Honesty Distributing getting off the ground, so that the attention at home could again be focused on me, on what I was doing at school, what I was thinking, how I was acting, where I was going. Inevitably my mother's scrutiny turned to the amount of time I spent in the company of "that American."

"Why I've heard from June that you even walk him home after school," she said, her face taut with distaste. "I've never heard the like. What *can* you be thinking of?"

"Oh, Mother, that's not even true," I said. "Sometimes after basketball practice my legs are sore and he said a brisk walk is good for the muscles, loosens them up. So I walk to the post office corner and then back home. Sometimes he's on his way home but usually I'm alone. Honestly, that's just Trudy telling her Mom stories because she's jealous, she wishes she were on the team and she's not. Honestly."

He had come back all tanned and crisp in his pale blue shirts and his hair seemed even more fair. But he was different, even more aloof than he had been in the spring. He never wanted to talk the way he had. "Just walk along like a good quiet friend," he would say, and we would take long strides together.

In early October Mayruth called me to sit with Nancy while they took the bus into the city for a Saturday matinee, and I could see immediately that the baby had not thrived during the summer. She seemed awfully puny and weak, and it was apparent now that she couldn't move properly, that she was going to be a cripple. When they came home Mayruth invited me to stay for supper but I said I had better go, my mother would be expecting me. "Come and see Nancy any time you like," she said at the door. "You can come and visit, you know, you don't have to wait to be called to babysit."

I looked down at her pale freckled face with much confusion. Was she saying this because she thought I was devoted to the baby? I wasn't; I didn't much like her, she made me feel far too much pity and guilt. Or was she asking me to be *her* friend? After all, there were barely six years between us, and she was desperately lonely and shy. But I couldn't. I couldn't be her friend because I loved her husband; it just wouldn't be right.

But I couldn't stop myself thinking about Mayruth's small sad face, her breathy, hesitant voice asking me something under the words. I could feel her plucking at me and eventually I knew I would give in. One afternoon, when there was no girls' basketball practice, I left school and walked directly to the wartime houses. It was unseasonably warm; I would offer to take Nancy out for a carriage stroll and that way make peace with myself.

It took a very long time for Mayruth to answer the door, but I rang the bell several times and waited, knowing that she must be there because she never went anywhere without her husband. Eventually the door opened, only a little. She had her hand over one side of her face.

"Oh, Elizabeth, it's you, come in. I wasn't sure who it might be, I look such a fright. . . ." Her voice trailed off and in an apologetic way she lowered her hand and I saw that the whole side of her face was a massive, yellowish bruise. "I didn't turn on the upstairs light and I tripped on a pile of laundry I'd left on the top step," she said. "What an idiot, eh? Well, I've learned my lesson, that's for sure. I'm just glad I didn't break my arm." And she showed me her elbow and upper arm, black and mauve like a summer storm sky. I felt my stomach heave and twist in revulsion; confronted by such clumsiness, such vulnerability, I only wanted to run away.

But I stayed, and shook little rattles at Nancy to make her laugh, and pretended that I thought she was a lovely baby. And I listened to Mayruth tell about how she'd been on a music scholarship to Oberlin and in her first year had met Mr. Wheeling. "Well, I guess I can call him Jerry in front of you, Elizabeth," she said. And she showed me some old photographs of what they'd looked like just four years before when they'd been going out to proms and football games together. He was lanky, awkward-looking in whatever clothes he wore, with hair cut so short he seemed nearly bald in black-and-white snapshots. She seemed always to be dressed in something full-skirted and tight-waisted, aiming a dimpled, adoring smile at his shoulder. In some pictures she held a plaid wool blanket over one arm and had a tassled toque pulled down over one eye. Flirtatious, raffish, coy. Only later do I think to comment how much her demeanour changed once married. Then, I only thought how much better I would have looked by his side, tall, straightforward and unafraid. And I thought how unfair it was, the way life worked itself out so badly.

That night at supper I told Mavis and Frank about what a nice time I'd had with Mrs. Wheeling that afternoon and how lonely she seemed. "We should have them over for dinner sometime, Mommy," I said. "She's awfully shy and they really don't ever go out with the baby. There's still that old crib in the basement we could bring up for Nancy, so they could bring her too."

I knew better than to pester, so that the next two or three weeks passed without any plans to have the Wheelings over. My father was usually out every evening with his hardware partners, working on their plans for a warehouse, and my mother said we would just have to wait until he wasn't so busy before we could invite company. And then it was too late. In November, I heard in the corridor at school that Mr. Wheeling wasn't in that day because his baby had died in the night.

"Crib death," said all the mothers of Garten, a chorus on the edge of the tragedy, eager to explain events in the light of their own experience. And sure enough, that's what Dr. Waddell's verdict was too. "We don't know *why* these poor little tykes die," he said to Mavis that same week during a bridge party she and Frank attended at the doctor's house. "But for some reason there are infants who simply stop breathing and pass away in their sleep. One of God's mysteries we still haven't solved."

It was the same explanation that Mr. Wheeling gave when he returned to school a week later, looking as if he had not slept himself during all that time for fear of his own life ending. I went to his room after classes, feeling as if I should make some gesture. I had, after all, been the babysitter for that frail little soul, and I should be mourning her death — even though I felt nothing except relief that she was gone.

"Elizabeth," he said when I came into his room, and I was horribly afraid he was going to cry. His face crumpled and reformed around my name and he finally said, "Mayruth said to thank you when I saw you for the card and the flowers. She's going to stay with her folks for a few weeks. She's taking the whole thing pretty hard."

"How are *you?*" I asked, emphasizing the last word with the implication that it was insensitive of sweet Mayruth to leave him alone during such a sad time. He looked startled, surprised no doubt by the personal tone of my question.

"Oh well, I'll make out," he said, and he suddenly smiled. "It was all for the best. You know that, don't you? It's just that Mayruth can't see it that way."

"I love you," I said suddenly, unaware I was going to say it until it had been said.

"I know that, Elizabeth," he said, his face becoming long and sombre again. "I know that. But we won't speak of it, not now."

I ran from the room, humiliated by his gentle tone. Later that afternoon I felt such embarrassment at the thought of facing him I told Mrs. Ridley that I had period cramps and couldn't stay for basketball practice. When I got home I told my mother I thought I was getting the flu, and went to my room where I sat on the bed, laying out cards for clock solitaire, until suppertime.

We didn't exchange words again until early December at the Christmas Couples' Dance, to which I had bribed Tommy Bauman to take me by promising him all that term's physics experiments. Mr. Wheeling had come to the dance alone and stood against the back wall with three other male teachers, neither talking nor dancing as he usually did. Tommy was the tallest boy in our class, which is why I had asked him, but he couldn't dance very well and he didn't much like me and so we shunted around the floor in an aimless, loosely held way, both miserable. All night long my body felt empty and concave as an open clam shell, wanting to be gathered up by Jerry Wheeling's long sad arms and crushed against his chest. Half an hour before the dance was over he came to where Tommy and I were standing in resentful silence and said, "Coach's choice, Tom." Tommy was one of his senior boys and would have died for him; giving up a dance with Elizabeth Kessler was pure pleasure. "Keep her as long as you want, Sir," he said, and ducked out the sidedoor of the gym.

We danced only one dance and I can't remember the song. My body was pulled up against his so tightly that my breasts felt flattened and bruised and the side of my face, where it touched his jaw, burned. He hummed in my ear, a low tuneless moan, and his fingers pressed into my back, each fingertip a separate, exquisite pressure. And I felt within myself a gathering sadness, a sorrow in the flesh, as if my body knew too much for the mind to bear, as if the blood humming up and down my limbs held more awful knowledge than it could tell.

He went to Ohio for the holidays, and we heard when he got back to school in January that he had come back to town with Mayruth. I kept meaning to go and see her but after school there was always basketball and I didn't want to go on the weekend in case he might be there. She, for her part, became even more reclusive than she'd been when Nancy was alive, and the neighbours said they never saw her out.

The basketball finals were in February that year and we expected to win. Mr. Wheeling had devoted himself to our team and we in return had mastered every intricate play and trick he had taught us. We had become experts at the fast pivot, feinting a pass one direction and then turning and throwing the ball another. The forwards had picked up his easy style of rising up off the floor just at the basket and flicking the wrist up and out so that the ball would flip sweetly up, out and down through the net. The guards became confidently aggressive and sly, always ahead of the game. I had turned into the kind of player I most admired — fast, light and totally unpredictable, always in control of the ball.

We won the game easily, and on the bus back home to the Celebration Dance at the school, Mrs. Ridley suggested to us girls that we go over and ask Mrs. Wheeling to join us, since she had given up her husband to the team for so many weeks. We all laughed and said what a good idea that was, and Karen and Diane volunteered to go. "Don't tell Mr. Wheeling," Mrs. Ridley said. "It'll be a nice surprise for him when she gets here."

When the bus arrived back at the school, the two girls went off on the run. They were back in half an hour, without her. "She came to the door like a scared little rabbit," Diane said. "And when she turned on the porch light we could see she had bandages on her face. She said she had been putting her suitcases away at the top of a closet and they all fell down on her, and she wouldn't think of coming out when she looks such a mess." Inwardly, we were all relieved, I think. We *all* wanted to keep Mr. Wheeling to ourselves that night, he had shown us the way to glory. But when he heard what had happened, that the girls had gone to see Mayruth, he decided to leave the dance and go home. I felt betrayed, and without him the celebration soured and died. Who cared, really, about winning, if he weren't there to say how terrific we were, how terrific, how neat.

Two weeks later it was all over.

Sweet Mayruth fled to the neighbours in the middle of the night, bleeding from the mouth and bruised all about her head and shoulders. Phone my parents, she is reported to have said. Have them come and take me home. Get me out of here before I die.

The neighbours, an elderly couple who were the caretakers for our church (and so Mavis got many of the details from the minister's wife), phoned not only her parents but the police, and Jerry Wheeling was arrested and booked for assault.

None of us ever saw him again. I wanted to testify at the trial but I was under sixteen and the lawyer, when I called him, said he would convey my best wishes to his client and hung up. I wanted to say, "Tell him I love him," but I knew he knew that already and it might have been the wrong thing to say to a lawyer.

My mother said she could sleep nights now that that man was locked up. "I never did trust him," she said, "and it used to make me quite ill, all the time you spent with him, Elizabeth. I shudder to think what might have happened." My father said that what could you expect, violence had always been part of the American character, and we should all just consider ourselves lucky he took it out on his wife.

There was some stirring of renewed interest in exactly how poor Nancy had died but Dr. Waddell stood by his original statement of natural causes and the matter was let alone. Mr. Wheeling's trial in the city wasn't until several months later, and although there were rumoured to be all manner of complications, he was eventually found guilty. The week he was sentenced to four years in jail, the Garten *Enterprise* had a big story on the front page, with a photo of him taken from the school yearbook. At the end of the story it mentioned that Mrs. Wheeling was suing for divorce.

My mother said there was no justice, that man should have been put away for life. My father just grunted and said he would read about it in the paper when he got back from the warehouse. My mother said, "At least when you were with the bank you were home some evenings." My father turned and looked at her with as pure a hate as I have ever seen.

He became a rich man, Frank Kessler. There are Honesty Distributing outlets across the province now, with plans for the Maritimes in the near future. He retired at 60, so that he and Mavis could enjoy his money in good health, spending half the winter in Florida, and the rest travelling across North America in their mobile home.

Jamaica Kincaid

Jamaica Kincaid's narrative voice — she favors the first person — is authentic and unsparing, and the reader cannot help feeling that the narrator is speaking directly to him or her, as in an intimate conversation or from the pages of a diary. She employs a straightforward, formal diction — much as the young narrator of Richard Ford's "Great Falls" does — and this lends an impression of earnestness to the writing, as if the narrator is sticking strictly to the rules of propriety because it is so very important to get everything just right. Most notably, her narrators rarely use the contractions or slang of casual speech, as, for example, in this passage from her 1996 novel, *The Autobiography of My Mother:* "My mother died at the moment I was born, and so for my whole life there was nothing standing between myself and eternity; at my back was always a bleak, black wind. I could not have known at the beginning of my life that this would be so; I only came to know this in the middle of life, just at the time when I was no longer young and realized that I had less of some of the things I used to have in abundance and more of some of the things I scarcely had at all." This is powerful and testamentary, and it is the voice that infuses all her narratives (as does the regret offered up by that "bleak, black wind").

Jamaica Kincaid is the author of the novels *Annie John, Lucy, My Brother,* and *Mr. Potter,* among others, and the nonfiction volume *A Small Place,* an unsentimental look at Antigua, the West Indian island on which she was born. I first came to her work with *Lucy* and was immediately taken with the power and directness of her narrative, which concerns the two great dislocations in a young girl's life — her estrangement from her mother and her encounter with a new culture. The first selection here, "Poor Visitor," is the opening chapter of that novel. It has the concision of a short story and speaks eloquently to the cultural misapprehensions of even the most well-intentioned. Too many of us judge people on first sight by color and class — pigeonhole them — but Lucy, with her firm sense of self, defies any attempt to limit or stereotype her. The second piece here, "Figures in the Distance," is also excerpted from a novel *(Annie John)*. It deals with a familiar rite of passage, a ten-year-old girl's first experience of death, but it does so with a clarity — and impishness — that makes the material new.

Poor Visitor

It was my first day. I had come the night before, a gray-black and cold night before — as it was expected to be in the middle of January, though I didn't know that at the time — and I could not see anything clearly on the way in from the airport, even though there were lights everywhere. As we drove along, someone would single out to me a famous building, an important street, a park, a bridge that when built was thought to be a spectacle. In a daydream I used to have, all these places were points of happiness to me; all these places were lifeboats to my small drowning soul, for I would imagine myself entering and leaving them, and just that — entering and leaving over and over again — would see me through a bad feeling I did not have a name for. I only knew it felt a little like sadness but heavier than that. Now that I saw these places, they looked ordinary, dirty, worn down by so many people entering and leaving them in real life, and it occurred to me that I could not be the only person in the world for whom they were a fixture of fantasy. It was not my first bout with the disappointment of reality and it would not be my last. The undergarments that I wore were all new, bought for my journey, and as I sat in the car, twisting this way and that to get a good view of the sights before me, I was reminded of how uncomfortable the new can make you feel.

I got into an elevator, something I had never done before, and then I was in an apartment and seated at a table, eating food just taken from a refrigerator. In the place I had just come from, I always lived in a house, and my house did not have a refrigerator in it. Everything I was experiencing — the ride in the elevator, being in an apartment, eating day-old food that had been stored in a refrigerator — was such a good idea that I could imagine I would grow used to it and like it very much, but at first it was all so new that I had to smile with my mouth turned down at the corners. I slept soundly that night, but it wasn't because I was happy and comfortable — quite the opposite; it was because I didn't want to take in anything else.

That morning, the morning of my first day, the morning that followed my first night, was a sunny morning. It was not the sort of bright sun-yellow making everything curl at the edges, almost in fright, that I was used to, but a pale-yellow sun, as if the sun had grown weak from trying too hard to shine; but still it was sunny, and that was nice and made me miss my home less. And so, seeing the sun, I got up and put on a dress, a gay dress made out of madras cloth, the same sort of dress that I would wear if I were at home and setting out for a day in the country. It was all wrong. The sun was shining but the air was cold. It was the middle of January, after all. But I did not know that the sun could shine and the air remain cold; no one had ever told me. What a feeling that was! How can I explain? Something I had always known — the way I knew my skin was the color brown of a nut rubbed repeatedly with a soft cloth, or the way I knew my own name — something I took completely for granted, "the sun is shining, the air is warm," was not so. I was no longer in a tropical zone, and this realization now entered my life like a flow of water dividing formerly dry and solid ground, creating two banks, one of which was my past — so familiar and predictable that even my unhappiness then made me happy now just to think of it — the other, my future, a gray blank, an overcast seascape on which rain was falling and no boats were in sight. I was no longer in a tropical zone and I felt cold inside and out, the first time such a sensation had come over me.

In books I had read — from time to time, when the plot called for it — someone would suffer from homesickness. A person would leave a not very nice situation and go somewhere else, somewhere a lot better, and then long to go back where it was not very nice. How impatient I would become with such a person, for I would feel that I was in a not very nice situation myself, and how I wanted to go somewhere else. But now I, too, felt that I wanted to be back where I came from. I understood it, I knew where I stood there. If I had had to draw a picture of my future then, it would have been a large gray patch surrounded by black, blacker, blackest.

What a surprise this was to me, that I longed to be back in the place that I came from, that I longed to sleep in a bed I had outgrown, that I longed to be with people whose smallest, most natural gesture would call up in me such a rage that I longed to see them all dead at my feet. Oh, I had imagined that with my one swift act — leaving home and coming to this new place — I could leave behind me, as if it were an old garment never to be worn again, my sad thoughts, my sad feelings, and my discontent with life in general as it presented itself to me. In the past, the thought of being in my present situation had been a comfort, but now I did not even have this to look forward to, and so I lay down on my bed and dreamt I was eating a bowl of pink mullet and green figs cooked in coconut milk, and it had been cooked by my grandmother, which was why the taste of it pleased me so, for she was the person I liked best in all the world and those were the things I liked best to eat also.

The room in which I lay was a small room just off the kitchen — the maid's room. I was used to a small room, but this was a different sort of small room. The ceiling was very high and the walls went all the way up to the ceiling, enclosing the room like a box — a box in which cargo traveling a long way should be shipped. But I was not cargo. I was only an unhappy young woman living in a maid's room, and I was not even the maid. I was the young girl who watches over the children and goes to school at night. How nice everyone was to me, though, saying that I should regard them as my family and make myself at home. I believed them to be sincere, for I knew that such a thing would not be said to a member of their real family. After all, aren't family the people who become the millstone around your life's neck? On the last day I spent at home, my cousin — a girl I had known all my life, an unpleasant person even before her parents forced her to become a Seventh-Day Adventist — made a farewell present to me of her own Bible, and with it she made a little speech about God and goodness and blessings. Now it sat before me on a dresser, and I remembered how when we were children we would sit under my house and terrify and torment each other by reading out loud passages from the Book of Revelation, and I wondered if ever in my whole life a day would go by when these people I had left behind, my own family, would not appear before me in one way or another.

There was also a small radio on this dresser, and I had turned it on. At that moment, almost as if to sum up how I was feeling, a song came on, some of the words of which were "Put yourself in my place, if only for a day; see if you can stand the awful emptiness inside." I sang these words to myself over and over, as if they were a lullaby, and I fell asleep again. I dreamt then that I was holding in my hands one of my old cotton-flannel nightgowns, and it was printed with beautiful scenes of children playing with Christmas-tree decorations. The scenes printed on my nightgown were so real that I could actually hear the children laughing. I felt compelled to know where this nightgown came from, and I started to examine it furiously, looking for the label. I found it just where a label usually is, in the back, and it read "Made in Australia." I was awakened from this dream by the actual maid, a woman who had let me know right away, on meeting me, that she did not like me, and gave as her reason the way I talked. I thought it was because of something else, but I did not know what. As I opened my eyes, the word "Australia" stood between our faces, and I remembered then that Australia was settled as a prison for bad people, people so bad that they couldn't be put in a prison in their own country.

※

My waking hours soon took on a routine. I walked four small girls to their school, and when they returned at midday I gave them a lunch of soup from a tin, and sandwiches. In the afternoon, I read to them and played with them. When they were away, I studied my books, and at night I went to school. I was unhappy. I looked at a map. An ocean stood between me and the place I came from, but would it have made a difference if it had been a teacup of water? I could not go back.

Outside, always it was cold, and everyone said that it was the coldest winter they had ever experienced; but the way they said it made me think they said this every time winter came around. And I couldn't blame them for not really remembering each year how unpleasant, how unfriendly winter weather could be. The trees with their bare, still limbs looked dead, and as if someone had just placed them there and planned to come back and get them later; all the windows of the houses were shut tight, the way windows are shut up when a house will be empty for a long time; when people walked on the streets they did it quickly, as if they were doing something behind someone's back, as if they didn't want to draw attention to themselves, as if being out in the cold too long would cause them to dissolve. How I longed to see someone lingering on a corner, trying to draw my attention to him, trying to engage me in conversation, someone complaining to himself in a voice I could overhear about a God whose love and mercy fell on the just and the unjust.

I wrote home to say how lovely everything was, and I used flourishing words and phrases, as if I were living life in a greeting card — the kind that has a satin ribbon on it, and quilted hearts and roses, and is expected to be so precious to the person receiving it that the manufacturer has placed a leaf of plastic on the front to protect it. Everyone I wrote to said how nice it was to hear from me, how nice it was to know that I was doing well, that I was very much missed, and that they couldn't wait until the day came when I returned.

One day the maid who said she did not like me because of the way I talked told me that she was sure I could not dance. She said that I spoke like a nun, I walked like one also, and that everything about me was so pious it made her feel at once sick to her stomach and sick with pity just to look at me. And so, perhaps giving way to the latter feeling, she said that we should dance, even though she was quite sure I didn't know how. There was a little portable record player in my room, the kind that when closed up looked like a ladies' vanity case, and she put on a record she had bought earlier that day. It was a song that was very popular at the time — three girls, not older than I was, singing in harmony and in a very insincere and artificial way about love and so on. It was very beautiful all the same, and it was beautiful because it was so insincere and artificial. She enjoyed this song, singing at the top of her voice, and she was a wonderful dancer — it amazed me to see the way in which she moved. I could not join her and I told her why: the melodies of her song were so shallow, and the words, to me, were meaningless. From her face, I could see she had only one feeling about me: how sick to her stomach I made her. And so I said that I knew songs, too, and I burst into a calypso about a girl who ran away to Port-of-Spain, Trinidad, and had a good time, with no regrets.

The household in which I lived was made up of a husband, a wife, and the four girl children. The husband and wife looked alike and their four children looked just like them. In photographs of themselves, which they placed all over the house, their six yellow-haired heads of various sizes were bunched as if they were a bouquet of flowers tied together by an unseen string. In the pictures, they smiled out at the world, giving the impression that they found everything in it unbearably wonderful. And it was not a farce, their smiles. From wherever they had gone, and they seemed to have been all over the world, they brought back some tiny memento, and they could each recite its history from its very beginnings. Even when a little rain fell, they would admire the way it streaked through the blank air.

At dinner, when we sat down at the table — and did not have to say grace (such a relief, as if they believed in a God that did not have to be thanked every time you turned around) — they said such nice things to each other, and the children were so happy. They would spill their food, or not eat any of it at all, or make up rhymes about it that would end with the words "smelt bad." How they made me laugh, and I wondered what sort of parents I must have had, for even to think of such words in their presence I would have been scolded severely, and I vowed that if I ever had children I would make sure that the first words out of their mouths were bad ones.

It was at dinner one night not long after I began to live with them that they began to call me the Visitor. They said I seemed not to be a part of things, as if I didn't live in their house with them, as if they weren't like a family to me, as if I were just passing through, just saying one long Hallo!, and soon would be saying a quick Goodbye! So long! It was very nice! For look at the way I stared at them as they ate, Lewis said. Had I never seen anyone put a forkful of French-cut green beans in his mouth before? This made Mariah laugh, but almost everything Lewis said made Mariah happy and so she would laugh. I didn't laugh, though, and Lewis looked at me, concern on his face. He said, "Poor Visitor, poor Visitor," over and over, a sympathetic tone to his voice, and then he told me a story about an uncle he had who had gone to Canada and raised monkeys, and of how after a while the uncle loved monkeys so much and was so used to being around them that he found actual human beings hard to take. He had told me this story about his uncle before, and while he was telling it to me this time I was remembering a dream I had had about them: Lewis was chasing me around the house. I wasn't wearing any clothes. The ground on which I was running was yellow, as if it had been paved with cornmeal. Lewis was chasing me around and around the house, and though he came close he could never catch up with me. Mariah stood at the open windows saying, Catch her, Lewis, catch her. Eventually I fell down a hole, at the bottom of which were some silver and blue snakes.

When Lewis finished telling his story, I told them my dream. When I finished, they both fell silent. Then they looked at me and Mariah cleared her throat, but it was obvious from the way she did it that her throat did not need clearing at all. Their two yellow heads swam toward each other and, in unison, bobbed up and down. Lewis made a clucking noise, then said, Poor, poor Visitor. And Mariah said, Dr. Freud for Visitor, and I wondered why she said that, for I did not know who Dr. Freud was. Then they laughed in a soft, kind way. I had meant by telling them my dream that I had taken them in, because only people who were very important to me had ever shown up in my dreams. I did not know if they understood that.

Figures in the Distance

For a short while during the year I was ten, I thought only people I did not know died. At the time I thought this I was on my summer holidays and we were living far out on Fort Road. Usually, we lived in our house on Dickenson Bay Street, a house my father built with his own hands, but just now it needed a new roof and so we were living in a house out on Fort Road. We had only two neighbors, Mistress Maynard and her husband. That summer, we had a pig that had just had piglets; some guinea fowl; and some ducks that laid enormous eggs that my mother said were big even for ducks. I hated to eat any food except for the enormous duck eggs, hardboiled. I had nothing to do every day except to feed the birds and the pig in the morning and in the evening. I spoke to no one other than my parents, and sometimes to Mistress Maynard, if I saw her when I went to pick up the peelings of vegetables which my mother had asked her to save for the pig, which was just the thing the pig really liked. From our yard, I could see the cemetery. I did not know it was the cemetery until one day when I said to my mother that sometimes in the evening, while feeding the pig, I could see various small, sticklike figures, some dressed in black, some dressed in white, bobbing up and down in the distance. I noticed, too, that sometimes the black and white sticklike figures appeared in the morning. My mother said that it was probably a child being buried, since children were always buried in the morning. Until then, I had not known that children died.

I was afraid of the dead, as was everyone I knew. We were afraid of the dead because we never could tell when they might show up again. Sometimes they showed up in a dream, but that wasn't so bad, because they usually only brought a warning, and in any case you wake up from a dream. But sometimes they would show up standing under a tree just as you were passing by. Then they might follow you home, and even though they might not be able to come into your house, they might wait for you and follow you wherever you went; in that case, they would never give up until you joined them. My mother knew of many people who had died in such a way. My mother knew of many people who had died, including her own brother.

After I found out about the cemetery, I would stand in my yard and wait for a funeral to come. Some days, there were no funerals. "No one died," I would say to my mother. Some days, just as I was about to give up and go inside, I would see the small specks appear. "What made them so late?" I would ask my mother. Probably someone couldn't bear to see the coffin lid put in place, and so as a favor the undertaker might let things go on too long, she said. The undertaker! On our way into town, we would pass the undertaker's workshop. Outside, a little sign read "STRAFFEE & SONS, UNDERTAKERS & CABINETMAKERS." I could always tell we were approaching this place, because of the smell of pitch pine and varnish in the air.

Later, we moved back to our house in town, and I no longer had a view of the cemetery. Still no one I knew had died. One day, a girl smaller than I, a girl whose mother was a friend of my mother's, died in my mother's arms. I did not know this girl at all, though I may have got a glimpse of her once or twice as I passed her and her mother coming out of our yard, and I tried to remember everything I had heard about her. Her name was Nalda; she had red hair; she was very bony; she did not like to eat any food. In fact, she liked to eat mud, and her mother always had to keep a strict eye on her to prevent her from doing that. Her father made bricks, and her mother dressed in a way that my father found unbecoming. I heard my mother describe to my father just how Nalda had died: She had a fever, they noticed a change in her breathing, so they called a car and were rushing her off to Dr. Bailey when, just as they were crossing over a bridge, she let out a long sigh and went limp. Dr. Bailey pronounced her dead, and when I heard that I was so glad he wasn't my doctor. My mother asked my father to make the coffin for Nalda, and he did, carving bunches of tiny flowers on the sides. Nalda's mother wept so much that my mother had to take care of everything, and since children were never prepared by under-takers, my mother had to prepare the little girl to be buried. I then began to look at my mother's hands differently. They had stroked the dead girl's forehead; they had bathed and dressed her and laid her in the coffin my father had made. My mother would come back from the dead girl's house smelling of bay rum — a scent that for a long time afterward would make me feel ill. For a while, though not for very long, I could not bear to have my mother caress me or touch my food or help me with my bath. I especially couldn't bear the sight of her hands lying still in her lap.

At school, I told all my friends about this death. I would take them aside individually, so I could repeat the details over and over again.

They would listen to me with their mouths open. In turn, they would tell me of someone they had known or heard of who had died. I would listen with my mouth open. One person had known very well a neighbor who had gone swimming after eating a big lunch at a picnic and drowned. Someone had a cousin who in the middle of something one day just fell down dead. Someone knew a boy who had died after eating some poisonous berries. "Fancy that," we said to each other.

I loved very much — and so used to torment until she cried — a girl named Sonia. She was smaller than I, even though she was almost two years older, and she was a dunce — the first real dunce I had ever met. She was such a dunce that sometimes she could not remember the spelling of her own name. I would try to get to school early and give her my homework, so that she could copy it, and in class I would pass her the answers to sums. My friends ignored her, and whenever I mentioned her name in a favorable way they would twist up their lips and make a sound to show their disdain. I thought her beautiful and I would say so. She had long, thick black hair that lay down flat on her arms and legs; and then running down the nape of her neck, down the middle of her back for as far as could be seen before it was swallowed up by her school uniform, was a line of the same long, thick black hair, only here it flared out as if a small breeze had come and parted it. At recess, I would buy her a sweet — something called a frozen joy — with money I had stolen from my mother's purse, and then we would go and sit under a tree in our schoolyard. I would then stare and stare at her, narrowing and opening wide my eyes until she began to fidget under my gaze. Then I would pull at the hair on her arms and legs — gently at first, and then awfully hard, holding it up taut with the tips of my fingers until she cried out. For a few weeks, she didn't appear in school, and we were told that her mother, who had been with child, had died suddenly. I couldn't ever again bring myself to speak to her, even though we spent two more years as classmates. She seemed such a shameful thing, a girl whose mother had died and left her alone in the world.

Not long after the little girl died in my mother's arms on the way to the doctor, Miss Charlotte, our neighbor across the street, collapsed and died while having a conversation with my mother. If my mother hadn't caught her, she would have fallen to the ground. When I came home from school that day, my mother said, "Miss Charlotte is dead." I had known Miss Charlotte very well, and I tried to imagine her dead. I couldn't. I did not know what someone looked like dead. I knew what Miss Charlotte looked like coming from market. I knew what she looked like going to church. I knew what she looked like when she told her dog not to frighten me by chasing me up and down the street. Once, when Miss Charlotte was sick, my mother asked me to take her a bowl with some food, so I saw her lying in her bed in her nightgown. Miss Charlotte was buried in a coffin my father did not make, and I was not allowed to go to the funeral.

At school, almost everyone I knew had seen a dead person, and not a spirit of a dead person but a real dead person. The girl who sat at the desk next to mine suddenly stopped sucking her thumb because her mother had washed it in water in which a dead person had been given a bath. I told her that her mother must have been playing a trick on her, that I was sure the water was plain water, since it was just the sort of trick my mother would play on me. But she had met my mother and she said she could see that my mother and her mother weren't alike at all.

I began to go to funerals. I didn't actually go to the funerals as an official mourner, since I didn't know any of the people who had died and I was going without my parents' permission. I visited the funeral parlors or the drawing rooms where the dead were laid out for viewing by the mourners. When I heard the church bell toll in the way it tolled when someone had died, I would try to find out who had died and where the funeral was to be — home or funeral parlor. The funeral parlor was in much the same direction as my route home, but sometimes to get to someone's house I would have to go in the opposite direction of my way home. At first, I didn't go in; I would just stand outside and watch the people come and go, hear the close relatives and friends let out incredible loud wails and moans, and then watch the procession march off to church. But then I began to go in and take a look. The first time I actually saw a dead person, I didn't know what to think. Since it wasn't someone I knew, I couldn't make a comparison. I had never seen the person laugh or smile or frown or shoo a chicken out of a garden. So I looked and looked for as long as I could without letting anyone know I was just there out of curiosity.

One day, a girl my own age died. I did not know her name or anything personal about her except that she was my own age and that she had a humpback. She attended another school, and on the day of her funeral her whole school got the day off. At my school, it was all we could talk about: "Did you know the humpbacked girl?" I remembered once standing behind her in a line to take out books at the library; then I saw a fly land on the collar of her uniform and walk up and down as the collar lay flat on her hump. On hearing that she was dead, I wished I had tapped the hump to see if it was hollow. I also remembered that her hair was parted into four plaits and that the parts were crooked. "She must have combed her hair herself," I said. At last, though, someone I knew was dead. The day of her funeral, I bolted from school as soon as we finished the last amen of our evening prayers, and I made my way to the funeral home. When I got there, the whole street was full of girls from her school, all in their white dress uniforms. It was a big crowd of them, and they were milling around, talking to each other quietly and looking very important. I didn't have time to stop and really envy them; I made my way to the door and entered the funeral parlor. There she was. She was lying in the regular pitch-pine, varnished coffin, on a bed of mauve-and-white lilacs. She wore a white dress, and it may have come all the way down to her ankles, but I didn't have time to look carefully. It was her face that I wanted to see. I remembered how she had looked the day in the library. Her face was just a plain face. She had black eyes, flat nostrils, broad lips. Lying there dead, she looked the same, except her eyes were closed and she was so still. I once had heard someone say about another dead person that it was as if the dead person were asleep. But I had seen a person asleep, and this girl did not look asleep. My parents had just bought me a View-Master. The View-Master came with pictures of the pyramids, the Taj Mahal, Mt. Everest, and scenes of the Amazon River. When the View-Master worked properly, all the scenes looked as if they were alive, as if we could just step into the View-Master and sail down the Amazon River or stand at the foot of the pyramids. When the View-Master didn't work properly, it was as if we were looking at an ordinary, colorful picture. When I looked at this girl, it was as if the View-Master wasn't working properly. I stared at her a long time — long enough so that I caused the line of people waiting to stop by the coffin to grow long and on the verge of impatience. Of course, as I stared I kept my fingers curled up tight against my palms, because I didn't want to make a mistake and point and then have them rot and drop off right there. I then went and sat among the mourners. Her family smiled at me, thinking, I am sure, that I was a school friend, even though I wore the uniform of another school. We sang a hymn — "All Things Bright and Beautiful" — and her mother said it was the first hymn the humpbacked girl had learned to sing by heart.

I walked home. By then, I was very late getting home from school, but I was too excited to worry about it. I wondered if one day while going somewhere alone I would see the humpbacked girl standing under a tree, and if she would try to get me to go for a swim or eat a piece of fruit, and the next thing my mother would know, she would be asking my father to make a coffin for me. Of course, he would be so overcome with grief he wouldn't be able to make my coffin and would have to ask Mr. Oatie to do it, and he just hated to ask Mr. Oatie to do him a favor, because, as I heard him tell my mother, Mr. Oatie was such a leech he tried to suck you dry by making you pay for everything twice.

When I got home, my mother asked me for the fish I was to have picked up from Mr. Earl, one of our fishermen, on the way home from school. But in my excitement I had completely forgotten. Trying to think quickly, I said that when I got to the market Mr. Earl told me that they hadn't gone to sea that day because the sea was too rough. "Oh?" said my mother, and uncovered a pan in which were lying, flat on their sides and covered with lemon juice and butter and onions, three fish: an angelfish for my father, a kanya fish for my mother, and a lady doctorfish for me — the special kind of fish each of us liked. While I was at the funeral parlor, Mr. Earl had got tired of waiting for me and had brought the fish to our house himself. That night, as a punishment, I ate my supper outside, alone, under the breadfruit tree, and my mother said that she would not be kissing me good night later, but when I climbed into bed she came and kissed me anyway.

Lorrie Moore

The first story Lorrie Moore ever sent out for publication — when she was a nineteen-year-old undergraduate at St. Lawrence — won first prize in *Seventeen* magazine's fiction contest. In an interview with Caryn James of the *The New York Times,* she said of that period in her life, "When I was 18 or 19, my favorite writer was Margaret Atwood. For the first time I read fiction about women who were not goddesses or winners. In some ways they were victims, but they weren't wimps. They were stylish about their victimization." Moore's heroines can be stylish and self-aware even as they are victimized — and ironic, funny, and obsessed with wordplay too. The narrator of "How to Be an Other Woman," the opening story of her first collection, *Self-Help,* adheres to the formula. She conducts an affair with a married man, an affair ritualistically doomed, but observes, with a kind of loopy grace, "When you were six you thought *mistress* meant to put your shoes on the wrong feet. Now you are older and know it can mean many things, but essentially it means to put your shoes on the wrong feet." There is an essential sadness leaking through the bright chirp of humor here — the dizzy, all-is-right-with-the-world tone of the self-improvement manual — that is the key to the strength and originality of Moore's stories. Like Flannery O'Connor, she is able to catch the reader off guard and turn light to darkness, laughter to tears.

"People Like That Are the Only People Here: Canonical Babbling in Peed Onk," from Moore's third collection, *Birds of America,* works in precisely this way. It gives us the archetypal figures of the Mother, the Father, and the Baby and uses a bright, almost hysterical humor as a way of distracting the characters from the grim reality of the situation. I love the story's terse, two-line ending — it wraps its fingers around the reader's throat and then pulls them tight. If it doesn't choke you up, I don't know what will. The second story here, "How to Become a Writer," from *Self-Help,* is a wicked satire that should delight anyone who has ever sat through a writing workshop (" 'But does it work?' 'Why should we care about this character?' 'Have you earned this cliché?' ").

People Like That Are the Only People Here: Canonical Babbling in Peed Onk

A beginning, an end: there seems to be neither. The whole thing is like a cloud that just lands and everywhere inside it is full of rain. A start: the Mother finds a blood clot in the Baby's diaper. What is the story? Who put this here? It is big and bright, with a broken khaki-colored vein in it. Over the weekend, the Baby had looked listless and spacey, clayey and grim. But today he looks fine — so what is this thing, startling against the white diaper, like a tiny mouse heart packed in snow? Perhaps it belongs to someone else. Perhaps it is something menstrual, something belonging to the Mother or to the Babysitter, something the Baby has found in a wastebasket and for his own de-mented baby reasons stowed away here. (Babies: they're crazy! What can you do?) In her mind, the Mother takes this away from his body and attaches it to someone else's. There. Doesn't that make more sense?

Still, she phones the clinic at the children's hospital. "Blood in the diaper," she says, and, sounding alarmed and perplexed, the woman on the other end says, "Come in now."

Such pleasingly instant service! Just say "blood." Just say "diaper." Look what you get!

In the examination room, pediatrician, nurse, head resident — all seem less alarmed and perplexed than simply perplexed. At first, stu-pidly, the Mother is calmed by this. But soon, besides peering and say-ing "Hmmmm," the pediatrician, nurse, and head resident are all drawing their mouths in, bluish and tight — morning glories sensing noon. They fold their arms across their white-coated chests, unfold them again and jot things down. They order an ultrasound. Bladder and kidneys. "Here's the card. Go downstairs; turn left."

In Radiology, the Baby stands anxiously on the table, naked against the Mother as she holds him still against her legs and waist, the Radi-ologist's cold scanning disc moving about the Baby's back. The Baby whimpers, looks up at the Mother. *Let's get out of here,* his eyes beg. *Pick me up!* The Radiologist stops, freezes one of the many swirls of oceanic gray, and clicks repeatedly, a single moment within the long, cavernous weather map that is the Baby's insides.

"Are you finding something?" asks the Mother. Last year, her uncle Larry had had a kidney removed for something that turned out to be benign. These imaging machines! They are like dogs, or metal detectors: they find everything, but don't know what they've found. That's where the surgeons come in. They're like the owners of the dogs. "Give me that," they say to the dog. "What the heck is that?"

"The surgeon will speak to you," says the Radiologist.

"Are you finding something?"

"The surgeon will speak to you," the Radiologist says again. "There seems to be something there, but the surgeon will talk to you about it."

"My uncle once had something on his kidney," says the Mother. "So they removed the kidney and it turned out the something was benign."

The Radiologist smiles a broad, ominous smile. "That's always the way it is," he says. "You don't know exactly what it is until it's in the bucket."

"'In the bucket,'" the Mother repeats.

The Radiologist's grin grows scarily wider — is that even possible? "That's doctor talk," he says.

"It's very appealing," says the Mother. "It's a very appealing way to talk." Swirls of bile and blood, mustard and maroon in a pail, the colors of an African flag or some exuberant salad bar: *in the bucket* — she imagines it all.

"The Surgeon will see you soon," he says again. He tousles the Baby's ringletty hair. "Cute kid," he says.

"Let's see now," says the Surgeon in one of his examining rooms. He has stepped in, then stepped out, then come back in again. He has crisp, frowning features, sharp bones, and a tennis-in-Bermuda tan. He crosses his blue-cottoned legs. He is wearing clogs.

The Mother knows her own face is a big white dumpling of worry. She is still wearing her long, dark parka, holding the Baby, who has pulled the hood up over her head because he always thinks it's funny to do that. Though on certain windy mornings she would like to think she could look vaguely romantic like this, like some French Lieutenant's Woman of the Prairie, in all of her saner moments she knows she doesn't. Ever. She knows she looks ridiculous — like one of those animals made out of twisted party balloons. She lowers the hood and slips one arm out of the sleeve. The Baby wants to get up and play with the light switch. He fidgets, fusses, and points.

"He's big on lights these days," explains the Mother.

"That's okay," says the Surgeon, nodding toward the light switch. "Let him play with it." The Mother goes and stands by it, and the Baby begins turning the lights off and on, off and on.

"What we have here is a Wilms' tumor," says the Surgeon, suddenly plunged into darkness. He says "tumor" as if it were the most normal thing in the world.

"Wilms'?" repeats the Mother. The room is quickly on fire again with light, then wiped dark again. Among the three of them here, there is a long silence, as if it were suddenly the middle of the night. "Is that apostrophe *s* or *s* apostrophe?" the Mother says finally. She is a writer and a teacher. Spelling can be important — perhaps even at a time like this, though she has never before been at a time like this, so there are barbarisms she could easily commit and not know.

The lights come on: the world is doused and exposed.

"*S* apostrophe," says the Surgeon. "I think." The lights go back out, but the Surgeon continues speaking in the dark. "A malignant tumor on the left kidney."

Wait a minute. Hold on here. The Baby is only a baby, fed on organic applesauce and soy milk — a little prince! — and he was standing so close to her during the ultrasound. How could he have this terrible thing? It must have been *her* kidney. A fifties kidney. A DDT kidney. The Mother clears her throat. "Is it possible it was my kidney on the scan? I mean, I've never heard of a baby with a tumor, and, frankly, I was standing very close." She would make the blood hers, the tumor hers; it would all be some treacherous, farcical mistake.

"No, that's not possible," says the Surgeon. The light goes back on.

"It's not?" says the Mother. Wait until it's *in the bucket,* she thinks. Don't be so sure. *Do we have to wait until it's in the bucket to find out a mistake has been made?*

"We will start with a radical nephrectomy," says the Surgeon, instantly thrown into darkness again. His voice comes from nowhere and everywhere at once. "And then we'll begin with chemotherapy after that. These tumors usually respond very well to chemo."

"I've never heard of a baby having chemo," the Mother says. *Baby* and *Chemo,* she thinks: they should never even appear in the same sentence together, let alone the same life. In her other life, her life before this day, she had been a believer in alternative medicine. Chemotherapy? Unthinkable. Now, suddenly, alternative medicine seems the wacko maiden aunt to the Nice Big Daddy of Conventional Treatment. How quickly the old girl faints and gives way, leaves one just standing there. Chemo? Of course: chemo! Why by all means: chemo. Absolutely! Chemo!

The Baby flicks the switch back on, and the walls reappear, big wedges of light checkered with small framed watercolors of the local lake. The Mother has begun to cry: all of life has led her here, to this moment. After this, there is no more life. There is something else, something stumbling and unlivable, something mechanical, something for robots, but not life. Life has been taken and broken, quickly, like a stick. The room goes dark again, so that the Mother can cry more freely. How can a baby's body be stolen so fast? How much can one heaven-sent and unsuspecting child endure? Why has he not been spared this inconceivable fate?

Perhaps, she thinks, she is being punished: too many baby-sitters too early on. ("Come to Mommy! Come to Mommy-Baby-sitter!" she used to say. But it was a joke!) Her life, perhaps, bore too openly the marks and wigs of deepest drag. Her unmotherly thoughts had all been noted: the panicky hope that his nap would last longer than it did; her occasional desire to kiss him passionately on the mouth (to make out with her baby!); her ongoing complaints about the very vocabulary of motherhood, how it degraded the speaker ("Is this a poopie onesie! Yes, it's a very poopie onesie!"). She had, moreover, on three occasions used the formula bottles as flower vases. She twice let the Baby's ears get fudgy with wax. A few afternoons last month, at snacktime, she placed a bowl of Cheerios on the floor for him to eat, like a dog. She let him play with the Dustbuster. Just once, before he was born, she said, "Healthy? I just want the kid to be rich." A joke, for God's sake! After he was born she announced that her life had become a daily sequence of mind-wrecking chores, the same ones over and over again, like a novel by Mrs. Camus. Another joke! These jokes will kill you! She had told too often, and with too much enjoyment, the story of how the Baby had said "Hi" to his high chair, waved at the lake waves, shouted "Goody-goody-goody" in what seemed to be a Russian accent, pointed at his eyes and said "Ice." And all that nonsensical baby talk: wasn't it a stitch? "Canonical babbling," the language experts called it. He recounted whole stories in it — totally made, she could tell. He embroidered; he fished; he exaggerated. What a card! To friends, she spoke of his eating habits (carrots yes, tuna no). She mentioned, too much, his sidesplitting giggle. Did she have to be so boring? Did she have no consideration for others, for the intellectual demands and courtesies of human society? Would she not even attempt to be more interesting? It was a crime against the human mind not even to try.

Now her baby, for all these reasons — lack of motherly gratitude, motherly judgment, motherly proportion — will be taken away.

The room is fluorescently ablaze again. The Mother digs around in her parka pocket and comes up with a Kleenex. It is old and thin, like a mashed flower saved from a dance; she dabs it at her eyes and nose.

"The Baby won't suffer as much as you," says the Surgeon.

And who can contradict? Not the Baby, who in his Slavic Betty Boop voice can say only *mama, dada, cheese, ice, bye-bye, outside, boogie-boogie, goody-goody, eddy-eddy,* and *car.* (Who is Eddy? They have no idea.) This will not suffice to express his mortal suffering. Who can say what babies do with their agony and shock? Not they themselves. (Baby talk: isn't it a stitch?) They put it all no place anyone can really see. They are like a different race, a different species: they seem not to experience pain the way *we* do. Yeah, that's it: their nervous systems are not as fully formed, and *they just don't experience pain the way we do.* A tune to keep one humming through the war. "You'll get through it," the Surgeon says.

"How?" asks the Mother. "How does one get through it?"

"You just put your head down and go," says the Surgeon. He picks up his file folder. He is a skilled manual laborer. The tricky emotional stuff is not to his liking. The babies. The babies! What can be said to console the parents about the babies? "I'll go phone the oncologist on duty to let him know," he says, and leaves the room.

"Come here, sweetie," the Mother says to the Baby, who has toddled off toward a gum wrapper on the floor. "We've got to put your jacket on." She picks him up and he reaches for the light switch again. Light, dark. Peekaboo: where's baby? Where did baby go?

At home, she leaves a message — "Urgent! Call me!" — for the Husband on his voice mail. Then she takes the Baby upstairs for his nap, rocks him in the rocker. The Baby waves good-bye to his little bears, then looks toward the window and says, "Bye-bye, outside." He has, lately, the habit of waving good-bye to everything, and now it seems as if he senses an imminent departure, and it breaks her heart to hear him. *Bye-bye!* She sings low and monotonously, like a small appliance, which is how he likes it. He is drowsy, dozy, drifting off. He has grown so much in the last year, he hardly fits in her lap anymore; his limbs dangle off like a pietà. His head rolls slightly inside the crook of her arm. She can feel him falling backward into sleep, his mouth round and open like the sweetest of poppies. All the lullabies in the world, all the melodies threaded through with maternal melancholy now become for her — abandoned as a mother can be by working men and napping babies — the songs of hard, hard grief. Sitting there, bowed and bobbing, the Mother feels the entirety of her love as worry and heartbreak.

A quick and irrevocable alchemy: there is no longer one unworried scrap left for happiness. "If you go," she keens low into his soapy neck, into the ranunculus coil of his ear, "we are going with you. We are nothing without you. Without you, we are a heap of rocks. We are gravel and mold. Without you, we are two stumps, with nothing any longer in our hearts. Wherever this takes you, we are following. We will be there. Don't be scared. We are going, too. That is that."

"Take Notes," says the Husband, after coming straight home from work, midafternoon, hearing the news, and saying all the words out loud — *surgery, metastasis, dialysis, transplant* — then collapsing in a chair in tears. "Take notes. We are going to need the money."

"Good God," cries the Mother. Everything inside her suddenly begins to cower and shrink, a thinning of bones. Perhaps this is a soldier's readiness, but it has the whiff of death and defeat. It feels like a heart attack, a failure of will and courage, a power failure: a failure of everything. Her face, when she glimpses it in a mirror, is cold and bloated with shock, her eyes scarlet and shrunk. She has already started to wear sunglasses indoors, like a celebrity widow. From where will her own strength come? From some philosophy? From some frigid little philosophy? She is neither stalwart nor realistic and has trouble with basic concepts, such as the one that says events move in one direction only and do not jump up, turn around, and take themselves back.

The Husband begins too many of his sentences with "What if." He is trying to piece everything together like a train wreck. He is trying to get the train to town.

"We'll just take all the steps, move through all the stages. We'll go where we have to go. We'll hunt; we'll find; we'll pay what we have to pay. What if we can't pay?"

"Sounds like shopping."

"I cannot believe this is happening to our little boy," he says, and starts to sob again. "Why didn't it happen to one of us? It's so unfair. Just last week, my doctor declared me in perfect health: the prostate of a twenty-year-old, the heart of a ten-year-old, the brain of an insect — or whatever it was he said. What a nightmare this is."

What words can be uttered? You turn just slightly and there it is: the death of your child. It is part symbol, part devil, and in your blind spot all along, until, if you are unlucky, it is completely upon you. Then it is a fierce little country abducting you; it holds you squarely inside itself like a cellar room — the best boundaries of you are the boundaries of it. Are there windows? Sometimes aren't there windows?

᭞

The Mother is not a shopper. She hates to shop, is generally bad at it, though she does like a good sale. She cannot stroll meaningfully through anger, denial, grief, and acceptance. She goes straight to bargaining and stays there. How much? she calls out to the ceiling, to some make-shift construction of holiness she has desperately, though not uncre-atively, assembled in her mind and prayed to; a doubter, never before given to prayer, she must now reap what she has not sown; she must assemble from scratch an entire altar of worship and begging. She tries for noble abstractions, nothing too anthropomorphic, just some Higher Morality, though if this particular Highness looks something like the manager at Marshall Field's, sucking a Frango mint, so be it. Amen. Just tell me what you want, requests the Mother. And how do you want it? More charitable acts? A billion starting now. Charitable thoughts? Harder, but of course! Of course! I'll do the cooking, honey; I'll pay the rent. Just tell me. *Excuse me?* Well, if not to you, to whom do I speak? Hello? To whom do I have to speak around here? A higher-up? A superior? Wait? I can wait. I've got all day. I've got the whole damn day.

The Husband now lies next to her in bed, sighing. "Poor little guy could survive all this, only to be killed in a car crash at the age of six-teen," he says.

The wife, bargaining, considers this. "We'll take the car crash," she says.

"What?"

"Let's Make a Deal! Sixteen Is a Full Life! We'll take the car crash. We'll take the car crash, in front of which Carol Merrill is now standing."

Now the Manager of Marshall Field's reappears. "To take the sur-prises out is to take the life out of life," he says.

The phone rings. The Husband gets up and leaves the room.

"But I don't want these surprises," says the Mother. "Here! You take these surprises!"

"To know the narrative in advance is to turn yourself into a machine," the Manager continues. "What makes humans human is precisely that they do not know the future. That is why they do the fateful and amus-ing things they do: who can say how anything will turn out? Therein lies the only hope for redemption, discovery, and — let's be frank — fun, fun, fun! There might be things people will get away with. And not just motel towels. There might be great illicit loves, enduring joy, faith-shaking accidents with farm machinery. But you have to not know in order to see what stories your life's efforts bring you. The mystery is all."

The Mother, though shy, has grown confrontational. "Is this the kind of bogus, random crap they teach at merchandising school? We would like fewer surprises, fewer efforts and mysteries, thank you. K through eight; can we just get K through eight?" It now seems like the luckiest, most beautiful, most musical phrase she's ever heard: K through eight. The very lilt. The very thought.

The Manager continues, trying things out. "I mean, the whole conception of 'the story,' of cause and effect, the whole idea that people have a clue as to how the world works is just a piece of laughable metaphysical colonialism perpetrated upon the wild country of time."

Did they own a gun? The Mother begins looking through drawers.

The Husband comes back into the room and observes her. "Ha! The Great Havoc that is the Puzzle of all Life!" he says of the Marshall Field's management policy. He has just gotten off a conference call with the insurance company and the hospital. The surgery will be Friday. "It's all just some dirty capitalist's idea of a philosophy."

"Maybe it's just a fact of narrative and you really can't politicize it," says the Mother. It is now only the two of them.

"Whose side are you on?"

"I'm on the Baby's side."

"Are you taking notes for this?"

"No."

"You're not?"

"No. I can't. Not this! I write fiction. This isn't fiction."

"Then write nonfiction. Do a piece of journalism. Get two dollars a word."

"Then it has to be true and full of information. I'm not trained. I'm not that skilled. Plus, I have a convenient personal principle about artists not abandoning art. One should never turn one's back on a vivid imagination. Even the whole memoir thing annoys me."

"Well, make things up, but pretend they're real."

"I'm not that insured."

"You're making me nervous."

"Sweetie, darling, I'm not that good. I can't *do this*. I can do — what can I do? I can do quasi-amusing phone dialogue. I can do succinct descriptions of weather. I can do screwball outings with the family pet. Sometimes I can do those. Honey, I only do what I can. I do *the careful ironies of daydream*. I do *the marshy ideas upon which intimate life is built*. But this? Our baby with cancer? I'm sorry. My stop was two stations back. This is irony at its most gaudy and careless. This is a Hieronymus Bosch of facts and figures and blood and graphs. This is a nightmare of narrative slop. This cannot be designed. This cannot even be noted in preparation for a design — "

"We're going to need the money."

"To say nothing of the moral boundaries of pecuniary recompense in a situation such as this — "

"What if the other kidney goes? What if he needs a transplant? Where are the moral boundaries there? What are we going to do, have bake sales?"

"We can sell the house. I hate this house. It makes me crazy."

"And we'll live — where again?"

"The Ronald McDonald place. I hear it's nice. It's the least McDonald's can do."

"You have a keen sense of justice."

"I try. What can I say?" She pauses. "Is all this really happening? I keep thinking that soon it will be over — the life expectancy of a cloud is supposed to be only twelve hours — and then I realize something has occurred that can never ever be over."

The Husband buries his face in his hands: "Our poor baby. How did this happen to him?" He looks over and stares at the bookcase that serves as the nightstand. "And do you think even one of these baby books is any help?" He picks up the Leach, the Spock, the *What to Expect.* "Where in the pages or index of any of these does it say 'chemotherapy' or 'Hickman catheter' or 'renal sarcoma'? Where does it say 'carcinogenesis'? You know what these books are obsessed with? *Holding a fucking spoon.*" He begins hurling the books off the night table and against the far wall.

"Hey," says the Mother, trying to soothe. "Hey, hey, hey." But compared to his stormy roar, her words are those of a backup singer — a Shondell, a Pip — a doo-wop ditty. Books, and now more books, continue to fly.

Take Notes.

Is *fainthearted* one word or two? Student prose has wrecked her spelling.

It's one word. Two words — *Faint Hearted* — what would that be? The name of a drag queen.

Take Notes. In the end, you suffer alone. But at the beginning you suffer with a whole lot of others. When your child has cancer, you are instantly whisked away to another planet: one of bald-headed little boys. Pediatric Oncology. Peed Onk. You wash your hands for thirty seconds in antibacterial soap before you are allowed to enter through the swinging doors. You put paper slippers on your shoes. You keep your voice down. A whole place has been designed and decorated for your nightmare. Here is where your nightmare will occur. We've got a room all ready for you. We have cots. We have refrigerators. "The children are almost entirely boys," says one of the nurses. "No one knows why. It's been documented, but a lot of people out there still don't realize it." The little boys are all from sweet-sounding places — Janesville and Appleton — little heartland towns with giant landfills, agricultural runoff, paper factories, Joe McCarthy's grave (Alone, a site of great toxicity, thinks the Mother. The soil should be tested).

All the bald little boys look like brothers. They wheel their IVs up and down the single corridor of Peed Onk. Some of the lively ones, feeling good for a day, ride the lower bars of the IV while their large, cheerful mothers whiz them along the halls. *Wheee!*

The Mother does not feel large and cheerful. In her mind, she is scathing, acid-tongued, wraith-thin, and chain-smoking out on a fire escape somewhere. Beneath her lie the gentle undulations of the Midwest, with all its aspirations to be — to be what? To be Long Island. How it has succeeded! Strip mall upon strip mall. Lurid water, poisoned potatoes. The Mother drags deeply, blowing clouds of smoke out over the disfigured cornfields. When a baby gets cancer, it seems stupid ever to have given up smoking. When a baby gets cancer, you think, Whom are we kidding? Let's all light up. When a baby gets cancer, you think, Who came up with *this* idea? What celestial abandon gave rise to *this*? Pour me a drink, so I can refuse to toast.

The Mother does not know how to be one of these other mothers, with their blond hair and sweatpants and sneakers and determined pleasantness. She does not think that she can be anything similar. She does not feel remotely like them. She knows, for instance, too many people in Greenwich Village. She mail-orders oysters and tiramisu from a shop in SoHo. She is close friends with four actual homosexuals. Her husband is asking her to Take Notes.

Where do these women get their sweatpants? She will find out.

She will start, perhaps, with the costume and work from there.

She will live according to the bromides. Take one day at a time. Take a positive attitude. *Take a hike!* She wishes that there were more interesting things that were useful and true, but it seems now that it's only the boring things that are useful and true. *One day at a time.* And *at least we have our health.* How ordinary. How obvious. One day at a time. You need a brain for that?

While the Surgeon is fine-boned, regal, and laconic — they have correctly guessed his game to be doubles — there is a bit of the mad, over-caffeinated scientist to the Oncologist. He speaks quickly. He knows a lot of studies and numbers. He can do the math. Good! Someone should be able to do the math! "It's a fast but wimpy tumor," he explains. "It typically metastasizes to the lung." He rattles off some numbers, time frames, risk statistics. Fast but wimpy: the Mother tries to imagine this combination of traits, tries to think and think, and can only come up with Claudia Osk from the fourth grade, who blushed and almost wept when called on in class, but in gym could outrun everyone in the quarter-mile fire-door-to-fence dash. The Mother thinks now of this tumor as Claudia Osk. They are going to get Claudia Osk, make her sorry. All right! Claudia Osk must die. Though it has never been mentioned before, it now seems clear that Claudia Osk should have died long ago. Who was she anyway? So conceited: not letting anyone beat her in a race. Well, hey, hey, hey: don't look now, Claudia!

The Husband nudges her. "Are you listening?"

"The chances of this happening even just to one kidney are one in fifteen thousand. Now given all these other factors, the chances on the second kidney are about one in eight."

"One in eight," says the Husband. "Not bad. As long as it's not one in fifteen thousand."

The Mother studies the trees and fish along the ceiling's edge in the Save the Planet wallpaper border. Save the Planet. Yes! But the windows in this very building don't open and diesel fumes are leaking into the ventilating system, near which, outside, a delivery truck is parked. The air is nauseous and stale.

"Really," the Oncologist is saying, "of all the cancers he could get, this is probably the best."

"We win," says the Mother.

"*Best,* I know, hardly seems the right word. Look, you two probably need to get some rest. We'll see how the surgery and histology go. Then we'll start with chemo the week following. A little light chemo: vincristine and — "

"Vincristine?" interrupts the Mother. "Wine of Christ?"

"The names are strange, I know. The other one we use is actinomycin-D. Sometimes called 'dactinomycin.' People move the *D* around to the front."

"They move the *D* around to the front," repeats the Mother.

"Yup!" the Oncologist says. "I don't know why — they just do!"

"Christ didn't survive his wine," says the Husband.

"But of course he did," says the Oncologist, and nods toward the Baby, who has now found a cupboard full of hospital linens and bandages and is yanking them all out onto the floor. "I'll see you guys tomorrow, after the surgery." And with that, the Oncologist leaves.

"Or, rather, Christ *was* his wine," mumbles the Husband. Everything he knows about the New Testament, he has gleaned from the sound track of *Godspell.* "His blood was the wine. What a great beverage idea."

"A little light chemo. Don't you like that one?" says the Mother. "*Eine kleine* dactinomycin. I'd like to see Mozart write that one up for a big wad o' cash."

"Come here, honey," the Husband says to the Baby, who has now pulled off both his shoes.

"It's bad enough when they refer to medical science as 'an inexact science,'" says the Mother. "But when they start referring to it as 'an art,' I get extremely nervous."

"Yeah. If we wanted art, Doc, we'd go to an art museum." The Husband picks up the Baby. "You're an artist," he says to the Mother, with the taint of accusation in his voice. "They probably think you find creativity reassuring."

The Mother sighs. "I just find it inevitable. Let's go get something to eat." And so they take the elevator to the cafeteria, where there is a high chair, and where, not noticing, they all eat a lot of apples with the price tags still on them.

Because his surgery is not until tomorrow, the Baby likes the hospital. He likes the long corridors, down which he can run. He likes everything on wheels. The flower carts in the lobby! ("Please keep your boy away from the flowers," says the vendor. "We'll buy the whole display," snaps the Mother, adding, "Actual children in a children's hospital — unbelievable, isn't it?") The Baby likes the other little boys. Places to go! People to see! Rooms to wander into! There is Intensive Care. There is the Trauma Unit. The Baby smiles and waves. What a little Cancer Personality! Bandaged citizens smile and wave back. In Peed Onk, there are the bald little boys to play with. Joey, Eric, Tim, Mort, and Tod (Mort! Tod!). There is the four-year-old, Ned, holding his little deflated rubber ball, the one with the intriguing curling hose. The Baby wants to play with it. "It's mine. Leave it alone," says Ned. "Tell the Baby to leave it alone."

"Baby, you've got to share," says the Mother from a chair some feet away.

Suddenly, from down near the Tiny Tim Lounge, comes Ned's mother, large and blond and sweatpanted. "Stop that! Stop it!" she cries out, dashing toward the Baby and Ned and pushing the Baby away. "Don't touch that!" she barks at the Baby, who is only a Baby and bursts into tears because he has never been yelled at like this before.

Ned's mom glares at everyone. "This is drawing fluid from Neddy's liver!" She pats at the rubber thing and starts to cry a little.

"Oh my God," says the Mother. She comforts the Baby, who is also crying. She and Ned, the only dry-eyed people, look at each other. "I'm so sorry," she says to Ned and then to his mother. "I'm so stupid. I thought they were squabbling over a toy."

"It does look like a toy," agrees Ned. He smiles. He is an angel. All the little boys are angels. Total, sweet, bald little angels, and now God is trying to get them back for himself. Who are they, mere mortal women, in the face of this, this powerful and overwhelming and inscrutable thing, God's will? They are the mothers, that's who. You can't have him! they shout every day. You dirty old man! *Get out of here! Hands off!*

"I'm so sorry," says the Mother again. "I didn't know."

Ned's mother smiles vaguely. "Of course you didn't know," she says, and walks back to the Tiny Tim Lounge.

The Tiny Tim Lounge is a little sitting area at the end of the Peed Onk corridor. There are two small sofas, a table, a rocking chair, a television and a VCR. There are various videos: *Speed, Dune,* and *Star Wars.* On one of the lounge walls there is a gold plaque with the singer Tiny Tim's name on it: his son was treated once at this hospital and so, five years ago, he donated money for this lounge. It is a cramped little lounge, which, one suspects, would be larger if Tiny Tim's son had actually lived. Instead, he died here, at this hospital and now there is this tiny room which is part gratitude, part generosity, part *fuck-you.*

Sifting through the videocassettes, the Mother wonders what science fiction could begin to compete with the science fiction of cancer itself — a tumor with its differentiated muscle and bone cells, a clump of wild nothing and its mad, ambitious desire to be something: something inside you, instead of you, another organism, but with a monster's architecture, a demon's sabotage and chaos. Think of leukemia, a tumor diabolically taking liquid form, better to swim about incognito in the blood. George Lucas, direct that!

Sitting with the other parents in the Tiny Tim Lounge, the night before the surgery, having put the Baby to bed in his high steel crib two rooms down, the Mother begins to hear the stories: leukemia in kindergarten, sarcomas in Little League, neuroblastomas discovered at summer camp. "Eric slid into third base, but then the scrape didn't heal." The parents pat one another's forearms and speak of other children's hospitals as if they were resorts. "You were at St. Jude's last winter? So were we. What did you think of it? We loved the staff." Jobs have been quit, marriages hacked up, bank accounts ravaged; the parents have seemingly endured the unendurable. They speak not of the *possibility* of comas brought on by the chemo, but of the *number* of them. "He was in his first coma last July," says Ned's mother. "It was a scary time, but we pulled through."

Pulling through is what people do around here. There is kind of bravery in their lives that isn't bravery at all. It is automatic, unflinching, a mix of man and machine, consuming and unquestionable obligation meeting illness move for move in a giant even-steven game of chess — an unending round of something that looks like shadowboxing, though between love and death, which is the shadow? "Everyone admires us for our courage," says one man. "They have no idea what they're talking about."

I could get out of here, thinks the Mother. I could just get on a bus and go, never come back. Change my name. A kind of witness relocation thing.

"Courage requires options," the man adds.

The Baby might be better off.

"There are options," says a woman with a thick suede headband. "You could give up. You could fall apart."

"No, you can't. Nobody does. I've never seen it," says the man. "Well, not *really* fall apart." Then the lounge falls quiet. Over the VCR someone has taped the fortune from a fortune cookie. "Optimism," it says, "is what allows a teakettle to sing though up to its neck in hot water." Underneath, someone else has taped a clipping from a summer horoscope. "Cancer rules!" it says. Who would tape this up? Somebody's twelve-year-old brother. One of the fathers — Joey's father — gets up and tears them both off, makes a small wad in his fist.

There is some rustling of magazine pages.

The Mother clears her throat. "Tiny Tim forgot the wet bar," she says.

Ned, who is still up, comes out of his room and down the corridor, whose lights dim at nine. Standing next to her chair, he says to the Mother, "Where are you from? What is wrong with your baby?"

In the tiny room that is theirs, she sleeps fitfully in her sweatpants, occasionally leaping up to check on the Baby. This is what the sweatpants are for: leaping. In case of fire. In case of anything. In case the difference between day and night starts to dissolve, and there is no difference at all, so why pretend? In the cot beside her, the Husband, who has taken a sleeping pill, is snoring loudly, his arms folded about his head in a kind of origami. How could either of them have stayed back at the house, with its empty high chair and empty crib? Occasionally the Baby wakes and cries out, and she bolts up, goes to him, rubs his back, rearranges the linens. The clock on the metal dresser shows that it is five after three. Then twenty to five. And then it is really morning, the beginning of this day, nephrectomy day. Will she be glad when it's over, or barely alive, or both? Each day this week has arrived huge, empty, and unknown, like a spaceship, and this one especially is lit a bright gray.

"He'll need to put this on," says John, one of the nurses, bright and early, handing the Mother a thin greenish garment with roses and teddy bears printed on it. A wave of nausea hits her; this smock, she thinks, will soon be splattered with — with what?

The Baby is awake but drowsy. She lifts off his pajamas. "Don't forget, *bubeleh,*" she whispers, undressing and dressing him. "We will be with you every moment, every step. When you think you are asleep and floating off far away from everybody, Mommy will still be there." If she hasn't fled on a bus. "Mommy will take care of you. And Daddy, too." She hopes the Baby does not detect her own fear and uncertainty, which she must hide from him, like a limp. He is hungry, not having been allowed to eat, and he is no longer amused by this new place, but worried about its hardships. Oh, my baby, she thinks. And the room starts to swim a little. The Husband comes in to take over. "Take a break," he says to her. "I'll walk him around for five minutes."

She leaves but doesn't know where to go. In the hallway, she is approached by a kind of social worker, a customer-relations person, who had given them a video to watch about the anesthesia: how the parent accompanies the child into the operating room, and how gently, nicely the drugs are administered.

"Did you watch the video?"

"Yes," says the Mother.

"Wasn't it helpful?"

"I don't know," says the Mother.

"Do you have any questions?" asks the video woman. "Do you have any questions?" asked of someone who has recently landed in this fearful, alien place seems to the Mother an absurd and amazing little courtesy. The very specificity of a question would give a lie to the overwhelming strangeness of everything around her.

"Not right now," says the Mother. "Right now, I think I'm just going to go to the bathroom."

When she returns to the Baby's room, everyone is there: the surgeon, the anesthesiologist, all the nurses, the social worker. In their blue caps and scrubs, they look like a clutch of forget-me-nots, and forget them, who could? The Baby, in his little teddy-bear smock, seems cold and scared. He reaches out and the Mother lifts him from the Husband's arms, rubs his back to warm him.

"Well, it's time!" says the Surgeon, forcing a smile.

"Shall we go?" says the Anesthesiologist.

What follows is a blur of obedience and bright lights. They take an elevator down to a big concrete room, the anteroom, the greenroom, the backstage of the operating room. Lining the walls are long shelves full of blue surgical outfits. "Children often become afraid of the color blue," says one of the nurses. But of course. Of course! "Now, which one of you would like to come into the operating room for the anesthesia?"

"I will," says the Mother.

"Are you sure?" asks the Husband.

"Yup." She kisses the Baby's hair. "Mr. Curlyhead," people keep calling him here, and it seems both rude and nice. Women look admiringly at his long lashes and exclaim, "Always the boys! Always the boys!"

Two surgical nurses put a blue smock and a blue cotton cap on the Mother. The Baby finds this funny and keeps pulling at the cap. "This way," says another nurse, and the Mother follows. "Just put the Baby down on the table."

In the video, the mother holds the baby and fumes are gently waved under the baby's nose until he falls asleep. Now, out of view of camera or social worker, the Anesthesiologist is anxious to get this under way and not let too much gas leak out into the room generally. The occupational hazard of this, his chosen profession, is gas exposure and nerve damage, and it has started to worry him. No doubt he frets about it to his wife every night. Now he turns the gas on and quickly clamps the plastic mouthpiece over the baby's cheeks and lips.

The Baby is startled. The Mother is startled. The Baby starts to scream and redden behind the plastic, but he cannot be heard. He thrashes. "Tell him it's okay," says the nurse to the Mother.

Okay? "It's okay," repeats the Mother, holding his hand, but she knows he can tell it's not okay, because he can see not only that she is still wearing that stupid paper cap but that her words are mechanical and swallowed, and she is biting her lips to keep them from trembling. Panicked, he attempts to sit. He cannot breathe; his arms reach up. *Bye-bye, outside.* And then, quite quickly, his eyes shut; he untenses and has fallen not *into* sleep but aside to sleep, an odd, kidnapping kind of sleep, his terror now hidden someplace deep inside him.

"How did it go?" asks the social worker, waiting in the concrete outer room. The Mother is hysterical. A nurse has ushered her out.

"It wasn't at all like the filmstrip!" she cries. "It wasn't like the filmstrip at all!"

"The filmstrip? You mean the video?" asks the social worker.

"It wasn't like that at all! It was brutal and unforgivable."

"Why, that's terrible," she says, her role now no longer misinformational but janitorial, and she touches the Mother's arm, though the Mother shakes it off and goes to find the Husband.

She finds him in the large mulberry Surgery Lounge, where he has been taken and where there is free hot chocolate in small Styrofoam cups. Red cellophane garlands festoon the doorways. She has totally forgotten it is as close to Christmas as this. A pianist in the corner is playing "Carol of the Bells," and it sounds not only unfestive but scary, like the theme from *The Exorcist.*

There is a giant clock on the far wall. It is a kind of porthole into the operating room, a way of assessing the Baby's ordeal: forty-five minutes for the Hickman implant; two and a half hours for the nephrectomy. And then, after that, three months of chemotherapy. The magazine on her lap stays open at a ruby-hued perfume ad.

"Still not taking notes," says the Husband.

"Nope."

"You know, in a way, this is the kind of thing you've *always* written about."

"You are really something, you know that? This is life. This isn't a 'kind of thing.'"

"But this is the kind of thing that fiction is: it's the unlivable life, the strange room tacked onto the house, the extra moon that is circling the earth unbeknownst to science."

"I told you that."

"I'm quoting you."

She looks at her watch, thinking of the Baby. "How long has it been?"

"Not long. Too long. In the end, maybe those're the same things."

"What do you suppose is happening to him right this second?"

Infection? Slipping knives? "I don't know. But you know what? I've gotta go. I've gotta just walk a bit." The Husband gets up, walks around the lounge, then comes back and sits down.

The synapses between the minutes are unswimmable. An hour is thick as fudge. The Mother feels depleted; she is a string of empty tin cans attached by wire, something a goat would sniff and chew, something now and then enlivened by a jolt of electricity.

She hears their names being called over the intercom. "Yes? Yes?" She stands up quickly. Her words have flown out before her, an exhalation of birds. The piano music has stopped. The pianist is gone. She and the Husband approach the main desk, where a man looks up at them and smiles. Before him is a xeroxed list of patients' names. "That's our little boy right there," says the Mother, seeing the Baby's name on the list and pointing at it. "Is there some word? Is everything okay?"

"Yes," says the man. "Your boy is doing fine. They've just finished with the catheter, and they are moving on to the kidney."

"But it's been two hours already! Oh my God, did something go wrong? What happened? What went wrong?"

"Did something go wrong?" The Husband tugs at his collar.

"Not really. It just took longer than they expected. I'm told everything is fine. They wanted you to know."

"Thank you," says the Husband. They turn and walk back toward where they were sitting.

"I'm not going to make it." The Mother sighs, sinking into a fake leather chair shaped somewhat like a baseball mitt. "But before I go, I'm taking half this hospital out with me."

"Do you want some coffee?" asks the Husband.

"I don't know," says the Mother. "No, I guess not. No. Do you?"

"Nah, I don't, either, I guess," he says.

"Would you like part of an orange?"

"Oh, maybe, I guess, if you're having one." She takes an orange from her purse and just sits there peeling its difficult skin, the flesh rupturing beneath her fingers, the juice trickling down her hands, stinging the hangnails. She and the Husband chew and swallow, discreetly spit the seeds into Kleenex, and read from photocopies of the latest medical research, which they begged from the intern. They read, and underline, and sigh and close their eyes, and after some time, the surgery is over. A nurse from Peed Onk comes down to tell them.

"Your little boy's in recovery right now. He's doing well. You can see him in about fifteen minutes."

How can it be described? How can any of it be described? The trip and the story of the trip are always two different things. The narrator is the one who has stayed home, but then, afterward, presses her mouth upon the traveler's mouth, in order to make the mouth work, to make the mouth say, say, say. One cannot go to a place and speak of it; one cannot both see and say, not really. One can go, and upon returning make a lot of hand motions and indications with the arms. The mouth itself, working at the speed of light, at the eye's instructions, is necessarily struck still; so fast, so much to report, it hangs open and dumb as a gutted bell. All that unsayable life! That's where the narrator comes in. The narrator comes with her kisses and mimicry and tidying up. The narrator comes and makes a slow, fake song of the mouth's eager devastation.

It is a horror and a miracle to see him. He is lying in his crib in his room, tubed up, splayed like a boy on a cross, his arms stiffened into cardboard "no-no's" so that he cannot yank out the tubes. There is the bladder catheter, the nasal-gastric tube, and the Hickman, which, beneath the skin, is plugged into his jugular, then popped out his chest wall and capped with a long plastic cap. There is a large bandage taped over his abdomen. Groggy, on a morphine drip, still he is able to look at her when, maneuvering through all the vinyl wiring, she leans to hold him, and when she does, he begins to cry, but cry silently, without motion or noise. She has never seen a baby cry without motion or noise. It is the crying of an old person: silent, beyond opinion, shattered. In someone so tiny, it is frightening and unnatural. She wants to pick up the Baby and run — out of there, out of there. She wants to whip out a gun: *No-no's, eh? This whole thing is what I call a no-no.* Don't you touch him! she wants to shout at the surgeons and the needle nurses. Not anymore! No more! No more! She would crawl up and lie beside him in the crib if she could. But instead, because of all his intricate wiring, she must lean and cuddle, sing to him, songs of peril and flight: "We gotta get out of this place, if it's the last thing we ever do. We gotta get out of this place. There's a better life for me and you."

Very 1967. She was eleven then and impressionable.

The Baby looks at her, pleadingly, his arms splayed out in surrender. To where? Where is there to go? Take me! Take me!

That night, postop night, the Mother and Husband lie afloat in the cot together. A fluorescent lamp near the crib is kept on in the dark. The Baby breathes evenly but thinly in his drugged sleep. The morphine in its first flooding doses apparently makes him feel as if he were falling backward — or so the Mother has been told — and it causes the Baby to jerk, to catch himself over and over, as if he were being dropped from a tree. "Is this right? Isn't there something that should be done?" The nurses come in hourly, different ones — the night shifts seem strangely short and frequent. If the Baby stirs or frets, the nurses give him more morphine through the Hickman catheter, then leave to tend to other patients. The Mother rises to check on him in the low light. There is gurgling from the clear plastic suction tube coming out of his mouth. Brownish clumps have collected in the tube. What is going on? The Mother rings for the nurse. Is it Renée or Sarah or Darcy? She's forgotten.

"What, what is it?" murmurs the Husband, waking up.

"Something is wrong," says the Mother. "It looks like blood in his N-G tube."

"What?" The Husband gets out of bed. He, too, is wearing sweatpants.

The nurse — Valerie — pushes open the heavy door to the room and enters quietly. "Everything okay?"

"There's something wrong here. The tube is sucking blood out of his stomach. It looks like it may have perforated his stomach and that now he's bleeding internally. Look!"

Valerie is a saint, but her voice is the standard hospital saint voice: an infuriating, pharmaceutical calm. It says, Everything is normal here. Death is normal. Pain is normal. Nothing is abnormal. So there is nothing to get excited about. "Well now, let's see." She holds up the plastic tube and tries to see inside it. "Hmmm," she says. "I'll call the attending physician."

Because this is a research and teaching hospital, all the regular doctors are at home sleeping in their Mission-style beds. Tonight, as is apparently the case every weekend night, the attending physician is a medical student. He looks fifteen. The authority he attempts to convey, he cannot remotely inhabit. He is not even in the same building with it. He shakes everyone's hands, then strokes his chin, a gesture no doubt gleaned from some piece of dinner theater his parents took him to once. As if there were an actual beard on that chin! As if beard growth on that chin were even possible! *Our Town! Kiss Me Kate! Barefoot in the Park!* He is attempting to convince, if not to impress.

"We're in trouble," the Mother whispers to the Husband. She is tired, tired of young people grubbing for grades. "We've got Dr. 'Kiss Me Kate,' here."

The Husband looks at her blankly, a mix of disorientation and divorce.

The medical student holds the tubing in his hands. "I don't really see anything," he says.

He flunks! "You don't?" The Mother shoves her way in, holds the clear tubing in both hands. "That," she says. "Right here and here." Just this past semester, she said to one of her own students, "If you don't see how this essay is better than that one, then I want you just to go out into the hallway and stand there until you do." Is it important to keep one's voice down? The Baby stays asleep. He is drugged and dreaming, far away.

"Hmmm," says the medical student. "Perhaps there's a little irritation in the stomach."

"A little irritation?" The Mother grows furious. "This is blood. These are clumps and clots. This stupid thing is sucking the life right out of him!" Life! She is starting to cry.

They turn off the suction and bring in antacids, which they feed into the Baby through the tube. Then they turn the suction on again. This time on low.

"What was it on before?" asks the Husband.

"High," says Valerie. "Doctor's orders, though I don't know why. I don't know why these doctors do a lot of the things they do."

"Maybe they're . . . not all that bright?" suggests the Mother. She is feeling relief and rage simultaneously: there is a feeling of prayer and litigation in the air. Yet essentially, she is grateful. Isn't she? She thinks she is. And still, and still: look at all the things you have to do to protect a child, a hospital merely an intensification of life's cruel obstacle course.

The Surgeon comes to visit on Saturday morning. He steps in and nods at the Baby, who is awake but glazed from the morphine, his eyes two dark unseeing grapes. "The boy looks fine," the Surgeon announces. He peeks under the Baby's bandage. "The stitches look good," he says. The Baby's abdomen is stitched all the way across like a baseball. "And the other kidney, when we looked at it yesterday face-to-face, looked fine. We'll try to wean him off the morphine a little, and see how he's doing on Monday." He clears his throat. "And now," he says, looking about the room at the nurses and medical students, "I would like to speak with the Mother, alone."

The Mother's heart gives a jolt. "Me?"

"Yes," he says, motioning, then turning.

She gets up and steps out into the empty hallway with him, closing the door behind her. What can this be about? She hears the Baby fretting a little in his crib. Her brain fills with pain and alarm. Her voice comes out as a hoarse whisper. "Is there something — "

"There is a particular thing I need from you," says the Surgeon, turning and standing there very seriously.

"Yes?" Her heart is pounding. She does not feel resilient enough for any more bad news.

"I need to ask a favor."

"Certainly," she says, attempting very hard to summon the strength and courage for this occasion, whatever it is; her throat has tightened to a fist.

From inside his white coat, the surgeon removes a thin paperback book and thrusts it toward her. "Will you sign my copy of your novel?"

The Mother looks down and sees that it is indeed a copy of a novel she has written, one about teenaged girls.

She looks up. A big, spirited grin is cutting across his face. "I read this last summer," he says, "and I still remember parts of it! Those girls got into such trouble!"

Of all the surreal moments of the last few days, this, she thinks, might be the most so.

"Okay," she says, and the Surgeon merrily hands her a pen.

"You can just write 'To Dr. — ' Oh, I don't need to tell you what to write."

The Mother sits down on a bench and shakes ink into the pen. A sigh of relief washes over and out of her. Oh, the pleasure of a sigh of relief, like the finest moments of love; has anyone properly sung the praises of sighs of relief? She opens the book to the title page. She breathes deeply. What is he doing reading novels about teenaged girls, anyway? And why didn't be buy the hardcover? She inscribes something grateful and true, then hands the book back to him.

"Is he going to be okay?"

"The boy? The boy is going to be fine," he says, then taps her stiffly on the shoulder. "Now you take care. It's Saturday. Drink a little wine."

Over the weekend, while the Baby sleeps, the Mother and Husband sit together in the Tiny Tim Lounge. The Husband is restless and makes cafeteria and sundry runs, running errands for everyone. In his absence, the other parents regale her further with their sagas. Pediatric cancer and chemo stories: the children's amputations, blood poisoning, teeth flaking like shale, the learning delays and disabilities caused by chemo frying the young, budding brain. But strangely optimistic codas are tacked on — endings as stiff and loopy as carpenter's lace, crisp and empty as lettuce, reticulate as a net — ah, words. "After all that business with the tutor, he's better now, and fitted with new incisors by my wife's cousin's husband, who did dental school in two and a half years, if you can believe that. We hope for the best. We take things as they come. Life is hard."

"Life's a big problem," agrees the Mother. Part of her welcomes and invites all their tales. In the few long days since this nightmare began, part of her has become addicted to disaster and war stories. She wants only to hear about the sadness and emergencies of others. They are the only situations that can join hands with her own; everything else bounces off her shiny shield of resentment and unsympathy. Nothing else can even stay in her brain. From this, no doubt, the philistine world is made, or should one say recruited? Together, the parents huddle all day in the Tiny Tim Lounge — no need to watch *Oprah*. They leave Oprah in the dust. Oprah has nothing on them. They chat matter-of-factly, then fall silent and watch *Dune* or *Star Wars,* in which there are bright and shiny robots, whom the Mother now sees not as robots at all but as human beings who have had terrible things happen to them.

⁂

Some of their friends visit with stuffed animals and soft greetings of "Looking good" for the dozing baby, though the room is way past the stuffed-animal limit. The Mother arranges, once more, a plateful of Mint Milano cookies and cups of take-out coffee for guests. All her nutso pals stop by — the two on Prozac, the one obsessed with the word *penis* in the word *happiness,* the one who recently had her hair foiled green. "Your friends put the *de* in *fin de siècle,*" says the husband. Overheard, or recorded, all marital conversation sounds as if someone must be joking, though usually no one is.

She loves her friends, especially loves them for coming, since there are times they all fight and don't speak for weeks. Is this friendship? For now and here, it must do and is, and is, she swears it is. For one, they never offer impromptu spiritual lectures about death, how it is part of life, its natural ebb and flow, how we all must accept that, or other such utterances that make her want to scratch out some eyes. Like true friends, they take no hardy or elegant stance loosely choreographed from some broad perspective. They get right in there and mutter "Jesus Christ!" and shake their heads. Plus, they are the only people who not only will laugh at her stupid jokes but offer up stupid ones of their own. *What do you get when you cross Tiny Tim with a pit bull?* A child's illness is a strain on the mind. They know how to laugh in a fluty, desperate way — unlike the people who are more her husband's friends and who seem just to deepen their sorrowful gazes, nodding their heads with Sympathy. How exiling and estranging are everybody's Sympathetic Expressions! When anyone laughs, she thinks, Okay! Hooray: a buddy. In disaster as in show business.

Nurses come and go; their chirpy voices both startle and soothe. Some of the other Peed Onk parents stick their heads in to see how the Baby is and offer encouragement.

Green Hair scratches her head. "Everyone's so friendly here. Is there someone in this place who isn't doing all this airy, scripted optimism — or are people like that the only people here?"

"It's Modern Middle Medicine meets the Modern Middle Family," says the Husband. "In the Modern Middle West."

Someone has brought in take-out lo mein, and they all eat it out in the hall by the elevators.

Parents are allowed use of the Courtesy Line.

"You've got to have a second child," says a different friend on the phone, a friend from out of town. "An heir and a spare. That's what we did. We had another child to ensure we wouldn't off ourselves if we lost our first."

"Really?"

"I'm serious."

"A formal suicide? Wouldn't you just drink yourself into a lifelong stupor and let it go at that?"

"Nope. I knew how I would do it even. For a while, until our second came along, I had it all planned."

"What did you plan?"

"I can't go into too much detail, because — Hi, honey! — the kids are here now in the room. But I'll spell out the general idea: R-O-P-E."

Sunday evening, she goes and sinks down on the sofa in the Tiny Tim Lounge next to Frank, Joey's father. He is a short stocky man with the currentless, flatlined look behind the eyes that all the parents eventually get here. He has shaved his head bald in solidarity with his son. His little boy has been battling cancer for five years. It is now in the liver, and the rumor around the corridor is that Joey has three weeks to live. She knows that Joey's mother, Heather, left Frank years ago, two years into the cancer, and has remarried and had another child, a girl named Brittany. The Mother sees Heather here sometimes with her new life — the cute little girl and the new, young, full-haired husband who will never be so maniacally and debilitatingly obsessed with Joey's illness the way Frank, her first husband, was. Heather comes to visit Joey, to say hello and now good-bye, but she is not Joey's main man. Frank is.

Frank is full of stories — about the doctors, about the food, about the nurses, about Joey. Joey, affectless from his meds, sometimes leaves his room and comes out to watch TV in his bathrobe. He is jaundiced and bald, and though he is nine, he looks no older than six. Frank has devoted the last four and a half years to saving Joey's life. When the cancer was first diagnosed, the doctors gave Joey a 20 percent chance of living six more months. Now here it is, almost five years later, and Joey's still here. It is all due to Frank, who, early on, quit his job as vice president of a consulting firm in order to commit himself totally to his son. He is proud of everything he's given up and done, but he is tired. Part of him now really believes things are coming to a close, that this is the end. He says this without tears. There are no more tears.

"You have probably been through more than anyone else on this corridor," says the Mother.

"I could tell you stories," he says. There is a sour odor between them, and she realizes that neither of them has bathed for days.

"Tell me one. Tell me the worst one." She knows he hates his ex-wife and hates her new husband even more.

"The worst? They're all the worst. Here's one: one morning, I went out for breakfast with my buddy — it was the only time I'd left Joey alone ever; left him for two hours is all — and when I came back, his N-G tube was full of blood. They had the suction on too high, and it was sucking the guts right out of him."

"Oh my God. That just happened to us," said the Mother.

"It did?"

"Friday night."

"You're kidding. They let that happen again? I gave them such a chewing-out about that!"

"I guess our luck is not so good. We get your very worst story on the second night we're here."

"It's not a bad place, though."

"It's not?"

"Naw. I've seen worse. I've taken Joey everywhere."

"He seems very strong." Truth is, at this point, Joey seems like a zombie and frightens her.

"Joey's a fucking genius. A biological genius. They'd given him six months, remember."

The Mother nods.

"Six months is not very long," says Frank. "Six months is nothing. He was four and a half years old."

All the words are like blows. She feels flooded with affection and mourning for this man. She looks away, out the window, out past the hospital parking lot, up toward the black marbled sky and the electric eyelash of the moon. "And now he's nine," she says. "You're his hero."

"And he's mine," says Frank, though the fatigue in his voice seems to overwhelm him. "He'll be that forever. Excuse me," he says, "I've got to go check. His breathing hasn't been good. Excuse me."

"Good news and bad," says the Oncologist on Monday. He has knocked, entered the room, and now stands there. Their cots are unmade. One wastebasket is overflowing with coffee cups. "We've got the pathologist's report. The bad news is that the kidney they removed had certain lesions, called 'rests,' which are associated with a higher risk for disease in the other kidney. The good news is that the tumor is stage one, regular cell structure, and under five hundred grams, which qualifies you for a national experiment in which chemotherapy isn't done but your boy is monitored with ultrasound instead. It's not all that risky, given that the patient's watched closely, but here is the literature on it. There are forms to sign, if you decide to do that. Read all this and we can discuss it further. You have to decide within four days."

Lesions? Rests? They dry up and scatter like M&M's on the floor. All she hears is the part about no chemo. Another sigh of relief rises up in her and spills out. In a life where there is only the bearable and the unbearable, a sigh of relief is an ecstasy.

"No chemo?" says the Husband. "Do you recommend that?"

The Oncologist shrugs. What casual gestures these doctors are permitted! "I know chemo. I like chemo," says the Oncologist. "But this is for you to decide. It depends how you feel."

The Husband leans forward. "But don't you think that now that we have the upper hand with this thing, we should keep going? Shouldn't we stomp on it, beat it, smash it to death with the chemo?"

The Mother swats him angrily and hard. "Honey, you're delirious!" She whispers, but it comes out as a hiss. "This is our lucky break!" Then she adds gently, "We don't want the Baby to have chemo."

The Husband turns back to the Oncologist. "What do *you* think?"

"It could be," he says, shrugging. "It could be that this is your lucky break. But you won't know for sure for five years."

The Husband turns back to the Mother. "Okay," he says. "Okay."

The Baby grows happier and strong. He begins to move and sit and eat. Wednesday morning, they are allowed to leave, and leave without chemo. The Oncologist looks a little nervous. "Are you nervous about this?" asks the Mother.

"Of course I'm nervous." But he shrugs and doesn't look that nervous. "See you in six weeks for the ultrasound," he says, waves and then leaves, looking at his big black shoes as he does.

The Baby smiles, even toddles around a little, the sun bursting through the clouds, an angel chorus crescendoing. Nurses arrive. The Hickman is taken out of the Baby's neck and chest; antibiotic lotion is dispensed. The Mother packs up their bags. The Baby sucks on a bottle of juice and does not cry.

"No chemo?" says one of the nurses. "Not even a *little* chemo?"

"We're doing watch and wait," says the Mother.

The other parents look envious but concerned. They have never seen any child get out of there with his hair and white blood cells intact.

"Will you be okay?" asks Ned's mother.

"The worry's going to kill us," says the Husband.

"But if all we have to do is worry," chides the Mother, "every day for a hundred years, it'll be easy. It'll be nothing. I'll take all the worry in the world, if it wards off the thing itself."

"That's right," says Ned's mother. "Compared to everything else, compared to all the actual events, the worry is nothing."

The Husband shakes his head. "I'm such an amateur," he moans.

"You're both doing admirably," says the other mother. "Your baby's lucky, and I wish you all the best."

The Husband shakes her hand warmly. "Thank you," he says. "You've been wonderful."

Another mother, the mother of Eric, comes up to them. "It's all very hard," she says, her head cocked to one side. "But there's a lot of collateral beauty along the way."

Collateral beauty? Who is entitled to such a thing? A child is ill. No one is entitled to any collateral beauty!

"Thank you," says the Husband.

Joey's father, Frank, comes up and embraces them both. "It's a journey," he says. He chucks the Baby on the chin. "Good luck, little man."

"Yes, thank you so much," says the Mother. "We hope things go well with Joey." She knows that Joey had a hard, terrible night.

Frank shrugs and steps back. "Gotta go," he says. "Goodbye!"

"Bye," she says, and then he is gone. She bites the inside of her lip, a bit tearily, then bends down to pick up the diaper bag, which is now stuffed with little animals; helium balloons are tied to its zipper. Shouldering the thing, the Mother feels she has just won a prize. All the parents have now vanished down the hall in the opposite direction. The Husband moves close. With one arm, he takes the Baby from her; with the other, he rubs her back. He can see she is starting to get weepy.

"Aren't these people nice? Don't you feel better hearing about their lives?" he asks.

Why does he do this, form clubs all the time; why does even this society of suffering soothe him? When it comes to death and dying, perhaps someone in this family ought to be more of a snob.

"All these nice people with their brave stories," he continues as they make their way toward the elevator bank, waving good-bye to the nursing staff as they go, even the Baby waving shyly. *Bye-bye! Bye-bye!* "Don't you feel consoled, knowing we're all in the same boat, that we're all in this together?"

But who on earth would want to be in this boat? the Mother thinks. This boat is a nightmare boat. Look where it goes: to a silver-and-white room, where, just before your eyesight and hearing and your ability to touch or be touched disappear entirely, you must watch your child die.

Rope! Bring on the rope.

"Let's make our own way," says the Mother, "and not in this boat."

Woman Overboard! She takes the Baby back from the Husband, cups the Baby's cheek in her hand, kisses his brow and then, quickly, his flowery mouth. The Baby's heart — she can hear it — drums with life. "For as long as I live," says the Mother, pressing the elevator button — up or down, everyone in the end has to leave this way — "I never want to see any of these people again."

There are the notes.

Now where is the money?

🌿 LORRIE MOORE

How to Become a Writer

First, try to be something, anything, else. A movie star/astronaut. A movie star/missionary. A movie star/kindergarten teacher. President of the World. Fail miserably. It is best if you fail at an early age — say, fourteen. Early, critical disillusionment is necessary so that at fifteen you can write long haiku sequences about thwarted desire. It is a pond, a cherry blossom, a wind brushing against sparrow wing leaving for mountain. Count the syllables. Show it to your mom. She is tough and practical. She has a son in Vietnam and a husband who may be having an affair. She believes in wearing brown because it hides spots. She'll look briefly at your writing, then back up at you with a face blank as a donut. She'll say: "How about emptying the dishwasher?" Look away. Shove the forks in the fork drawer. Accidentally break one of the free-bie gas station glasses. This is the required pain and suffering. This is only for starters.

In your high school English class look at Mr. Killian's face. Decide faces are important. Write a villanelle about pores. Struggle. Write a sonnet. Count the syllables: nine, ten, eleven, thirteen. Decide to experiment with fiction. Here you don't have to count syllables. Write a short story about an elderly man and woman who accidentally shoot each other in the head, the result of an inexplicable malfunction of a shotgun which appears mysteriously in their living room one night. Give it to Mr. Killian as your final project. When you get it back, he has written on it: "Some of your images are quite nice, but you have no sense of plot." When you are home, in the privacy of your own room, faintly scrawl in pencil beneath his black-inked comments: "Plots are for dead people, pore-face."

Take all the babysitting jobs you can get. You are great with kids. They love you. You tell them stories about old people who die idiot deaths. You sing them songs like "Blue Bells of Scotland," which is their favorite. And when they are in their pajamas and have finally stopped pinching each other, when they are fast asleep, you read every sex manual in the house, and wonder how on earth anyone could ever do those things with someone they truly loved. Fall asleep in a chair reading Mr. McMurphy's *Playboy.* When the McMurphys come home, they will tap you on the shoulder, look at the magazine in your lap, and grin. You will want to die. They will ask you if Tracey took her medicine all right. Explain, yes, she did, that you promised her a story if she would take it like a big girl and that seemed to work out just fine. "Oh, marvelous," they will exclaim.

Try to smile proudly.

Apply to college as a child psychology major.

As a child psychology major, you have some electives. You've always liked birds. Sign up for something called "The Ornithological Field Trip." It meets Tuesdays and Thursdays at two. When you arrive at Room 134 on the first day of class, everyone is sitting around a seminar table talking about metaphors. You've heard of these. After a short, excruciating while, raise your hand and say diffidently, "Excuse me, isn't this Birdwatching One-oh-one?" The class stops and turns to look at you. They seem to all have one face — giant and blank as a vandalized clock. Someone with a beard booms out, "No, this is Creative Writing." Say: "Oh — right," as if perhaps you knew all along. Look down at your schedule. Wonder how the hell you ended up here. The computer, apparently, has made an error. You start to get up to leave and then don't. The lines at the registrar this week are huge. Perhaps you should stick with this mistake. Perhaps your creative writing isn't all that bad. Perhaps it is fate. Perhaps this is what your dad meant when he said, "It's the age of computers, Francie, it's the age of computers."

Decide that you like college life. In your dorm you meet many nice people. Some are smarter than you. And some, you notice, are dumber than you. You will continue, unfortunately, to view the world in exactly these terms for the rest of your life.

The assignment this week in creative writing is to narrate a violent happening. Turn in a story about driving with your Uncle Gordon and another one about two old people who are accidentally electrocuted when they go to turn on a badly wired desk lamp. The teacher will hand them back to you with comments: "Much of your writing is smooth and energetic. You have, however, a ludicrous notion of plot." Write another story about a man and a woman who, in the very first paragraph, have their lower torsos accidentally blitzed away by dynamite. In the second paragraph, with the insurance money, they buy a frozen yogurt stand together. There are six more paragraphs. You read the whole thing out loud in class. No one likes it. They say your sense of plot is outrageous and incompetent. After class someone asks you if you are crazy.

Decide that perhaps you should stick to comedies. Start dating someone who is funny, someone who has what in high school you called a "really great sense of humor" and what now your creative writing class calls "self-contempt giving rise to comic form." Write down all of his jokes, but don't tell him you are doing this. Make up anagrams of his old girlfriend's name and name all of your socially handicapped characters with them. Tell him his old girlfriend is in all of your stories and then watch how funny he can be, see what a really great sense of humor he can have.

Your child psychology advisor tells you you are neglecting courses in your major. What you spend the most time on should be what you're majoring in. Say yes, you understand.

In creative writing seminars over the next two years, everyone continues to smoke cigarettes and ask the same things: "But does it work?" "Why should we care about this character?" "Have you earned this cliché?" These seem like important questions.

On days when it is your turn, you look at the class hopefully as they scour your mimeographs for a plot. They look back up at you, drag deeply, and then smile in a sweet sort of way.

You spend too much time slouched and demoralized. Your boyfriend suggests bicycling. Your roommate suggests a new boyfriend. You are said to be self-mutilating and losing weight, but you continue writing. The only happiness you have is writing something new, in the middle of the night, armpits damp, heart pounding, something no one has yet seen. You have only those brief, fragile, untested moments of exhilaration when you know: you are a genius. Understand what you must do. Switch majors. The kids in your nursery project will be disappointed, but you have a calling, an urge, a delusion, an unfortunate habit. You have, as your mother would say, fallen in with a bad crowd.

Why write? Where does writing come from? These are questions to ask yourself. They are like: Where does dust come from? Or: Why is there war? Or: If there's a God, then why is my brother now a cripple?

These are questions that you keep in your wallet, like calling cards. These are questions, your creative writing teacher says, that are good to address in your journals but rarely in your fiction.

The writing professor this fall is stressing the Power of the Imagination. Which means he doesn't want long descriptive stories about your camping trip last July. He wants you to start in a realistic context but then to alter it. Like recombinant DNA. He wants you to let your imagination sail, to let it grow big-bellied in the wind. This is a quote from Shakespeare.

Tell your roommate your great idea, your great exercise of imaginative power: a transformation of Melville to contemporary life. It will be about monomania and the fish-eat-fish world of life insurance in Rochester, New York. The first line will be "Call me Fishmeal," and it will feature a menopausal suburban husband named Richard, who because he is so depressed all the time is called "Mopey Dick" by his witty wife Elaine. Say to your roommate: "Mopey Dick, get it?" Your roommate looks at you, her face blank as a large Kleenex. She comes up to you, like a buddy, and puts an arm around your burdened shoulders. "Listen, Francie," she says, slow as speech therapy. "Let's go out and get a big beer."

The seminar doesn't like this one either. You suspect they are beginning to feel sorry for you. They say: "You have to think about what is happening. Where is the story here?"

The next semester the writing professor is obsessed with writing from personal experience. You must write from what you know, from what has happened to you. He wants deaths, he wants camping trips. Think about what has happened to you. In three years there have been three things: you lost your virginity; your parents got divorced; and your brother came home from a forest ten miles from the Cambodian border with only half a thigh, a permanent smirk nestled into one corner of his mouth.

About the first you write: "It created a new space, which hurt and cried in a voice that wasn't mine, 'I'm not the same anymore, but I'll be okay.'"

About the second you write an elaborate story of an old married couple who stumble upon an unknown land mine in their kitchen and accidentally blow themselves up. You call it: "For Better or for Liverwurst."

About the last you write nothing. There are no words for this. Your typewriter hums. You can find no words.

At undergraduate cocktail parties, people say, "Oh, you write? What do you write about?" Your roommate, who has consumed too much wine, too little cheese, and no crackers at all, blurts: "Oh, my god, she always writes about her dumb boyfriend."

Later on in life you will learn that writers are merely open, helpless texts with no real understanding of what they have written and therefore must half-believe anything and everything that is said of them. You, however, have not yet reached this stage of literary criticism. You stiffen and say, "I do not," the same way you said it when someone in the fourth grade accused you of really liking oboe lessons and your parents really weren't just making you take them.

Insist you are not very interested in any one subject at all, that you are interested in the music of language, that you are interested in — in — syllables, because they are the atoms of poetry, the cells of the mind, the breath of the soul. Begin to feel woozy. Stare into your plastic wine cup.

"Syllables?" you will hear someone ask, voice trailing off, as they glide slowly toward the reassuring white of the dip.

Begin to wonder what you do write about. Or if you have anything to say. Or if there even is such a thing as a thing to say. Limit these thoughts to no more than ten minutes a day; like sit-ups, they can make you thin.

You will read somewhere that all writing has to do with one's genitals. Don't dwell on this. It will make you nervous.

Your mother will come visit you. She will look at the circles under your eyes and hand you a brown book with a brown briefcase on the cover. It is entitled: *How to Become a Business Executive.* She has also brought the *Names for Baby* encyclopedia you asked for; one of your characters, the aging clown school teacher, needs a new name. Your mother will shake her head and say: "Francie, Francie, remember when you were going to be a child psychology major?"

Say: "Mom, I like to write."

She'll say: "Sure you like to write. Of course. Sure you like to write."

Write a story about a confused music student and title it: "Schubert Was the One with the Glasses, Right?" It's not a big hit, although your roommate likes the part where the two violinists accidentally blow themselves up in a recital room. "I went out with a violinist once," she says, snapping her gum.

Thank god you are taking other courses. You can find sanctuary in nineteenth-century ontological snags and invertebrate courting rituals. Certain globular mollusks have what is called "Sex by the Arm." The male octopus, for instance, loses the end of one arm when placing it inside the female body during intercourse. Marine biologists call it "Seven Heaven." Be glad you know these things. Be glad you are not just a writer. Apply to law school.

From here on in, many things can happen. But the main one will be this: you decide not to go to law school after all, and, instead, you spend a good, big chunk of your adult life telling people how you decided not to go to law school after all. Somehow you end up writing again. Perhaps you go to graduate school. Perhaps you work odd jobs and take writing courses at night. Perhaps you are working on a novel and writing down all the clever remarks and intimate personal confessions you hear during the day. Perhaps you are losing your pals, your acquaintances, your balance.

You have broken up with your boyfriend. You now go out with men who, instead of whispering "I love you," shout: "Do it to me, baby." This is good for your writing.

Sooner or later you have a finished manuscript more or less. People look at it in a vaguely troubled sort of way and say, "I'll bet becoming a writer was always a fantasy of yours, wasn't it?" Your lips dry to salt. Say that of all the fantasies possible in the world, you can't imagine being a writer even making the top twenty. Tell them you were going to be a child psychology major. "I bet," they always sigh, "you'd be great with kids." Scowl fiercely. Tell them you're a walking blade.

Quit classes. Quit jobs. Cash in old savings bonds. Now you have time like warts on your hands. Slowly copy all of your friends' addresses into a new address book.

Vacuum. Chew cough drops. Keep a folder full of fragments.

An eyelid darkening sideways.
World as conspiracy.
Possible plot? A woman gets on a bus.
Suppose you threw a love affair and nobody came.

At home drink a lot of coffee. At Howard Johnson's order the cole slaw. Consider how it looks like the soggy confetti of a map: where you've been, where you're going — "You Are Here," says the red star on the back of the menu.

Occasionally a date with a face blank as a sheet of paper asks you whether writers often become discouraged. Say that sometimes they do and sometimes they do. Say it's a lot like having polio.

"Interesting," smiles your date, and then he looks down at his arm hairs and starts to smooth them, all, always, in the same direction.

Joyce Carol Oates

Joyce Carol Oates is America's foremost woman of letters, having published collections of poetry, literary essays, and short fiction, as well as drama, novels, and journalism. Among my favorite Oates titles (she is the author, to date, of ninety-four books) are her 1987 volume of essays, *On Boxing,* in which she examines the sport as both a fan and a sociologist; her early novel *them,* for which she won the National Book Award; *Bellefleur,* a Gothic tale infused with the magical realism of García Márquez; and *Zombie,* her chilling take on the mentality of a serial killer. Like Lorrie Moore, Oates published early, winning the *Mademoiselle* fiction contest when she was an undergraduate at Syracuse University, and she has been staggeringly productive ever since. According to her biographer, she keeps a quote from Henry James on the bulletin board above her desk for inspiration, a quote that speaks to her methodology: "We work in the dark — we do what we can — we give what we have. Our doubt is our passion, and our passion is our task. The rest is the madness of art."

The two stories I've chosen for this volume are from *The Assignation,* a collection of experimental pieces, some so brief as to call into question just what the essential elements of a story are ("One Flesh" is a mere paragraph in length, and yet it manages to create a vivid tableau and a palpable tension; the story that succeeds it, "Slow," compacts its drama into seventeen lines). "Tick," reprinted here, is likewise a marvel of compression. It begins, "She said, I can't live with you under these conditions, and her husband said, But these *are* the conditions. And moved out." From there, we are left to see how this "shy cold girl" deals with her independence, with the ringing telephone she no longer bothers to answer, and with one of those unexpected little contingencies that arises when the natural world intrudes on our own. "The Abduction," like Coover's "The Brother," is told in a minimally punctuated rush of perception, the first frantic long run-on sentence closing finally with this: ". . . then she knew she'd made the worst mistake of her life climbing into a car with a crazy man and was he going to rape her? was he going to murder her?" The story turns neatly on the psychology of the victim and the way in which this transformative experience has affected her.

Tick

She said, I can't live with you under these conditions, and her husband said, But these *are* the conditions. And moved out. And did not telephone her for several days. And when he did call she told him quickly, I'm happy here alone — I've gotten through the worst of it. Don't spoil my happiness again.

Since then the telephone rings at odd hours and she never answers. She will never answer — it's that simple. She does her work in the apartment spreading her books and papers out on the dining room table and she is working well, better than she has in years but it's all precarious, she knows it's precarious, not the temptation to kill herself — she understands this is an adolescent fantasy and would never act upon it — but the temptation to succumb to thoughts of despair, self-hatred. Easier, she thinks, to hate yourself than to respect yourself: it involves less imagination.

Tonight, contemplating these matters, she runs her fingers through her hair and comes upon a small bump on her head, the very crown of her head. A pimple, except it isn't a pimple. A mysterious hardness, shell-like. Could it be a tiny pebble embedded in her scalp? But how? She tries gently to dislodge it with her fingernails but it is stuck fast. What can it be? — she's fastidious about grooming, shampooing her hair every morning when she showers.

She tries to comb the thing out of her hair first with a plastic comb and then with a fine-toothed steel comb her husband left behind. It won't budge. Perhaps it is a tiny wound, a tiny scab, she thinks, and then she thinks, It's alive, it has its jaws in me. And she realizes it must be a tick.

Since her husband moved out and it is possible for her to go for days without seeing anyone she has made a conscientious effort to be better groomed than she has ever been in her life. Shaves her underarms before the harsh stubble appears, keeps her legs smooth and hairless. Always dresses no matter the black rain falling against the windows in the early morning and the faint odors of garbage and wet ashes pervading the apartment building. Puts on lipstick, sometimes even a touch of cologne on her wrist, behind her ear. Pride! she thinks, winking in the mirror. Self-reliance! There you go!

She's in the bathroom trying desperately to inspect the top of her head in the medicine cabinet mirror. Roughly parting her hair, stooping, her eyes rolling up in their sockets. But she can't see — it's impossible. She runs for a hand mirror and holds it at such an angle that she can see into the cabinet mirror where she parts her hair clumsily with the fingers of one hand and she gives a little scream and nearly drops the mirror: it *is* a tick, bloated and purplish-black, stuck fast in her scalp.

She instructs herself to be calm. Not to panic. Not to give in to nausea, gagging. It's only an insect after all, one of those tiny black spiderlike things, parasites that suck animal and human blood, it's said the woods and fields are filled with them because of the rain this spring, and the heat, or is it because of the dryness and the heat, they're remarkably quick, darting and leaping and flying, raining from the trees onto unknowing human heads which is how she must have picked this one up — walking through the park the other morning, forcing herself to look and to really *see* the beauty of the natural world which she'd lost these past several months or has it been these past several years, embarked upon the precarious enterprise of adulthood, wifehood, loneliness.

She recalls that ticks secrete an anesthetic when they bite so you can't feel the bite. She recalls they're so hardy they can't be killed by ordinary methods, can't be squashed — the most practical method is to flush them down the toilet.

She is digging furiously at her scalp with her nails and the sink is flecked with blood, her blood, and a number of hairs. No reason to panic but she can't stop the frantic digging, she's bent low over the sink, panting, cursing, blood beating in her eyeballs and rivulets of sweat running down her back. She feels a sensation of nausea, a taste of something hot and acid at the back of her mouth but she manages to swallow it down. She thinks of the book she'd been planning to read this evening and the piano pieces by a contemporary composer whose work she admires she'd planned to study and work out though she hasn't a piano in the apartment yet (she intends to buy one, or rent one, soon, now that she'll have more time for it, and more energy) and these activities strike her suddenly as remote, preposterous.

Her husband once had a medical handbook, she goes to look for it in the bedroom in a pile of books he left behind but can't find it, she tries the bookshelves in the living room then the stack of books in the kitchen beside the refrigerator, mostly paperbacks and shamelessly dusty, and when she's about to give up she discovers it, *The Family Medical Companion,* thank God her husband was so angry and hurt, so eager to get away from her, he'd left it behind. With trembling fingers she opens it to the section "Insects" that begins, "Insects are both friends and enemies of man. Some simply annoy by their bites and stings, but a few carry disease-bearing microbes."

The paragraph on ticks is disappointingly brief. She reads that she should not try to yank the tick out of her skin since ticks embed themselves so snugly, part of its body will very likely remain and there's the chance of infection. She has her choice of several procedures: she can hold a lighted match or cigarette against the tick's back until it wriggles free; she can coat it with Vaseline, gasoline, kerosene, or turpentine; she can pick the tick off gently with a tweezers.

She tries the tweezers. Tries repeatedly, a dozen times or more, at the bathroom sink, until the tweezers slips from her numbed fingers. She's crying. Her face is flushed as if with sunstroke, her eyes in the mirror are those of a deranged woman. To her horror she feels, or believes she feels, the tick stirring in her scalp — enlivened, enraged, burrowing more deeply into her flesh. She wonders if it has the power to pierce the bone, to embed itself in her very brain.

She jams her knuckles into her mouth to muffle her screaming.

She's close to hysteria so she leaves the bathroom and paces about the apartment, from one room to another, one room to another, in an effort to calm herself. Minutes pass: she has no idea how many. She beats her hands softly together, the fleshy parts of the palms, she tries to breathe deeply and rhythmically, after all this is such a minor problem, hardly a matter of life and death, if worse comes to worst she can take a taxi to a hospital to an emergency room but what if they laugh at her there? — what if they're furious with her there? — her with her face like death, trembling and panting as if she'd been physically assaulted, *a mere tick embedded in her scalp.* More plausibly, she might go next door and ask for help from her neighbor — but when she envisions knocking at the door, handing the astonished young woman the tweezers and begging her to extricate the thing in her head, she knows she can't do it. She isn't acquainted with the woman even casually — she's a shy cold girl very like herself. When they meet in the foyer or in the elevator each smiles faintly and pointedly looks away thinking, *Don't talk to me. Please. Not right now.*

Perhaps she should kill herself after all — it would be the easiest solution to all her problems.

By this time she's walking fast, on the verge of breaking into a run, can't stop! can't sit down! her heart beating wildly and her breath audible. At the crown of her head there's a hot piercing throbbing pain. Her fingernails are edged with blood. She's rushing from room to room, pacing, turning in tight corners like a trapped animal, hardly seeing where she's careening, her eyes filled with tears of hurt, rage, frustration, shame — this is what it comes to, she's thinking, this is all it comes to, and she's leaning in a doorway trying to get her breath trying to stave off an attack of faintness when she hears the telephone ring and understands it has been ringing for some time.

She heads for it like a sleepwalker, propelled by a rough shove. She foresees a reconciliation, lovemaking both anguished and tender. She foresees starting a child. It's time.

The Abduction

She was seventeen years old and mature for her age and she'd known of course what the word meant but would not have applied it to what happened to her one afternoon when, not exactly hitchhiking along the highway by the shopping mall, just walking there, alone, her shoulders hunched against the wind, she was asked by this man driving a low-slung rust-speckled Cadillac would she like a ride, so she said sure, and got in the car, and it wasn't actually right away that she understood something was wrong though that's what she would say afterward and perhaps even, with the passage of days, weeks, months, come eventually to believe, but when he started in talking kind of strange and making little jokes hardly talking *to* her or asking questions of the kind she and her girlfriends usually were asked by guys like this, meaning men that were older, clearly past thirty and in this case (she'd looked at him climbing in, got a good clear look at him and wasn't put off by what she saw, just a guy with a pocked or pitted skin the kind you naturally feel sorry for, and hair going thin on top this gunmetal-gray like her father's wetted down and combed carefully so the balding spots didn't show, or didn't show much, and some sort of twitchy little moustache she'd have laughed at with her girlfriends but he was wearing what looked like a nice topcoat and had a tie on, and a white shirt which men hardly wear anymore not even the men teachers at the high school, and there was something about, what was it, his hands, his fingers, the nails that were specially clean, clipped short and neat and filed) — when he kept on talking in this queer voice like he was making an effort not to talk too fast or get too excited and wasn't paying all that much attention where he was driving, which lane exactly was he in, and which speed he wanted — fast, or slow — and the things he was saying didn't make all that much sense if you tried actually to listen to them (he seemed to be angry about the U.S. Government because he'd been cheated, he said, of something, or somebody had betrayed him, and there was a lot too about Christmas and this time of year and ghosts out of the ancestral past pushing forth he said in the genes of the living, the genes and chromosomes — which she picked up on because they'd been studying that kind of thing in biology) then she knew she'd made the worst mistake of her life climbing into a car

with a crazy man and was he going to rape her? was he going to murder her? Her blood did truly run cold, icy-cold, all that stuff is true
when you're scared to death, her fingers and her toes cold like a
corpse's and her heart, dear God her heart was beating so hard and fast
it seemed like it was going to push out of her chest rocking her entire
body while she sat there trying to smile listening to this madman talking and talking and talking as he'd do for the next hour and twenty
minutes though she tried to tell him she wanted to get out of the car,
she had to get home where they were waiting for her and he was taking her out of her way please she begged please mister would he stop
and let her out starting to cry a little so he reached over and touched
her for the first time which almost freaked her out but he was saying
how he wouldn't hurt her for the world, he was a pacifist and would
never hurt another living sentient being unless he was forced but she
would have to sit still she couldn't make him nervous while he was
driving or they might have a fatal accident so she sat as quiet as possible staring straight ahead but not really seeing anything for a while
so it came as a kind of surprise when she realized they weren't on
Route 1 anymore but on I-95 going over into Pennsylvania and he was
talking like before but talking faster with this excitement you could
almost feel in the air around him like radiant heat, the moral crimes of
the U.S. Government and certain curses out of the ancestral past, and
he was weaving from one lane to another so she thought they'd have an
accident and both be killed, then what was worse he suddenly got
sleepy yawning and shaking his head and slapping at his cheeks to
keep awake and he told her it was fatigue like battle fatigue, trench
warfare fatigue had she ever heard of that? and she said no and he said
Well it's a phenomenon of mental life you're in the trenches in the
foremost line of fire and you fall asleep so maybe she should sing to
him to keep him awake to keep from having an accident and she asked
why didn't he put on the radio and he said he didn't have a radio, so
she tried to sing, her voice faint and sickish and her throat scratchy so
the words died out after a few minutes but he didn't seem to notice,
maybe hadn't been listening, still yawning and slapping at his cheeks
smelling of sweat giving off this weird heat and they were going
eighty miles an hour so fast the car rattled over the bridge over the
Delaware into Pennsylvania then toward Philadelphia and she was
wondering could she signal somehow for help, could anyone guess the
situation she was in or would they just naturally think she was a girl in
a car with her father, even if she was crying, looking so scared, but if
anybody glanced at her they didn't actually see her, it was clear they
didn't give a damn about her, barreling along in this guy's old Caddie
past Philadelphia and past Wilmington, Delaware, and into Maryland

halfway to Baltimore when the gas gauge showed empty and the little red light went on in warning and he said he would have to stop for gas and would she promise him to stay still in the car and not cause him to hurt her and she said yes she promised but he didn't exit at the next exit as she'd expected, kept driving despite the red light blinking on and off and on again until finally he had to stop, pulled into one of the service stations and up to the gas pumps and she said she had to use the restroom (which was true enough) and he said would she promise him she'd come back and she said yes she'd only be gone a minute or two and she was smiling to show him she was telling the truth seeing how sweaty he was, the poor guy, hair gummy on his forehead and some of it coming loose so you could see the bald places, him saying she'd been so kind and patient and he could see in her eyes her special quality, hers was to be a special destiny he said so it was imperative *she return to him* and she said yes she would her fingers closing around the door handle and by this time the gas station attendant was rapping at his window and it was like a moment in a dream when something terrible and wonderful is happening, and so easily — she opened the door and climbed out and started to run sobbing and screaming for help and that was the way it ended, the abduction as it was called by police and in the newspapers and on the 6:00 P.M. Trenton news that very night and the next night too when she was a guest on the show interviewed live telling her story breathless and pretty remembering to look directly at the camera as they'd instructed her, the camera with the red light is the one that's on, were you frightened, did you think he would kill you, what sorts of things did he say to you, what sorts of things were going through your mind? and she answered as truthfully as possible as, in the days, weeks, months, and eventually years to come she would tell of that event in her life that was like nothing before it and nothing to follow when she'd known she was marked for a special destiny and a special happiness — about which, out of very gratitude, she dared not speak.

Tim O'Brien

Tim O'Brien served in Vietnam in 1969–70, and much of his writing has grown out of that experience. His first book, *If I Die in a Combat Zone*, was a clear-eyed memoir of that time, and his second, the dreamlike novel *Going After Cacciato* (1978), won the National Book Award for its surrealistic portrayal of the dislocations of war. He returned to the subject of Vietnam in his novel *In the Lake of the Woods* and in what is perhaps his best-known work, *The Things They Carried*, a collection of interconnected stories published in 1990. What I especially like about O'Brien's stories is their richness and immediacy — more than any other writer, he has the uncanny ability to put you into the scene, to make you see, hear, smell, and taste what it is like to trudge through the lowering forests of an alien country or to crawl into a wet foxhole while bombs explode in the night. There is a confidentiality too, the sense of being let in on a secret, that illuminates his stories. "On the Rainy River," for instance, begins, "This is one story I've never told before. Not to anyone. Not to my parents, not to my brother or sister, not even to my wife. To go into it, I've always thought, would only cause embarrassment for all of us, a sudden need to be elsewhere, which is the natural response to a confession."

The title story from *The Things They Carried* is much anthologized elsewhere, but I include it here because it is one of the essential stories of our time. The genius of the piece lies in the title trope — what they carried was a physical load, surely, as we learn in precise detail after the first scene break, but it was a psychological burden too, and therein lies the power of the story. The second piece here, "Sweetheart of the Song Tra Bong," creates a sustaining myth — the story of Mary Anne Bell, the all-American girl every grunt was fighting for sprung to miraculous life on the battlefield — even as it reveals how innocence is corrupted by the seductive tug of combat. It is one of the best of the twenty-two superb stories that constitute *The Things They Carried*, and I like it all the more for its departure from the realism of the other pieces.

The Things They Carried

First Lieutenant Jimmy Cross carried letters from a girl named Martha, a junior at Mount Sebastian College in New Jersey. They were not love letters, but Lieutenant Cross was hoping, so he kept them folded in plastic at the bottom of his rucksack. In the late afternoon, after a day's march, he would dig his foxhole, wash his hands under a canteen, unwrap the letters, hold them with the tips of his fingers, and spend the last hour of light pretending. He would imagine romantic camping trips into the White Mountains in New Hampshire. He would sometimes taste the envelope flaps, knowing her tongue had been there. More than anything, he wanted Martha to love him as he loved her, but the letters were mostly chatty, elusive on the matter of love. She was a virgin, he was almost sure. She was an English major at Mount Sebastian, and she wrote beautifully about her professors and roommates and midterm exams, about her respect for Chaucer and her great affection for Virginia Woolf. She often quoted lines of poetry; she never mentioned the war, except to say Jimmy, take care of yourself. The letters weighed 10 ounces. They were signed Love, Martha, but Lieutenant Cross understood that Love was only a way of signing and did not mean what he sometimes pretended it meant. At dusk, he would carefully return the letters to his rucksack. Slowly, a bit distracted, he would get up and move among his men, checking the perimeter, then at full dark he would return to his hole and watch the night and wonder if Martha was a virgin.

The things they carried were largely determined by necessity. Among the necessities or near-necessities were P-38 can openers, pocket knives, heat tabs, wristwatches, dog tags, mosquito repellent, chewing gum, candy, cigarettes, salt tablets, packets of Kool-Aid, lighters, matches, sewing kits, Military Payment Certificates, C rations, and two or three canteens of water. Together, these items weighed between 15 and 20 pounds, depending upon a man's habits or rate of metabolism. Henry Dobbins, who was a big man, carried extra rations; he was especially fond of canned peaches in heavy syrup over pound cake. Dave Jensen, who practiced field hygiene, carried a toothbrush, dental floss, and several hotel-sized bars of soap he'd stolen on R&R in Sydney, Australia.

Ted Lavender, who was scared, carried tranquilizers until he was shot in the head outside the village of Than Khe in mid-April. By necessity, and because it was SOP, they all carried steel helmets that weighed 5 pounds including the liner and camouflage cover. They carried the standard fatigue jackets and trousers. Very few carried underwear. On their feet they carried jungle boots — 2.1 pounds — and Dave Jensen carried three pairs of socks and a can of Dr. Scholl's foot powder as a precaution against trench foot. Until he was shot, Ted Lavender carried 6 or 7 ounces of premium dope, which for him was a necessity. Mitchell Sanders, the RTO, carried condoms. Norman Bowker carried a diary. Rat Kiley carried comic books. Kiowa, a devout Baptist, carried an illustrated New Testament that had been presented to him by his father, who taught Sunday school in Oklahoma City, Oklahoma. As a hedge against bad times, however, Kiowa also carried his grandmother's distrust of the white man, his grandfather's old hunting hatchet. Necessity dictated. Because the land was mined and booby-trapped, it was SOP for each man to carry a steel-centered, nylon-covered flak jacket, which weighed 6.7 pounds, but which on hot days seemed much heavier. Because you could die so quickly, each man carried at least one large compress bandage, usually in the helmet band for easy access. Because the nights were cold, and because the monsoons were wet, each carried a green plastic poncho that could be used as a raincoat or groundsheet or makeshift tent. With its quilted liner, the poncho weighed almost 2 pounds, but it was worth every ounce. In April, for instance, when Ted Lavender was shot, they used his poncho to wrap him up, then to carry him across the paddy, then to lift him into the chopper that took him away.

They were called legs or grunts.

To carry something was to hump it, as when Lieutenant Jimmy Cross humped his love for Martha up the hills and through the swamps. In its intransitive form, to hump meant to walk, or to march, but it implied burdens far beyond the intransitive.

Almost everyone humped photographs. In his wallet, Lieutenant Cross carried two photographs of Martha. The first was a Kodacolor snapshot signed Love, though he knew better. She stood against a brick wall. Her eyes were gray and neutral, her lips slightly open as she stared straight-on at the camera. At night, sometimes, Lieutenant Cross wondered who had taken the picture, because he knew she had boyfriends, because he loved her so much, and because he could see the shadow of the picture-taker spreading out against the brick wall. The second photograph had been clipped from the 1968 Mount Sebastian yearbook. It was an action shot — women's volleyball — and Martha was bent horizontal to the floor, reaching, the palms of her hands in sharp focus, the tongue taut, the expression frank and competitive. There was no visible sweat. She wore white gym shorts. Her legs, he thought, were almost certainly the legs of a virgin, dry and without hair, the left knee cocked and carrying her entire weight, which was just over 100 pounds. Lieutenant Cross remembered touching that left knee. A dark theater, he remembered, and the movie was *Bonnie and Clyde,* and Martha wore a tweed skirt, and during the final scene, when he touched her knee, she turned and looked at him in a sad, sober way that made him pull his hand back, but he would always remember the feel of the tweed skirt and the knee beneath it and the sound of the gunfire that killed Bonnie and Clyde, how embarrassing it was, how slow and oppressive. He remembered kissing her good night at the dorm door. Right then, he thought, he should've done something brave. He should've carried her up the stairs to her room and tied her to the bed and touched that left knee all night long. He should've risked it. Whenever he looked at the photographs, he thought of new things he should've done.

What they carried was partly a function of rank, partly of field specialty.

As a first lieutenant and platoon leader, Jimmy Cross carried a compass, maps, code books, binoculars, and a .45-caliber pistol that weighed 2.9 pounds fully loaded. He carried a strobe light and the responsibility for the lives of his men.

As an RTO, Mitchell Sanders carried the PRC-25 radio, a killer, 26 pounds with its battery.

As a medic, Rat Kiley carried a canvas satchel filled with morphine and plasma and malaria tablets and surgical tape and comic books and all the things a medic must carry, including M&M's for especially bad wounds, for a total weight of nearly 20 pounds.

As a big man, therefore a machine gunner, Henry Dobbins carried the M-60, which weighed 23 pounds unloaded, but which was almost always loaded. In addition, Dobbins carried between 10 and 15 pounds of ammunition draped in belts across his chest and shoulders.

As PFCs or Spec 4s, most of them were common grunts and carried the standard M-16 gas-operated assault rifle. The weapon weighed 7.5 pounds unloaded, 8.2 pounds with its full 20-round magazine. Depending on numerous factors, such as topography and psychology, the riflemen carried anywhere from 12 to 20 magazines, usually in cloth bandoliers, adding on another 8.4 pounds at minimum, 14 pounds at maximum. When it was available, they also carried M-16 maintenance gear — rods and steel brushes and swabs and tubes of LSA oil — all of which weighed about a pound. Among the grunts, some carried the

M-79 grenade launcher, 5.9 pounds unloaded, a reasonably light weapon except for the ammunition, which was heavy. A single round weighed 10 ounces. The typical load was 25 rounds. But Ted Lavender, who was scared, carried 34 rounds when he was shot and killed outside Than Khe, and he went down under an exceptional burden, more than 20 pounds of ammunition, plus the flak jacket and helmet and rations and water and toilet paper and tranquilizers and all the rest, plus the un-weighed fear. He was dead weight. There was no twitching or flopping. Kiowa, who saw it happen, said it was like watching a rock fall, or a big sandbag or, something — just boom, then down — not like the movies where the dead guy rolls around and does fancy spins and goes ass over teakettle — not like that, Kiowa said, the poor bastard just flat-fuck fell. Boom. Down. Nothing else. It was a bright morning in mid-April. Lieutenant Cross felt the pain. He blamed himself. They stripped off Lavender's canteens and ammo, all the heavy things, and Rat Kiley said the obvious, the guy's dead, and Mitchell Sanders used his radio to report one U.S. KIA and to request a chopper. Then they wrapped Lavender in his poncho. They carried him out to a dry paddy, established security, and sat smoking the dead man's dope until the chopper came. Lieutenant Cross kept to himself. He pictured Martha's smooth young face, thinking he loved her more than anything, more than his men, and now Ted Lavender was dead because he loved her so much and could not stop thinking about her. When the dustoff arrived, they carried Lavender aboard. Afterward they burned Than Khe. They marched until dusk, then dug their holes, and that night Kiowa kept explaining how you had to be there, how fast it was, how the poor guy just dropped like so much concrete. Boom-down, he said. Like cement.

In addition to the three standard weapons — the M-60, M-16, and M-79 — they carried whatever presented itself, or whatever seemed appropriate as a means of killing or staying alive. They carried catch-as-catch-can. At various times, in various situations, they carried M-14s and CAR-15s and Swedish Ks and grease guns and captured AK-47s and Chi-Coms and RPGs and Simonov carbines and black market Uzis and .38-caliber Smith & Wesson handguns and 66 mm LAWs and shot-guns and silencers and blackjacks and bayonets and C-4 plastic explosives. Lee Strunk carried a slingshot; a weapon of last resort, he called it. Mitchell Sanders carried brass knuckles. Kiowa carried his grand-father's feathered hatchet. Every third or fourth man carried a Claymore antipersonnel mine — 3.5 pounds with its firing device. They all carried fragmentation grenades — 14 ounces each. They all carried at least one M-18 colored smoke grenade — 24 ounces. Some carried CS or tear gas grenades. Some carried white phosphorus grenades. They carried all they could bear, and then some, including a silent awe for the terrible power of the things they carried.

In the first week of April, before Lavender died, Lieutenant Jimmy Cross received a good-luck charm from Martha. It was a simple pebble, an ounce at most. Smooth to the touch, it was a milky white color with flecks of orange and violet, oval-shaped, like a miniature egg. In the accompanying letter, Martha wrote that she had found the pebble on the Jersey shoreline, precisely where the land touched water at high tide, where things came together but also separated. It was this separate-but-together quality, she wrote, that had inspired her to pick up the pebble and to carry it in her breast pocket for several days, where it seemed weightless, and then to send it through the mail, by air, as a token of her truest feelings for him. Lieutenant Cross found this romantic. But he wondered what her truest feelings were, exactly, and what she meant by separate-but-together. He wondered how the tides and waves had come into play on that afternoon along the Jersey shoreline when Martha saw the pebble and bent down to rescue it from geology. He imagined bare feet. Martha was a poet, with the poet's sensibilities, and her feet would be brown and bare, the toenails unpainted, the eyes chilly and somber like the ocean in March, and though it was painful, he wondered who had been with her that afternoon. He imagined a pair of shadows moving along the strip of sand where things came together but also separated. It was phantom jealousy, he knew, but he couldn't help himself. He loved her so much. On the march, through the hot days of early April, he carried the pebble in his mouth, turning it with his tongue, tasting sea salt and moisture. His mind wandered. He had difficulty keeping his attention on the war. On occasion he would yell at his men to spread out the column, to keep their eyes open, but then he would slip away into daydreams, just pretending, walking barefoot along the Jersey shore, with Martha, carrying nothing. He would feel himself rising. Sun and waves and gentle winds, all love and lightness.

What they carried varied by mission.

When a mission took them to the mountains, they carried mosquito netting, machetes, canvas tarps, and extra bug juice.

If a mission seemed especially hazardous, or if it involved a place they knew to be bad, they carried everything they could. In certain heavily mined AOs, where the land was dense with Toe Poppers and Bouncing Betties, they took turns humping a 28-pound mine detector. With its headphones and big sensing plate, the equipment was a stress on the lower back and shoulders, awkward to handle, often useless because of the shrapnel in the earth, but they carried it anyway, partly for safety, partly for the illusion of safety.

On ambush, or other night missions, they carried peculiar little odds and ends. Kiowa always took along his New Testament and a pair of moccasins for silence. Dave Jensen carried night-sight vitamins high in carotene. Lee Strunk carried his slingshot; ammo, he claimed, would never be a problem. Rat Kiley carried brandy and M&Ms candy. Until he was shot, Ted Lavender carried the starlight scope, which weighed 6.3 pounds with its aluminum carrying case. Henry Dobbins carried his girlfriend's pantyhose wrapped around his neck as a comforter. They all carried ghosts. When dark came, they would move out single file across the meadows and paddies to their ambush coordinates, where they would quietly set up the Claymores and lie down and spend the night waiting.

Other missions were more complicated and required special equipment. In mid-April, it was their mission to search out and destroy the elaborate tunnel complexes in the Than Khe area south of Chu Lai. To blow the tunnels, they carried one-pound blocks of pentrite high explosives, four blocks to a man, 68 pounds in all. They carried wiring, detonators, and battery-powered clackers. Dave Jensen carried earplugs. Most often, before blowing the tunnels, they were ordered by higher command to search them, which was considered bad news, but by and large they just shrugged and carried out orders. Because he was a big man, Henry Dobbins was excused from tunnel duty. The others would draw numbers. Before Lavender died there were 17 men in the platoon, and whoever drew the number 17 would strip off his gear and crawl in headfirst with a flashlight and Lieutenant Cross's .45-caliber pistol. The rest of them would fan out as security. They would sit down or kneel, not facing the hole, listening to the ground beneath them, imagining cobwebs and ghosts, whatever was down there — the tunnel walls squeezing in — how the flashlight seemed impossibly heavy in the hand and how it was tunnel vision in the very strictest sense, compression in all ways, even time, and how you had to wiggle in — ass and elbows — a swallowed-up feeling — and how you found yourself worrying about odd things: Will your flashlight go dead? Do rats carry rabies? If you screamed, how far would the sound carry? Would your buddies hear it? Would they have the courage to drag you out? In some respects, though not many, the waiting was worse than the tunnel itself. Imagination was a killer.

On April 16, when Lee Strunk drew the number 17, he laughed and muttered something and went down quickly. The morning was hot and very still. Not good, Kiowa said. He looked at the tunnel opening, then out across a dry paddy toward the village of Than Khe. Nothing moved. No clouds or birds or people. As they waited, the men smoked and drank Kool-Aid, not talking much, feeling sympathy for Lee Strunk but also feeling the luck of the draw. You win some, you lose some, said Mitchell Sanders, and sometimes you settle for a rain check. It was a tired line and no one laughed.

Henry Dobbins ate a tropical chocolate bar. Ted Lavender popped a tranquilizer and went off to pee.

After five minutes, Lieutenant Jimmy Cross moved to the tunnel, leaned down, and examined the darkness. Trouble, he thought — a cave-in maybe. And then suddenly, without willing it, he was thinking about Martha. The stresses and fractures, the quick collapse, the two of them buried alive under all that weight. Dense, crushing love. Kneeling, watching the hole, he tried to concentrate on Lee Strunk and the war, all the dangers, but his love was too much for him, he felt paralyzed, he wanted to sleep inside her lungs and breathe her blood and be smothered. He wanted her to be a virgin and not a virgin, all at once. He wanted to know her. Intimate secrets: Why poetry? Why so sad? Why that grayness in her eyes? Why so alone? Not lonely, just alone — riding her bike across campus or sitting off by herself in the cafeteria — even dancing, she danced alone — and it was the aloneness that filled him with love. He remembered telling her that one evening. How she nodded and looked away. And how, later, when he kissed her, she received the kiss without returning it, her eyes wide open, not afraid, not a virgin's eyes, just flat and uninvolved.

Lieutenant Cross gazed at the tunnel. But he was not there. He was buried with Martha under the white sand at the Jersey shore. They were pressed together, and the pebble in his mouth was her tongue. He was smiling. Vaguely, he was aware of how quiet the day was, the sullen paddies, yet he could not bring himself to worry about matters of security. He was beyond that. He was just a kid at war, in love. He was twenty-four years old. He couldn't help it.

A few moments later Lee Strunk crawled out of the tunnel. He came up grinning, filthy but alive. Lieutenant Cross nodded and closed his eyes while the others clapped Strunk on the back and made jokes about rising from the dead.

Worms, Rat Kiley said. Right out of the grave. Fuckin' zombie.

The men laughed. They all felt great relief.

Spook city, said Mitchell Sanders.

Lee Strunk made a funny ghost sound, a kind of moaning, yet very happy, and right then, when Strunk made that high happy moaning sound, when he went *Ahhooooo,* right then Ted Lavender was shot in the head on his way back from peeing. He lay with his mouth open. The teeth were broken. There was a swollen black bruise under his left eye. The cheekbone was gone. Oh shit, Rat Kiley said, the guy's dead. The guy's dead, he kept saying, which seemed profound — the guy's dead. I mean really.

The things they carried were determined to some extent by superstition. Lieutenant Cross carried his good-luck pebble. Dave Jensen carried a rabbit's foot. Norman Bowker, otherwise a very gentle person, carried a thumb that had been presented to him as a gift by Mitchell Sanders. The thumb was dark brown, rubbery to the touch, and weighed 4 ounces at most. It had been cut from a VC corpse, a boy of fifteen or sixteen. They'd found him at the bottom of an irrigation ditch, badly burned, flies in his mouth and eyes. The boy wore black shorts and sandals. At the time of his death he had been carrying a pouch of rice, a rifle, and three magazines of ammunition.

You want my opinion, Mitchell Sanders said, there's a definite moral here.

He put his hand on the dead boy's wrist. He was quiet for a time, as if counting a pulse, then he patted the stomach, almost affectionately, and used Kiowa's hunting hatchet to remove the thumb.

Henry Dobbins asked what the moral was.

Moral?

You know. *Moral.*

Sanders wrapped the thumb in toilet paper and handed it across to Norman Bowker. There was no blood. Smiling, he kicked the boy's head, watched the flies scatter, and said, It's like with that old TV show — Paladin. Have gun, will travel.

Henry Dobbins thought about it.

Yeah, well, he finally said. I don't see no moral.

There it *is,* man.

Fuck off.

They carried USO stationery and pencils and pens. They carried Sterno, safety pins, trip flares, signal flares, spools of wire, razor blades, chewing tobacco, liberated joss sticks and statuettes of the smiling Buddha, candles, grease pencils, *The Stars and Stripes,* fingernail clippers, Psy Ops leaflets, bush hats, bolos, and much more. Twice a week, when the resupply choppers came in, they carried hot chow in green mermite cans and large canvas bags filled with iced beer and soda pop. They carried plastic water containers, each with a 2-gallon capacity. Mitchell Sanders carried a set of starched tiger fatigues for special occasions. Henry Dobbins carried Black Flag insecticide. Dave Jensen carried empty sandbags that could be filled at night for added protection. Lee

Strunk carried tanning lotion. Some things they carried in common. Taking turns, they carried the big PRC-77 scrambler radio, which weighed 30 pounds with its battery. They shared the weight of memory. They took up what others could no longer bear. Often, they carried each other, the wounded or weak. They carried infections. They carried chess sets, basketballs, Vietnamese-English dictionaries, insignia of rank, Bronze Stars and Purple Hearts, plastic cards imprinted with the Code of Conduct. They carried diseases, among them malaria and dysentery. They carried lice and ringworm and leeches and paddy algae and various rots and molds. They carried the land itself — Vietnam, the place, the soil — a powdery orange-red dust that covered their boots and fatigues and faces. They carried the sky. The whole atmosphere, they carried it, the humidity, the monsoons, the stink of fungus and decay, all of it, they carried gravity. They moved like mules. By daylight they took sniper fire, at night they were mortared, but it was not battle, it was just the endless march, village to village, without purpose, nothing won or lost. They marched for the sake of the march. They plodded along slowly, dumbly, leaning forward against the heat, unthinking, all blood and bone, simple grunts, soldiering with their legs, toiling up the hills and down into the paddies and across the rivers and up again and down, just humping, one step and then the next and then another, but no volition, no will, because it was automatic, it was anatomy, and the war was entirely a matter of posture and carriage, the hump was everything, a kind of inertia, a kind of emptiness, a dullness of desire and intellect and conscience and hope and human sensibility. Their principles were in their feet. Their calculations were biological. They had no sense of strategy or mission. They searched the villages without knowing what to look for, not caring, kicking over jars of rice, frisking children and old men, blowing tunnels, sometimes setting fires and sometimes not, then forming up and moving on to the next village, then other villages, where it would always be the same. They carried their own lives. The pressures were enormous. In the heat of early afternoon, they would remove their helmets and flak jackets, walking bare, which was dangerous but which helped ease the strain. They would often discard things along the route of march. Purely for comfort, they would throw away rations, blow their Claymores and grenades, no matter, because by nightfall the resupply choppers would arrive with more of the same, then a day or two later still more, fresh watermelons and crates of ammunition and sunglasses and woolen sweaters — the resources were stunning — sparklers for the Fourth of July, colored eggs for Easter — it was the great American war chest — the fruits of science, the smokestacks, the canneries, the arsenals at Hartford, the Minnesota forests, the machine shops, the vast fields of corn and wheat — they carried like freight trains; they carried it on their backs and shoulders — and for all the ambiguities of Vietnam, all the mysteries and unknowns, there was at least the single abiding certainty that they would never be at a loss for things to carry.

After the chopper took Lavender away, Lieutenant Jimmy Cross led his men into the village of Than Khe. They burned everything. They shot chickens and dogs, they trashed the village well, they called in artillery and watched the wreckage, then they marched for several hours through the hot afternoon, and then at dusk, while Kiowa explained how Lavender died, Lieutenant Cross found himself trembling.

He tried not to cry. With his entrenching tool, which weighed 5 pounds, he began digging a hole in the earth.

He felt shame. He hated himself. He had loved Martha more than his men, and as a consequence Lavender was now dead, and this was something he would have to carry like a stone in his stomach for the rest of the war.

All he could do was dig. He used his entrenching tool like an ax, slashing, feeling both love and hate, and then later, when it was full dark, he sat at the bottom of his foxhole and wept. It went on for a long while. In part, he was grieving for Ted Lavender, but mostly it was for Martha, and for himself, because she belonged to another world, which was not quite real, and because she was a junior at Mount Sebastian College in New Jersey, a poet and a virgin and uninvolved, and because he realized she did not love him and never would.

Like cement, Kiowa whispered in the dark. I swear to God — boom, down. Not a word.

I've heard this, said Norman Bowker.

A pisser, you know? Still zipping himself up. Zapped while zipping.

All right, fine. That's enough.

Yeah, but you had to see it, the guy just —

I *heard,* man. Cement. So why not shut the fuck *up?*

Kiowa shook his head sadly and glanced over at the hole where Lieutenant Jimmy Cross sat watching the night. The air was thick and wet. A warm dense fog had settled over the paddies and there was the stillness that precedes rain.

After a time Kiowa sighed.

One thing for sure, he said. The lieutenant's in some deep hurt. I mean that crying jag — the way he was carrying on — it wasn't fake or anything, it was real heavy-duty hurt. The man cares.

Sure, Norman Bowker said.

Say what you want, the man does care.

We all got problems.

Not Lavender.

No, I guess not, Bowker said. Do me a favor, though.

Shut up?

That's a smart Indian. Shut up.

Shrugging, Kiowa pulled off his boots. He wanted to say more, just to lighten up his sleep, but instead he opened his New Testament and arranged it beneath his head as a pillow. The fog made things seem hollow and unattached. He tried not to think about Ted Lavender, but then he was thinking how fast it was, no drama, down and dead, and how it was hard to feel anything except surprise. It seemed unchristian. He wished he could find some great sadness, or even anger, but the emotion wasn't there and he couldn't make it happen. Mostly he felt pleased to be alive. He liked the smell of the New Testament under his cheek, the leather and ink and paper and glue, whatever the chemicals were. He liked hearing the sounds of night. Even his fatigue, it felt fine, the stiff muscles and the prickly awareness of his own body, a floating feeling. He enjoyed not being dead. Lying there, Kiowa admired Lieutenant Jimmy Cross's capacity for grief. He wanted to share the man's pain, he wanted to care as Jimmy Cross cared. And yet when he closed his eyes, all he could think was Boom-down, and all he could feel was the pleasure of having his boots off and the fog curling in around him and the damp soil and the Bible smells and the plush comfort of night.

After a moment Norman Bowker sat up in the dark.

What the hell, he said. You want to talk, *talk.* Tell it to me.

Forget it.

No, man, go on. One thing I hate, it's a silent Indian.

For the most part they carried themselves with poise, a kind of dignity. Now and then, however, there were times of panic, when they squealed or wanted to squeal but couldn't, when they twitched and made moaning sounds and covered their heads and said Dear Jesus and flopped around on the earth and fired their weapons blindly and cringed and sobbed and begged for the noise to stop and went wild and made stupid promises to themselves and to God and to their mothers and fathers, hoping not to die. In different ways, it happened to all of them. Afterward, when the firing ended, they would blink and peek up. They would touch their bodies, feeling shame, then quickly hiding it. They would force themselves to stand. As if in slow motion, frame by frame, the world would take on the old logic — absolute silence, then the wind, then sunlight, then voices. It was the burden of being alive. Awkwardly, the men would reassemble themselves, first in private, then in groups, becoming soldiers again. They would repair the leaks in their eyes. They would check for casualties, call in dustoffs, light cigarettes, try to smile, clear their throats and spit and begin cleaning their weapons. After a time someone would shake his head and say, No lie, I almost shit my pants, and someone else would laugh, which meant it was bad, yes, but the guy had obviously not shit his pants, it wasn't that bad, and in any case nobody would ever do such a thing and then go ahead and talk about it. They would squint into the dense, oppressive sunlight. For a few moments, perhaps, they would fall silent, lighting a joint and tracking its passage from man to man, inhaling, holding in the humiliation. Scary stuff, one of them might say. But then someone else would grin or flick his eyebrows and say, Roger-dodger, almost cut me a new asshole, *almost.*

There were numerous such poses. Some carried themselves with a sort of wistful resignation, others with pride or stiff soldierly discipline or good humor or macho zeal. They were afraid of dying but they were even more afraid to show it.

They found jokes to tell.

They used a hard vocabulary to contain the terrible softness. *Greased* they'd say. *Offed, lit up, zapped while zipping.* It wasn't cruelty, just stage presence. They were actors. When someone died, it wasn't quite dying, because in a curious way it seemed scripted, and because they had their lines mostly memorized, irony mixed with tragedy, and because they called it by other names, as if to encyst and destroy the reality of death itself. They kicked corpses. They cut off thumbs. They talked grunt lingo. They told stories about Ted Lavender's supply of tranquilizers, how the poor guy didn't feel a thing, how incredibly tranquil he was.

There's a moral here, said Mitchell Sanders.

They were waiting for Lavender's chopper, smoking the dead man's dope.

The moral's pretty obvious, Sanders said, and winked. Stay away from drugs. No joke, they'll ruin your day every time.

Cute, said Henry Dobbins.

Mind blower, get it? Talk about wiggy. Nothing left, just blood and brains.

They made themselves laugh.

There it is, they'd say. Over and over — there it is, my friend, there it is — as if the repetition itself were an act of poise, a balance between crazy and almost crazy, knowing without going, there it is, which meant be cool, let it ride, because Oh yeah, man, you can't change what can't be changed, there it is, there it absolutely and positively and fucking well *is.*

They were tough.

They carried all the emotional baggage of men who might die. Grief, terror, love, longing — these were intangibles, but the intangibles had their own mass and specific gravity, they had tangible weight. They carried shameful memories. They carried the common secret of coward-ice barely restrained, the instinct to run or freeze or hide, and in many respects this was the heaviest burden of all, for it could never be put down, it required perfect balance and perfect posture. They carried their reputations. They carried the soldier's greatest fear, which was the fear of blushing. Men killed, and died, because they were embarrassed not to. It was what had brought them to the war in the first place, nothing positive, no dreams of glory or honor, just to avoid the blush of dis-honor. They died so as not to die of embarrassment. They crawled into tunnels and walked point and advanced under fire. Each morning, despite the unknowns, they made their legs move. They endured. They kept humping. They did not submit to the obvious alternative, which was simply to close the eyes and fall. So easy, really. Go limp and tumble to the ground and let the muscles unwind and not speak and not budge until your buddies picked you up and lifted you into the chopper that would roar and dip its nose and carry you off to the world. A mere matter of falling, yet no one ever fell. It was not courage, exactly; the object was not valor. Rather, they were too frightened to be cowards.

By and large they carried these things inside, maintaining the masks of composure. They sneered at sick call. They spoke bitterly about guys who had found release by shooting off their own toes or fin-gers. Pussies, they'd say. Candy-asses. It was fierce, mocking talk, with only a trace of envy or awe, but even so the image played itself out be-hind their eyes.

They imagined the muzzle against flesh. So easy: squeeze the trig-ger and blow away a toe. They imagined it. They imagined the quick, sweet pain, then the evacuation to Japan, then a hospital with warm beds and cute geisha nurses.

And they dreamed of freedom birds.

At night, on guard, staring into the dark, they were carried away by jumbo jets. They felt the rush of takeoff. *Gone!* they yelled. And then velocity — wings and engines — a smiling stewardess — but it was more than a plane, it was a real bird, a big sleek silver bird with feathers and talons and high screeching. They were flying. The weights fell off; there was nothing to bear. They laughed and held on tight, feeling the cold slap of wind and altitude, soaring, thinking *It's over, I'm gone!* — they were naked, they were light and free — it was all lightness, bright and fast and buoyant, light as light, a helium buzz in the brain, a giddy bubbling in the lungs as they were taken up over the clouds and the war, beyond duty, beyond gravity and mortification and global entanglements — *Sin loi!* they yelled. *I'm sorry, motherfuckers, but I'm out of it, I'm goofed, I'm on a space cruise, I'm gone!* — and it was a restful, unencumbered sensation, just riding the light waves, sailing that big silver freedom bird over the mountains and oceans, over America, over the farms and great sleeping cities and cemeteries and highways and the golden arches of McDonald's, it was flight, a kind of fleeing, a kind of falling, falling higher and higher, spinning off the edge of the earth and beyond the sun and through the vast, silent vacuum where there were no burdens and where everything weighed exactly nothing — *Gone!* they screamed. *I'm sorry but I'm gone!* — and so at night, not quite dreaming, they gave themselves over to lightness, they were carried, they were purely borne.

On the morning after Ted Lavender died, First Lieutenant Jimmy Cross crouched at the bottom of his foxhole and burned Martha's letters. Then he burned the two photographs. There was a steady rain falling, which made it difficult, but he used heat tabs and Sterno to build a small fire, screening it with his body, holding the photographs over the tight blue flame with the tips of his fingers.

He realized it was only a gesture. Stupid, he thought. Sentimental, too, but mostly just stupid.

Lavender was dead. You couldn't burn the blame.

Besides, the letters were in his head. And even now, without photographs, Lieutenant Cross could see Martha playing volleyball in her white gym shorts and yellow T-shirt. He could see her moving in the rain.

When the fire died out, Lieutenant Cross pulled his poncho over his shoulders and ate breakfast from a can.

There was no great mystery, he decided.

In those burned letters Martha had never mentioned the war, except to say, Jimmy, take care of yourself. She wasn't involved. She signed the letters Love, but it wasn't love, and all the fine lines and technicalities did not matter. Virginity was no longer an issue. He hated her. Yes, he did. He hated her. Love, too, but it was a hard, hating kind of love.

The morning came up wet and blurry. Everything seemed part of everything else, the fog and Martha and the deepening rain.

He was a soldier, after all.

Half smiling, Lieutenant Jimmy Cross took out his maps. He shook his head hard, as if to clear it, then bent forward and began planning the day's march. In ten minutes, or maybe twenty, he would rouse the men and they would pack up and head west, where the maps showed the country to be green and inviting. They would do what they had always done. The rain might add some weight, but otherwise it would be one more day layered upon all the other days.

He was realistic about it. There was that new hardness in his stomach. He loved her but he hated her.

No more fantasies, he told himself.

Henceforth, when he thought about Martha, it would be only to think that she belonged elsewhere. He would shut down the daydreams. This was not Mount Sebastian, it was another world, where there were no pretty poems or midterm exams, a place where men died because of carelessness and gross stupidity. Kiowa was right. Boom-down, and you were dead, never partly dead.

Briefly, in the rain, Lieutenant Cross saw Martha's gray eyes gazing back at him.

He understood.

It was very sad, he thought. The things men carried inside. The things men did or felt they had to do.

He almost nodded at her, but didn't.

Instead he went back to his maps. He was now determined to perform his duties firmly and without negligence. It wouldn't help Lavender, he knew that, but from this point on he would comport himself as an officer. He would dispose of his good-luck pebble. Swallow it, maybe, or use Lee Strunk's slingshot, or just drop it along the trail. On the march he would impose strict field discipline. He would be careful to send out flank security, to prevent straggling or bunching up, to keep his troops moving at the proper pace and at the proper interval. He would insist on clean weapons. He would confiscate the remainder of Lavender's dope. Later in the day, perhaps, he would call the men together and speak to them plainly. He would accept the blame for what had happened to Ted Lavender. He would be a man about it. He would look them in the eyes, keeping his chin level, and he would issue the new SOPs in a calm, impersonal tone of voice, a lieutenant's voice, leaving no room for argument or discussion. Commencing immediately, he'd tell them, they would no longer abandon equipment along the route of march. They would police up their acts. They would get their shit together, and keep it together, and maintain it neatly and in good working order.

He would not tolerate laxity. He would show strength, distancing himself.

Among the men there would be grumbling, of course, and maybe worse, because their days would seem longer and their loads heavier, but Lieutenant Jimmy Cross reminded himself that his obligation was not to be loved but to lead. He would dispense with love; it was not now a factor. And if anyone quarreled or complained, he would simply tighten his lips and arrange his shoulders in the correct command posture. He might give a curt little nod. Or he might not. He might just shrug and say, Carry on, then they would saddle up and form into a column and move out toward the villages west of Than Khe.

Sweetheart of the Song Tra Bong

Vietnam was full of strange stories, some improbable, some well beyond that, but the stories that will last forever are those that swirl back and forth across the border between trivia and bedlam, the mad and the mundane. This one keeps returning to me. I heard it from Rat Kiley, who swore up and down to its truth, although in the end, I'll admit, that doesn't amount to much of a warranty. Among the men in Alpha Company, Rat had a reputation for exaggeration and overstatement, a compulsion to rev up the facts, and for most of us it was normal procedure to discount sixty or seventy percent of anything he had to say. If Rat told you, for example, that he'd slept with four girls one night, you could figure it was about a girl and a half. It wasn't a question of deceit. Just the opposite: he wanted to heat up the truth, to make it burn so hot that you would feel exactly what he felt. For Rat Kiley, I think, facts were formed by sensation, not the other way around, and when you listened to one of his stories, you'd find yourself performing rapid calculations in your head, subtracting superlatives, figuring the square root of an absolute and then multiplying by maybe.

Still, with this particular story, Rat never backed down. He claimed to have witnessed the incident with his own eyes, and I remember how upset he became one morning when Mitchell Sanders challenged him on its basic premise.

"It can't happen," Sanders said. "Nobody ships his honey over to Nam. It don't ring true. I mean, you just can't import your own personal poontang."

Rat shook his head. "I *saw* it, man. I was right there. This guy did it."

"His girlfriend?"

"Straight on. It's a fact." Rat's voice squeaked a little. He paused and looked at his hands. "Listen, the guy sends her the money. Flies her over. This cute blonde — just a kid, just barely out of high school — she shows up with a suitcase and one of those plastic cosmetic bags. Comes right out to the boonies. I swear to God, man, she's got on culottes. White culottes and this sexy pink sweater. There she *is*."

I remember Mitchell Sanders folding his arms. He looked over at me for a second, not quite grinning, not saying a word, but I could read the amusement in his eyes.

Rat saw it, too.

"No lie," he muttered. "Culottes."

When he first arrived in-country, before joining Alpha Company, Rat had been assigned to a small medical detachment up in the mountains west of Chu Lai, near the village of Tra Bong, where along with eight other enlisted men he ran an aid station that provided basic emergency and trauma care. Casualties were flown in by helicopter, stabilized, then shipped out to hospitals in Chu Lai or Danang. It was gory work, Rat said, but predictable. Amputations, mostly — legs and feet. The area was heavily mined, thick with Bouncing Betties and homemade booby traps. For a medic, though, it was ideal duty, and Rat counted himself lucky. There was plenty of cold beer, three hot meals a day, a tin roof over his head. No humping at all. No officers, either. You could let your hair grow, he said, and you didn't have to polish your boots or snap off salutes or put up with the usual rear-echelon nonsense. The highest ranking NCO was an E-6 named Eddie Diamond, whose pleasures ran from dope to Darvon, and except for a rare field inspection there was no such thing as military discipline.

As Rat described it, the compound was situated at the top of a flat-crested hill along the northern outskirts of Tra Bong. At one end was a small dirt helipad; at the other end, in a rough semicircle, the mess hall and medical hootches overlooked a river called the Song Tra Bong. Surrounding the place were tangled rolls of concertina wire, with bunkers and reinforced firing positions at staggered intervals, and base security was provided by a mixed unit of RFs, PFs, and ARVN infantry. Which is to say virtually no security at all. As soldiers, the ARVNs were useless; the Ruff-and-Puffs were outright dangerous. And yet even with decent troops the place was clearly indefensible. To the north and west the country rose up in thick walls of wilderness, triple-canopied jungle, mountains unfolding into higher mountains, ravines and gorges and fast-moving rivers and waterfalls and exotic butterflies and steep cliffs and smoky little hamlets and great valleys of bamboo and elephant grass. Originally, in the early 1960s, the place had been set up as a Special Forces outpost, and when Rat Kiley arrived nearly a decade later, a squad of six Green Berets still used the compound as a base of operations. The Greenies were not social animals. Animals, Rat said, but far from social. They had their own hootch at the edge of the perimeter, fortified with sandbags and a metal fence, and except for the bare essentials they avoided contact with the medical detachment. Secretive and suspicious, loners by nature, the six Greenies would sometimes vanish for days at a time, or even weeks, then late in the night they would just as magically reappear, moving like shadows through the moonlight, filing in silently from the dense rain forest off to the west. Among the medics there were jokes about this, but no one asked questions.

While the outpost was isolated and vulnerable, Rat said, he always felt a curious sense of safety there. Nothing much ever happened. The place was never mortared, never taken under fire, and the war seemed to be somewhere far away. On occasion, when casualties came in, there were quick spurts of activity, but otherwise the days flowed by without incident, a smooth and peaceful time. Most mornings were spent on the volleyball court. In the heat of midday the men would head for the shade, lazing away the long afternoons, and after sundown there were movies and card games and sometimes all-night drinking sessions.

It was during one of those late nights that Eddie Diamond first brought up the tantalizing possibility. It was an offhand comment. A joke, really. What they should do, Eddie said, was pool some bucks and bring in a few mamasans from Saigon, spice things up, and after a moment one of the men laughed and said, "Our own little EM club," and somebody else said, "Hey, yeah, we pay our fuckin' dues, don't we?" It was nothing serious. Just passing time, playing with the possibilities, and so for a while they tossed the idea around, how you could actually get away with it, no officers or anything, nobody to clamp down, then they dropped the subject and moved on to cars and baseball.

Later in the night, though, a young medic named Mark Fossie kept coming back to the subject.

"Look, if you think about it," he said, "it's not that crazy. You could actually do it."

"Do what?" Rat said.

"You know. Bring in a girl. I mean, what's the problem?"

Rat shrugged. "Nothing. A war."

"Well, see, that's the thing," Mark Fossie said. "No war *here*. You could really do it. A pair of solid brass balls, that's all you'd need."

There was some laughter, and Eddie Diamond told him he'd best strap down his dick, but Fossie just frowned and looked at the ceiling for a while and then went off to write a letter.

Six weeks later his girlfriend showed up.

The way Rat told it, she came in by helicopter along with the daily resupply shipment out of Chu Lai. A tall, big-boned blonde. At best, Rat said, she was seventeen years old, fresh out of Cleveland Heights Senior High. She had long white legs and blue eyes and a complexion like strawberry ice cream. Very friendly, too.

At the helipad that morning, Mark Fossie grinned and put his arm around her and said, "Guys, this is Mary Anne."

The girl seemed tired and somewhat lost, but she smiled.

There was a heavy silence. Eddie Diamond, the ranking NCO, made a small motion with his hand, and some of the others murmured a word or two, then they watched Mark Fossie pick up her suitcase and lead her by the arm down to the hootches. For a long while the men were quiet.

"That fucker," somebody finally said.

At evening chow Mark Fossie explained how he'd set it up. It was expensive, he admitted, and the logistics were complicated, but it wasn't like going to the moon. Cleveland to Los Angeles, LA to Bangkok, Bangkok to Saigon. She'd hopped a C-130 up to Chu Lai and stayed overnight at the USO and the next morning hooked a ride west with the resupply chopper.

"A cinch," Fossie said, and gazed down at his pretty girlfriend. "Thing is, you just got to *want* it enough."

Mary Anne Bell and Mark Fossie had been sweethearts since grammar school. From the sixth grade on they had known for a fact that someday they would be married, and live in a fine gingerbread house near Lake Erie, and have three healthy yellow-haired children, and grow old together, and no doubt die in each other's arms and be buried in the same walnut casket. That was the plan. They were very much in love, full of dreams, and in the ordinary flow of their lives the whole scenario might well have come true.

On the first night they set up house in one of the bunkers along the perimeter, near the Special Forces hootch, and over the next two weeks they stuck together like a pair of high school steadies. It was almost disgusting, Rat said, the way they mooned over each other. Always holding hands, always laughing over some private joke. All they needed, he said, were a couple of matching sweaters. But among the medics there was some envy. It was Vietnam, after all, and Mary Anne Bell was an attractive girl. Too wide in the shoulders, maybe, but she had terrific legs, a bubbly personality, a happy smile. The men genuinely liked her. Out on the volleyball court she wore cut-off blue jeans and a black swimsuit top, which the guys appreciated, and in the evenings she liked to dance to music from Rat's portable tape deck. There was a novelty to it; she was good for morale. At times she gave off a kind of come-get-me energy, coy and flirtatious, but apparently it never bothered Mark Fossie. In fact he seemed to enjoy it, just grinning at her, because he was so much in love, and because it was the sort of show that a girl will sometimes put on for her boyfriend's entertainment and education.

Though she was young, Rat said, Mary Anne Bell was no timid child. She was curious about things. During her first days in-country she liked to roam around the compound asking questions: What exactly was a trip flare? How did a Claymore work? What was behind those

scary green mountains to the west? Then she'd squint and listen quietly while somebody filled her in. She had a good quick mind. She
paid attention. Often, especially during the hot afternoons, she would
spend time with the ARVNs out along the perimeter, picking up little
phrases of Vietnamese, learning how to cook rice over a can of Sterno,
how to eat with her hands. The guys sometimes liked to kid her about
it — our own little native, they'd say — but Mary Anne would just
smile and stick out her tongue. "I'm here," she'd say, "I might as well
learn something."

The war intrigued her. The land, too, and the mystery. At the beginning of her second week she began pestering Mark Fossie to take
her down to the village at the foot of the hill. In a quiet voice, very patiently, he tried to tell her that it was a bad idea, way too dangerous,
but Mary Anne kept after him. She wanted to get a feel for how people
lived, what the smells and customs were. It did not impress her that
the VC owned the place.

"Listen, it can't be that bad," she said. "They're human beings, aren't
they? Like everybody else?"

Fossie nodded. He loved her.

And so in the morning, Rat Kiley and two other medics tagged
along as security while Mark and Mary Anne strolled through the ville
like a pair of tourists. If the girl was nervous, she didn't show it. She
seemed comfortable and entirely at home; the hostile atmosphere did
not seem to register. All morning Mary Anne chattered away about
how quaint the place was, how she loved the thatched roofs and naked
children, the wonderful simplicity of village life. A strange thing to
watch, Rat said. This seventeen-year-old doll in her goddamn culottes,
perky and fresh-faced, like a cheerleader visiting the opposing team's
locker room. Her pretty blue eyes seemed to glow. She couldn't get
enough of it. On their way back up to the compound she stopped for a
swim in the Song Tra Bong, stripping down to her underwear, showing off her legs while Fossie tried to explain to her about things like
ambushes and snipers and the stopping power of an AK-47.

The guys, though, were impressed.

"A real tiger," said Eddie Diamond. "D-cup guts, trainer-bra brains."

"She'll learn," somebody said.

Eddie Diamond gave a solemn nod. "There's the scary part. I promise you, this girl will most definitely learn."

In parts, at least, it was a funny story, and yet to hear Rat Kiley tell it
you'd almost think it was intended as straight tragedy. He never
smiled. Not even at the crazy stuff. There was always a dark, far-off
look in his eyes, a kind of sadness, as if he were troubled by something

sliding beneath the story's surface. Whenever we laughed, I remember, he'd sigh and wait it out, but the one thing he could not tolerate was disbelief. He'd get edgy if someone questioned one of the details. "She *wasn't* dumb," he'd snap. "I never said that. Young, that's all I said. Like you and me. A *girl,* that's the only difference, and I'll tell you something: it didn't amount to jack. I mean, when we first got here — all of us — we were real young and innocent, full of romantic bullshit, but we learned pretty damn quick. And so did Mary Anne."

Rat would peer down at his hands, silent and thoughtful. After a moment his voice would flatten out.

"You don't believe it?" he'd say. "Fine with me. But you don't know human nature. You don't know Nam."

Then he'd tell us to listen up.

A good sharp mind, Rat said. True, she could be silly sometimes, but she picked up on things fast. At the end of the second week, when four casualties came in, Mary Anne wasn't afraid to get her hands bloody. At times, in fact, she seemed fascinated by it. Not the gore so much, but the adrenaline buzz that went with the job, that quick hot rush in your veins when the choppers settled down and you had to do things fast and right. No time for sorting through options, no thinking at all; you just stuck your hands in and started plugging up holes. She was quiet and steady. She didn't back off from the ugly cases. Over the next day or two, as more casualties trickled in, she learned how to clip an artery and pump up a plastic splint and shoot in morphine. In times of action her face took on a sudden new composure, almost serene, the fuzzy blue eyes narrowing into a tight, intelligent focus. Mark Fossie would grin at this. He was proud, yes, but also amazed. A different person, it seemed, and he wasn't sure what to make of it.

Other things, too. The way she quickly fell into the habits of the bush. No cosmetics, no fingernail filing. She stopped wearing jewelry, cut her hair short and wrapped it in a dark green bandanna. Hygiene became a matter of small consequence. In her second week Eddie Diamond taught her how to disassemble an M-16, how the various parts worked, and from there it was a natural progression to learning how to use the weapon. For hours at a time she plunked away at C-ration cans, a bit unsure of herself, but as it turned out she had a real knack for it. There was a new confidence in her voice, a new authority in the way she carried herself. In many ways she remained naive and immature, still a kid, but Cleveland Heights now seemed very far away.

Once or twice, gently, Mark Fossie suggested that it might be time to think about heading home, but Mary Anne laughed and told him to forget it. "Everything I want," she said, "is right here."

She stroked his arm, and then kissed him.

On one level things remained the same between them. They slept together. They held hands and made plans for after the war. But now there was a new imprecision in the way Mary Anne expressed her thoughts on certain subjects. Not necessarily three kids, she'd say. Not necessarily a house on Lake Erie. "Naturally we'll still get married," she'd tell him, "but it doesn't have to be right away. Maybe travel first. Maybe live together. Just test it out, you know?"

Mark Fossie would nod at this, even smile and agree, but it made him uncomfortable. He couldn't pin it down. Her body seemed foreign somehow — too stiff in places, too firm where the softness used to be. The bubbliness was gone. The nervous giggling, too. When she laughed now, which was rare, it was only when something struck her as truly funny. Her voice seemed to reorganize itself at a lower pitch. In the evenings, while the men played cards, she would sometimes fall into long elastic silences, her eyes fixed on the dark, her arms folded, her foot tapping out a coded message against the floor. When Fossie asked about it one evening, Mary Anne looked at him for a long moment and then shrugged. "It's nothing," she said. "Really nothing. To tell the truth, I've never been happier in my whole life. Never."

Twice, though, she came in late at night. Very late. And then finally she did not come in at all.

Rat Kiley heard about it from Fossie himself. Before dawn one morning, the kid shook him awake. He was in bad shape. His voice seemed hollow and stuffed up, nasal-sounding, as if he had a bad cold. He held a flashlight in his hand, clicking it on and off.

"Mary Anne," he whispered, "I can't *find* her."

Rat sat up and rubbed his face. Even in the dim light it was clear that the boy was in trouble. There were dark smudges under his eyes, the frayed edges of somebody who hadn't slept in a while.

"Gone," Fossie said. "Rat, listen, she's sleeping with somebody. Last night, she didn't even . . . I don't know what to *do*."

Abruptly then, Fossie seemed to collapse. He squatted down, rocking on his heels, still clutching the flashlight. Just a boy — eighteen years old. Tall and blond. A gifted athlete. A nice kid, too, polite and good-hearted, although for the moment none of it seemed to be serving him well.

He kept clicking the flashlight on and off.

"All right, start at the start," Rat said. "Nice and slow. Sleeping with who?"

"I don't know who. Eddie Diamond."

"Eddie?"

"Has to be. The guy's always there, always hanging on her."

Rat shook his head. "Man, I don't know. Can't say it strikes a right note, not with Eddie."

"Yes, but he's — "

"Easy does it," Rat said. He reached out and tapped the boy's shoulder. "Why not just check some bunks? We got nine guys. You and me, that's two, so there's seven possibles. Do a quick body count."

Fossie hesitated. "But I can't . . . If she's there, I mean, if she's with somebody — "

"Oh, Christ."

Rat pushed himself up. He took the flashlight, muttered something, and moved down to the far end of the hootch. For privacy, the men had rigged up curtained walls around their cots, small makeshift bedrooms, and in the dark Rat went quickly from room to room, using the flashlight to pluck out the faces. Eddie Diamond slept a hard deep sleep — the others, too. To be sure, though, Rat checked once more, very carefully, then he reported back to Fossie.

"All accounted for. No extras."

"Eddie?"

"Darvon dreams." Rat switched off the flashlight and tried to think it out. "Maybe she just — I don't know — maybe she camped out tonight. Under the stars or something. You search the compound?"

"Sure I did."

"Well, come on," Rat said. "One more time."

Outside, a soft violet light was spreading out across the eastern hillsides. Two or three ARVN soldiers had built their breakfast fires, but the place was mostly quiet and unmoving. They tried the helipad first, then the mess hall and supply hootches, then they walked the entire six hundred meters of perimeter.

"Okay," Rat finally said. "We got a problem."

When he first told the story, Rat stopped there and looked at Mitchell Sanders for a time.

"So what's your vote? Where was she?"

"The Greenies," Sanders said.

"Yeah?"

Sanders smiled. "No other option. That stuff about the Special Forces — how they used the place as a base of operations, how they'd glide in and out — all that had to be there for a *reason.* That's how stories work, man."

Rat thought about it, then shrugged.

"All right, sure, the Greenies. But it's not what Fossie thought. She wasn't sleeping with any of them. At least not exactly. I mean, in a way she was sleeping with *all* of them, more or less, except it wasn't sex or anything. They was just lying together, so to speak, Mary Anne and these six grungy weirded-out Green Berets."

"Lying down?" Sanders said.

"You got it."

"Lying down how?"

Rat smiled. "Ambush. All night long, man, Mary Anne's out on fuckin' *ambush*."

Just after sunrise, Rat said, she came trooping in through the wire, tired-looking but cheerful as she dropped her gear and gave Mark Fossie a brisk hug. The six Green Berets did not speak. One of them nodded at her, and the others gave Fossie a long stare, then they filed off to their hootch at the edge of the compound.

"Please," she said. "Not a word."

Fossie took a half step forward and hesitated. It was as though he had trouble recognizing her. She wore a bush hat and filthy green fatigues; she carried the standard M-16 automatic assault rifle; her face was black with charcoal.

Mary Anne handed him the weapon. "I'm exhausted," she said. "We'll talk later."

She glanced over at the Special Forces area, then turned and walked quickly across the compound toward her own bunker. Fossie stood still for a few seconds. A little dazed, it seemed. After a moment, though, he set his jaw and whispered something and went after her with a hard, fast stride.

"Not later!" he yelled. "Now!"

What happened between them, Rat said, nobody ever knew for sure. But in the mess hall that evening it was clear that an accommodation had been reached. Or more likely, he said, it was a case of setting down some new rules. Mary Anne's hair was freshly shampooed. She wore a white blouse, a navy blue skirt, a pair of plain black flats. Over dinner she kept her eyes down, poking at her food, subdued to the point of silence. Eddie Diamond and some of the others tried to nudge her into talking about the ambush — What was the feeling out there? What exactly did she see and hear? — but the questions seemed to give her trouble. Nervously, she'd look across the table at Fossie. She'd wait a moment, as if to receive some sort of clearance, then she'd bow her head and mumble out a vague word or two. There were no real answers.

Mark Fossie, too, had little to say.

"Nobody's business," he told Rat that night. Then he offered a brief smile. "One thing for sure, though, there won't be any more ambushes. No more late nights."

"You laid down the law?"

"Compromise," Fossie said. "I'll put it this way — we're officially engaged."

Rat nodded cautiously.

"Well hey, she'll make a sweet bride," he said. "Combat ready."

Over the next several days there was a strained, tightly wound quality to the way they treated each other, a rigid correctness that was enforced by repetitive acts of willpower. To look at them from a distance, Rat said, you would think they were the happiest two people on the planet. They spent the long afternoons sunbathing together, stretched out side by side on top of their bunker, or playing backgammon in the shade of a giant palm tree, or just sitting quietly. A model of togetherness, it seemed. And yet at close range their faces showed the tension. Too polite, too thoughtful. Mark Fossie tried hard to keep up a self-assured pose, as if nothing had ever come between them, or ever could, but there was a fragility to it, something tentative and false. If Mary Anne happened to move a few steps away from him, even briefly, he'd tighten up and force himself not to watch her. But then a moment later he'd be watching.

In the presence of others, at least, they kept on their masks. Over meals they talked about plans for a huge wedding in Cleveland Heights — a two-day bash, lots of flowers. And yet even then their smiles seemed too intense. They were too quick with their banter; they held hands as if afraid to let go.

It had to end, and eventually it did.

Near the end of the third week Fossie began making arrangements to send her home. At first, Rat said, Mary Anne seemed to accept it, but then after a day or two she fell into a restless gloom, sitting off by herself at the edge of the perimeter. She would not speak. Shoulders hunched, her blue eyes opaque, she seemed to disappear inside herself. A couple of times Fossie approached her and tried to talk it out, but Mary Anne just stared out at the dark green mountains to the west. The wilderness seemed to draw her in. A haunted look, Rat said — partly terror, partly rapture. It was as if she had come up on the edge of something, as if she were caught in that no-man's-land between Cleveland Heights and deep jungle. Seventeen years old. Just a child, blond and innocent, but then weren't they all?

The next morning she was gone. The six Greenies were gone, too.

In a way, Rat said, poor Fossie expected it, or something like it, but that did not help much with the pain. The kid couldn't function. The grief took him by the throat and squeezed and would not let go.

"Lost," he kept whispering.

✹

It was nearly three weeks before she returned. But in a sense she never returned. Not entirely, not all of her.

By chance, Rat said, he was awake to see it. A damp misty night, he couldn't sleep, so he'd gone outside for a quick smoke. He was just standing there, he said, watching the moon, and then off to the west a column of silhouettes appeared as if by magic at the edge of the jungle. At first he didn't recognize her — a small, soft shadow among six other shadows. There was no sound. No real substance either. The seven silhouettes seemed to float across the surface of the earth, like spirits, vaporous and unreal. As he watched, Rat said, it made him think of some weird opium dream. The silhouettes moved without moving. Silently, one by one, they came up the hill, passed through the wire, and drifted in a loose file across the compound. It was then, Rat said, that he picked out Mary Anne's face. Her eyes seemed to shine in the dark — not blue, though, but a bright glowing jungle green. She did not pause at Fossie's bunker. She cradled her weapon and moved swiftly to the Special Forces hootch and followed the others inside.

Briefly, a light came on, and someone laughed, then the place went dark again.

Whenever he told the story, Rat had a tendency to stop now and then, interrupting the flow, inserting little clarifications or bits of analysis and personal opinion. It was a bad habit, Mitchell Sanders said, because all that matters is the raw material, the stuff itself, and you can't clutter it up with your own half-baked commentary. That just breaks the spell. It destroys the magic. What you have to do, Sanders said, is trust your own story. Get the hell out of the way and let it tell itself.

But Rat Kiley couldn't help it. He wanted to bracket the full range of meaning.

"I know it sounds far-out," he'd tell us, "but it's not like *impossible* or anything. We all heard plenty of wackier stories. Some guy comes back from the bush, tells you he saw the Virgin Mary out there, she was riding a goddamn goose or something. Everybody buys it. Everybody smiles and asks how fast was they going, did she have spurs on. Well, it's not like that. This Mary Anne wasn't no virgin but at least she was real. I saw it. When she came in through the wire that night, I was right there, I saw those eyes of hers, I saw how she wasn't even the same person no more. What's so impossible about that? She was a girl, that's all. I mean, if it was a guy, everybody'd say, Hey, no big deal, he got caught up in the Nam shit, he got seduced by the Greenies. See what I mean? You got these blinders on about women. How gentle and peaceful they are. All that crap about how if we had a pussy for president there wouldn't be no more wars. Pure garbage. You got to get rid of that sexist attitude."

Rat would go on like that until Mitchell Sanders couldn't tolerate it any longer. It offended his inner ear.

"The story," Sanders would say. "The whole tone, man, you're wrecking it."

"Tone?"

"The *sound*. You need to get a consistent sound, like slow or fast, funny or sad. All these digressions, they just screw up your story's *sound*. Stick to what happened."

Frowning, Rat would close his eyes.

"Tone?" he'd say. "I didn't know it was all that complicated. The girl joined the zoo. One more animal — end of story."

"Yeah, fine. But tell it right."

At daybreak the next morning, when Mark Fossie heard she was back, he stationed himself outside the fenced-off Special Forces area. All morning he waited for her, and all afternoon. Around dusk Rat brought him something to eat.

"She has to come out," Fossie said. "Sooner or later, she has to."

"Or else what?" Rat said.

"I go get her. I bring her out."

Rat shook his head. "Your decision. I was you, though, no way I'd mess around with any Greenie types, not for nothing."

"It's Mary Anne in there."

"Sure, I know that. All the same, I'd knock real extra super polite."

Even with the cooling night air Fossie's face was slick with sweat. He looked sick. His eyes were bloodshot; his skin had a whitish, almost colorless cast. For a few minutes Rat waited with him, quietly watching the hootch, then he patted the kid's shoulder and left him alone.

It was after midnight when Rat and Eddie Diamond went out to check on him. The night had gone cold and steamy, a low fog sliding down from the mountains, and somewhere out in the dark they heard music playing. Not loud but not soft either. It had a chaotic, almost unmusical sound, without rhythm or form or progression, like the noise of nature. A synthesizer, it seemed, or maybe an electric organ. In the background, just audible, a woman's voice was half singing, half chanting, but the lyrics seemed to be in a foreign tongue.

They found Fossie squatting near the gate in front of the Special Forces area. Head bowed, he was swaying to the music, his face wet and shiny. As Eddie bent down beside him, the kid looked up with dull eyes, ashen and powdery, not quite in register.

"Hear that?" he whispered. "You *hear*? It's Mary Anne."

Eddie Diamond took his arm. "Let's get you inside. Somebody's radio, that's all it is. Move it now."

"Mary Anne. Just listen."

"Sure, but — "

"Listen!"

Fossie suddenly pulled away, twisting sideways, and fell back against the gate. He lay there with his eyes closed. The music — the noise, whatever it was — came from the hootch beyond the fence. The place was dark except for a small glowing window, which stood partly open, the panes dancing in bright reds and yellows as though the glass were on fire. The chanting seemed louder now. Fiercer, too, and higher pitched.

Fossie pushed himself up. He wavered for a moment then forced the gate open.

"That voice," he said. "Mary Anne."

Rat took a step forward, reaching out for him, but Fossie was already moving fast toward the hootch. He stumbled once, caught himself, and hit the door hard with both arms. There was a noise — a short screeching sound, like a cat — and the door swung in and Fossie was framed there for an instant, his arms stretched out, then he slipped inside. After a moment Rat and Eddie followed quietly. Just inside the door they found Fossie bent down on one knee. He wasn't moving.

Across the room a dozen candles were burning on the floor near the open window. The place seemed to echo with a weird deep-wilderness sound — tribal music — bamboo flutes and drums and chimes. But what hit you first, Rat said, was the smell. Two kinds of smells. There was a topmost scent of joss sticks and incense, like the fumes of some exotic smokehouse, but beneath the smoke lay a deeper and much more powerful stench. Impossible to describe, Rat said. It paralyzed your lungs. Thick and numbing, like an animal's den, a mix of blood and scorched hair and excrement and the sweet-sour odor of moldering flesh — the stink of the kill. But that wasn't all. On a post at the rear of the hootch was the decayed head of a large black leopard; strips of yellow-brown skin dangled from the overhead rafters. And bones. Stacks of bones — all kinds. To one side, propped up against a wall, stood a poster in neat black lettering: ASSEMBLE YOUR OWN GOOK!! FREE SAMPLE KIT!! The images came in a swirl, Rat said, and there was no way you could process it all. Off in the gloom a few dim figures lounged in hammocks, or on cots, but none of them moved or spoke.

The background music came from a tape deck near the circle of candles, but the high voice was Mary Anne's.

After a second Mark Fossie made a soft moaning sound. He started to get up but then stiffened.

"Mary Anne?" he said.

Quietly then, she stepped out of the shadows. At least for a moment she seemed to be the same pretty young girl who had arrived a few weeks earlier. She was barefoot. She wore her pink sweater and a white blouse and a simple cotton skirt.

For a long while the girl gazed down at Fossie, almost blankly, and in the candlelight her face had the composure of someone perfectly at peace with herself. It took a few seconds, Rat said, to appreciate the full change. In part it was her eyes: utterly flat and indifferent. There was no emotion in her stare, no sense of the person behind it. But the grotesque part, he said, was her jewelry. At the girl's throat was a necklace of human tongues. Elongated and narrow, like pieces of blackened leather, the tongues were threaded along a length of copper wire, one overlapping the next, the tips curled upward as if caught in a final shrill syllable.

Briefly, it seemed, the girl smiled at Mark Fossie.

"There's no sense talking," she said. "I know what you think, but it's not . . . it's not *bad*."

"Bad?" Fossie murmured.

"It's not."

In the shadows there was laughter.

One of the Greenies sat up and lighted a cigar. The others lay silent.

"You're in a place," Mary Anne said softly, "where you don't belong."

She moved her hand in a gesture that encompassed not just the hootch but everything around it, the entire war, the mountains, the mean little villages, the trails and trees and rivers and deep misted-over valleys.

"You just don't *know*," she said. "You hide in this little fortress, behind wire and sandbags, and you don't know what it's all about. Sometimes I want to *eat* this place. Vietnam. I want to swallow the whole country — the dirt, the death — I just want to eat it and have it there inside me. That's how I feel. It's like . . . this appetite. I get scared sometimes — lots of times — but it's not *bad*. You know? I feel close to myself. When I'm out there at night, I feel close to my own body, I can feel my blood moving, my skin and my fingernails, everything, it's like I'm full of electricity and I'm glowing in the dark — I'm on fire almost — I'm burning away into nothing — but it doesn't matter because I know exactly who I am. You can't feel like that anywhere else."

All this was said softly, as if to herself, her voice slow and impassive. She was not trying to persuade. For a few moments she looked at Mark Fossie, who seemed to shrink away, then she turned and moved back into the gloom.

There was nothing to be done.

Rat took Fossie's arm, helped him up, and led him outside. In the darkness there was that weird tribal music, which seemed to come from the earth itself, from the deep rain forest, and a woman's voice rising up in a language beyond translation.

Mark Fossie stood rigid.

"Do something," he whispered. "I can't just let her go like that."

Rat listened for a time, then shook his head.

"Man, you must be deaf. She's already gone."

Rat Kiley stopped there, almost in midsentence, which drove Mitchell Sanders crazy.

"What next?" he said.

"Next?"

"The girl. What happened to her?"

Rat made a small, tired motion with his shoulders. "Hard to tell for sure. Maybe three, four days later I got orders to report here to Alpha Company. Jumped the first chopper out, that's the last I ever seen of the place. Mary Anne, too."

Mitchell Sanders stared at him.

"You can't do that."

"Do what?"

"Jesus Christ, it's against the *rules*," Sanders said. "Against human *nature*. This elaborate story, you can't say, Hey, by the way, I don't know the *ending*. I mean, you got certain obligations."

Rat gave a quick smile. "Patience, man. Up to now, everything I told you is from personal experience, the exact truth, but there's a few other things I heard secondhand. Thirdhand, actually. From here on it gets to be . . . I don't know what the word is."

"Speculation."

"Yeah, right." Rat looked off to the west, scanning the mountains, as if expecting something to appear on one of the high ridgelines. After a second he shrugged. "Anyhow, maybe two months later I ran into Eddie Diamond over in Bangkok — I was on R&R, just this fluke thing — and he told me some stuff I can't vouch for with my own eyes. Even Eddie didn't really see it. He heard it from one of the Greenies, so you got to take this with a whole shakerful of salt."

Once more, Rat searched the mountains, then he sat back and closed his eyes.

"You know," he said abruptly, "I loved her."

"Say again?"

"A lot. We all did, I guess. The way she looked, Mary Anne made you think about those girls back home, how clean and innocent they all are, how they'll never understand any of this, not in a billion years. Try to tell them about it, they'll just stare at you with those big round candy eyes. They won't understand zip. It's like trying to tell somebody what chocolate tastes like."

Mitchell Sanders nodded. "Or shit."

"There it is, you got to taste it, and that's the thing with Mary Anne. She was *there*. She was up to her eyeballs in it. After the war, man, I promise you, you won't find nobody like her."

Suddenly, Rat pushed up to his feet, moved a few steps away from us, then stopped and stood with his back turned. He was an emotional guy.

"Got hooked, I guess," he said. "I loved her. So when I heard from Eddie about what happened, it almost made me . . . Like you say, it's pure speculation."

"Go on," Mitchell Sanders said. "Finish up."

What happened to her, Rat said, was what happened to all of them. You come over clean and you get dirty and then afterward it's never the same. A question of degree. Some make it intact, some don't make it at all. For Mary Anne Bell, it seemed, Vietnam had the effect of a powerful drug: that mix of unnamed terror and unnamed pleasure that comes as the needle slips in and you know you're risking something. The endorphins start to flow, and the adrenaline, and you hold your breath and creep quietly through the moonlit nightscapes; you become intimate with danger; you're in touch with the far side of yourself, as though it's another hemisphere, and you want to string it out and go wherever the trip takes you and be host to all the possibilities inside yourself. Not *bad,* she'd said. Vietnam made her glow in the dark. She wanted more, she wanted to penetrate deeper into the mystery of herself, and after a time the wanting became needing, which turned then to craving.

According to Eddie Diamond, who heard it from one of the Greenies, she took a greedy pleasure in night patrols. She was good at it; she had the moves. All camouflaged up, her face smooth and vacant, she seemed to flow like water through the dark, like oil, without sound or center. She went barefoot. She stopped carrying a weapon. There were times, apparently, when she took crazy, death-wish chances — things that even the Greenies balked at. It was as if she were taunting some wild creature out in the bush, or in her head, inviting it to show itself, a curious game of hide-and-go-seek that was played out in the dense terrain of a nightmare. She was lost inside herself. On occasion, when they were taken under fire, Mary Anne would stand quietly and watch the tracer rounds snap by, a little smile at her lips, intent on some private transaction with the war. Other times she would simply vanish altogether — for hours, for days.

And then one morning, all alone, Mary Anne walked off into the mountains and did not come back.

No body was ever found. No equipment, no clothing. For all he knew, Rat said, the girl was still alive. Maybe up in one of the high mountain villes, maybe with the Montagnard tribes. But that was guesswork.

There was an inquiry, of course, and a week-long air search, and for a time the Tra Bong compound went crazy with MP and CID types. In the end, however, nothing came of it. It was a war and the war went on. Mark Fossie was busted to PFC, shipped back to a hospital in the States, and two months later received a medical discharge. Mary Anne Bell joined the missing.

But the story did not end there. If you believed the Greenies, Rat said, Mary Anne was still somewhere out there in the dark. Odd movements, odd shapes. Late at night, when the Greenies were out on ambush, the whole rain forest seemed to stare in at them — a watched feeling — and a couple of times they almost saw her sliding through the shadows. Not quite, but almost. She had crossed to the other side. She was part of the land. She was wearing her culottes, her pink sweater, and a necklace of human tongues. She was dangerous. She was ready for the kill.

Flannery O'Connor

The contemporary American story begins with Flannery O'Connor (1925–1964). Her influence can be seen in the work of many of the writers in this collection, including Ellen Gilchrist, Lorrie Moore, Stacey Richter, and Annie Proulx. O'Connor was able to combine a flawless sense of comic timing with moral outrage and a hard-nosed awareness of the presence of corruption warring with the bland platitudes about redemption and brotherly love that narcotized her society. Her characters are often seen as grotesques — Hazel Motes, the self-flagellating protagonist of her first novel, *Wise Blood,* is an example, as is his alter ego, Enoch Emery — and they exhibit obsessive-compulsive behavior because the moral ground on which they stand is so uncertain. Like Cheever, she was concerned above all with ethics, Christian ethics, with issues of right and wrong in a morally ambivalent society, and her allegorical satires are, as a result, infused with a depth and mystery all her own.

For this anthology, I've selected two of O'Connor's most celebrated stories. The first, "A Good Man Is Hard to Find," is remarkable for its blend of the comic and the tragic. We laugh at the grandmother for her conventional thinking, her inane chatter, and her slapstick interference with her son's driving, and yet her fate — and the fate of her family — is utterly chilling. And how exactly do we judge her? Is it true, as The Misfit says, that "she would of been a good woman . . . if it had been somebody there to shoot her every minute of her life"? "Good Country People" also makes use of comedy in the service of something darker, and it stands as an example of the sort of fiction that discovers its own meanings in the process of its composition. As O'Connor said of this story, "I wouldn't want you to think that . . . I sat down and said, 'I am now going to write a story about a Ph.D. with a wooden leg, using the wooden leg as a symbol for another kind of affliction.'" And further: "As the story progressed, I brought in the Bible salesman, but I had no idea what I was going to do with him. I didn't know he was going to steal that wooden leg until ten or twelve lines before he did it . . ." In other words, stories happen, like thunderstorms or murders. We should all take heart.

A Good Man Is Hard to Find

The grandmother didn't want to go to Florida. She wanted to visit some of her connections in east Tennessee and she was seizing at every chance to change Bailey's mind. Bailey was the son she lived with, her only boy. He was sitting on the edge of his chair at the table, bent over the orange sports section of the *Journal*. "Now look here, Bailey," she said, "see here, read this," and she stood with one hand on her thin hip and the other rattling the newspaper at his bald head. "Here this fellow that calls himself The Misfit is aloose from the Federal Pen and headed toward Florida and you read here what it says he did to these people. Just you read it. I wouldn't take my children in any direction with a criminal like that aloose in it. I couldn't answer to my conscience if I did."

Bailey didn't look up from his reading so she wheeled around then and faced the children's mother, a young woman in slacks, whose face was as broad and innocent as a cabbage and was tied around with a green head-kerchief that had two points on the top like a rabbit's ears. She was sitting on the sofa, feeding the baby his apricots out of a jar. "The children have been to Florida before," the old lady said. "You all ought to take them somewhere else for a change so they would see different parts of the world and be broad. They never have been to east Tennessee."

The children's mother didn't seem to hear her but the eight-year-old boy, John Wesley, a stocky child with glasses, said, "If you don't want to go to Florida, why dontcha stay at home?" He and the little girl, June Star, were reading the funny papers on the floor.

"She wouldn't stay at home to be queen for a day," June Star said without raising her yellow head.

"Yes and what would you do if this fellow, The Misfit, caught you?" the grandmother asked.

"I'd smack his face," John Wesley said.

"She wouldn't stay at home for a million bucks," June Star said. "Afraid she'd miss something. She has to go everywhere we go."

"All right, Miss," the grandmother said. "Just remember that the next time you want me to curl your hair."

June Star said her hair was naturally curly.

The next morning the grandmother was the first one in the car, ready to go. She had her big black valise that looked like the head of a hippopotamus in one corner, and underneath it she was hiding a basket with Pitty Sing, the cat, in it. She didn't intend for the cat to be left alone in the house for three days because he would miss her too much and she was afraid he might brush against one of the gas burners and accidentally asphyxiate himself. Her son, Bailey, didn't like to arrive at a motel with a cat.

She sat in the middle of the back seat with John Wesley and June Star on either side of her. Bailey and the children's mother and the baby sat in front and they left Atlanta at eight forty-five with the mileage on the car at 55890. The grandmother wrote this down because she thought it would be interesting to say how many miles they had been when they got back. It took them twenty minutes to reach the outskirts of the city.

The old lady settled herself comfortably, removing her white cotton gloves and putting them up with her purse on the shelf in front of the back window. The children's mother still had on slacks and still had her head tied up in a green kerchief, but the grandmother had on a navy blue straw sailor hat with a bunch of white violets on the brim and a navy blue dress with a small white dot in the print. Her collars and cuffs were white organdy trimmed with lace and at her neckline she had pinned a purple spray of cloth violets containing a sachet. In case of an accident, anyone seeing her dead on the highway would know at once that she was a lady.

She said she thought it was going to be a good day for driving, neither too hot nor too cold, and she cautioned Bailey that the speed limit was fifty-five miles an hour and that the patrolmen hid themselves behind billboards and small clumps of trees and sped out after you before you had a chance to slow down. She pointed out interesting details of the scenery: Stone Mountain; the blue granite that in some places came up to both sides of the highway; the brilliant red clay banks slightly streaked with purple; and the various crops that made rows of green lace-work on the ground. The trees were full of silver-white sunlight and the meanest of them sparkled. The children were reading comic magazines and their mother had gone back to sleep.

"Let's go through Georgia fast so we won't have to look at it much," John Wesley said.

"If I were a little boy," said the grandmother, "I wouldn't talk about my native state that way. Tennessee has the mountains and Georgia has the hills."

"Tennessee is just a hillbilly dumping ground," John Wesley said, "and Georgia is a lousy state too."

"You said it," June Star said.

"In my time," said the grandmother, folding her thin veined fingers, "children were more respectful of their native states and their parents and everything else. People did right then. Oh look at the cute little pickaninny!" she said and pointed to a Negro child standing in the door of a shack. "Wouldn't that make a picture, now?" she asked and they all turned and looked at the little Negro out of the back window. He waved.

"He didn't have any britches on," June Star said.

"He probably didn't have any," the grandmother explained. "Little niggers in the country don't have things like we do. If I could paint, I'd paint that picture," she said.

The children exchanged comic books.

The grandmother offered to hold the baby and the children's mother passed him over the front seat to her. She set him on her knee and bounced him and told him about the things they were passing. She rolled her eyes and screwed up her mouth and stuck her leathery thin face into his smooth bland one. Occasionally he gave her a faraway smile. They passed a large cotton field with five or six graves fenced in the middle of it, like a small island.

"Look at the graveyard!" the grandmother said, pointing it out. "That was the old family burying ground. That belonged to the plantation."

"Where's the plantation?" John Wesley asked.

"Gone With the Wind," said the grandmother. "Ha. Ha."

When the children finished all the comic books they had brought, they opened the lunch and ate it. The grandmother ate a peanut butter sandwich and an olive and would not let the children throw the box and the paper napkins out the window. When there was nothing else to do they played a game by choosing a cloud and making the other two guess what shape it suggested. John Wesley took one the shape of a cow and June Star guessed a cow and John Wesley said, no, an automobile, and June Star said he didn't play fair, and they began to slap each other over the grandmother.

The grandmother said she would tell them a story if they would keep quiet. When she told a story, she rolled her eyes and waved her head and was very dramatic. She said once when she was a maiden lady she had been courted by a Mr. Edgar Atkins Teagarden from Jasper, Georgia. She said he was a very good-looking man and a gentleman and that he brought her a watermelon every Saturday afternoon with his initials cut in it, E. A. T. Well, one Saturday, she said, Mr. Teagarden brought the watermelon and there was nobody at home and he left it on the front porch and returned in his buggy to Jasper, but she never got the watermelon, she said, because a nigger boy ate it when he saw the initials, E. A. T.! This story tickled John Wesley's funny bone and he giggled and giggled but June Star didn't think it was any good. She said she wouldn't marry a man that just brought her a watermelon on Saturday. The grandmother said she would have done well to marry Mr. Teagarden because he was a gentleman and had bought Coca-Cola stock when it first came out and that he had died only a few years ago, a very wealthy man.

They stopped at The Tower for barbecued sandwiches. The Tower was a part stucco and part wood filling station and dance hall set in a clearing outside of Timothy. A fat man named Red Sammy Butts ran it and there were signs stuck here and there on the building and for miles up and down the highway saying, TRY RED SAMMY'S FAMOUS BARBECUE. NONE LIKE FAMOUS RED SAMMY'S! RED SAM! THE FAT BOY WITH THE HAPPY LAUGH! A VETERAN! RED SAMMY'S YOUR MAN!

Red Sammy was lying on the bare ground outside The Tower with his head under a truck while a gray monkey about a foot high, chained to a small chinaberry tree, chattered nearby. The monkey sprang back into the tree and got on the highest limb as soon as he saw the children jump out of the car and run toward him.

Inside, The Tower was a long dark room with a counter at one end and tables at the other and dancing space in the middle. They all sat down at a board table next to the nickelodeon and Red Sam's wife, a tall burnt-brown woman with hair and eyes lighter than her skin, came and took their order. The children's mother put a dime in the machine and played "The Tennessee Waltz," and the grandmother said that tune always made her want to dance. She asked Bailey if he would like to dance but he only glared at her. He didn't have a naturally sunny disposition like she did and trips made him nervous. The grandmother's brown eyes were very bright. She swayed her head from side to side and pretended she was dancing in her chair. June Star said play something she could tap to so the children's mother put in another dime and played a fast number and June Star stepped out onto the dance floor and did her tap routine.

"Ain't she cute?" Red Sam's wife said, leaning over the counter. "Would you like to come be my little girl?"

"No I certainly wouldn't," June Star said. "I wouldn't live in a broken-down place like this for a million bucks!" and she ran back to the table.

"Ain't she cute?" the woman repeated, stretching her mouth politely.

"Aren't you ashamed?" hissed the grandmother.

Red Sam came in and told his wife to quit lounging on the counter and hurry up with these people's order. His khaki trousers reached just to his hip bones and his stomach hung over them like a sack of meal swaying under his shirt. He came over and sat down at a table nearby and let out a combination sigh and yodel. "You can't win," he said. "You can't win," and he wiped his sweating red face off with a gray handkerchief. "These days you don't know who to trust," he said. "Ain't that the truth?"

"People are certainly not nice like they used to be," said the grandmother.

"Two fellers come in here last week," Red Sammy said, "driving a Chrysler. It was a old beat-up car but it was a good one and these boys looked all right to me. Said they worked at the mill and you know I let them fellers charge the gas they bought? Now why did I do that?"

"Because you're a good man!" the grandmother said at once.

"Yes'm, I suppose so," Red Sam said as if he were struck with this answer.

His wife brought the orders, carrying the five plates all at once without a tray, two in each hand and one balanced on her arm. "It isn't a soul in this green world of God's that you can trust," she said. "And I don't count nobody out of that, not nobody," she repeated, looking at Red Sammy.

"Did you read about that criminal, The Misfit, that's escaped?" asked the grandmother.

"I wouldn't be a bit surprised if he didn't attact this place right here," said the woman. "If he hears about it being here, I wouldn't be none surprised to see him. If he hears it's two cent in the cash register, I wouldn't be a tall surprised if he . . ."

"That'll do," Red Sam said. "Go bring these people their Co'Colas," and the woman went off to get the rest of the order.

"A good man is hard to find," Red Sammy said. "Everything is getting terrible. I remember the day you could go off and leave your screen door unlatched. Not no more."

He and the grandmother discussed better times. The old lady said that in her opinion Europe was entirely to blame for the way things were now. She said the way Europe acted you would think we were made of money and Red Sam said it was no use talking about it, she was exactly right. The children ran outside into the white sunlight and looked at the monkey in the lacy chinaberry tree. He was busy catching fleas on himself and biting each one carefully between his teeth as if it were a delicacy.

They drove off again into the hot afternoon. The grandmother took cat naps and woke up every few minutes with her own snoring. Outside of Toombsboro she woke up and recalled an old plantation that she had visited in this neighborhood once when she was a young lady.

She said the house had six white columns across the front and that there was an avenue of oaks leading up to it and two little wooden trellis arbors on either side in front where you sat down with your suitor after a stroll in the garden. She recalled exactly which road to turn off to get to it. She knew that Bailey would not be willing to lose any time looking at an old house, but the more she talked about it, the more she wanted to see it once again and find out if the little twin arbors were still standing. "There was a secret panel in this house," she said craftily, not telling the truth but wishing that she were, "and the story went that all the family silver was hidden in it when Sherman came through but it was never found . . ."

"Hey!" John Wesley said. "Let's go see it! We'll find it! We'll poke all the woodwork and find it! Who lives there? Where do you turn off at? Hey Pop, can't we turn off there?"

"We never have seen a house with a secret panel!" June Star shrieked. "Let's go to the house with the secret panel! Hey Pop, can't we go see the house with the secret panel!"

"It's not far from here, I know," the grandmother said. "It wouldn't take over twenty minutes."

Bailey was looking straight ahead. His jaw was as rigid as a horseshoe. "No," he said.

The children began to yell and scream that they wanted to see the house with the secret panel. John Wesley kicked the back of the front seat and June Star hung over her mother's shoulder and whined desperately into her ear that they never had any fun even on their vacation, that they could never do what THEY wanted to do. The baby began to scream and John Wesley kicked the back of the seat so hard that his father could feel the blows in his kidney.

"All right!" he shouted and drew the car to a stop at the side of the road. "Will you all shut up? Will you all just shut up for one second? If you don't shut up, we won't go anywhere."

"It would be very educational for them," the grandmother murmured.

"All right," Bailey said, "but get this: this is the only time we're going to stop for anything like this. This is the one and only time."

"The dirt road that you have to turn down is about a mile back," the grandmother directed. "I marked it when we passed."

"A dirt road," Bailey groaned.

After they had turned around and were headed toward the dirt road, the grandmother recalled other points about the house, the beautiful glass over the front doorway and the candle-lamp in the hall. John Wesley said that the secret panel was probably in the fireplace.

"You can't go inside this house," Bailey said. "You don't know who lives there."

"While you all talk to the people in front, I'll run around behind and get in a window," John Wesley suggested.

"We'll all stay in the car," his mother said.

They turned onto the dirt road and the car raced roughly along in a swirl of pink dust. The grandmother recalled the times when there were no paved roads and thirty miles was a day's journey. The dirt road was hilly and there were sudden washes in it and sharp curves on dangerous embankments. All at once they would be on a hill, looking down over the blue tops of trees for miles around, then the next minute, they would be in a red depression with the dust-coated trees looking down on them.

"This place had better turn up in a minute," Bailey said, "or I'm going to turn around."

The road looked as if no one had traveled on it in months.

"It's not much farther," the grandmother said and just as she said it, a horrible thought came to her. The thought was so embarrassing that she turned red in the face and her eyes dilated and her feet jumped up, upsetting her valise in the corner. The instant the valise moved, the newspaper top she had over the basket under it rose with a snarl and Pitty Sing, the cat, sprang onto Bailey's shoulder.

The children were thrown to the floor and their mother, clutching the baby, was thrown out the door onto the ground; the old lady was thrown into the front seat. The car turned over once and landed right-side-up in a gulch off the side of the road. Bailey remained in the driver's seat with the cat — gray-striped with a broad white face and an orange nose — clinging to his neck like a caterpillar.

As soon as the children saw they could move their arms and legs, they scrambled out of the car, shouting, "We've had an ACCIDENT!" The grandmother was curled up under the dashboard, hoping she was injured so that Bailey's wrath would not come down on her all at once. The horrible thought she had had before the accident was that the house she had remembered so vividly was not in Georgia but in Tennessee.

Bailey removed the cat from his neck with both hands and flung it out the window against the side of a pine tree. Then he got out of the car and started looking for the children's mother. She was sitting against the side of the red gutted ditch, holding the screaming baby, but she only had a cut down her face and a broken shoulder. "We've had an ACCIDENT!" the children screamed in a frenzy of delight.

"But nobody's killed," June Star said with disappointment as the grandmother limped out of the car, her hat still pinned to her head but the broken front brim standing up at a jaunty angle and the violet spray hanging off the side. They all sat down in the ditch, except the children, to recover from the shock. They were all shaking.

"Maybe a car will come along," said the children's mother hoarsely.

"I believe I have injured an organ," said the grandmother, pressing her side, but no one answered her. Bailey's teeth were clattering. He had on a yellow sport shirt with bright blue parrots designed in it and his face was as yellow as the shirt. The grandmother decided that she would not mention that the house was in Tennessee.

The road was about ten feet above and they could see only the tops of the trees on the other side of it. Behind the ditch they were sitting in there were more woods, tall and dark and deep. In a few minutes they saw a car some distance away on top of a hill, coming slowly as if the occupants were watching them. The grandmother stood up and waved both arms dramatically to attract their attention. The car continued to come on slowly, disappeared around a bend and appeared again, moving even slower, on top of the hill they had gone over. It was a big black battered hearse-like automobile. There were three men in it.

It came to a stop just over them and for some minutes, the driver looked down with a steady expressionless gaze to where they were sitting, and didn't speak. Then he turned his head and muttered something to the other two and they got out. One was a fat boy in black trousers and a red sweat shirt with a silver stallion embossed on the front of it. He moved around on the right side of them and stood staring, his mouth partly open in a kind of loose grin. The other had on khaki pants and a blue striped coat and a gray hat pulled down very low, hiding most of his face. He came around slowly on the left side. Neither spoke.

The driver got out of the car and stood by the side of it, looking down at them. He was an older man than the other two. His hair was just beginning to gray and he wore silver-rimmed spectacles that gave him a scholarly look. He had a long creased face and didn't have on any shirt or undershirt. He had on blue jeans that were too tight for him and was holding a black hat and a gun. The two boys also had guns.

"We've had an ACCIDENT!" the children screamed.

The grandmother had the peculiar feeling that the bespectacled man was someone she knew. His face was as familiar to her as if she had known him all her life but she could not recall who he was. He moved away from the car and began to come down the embankment, placing his feet carefully so that he wouldn't slip. He had on tan and white shoes and no socks, and his ankles were red and thin. "Good afternoon," he said. "I see you all had you a little spill."

"We turned over twice!" said the grandmother.

"Oncet," he corrected. "We seen it happen. Try their car and see will it run, Hiram," he said quietly to the boy with the gray hat.

"What you got that gun for?" John Wesley asked. "Whatcha gonna do with that gun?"

"Lady," the man said to the children's mother, "would you mind calling them children to sit down by you? Children make me nervous. I want all you all to sit down right together there where you're at."

"What are you telling US what to do for?" June Star asked.

Behind them the line of woods gaped like a dark open mouth. "Come here," said their mother.

"Look here now," Bailey began suddenly, "we're in a predicament! We're in . . ."

The grandmother shrieked. She scrambled to her feet and stood staring. "You're The Misfit!" she said. "I recognized you at once!"

"Yes'm," the man said, smiling slightly as if he were pleased in spite of himself to be known, "but it would have been better for all of you, lady, if you hadn't of reckernized me."

Bailey turned his head sharply and said something to his mother that shocked even the children. The old lady began to cry and The Misfit reddened.

"Lady," he said, "don't you get upset. Sometimes a man says things he don't mean. I don't reckon he meant to talk to you thataway."

"You wouldn't shoot a lady, would you?" the grandmother said and removed a clean handkerchief from her cuff and began to slap at her eyes with it.

The Misfit pointed the toe of his shoe into the ground and made a little hole and then covered it up again. "I would hate to have to," he said.

"Listen," the grandmother almost screamed, "I know you're a good man. You don't look a bit like you have common blood. I know you must come from nice people!"

"Yes mam," he said, "finest people in the world." When he smiled he showed a row of strong white teeth. "God never made a finer woman than my mother and my daddy's heart was pure gold," he said. The boy with the red sweat shirt had come around behind them and was standing with his gun at his hip. The Misfit squatted down on the ground. "Watch them children, Bobby Lee," he said. "You know they make me nervous." He looked at the six of them huddled together in front of him and he seemed to be embarrassed as if he couldn't think of anything to say. "Ain't a cloud in the sky," he remarked, looking up at it. "Don't see no sun but don't see no cloud neither."

"Yes, it's a beautiful day," said the grandmother. "Listen," she said, "you shouldn't call yourself The Misfit because I know you're a good man at heart. I can just look at you and tell."

"Hush!" Bailey yelled. "Hush! Everybody shut up and let me handle this!" He was squatting in the position of a runner about to sprint forward but he didn't move.

"I pre-chate that, lady," The Misfit said and drew a little circle in the ground with the butt of his gun.

"It'll take a half a hour to fix this here car," Hiram called, looking over the raised hood of it.

"Well, first you and Bobby Lee get him and that little boy to step over yonder with you," The Misfit said, pointing to Bailey and John Wesley. "The boys want to ast you something," he said to Bailey. "Would you mind stepping back in them woods there with them?"

"Listen," Bailey began, "we're in a terrible predicament! Nobody realizes what this is," and his voice cracked. His eyes were as blue and intense as the parrots in his shirt and he remained perfectly still.

The grandmother reached up to adjust her hat brim as if she were going to the woods with him but it came off in her hand. She stood staring at it and after a second she let it fall on the ground. Hiram pulled Bailey up by the arm as if he were assisting an old man. John Wesley caught hold of his father's hand and Bobby Lee followed. They went off toward the woods and just as they reached the dark edge, Bailey turned and supporting himself against a gray naked pine trunk, he shouted, "I'll be back in a minute, Mamma, wait on me!"

"Come back this instant!" his mother shrilled but they all disappeared into the woods.

"Bailey Boy!" the grandmother called in a tragic voice but she found she was looking at The Misfit squatting on the ground in front of her. "I just know you're a good man," she said desperately. "You're not a bit common!"

"Nome, I ain't a good man," The Misfit said after a second as if he had considered her statement carefully, "but I ain't the worst in the world neither. My daddy said I was a different breed of dog from my brothers and sisters. 'You know,' Daddy said, 'it's some that can live their whole life out without asking about it and it's others has to know why it is, and this boy is one of the latters. He's going to be into everything!'" He put on his black hat and looked up suddenly and then away deep into the woods as if he were embarrassed again. "I'm sorry I don't have on a shirt before you ladies," he said, hunching his shoulders slightly. "We buried our clothes that we had on when we escaped and we're just making do until we can get better. We borrowed these from some folks we met," he explained.

"That's perfectly all right," the grandmother said. "Maybe Bailey has an extra shirt in his suitcase."

"I'll look and see terrectly," The Misfit said.

"Where are they taking him?" the children's mother screamed.

"Daddy was a card himself," The Misfit said. "You couldn't put anything over on him. He never got in trouble with the Authorities though. Just had the knack of handling them."

"You could be honest too if you'd only try," said the grandmother. "Think how wonderful it would be to settle down and live a comfortable life and not have to think about somebody chasing you all the time."

The Misfit kept scratching in the ground with the butt of his gun as if he were thinking about it. "Yes'm, somebody is always after you," he murmured.

The grandmother noticed how thin his shoulder blades were just behind his hat because she was standing up looking down on him. "Do you ever pray?" she asked.

He shook his head. All she saw was the black hat wiggle between his shoulder blades. "Nome," he said.

There was a pistol shot from the woods, followed closely by another. Then silence. The old lady's head jerked around. She could hear the wind move through the tree tops like a long satisfied insuck of breath. "Bailey Boy!" she called.

"I was a gospel singer for a while," The Misfit said. "I been most everything. Been in the arm service, both land and sea, at home and abroad, been twict married, been an undertaker, been with the railroads, plowed Mother Earth, been in a tornado, seen a man burnt alive oncet," and looked up at the children's mother and the little girl who were sitting close together, their faces white and their eyes glassy; "I even seen a woman flogged," he said.

"Pray, pray," the grandmother began, "pray, pray . . ."

"I never was a bad boy that I remember of," The Misfit said in an almost dreamy voice, "but somewheres along the line I done something wrong and got sent to the penitentiary. I was buried alive," and he looked up and held her attention to him by a steady stare.

"That's when you should have started to pray," she said. "What did you do to get sent to the penitentiary that first time?"

"Turn to the right, it was a wall," The Misfit said, looking up again at the cloudless sky. "Turn to the left, it was a wall. Look up it was a ceiling, look down it was a floor. I forget what I done, lady. I set there and set there, trying to remember what it was I done and I ain't recalled it to this day. Oncet in a while, I would think it was coming to me, but it never come."

"Maybe they put you in by mistake," the old lady said vaguely.

"Nome," he said. "It wasn't no mistake. They had the papers on me."

"You must have stolen something," she said.

The Misfit sneered slightly. "Nobody had nothing I wanted," he said. "It was a head-doctor at the penitentiary said what I had done was kill my daddy but I known that for a lie. My daddy died in nineteen ought nineteen of the epidemic flu and I never had a thing to do with it. He was buried in the Mount Hopewell Baptist churchyard and you can go there and see for yourself."

"If you would pray," the old lady said, "Jesus would help you."

"That's right," The Misfit said.

"Well then, why don't you pray?" she asked trembling with delight suddenly.

"I don't want no hep," he said. "I'm doing all right by myself."

Bobby Lee and Hiram came ambling back from the woods. Bobby Lee was dragging a yellow shirt with bright blue parrots in it.

"Thow me that shirt, Bobby Lee," The Misfit said. The shirt came flying at him and landed on his shoulder and he put it on. The grandmother couldn't name what the shirt reminded her of. "No, lady," The Misfit said while he was buttoning it up, "I found out the crime don't matter. You can do one thing or you can do another, kill a man or take a tire off his car, because sooner or later you're going to forget what it was you done and just be punished for it."

The children's mother had begun to make heaving noises as if she couldn't get her breath. "Lady," he asked, "would you and that little girl like to step off yonder with Bobby Lee and Hiram and join your husband?"

"Yes, thank you," the mother said faintly. Her left arm dangled helplessly and she was holding the baby, who had gone to sleep, in the other. "Hep that lady up, Hiram," The Misfit said as she struggled to climb out of the ditch, "and Bobby Lee, you hold onto that little girl's hand."

"I don't want to hold hands with him," June Star said. "He reminds me of a pig."

The fat boy blushed and laughed and caught her by the arm and pulled her off into the woods after Hiram and her mother.

Alone with The Misfit, the grandmother found that she had lost her voice. There was not a cloud in the sky nor any sun. There was nothing around her but woods. She wanted to tell him that he must pray. She opened and closed her mouth several times before anything came out. Finally she found herself saying, "Jesus, Jesus," meaning, Jesus will help you, but the way she was saying it, it sounded as if she might be cursing.

"Yes'm," The Misfit said as if he agreed. "Jesus thown everything off balance. It was the same case with Him as with me except He hadn't committed any crime and they could prove I had committed one because they had the papers on me. Of course," he said, "they never shown me my papers. That's why I sign myself now. I said long ago, you get you a signature and sign everything you do and keep a copy of it. Then you'll know what you done and you can hold up the crime to the pun-ishment and see do they match and in the end you'll have something to prove you ain't been treated right. I call myself The Misfit," he said, "because I can't make what all I done wrong fit what all I gone through in punishment."

There was a piercing scream from the woods, followed closely by a pistol report. "Does it seem right to you, lady, that one is punished a heap and another ain't punished at all?"

"Jesus!" the old lady cried. "You've got good blood! I know you wouldn't shoot a lady! I know you come from nice people! Pray! Jesus, you ought not to shoot a lady. I'll give you all the money I've got!"

"Lady," The Misfit said, looking beyond her far into the woods, "there never was a body that give the undertaker a tip."

There were two more pistol reports and the grandmother raised her head like a parched old turkey hen crying for water and called, "Bailey Boy, Bailey Boy!" as if her heart would break.

"Jesus was the only One that ever raised the dead." The Misfit con-tinued, "and He shouldn't have done it. He thown everything off bal-ance. If He did what He said, then it's nothing for you to do but thow away everything and follow Him, and if He didn't, then it's nothing for you to do but enjoy the few minutes you got left the best way you can — by killing somebody or burning down his house or doing some other meanness to him. No pleasure but meanness," he said and his voice had become almost a snarl.

"Maybe He didn't raise the dead," the old lady mumbled, not know-ing what she was saying and feeling so dizzy that she sank down in the ditch with her legs twisted under her.

"I wasn't there so I can't say He didn't," The Misfit said. "I wisht I had of been there," he said, hitting the ground with his fist. "It ain't right I wasn't there because if I had of been there I would of known. Listen lady," he said in a high voice, "if I had of been there I would of known and I wouldn't be like I am now." His voice seemed about to crack and the grandmother's head cleared for an instant. She saw the man's face twisted close to her own as if he were going to cry and she murmured, "Why you're one of my babies. You're one of my own chil-dren!" She reached out and touched him on the shoulder. The Misfit sprang back as if a snake had bitten him and shot her three times through the chest. Then he put his gun down on the ground and took off his glasses and began to clean them.

Hiram and Bobby Lee returned from the woods and stood over the ditch, looking down at the grandmother who half sat and half lay in a puddle of blood with her legs crossed under her like a child's and her face smiling up at the cloudless sky.

Without his glasses, The Misfit's eyes were red-rimmed and pale and defenseless-looking. "Take her off and throw her where you thrown the others," he said, picking up the cat that was rubbing itself against his leg.

"She was a talker, wasn't she?" Bobby Lee said, sliding down the ditch with a yodel.

"She would of been a good woman," The Misfit said, "if it had been somebody there to shoot her every minute of her life."

"Some fun!" Bobby Lee said.

"Shut up, Bobby Lee," The Misfit said. "It's no real pleasure in life."

Good Country People

Besides the neutral expression that she wore when she was alone, Mrs. Freeman had two others, forward and reverse, that she used for all her human dealings. Her forward expression was steady and driving like the advance of a heavy truck. Her eyes never swerved to left or right but turned as the story turned as if they followed a yellow line down the center of it. She seldom used the other expression because it was not often necessary for her to retract a statement, but when she did, her face came to a complete stop, there was an almost imperceptible movement of her black eyes, during which they seemed to be receding, and then the observer would see that Mrs. Freeman, though she might stand there as real as several grain sacks thrown on top of each other, was no longer there in spirit. As for getting anything across to her when this was the case, Mrs. Hopewell had given it up. She might talk her head off. Mrs. Freeman could never be brought to admit herself wrong on any point. She would stand there and if she could be brought to say anything, it was something like, "Well, I wouldn't of said it was and I wouldn't of said it wasn't," or letting her gaze range over the top kitchen shelf where there was an assortment of dusty bottles, she might remark, "I see you ain't ate many of them figs you put up last summer."

They carried on their most important business in the kitchen at breakfast. Every morning Mrs. Hopewell got up at seven o'clock and lit her gas heater and Joy's. Joy was her daughter, a large blonde girl who had an artificial leg. Mrs. Hopewell thought of her as a child though she was thirty-two years old and highly educated. Joy would get up while her mother was eating and lumber into the bathroom and slam the door, and before long, Mrs. Freeman would arrive at the back door. Joy would hear her mother call, "Come on in," and then they would talk for a while in low voices that were indistinguishable in the bathroom. By the time Joy came in, they had usually finished the weather report and were on one or the other of Mrs. Freeman's daughters, Glynese or Carramae, Joy called them Glycerin and Caramel. Glynese, a redhead, was eighteen and had many admirers; Carramae, a blonde, was only fifteen but already married and pregnant. She could not keep anything on her stomach. Every morning Mrs. Freeman told Mrs. Hopewell how many times she had vomited since the last report.

Mrs. Hopewell liked to tell people that Glynese and Carramae were two of the finest girls she knew and that Mrs. Freeman was a *lady* and that she was never ashamed to take her anywhere or introduce her to anybody they might meet. Then she would tell how she had happened to hire the Freemans in the first place and how they were a godsend to her and how she had had them four years. The reason for her keeping them so long was that they were not trash. They were good country people. She had telephoned the man whose name they had given as a reference and he had told her that Mr. Freeman was a good farmer but that his wife was the nosiest woman ever to walk the earth. "She's got to be into everything," the man said. "If she don't get there before the dust settles, you can bet she's dead, that's all. She'll want to know all your business. I can stand him real good," he had said, "but me nor my wife neither could have stood that woman one more minute on this place." That had put Mrs. Hopewell off for a few days.

She had hired them in the end because there were no other applicants but she had made up her mind beforehand exactly how she would handle the woman. Since she was the type who had to be into everything, then, Mrs. Hopewell had decided, she would not only let her be into everything, she would *see to it* that she was into everything — she would give her the responsibility of everything, she would put her in charge. Mrs. Hopewell had no bad qualities of her own but she was able to use other people's in such a constructive way that she never felt the lack. She had hired the Freemans and she had kept them four years.

Nothing is perfect. This was one of Mrs. Hopewell's favorite sayings. Another was: that is life! And still another, the most important, was: well, other people have their opinions too. She would make these statements, usually at the table, in a tone of gentle insistence as if no one held them but her, and the large hulking Joy, whose constant outrage had obliterated every expression from her face, would stare just a little to the side of her, her eyes icy blue, with the look of someone who has achieved blindness by an act of will and means to keep it.

When Mrs. Hopewell said to Mrs. Freeman that life was like that, Mrs. Freeman would say, "I always said so myself." Nothing had been arrived at by anyone that had not first been arrived at by her. She was quicker than Mr. Freeman. When Mrs. Hopewell said to her after they had been on the place a while, "You know, you're the wheel behind the wheel," and winked, Mrs. Freeman had said, "I know it. I've always been quick. It's some that are quicker than others."

"Everybody is different," Mrs. Hopewell said.

"Yes, most people is," Mrs. Freeman said.

"It takes all kinds to make the world."

"I always said it did myself."

The girl was used to this kind of dialogue for breakfast and more of it for dinner; sometimes they had it for supper too. When they had no guest they ate in the kitchen because that was easier. Mrs. Freeman always managed to arrive at some point during the meal and to watch them finish it. She would stand in the doorway if it were summer but in the winter she would stand with one elbow on top of the refrigerator and look down on them, or she would stand by the gas heater, lifting the back of her skirt slightly. Occasionally she would stand against the wall and roll her head from side to side. At no time was she in any hurry to leave. All this was very trying on Mrs. Hopewell but she was a woman of great patience. She realized that nothing is perfect and that in the Freemans she had good country people and that if, in this day and age, you get good country people, you had better hang onto them.

She had had plenty of experience with trash. Before the Freemans she had averaged one tenant family a year. The wives of these farmers were not the kind you would want to be around you for very long. Mrs. Hopewell, who had divorced her husband long ago, needed someone to walk over the fields with her; and when Joy had to be impressed for these services, her remarks were usually so ugly and her face so glum that Mrs. Hopewell would say, "If you can't come pleasantly, I don't want you at all," to which the girl, standing square and rigid-shouldered with her neck thrust slightly forward, would reply, "If you want me, here I am — LIKE I AM."

Mrs. Hopewell excused this attitude because of the leg (which had been shot off in a hunting accident when Joy was ten). It was hard for Mrs. Hopewell to realize that her child was thirty-two now and that for more than twenty years she had had only one leg. She thought of her still as a child because it tore her heart to think instead of the poor stout girl in her thirties who had never danced a step or had any *normal* good times. Her name was really Joy but as soon as she was twenty-one and away from home, she had had it legally changed. Mrs. Hopewell was certain that she had thought and thought until she had hit upon the ugliest name in any language. Then she had gone and had the beautiful name, Joy, changed without telling her mother until after she had done it. Her legal name was Hulga.

When Mrs. Hopewell thought the name, Hulga, she thought of the broad blank hull of a battleship. She would not use it. She continued to call her Joy to which the girl responded but in a purely mechanical way.

Hulga had learned to tolerate Mrs. Freeman who saved her from taking walks with her mother. Even Glynese and Carramae were useful when they occupied attention that might otherwise have been directed at her. At first she had thought she could not stand Mrs. Freeman for she had found that it was not possible to be rude to her. Mrs. Freeman would take on strange resentments and for days together she would be sullen but the source of her displeasure was always obscure; a direct attack, a positive leer, blatant ugliness to her face — these never touched her. And without warning one day she began calling her Hulga.

She did not call her that in front of Mrs. Hopewell who would have been incensed but when she and the girl happened to be out of the house together, she would say something and add the name Hulga to the end of it, and the big spectacled Joy-Hulga would scowl and redden as if her privacy had been intruded upon. She considered the name her personal affair. She had arrived at it first purely on the basis of its ugly sound and then the full genius of its fitness had struck her. She had a vision of the name working like the ugly sweating Vulcan who stayed in the furnace and to whom, presumably, the goddess had to come when called. She saw it as the name of her highest creative act. One of her major triumphs was that her mother had not been able to turn her dust into Joy, but the greater one was that she had been able to turn it herself into Hulga. However, Mrs. Freeman's relish for using the name only irritated her. It was as if Mrs. Freeman's beady steel-pointed eyes had penetrated far enough behind her face to reach some secret fact. Something about her seemed to fascinate Mrs. Freeman and then one day Hulga realized that it was the artificial leg. Mrs. Freeman had a special fondness for the details of secret infections, hidden deformities, assaults upon children. Of diseases, she preferred the lingering or incurable. Hulga had heard Mrs. Hopewell give her the details of the hunting accident, how the leg had been literally blasted off, how she had never lost consciousness. Mrs. Freeman could listen to it any time as if it had happened an hour ago.

When Hulga stumped into the kitchen in the morning (she could walk without making the awful noise but she made it — Mrs. Hopewell was certain — because it was ugly-sounding), she glanced at them and did not speak. Mrs. Hopewell would be in her red kimono with her hair tied around her head in rags. She would be sitting at the table, finishing her breakfast and Mrs. Freeman would be hanging by her elbow outward from the refrigerator, looking down at the table. Hulga always put her eggs on the stove to boil and then stood over them with her arms folded, and Mrs. Hopewell would look at her — a kind of indirect gaze divided between her and Mrs. Freeman — and would think that if she would only keep herself up a little, she wouldn't be so bad looking. There was nothing wrong with her face that a pleasant expression wouldn't help. Mrs. Hopewell said that people who looked on the bright side of things would be beautiful even if they were not.

Whenever she looked at Joy this way, she could not help but feel that it would have been better if the child had not taken the Ph.D. It had certainly not brought her out any and now that she had it, there was no more excuse for her to go to school again. Mrs. Hopewell thought it was nice for girls to go to school to have a good time but Joy had "gone through." Anyhow, she would not have been strong enough to go again. The doctors had told Mrs. Hopewell that with the best of care, Joy might see forty-five. She had a weak heart. Joy had made it plain that if it had not been for this condition, she would be far from these red hills and good country people. She would be in a university lecturing to people who knew what she was talking about. And Mrs. Hopewell could very well picture her there, looking like a scarecrow and lecturing to more of the same. Here she went about all day in a six-year-old skirt and a yellow sweat shirt with a faded cowboy on a horse embossed on it. She thought this was funny; Mrs. Hopewell thought it was idiotic and showed simply that she was still a child. She was brilliant but she didn't have a grain of sense. It seemed to Mrs. Hopewell that every year she grew less like other people and more like herself — bloated, rude, and squint-eyed. And she said such strange things! To her own mother she had said — without warning, without excuse, standing up in the middle of a meal with her face purple and her mouth half full — "Woman! do you ever look inside? Do you ever look inside and see what you are *not*? God!" she had cried sinking down again and staring at her plate, "Malebranche was right: we are not our own light. We are not our own light!" Mrs. Hopewell had no idea to this day what brought that on. She had only made the remark, hoping Joy would take it in, that a smile never hurt anyone.

The girl had taken the Ph.D. in philosophy and this left Mrs. Hopewell at a complete loss. You could say, "My daughter is a nurse," or "My daughter is a schoolteacher," or even, "My daughter is a chemical engineer." You could not say, "My daughter is a philosopher." That was something that had ended with the Greeks and Romans. All day Joy sat on her neck in a deep chair, reading. Sometimes she went for walks but she didn't like dogs or cats or birds or flowers or nature or nice young men. She looked at nice young men as if she could smell their stupidity.

One day Mrs. Hopewell had picked up one of the books the girl had just put down and opening it at random, she read, "Science, on the other hand, has to assert its soberness and seriousness afresh and declare that it is concerned solely with what-is. Nothing — how can it be for science anything but a horror and a phantasm? If science is right, then one thing stands firm: science wishes to know nothing of nothing. Such is after all the strictly scientific approach to Nothing. We know it by wishing to know nothing of Nothing." These words had been underlined with a blue pencil and they worked on Mrs. Hopewell like some evil incantation in gibberish. She shut the book quickly and went out of the room as if she were having a chill.

This morning when the girl came in, Mrs. Freeman was on Carramae. "She thrown up four times after supper," she said, "and was up twict in the night after three o'clock. Yesterday she didn't do nothing but ramble in the bureau drawer. All she did. Stand up there and see what she could run up on."

"She's got to eat," Mrs. Hopewell muttered, sipping her coffee, while she watched Joy's back at the stove. She was wondering what the child had said to the Bible salesman. She could not imagine what kind of a conversation she could possibly have had with him.

He was a tall gaunt hatless youth who had called yesterday to sell them a Bible. He had appeared at the door, carrying a large black suitcase that weighted him so heavily on one side that he had to brace himself against the door facing. He seemed on the point of collapse but he said in a cheerful voice, "Good morning, Mrs. Cedars!" and set the suitcase down on the mat. He was not a bad-looking young man though he had on a bright blue suit and yellow socks that were not pulled up far enough. He had prominent face bones and a streak of sticky-looking brown hair falling across his forehead.

"I'm Mrs. Hopewell," she said.

"Oh!" he said, pretending to look puzzled but with his eyes sparkling, "I saw it said 'The Cedars' on the mailbox so I thought you was Mrs. Cedars!" and he burst out in a pleasant laugh. He picked up the satchel and under cover of a pant, he fell forward into her hall. It was rather as if the suitcase had moved first, jerking him after it. "Mrs. Hopewell!" he said and grabbed her hand. "I hope you are well!" and he laughed again and then all at once his face sobered completely. He paused and gave her a straight earnest look and said, "Lady, I've come to speak of serious things."

"Well, come in," she muttered, none too pleased because her dinner was almost ready. He came into the parlor and sat down on the edge of a straight chair and put the suitcase between his feet and glanced around the room as if he were sizing her up by it. Her silver gleamed on the two sideboards; she decided he had never been in a room as elegant as this.

"Mrs. Hopewell," he began, using her name in a way that sounded almost intimate, "I know you believe in Chrustian service."

"Well yes," she murmured.

"I know," he said and paused, looking very wise with his head cocked on one side, "that you're a good woman. Friends have told me."

Mrs. Hopewell never liked to be taken for a fool. "What are you selling?" she asked.

"Bibles," the young man said and his eye raced around the room before he added, "I see you have no family Bible in your parlor, I see that is the one lack you got!"

Mrs. Hopewell could not say, "My daughter is an atheist and won't let me keep the Bible in the parlor." She said, stiffening slightly, "I keep my Bible by my bedside." This was not the truth. It was in the attic somewhere.

"Lady," he said, "the word of God ought to be in the parlor."

"Well, I think that's a matter of taste," she began. "I think . . ."

"Lady," he said, "for a Chrustian, the word of God ought to be in every room in the house besides in his heart. I know you're a Chrustian because I can see it in every line of your face."

She stood up and said, "Well, young man, I don't want to buy a Bible and I smell my dinner burning."

He didn't get up. He began to twist his hands and looking down at them, he said softly, "Well lady, I'll tell you the truth — not many people want to buy one nowadays and besides, I know I'm real simple. I don't know how to say a thing but to say it. I'm just a country boy." He glanced up into her unfriendly face. "People like you don't like to fool with country people like me!"

"Why!" she cried, "good country people are the salt of the earth! Besides, we all have different ways of doing, it takes all kinds to make the world go 'round. That's life!"

"You said a mouthful," he said.

"Why, I think there aren't enough good country people in the world!" she said, stirred. "I think that's what's wrong with it!"

His face had brightened. "I didn't inraduce myself," he said. "I'm Manley Pointer from out in the country around Willohobie, not even from a place, just from near a place."

"You wait a minute," she said. "I have to see about my dinner." She went out to the kitchen and found Joy standing near the door where she had been listening.

"Get rid of the salt of the earth," she said, "and let's eat."

Mrs. Hopewell gave her a pained look and turned the heat down under the vegetables. "*I* can't be rude to anybody," she murmured and went back into the parlor.

He had opened the suitcase and was sitting with a Bible on each knee.

"You might as well put those up," she told him. "I don't want one."

"I appreciate your honesty," he said. "You don't see any more real honest people unless you go way out in the country."

"I know," she said, "real genuine folks!" Through the crack in the door she heard a groan.

"I guess a lot of boys come telling you they're working their way through college," he said, "but I'm not going to tell you that. Somehow," he said, "I don't want to go to college. I want to devote my life to Chrustian service. See," he said, lowering his voice, "I got this heart condition. I may not live long. When you know it's something wrong with you and you may not live long, well then, lady . . ." He paused, with his mouth open, and stared at her.

He and Joy had the same condition! She knew that her eyes were filling with tears but she collected herself quickly and murmured, "Won't you stay for dinner? We'd love to have you!" and was sorry the instant she heard herself say it.

"Yes mam," he said in an abashed voice, "I would sher love to do that!"

Joy had given him one look on being introduced to him and then throughout the meal had not glanced at him again. He had addressed several remarks to her, which she had pretended not to hear. Mrs. Hopewell could not understand deliberate rudeness, although she lived with it, and she felt she had always to overflow with hospitality to make up for Joy's lack of courtesy. She urged him to talk about himself and he did. He said he was the seventh child of twelve and that his father had been crushed under a tree when he himself was eight year old. He had been crushed very badly, in fact, almost cut in two and was practically not recognizable. His mother had got along the best she could by hard working and she had always seen that her children went to Sunday School and that they read the Bible every evening. He was now nineteen year old and he had been selling Bibles for four months. In that time he had sold seventy-seven Bibles and had the promise of two more sales. He wanted to become a missionary because he thought that was the way you could do most for people. "He who losest his life shall find it," he said simply and he was so sincere, so genuine and earnest that Mrs. Hopewell would not for the world have smiled. He prevented his peas from sliding onto the table by blocking them with a piece of bread which he later cleaned his plate with. She could see Joy observing sidewise how he handled his knife and fork and she saw too that every few minutes, the boy would dart a keen appraising glance at the girl as if he were trying to attract her attention.

After dinner Joy cleared the dishes off the table and disappeared and Mrs. Hopewell was left to talk with him. He told her again about his childhood and his father's accident and about various things that had happened to him. Every five minutes or so she would stifle a yawn. He sat for two hours until finally she told him she must go because she had an appointment in town. He packed his Bibles and thanked her and prepared to leave, but in the doorway he stopped and wrung her hand and said that not on any of his trips had he met a lady as nice as her and he asked if he could come again. She had said she would always be happy to see him.

Joy had been standing in the road, apparently looking at something in the distance, when he came down the steps toward her, bent to the side with his heavy valise. He stopped where she was standing and confronted her directly. Mrs. Hopewell could not hear what he said but she trembled to think what Joy would say to him. She could see that after a minute Joy said something and that then the boy began to speak again, making an excited gesture with his free hand. After a minute Joy said something else at which the boy began to speak once more. Then to her amazement, Mrs. Hopewell saw the two of them walk off together, toward the gate. Joy had walked all the way to the gate with him and Mrs. Hopewell could not imagine what they had said to each other, and she had not yet dared to ask.

Mrs. Freeman was insisting upon her attention. She had moved from the refrigerator to the heater so that Mrs. Hopewell had to turn and face her in order to seem to be listening. "Glynese gone out with Harvey Hill again last night," she said. "She had this sty."

"Hill," Mrs. Hopewell said absently, "is that the one who works in the garage?"

"Nome, he's the one that goes to chiropracter school," Mrs. Freeman said. "She had this sty. Been had it two days. So she says when he brought her in the other night he says, 'Lemme get rid of that sty for you,' and she says, 'How?' and he says, 'You just lay yourself down acrost the seat of that car and I'll show you.' So she done it and he popped her neck. Kept on a-popping it several times until she made him quit. This morning," Mrs. Freeman said, "she ain't got no sty. She ain't got no traces of a sty."

"I never heard of that before," Mrs. Hopewell said.

"He ast her to marry him before the Ordinary," Mrs. Freeman went on, "and she told him she wasn't going to be married in no *office*."

"Well, Glynese is a fine girl," Mrs. Hopewell said. "Glynese and Carramae are both fine girls."

"Carramae said when her and Lyman was married Lyman said it sure felt sacred to him. She said he said he wouldn't take five hundred dollars for being married by a preacher."

"How much would he take?" the girl asked from the stove.

"He said he wouldn't take five hundred dollars," Mrs. Freeman repeated.

"Well we all have work to do," Mrs. Hopewell said.

"Lyman said it just felt more sacred to him," Mrs. Freeman said. "The doctor wants Carramae to eat prunes. Says instead of medicine. Says them cramps is coming from pressure. You know where I think it is?"

"She'll be better in a few weeks," Mrs. Hopewell said.

"In the tube," Mrs. Freeman said. "Else she wouldn't be as sick as she is."

Hulga had cracked her two eggs into a saucer and was bringing them to the table along with a cup of coffee that she had filled too full. She sat down carefully and began to eat, meaning to keep Mrs. Freeman there by questions if for any reason she showed an inclination to leave. She could perceive her mother's eye on her. The first round-about question would be about the Bible salesman and she did not wish to bring it on. "How did he pop her neck?" she asked.

Mrs. Freeman went into a description of how he had popped her neck. She said he owned a '55 Mercury but that Glynese said she would rather marry a man with only a '36 Plymouth who would be married by a preacher. The girl asked what if he had a '32 Plymouth and Mrs. Freeman said what Glynese had said was a '36 Plymouth.

Mrs. Hopewell said there were not many girls with Glynese's common sense. She said what she admired in those girls was their common sense. She said that reminded her that they had had a nice visitor yesterday, a young man selling Bibles. "Lord," she said, "he bored me to death but he was so sincere and genuine I couldn't be rude to him. He was just good country people, you know," she said, "— just the salt of the earth."

"I seen him walk up," Mrs. Freeman said, "and then later — I seen him walk off," and Hulga could feel the slight shift in her voice, the slight insinuation, that he had not walked off alone, had he? Her face remained expressionless but the color rose into her neck and she seemed to swallow it down with the next spoonful of egg. Mrs. Freeman was looking at her as if they had a secret together.

"Well, it takes all kinds of people to make the world go 'round," Mrs. Hopewell said. "It's very good we aren't all alike."

"Some people are more alike than others," Mrs. Freeman said.

Hulga got up and stumped, with about twice the noise that was necessary, into her room and locked the door. She was to meet the Bible salesman at ten o'clock at the gate. She had thought about it half the night. She had started thinking of it as a great joke and then she had begun to see profound implications in it. She had lain in bed imagining dialogues for them that were insane on the surface but that reached below to depths that no Bible salesman would be aware of. Their conversation yesterday had been of this kind.

He had stopped in front of her and had simply stood there. His face was bony and sweaty and bright, with a little pointed nose in the center of it, and his look was different from what it had been at the dinner table. He was gazing at her with open curiosity, with fascination, like a child watching a new fantastic animal at the zoo, and he was breathing as if he had run a great distance to reach her. His gaze seemed somehow familiar but she could not think where she had been regarded with it before. For almost a minute he didn't say anything. Then on what seemed an insuck of breath, he whispered, "You ever ate a chicken that was two days old?"

The girl looked at him stonily. He might have just put this question up for consideration at the meeting of a philosophical association. "Yes," she presently replied as if she had considered it from all angles.

"It must have been mighty small!" he said triumphantly and shook all over with little nervous giggles, getting very red in the face, and subsiding finally into his gaze of complete admiration, while the girl's expression remained exactly the same.

"How old are you?" he asked softly.

She waited some time before she answered. Then in a flat voice she said, "Seventeen."

His smiles came in succession like waves breaking on the surface of a little lake. "I see you got a wooden leg," he said. "I think you're brave. I think you're real sweet."

The girl stood blank and solid and silent.

"Walk to the gate with me," he said. "You're a brave sweet little thing and I liked you the minute I seen you walk in the door."

Hulga began to move forward.

"What's your name?" he asked, smiling down on the top of her head.

"Hulga," she said.

"Hulga," he murmured, "Hulga. Hulga. I never heard of anybody name Hulga before. You're shy, aren't you, Hulga?" he asked.

She nodded, watching his large red hand on the handle of the giant valise.

"I like girls that wear glasses," he said. "I think a lot. I'm not like these people that a serious thought don't ever enter their heads. It's because I may die."

"I may die too," she said suddenly and looked up at him. His eyes were very small and brown, glittering feverishly.

"Listen," he said, "don't you think some people was meant to meet on account of what all they got in common and all? Like they both think serious thoughts and all?" He shifted the valise to his other hand so that the hand nearest her was free. He caught hold of her elbow and shook it a little. "I don't work on Saturday," he said. "I like to walk in the woods and see what Mother Nature is wearing. O'er the hills and far away. Pic-nics and things. Couldn't we go on a pic-nic tomorrow? Say yes, Hulga," he said and gave her a dying look as if he felt his insides about to drop out of him. He had even seemed to sway slightly toward her.

During the night she had imagined that she seduced him. She imagined that the two of them walked on the place until they came to the storage barn beyond the two back fields and there, she imagined, that things came to such a pass that she very easily seduced him and that then, of course, she had to reckon with his remorse. True genius can get an idea across even to an inferior mind. She imagined that she took his remorse in hand and changed it into a deeper understanding of life. She took all his shame away and turned it into something useful.

She set off for the gate at exactly ten o'clock, escaping without drawing Mrs. Hopewell's attention. She didn't take anything to eat, forgetting that food is usually taken on a picnic. She wore a pair of slacks and a dirty white shirt, and as an afterthought, she had put some Vapex on the collar of it since she did not own any perfume. When she reached the gate no one was there.

She looked up and down the empty highway and had the furious feeling that she had been tricked, that he had only meant to make her walk to the gate after the idea of him. Then suddenly he stood up, very tall, from behind a bush on the opposite embankment.

Smiling, he lifted his hat which was new and wide-brimmed. He had not worn it yesterday and she wondered if he had bought it for the occasion. It was toast-colored with a red and white band around it and was slightly too large for him. He stepped from behind the bush still carrying the black valise. He had on the same suit and the same yellow socks sucked down in his shoes from walking. He crossed the highway and said, "I knew you'd come!"

The girl wondered acidly how he had known this. She pointed to the valise and asked, "Why did you bring your Bibles?"

He took her elbow, smiling down on her as if he could not stop. "You can never tell when you'll need the word of God, Hulga," he said. She had a moment in which she doubted that this was actually happening and then they began to climb the embankment. They went down into the pasture toward the woods. The boy walked lightly by her side, bouncing on his toes. The valise did not seem to be heavy today; he even swung it. They crossed half the pasture without saying anything and then, putting his hand easily on the small of her back, he asked softly, "Where does your wooden leg join on?"

She turned an ugly red and glared at him and for an instant the boy looked abashed. "I didn't mean you no harm," he said. "I only meant you're so brave and all. I guess God takes care of you."

"No," she said, looking forward and walking fast, "I don't even believe in God."

At this he stopped and whistled. "No!" he exclaimed as if he were too astonished to say anything else.

She walked on and in a second he was bouncing at her side, fanning with his hat. "That's very unusual for a girl," he remarked, watching her out of the corner of his eye. When they reached the edge of the wood, he put his hand on her back again and drew her against him without a word and kissed her heavily.

The kiss, which had more pressure than feeling behind it, produced that extra surge of adrenalin in the girl that enables one to carry a packed trunk out of a burning house, but in her, the power went at once to the brain. Even before he released her, her mind, clear and detached and ironic anyway, was regarding him from a great distance, with amusement but with pity. She had never been kissed before and she was pleased to discover that it was an unexceptional experience and all a matter of the mind's control. Some people might enjoy drain water if they were told it was vodka. When the boy, looking expectant but uncertain, pushed her gently away, she turned and walked on, saying nothing as if such business, for her, were common enough.

He came along panting at her side, trying to help her when he saw a root that she might trip over. He caught and held back the long swaying blades of thorn vine until she had passed beyond them. She led the way and he came breathing heavily behind her. Then they came out on a sunlit hillside, sloping softly into another one a little smaller. Beyond, they could see the rusted top of the old barn where the extra hay was stored.

The hill was sprinkled with small pink weeds. "Then you ain't saved?" he asked suddenly, stopping.

The girl smiled. It was the first time she had smiled at him at all. "In my economy," she said, "I'm saved and you are damned but I told you I didn't believe in God."

Nothing seemed to destroy the boy's look of admiration. He gazed at her now as if the fantastic animal at the zoo had put its paw through the bars and given him a loving poke. She thought he looked as if he wanted to kiss her again and she walked on before he had the chance.

"Ain't there somewheres we can sit down sometime?" he murmured, his voice softening toward the end of the sentence.

"In that barn," she said.

They made for it rapidly as if it might slide away like a train. It was a large two-story barn, cool and dark inside. The boy pointed up the ladder that led into the loft and said, "It's too bad we can't go up there."

"Why can't we?" she asked.

"Yer leg," he said reverently.

The girl gave him a contemptuous look and putting both hands on the ladder, she climbed it while he stood below, apparently awestruck. She pulled herself expertly through the opening and then looked down at him and said, "Well, come on if you're coming," and he began to climb the ladder, awkwardly bringing the suitcase with him.

"We won't need the Bible," she observed.

"You never can tell," he said, panting. After he had got into the loft, he was a few seconds catching his breath. She had sat down in a pile of straw. A wide sheath of sunlight, filled with dust particles, slanted over her. She lay back against a bale, her face turned away, looking out the front opening of the barn where hay was thrown from a wagon into the loft. The two pink-speckled hillsides lay back against a dark ridge of woods. The sky was cloudless and cold blue. The boy dropped down by her side and put one arm under her and the other over her and began methodically kissing her face, making little noises like a fish. He did not remove his hat but it was pushed far enough back not to interfere. When her glasses got in his way, he took them off of her and slipped them into his pocket.

The girl at first did not return any of the kisses but presently she began to and after she had put several on his cheek, she reached his lips and remained there, kissing him again and again as if she were trying to draw all the breath out of him. His breath was clear and sweet like a child's and the kisses were sticky like a child's. He mumbled about loving her and about knowing when he first seen her that he loved her, but the mumbling was like the sleepy fretting of a child being put to sleep by his mother. Her mind, throughout this, never stopped or lost itself for a second to her feelings. "You ain't said you loved me none," he whispered finally, pulling back from her. "You got to say that."

She looked away from him off into the hollow sky and then down at a black ridge and then down farther into what appeared to be two green swelling lakes. She didn't realize he had taken her glasses but this landscape could not seem exceptional to her for she seldom paid any close attention to her surroundings.

"You got to say it," he repeated. "You got to say you love me."

She was always careful how she committed herself. "In a sense," she began, "if you use the word loosely, you might say that. But it's not a word I use. I don't have illusions. I'm one of those people who see *through* to nothing."

The boy was frowning. "You got to say it. I said it and you got to say it," he said.

The girl looked at him almost tenderly. "You poor baby," she murmured. "It's just as well you don't understand," and she pulled him by the neck, face-down, against her. "We are all damned," she said, "but some of us have taken off our blindfolds and see that there's nothing to see. It's a kind of salvation."

The boy's astonished eyes looked blankly through the ends of her hair. "Okay," he almost whined, "but do you love me or don'tcher?"

"Yes," she said and added, "in a sense. But I must tell you something. There mustn't be anything dishonest between us." She lifted his head and looked him in the eye. "I am thirty years old," she said. "I have a number of degrees."

The boy's look was irritated but dogged. "I don't care," he said. "I don't care a thing about what all you done. I just want to know if you love me or don'tcher?" and he caught her to him and wildly planted her face with kisses until she said, "Yes, yes."

"Okay then," he said, letting her go. "Prove it."

She smiled, looking dreamily out on the shifty landscape. She had seduced him without even making up her mind to try. "How?" she asked, feeling that he should be delayed a little.

He leaned over and put his lips to her ear. "Show me where your wooden leg joins on," he whispered.

The girl uttered a sharp little cry and her face instantly drained of color. The obscenity of the suggestion was not what shocked her. As a child she had sometimes been subject to feelings of shame but education had removed the last traces of that as a good surgeon scrapes for cancer; she would no more have felt it over what he was asking than she would have believed in his Bible. But she was as sensitive about the artificial leg as a peacock about his tail. No one ever touched it but her. She took care of it as someone else would his soul, in private and almost with her own eyes turned away. "No," she said.

"I known it," he muttered, sitting up. "You're just playing me for a sucker."

"Oh no no!" she cried. "It joins on at the knee. Only at the knee. Why do you want to see it?"

The boy gave her a long penetrating look. "Because," he said, "it's what makes you different. You ain't like anybody else."

She sat staring at him. There was nothing about her face or her round freezing-blue eyes to indicate that this had moved her; but she felt as if her heart had stopped and left her mind to pump her blood.

She decided that for the first time in her life she was face to face with real innocence. This boy, with an instinct that came from beyond wisdom, had touched the truth about her. When after a minute, she said in a hoarse high voice, "All right," it was like surrendering to him completely. It was like losing her own life and finding it again, miraculously, in his.

Very gently he began to roll the slack leg up. The artificial limb, in a white sock and brown flat shoe, was bound in a heavy material like canvas and ended in an ugly jointure where it was attached to the stump. The boy's face and his voice were entirely reverent as he uncovered it and said, "Now show me how to take it off and on."

She took it off for him and put it back on again and then he took it off himself, handling it as tenderly as if it were a real one. "See!" he said with a delighted child's face, "Now I can do it myself!"

"Put it back on," she said. She was thinking that she would run away with him and that every night he would take the leg off and every morning put it back on again. "Put it back on," she said.

"Not yet," he murmured, setting it on its foot out of her reach. "Leave it off for a while. You got me instead."

She gave a little cry of alarm but he pushed her down and began to kiss her again. Without the leg she felt entirely dependent on him. Her brain seemed to have stopped thinking altogether and to be about some other function that it was not very good at. Different expressions raced back and forth over her face. Every now and then the boy, his eyes like two steel spikes, would glance behind him where the leg stood. Finally she pushed him off and said, "Put it back on me now."

"Wait," he said. He leaned the other way and pulled the valise toward him and opened it. It had a pale blue spotted lining and there were only two Bibles in it. He took one of these out and opened the cover of it. It was hollow and contained a pocket flask of whiskey, a pack of cards, and a small blue box with printing on it. He laid these out in front of her one at a time in an evenly-spaced row, like one presenting offerings at the shrine of a goddess. He put the blue box in her hand. THIS PRODUCT TO BE USED ONLY FOR THE PREVENTION OF DISEASE, she read, and dropped it. The boy was unscrewing the top of the flask. He stopped and pointed, with a smile, to the deck of cards. It was not an ordinary deck but one with an obscene picture on the back of each card. "Take a swig," he said, offering her the bottle first. He held it in front of her, but like one mesmerized, she did not move.

Her voice when she spoke had an almost pleading sound. "Aren't you," she murmured, "aren't you just good country people?"

The boy cocked his head. He looked as if he were just beginning to understand that she might be trying to insult him. "Yeah," he said, curling his lip slightly, "but it ain't held me back none. I'm as good as you any day in the week."

"Give me my leg," she said.

He pushed it farther away with his foot. "Come on now, let's begin to have us a good time," he said coaxingly. "We ain't got to know one another good yet."

"Give me my leg!" she screamed and tried to lunge for it but he pushed her down easily.

"What's the matter with you all of a sudden?" he asked, frowning as he screwed the top on the flask and put it quickly back inside the Bible. "You just a while ago said you didn't believe in nothing. I thought you was some girl!"

Her face was almost purple. "You're a Christian!" she hissed. "You're a fine Christian! You're just like them all — say one thing and do another. You're a perfect Christian, you're . . ."

The boy's mouth was set angrily. "I hope you don't think," he said in a lofty indignant tone, "that I believe in that crap! I may sell Bibles but I know which end is up and I wasn't born yesterday and I know where I'm going!"

"Give me my leg!" she screeched. He jumped up so quickly that she barely saw him sweep the cards and the blue box into the Bible and throw the Bible into the valise. She saw him grab the leg and then she saw it for an instant slanted forlornly across the inside of the suitcase with a Bible at either side of its opposite ends. He slammed the lid shut and snatched up the valise and swung it down the hole and then stepped through himself.

When all of him had passed but his head, he turned and regarded her with a look that no longer had any admiration in it. "I've gotten a lot of interesting things," he said. "One time I got a woman's glass eye this way. And you needn't to think you'll catch me because Pointer ain't really my name. I use a different name at every house I call at and don't stay nowhere long. And I'll tell you another thing, Hulga," he said, using the name as if he didn't think much of it, "you ain't so smart. I been believing in nothing ever since I was born!" and then the toast-colored hat disappeared down the hole and the girl was left, sitting on the straw in the dusty sunlight. When she turned her churning face toward the opening, she saw his blue figure struggling successfully over the green speckled lake.

Mrs. Hopewell and Mrs. Freeman, who were in the back pasture, digging up onions, saw him emerge a little later from the woods and head across the meadow toward the highway. "Why, that looks like that nice dull young man that tried to sell me a Bible yesterday," Mrs. Hopewell said, squinting. "He must have been selling them to the Negroes back in there. He was so simple," she said, "but I guess the world would be better off if we were all that simple."

Mrs. Freeman's gaze drove forward and just touched him before he disappeared under the hill. Then she returned her attention to the evil-smelling onion shoot she was lifting from the ground. "Some can't be that simple," she said. "I know I never could."

Annie Proulx

Annie Proulx's characters—the deformed, the lame, the visionary, and the mad—have a lot in common with Flannery O'Connor's, though Proulx's outlook is at once more antic and bleak. Quoyle, the hapless hero of her second novel, *The Shipping News,* takes as much undeserved abuse as anyone since Job, and there is a penetrating sadness to the fates of the characters in her most recent collection, *Close Range.* Proulx has a fondness for odd comic names that hearkens back to the work of Dickens and Fielding (Mavis Bangs, Diddy Shovel, Beety Nutbeem, Alvin Yark, and Billy Pretty, all from the supporting cast of *The Shipping News* alone), and her rural locales and the dense poetry of her regional language bring Faulkner to mind. One of the stories in *Close Range,* "55 Miles to the Gas Pump," is a soaring, two-paragraph-and-a-tag-line variant on "A Rose for Miss Emily," in which we find the Widow Croom making certain unsavory discoveries about her dead husband: ". . . just as she thought: the corpses of Mr. Croom's paramours . . . some desiccated as jerky and much the same color, some moldy from lying beneath roof leaks, and all of them used hard, covered with tarry handprints, the marks of boot heels, some bright blue with the remnants of paint used on the shutters years ago, one wrapped in newspaper nipple to knee." And the conclusion? "When you live way out you make your own fun."

Proulx came to fiction relatively late, publishing her first collection at the age of fifty-four and her first novel three years later. Since then, she's become a major voice in American letters, prized for her experiments with language and her narrative fervor. The first story here, "The Half-Skinned Steer," a tall tale that became an instant classic, exacts the ultimate penalty from its protagonist, Mero, for having deserted the high plains of Wyoming for the comforts of the East. The second piece, "The Blood Bay," is also a tall tale, but grimmer, funnier, and with a punch line that speaks to the ethos of hard times and survival in an environment both capricious and indifferent.

The Half-Skinned Steer

In the long unfurling of his life, from tight-wound kid hustler in a wool suit riding the train out of Cheyenne to geriatric limper in this spooled-out year, Mero had kicked down thoughts of the place where he began, a so-called ranch on strange ground at the south hinge of the Big Horns. He'd got himself out of there in 1936, had gone to a war and come back, married and married again (and again), made money in boilers and air-duct cleaning and smart investments, retired, got into local politics and out again without scandal, never circled back to see the old man and Rollo bankrupt and ruined because he knew they were.

They called it a ranch and it had been, but one day the old man said it was impossible to run cows in such tough country where they fell off cliffs, disappeared into sinkholes, gave up large numbers of calves to marauding lions, where hay couldn't grow but leafy spurge and Canada thistle throve, and the wind packed enough sand to scour windshields opaque. The old man wangled a job delivering mail, but looked guilty fumbling bills into his neighbors' mailboxes.

Mero and Rollo saw the mail route as a defection from the work of the ranch, work that fell on them. The breeding herd was down to eighty-two and a cow wasn't worth more than fifteen dollars, but they kept mending fence, whittling ears and scorching hides, hauling cows out of mudholes and hunting lions in the hope that sooner or later the old man would move to Ten Sleep with his woman and his bottle and they could, as had their grandmother Olive when Jacob Corn disappointed her, pull the place taut. That bird didn't fly and Mero wound up sixty years later as an octogenarian vegetarian widower pumping an Exercycle in the living room of a colonial house in Woolfoot, Massachusetts.

One of those damp mornings the nail-driving telephone voice of a woman said she was Louise, Tick's wife, and summoned him back to Wyoming. He didn't know who she was, who Tick was, until she said, Tick Corn, your brother Rollo's son, and that Rollo had passed on, killed by a waspy emu though prostate cancer was waiting its chance. Yes, she said, you bet Rollo still owned the ranch. Half of it anyway. Me and Tick, she said, we been pretty much running it the last ten years.

An emu? Did he hear right?

Yes, she said. Well, of course you didn't know. You heard of Down Under Wyoming?

He had not. And thought, what kind of name was Tick? He recalled the bloated grey insects pulled off the dogs. This tick probably thought he was going to get the whole damn ranch and bloat up on it. He said, what the hell was this about an emu? Were they all crazy out there?

That's what the ranch was now, she said, Down Under Wyoming. Rollo'd sold the place way back when to the Girl Scouts, but one of the girls was dragged off by a lion and the G.S.A. sold out to the Banner ranch next door who ran cattle on it for a few years, then unloaded it on a rich Australian businessman who started Down Under Wyoming but it was too much long-distance work and he'd had bad luck with his manager, a feller from Idaho with a pawnshop rodeo buckle, so he'd looked up Rollo and offered to swap him a half-interest if he'd run the place. That was back in 1978. The place had done real well. Course we're not open now, she said, it's winter and there's no tourists. Poor Rollo was helping Tick move the emus to another building when one of them turned on a dime and come right for him with its big razor claws. Emus is bad for claws.

I know, he said. He watched the nature programs on television.

She shouted as though the telephone lines were down all across the country, Tick got your number off the computer. Rollo always said he was going to get in touch. He wanted you to see how things turned out. He tried to fight it off with his cane but it laid him open from belly to breakfast.

Maybe, he thought, things hadn't finished turning out. Impatient with this game he said he would be at the funeral. No point talking about flights and meeting him at the airport, he told her, he didn't fly, a bad experience years ago with hail, the plane had looked like a waffle iron when it landed. He intended to drive. Of course he knew how far it was. Had a damn fine car, Cadillac, always drove Cadillacs, Gislaved tires, interstate highways, excellent driver, never had an accident in his life knock on wood, four days, he would be there by Saturday afternoon. He heard the amazement in her voice, knew she was plotting his age, figuring he had to be eighty-three, a year or so older than Rollo, figuring he must be dotting around on a cane too, drooling the tiny days away, she was probably touching her own faded hair. He flexed his muscular arms, bent his knees, thought he could dodge an emu. He would see his brother dropped in a red Wyoming hole. That event could jerk him back; the dazzled rope of lightning against the cloud is not the downward bolt, but the compelled upstroke through the heated ether.

✳

He had pulled away at the sudden point when it seemed the old man's
girlfriend — now he couldn't remember her name — had jumped the
track, Rollo goggling at her bloody bitten fingers, nails chewed to the
quick, neck veins like wires, the outer forearms shaded with hairs, and
the cigarette glowing, smoke curling up, making her wink her bulged
mustang eyes, a teller of tales of hard deeds and mayhem. The old
man's hair was falling out, Mero was twenty-three and Rollo twenty
and she played them all like a deck of cards. If you admired horses
you'd go for her with her arched neck and horsy buttocks, so high and
haunchy you'd want to clap her on the rear. The wind bellowed around
the house, driving crystals of snow through the cracks of the warped
log door and all of them in the kitchen seemed charged with some intensity of purpose. She'd balanced that broad butt on the edge of the
dog food chest, looking at the old man and Rollo, now and then
rolling her glossy eyes over at Mero, square teeth nipping a rim of nail,
sucking the welling blood, drawing on her cigarette.

The old man drank his Everclear stirred with a peeled willow stick
for the bitter taste. The image of him came sharp in Mero's mind as he
stood at the hall closet contemplating his hats; should he bring one for
the funeral? The old man had had the damnedest curl to his hat brim,
a tight roll on the right where his doffing or donning hand gripped it
and a wavering downslope on the left like a shed roof. You could recognize him two miles away. He wore it at the table listening to the
woman's stories about Tin Head, steadily emptying his glass until he
was nine-times-nine drunk, his gangstery face loosening, the crushed
rodeo nose and scar-crossed eyebrows, the stub ear dissolving as he drank.
Now he must be dead fifty years or more, buried in the mailman sweater.

The girlfriend started a story, yeah, there was this guy named Tin
Head down around Dubois when my dad was a kid. Had a little ranch,
some horses, cows, kids, a wife. But there was something funny about
him. He had a metal plate in his head from falling down some cement
steps.

Plenty of guys has them, said Rollo in a challenging way.

She shook her head. Not like his. His was made out of galvy and it
eat at his brain.

The old man held up the bottle of Everclear, raised his eyebrows at
her: Well, darlin?

She nodded, took the glass from him and knocked it back in one
swallow. Oh, that's not gonna slow *me* down, she said.

Mero expected her to neigh.

So what then, said Rollo, picking at the horse shit under his boot heel. What about Tin Head and his galvanized skull-plate?

I heard it this way, she said. She held out her glass for another shot of Everclear and the old man poured it and she went on.

Mero had thrashed all that ancient night, dreamed of horse breeding or hoarse breathing, whether the act of sex or bloody, cut-throat gasps he didn't know. The next morning he woke up drenched in stinking sweat, looked at the ceiling and said aloud, it could go on like this for some time. He meant cows and weather as much as anything, and what might be his chances two or three states over in any direction. In Woolfoot, riding the Exercycle, he thought the truth was somewhat different: he'd wanted a woman of his own without scrounging the old man's leftovers.

What he wanted to know now, tires spanking the tar-filled road cracks and potholes, funeral homburg sliding on the backseat, was if Rollo had got the girlfriend away from the old man, thrown a saddle on her and ridden off into the sunset?

The interstate, crippled by orange pylons, forced traffic into single lanes, broke his expectation of making good time. His Cadillac, boxed between semis with hissing air brakes, snuffled huge rear tires, framed a looming Peterbilt in the back window. His thoughts clogged as if a comb working through his mind had stuck against a snarl. When the traffic eased and he tried to cover some ground the highway patrol pulled him over. The cop, a pimpled, mustached specimen with mismatched eyes, asked his name, where he was going. For the minute he couldn't think what he was doing there. The cop's tongue dapped at the scraggy mustache while he scribbled.

Funeral, he said suddenly. Going to my brother's funeral.

Well you take it easy, Gramps, or they'll be doing one for you.

You're a little polecat, aren't you, he said, staring at the ticket, at the pathetic handwriting, but the mustache was a mile gone, peeling through the traffic as Mero had peeled out of the ranch road that long time ago, squinting through the abraded windshield. He might have made a more graceful exit but urgency had struck him as a blow on the humerus sends a ringing jolt up the arm. He believed it was the horse-haunched woman leaning against the chest and Rollo fixed on her, the old man swilling Everclear and not noticing or, if noticing, not caring, that had worked in him like a key in an ignition. She had long grey-streaked braids, Rollo could use them for reins.

❊

Yah, she said, in her low and convincing liar's voice. I'll tell you, on Tin Head's ranch things went wrong. Chickens changed color overnight, calves was born with three legs, his kids was piebald and his wife always crying for blue dishes. Tin Head never finished nothing he started, quit halfway through a job every time. Even his pants was half-buttoned so his wienie hung out. He was a mess with the galvy plate eating at his brain and his ranch and his family was a mess. But, she said. They had to eat, didn't they, just like anybody else?

I hope they eat pies better than the ones you make, said Rollo, who didn't like the mouthful of pits that came with the chokecherries.

His interest in women began a few days after the old man had said, take this guy up and show him them Indan drawrings, jerking his head at the stranger. Mero had been eleven or twelve at the time, no older. They rode along the creek and put up a pair of mallards who flew downstream and then suddenly reappeared, pursued by a goshawk who struck the drake with a sound like a handclap. The duck tumbled through the trees and into deadfall trash and the hawk shot as swiftly away as it had come.

They climbed through the stony landscape, limestone beds eroded by wind into fantastic furniture, stale gnawed breadcrusts, tumbled bones, stacks of dirty folded blankets, bleached crab claws and dog teeth. He tethered the horses in the shade of a stand of limber pine and led the anthropologist up through the stiff-branched mountain ma-hogany to the overhang. Above them reared corroded cliffs brilliant with orange lichen, pitted with holes and ledges darkened by millennia of raptor feces.

The anthropologist moved back and forth scrutinizing the stone gallery of red and black drawings: bison skulls, a line of mountain sheep, warriors carrying lances, a turkey stepping into a snare, a stick man upside-down dead and falling, red ochre hands, violent figures with rakes on their heads that he said were feather headdresses, a great red bear dancing forward on its hind legs, concentric circles and crosses and latticework. He copied the drawings in his notebook, saying rubba-dubba a few times.

That's the sun, said the anthropologist who resembled an unfin-ished drawing himself, pointing at an archery target, ramming his pen-cil into the air as though tapping gnats. That's an atlatl and that's a dragonfly. There we go. You know what this is; and he touched a cloven oval, rubbing the cleft with his dusty fingers. He got down on his hands and knees, pointed out more, a few dozen.

A horseshoe?

A horseshoe! The anthropologist laughed. No boy, it's a vulva. That's what all of these are. You don't know what that is, do you? You go to school on Monday and look it up in the dictionary.

It's a symbol, he said. You know what a symbol is?

Yes, said Mero, who had seen them clapped together in the high school marching band. The anthropologist laughed and told him he had a great future, gave him a dollar for showing him the place. Listen, kid, the Indians did it just like anybody else, he said.

He had looked the word up in the school dictionary, slammed the book closed in embarrassment, but the image was fixed for him (with the brassy background sound of a military march), blunt ochre tracing on stone, and no fleshy examples ever conquered his belief in the subterranean stony structure of female genitalia, the pubic bone a proof, except for the old man's girlfriend whom he imagined down on all fours, entered from behind and whinnying like a mare, a thing not of geology but flesh.

Thursday night, balked by detours and construction, he was on the outskirts of Des Moines and no farther. In the cinderblock motel room he set the alarm but his own stertorous breathing woke him before it rang. He was up at five-fifteen, eyes aflame, peering through the vinyl drapes at his snow-hazed car flashing blue under the motel sign SLEEP SLEEP. In the bathroom he mixed the packet of instant motel coffee and drank it black without ersatz sugar or chemical cream. He wanted the caffeine. The roots of his mind felt withered and punky.

A cold morning, light snow slanting down: he unlocked the Cadillac, started it and curved into the vein of traffic, all semis, double- and triple-trailers. In the headlights' red glare he missed the westbound ramp and got into torn-up muddy streets, swung right and right again, using the motel's SLEEP sign as a landmark, but he was on the wrong side of the interstate and the sign belonged to a different motel.

Another mudholed lane took him into a traffic circle of commuters sucking coffee from insulated cups, pastries sliding on dashboards. Halfway around the hoop he spied the interstate entrance ramp, veered for it, collided with a panel truck emblazoned STOP SMOKING! HYPNOSIS THAT WORKS!, was rammed from behind by a stretch limo, the limo in its turn rear-ended by a yawning hydroblast operator in a company pickup.

He saw little of this, pressed into his seat by the air bag, his mouth full of a rubbery, dusty taste, eyeglasses cutting into his nose. His first thought was to blame Iowa and those who lived in it. There were a few round spots of blood on his shirt cuff.

A star-spangled Band-Aid over his nose, he watched his crumpled car, pouring dark fluids onto the highway, towed away behind a wrecker. A taxi took him, his suitcase, the homburg funeral hat, in the other direction to Posse Motors where lax salesmen drifted like disorbited satellites and where he bought a secondhand Cadillac, black like the wreck, but three years older and the upholstery not cream leather but sun-faded velour. He had the good tires from the wreck brought over and mounted. He could do that if he liked, buy cars like packs of cigarettes and smoke them up. He didn't care for the way it handled out on the highway, throwing itself abruptly aside when he twitched the wheel and he guessed it might have a bent frame. Damn, he'd buy another for the return trip. He could do what he wanted.

He was half an hour past Kearney, Nebraska, when the full moon rose, an absurd visage balanced in his rearview mirror, above it a curled wig of a cloud, filamented edges like platinum hairs. He felt his swollen nose, palped his chin, tender from the stun of the air bag. Before he slept that night he swallowed a glass of hot tap water enlivened with whiskey, crawled into the damp bed. He had eaten nothing all day yet his stomach coiled at the thought of road food.

He dreamed that he was in the ranch house but all the furniture had been removed from the rooms and in the yard troops in dirty white uniforms fought. The concussive reports of huge guns were breaking the window glass and forcing the floorboards apart so that he had to walk on the joists and below the disintegrating floors he saw galvanized tubs filled with dark, coagulated fluid.

On Saturday morning, with four hundred miles in front of him, he swallowed a few bites of scorched eggs, potatoes painted with canned *salsa verde,* a cup of yellow coffee, left no tip, got on the road. The food was not what he wanted. His breakfast habit was two glasses of mineral water, six cloves of garlic, a pear. The sky to the west hulked sullen, behind him smears of tinselly orange shot through with blinding streaks. The thick rim of sun bulged against the horizon.

He crossed the state line, hit Cheyenne for the second time in sixty years. There was neon, traffic and concrete, but he knew the place, a railroad town that had been up and down. That other time he had been painfully hungry, had gone into the restaurant in the Union Pacific station although he was not used to restaurants and ordered a steak, but when the woman brought it and he cut into the meat the blood spread across the white plate and he couldn't help it, he saw the beast, mouth agape in mute bawling, saw the comic aspects of his revulsion as well, a cattleman gone wrong.

Now he parked in front of a phone booth, locked the car although he stood only seven feet away, and telephoned the number Tick's wife had given him. The ruined car had had a phone. Her voice roared out of the earpiece.

We didn't hear so we wondered if you changed your mind.

No, he said, I'll be there late this afternoon. I'm in Cheyenne now.

The wind's blowing pretty hard. They're saying it could maybe snow. In the mountains. Her voice sounded doubtful.

I'll keep an eye on it, he said.

He was out of town and running north in a few minutes.

The country poured open on each side, reduced the Cadillac to a finger-snap. Nothing had changed, not a goddamn thing, the empty pale place and its roaring wind, the distant antelope as tiny as mice, landforms shaped true to the past. He felt himself slip back, the calm of eighty-three years sheeted off him like water, replaced by a young man's scalding anger at a fool world and the fools in it. What a damn hard time it had been to hit the road. You don't know what it was like, he told his ex-wives until they said they did know, he'd pounded it into their ears two hundred times, the poor youth on the street holding up a sign asking for work, and the job with the furnace man, *yatata yatata ya.* Thirty miles out of Cheyenne he saw the first billboard, DOWN UNDER WYOMING, *Western Fun the Western Way,* over a blown-up photograph of kangaroos hopping through the sagebrush and a blond child grinning in a manic imitation of pleasure. A diagonal banner warned, *Open May 31.*

So what, Rollo had said to the old man's girlfriend, what about that Mr. Tin Head? Looking at her, not just her face, but up and down, eyes moving over her like an iron over a shirt and the old man in his mailman's sweater and lopsided hat tasting his Everclear and not noticing or not caring, getting up every now and then to lurch onto the porch and water the weeds. When he left the room the tension ebbed and they were only ordinary people to whom nothing happened. Rollo looked away from the woman, leaned down to scratch the dog's ears, saying, Snarleyow Snapper, and the woman brought a dish to the sink and ran water on it, yawning. When the old man came back to his chair, the Everclear like sweet oil in his glass, glances resharpened and inflections of voice again carried complex messages.

Well well, she said, tossing her braids back, every year Tin Head butchers one of his steers, and that's what they'd eat all winter long, boiled, fried, smoked, fricasseed, burned and raw. So one time he's out there by the barn and he hits the steer a good one with the axe and it drops stun down. He ties up the back legs, hoists it up and sticks it, shoves the tub under to catch the blood. When it's bled out pretty good he lets it down and starts skinning it, starts with the head, cuts back of the poll down past the eye to the nose, peels the hide back. He don't cut the head off but keeps on skinning, dewclaws to hock up the inside of the thigh and then to the cod and down the middle of the belly to brisket to tail. Now he's ready to start siding, working that tough old skin off. But siding is hard work — (the old man nodded) — and he gets the hide off about halfway and starts thinking about dinner. So he leaves the steer half-skinned there on the ground and he goes into the kitchen, but first he cuts out the tongue which is his favorite dish all cooked up and eat cold with Mrs. Tin Head's mustard in a forget-me-not teacup. Sets it on the ground and goes in to dinner. Dinner is chicken and dumplins, one of them changed-color chickens started out white and ended up blue, yessir, blue as your old daddy's eyes.

She was a total liar. The old man's eyes were murk brown.

Onto the high plains sifted the fine snow, delicately clouding the air, a rare dust, beautiful, he thought, silk gauze, but there was muscle in the wind rocking the heavy car, a great pulsing artery of the jet stream swooping down from the sky to touch the earth. Plumes of smoke rose hundreds of feet into the air, elegant fountains and twisting snow devils, shapes of veiled Arab women and ghost riders dissolving in white fume. The snow snakes writhing across the asphalt straightened into rods. He was driving in a rushing river of cold whiteout foam. He could see nothing, trod on the brake, the wind buffeting the car, a bitter, hard-flung dust hissing over metal and glass. The car shuddered. And as suddenly as it had risen the wind dropped and the road was clear; he could see a long, empty mile.

How do you know when there's enough of anything? What trips the lever that snaps up the STOP sign? What electrical currents fizz and crackle in the brain to shape the decision to quit a place? He had listened to her damn story and the dice had rolled. For years he believed he had left without hard reason and suffered for it. But he'd learned from television nature programs that it had been time for him to find his own territory and his own woman. How many women were out there! He had married three or four of them and sampled plenty.

With the lapping subtlety of incoming tide the shape of the ranch began to gather in his mind; he could recall the intimate fences he'd made, taut wire and perfect corners, the draws and rock outcrops, the watercourse valley steepening, cliffs like bones with shreds of meat on them rising and rising, and the stream plunging suddenly underground, disappearing into subterranean darkness of blind fish, shooting out of the mountain ten miles west on a neighbor's place, but leaving their ranch some badland red country as dry as a cracker, steep canyons with high caves suited to lions. He and Rollo had shot two early in that winter close to the overhang with the painted vulvas. There were good caves up there from a lion's point of view.

He traveled against curdled sky. In the last sixty miles the snow began again. He climbed out of Buffalo. Pallid flakes as distant from each other as galaxies flew past, then more and in ten minutes he was crawling at twenty miles an hour, the windshield wipers thumping like a stick dragged down the stairs.

The light was falling out of the day when he reached the pass, the blunt mountains lost in snow, the greasy hairpin turns ahead. He drove slowly and steadily in a low gear; he had not forgotten how to drive a winter mountain. But the wind was up again, rocking and slapping the car, blotting out all but whipping snow and he was sweating with the anxiety of keeping to the road, dizzy with the altitude. Twelve more miles, sliding and buffeted, before he reached Ten Sleep where streetlights glowed in revolving circles like Van Gogh's sun. There had not been electricity when he left the place. In those days there were seventeen black, lightless miles between the town and the ranch, and now the long arch of years compressed into that distance. His headlights picked up a sign: 20 MILES TO DOWN UNDER WYOMING. Emus and bison leered above the letters.

He turned onto the snowy road marked with a single set of tracks, faint but still discernible, the heater fan whirring, the radio silent, all beyond the headlights blurred. Yet everything was as it had been, the shape of the road achingly familiar, sentinel rocks looming as they had in his youth. There was an eerie dream quality in seeing the deserted Farrier place leaning east as it had leaned sixty years ago, the Banner ranch gate, where the companionable tracks he had been following turned off, the gate ghostly in the snow but still flying its wrought iron flag, unmarked by the injuries of weather, and the taut five-strand fences and dim shifting forms of cattle. Next would come the road to their ranch, a left-hand turn just over the crest of a rise. He was running now on the unmarked road through great darkness.

Winking at Rollo the girlfriend said, yes, she had said, yes sir, Tin Head eats half his dinner and then he has to take a little nap. After a while he wakes up again and goes outside stretching his arms and yawning, says, guess I'll finish skinning out that steer. But the steer ain't there. It's gone. Only the tongue, laying on the ground all covered with dirt and straw, and the tub of blood and the dog licking at it.

It was her voice that drew you in, that low, twangy voice, wouldn't matter if she was saying the alphabet, what you heard was the rustle of hay. She could make you smell the smoke from an unlit fire.

How could he not recognize the turnoff to the ranch? It was so clear and sharp in his mind: the dusty crimp of the corner, the low section where the snow drifted, the run where willows slapped the side of the truck. He went a mile, watching for it, but the turn didn't come up, then watched for the Bob Kitchen place two miles beyond, but the distance unrolled and there was nothing. He made a three-point turn and backtracked. Rollo must have given up the old entrance road, for it wasn't there. The Kitchen place was gone to fire or wind. If he didn't find the turn it was no great loss; back to Ten Sleep and scout a motel. But he hated to quit when he was close enough to spit, hated to retrace black miles on a bad night when he was maybe twenty minutes away from the ranch.

He drove very slowly, following his tracks, and the ranch entrance appeared on the right although the gate was gone and the sign down. That was why he'd missed it, that and a clump of sagebrush that obscured the gap.

He turned in, feeling a little triumph. But the road under the snow was rough and got rougher until he was bucking along over boulders and slanted rock and knew wherever he was it was not right.

He couldn't turn around on the narrow track and began backing gingerly, the window down, craning his stiff neck, staring into the redness cast by the taillights. The car's right rear tire rolled up over a boulder, slid and sank into a quaggy hole. The tires spun in the snow, but he got no purchase.

I'll sit here, he said aloud. I'll sit here until it's light and then walk down to the Banner place and ask for a cup of coffee. I'll be cold but I won't freeze to death. It played like a joke the way he imagined it with Bob Banner opening the door and saying, why, it's Mero, come on in and have some java and a hot biscuit, before he remembered that Bob Banner would have to be 120 years old to play that role. He was maybe three miles from Banner's gate, and the Banner ranch house was another seven miles beyond the gate. Say a ten-mile hike at altitude in a snowstorm. On the other hand he had half a tank of gas. He could run the car for a while, then turn it off, start it again all through the night. It was bad luck, but that's all. The trick was patience.

He dozed half an hour in the wind-rocked car, woke shivering and cramped. He wanted to lie down. He thought perhaps he could put a flat rock under the goddamn tire. Never say die, he said, feeling around the passenger-side floor for the flashlight in his emergency bag, then remembering the wrecked car towed away, the flares and car phone and AAA card and flashlight and matches and candle and Power Bars and bottle of water still in it, and probably now in the damn tow-driver's damn wife's car. He might get a good enough look anyway in the snow-reflected light. He put on his gloves and the heavy overcoat, got out and locked the car, sidled around to the rear, bent down. The tail-lights lit the snow beneath the rear of the car like a fresh bloodstain. There was a cradle-sized depression eaten out by the spinning tire. Two or three flat ones might get him out, or small round ones, he was not going to insist on the perfect stone. The wind tore at him, the snow was certainly drifting up. He began to shuffle on the road, feeling with his feet for rocks he could move, the car's even throbbing promising motion and escape. The wind was sharp and his ears ached. His wool cap was in the damn emergency bag.

My lord, she continued, Tin Head is just startled to pieces when he don't see that steer. He thinks somebody, some neighbor don't like him, plenty of them, come and stole it. He looks around for tire marks or footprints but there's nothing except old cow tracks. He puts his hand up to his eyes and stares away. Nothing in the north, the south, the east, but way over there in the west on the side of the mountain he sees something moving stiff and slow, stumbling along. It looks raw and it's got something bunchy and wet hanging down over its hind-quarters. Yah, it was the steer, never making no sound. And just then it stops and it looks back. And all that distance Tin Head can see the raw meat of the head and the shoulder muscles and the empty mouth without no tongue open wide and its red eyes glaring at him, pure tee-total hate like arrows coming at him, and he knows he is done for and all of his kids and their kids is done for, and that his wife is done for and that every one of her blue dishes has got to break, and the dog that licked the blood is done for, and the house where they lived has to blow away or burn up and every fly or mouse in it.

There was a silence and she added, that's it. And it all went against him, too.

That's it? said Rollo. That's all there is to it?

Yet he knew he was on the ranch, he felt it and he knew this road, too. It was not the main ranch road but some lower entrance he could not quite recollect that cut in below the river. Now he remembered that the main entrance gate was on a side road that branched off well before the Banner place. He found a good stone, another, wondering which track this could be; the map of the ranch in his memory was not as bright now, but scuffed and obliterated as though trodden. The remembered gates collapsed, fences wavered, while the badland features swelled into massive prominence. The cliffs bulged into the sky, lions snarled, the river corkscrewed through a stone hole at a tremendous rate and boulders cascaded from the heights. Beyond the barbwire something moved.

He grasped the car door handle. It was locked. Inside, by the dashboard glow, he could see the gleam of the keys in the ignition where he'd left them to keep the car running. It was almost funny. He picked up a big two-handed rock and smashed it on the driver's-side window, slipped his arm in through the hole, into the delicious warmth of the car, a contortionist's reach, twisting behind the steering wheel and down, and had he not kept limber with exercise and nut cutlets and green leafy vegetables he never could have reached the keys. His fingers grazed and then grasped the keys and he had them. This is how they sort the men out from the boys, he said aloud. As his fingers closed on the keys he glanced at the passenger door. The lock button stood high. And even had it been locked as well, why had he strained to reach the keys when he had only to lift the lock button on the driver's side? Cursing, he pulled out the rubber floor mats and arranged them over the stones, stumbled around the car once more. He was dizzy, tremendously thirsty and hungry, opened his mouth to snowflakes. He had eaten nothing for two days but the burned eggs that morning. He could eat a dozen burned eggs now.

The snow roared through the broken window. He put the car in reverse and slowly trod the gas. The car lurched and steadied in the track and once more he was twisting his neck, backing in the red glare, twenty feet, thirty, but slipping and spinning; there was too much snow. He was backing up an incline that had seemed level on the way in but showed itself now as a remorselessly long hill studded with rocks and deep in snow. His incoming tracks twisted like rope. He forced out another twenty feet spinning the tires until they smoked, and the rear wheels slewed sideways off the track and into a two-foot ditch, the engine died and that was it. It was almost a relief to have reached this point where the celestial fingernails were poised to nip his thread. He dismissed the ten-mile distance to the Banner place: it might not be that far, or maybe they had pulled the ranch closer to the main road. A truck might come by. Shoes slipping, coat buttoned awry, he might find the mythical Grand Hotel in the sagebrush.

On the main road his tire tracks showed as a faint pattern in the pearly apricot light from the risen moon, winking behind roiling clouds of snow. His blurred shadow strengthened whenever the wind eased. Then the violent country showed itself, the cliffs rearing at the moon, the snow smoking off the prairie like steam, the white flank of the ranch slashed with fence cuts, the sagebrush glittering and along the creek black tangles of willow bunched like dead hair. There were cattle in the field beside the road, their plumed breaths catching the moony glow like comic strip dialogue balloons.

He walked against the wind, his shoes filled with snow, feeling as easy to tear as a man cut from paper. As he walked he noticed one from the herd inside the fence was keeping pace with him. He walked more slowly and the animal lagged. He stopped and turned. It stopped as well, huffing vapor, regarding him, a strip of snow on its back like a linen runner. It tossed its head and in the howling, wintry light he saw he'd been wrong again, that the half-skinned steer's red eye had been watching for him all this time.

ANNIE PROULX

The Blood Bay

For Buzzy Malli

The winter of 1886–87 was terrible. Every goddamn history of the high plains says so. There were great stocks of cattle on overgrazed land during the droughty summer. Early wet snow froze hard so the cattle could not break through the crust to the grass. Blizzards and freeze-eye cold followed, the gant bodies of cattle piling up in draws and coulees.

A young Montana cowboy, somewhat vain, had skimped on coat and mittens and put all his wages into a fine pair of handmade boots. He crossed into Wyoming Territory thinking it would be warmer, for it was south of where he was. That night he froze to death on Powder River's bitter west bank, that stream of famous dimensions and direction — an inch deep, a mile wide and she flows uphill from Texas.

The next afternoon three cowpunchers from the Box Spring outfit near Suggs rode past his corpse, blue as a whetstone and half-buried in snow. They were savvy and salty. They wore blanket coats, woolly chaps, grease-wool scarves tied over their hats and under their bristled chins, sheepskin mitts and two of them were fortunate enough to park their feet in good boots and heavy socks. The third, Dirt Sheets, a cross-eyed drinker of hair-oil, was all right on top but his luck was running muddy near the bottom, no socks and curl-toe boots cracked and holed.

"That can a corn beef's wearin my size boots," Sheets said and got off his horse for the first time that day. He pulled at the Montana cowboy's left boot but it was frozen on. The right one didn't come off any easier.

"Son of a sick steer in a snowbank," he said, "I'll cut em off and thaw em after supper." Sheets pulled out a Bowie knife and sawed through Montana's shins just above the boot tops, put the booted feet in his saddlebags, admiring the tooled leather and topstitched hearts and clubs. They rode on down the river looking for strays, found a dozen bogged in deep drifts and lost most of the daylight getting them out.

"Too late to try for the bunkhouse. Old man Grice's shack is somewheres up along. He's bound a have dried prunes or other dainties or at least a hot stove." The temperature was dropping, so cold that spit crackled in the air and a man didn't dare to piss for fear he'd be rooted fast until spring. They agreed it must be forty below and more, the wind scything up a nice Wyoming howler.

They found the shack four miles north. Old man Grice opened the door a crack.

"Come on in, puncher or rustler, I don't care."

"We'll put our horses up. Where's the barn."

"Barn. Never had one. There's a lean-to out there behind the woodpile should keep em from blowin away or maybe freezin. I got my two horses in here beside the dish cupboard. I pamper them babies somethin terrible. Sleep where you can find a space, but I'm tellin you don't bother that blood bay none, he will mull you up and spit you out. He's a spirited steed. Pull up a chair and have some a this son-of-a-bitch stew. And I got plenty conversation juice a wash it down. Hot biscuits just comin out a the oven."

It was a fine evening, eating, drinking and playing cards, swapping lies, the stove kicking out heat, old man Grice's spoiled horses sighing in comfort. The only disagreeable tone to the evening from the waddies' point of view was the fact that their host cleaned them out, took them for three dollars and four bits. Around midnight Grice blew out the lamp and got in his bunk and the three punchers stretched out on the floor. Sheets set his trophies behind the stove, laid his head on his saddle and went to sleep.

He woke half an hour before daylight, recalled it was his mother's birthday and if he wanted to telegraph a filial sentiment to her he would have to ride faster than chain lightning with the links snapped, for the Overland office closed at noon. He checked his grisly trophies, found them thawed and pulled the boots and socks off the originals, drew them onto his own pedal extremities. He threw the bare Montana feet and his old boots in the corner near the dish cupboard, slipped out like a falling feather, saddled his horse and rode away. The wind was low and the fine cold air refreshed him.

Old man Grice was up with the sun grinding coffee beans and frying bacon. He glanced down at his rolled-up guests and said, "Coffee's ready." The blood bay stamped and kicked at something that looked like a man's foot. Old man Grice took a closer look.

"There's a bad start to the day," he said, "it is a man's foot and there's the other." He counted the sleeping guests. There were only two of them.

"Wake up, survivors, for god's sake wake up and get up."

The two punchers rolled out, stared wild-eyed at the old man who was fairly frothing, pointing at the feet on the floor behind the blood bay.

"He's ate Sheets. Ah, I knew he was a hard horse, but to eat a man whole. You savage bugger," he screamed at the blood bay and drove him out into the scorching cold. "You'll never eat human meat again. You'll sleep out with the blizzards and wolves, you hell-bound fiend." Secretly he was pleased to own a horse with the sand to eat a raw cowboy.

The leftover Box Spring riders were up and drinking coffee. They squinted at old man Grice, hitched at their gun belts.

"Ah, boys, for god's sake, it was a terrible accident. I didn't know what a brute of a animal was that blood bay. Let's keep this to ourselves. Sheets was no prize and I've got forty gold dollars says so and the three and four bits I took off a you last night. Eat your bacon, don't make no trouble. There's enough trouble in the world without no more."

No, they wouldn't make trouble and they put the heavy money in their saddlebags, drank a last cup of hot coffee, saddled up and rode out into the grinning morning.

When they saw Sheets that night at the bunkhouse they nodded, congratulated him on his mother's birthday but said nothing about blood bays or forty-three dollars and four bits. The arithmetic stood comfortable.

Stacey Richter

Stacey Richter's stories are driven by a big beat — she is adept, daring, and funny, and she manages to hit all the drums all the time. These are stories fueled by drugs, teen angst, and rock and roll, and they are alternately cheerful, absurd, droll, sad, and affecting. In evidence, I quote the opening of "Prom Night," one of the thirteen narratives that compose her first collection, *My Date with Satan*: "In the beginning was everything, and it was promised to us, but we didn't possess anything of it yet. There was, for example, a gorgeous night perfumed with citrus blossoms, and we were in our gowns, driving drunk and on drugs. Somewhere there was a prom, and we wanted to go there. Our parents were so old that within their lifetimes they had put rubber bands around their kitchen doorknobs and watched them decay and fall off. I personally did not intend to live that long." Tone and attitude are everything here — they carry the piece into the maelstrom of the prom and a disillusionment that is precisely tuned to the opening observations. The narrator of "Goal 666" is a member of a posturing Scandinavian satanic metal band: "We must love nature, and we must rape nature for Satan!" In "Rats Eat Cats," the speaker is a young woman whose object in life is to become a "Cat Lady," "an old woman who lives 'by herself' with as many as seventy-five cats in a one-bedroom apartment."

What I admire in Richter's work is her effortless blend of the comedic and the poignant, her insistence that a story can emanate from even the most bizarre situations and yet remain true to the highest aesthetic standards. People often distinguish between the comic and the serious in literature, but the best comedy is very serious indeed, as "The Beauty Treatment" illustrates. For all its concern with fads and brand names, for all its very funny lines, the story is intense and revealing (and it bears comparison with Junot Díaz's "The Brief Wondrous Life of Oscar Wao" for its investment in pop culture — will the specificity date these stories? What of the allusions to another period in Beattie's "The Burning House"?). The second story here, "The Cavemen in the Hedges," begins with a whimsical premise and twists it round till the absurd world it creates reflects on the one we live in, and the hapless cavemen, sleeping beneath bridges and in the bushes behind our suburban houses, become succedanea for the homeless, the refugees, for the lost and bewildered legions who live close to the earth because they have no other choice.

The Beauty Treatment

She smiled when she saw me coming, the Bitch, she smiled and stuck her fingers in her mouth like she was plucking gum out of her dental work. Then, with a little pout, like a kiss, I saw a line of silver slide toward my face. I swear to God, I thought she'd pried off her braces. I thought she'd worked one of those bands free and was holding it up to show me how proud she was to have broken loose of what we referred to, in our charming teenage banter, as oral bondage. The next thing I know there's blood all over my J. Crew linen fitted blouse, in edelweiss — a very delicate, almost ecru shade of white, ruined now. There's blood all over the tops of my tits where they pushed out my J. Crew edelweiss linen shirt and a loose feeling around my mouth when I screamed. My first thought was Fuck, how embarrassing, then I ran into the girls' room and saw it: a red gash parted my cheek from my left temple to the corner of my lip. A steady stream of blood dripped off my jawline into the sink. One minute later, Cyndy Dashnaw found the razor blade on the concrete floor of the breezeway, right where the Bitch had dropped it.

Elizabeth Beecher and Kirsty Moseley run into the bathroom and go Oh my God, then drag me screaming hysterically, all three of us screaming hysterically, to Ms. B. Meanwhile, the Bitch slides into her Mercedes 450SL, lime green if you can believe that — the A-1 primo daddylac of all time — and drives off smoking Kools. I'm in the nurse's office screaming with Ms. B. calmly applying pressure and ordering Mr. Pierce, the principal, to get in gear and haul my ass to the emergency room. This is what you get from watching too much TV, I'm thinking, and believing your workaholic father when he tells you during one of his rare appearances that you're the Princess of the Universe to which none can compare. And then watching teenage girls from Detroit on *Montel,* for God's sake — the *inner city* — froth and brag about hiding razors under their tongues and cutting up some ho because she glanced sideways at the boyfriend: I mean, help me. This is the twentieth century. My father's a doctor. The Bitch's father is a developer who's covered half of Scottsdale with lifestyle condos. We consume the most expensive drugs, cosmetics, and coffee known to man. Tell me: what was she thinking?

I went to the emergency room where the nurse gave me a shot to stop the screaming and eventually my mother came down and the nurse had to give her a pill to stop her from screaming too. Once Mother had sufficiently calmed she paged Dr. Wohl, who'd done her tits, and had him run down and stitch me up with some special Indonesian silk that would make me look, he promised, like a slightly rakish movie star. Afterward, during the healing process, was when my mother really started broadcasting the wonders of Smith College and Mount Holyoke or, if worse came to worse, Mills. Women's colleges were so liberating, she said, waving her tennis elbow around to signify freedom. It was such a blessing, she said, to study without all that nasty competition and distraction from boys. That's when I knew I was in for it. If my mother, who wanted nothing more than for me to marry a Jewish doctor like she had — to duplicate her glorious life and live bored and frustrated in the suburbs and flirt with the other bald, wrinkled, fat, ugly doctors at the tennis club on Wednesday afternoons — if *this* mother was trying to usher me away from the prying eyes of young, male, pre-med students, I knew it was all over for me. I knew my looks were shot.

And another thing — as if I'd relish the thought of living with a bunch of chicks in hormonal flux after a prime example, the Bitch, my best friend, sliced a gill into my cheek for no apparent reason. Why did she do it? they kept asking. What happened between you? Ask her yourself, I replied. Ask the Bitch. But I knew she would never tell. How could she? It was bad enough that they took her down to the police station and put her in a cell without air-conditioning until her daddy showed up with *two* lawyers and escorted her out of there like she was Queen of the May Parade. It was bad enough that she got kicked out of Phoenix Country Day and had to go to Judson — *Judson,* where bad kids from California with parents who didn't want them were sent to board. At Judson, even the high school students had to wear uniforms.

Uniforms, ha ha, it served her right. After The Accident as my mother called it, or The Beauty Treatment, as my father referred to it, I was treated like that guy my verbal teacher at Princeton Review told us about, the prodigal son, but a female version. Did I shop? I shopped till I dropped. I had all the latest stuff from the stores *and* the catalogs. I had six pairs of Doc Martens, a set of sterling flatware (for my dowry), and a Chanel suit. We flew to New York to get the suit. All this accompanied by the message — through word and gesture of Arthur and Judi, doting parents — that no matter what I had, I could not have enough. Not only did I deserve this, I deserved this and more. I had suffered, and every available style of Swatch would bring relief.

The Bitch, meanwhile, was slogging through her days in a tartan skirt and knee socks. She was locked in a world without jewelry, hand-bags, or accessories. White shirt, button-down collar — no patterns, no decorations, no excuses. They couldn't even wear a demure white-on-white check. We got the lowdown from the Judson Cactus Wrens at soccer matches — big, bitter girls who charged the ball with clenched teeth and didn't even talk among themselves at half-time. They told us about the uniform requirements with a weird, stiff pride, like they were army recruits. Talk about future sadistic Phys Ed instructors, those Wrens were hard. Every time we had a game against them, half the Country Day girls got convenience periods and skipped out on a nurse's pass.

Even when I really did have my period, I never got a pass. I wasn't afraid of anything anymore, as long as the Bitch wasn't on the Judson soccer team, which she wasn't. I mean, what could happen that would be worse than what I had already gone through? Getting kicked in the shin? A torn earlobe? Being snubbed by Bobby English? Give me a break. I'd seen pain and passed through it. I was a superhero. I was a goddamn Jewish Joan of Arc riding a convertible Volkswagen Rabbit in a lemon yellow Chanel suit. After a few months, so many people had asked me what was wrong with my face that it stopped bothering me and I began to have fun with it. I even managed to work in some of my vocabulary words.

"I was on the back of Johnny Depp's motorcycle. He tried to feel me up, like the callow youth he is, and we wiped out."

And, "I was wearing Lee press-on nails and had the most vehement itch."

Or my personal favorite, "My father did it by accident, whilst beat-ing me zealously," which got horrified looks, especially from medical personnel.

All in all, things weren't so bad. Everyone at school was being really nice, and I was getting extra time to make up my homework. This while the Bitch had to either go straight home from school or go directly to the shrink. Even her stupid, doting mother thought she was crazy for a day or two; I know because her mom and my mom are friends, though I must say the relationship is, oh, a bit *strained.* The Bitch must have put them off with a fake story because if she ever told the truth they'd put her in the nuthouse with her schizophrenic brother where she probably belongs. She must have told them that I had stolen her boyfriend or shafted her on a dope deal. She must have told them something that would have sounded plausible on *Oprah* or *Montel,* something gritty and real — the kind of thing they wanted. When the truth is the Bitch started hating me one day out of the clear blue after we'd been friends for six years, since we were ten years old, because I wanted to go into a store and buy the sheet music for "Brokenhearted," a song made famous by the singer Brandy.

The Bitch hated Brandy. The Bitch was going through what Mr. Nesbit, our school counselor, referred to as a *phase*. The Bitch, natural born white girl, with a special pair of Mormon panties in her dresser and her own frequent flyer miles on her own credit card, wanted to be a homegirl. She had her dishwater hair done up in scrawny braids and got paste-on acrylic nails with a charm on the ring finger that said "Nubian." She wore deep brown lipstick from the Soul Collection at Walgreen's. When her braids got frizzy, which didn't take long, she slicked them back with Afro Sheen.

I, on the other hand, did not wish to be a homegirl. I figured it was my lot to try to survive as a rich, white Jewish girl who could not do the splits and therefore would never be a cheerleader and it would be fruitless to reach for anything else. I had nothing against black people, though it's true I didn't know any. Was it my fault there weren't any black families clamoring to send their children to Phoenix Country Day? Was it my fault my parents trundled me off to a snooty private school? Hell no! I was a pawn, a child, and the worst sin I was guilty of, according to those tablets Moses obtained, was taking off my bra for Bobby English and ridiculing my loving parents whenever I got a chance. Thus, I had no longings to be a homegirl, and it pissed the Bitch off. She said I was spoiled. She said we should be tough. She said black chicks were the coolest and saw the world for what it really was — a jungle; a merciless, dog-eat-dog world.

Which struck me as strange, especially considering the Bitch had the sweetest dog in the world named, perhaps ironically, Blackie. Blackie was getting pretty old but still had some spunk. Right up to the day of the razor incident, the Bitch and I would take her out to the golf course in the evenings and let her bite streams of water shooting from the sprinklers. That dog was great. We both loved Blackie and urged her to go get the sprinklers, to really kill 'em; then she would lie down panting in the wet grass and act like she was never going to get up. The Bitch and I frequently discussed what we would do if tragedy struck and the dog died. Blackie was fourteen and had been the Bitch's companion almost her entire life. The void, the terrible void that would be left behind. We discussed filling it with taxidermy. She would have her stuffed, the Bitch said, in the sprinkler-biting posture, because that was when Blackie was the happiest, and we were the happiest sharing in her joy. She would put it on her credit card.

The loss of Blackie loomed all the more ominous, I suppose, since the Bitch's adoring father basically never came home from work and the Bitch's mother was preoccupied trying to get the schizophrenic brother either into or out of commitment. The brother was smoking a lot of pot and talking to little guys from Canada or Planet Centaur, it just depended. On occasion he'd be struck by the notion that the Bitch was the Bride of Pure Evil and one day he stuck a fork in her thigh. In return, she bit him, then took off her shirt and showed him her tits, which mortified him so much he ran around the house for a while, then curled up in the corner. After that, if he was slipping, she'd wear a nursing bra at home so she could flash him when he got out of line.

All the while Blackie padded around after the Bitch, hoping for attention. She was a nuzzler, and even if the Bitch was busy doing something else she would insinuate her nose underneath one of her hands and just freeze there, pretending to be petted. It was touching. At night she would fall into a twitchy sleep beside the Bitch's bed. Every now and then she'd struggle to her feet and go stick her nose under the Bitch's arm or foot for a minute and hold it there. It was like she had to touch the Bitch every so often to make sure she was still okay. That dog was great. In fact, Blackie was probably the one creature she could count on, aside from me, and I could see why her decrepitude made the Bitch nervous.

Around the time Blackie was fading and her brother was going insane, the Bitch started acting even more homegirl and tough and was irked to high hell that I wouldn't get with the program. She was listening to all this gangsta rap in her Mercedes and never taking off her wraparound shades until the teacher made a specific and pointed request. I mean, even our favorite teacher, Mrs. DeMarzo, who talked like Katharine Hepburn, had to tell her to take them off. She had all these garments from the mall in extra large sizes which she referred to as "dope." Of course, do I have to mention the Bitch is not one iota interested in *actually* hanging with the homegirls? I mean, she's not driving down to the South Side and having her Alpine stereo gouged from her dashboard while she rounds up some sistahs to talk jive with, or whatever. She is hanging with me and the other fair students of Phoenix Country Day School as always, but she's acting like she's too cool for us, like she's doing us a favor.

She was annoying, but I never considered dumping her. With me, in private, she wasn't so bad. I mean, the Bitch lived right down the street and we'd been best friends since fourth grade, when being best friends really meant something. I'd only seen one miracle in my sixteen years of life and the Bitch had been its agent. The miracle wasn't much, but it was enough to make me believe that there was some kind of power floating around in the universe and that the Bitch had a little influence with it. I figured that if I stuck close to her, my life would periodically be visited by blessings and magic, like in fairy tales. What happened was this: we were eleven years old, sitting in my room on top of the rainbow Marimekko print comforter, beneath the Olympische Spiele München posters, talking animatedly and intimately about whatever. Suddenly, the Bitch gasped and pointed to the candy-colored Venetian glass chandelier my mother brought back on the trip to Europe she took without my father. A beat of time passed. And then the chandelier winked out.

Actually, the power had gone out in the whole neighborhood. If there'd been a sound or a pulse in the light, I hadn't noticed it, and when I asked the Bitch why she'd pointed at the chandelier, she said, "Because I knew something was going to happen." Oh my God, was I a bored little girl. Did I ever want to hitch my star to someone who knew something was going to happen.

So I overlooked her flaws, her erratic behavior, her insistence I smoke Kools and endure the strains of gangsta rappers calling me a bee-atch because at least around her, things were interesting. I tried to make light of her attitude, figuring it would pass, but I wasn't sacrificing anything of myself, understand? I mean, I wanted that Brandy sheet music. I didn't care that I couldn't play the piano or any other musical instrument. That wasn't the point. I wanted "Brokenhearted" because it had this great picture of Brandy, a beautiful girl, on the cover and I thought it was cool. Me, *I* thought it was cool. Well, the Bitch was just not having any of this. For one thing, Brandy's black, which apparently is her territory and she's the big fucking expert. For another thing, she says Brandy is "an ugly little crossover wimp" and not a real homegirl and I'm an asshole if I like her. I mean, so what? So, I like Brandy. So shoot me. So pitch a fit, which she did, peeling out in her 450SL and leaving me in the parking lot of a C-mall. So slice my face with a fucking razor blade.

Which she did the next time I saw her and I haven't seen her since, except for that one time at her shrink's office. This was after my mother had gotten all high and mighty because I'd only scored 590 on the quantitative part of the SAT, since math was right after lunch and frequently, I attended stoned. Of course, Judi couldn't give a shit if I did math or not; she hires an accountant to balance her checkbook, but since my youthful beauty was trampled she'd reasoned that I should fall back on my next best asset — the mind. Oh those smart girls! Do men ever love those clever girls! She said it over and over, with a fake, bright smile, when she thought I wasn't paying close attention.

I wasn't half as worried about my sullied good looks as she was. Doctor Wohl said we could smooth out the lumps with dermabrasion, plus he wasn't entirely wrong about the rakish charm. I'd begun wearing black Anna Sui numbers and hanging out at The Coffee Plantation in Biltmore Fashion Square, where the neo-beatnik kids considered me sort of a god. I rarely spoke and they were under the impression I had a boyfriend in France. I'd also realized the scar sort of went with the curves of my face, it cupped my cheekbone — I mean, if you're going to have a major facial scar, this was the one to have. One girl with piercings all over her nose came up to me and asked where I had it done.

It wasn't like I looked normal, but I was learning to adjust. I was feeling okay about myself — I rented *The Big Heat,* where the heroine gets coffee flung in her face, and I was beginning to feel like being maimed was kind of romantic. I mean, I got noticed, and I looked just fine from the right side. Still, Judi was putting all bets on the intellect and had dragged Arthur into her camp. Together they forced me to take a Princeton Review class to get my test scores up. I hated it all except vocabulary: *Perfidy:* betrayal, the deliberate breaking of trust. *Refractory:* resisting treatment, unmanageable. My verbal was 780. 780 — that's almost perfect! I couldn't believe they were making me. It had been years since they'd forced me to do anything. It was cutting into my spare time, and it wasn't only me who suffered: I knew the neo-beatniks would be lost without their tragic center. Finally I went on strike and refused to eat in the dining room. I just took a plate, retired to my room, locked the door, and put on my headphones. A couple days of this, I thought, and they'll go into serious parenting withdrawal.

The second day Mom caved and weaseled her way in. She said I could quit the class if I'd do something for her. She said she'd talked to the Bitch's mother, and she'd said her therapist had recommended I go to one of the Bitch's sessions. She "wasn't happy," Judi said; she was "having trouble adjusting." This was like one of those moments when my mother gets all doe-eyed and yearns to save the environment, but a second later it's *snap!* time for a manicure. But she was dead serious, and I knew this was my chance to get out of that fucking class. Even so, I wouldn't have done it. I wasn't scared of anything then except the Bitch. I thought I saw her a million times, in the mall or the cineplex; I saw her big, smiling head gliding through the crowd, and then a swish of silver. At the last minute it was never her — the big head always morphed into some alternate head — but whether I created it or not, I felt like I was being stalked. Then I had these dreams where the Bitch and I were just hanging out, dancing to Chaka Khan, just hanging out like before when everything was normal — and those really gave me the creeps. I did not want to see her. No Bitch for me.

But then I changed my mind. Young and foolish I am. Also, I loved the idea of going to see the Bitch's shrink. I pictured a distinguished man with gray at his temples gasping at the sight of my scar when I walked in the room. Then, he would look at me with infinite compassion. I would take a seat on the leather lounger. My outfit is DKNY. My shoes are Kenneth Cole. The Bitch would be sitting in a straight-backed chair, her hair in cornrows. The Doctor would shake his head reproachfully.

"I never dreamed the wound was so dramatic," he says.

The Bitch would blush. I notice her body racked by waves of contrition. In her arms is an album by Brandy. A CD would be more practical but I like the way an album fills up her arms.

"This is for you," she'd say. "I've learned that it's okay for us to like different things. I celebrate your appreciation of Brandy."

I thank her. The Doctor looks on approvingly. I can tell by his glance that he thinks I'm a brave and noble girl. A few minutes later I leave. The Bitch is weeping softly. I feel a light, crisp sense of forgiveness. The Doctor has offered me free therapy, if I should ever want to share my burdens.

Well I'm here to tell you, buddy, it wasn't like that at all. First, there's no lounger, and the doctor is a streaked blond chick about my mother's age. I arrive late and she shows me to the office where the Bitch is already sitting on a swivel chair. She barely looks up when I enter the room. My dress is DKNY. The Bitch is dressed like white trash in jeans and a T-shirt of normal proportions. She looks like hell. I mean, *I* look better than she does. I was always prettier than she was but she used to seem intriguing. Before, if she was in a room, you felt her presence immediately. The girl knew how to occupy space. Something came out of her — a lot of pesky teen rage but at times, something nicer. She had that glow, at least to me; she had a sense of excitement and wonder. But in the office she seems dulled, and the truth is, right away I feel sorry for the Bitch.

The Shrink looks like she came straight out of a Smith alumnae magazine — Ann Taylor suit, minimal makeup, low-heeled leather shoes. The picture of emotional efficiency. Her office, too, is a symphony in earth tones. She checks me and the Bitch out, then says something like, "Katie's been grappling with the conflict that occurred between the two of you, and now she needs to know how you feel about it."

She does not blink twice at my scar. She does not look at me with infinite compassion. I realize whose turf I'm on. She's an employee, and the Bitch's father writes the paychecks.

"I feel okay," I say. I keep trying not to look at the Bitch, but she's unavoidable. After hallucinating her face a million times, it's unnerving how unfamiliar she seems. She's gained weight, but it seems like she's not really there. There's something inert and lumpen about her. No rage, no nail charms. Nothing extreme. She's just examining her shoes — for God's sake — clogs.

"Just okay? Because Katie and I have been discussing the impact of the cutting, and for her it's really been quite profound."

The Bitch does not say anything. The Bitch is not looking at me. The Bitch is sitting with her head down and her mouth closed like the first day she came to school with braces. Then I realize something. "She's not even looking at it," I say. "She won't even check out the scar!"

I look at the Shrink like she's some kind of referee. She, apparently, is having none of that, and sits quite calmly glancing at the Bitch and me as though we were a light piece of entertainment intended to gaily pass the time. This goes on for a while. The Bitch looks at her clogs and a brown spot on the carpet. I look at the Bitch for as long as I can, then start reading the spines of the Shrink's books. *Personality Disorders* — ha, that should come in handy. I can hear the Bitch breathing, which is odd, because in all the years we hung out together I never noticed her breathing. It's like she's alive in some weird, biological way — the way those pithed frogs were alive in science class. Alive but damaged.

Finally, the Bitch clears her throat. She raises her head until her eyes hit the scar. She starts to wince, then freezes. I can tell she's trying to control her expression, but all the color drains out of her face in a smooth, descending line, like she's been pumped full of pink fluid and someone has pulled the plug.

That was when I knew for sure that I looked like shit, absolutely and for certain. I'd been fooling myself, believing I looked dashing and rascally, but in the shock on my best friend's face I saw the truth. I was ruined.

The Bitch started to cry. I started to cry. The Shrink tried to glance calmly at us as if we were a light piece of entertainment but you could sense the strain. I pulled a Kool out of my bag and lit it. The Shrink finally cracked and shot me a dirty look but I was beyond caring. I realized, after all I'd been through, that I still smoked Kools, just like the Bitch always had, like she'd encouraged me to, and the thought of that made me cry even harder. Something switched then and I wasn't crying about my face anymore. I was crying because the Bitch was the Bitch, and the friend I'd had since I was a kid, the friend who knew for certain something was going to happen to us, something magical and vivid, was lost forever. She was lost to us both. The wonder had been extinguished.

Eventually I got ahold of myself and squashed the Kool out in a piece of damp Kleenex. The Bitch had slumped over in her swivel chair and I didn't even want to look at her. My thoughts: fuck, shit, etc. It was weird. I began to feel practically like she was my friend again, us having had a simultaneous cry. I did not want that. I wanted her to stay the Bitch.

"Oh God," she says, unprompted by the Shrink.

I notice her braces are off. She's not looking at me. It's too much for her.

"Fuck," she says, to a spot on the carpet, "I'm really sorry."

Okay: I'm a girl who's going to Smith College. I'm going to Smith and then I'm going to law school to become a criminal lawyer who champions the rights of the victimized and oppressed. I'm going to have two cars, a Volvo for transportation and a Jag for thrills. I'll cut a feline figure in my Agnès B. clothes and I'll have a drawerful of jewels. Maybe I'll even get married to some average-looking dork, but I will never be pretty and I will never be loved by the handsome men who roam this earth. My dear mother told me long ago that youth and beauty will get you everything. Well, mine's fucked up and now I'll never have Everything. No magic, no wonder, no fairy tales.

My plan was to walk out of there with a light, crisp sense of forgiveness, but help me. I sat in a sea of beige and looked at the Bitch in her clogs, fat, miserable, and afraid, and I knew: if I really forgave her, something vast and infinite would open up inside me, some place wide and blue, and I couldn't enter such a place. It would be like some kind of health spa — where you go in naked, without any things. God, would I ever be lost in a place like that.

So I said, Oh Katie, that's okay, babe! No problema! I forgive you! with a hint of fake innocence in my voice — a little dose of manufactured niceness. She turned white again and the Shrink started urging me to get in touch with my feelings but you know, I had my finger right on them.

Later, when I got home, I went into the bathroom and stared at myself in the mirror for a while. It was the same mirror Katie and I used to stare at in the pitch black while chanting "Bloody Mary, Bloody Mary" over and over until we hallucinated the beheaded head of Mary Queen of Scots emerging in reflection, dripping like a porterhouse steak. She fought her way up from the land of the dead to punish us for tempting the dark with the sight of her terrible wound. Mary with her disgusting necklace of blood — she was a perfidious one! I didn't look anything like her. In fact, I had a certain glow about me. I was so radiant I looked almost pretty. From the right side, I actually was pretty.

The Cavemen in the Hedges

There are cavemen in the hedges again. I take the pellet gun from the rack beside the door and go out back and try to run them off. These cavemen are tough sons of bitches who are impervious to pain, but they love anything shiny, so I load the gun up with golden Mardi Gras beads my girlfriend, Kim, keeps in a bowl on the dresser and aim toward their ankles. There are two of them, hairy and squat, grunting around inside a privet hedge I have harassed with great labor into a series of rectilinear shapes. It takes the cavemen a while to register the beads. It's said that they have poor eyesight, and of all the bullshit printed in the papers about the cavemen in the past few months, this at least seems to be true. They crash through the branches, doing something distasteful. Maybe they're eating garbage. After a while they notice the beads and crawl out, covered in leaves, and start loping after them. They chase them down the alley, occasionally scooping up a few and whining to each other in that high-pitched way they have when they get excited, like little kids complaining.

I take a few steps off the edge of the patio and aim toward the Anderson's lot. The cavemen scramble after the beads, their matted backs receding into the distance.

"What is it?" Kim stands behind me and touches my arm. She's been staying indoors a lot lately, working on the house, keeping to herself. She hasn't said so, but it's pretty obvious the cavemen scare her.

"A couple of furry motherfuckers."

"I think they are," she says.

"What?"

"Motherfuckers. Without taboos. It's disgusting." She shivers and heads back inside.

After scanning the treetops, I follow. There haven't been any climbers reported so far, but they are nothing if not unpredictable. Inside, I find Kim sitting on the kitchen floor, arranging our spices alphabetically. She's transferring them out of their grocery-store bottles and into nicer ones, plain glass, neatly labeled. Kim has been tirelessly arranging things for the last four years — first the contents of our apartment on Pine Avenue, then, as her interior decorating business took off, other people's places, and lately our own house, since we took the plunge and bought it together last September. She finishes with fenugreek and picks up the galanga.

I go to the living room and put on some music. It's a nice, warm Saturday and if it weren't for the cavemen, we'd probably be spending it outdoors.

"Did you lock it?"

I tell her yes. I get a beer from the fridge and watch her. She's up to Greek seasonings. Her slim back is tense under her stretchy black top. The music kicks in and we don't say much for a few minutes. The band is D.I., and they're singing: "Johnny's got a problem and it's out of control!" We used to be punk rockers, Kim and I, back in the day. Now we are homeowners. When the kids down the street throw loud parties, we immediately dial 911.

"The thing that gets me," I say, "is how puny they are."

"What do they want?" asks Kim. Her hair is springing out of its plastic clamp, and she looks like she's going to cry. "What the fuck do they want with us?"

When the cavemen first appeared, they were assumed to be homeless examples of modern man. But it soon became obvious that even the most broken-down and mentally ill homeless guy wasn't *this* hairy. Or naked, hammer-browed, and short. And they didn't rummage through garbage cans and trash piles with an insatiable desire for spherical, shiny objects, empty shampoo bottles, and foam packing peanuts.

A reporter from KUTA had a hunch and sent a paleontologist from the university out to do a little fieldwork. For some reason I was watching the local news that night, and I remember this guy — typical academic, bad haircut, bad teeth — holding something in a take-out box. He said it was *scat*. Just when you think the news can't get any more absurd, there's a guy on TV, holding a turd in his hands, telling you the hairy people scurrying around the bike paths and Dumpsters of our fair burg are probably Neanderthal, from the Middle Paleolithic period, and that they have been surviving on a diet of pizza crusts, unchewed insects, and pigeon eggs.

People started calling them cavemen, though they were both male and female and tended to live in culverts, heavy brush, and freeway underpasses, rather than caves. Or they lived wherever — they turned up in weird places. The security guard at the Ice-O-Plex heard an eerie yipping one night. He flipped on the lights and found a half dozen of them sliding around the rink like otters. At least we knew another thing about them. They loved ice.

Facts about the cavemen have been difficult to establish. It is unclear if they're protected by the law. It is unclear if they are responsible for their actions. It *has* been determined that they're a nuisance to property and a threat to themselves. They will break into cars and climb fences to gain access to swimming pools, where they drop to all fours to drink. They will snatch food out of trucks or bins and eat out of trash cans. They avoid modern man as a general rule but are becoming bolder by the hour. The university students attempting to study them have had difficulties, though they've managed to discover that the cavemen cannot be taught or tamed and are extremely difficult to contain. They're strong for their size. It's hard to hurt them but they're simple to distract. They love pink plastic figurines and all things little-girl pretty. They love products perfumed with synthetic woodsy or herbal scents. You can shoot at them with rubber bullets all day and they'll just stand there, scratching their asses, but if you wave a little bottle of Barbie bubble bath in front of them they'll follow you around like a dog. They do not understand deterrence. They understand desire.

Fathers, lock up your daughters.

Kim sits across from me at the table, fingering the stem of her wine-glass and giving me The Look. She gets The Look whenever I confess that I'm not ready to get married yet. The Look is a peculiar expression, pained and brave, like Kim has swallowed a bee but she isn't going to let on.

"It's fine," she says. "It's not like I'm all goddamn *ready* either."

I drain my glass and sigh. Tonight she's made a fennel-basil lasagna, lit candles, and scratched the price tag off the wine. Kim and I have been together for ten years, since we were twenty-three, and she's still a real firecracker, brainy, blonde, and bitchy. What I have in Kim is one of those cute little women with a swishy ponytail who cuts people off in traffic while swearing like a Marine. She's a fierce one, grinding her teeth all night long, grimly determined, though the object of her determination is usually vague or unclear. I've never wanted anyone else. And I've followed her instructions. I've nested. I mean, we bought a house together. We're co-borrowers on a thirty-year mortgage. Isn't that commitment enough?

Oh no, I can see it is not. She shoots me The Look a couple more times and begins grabbing dishes off the table and piling them in the sink. Kim wants the whole ordeal: a white dress, bridesmaids stuffed into taffeta, a soft rain of cherry blossoms. I want none of it. The whole idea of marriage makes me want to pull a dry cleaning bag over my head. I miss our punk rock days, Kim and me and our loser friends playing in bands, hawking spit at guys in BMWs, shooting drugs . . . and living in basements with anarchy tattoos poking through the rips in our clothing. Those times are gone and we've since established real credit ratings, I had the circled-A tattoo lasered off my neck, but. But. I feel like marriage would exterminate the last shred of the rebel in me. For some reason, I think of marriage as a living death.

Or, I don't know, maybe I'm just a typical guy, don't want to pay for the cow if I can get the milk for free.

Kim is leaning in the open doorway, gazing out at the street, sucking on a cigarette. She doesn't smoke much anymore, but every time I tell her I'm not ready she rips through a pack in a day and a half. "They'd probably ruin it anyway," she says, watching a trio of cavemen out on the street, loping along, sniffing the sidewalk. They fan out and then move back together to briefly touch one another's ragged, dirty brown fur with their noses. The one on the end, lighter-boned with small, pale breasts poking out of her chest hair, stops dead in her tracks and begins making a cooing sound at the sky. It must be a full moon. Then she squats and pees a silver puddle onto the road.

Kim stares at her. She forgets to take a drag and ash builds on the end of her cigarette. I know her; I know what she's thinking. She's picturing hordes of cavemen crashing the reception, grabbing canapés with their fists, rubbing their crotches against the floral arrangements. That would never do. She's too much of a perfectionist to ever allow that.

When I first saw the cavemen scurrying around town, I have to admit I was horrified. It was like when kids started to wear those huge pants — I couldn't get used to it, I couldn't get over the shock. But now I have hopes Kim will let the marriage idea slide for a while. For this reason I am somewhat grateful to the cavemen.

It rains for three days and the railroad underpasses flood. The washes are all running and on the news there are shots of SUVs bobbing in the current because some idiot ignored the DO NOT ENTER WHEN FLOODED sign and tried to gun it through four feet of rushing water. A lot of cavemen have been driven out of their nests and the incident level is way up. They roam around the city hungry and disoriented. We keep the doors locked at all times. Kim has a few stashes of sample-sized shampoo bottles around the house. She says she'll toss them out like trick-or-treat candy if any cavemen come around hassling her. So far, we haven't had any trouble.

Our neighbors, the Schaefers, haven't been so lucky. Kim invites them over for dinner one night, even though she knows I can't stand them. The Schaefers are these lonely, New Age hippies who are always staggering toward us with eager, too-friendly looks on their faces, arms outstretched, like they're going to grab our necks and start sucking. I beg Kim not to invite them, but at this stage in the game she seems to relish annoying me. They arrive dressed in gauzy robes. It turns out

Winsome has made us a hammock out of hemp in a grasping attempt to secure our friendship. I tell her it's terrific and take it into the spare room where I stuff it in a closet, fully aware that by morning all of our coats are going to smell like bongwater.

When I return, everyone is sipping wine in the living room while the storm wets down the windows. Winsome is describing how she found a dead cavebaby in their backyard.

"It must not have been there for long," she says, her huge, oil-on-velvet eyes welling up with tears, "because it just looked like it was sleeping, and it wasn't very stiff. Its mother had wrapped it in tinsel, like for Christmas."

"Ick," says Kim. "How can you cry for those things?"

"It looked so vulnerable." Winsome leans forward and touches Kim's knee. "I sensed it had a spirit. I mean, they're human or proto-human or whatever."

"I don't care," says Kim, "I think they're disgusting."

"Isn't that kind of judgmental?"

"I think we should try to understand them," chimes in Evan, smoothing down his smock — every inch the soulful, sandal-wearing, sensitive man. "In a sense, they're *us*. If we understood why that female caveman wrapped her baby in tinsel, perhaps we'd know a little more about ourselves."

"I don't see why people can't just say 'cavewoman,'" snaps Kim. "'Female caveman' is weird, like 'male nurse.' Besides, they are *not* us. We're supposed to have won. You know, survival of the fittest."

"It might be that it's time we expanded our definition of 'humanity,'" intones Evan. "It might be that it's time we welcome all creatures on planet Earth."

I'm so incredibly annoyed by Evan that I have to go into the bathroom and splash cold water on my face. When I get back, Kim has herded the Schaefers into the dining room, where she proceeds to serve us a deluxe vegetarian feast: little kabobs of tofu skewered along with baby turnips, green beans, rice, and steamed leaf of something or other. Everything is lovely, symmetrical, and delicious, as always. The house looks great. Kim has cleaned and polished and organized the contents of each room until it's like living in a furniture store. The Schaefers praise everything and Kim grumbles her thanks. The thing about Kim is she's a wonderful cook, a great creator of ambiance, but she has a habit of getting annoyed with her guests, as if no one could ever be grateful enough for her efforts. We drain a couple more bottles of wine and after a while I notice that Kim has become fed up with the Schaefers too. She starts giving them The Look.

"Seriously," she begins, "do you two even like being married?"

They exchange a glance.

"No, c'mon, really. It's overrated, right?" Kim pulls the hair off her face and I can see how flushed she is, how infuriated. "I think all that crap about biological clocks and baby lust, it's all sexist propaganda meant to keep women in line."

"Well, I haven't noticed any conspiracy," offers Winsome, checking everyone's face to make sure she's not somehow being disagreeable. "I think marriage is just part of the journey."

"Ha," says Kim. "Ha ha ha." She leans across the table, swaying slightly. "I know," she pronounces, "that you don't believe that hippie shit. I can tell," she whispers, "how fucking lost you really are."

Then she stands, picks up her glass, and weaves toward the back door. "I have to go check the basement."

We stare at the space where Kim was for a while. Winsome is blinking rapidly and Evan keeps clearing his throat. I explain we have an unfinished basement that's been known to fill with water when it rains, and that the only entrance to it is outside in the yard, and that Kim probably wants to make sure that everything's okay down there. They nod vigorously. I can tell they're itching to purify our home with sticks of burning sage.

While Kim is gone I take them into the living room and show them my collection of LPs. I pull out my rare purple vinyl X-Ray Specs record, and after considering this for a while, Winsome informs me that purple is a healing color. We hear a couple of bangs under the house. I toy with the idea of checking on Kim, but then I recall the early days of our courtship, before all this house-beautiful crap, when Kim used to hang out the window of my 1956 hearse, which was also purple, and scream "Anarchy now!" and "Destroy!" while lobbing rocks through smoked glass windows into corporate lobbies. It's difficult to worry about a girl like that.

It doesn't take long for the Schaefers and me to run out of small talk. I have no idea how to get them to go home; social transitions are Kim's jurisdiction. We sit there nodding at each other like idiots until Kim finally straggles back inside. She's muddy, soaked to the bone, and strangely jolly. She says there's about a foot of water in the basement and that she was walking around in there and it's like a big honking wading pool. She giggles. The Schaefers stare with horror at the puddle spreading around her feet onto our nice oak floors. I put my arm around her and kiss her hair. She smells like wet dog.

I come home from work a few days later and find Kim unloading a Toys "R" Us bag. I notice a diamond tiara/necklace set with huge, divorcée-sized fake jewels stuck to a panel of pink cardboard. Again, she seems happy, which is odd for Kim. In fact, she's taken to singing around the house in this new style where she doesn't sing actual words, she goes "nar nar nar" like some demented little kid. It drives me crazy, in particular when the game is on, so I tell her to fucking please cut it out. She glares at me and storms off into the backyard. I let her pout for a while, but I'm in the mood to make an effort, so I eventually go out and find her standing on a chair, hanging over the hedge, gazing at the alley. I lean in beside her and see a caveman shambling off with a red bandana tied around his neck, like a puppy.

"That's weird."

"Look at his butt."

I look. There's a big blob of pink bubble gum stuck in his fur.

"God," says Kim, "isn't that pitiful?"

I ask her what we're having for dinner. She looks at me blankly and says I don't know, what are we having for dinner. I tell her I'll cook, and when I get back from picking up the pizza she's nowhere to be found. I walk from one empty room to another while the hairs on my arms start to tingle. I have to say, there's a peculiar feeling building in the household. Things are in a state of slight disarray. There's a candy bar wrapper on the coffee table, and the bag from the toy store is on the kitchen floor. I yell Kim's name. When she doesn't appear I turn on the TV and eat a few slices straight from the box. For some reason that starts to bother me, so I get up and get a plate, silverware, and a paper napkin. Kim walks in a little while later. She's wet from the waist down and all flushed, as if she's been doing calisthenics.

"I was bailing out the basement!" she says, with great verve, like basement bailing is a terrific new sport. Her hair is tangled around her head and she's sucking on a strand of it. She is smiling away. She says: "I'm worried about letting all that water just stand down there!"

But she doesn't look worried.

On the news one night, a psychic with a flashlight shining up under his chin explains there's a time portal in the condemned Pizza Hut by the freeway. Though the mayor whines he wasn't elected to buckle to the whim of every nutbar with an opinion, there are televised protests featuring people shaking placards proclaiming the Pizza Hut ground zero of unnatural evil, and finally they just bulldoze it to shut everyone up. A while after that, the incident levels start to drop. It seems that the cavemen are thinning out. They are not brainy enough for our world, and they can't stop extinguishing themselves. They tumble into swimming pools and drown. They walk through plate glass windows and sever their arteries. They fall asleep under eighteen-wheelers and wander onto runways and get mauled by pit bulls.

It looks like we're the dominant species after all; rock smashes scissors, *Homo sapiens* kicks *Homo sapiens neanderthalensis's* ass.

As the caveman population drops, the ominous feeling around town begins to lift. You can feel it in the air: women jog by themselves instead of in pairs. People barbecue large cuts of meat at dusk. The cavemen, it seems, are thinning out everywhere except around our house. I come home from work and walk through the living room and peek out the back window just in time to see a tough, furry leg disappear through a hole in the hedge. The hole is new. When I go outside and kick around in the landscaping, I find neat little stashes of rhinestones and fake pearls, Barbie shoes, and folded squares of foil wrapping paper. They can't see that well, but have the ears of a dog and flee as soon as I rustle the window shades. One time, though, I peel back the shade silently and catch a pair skipping in circles around the clothesline. One of them is gripping something purple and hairy, and when I go out there later I find a soiled My Little Pony doll on the ground. They are not living up to their reputation as club-swinging brutes. More than anything, they resemble feral little girls.

Also, our house has become an unbelievable mess. Kim walks through the door and drops the mail on the coffee table, where it remains for days until I remove it. There are panties on the bathroom floor and water glasses on top of the television and scraps of food on the kitchen counter. I ask Kim what's going on and she just says she's sick of that anal constant-housekeeping-bullshit, and if I want it clean, I can clean it myself. She looks straight at me and says this, without flinching, without any signs of deference or anger or subtle backing away that had always let me know, in nonverbal but gratifying ways, that I had the upper hand in the relationship. She tosses an orange peel on the table before marching outside and descending into the basement.

I stand there in the kitchen, which smells like sour milk, shaking my head and trying to face up to the increasingly obvious fact that my girlfriend of ten years is having an affair, and that her lover is a Neanderthal man from the Pleistocene epoch. They rendezvous in our moldy, water-stained basement where he takes her on the cement floor beneath a canopy of spiderwebs, grunting over her with his animal-like body, or perhaps behind her, so that when she comes back inside there are thick, dark hairs stuck all over her shirt and she smells like a cross between some musky, woodland animal gland and Herbal Essences shampoo. Furthermore, she's stopped shaving her legs.

The next day, I duck out of the office claiming I have a doctor's appointment and zip back home around noon. I open the door with my key and creep inside. I don't know what I'm looking for. I think I half expect to find Kim in bed with one of those things, and that he'll pop up and start "trying to reason" with me in a British accent. What I find instead is an empty house. Kim's car is gone. I poke around, stepping over mounds of dirty clothes, then head out back and take the stairs to the basement. When I pull the door open, the first thing to hit me is the smell of mold and earth. I pace from one side to the other and shine my flashlight around, but I don't see anything suspicious, just an old metal weight-lifting bench with a plastic bucket sitting on top. Maybe, I think, I'm making this whole thing up in my head. Maybe Kim just goes down there because she needs some time to herself.

But then on my way out, I spot something. On the concrete wall beside the door, several feet up, my flashlight picks out a pattern of crude lines. They appear to have been made with charcoal or maybe some type of crayon. When I take a few steps back, I can see it's a drawing, a cave painting of some sort. It's red and black with the occasional pom-pom of dripping orange that looks like it was made by someone who doesn't understand spray paint.

I stand there for two or three minutes trying to figure out what the painting is about, then spend another fifteen trying to convince myself my interpretation is wrong. The picture shows half a dozen cars in a V-shaped formation bearing down on a group of cavemen. The cavemen's flailing limbs suggest flight or panic; obviously, they're in danger of being flattened by the cars. Above them, sketched in a swift, forceful manner, floats a huge, God-like figure with very long arms. One arm cradles the fleeing cavemen while the other blocks the cars. This figure is flowing and graceful and has a big ponytail sprouting from the top of her head. Of course, it's meant to be Kim. Who else?

I go upstairs and sit at the kitchen table, elbowing away half a moldy cantaloupe, and hold my head in my hands. I was hoping it was nothing — a casual flirtation at most — but a guy who makes a cave painting for a girl is probably in love with the girl. And girls love to be loved, even high-strung ones like Kim. I admit I'm hurt, but my hurt switches to anger and my anger to resolve. I can fight this thing. I can win her back. I know her; I know what to do.

I put on rubber gloves and start cleaning everything, thoroughly and with strong-smelling products, the way Kim likes things cleaned. I do the laundry and iron our shirts and line everything up neatly in the closet. I get down on my knees and wipe the baseboards, then up on a chair to dust the lightbulbs. I pull a long clot of hair out of the drain. There's a picture of us in Mexico in a silver frame on top of the medicine cabinet. I pick it up and think: that is my woman! It's civilization versus base instinct, and I vow to deploy the strongest weapon at my disposal: my evolutionarily superior traits. I will use my patience, my facility with machinery and tools, my complex problem-solving skills. I will bathe often and floss my teeth. I will cook with gas.

A little after five Kim walks in and drops the mail on the coffee table. She looks around the house, at the gleaming neatness, smiling slightly and going "nar nar nar" to the tune of "Nobody Does It Better." I stand there in my cleanest suit with my arms hanging at my sides and gaze at her, in her little professional outfit, pretty and sexy in an I-don't-know-it-but-I-do way, clutching her black purse, her hair pulled back with one of those fabric hair things.

"God, I can't believe you cleaned," she says, and walks through the kitchen and out of the house into the yard and slams the basement door behind her.

Kim is so happy. The worst part is she's so disgustingly happy and I could never make her happy all by myself and I don't particularly like her this way. For a couple of weeks she walks around in a delirious haze. She spins around on the porch with her head thrown back and comments on the shape of the clouds. She asks why haven't I bothered to take in the pretty, pretty sunset, all blue and gold. Like I fucking care, I say, forgetting my pledge to be civil. It's as though someone has dumped a bottle of pancake syrup over her head — she has no nastiness left, no edge, no resentment. Her hair is hanging loose and she has dirty feet and bad breath. She smiles all the time. This is not the girl I originally took up with.

Of course, I'm heartsick; I'm torn up inside. Even so, I do my best to act all patient and evolutionarily superior. I keep the house clean enough to lick. I start to cook elaborate meals the minute I get home from work. I groom myself until I'm sleek as a goddamn seal. I aim for a Fred Astaire/James Bond hybrid: smooth, sophisticated, oozing suaveness around the collar and cuffs — the kind of guy who would never fart in front of a woman, at least not audibly. She has a big, inarticulate lug already. I want to provide her with an option.

Kim takes it all for granted, coming and going as she pleases, wandering away from the house without explanation, hanging out in the basement with the door locked and brushing off my questions about what the hell she's doing down there, and with whom. She doesn't listen when I talk to her and eats standing in front of the refrigerator with the door open, yelling between bites that it's time for me to go to the store and get more milk. One evening I watch her polish off a plate of appetizers I have made for her, melon balls wrapped in prosciutto, downing them one after another like airline peanuts. When she's finished, she unbuttons the top button of her pants and ambles out the door and lets it slam without so much as a glance back at me. Without so much as a thank you.

I trot out after her, figuring it's about time I give her a suave, patient lecture, but I'm not fast enough and she slams the basement door in my face. I pound and scream for a while before giving up and going up into the yard to wait. The night is very still. There's a full moon and the hedges glow silver on the top and then fade to blue at the bottom. I get a glass of iced tea and pull a chair off the patio, thinking to myself that she can't stay down there forever. I think about how maybe I'll catch the caveguy when he comes out too. Maybe I can tie on an apron and offer them both baby wieners on a toothpick.

After a while I hear a rustling in the hedges. At that moment I'm too miserable to be aware of the specifics of what's going on around me, so I'm startled as hell when a cavegirl pops out of the hedge, backlit in the moonlight, and begins walking toward me with a slow, hesitant gait. I sit there, taking shallow breaths, not sure whether or not I should be afraid. She has a low brow and a tucked, abbreviated chin, like Don Knotts's, but her limbs are long and sinewy. When she gets closer I see that she looks a lot stronger than a human woman does, and of course she's naked. Her breasts are like perfect human pinup breasts with bunny fur growing all over them. I can't unstick my eyes from them as they bob toward me, moving closer, until they come to a stop less than an arm's length from my chin. They are simultaneously furry and plump and I really want to bite them. But not hard.

She leans in closer. I hold very still as she reaches out with a leathery hand and begins to stroke my lapel. She lowers her head to my neck and sniffs. On the exhale I discover that cavegirl breath smells just like moss. She prods me a few times with her fingertips; after she's had enough of that she just rubs the fabric of my suit and sniffs my neck while sort of kneading me rhythmically, like a purring cat. It's pretty obvious she likes my suit — a shiny sharkskin number I've hauled out of the back of the closet in the interest of wooing Kim — and I guess she likes my cologne too. For a minute I feel special and chosen, but then it occurs to me that there's something sleazy and impersonal about her attention. I'm probably just a giant, shiny, sandalwood-scented object to her. The moon is behind her so I can't see her that clearly, but then she shifts and I get a better view of her face and I realize she's young. Really young. I feel like a creep for wanting to feel her up, more because she's about fourteen than because she's a Neanderthal.

She swings a leg over and settles her rump onto my thigh, lapdance-style.

I say: "Whoa there, Jailbait."

The cavegirl leaps up like she's spring-loaded. She stops a few feet away and stares at me. I stare back. She tilts her head from side to side in puzzlement. The moon shines down. I reach into my glass and draw out a crescent-shaped piece of ice, moving with aching slowness, and offer it to her on a flat palm. She considers this ice cube for a good long time. I hold my arm as still as possible while freezing water trickles off my elbow and my muscles start to seize. Then, after a few false lunges, she snatches it from my hand.

"Nar," she says. Just that. Then she darts back into the hedge with her prize.

I remain in the moonlight for a while, shaking with excitement. I feel almost high. It's like I've touched a wild animal; I've communicated with it — an animal that's somehow human, somehow like me. I'm totally giddy.

This is probably how it was with Kim and her guy when they first met.

I guess I'm a complete failure with every category of female because the cavegirl does not come back. Even worse, Kim continues to treat me like I'm invisible. It's painfully clear that my strategy of suaveness isn't working. So I say screw evolution. What's it ever done for me? I go out drinking with the guys and allow the house to return to a state of nature. The plates in the sink turn brown. I shower every other day, every third. Kim and I go days without speaking to each other. By this time there are hardly any cavemen left around town; the count is running at one or two dozen. I go to the bars and everyone is lounging with their drinks, all relaxed and relieved that the cavemen aren't really an issue anymore, while I continue to stew in my own miserable interspecies soap opera. I don't even want to talk to anyone about it. What could I say? Hey buddy, did I mention my girlfriend has thrown me over for the Missing Link? It's humiliating.

One hungover afternoon I decide to skip the bars and come straight home from the office. Kim, naturally, is not around, though this barely registers. I've lost interest in tracking her whereabouts. But when I go into the kitchen, I catch sight of her through the window, standing outside, leaning against the chinaberry tree. It looks like she's sick or something. She's trying to hold herself up but keeps doubling over anyway. I go outside and find her braced against the tree, sobbing from deep in her belly while a string of snot swings from her nose. She's pale and spongy and smudged with dirt and I get the feeling she's been standing there crying all afternoon. She's clutching something. A red bandana. So it was him. The one with gum on his butt.

"Where is he?"

"He's gone," she whispers, and gives me a sad, dramatic, miniseries smile. "They're all gone."

Her sobs begin anew. I pat her on the back.

So she's curled over crying and I'm patting her thinking well, well; now that the other boyfriend is gone she's all mine again. Immediately I'm looking forward to putting the whole caveman ordeal behind us and having a regular life like we had before. I see all sorts of normal activities looming in the distance like a mirage, including things we always made fun of, like procreating and playing golf. She blows her nose in the bandana. I put my arm around her. She doesn't shake it off.

I should wait I know, I should go slow; but I can see the opening, the niche all vacant and waiting for me. I feel absolutely compelled to exploit it right away, before some other guy does. I turn to Kim and say: "Babe, let's just forget about this whole caveman thing and go back to the way it was before. I'm willing to forgive you. Let's have a normal life without any weird creatures in it, okay?"

She's still hiccuping and wiping her nose but I observe a knot of tension building in her shoulders, the little wrinkles of a glare starting around the edge of her eyes. I realize I'm in grave danger of eliciting The Look. It dawns on me that my strategy is a failure and I'd better think fast. So I bow to the inevitable. I've always known I couldn't put it off forever.

I take a deep breath and drop to one knee and tell her I love her and I can't live without her and beg her to marry me while kissing her hand. She's hiccuping and trying to pull her hand away, but in the back of my mind I'm convinced that this is going to work and of course she'll say yes. I've never made an effort like this before; I've only told her I love her two or three times total, in my life. It's inconceivable that this effort won't be rewarded. Plus, I know her. She lives for this. This is exactly what she wants.

I look up at her from my kneeling position. Her hair is greasy and her face is smeared with dirt and snot, but she's stopped crying. I see that she has created a new Look. It involves a shaking of the head while simultaneously pushing the lips outward, like she's crushed a wasp between her teeth and is about to spit it out. It's a look of pity, pity mixed with superiority; pity mixed with superiority and blended with dislike.

"I don't want a normal life without any creatures in it," Kim says, her voice ragged from crying, but contemptuous nonetheless. "I want an extraordinary life, with everything in it."

The Look fades. She brings her dirty, snotty face to mine and kisses me on the forehead and turns and walks away, leaving me on my knees.

I stumble into the house after her. I can smell a trail of scent where she's passed by, cinnamon and sweat and fabric softener, but though I run through the house after her, and out into the street, I don't see her anywhere, not all night. Not the night after that. Never again.

Some psychic with a towel on his head says the cavemen passed through his drive-through palm reading joint on their way back to the Pleistocene epoch, and I finally go over and ask him if he saw Kim with them. He has me write him a check and then says, Oh *yeah,* I did see her! She was at the front of this line of female cavemen and she was all festooned with beads and tinsel, like she was some sort of goddess! He says it in this bullshit way, but after some reflection I decide even charlatans may see strange and wondrous things, as we all had during the time the cavemen were with us, and then report them so that they sound like a totally improbable lie.

It's bizarre, the way time changes things. Now that the cavemen are gone, it seems obvious that their arrival was the kind of astonishing event people measure their entire lives by; and now that Kim is gone it seems clear that she was astonishing too, regal and proud, like she's represented in the cave painting. I once thought of her as sort of a burden, a pain-in-the-ass responsibility, but now I think of her as the one good thing I had in my life, an intense woman with great reserves of strength, forever vanished.

Or, I don't know; maybe I'm just a typical guy, don't know what I have until it walks out on me.

I've been trying to get over her, but I can't stop wallowing in it. One night we hold a drum circle on the site of the old Pizza Hut, and I swear that after this night, I'll force myself to stop thinking about her. This drum circle is the largest yet, maybe a couple of hundred people milling around, having the kind of conversations people have these days — you know, they were annoyed and frightened by the cavemen when they were here, but now that they're gone they just want them back, they want that weird, vivid feeling, the newness of the primitive world, et cetera. My job is to tend the fire. There's a six-foot pyramid of split pine in the middle of the circle, ready to go. At the signal I throw on a match. The wood is soaked in lighter fluid and goes up with a whoosh. Everyone starts to bang on their drums, or garbage can lids, or whatever percussive dingus they've dragged along, while I stand there poking the flames, periodically squirting in plumes of lighter fluid, as the participants wail and drum and cry and dance.

We are supposedly honoring the cavemen with this activity, but in truth no one ever saw the cavemen making fires or dancing or playing any sort of musical instrument. Apparently the original Neanderthal did these things; they also ate one another's brains and worshipped the skulls of bears, though no one seems anxious to resurrect these particular hobbies. Still, I admit I get kind of into it. Standing there in the middle, sweating, with the sound of the drumming surrounding me while the fire crackles and pops, it's easy to zone out. For a moment I imagine what it might be like to live in an uncivilized haze of sweat and hunger and fear and desire, to never plan, to never speak or think in words — but then the smell of lighter fluid snaps me back to how artificial this whole drum circle is, how prearranged and ignited with gas.

Later, when the fire has burned out, some New Age hardcores roll around in the ashes and pray for the cavemen to come back, our savage brothers, our hairy predecessors, et cetera, but of course they don't come back. Those guys look stupid, covered in ash. When the sun comes up, everyone straggles away. I get into my hatchback and listen to bad news on the radio as I drive home.

George Saunders

Transpose Kafka to *fin de siècle* America, with its malls and theme parks
and stenographic speech, throw in a pinch of Borgesian wit and the
sheer love of literary play of Nabokov, and you have a sense of the territory George Saunders is mapping out for himself in his surreal, satiric
stories. His first collection, *CivilWarLand in Bad Decline,* published in
1996, shows off his genius for parodying the banal everyday speech patterns of a society in which everything is for sale and the jargon of the
self-help movement passes for wisdom. The title story is set in a historical theme park replete with teenage gangs, corporate line-toers, and the
ghosts of bewildered pioneers. "Pastoralia," the title piece of his second
collection, features a narrator paid to sit in a caveman exhibit and skin
and roast goat all day long for the edification of archaeologically
minded tourists. His mate, Janet, is so frustrated with the routine that
she reverts to English, instead of the gruntology they are required to
employ: "'Jeez,' she says first thing this morning. 'I'm so tired of roast
goat I could scream.'" What Saunders is getting at here and in a number of his other stories as well — "Sea Oak," set in a theme restaurant,
is another example — is not simply the artificiality of contemporary
American culture, but a critique of corporate rule and the deep disaf-
fection it breeds among its retainers.

The first story I've selected for this volume, "The Barber's Unhappiness," succeeds in taking a familiar type — the middle-aged mama's
boy — and giving him as rich a fantasy life as Walter Mitty's. The story
is painfully funny, the barber self-deluded, pathetic even, and yet it
achieves real poignancy through its rich and complex close third-person
point of view. Saunders's gift for the nuances of colloquial language is
on display here, as well as his keen satiric eye (witness the scene at Driving School), and the drop-off ending pulls us back into the story. Why
end here? Is the barber doomed to unhappiness, as the title indicates?
Or does the ending invite the reader to speculate about another possibility altogether? The second piece, "I CAN SPEAK!™," is a tour de force
parody of corporatese and the notion that everything is available to us
if only we can find the right product.

The Barber's Unhappiness

1.

Mornings the barber left his stylists inside and sat out front of his shop, drinking coffee and ogling every woman in sight. He ogled old women and pregnant women and women whose photographs were passing on the sides of buses and, this morning, a woman with close-cropped black hair and tear-stained cheeks, who wouldn't be half bad if she'd just make an effort, clean up her face a little and invest in some decent clothes, some white tights and a short skirt maybe, knee boots and a cowboy hat and a cigarillo, say, and he pictured her kneeling on a crude Mexican sofa, in a little mud hut, daring him to take her, and soon they'd screwed their way into some sort of beanfield while some gaucho guys played soft guitars, although actually he'd better put the gaucho guys behind some trees or a rock wall so they wouldn't get all hot and bothered from watching the screwing and swoop down and stab him and have their way with Miss Hacienda as he bled to death, and come to think of it, forget the gauchos altogether, he'd just put some soft guitars on the stereo in the hut and leave the door open, although actually what was a stereo doing in a Mexican hut? Were there outlets? Plus how could he meet her? He could compliment her hair, then ask her out for coffee. He could say that as a hair-care professional, he knew a little about hair, and boy did she ever have great hair, and by the way did she like coffee? Except they always said no. Lately no no no was all he got. Plus he had zero access to a beanfield or mud hut. They could do it in his yard but it wouldn't be the same because Jeepers had basically made of it a museum of poop, plus Ma would call 911 at the first hint of a sexy moan.

Now those, those on that meter maid, those were some serious hooters. Although her face was sort of beat. But if you could take those hooters and slap them on Miss Hacienda, wow, then you'd be talking. Just the meter maid's hooters and some decent clothes and a lip wax and the super sexy voice of the librarian who looked away whenever he ogled her, and you'd have his perfect woman, and wow would they ever be happy together forever, as long as she kept a positive attitude, which come to think of it might be an issue, because why the heck was she crying in public?

Miss Hacienda passed through a gap in a hedge and disappeared into the Episcopal church.

Why was she going into church on a weekday? Maybe she had a problem. Maybe she was knocked up. Maybe if he followed her into the church and told her he knew a little about problems, having been born with no toes, she'd have coffee with him. He was tired of going home to just Ma. Lately she'd been falling asleep with her head on his shoulder while they watched TV. Sometimes he worried that somebody would look in the window and wonder why he'd married such an old lady. Plus sometimes he worried that Ma would wake up and catch him watching the black girl in the silver bikini riding her horse through that tidal pool in slow motion on 1-900-DREMGAL.

He wondered how Miss Hacienda would look in a silver bikini in slow motion. Although if she was knocked up she shouldn't he riding a horse. She should be sitting down, taking it easy. Somebody should be bringing her a cup of tea. She should move in with him and Ma. He wouldn't rub it in that she was knocked up. He'd be loving about it. He'd be a good friend to her and wouldn't even try to screw her, and pretty soon she'd start wondering why not and start really wanting him. He'd be her labor coach and cheerfully change diapers in the wee hours and finally when she'd lost all the weight she'd come to his bed and screw his brains out in gratitude, after which he'd have a meditative smoke by the window and decide to marry her. He nearly got tears in his eyes thinking of how she'd get tears in her eyes as he went down on one knee to pop the question, a nice touch the dolt who'd knocked her up wouldn't have thought of in a million years, the nimrod, and that SOB could drive by as often as he wanted, deeply regretting his foolishness as the baby frolicked in the yard, it was too late, they were a family, and nothing would ever break them up.

But he'd have to remember to stick a towel under the door while meditatively smoking or Ma would have a cow, because after he smoked she always claimed everything smelled like smoke, and made him wash every piece of clothing in the house. And they'd better screw quietly if they weren't married, because Ma was old-fashioned. It was sort of a pain living with Ma. But Miss Hacienda had better be prepared to tolerate Ma, who was actually pretty good company when she stayed on her meds, and so what if she was nearly eighty and went around the house flossing in her bra? It was her damn house. He'd better never hear Miss Hacienda say a word against Ma, who'd paid his way through barber college, like for example asking why Ma had thick sprays of gray hair growing out of her ears, because that would kill Ma, who was always reminding the gas man she'd been a dish in high school. How would Miss Hacienda like it if after a lifetime of hard work she got wrinkled and forgetful and some knocked-up slut dressed like a Mexican cowgirl moved in and started complaining about her ear hair? Who did Miss Hacienda think she was, the Queen of Sheba? She could go into labor in the damn Episcopal church for all he cared, he'd keep wanking it in the pantry on the little milking stool for the rest of his life before he'd let Ma be hurt, and that was final.

As Miss Hacienda came out of the church she saw a thick-waisted, beak-nosed, middle-aged man rise angrily from a wooden bench and stomp into Mickey's Hairport, slamming the door behind him.

2.

Next morning Ma wanted an omelet. When he said he was running late she said never mind in a tone that made it clear she was going to accidentally/on purpose burn herself again while ostensibly making her own omelet. So he made the omelet. When he asked was it good, she said it was fine, which meant it was bad and he had to make pancakes. So he made pancakes. Then he kissed her cheek and flew out the door, very very late for Driving School.

Driving School was being held in what had been a trendy office park in the Carter years and was now a flat white overgrown stucco bunker with tinted windows and a towable signboard that said: *Dirving School.* Inside was a conference table that filled most of a room that smelled like a conference table sitting in direct sunlight with some spilled burned coffee on it.

"Latecomers will be beaten," said the Driving School instructor.

"Sorry," said the barber.

"Joking!" said the instructor, thrusting a disorderly wad of handouts at the barber, who was trying to get his clip-ons off. "What I was just saying was that, our aim is, we're going to be looking at some things or aspects, in terms of driving? Meaning safety, meaning, is speeding something we do in a vacuum, or could it involve a pedestrian or fatality or a family out for a fun drive, and then here you come, speeding, with the safety or destiny of that family not held firmly in your mind, and what happens next? Who knows?"

"A crash?" said someone.

"An accident?" said someone else.

"Crash or accident both could," said the instructor. "Either one might or may. Because I've seen, in my CPR role, as a paramedic, when many times, and I'm sorry if you find this gross or too much, I've had to sit in our rescue vehicle with a cut-off arm or hand, even of a kid, a really small arm or even limb, just weeping as if I hadn't been thoroughly trained, as I know none of you have, but I have, and why was I holding that small arm or limb and bawling? Because of someone like you yourselves, good people, I know you are, I'm not saying that, but you decided what? What did you decide? Or they. That person who cut off that kid's arm I was carrying that day I was just saying?"

No one knew.

"They decided to speed is what you did," said the instructor sadly, with pity for both the armless child and the otherwise good people who on that fateful day had decided to speed, and now sat before him, lives ruined.

"I didn't hit nobody," said a girl in a T-shirt that said *Buggin'*. "Cop just stopped me."

"But I'm talking the possibility aspect?" the instructor said kindly. "I'm talking what happens if you walk away from here a man or woman not changed in her thought patterns by the material I'm about to present you in terms of the visuals and graphics? Which some of the things are crashes and some are working wounds I myself have personally dressed and some are wounds we downloaded off the Internet so you could have a chance to see wounds that are national? Because why? Because consequences. Because are we on this earth or an island?"

"Oh," said the Buggin' girl, who now seemed chastened and convinced.

Outside the tinted window were a little forest and a stream and an insurance agency and a FedEx drop-off tilted by some pipeline digging. There were six students. One was the barber. One was a country boy with a briefcase, who took laborious notes and kept asking questions with a furrowed brow, as if, having been caught speeding, he was now considering a career in law enforcement. Did radar work via sonar beams? How snotty did someone have to get before you could stun them with your stun gun? Next to the country boy was the Buggin' girl. Next to the Buggin' girl was a very very happy crew-cut older man in a cowboy shirt and bolo tie who laughed at everything and seemed to consider it a great privilege to be here at the Driving School on this particular day with this particular bunch of excellent people, and who by the end of the session had proposed holding a monthly barbecue at his place so they wouldn't lose touch. Across the table from the Happy Man was a white-haired woman about the barber's age, who kept making sly references to films and books the barber had never heard of and rolling her eyes at things the instructor said, while writing *Help Me!* and *Beam Me Up!* on her notepad and shoving it across the table for the Happy Man to read, which seemed to make the Happy Man uncomfortable.

Next to the white-haired woman was a pretty girl. A very pretty girl. Wow. One of the prettiest girls the barber had ever seen. Boy was she pretty. Her hair was crimped and waist-length and her eyes were doelike and Egyptian and about her there was a sincerity and intelligence that made it hard for him to look away. She certainly looked out of place here at the conference table, with one hand before her in a strip of sunlight that shone on a very pretty turquoise ring that seemed to confirm her as someone exotic and darkish and schooled in things Eastern, someone you could easily imagine making love to on a barge on the Nile, say, surrounded by thousands of candles that smelled weird, or come to think of it maybe she was American Indian, and he saw her standing at the door of a tipi wearing that same sincere and intelligent expression as he came home from the hunt with a long string of dead rabbits, having been accepted into the tribe at her request after killing a cute white rabbit publicly to prove he was a man of the woods, or actually they had let him skip the rabbit part because he had spoken to them so frankly about the white man's deviousness and given them secret information about an important fort after first making them promise not to kill any women or children. He pictured one of the braves saying to her, as she rubbed two corncobs together in the dying sunlight near a spectacular mesa, that she was lucky to have the barber, who had powerful medicine in terms of being a powerful medicine man, and silently she smiled, rubbing the corncobs together perhaps a little faster, remembering the barber naked in their tipi, although on closer inspection it appeared she was actually probably Italian.

The girl looked up and caught him staring at her. He dropped his eyes and began leafing through his course materials.

After a number of slides of terrible wounds, the instructor asked did anyone know how many g's a person pulled when he or she went through a windshield at eighty miles per after hitting a bridge abutment or cow. No one knew. The instructor said quite a few. The Happy Man said he'd had a feeling it was quite a few; which was why, wasn't it, that people died? The instructor said either that or flying debris or having one's torso absolutely crushed.

"I guess that would do it," said the Happy Man, grinning.

"So what's my point?" the instructor said, pointing with his pointer to an overhead of a cartoon man driving a little car toward a tombstone while talking gaily on a car phone. "Say we're feeling good, very good, or bad, which is the opposite, say we've just had a death or a promotion or the birth of a child or a fight with our wife or spouse, but my point is, we're experiencing an emotional peak? Because what we then maybe forget, whether happy or fighting or sad or glad, whatever, is that two tons of car is what, is the thing you are in, inside of, driving, and I hope not speeding or otherwise, although for the sake of this pretend example I'm afraid we have to assume yes, you are, which is how this next bad graphic occurs."

Now on the overhead the cartoon man's body parts were scattered and his car phone was flying up to heaven on little angel wings. The barber looked at the pretty girl again. She smiled at him. His heart began to race. This never happened. They never smiled back. Well, she was young. Maybe she didn't know better than to smile back at an older guy you didn't want. Or maybe she wanted him. It was possible. Maybe she'd had it with young horny guys just out for quick rolls in the hay. Maybe she wanted someone old enough to really appreciate her, who didn't come too quickly and owned his own business and knew how to pick up after himself. He hoped she was a very strict religious virgin who'd never even had a roll in the hay. Not that he hoped she was frigid. He hoped she was the kind of strict religious virgin who, once married, would let it all hang out, and when not letting it all hang out would move with quiet dignity in conservative clothes so that no one would suspect how completely and totally she could let it all hang out when she chose to, and that she came from a poor family and could therefore really appreciate the hard work that went into running a small business, and maybe even had some accounting experience and could help with the books. Although truthfully, even if she'd had hundreds of rolls in the hay and couldn't add a stinking row of figures, he didn't care, she was so pretty, they'd work it out, assuming of course she'd have him, and with a sinking heart he remembered his missing toes. He remembered that day at the lake with Mary Ellen Kovski, when it had been over a hundred and he'd sat on a beach chair fully dressed, claiming to be chilly. A crowd of Mary Ellen's friends had gathered to help her undress him and throw him in, and in desperation he'd whispered to her about his toes, and she'd gone white and called off her friends and two months later married Phil Anpesto, that idiotic beanpole. Oh, he was tired of hiding his toes. He wanted to be open about them. He wanted to be loved in spite of them. Maybe this girl had a wisdom beyond her years. Maybe her father had a deformity, a glass eye or facial scar, maybe through long years of loving this kindly but deformed man she had come to almost need the man she loved to be somewhat deformed. Not that he liked the idea of her trotting after a bunch of deformed guys, and also not that he considered himself deformed, exactly, although, admittedly, ten barely discernible bright-pink nubs were no picnic. He pictured her lying nude in front of a fireplace, so comfortable with his feet that she'd given each nub a pet name, and maybe sometimes during lovemaking she got a little carried away and tried to kiss or lick his nubs, although certainly he didn't expect that, and in fact found it sort of disgusting, and for a split second thought somewhat less of her, then pictured himself gently pulling her up, away from his feet, and the slightly shamed look on her face made him forgive her completely for the disgusting thing she'd been about to do out of her deep deep love for him.

The instructor held up a small bloodied baby doll, which he then tossed across the room into a trunk.

"Blammo," he said. "Let's let that trunk represent a crypt or tomb, and it's your fault, from speeding, how then do you feel?"

"Bad," said the Buggin' girl.

The pretty girl passed the barber the Attendance Log, which had to be signed to obtain Course Credit and Associated Conviction Waivers/ Point Reductions.

They looked frankly at each other for what felt like a very long time.

"Hokay!" the instructor said brightly. "I suppose I don't have to grind you into absolute putty, so now it's a break, so you don't view me as some sort of Marquis de Sade or harsh taskmaster requiring you to watch gross visuals and graphics until your mind rots out."

The barber took a deep breath. He would speak to her. Maybe buy her a soda. The girl stood up. The barber got a shock. Her face was the same lovely exotic intelligent slim Cleopatran face, but her body seemed scaled to a head twice the size of the one she had. She was a big girl. Her arms were round and thick. Her mannerisms were a big girl's mannerisms. She hunched her shoulders and tugged at her smock. He felt a little miffed at her for having misled him and a little miffed at himself for having ogled such a fatty. Well, not a fatty, exactly, her body was okay, it seemed solid enough, it was just too big for her head. If you could somehow reduce the body to put it in scale with the head, or enlarge the head and shrink down the entire package, then you'd have a body that would do justice to that beautiful beautiful face that, even now, tidying up his handouts, he was regretting having lost.

"Hi," she said.

"Hello," he said, and went outside and sat in his car, and when she came out with two Cokes pretended to be cleaning the ashtrays until she went away.

3.

Later that month the barber sat stiffly at a wedding reception at the edge of a kind of mock Japanese tearoom at the Hilton while some goofball inside a full-body PuppetPlayers groom costume, complete with top hat and tails and a huge yellow felt head and three-fingered yellow felt hands, made vulgar thrusting motions with his hips in the barber's direction, as if to say: Do you like to do this? Have you done this? Can you show me how to do this, because soon I'm going to have to do this with that PuppetPlayers bride over there who is right now flirting — hey! — flirting with that bass player! and the PuppetPlayers groom sprinted across the dance floor and began romping pugilistically around the bass player who'd been trying to cuckold him. Everyone was laughing and giving the barber inexplicable thumbs-ups as the PuppetPlayers groom dragged the PuppetPlayers bride across the dance floor and introduced her to the barber, and she appeared to be very taken with him, and sat on his lap and forced his head into her yellow felt cleavage, which was stained with wine and had a cigarette burn at the neckline. With many gestures she bade the barber look under her skirts, and overcome with embarrassment he did so, eventually finding a wrapped box which, when opened, revealed a wrapped cylinder which, when opened, shot a banner across the dance floor, and on the banner was written: BEST O' LUCK ARNIE & EVELYN FROM MOM AND POP. The PuppetPlayers newlyweds sprinted across the room and bowed low before Arnie and Evelyn, who were sitting sullenly on the bandstand, apparently in the middle of a snit.

"Mickey!" Uncle Edgar shouted to the barber. "Mickey, you should've boffed that puppet broad! So what if she's a puppet! You're no prize! You're going to be choosy? Think of it! Think of it! Arnie's half your age!"

"Edgar for Christ's sake you're embarrassing him!" shouted Aunt Jean. "It's like you're saying he's old! It's like you're saying he's an old maid, only he's a guy! See what I mean? You think that's nice?"

"I am!" shouted Uncle Edgar, "I am saying that! He's a damned old lady! I don't mean no offense! I'm just saying get out and live! I love him! That's why I'm saying! The sun's setting! Pork some young babe, and if you like it, if you like the way she porks, what the hell, put down roots! What do you care? Love you can learn! But you gotta start somewhere! I mean my God, even these little so-and-sos here are try-ing to get some of it!"

And Uncle Edgar threw a dinner roll at a group of four adolescent boys the barber vaguely remembered having once pulled around the block in a little red wagon. The boys gave Uncle Edgar the finger and confirmed that not only were they trying to get some of it, they were actually getting some of it, and not always from the same chick, and sometimes more than once a day, and sometimes right after football practice, and quite possibly in the near future from a very hot Shop teacher they had reason to believe would probably give it to all of them at once if only they approached it the right way.

"Holy cow!" shouted Uncle Edgar. "Let me go to that school!"

"Edgar, you pig, be logical!" shouted Aunt Jean. "Just because Mickey's not married don't mean he ain't getting any! He could be getting some from a lady friend, or several lady friends, lady friends his own age, who already know the score, whose kids are full-grown! You don't know what goes on in his bed at night!"

"At least I don't think he's queer!" Uncle Edgar shouted to the adolescents the barber now remembered having loaded sleeping into a minivan on the evening of the day, years before, when he'd pulled them in the red wagon.

"If he is we don't give a rat's ass," said one of the adolescents. "That's his business."

"We learned that in school," said another. "Who You Do Is Up to You. We had a mini-session."

Now the PuppetPlayers groom was trying to remove the real bride's garter, and some little suited boys were walking a ledge along a goldfish stream that separated the Wedding Area from Okinawa Memories, where several clearly non-Japanese women in kimonos hustled drinks, sounding a huge metal gong whenever anyone ordered a double, at which time a bartender dressed like a sumo sent a plastic sparrow across the room on a guy wire. The little suited boys began prying up the screen that kept the goldfish from going over a tiny waterfall, to see if they would die in a shallow pond near the Vending Area.

"For example those kids torturing those fish," shouted Uncle Edgar. "You know who those kids are? Them are Brendan's kids. You know who Brendan is? He's Dick's kid. You remember who Dick is? Your second cousin the same age as you, man! Remember I took you guys to the ballgame and he threw up in my Rambler? So them kids are Dick's grandkids and here Dick's the same age as you, which means you're old enough to be a grandpa, grandpa, but you ain't even a pa yet, which I don't know how you feel about it but I think is sort of sad or weird!"

"You do but maybe he don't!" shouted Aunt Jean. "Why do you think everything you think is everything everybody else thinks? Plus Dick's no saint and neither are those kids! Dick was a teen dad and Brendan was a teen dad and probably those kids on that ledge are going to be teen dads as soon as they finish killing those poor fish!"

"Agreed!" shouted Uncle Edgar. "Hey, I got no abiding love for Dick! You want to have a fight with me at a wedding over my feelings for Dick, who throwing up in my Rambler was just the start of the crap he's pulled on me? All's I'm saying is, there's no danger of Mickey here being a teen dad, and he better think about what I'm saying and get on the stick before his shooter ain't a viable shooter anymore!"

"I'm sure you start talking about the poor guy's shooter at a wedding!" shouted Aunt Jean. "You're drunk!"

"Who ain't?" shouted Uncle Edgar, and the table exploded in laughter and one of the adolescents fell mock-drunk off his chair and when this got a laugh all the other adolescents fell mock-drunk off their chairs.

The barber excused himself and walked quickly out of the Wedding Area past three stunning girls in low-cut white gowns, who stood in what would have been shade from the fake overhanging Japanese cherry trees had the trees been outside and had it been daytime.

In the bathroom the Oriental theme receded and all was shiny chrome. The barber peed, mentally defending himself against Uncle Edgar. First off, he'd had plenty of women. Five. Five wasn't bad. Five was more than most guys, and for sure it was more than Uncle Edgar, who'd married Jean right out of high school and had a lower lip like a fish. Who would Uncle Edgar have had him marry? Sara DelBianco, with her little red face? Ellen Wiest, that tall drink of water? Ann De-Mann, who was swaybacked and had claimed he was a bad screw? Why in the world was he, a successful small businessman, expected to take advice from someone who'd spent the best years of his life transferring partial flanges from one conveyor belt to another while spraying them with a protective solvent mist? Uncle Edgar could take a flying leap, that drunk, why didn't he mind his own beeswax and spray himself with a protective solvent mist and leave the ambitious entrepreneurs of the world alone, the lush?

The barber wet his comb the way he'd been wetting his comb since high school and prepared to slick back his hair. A big vital man with a sweaty face came in and whacked the barber on the back as if they were old pals. In the mirror was a skeletal mask of blue and purple and pink that the barber knew was his face but couldn't quite believe was his face, because in the past his face had always risen to the occasion. In the past his face could always be counted on to amount to more than the sum of its parts when he smiled winningly, but now when he smiled winningly he looked like a corpse trying to appear cheerful in a wind tunnel. His eyes bulged, his lips were thin, his forehead wrinkles were deep as sticklines in mud. It had to be the lighting. He was ugly. He was old. How had this happened? Who would want him now?

"You look like hell," thundered the big man from a stall, and the barber fled the mirror without slicking back his hair.

As he rushed past the stunning girls, a boy in a fraternity sweatshirt came over. Seeing the barber, he made a comic geriatric coughing noise in his throat, and one of the girls giggled and adjusted her shoulder strap as if to keep the barber from seeing down her dress.

4.

A few weeks before the wedding, the barber had received in the mail a greeting card showing a cowboy roping a steer. The barber's name was scrawled across the steer's torso, and *Me (Mr. Jenks)* across the cowboy.

Here's hoping you will remember me from our driving school, said a note inside, *and attend a small barbecue at my home. My hope being to renew those acquaintances we started back then, which I found enjoyable and which since the loss of my wife I've had far too few of. Please come and bring nothing. As you can see from the cover, I am roping you in, not to brand you, but only to show you my hospitality, I hope. Your friend, Larry Jenks.*

Who was Jenks? Was Jenks the Happy Man? The barber threw the card in the bathroom trash, imagining the Driving School kooks seated glumly on folding chairs in a trailer house. For a week or so the card sat there, cowboy-side up, vaguely reproaching him. Then he took out the trash.

A few days after the wedding he received a second card from Jenks, with a black flower on the front.

A good time was had by all, it said. *Sorry you were unable to attend. Even the younger folks, I think, enjoyed. Many folks took home quite a few sodas, because as I am alone now, I never could have drank that many sodas in my life. This note, on a sadder note, and that is why the black flower, is to inform you that Eldora Ronsen is moving to Seattle. You may remember her as the older woman to your immediate right. She is high up in her company and just got higher, which is good for her, but bad for us, as she is such a super gal. Please join us Tuesday next, Corrigan's Pub, for farewell drinks, map enclosed, your friend, Larry Jenks.*

Tuesday next was tomorrow.

"Well, you can't go," Ma said. "The girls are coming over."

The girls were the Altar and Rosary Society. When they came over he had to wait on them hand and foot while they talked about which priest they would marry if only the priests weren't priests. When one lifted her blouse to show her recent scar, he had to say it was the worst scar ever. When one asked if her eye looked rheumy he had to get very close to her rheumy eye and say it looked non-rheumy to him.

"Well, I think I might want to go," he said.

"I just said you can't," she said. "The girls are coming."

She was trying to guilt him. She was always trying to guilt him. Once she'd faked a seizure when he tried to go to Detroit for a hair show. No wonder he had no friends. Not that he had no friends. He had plenty of friends. He had Rick the mailman. Every day when Rick the mailman came in, he asked the barber how it was hanging, and the barber said it was hanging fine. He had old Mr. Mellon, at Mellon Drugs, next door to the shop, who, though sort of deaf, was still a good friend, when not hacking phlegm into his little red cup.

"Ma," he said. "I'm going."

"Mr. Bigshot," she said. "Bullying an old lady."

"I'm not bullying you," he said. "And you're not old."

"Oh, I'm young, I'm a tiny baby," she said, tapping her dentures.

That night he dreamed of the pretty but heavy girl. In his dream she was all slimmed down. Her body looked like the body of Daisy Mae in the Li'l Abner cartoon, who he had always found somewhat attractive. She came into the shop in cut-off jeans, chewing a blade of grass, and said she found his accomplishments amazing, especially considering the hardships he'd had to overcome, like his dad dying young and his mother being so nervous, and then she took the blade of grass out of her mouth and put it on the magazine table and stretched out across the Waiting Area couch while he undressed, and seeing his unit she said it was the biggest unit she'd ever seen, and arched her back in a sexy way, and then she called him over and gave him a deep warm kiss on the mouth that was so much like the kiss he'd been waiting for all his life that it abruptly woke him.

Sitting up in bed, he missed her. He missed how much she loved and understood him. She knew everything about him and yet still liked him. His gut sort of ached with wanting.

In his boyhood mirror he caught sight of himself and flexed his chest the way he used to flex his chest in the weightlifting days, and looked so much like a little old man trying to take a dump in his bed that he hopped up and stood panting on the round green rug.

Ma was blundering around in the hallway. Because of the dream he had a partial bone. To hide his partial bone, he kept his groin behind the door as he thrust his head into the hall.

"I was walking in my sleep," Ma said. "I'm so worried I was walking in my sleep."

"What are you worried about?" he said.

"I'm worried about when the girls come," she said.

"Well, don't worry," he said. "It'll be fine."

"Thanks a million," she said, going back into her room. "Very reassuring."

Well, it would be fine. If they ran out of coffee, one of the old ladies could make coffee, if they ran out of snacks they could go a little hungry, if something really disastrous happened they could call him at Corrigan's, he'd leave Ma the number.

Because he was going.

In the morning he called Jenks and accepted the invitation, while Ma winced and clutched her stomach and pulled over a heavy wooden chair and collapsed into it.

5.

Corrigan's was meant to feel like a pub at the edge of a Scottish golf course, there was a roaring fire, and many ancient-looking golf clubs hanging above tremendous tables of a hard plastic material meant to appear gnarled and scarred, and kilted waitresses with names like Heather and Zoe were sloshing chicken wings and fried cheese and lobster chunks into metal vats near an aerial photo of the Old Course at St. Andrews, Scotland.

The barber was early. He liked to be early. He felt it was polite to be early, except when he was late, at which time he felt being early was anal. Where the heck was everybody? They weren't very polite. He looked down at his special shoes. They were blocky and black and had big removable metal stays in the sides and squeaked when he walked. Well if anybody said anything about his shoes they could go to hell, he hadn't asked to be born with no toes, and besides, the special shoes looked nice with khakis.

"Sorry we're late!" Mr. Jenks shouted, and the Driving School group settled in around the long gnarled table.

The pretty but heavy girl hung her purse across the back of her chair. Her hair looked like her hair in the dream and her eyes looked like her eyes in the dream, and as for her body, he couldn't tell, she was wearing a mumu. But certainly facially she was pretty. Facially she was very possibly the prettiest girl here. Was she? If aliens came down and forced each man to pick one woman to reproduce with in a chain-link enclosure while they took notes, would he choose her, based solely on face? Here was a woman with a good rear but a doglike face, here was a woman with a nice perm but a blop at the end of her nose, here was the Buggin' girl, who looked like a chicken, here was the white-haired woman, whose face was all wrinkled, here was the pretty but heavy girl. Was she the prettiest? Facially? He thought she very possibly was.

He regarded her fondly from across the table, waiting for her to catch him regarding her fondly, so he could quickly avert his eyes, so she'd know he was still possibly interested, and then she dropped her menu and bent to retrieve it and the barber had a chance to look briefly down her dress.

Well she definitely had something going on in the chest category. So facially she was the prettiest in the room, plus she had decent boobs. Attractive breasts. The thing was, would she want him? He was old. Oldish. When he stood up too fast his knee joints popped. Lately his gums had started to bleed. Plus he had no toes. Although why sell himself short? He owned his own small business. He had a bit of a gut, yes, and his hair was somewhat thin, but then again his shoulders and chest were broad, so that the overall effect, even with the gut, was of power, which girls liked, and at least his head was properly sized for his body, which was more than she could say, although then again he still lived with his mother.

Well, who was perfect? He wasn't perfect and she wasn't perfect but they obviously had some sort of special chemistry, based on what had happened at the Driving School, and anyway, what the heck, he wasn't proposing, he was just considering possibly trying to get to know her somewhat better.

In this way he decided to ask the pretty but heavy girl out.

How to do it, that was the thing. How to ask her. He could get her alone and say her hair looked super. While saying it looked super he could run a curl through his fingers in a professional way, as if looking for split ends. He could say he'd love a chance to cut such excellent hair, then slip her a card for One Free Cut and Coffee. That could work. That had worked in the past. It had worked with Sylvia Reynolds, a bank teller with crow's-feet and a weird laugh who turned out to be an excellent kisser. When she'd come in for her Free Cut and Coffee, he'd claimed they were out of coffee, and taken her to Bean Men Roasters. A few dates later they'd gotten carried away, unfortunately, because of her excellent kissing, and done more, much more actually, than he ever would've imagined doing with someone with crow's-feet and a weird laugh and strangely wide hips, and when he'd gotten home that night and had a good hard look at the locket she'd given him after they'd done it, he'd instantly felt bad, because wow could you ever see the crow's-feet in that picture. As he looked at Sylvia standing in that bright sunlit meadow in the picture, her head thrown back, joyfully laughing, her crow's-feet so very pronounced, a spontaneous image had sprung into his mind of her coming wide-hipped toward him while holding a baby, and suddenly he'd been deeply disappointed in himself for doing it with someone so unusual-looking, and to ensure that he didn't make matters worse by inadvertently doing it with her a second time, he'd sort of never called her again, and had even switched banks.

He glanced at the pretty but heavy girl and found her making her way toward the Ladies'.

Now was as good a time as any.

He waited a few minutes, then excused himself and stood outside the Ladies' reading ads posted on a corkboard until the pretty but heavy girl came out.

He cleared his throat and asked was she having fun?

She said yes.

Then he said wow did her hair look great. And in terms of great hair, he knew what he was talking about, he was a professional. Where did she have it cut? He ran one of her curls through his fingers, as if looking for split ends, and said he'd love the chance to work with such dynamite hair, and took from his shirt pocket the card for One Free Cut and Coffee.

"Maybe you could stop by sometime," he said.

"That's nice of you," she said, and blushed.

So she was a shy girl. Sort of cutely nerdy. Not exactly confident. That was too bad. He liked confidence. He found it sexy. On the other hand, who could blame her, he could sometimes be very intimidating. Also her lack of confidence indicated he could perhaps afford to be a little bit bold.

"Like, say, tomorrow?" he said. "Like, say, tomorrow at noon?"

"Ha," she said. "You move quick."

"Not too quick, I hope," he said.

"No," she said. "Not too quick."

So he had her. By saying he wasn't moving too quick, wasn't she implicitly implying that he was moving at exactly the right speed? All he had to do now was close the deal.

"I'll be honest," he said. "I've been thinking about you since Driving School."

"You have?" she said.

"I have," he said.

"So you're saying tomorrow?" she said, blushing again.

"If that's okay for you," he said.

"It's okay for me," she said.

Then she started uncertainly back to the table and the barber raced into the Men's. Yes! Yes yes yes. It was a date. He had her. He couldn't believe it. He'd really played that smart. What had he been worried about? He was cute, women had always considered him cute, never mind the thin hair and minor gut, there was just something about him women liked.

Wow she was pretty, he had done very very well for himself.

Back at the table Mr. Jenks was taking Polaroids. He announced his intention of taking six shots of the Driving School group, one for each member to keep, and the barber stood behind the pretty but heavy girl, with his hands on her shoulders, and she reached up and gave his wrist a little squeeze.

6.

At home old-lady cars were in the driveway and old-lady coats were piled on the couch and the house smelled like old lady and the members of the Altar and Rosary Society were gathered around the dining room table looking frail. They all looked the same to the barber, he could never keep them straight, there was a crone in a lime pantsuit and a crone in a pink pantsuit and two crones in blue pantsuits. As he came in they began asking Ma where he had been, why was he out so late, why hadn't he been here to help, wasn't he normally a fairly good son? And Ma said yes, he was normally a fairly good son, except he hadn't given her any grandkids yet and often wasted water by bathing twice a day.

"My son had that problem," said one of the blue crones. "His wife once pulled me aside."

"Has his wife ever pulled you aside?" the pink crone said to Ma.

"He's not married," said Ma.

"Maybe the not-married is related to the bathing-too-often," said the lime crone.

"Maybe he holds himself aloof from others," said the blue crone. "My son held himself aloof from others."

"My daughter holds herself aloof from others," said the pink crone.

"Does she bathe too often?" said Ma.

"She doesn't bathe too often," said the pink crone. "She just thinks she's smarter than everyone."

"Do you think you're smarter than everyone?" asked the lime crone severely, and thank God at that moment Ma reached up and pulled him down by the shirt and roughly kissed his cheek.

"Have a good time?" she said, and the group photo fell out of his pocket and into the dip.

"Very nice," he said.

"Who are these people?" she said, wiping a bit of dip off the photo with her finger. "Are these the people you went to meet? Who is this you're embracing? This big one."

"I'm not embracing her, Ma," he said. "I'm just standing behind her. She's a friend."

"She's big," Ma said. "You smell like beer."

"Did you girls see Mrs. Link last Sunday?" said the lime crone. "Mrs. Link should never wear slacks. When she wears slacks her hips look wide. Her hips are all you see."

"They almost seem to precede her into the church," said the pink crone.

"It's as if she is being accompanied by her own hips," said the lime crone.

"Some men like them big," said one of the blue crones.

"Look at his face," said the other blue crone. "He likes them big."

"The cat who ate the canary," said the lime crone.

"Actually I don't consider her big," said the barber, in a tone of disinterested interest, looking down over the pink crone's shoulder at the photo.

"Whatever you say," said the lime crone.

"He's been drinking," said Ma.

Oh he didn't care what they thought, he was happy. He jokingly snatched the photo away and dashed up to his room, taking two stairs at a time. These poor old farts, they were all superlonely, which was why they were so damn mean.

Gabby Gabby Gabby, her name was Gabby, short for Gabrielle.

Tomorrow they had a date for lunch.

Breakfast, rather. They'd moved it up to breakfast. While they'd been kissing against her car she'd said she wasn't sure she could wait until lunch to see him again. He felt the same way. Even breakfast seemed a long time to wait. He wished she was sitting next to him on the bed right now, holding his hand, listening through the tiny vined window to the sounds of the crones cackling as they left. In his mind he stroked her hair and said he was glad he'd finally found her, and she said she was glad to have been found, she'd never dreamed that someone so distinguished, with such a broad chest and wide shoulders, could love a girl like her. Was she happy? he tenderly asked. Oh she was so happy, she said, so happy to be sitting next to this accomplished, distinguished man in this amazing house, which in his mind was not the current house, a peagreen ranch with a tilted cracked sidewalk, but a mansion, on a lake, with a smaller house nearby for Ma, down a very very long wooded path, and he'd paid cash for the mansion with money he'd made from his international chain of barbershops, each of which was an exact copy of his current barbershop, and when he and Gabby visited his London England shop, leaving Ma behind in the little house, his English barbers would always burst into applause and say Jolly Good Jolly Good as the happy couple walked in the door.

"I'm leaving you the dishes, Romeo," Ma shouted from the bottom of the stairs.

7.

Early next morning he sat in the bath, getting ready for his date. Here was his floating wienie, like some kind of sea creature, here were his nubs on the green tile. He danced them nervously around a bit, like Fred Astaire dancing on a wall, and swirled the washrag through the water, holding it by one corner, so that it too was like a sea creature, a blue ray, a blue monogrammed ray that now crossed the land that was his belly and attacked the sea creature that was his wienie, and remembering what Uncle Edgar had said at the wedding about his shooter not being viable, he gave his shooter a good, hard, reassuring shake, as if congratulating it for being so very viable. It was a great shooter, very good, perfectly fine, in spite of what Ann DeMann had once said about him being a bad screw, it had gotten hard quick last night and stayed hard throughout the kissing, and as far as being queer, that was laughable, he wished Uncle Edgar could have seen that big boner.

Oh he felt good, in spite of a slight hangover he was very happy.

Flipping his unit carelessly from side to side with thumb and forefinger, he looked at the group Polaroid, which he'd placed near the sink. God, she was pretty. He was so lucky. He had a date with a pretty young girl. Those crones were nuts, she wasn't big, no bigger than any other girl. Not much bigger anyway. How wide were her shoulders compared to, say, the shoulders of the Buggin' girl? Well, he wasn't going to dignify that with a response. She was perfect just the way she was. He leaned out of the tub to look closer at the photo. Well, Gabby's shoulders were maybe a little wider than the Buggin' girl's shoulders. Definitely wider. Were they wider than the shoulders of the white-haired woman? Actually in the photo they were even wider than the shoulders of the country boy.

Oh, he didn't care, he just really liked her. He liked her laugh and the way she had of raising one eyebrow when skeptical, he liked the way that, when he moved his hand to her boob as they leaned against her car, she let out a happy little sigh. He liked how, after a few minutes of kissing her while feeling her boobs, which were super, very firm, when he dropped his hand down between her legs, she said she thought that was probably enough for one night, which was good, it showed good morals, it showed she knew when to call it quits.

Ma was in her room, banging things around.

Because for a while there he'd been worried. Worried she wasn't going to stop him. Which would have been disappointing. Because she barely knew him. He could've been anybody. For a few minutes there against the car he'd wondered if she wasn't a little on the easy side. He wondered this now. Did he? Did he wonder this now? Did he want to wonder this now? Wasn't that sort of doubting her? Wasn't that sort of disloyal? No, no, it was fine, there was no sin in looking at things honestly. So was she? Too easy? In other words, why so sort of desperate? Why had she so quickly agreed to go out with him? Why so willing to give it away so easily to some old guy she barely knew? Well, he thought he might know why. Possibly it was due to her size. Possibly the guys her own age had passed her by, due to the big bod, and nearing thirty, she'd heard her biologic clock ticking and decided it was time to lower her standards, which, possibly, was where he came in. Possibly, seeing him at the Driving School, she'd thought: Since all old guys like young girls, big bods notwithstanding, this old pear-shaped balding guy can ergo be had no problem.

Was that it? Was that how it was?

"Some girl just called," Ma said, leaning heavily against the bathroom door. "Some girl, Gabby or Tabby or something? Said you had a date. Wanted you to know she's running late. Is that the same girl? The same fat girl you were embracing?"

Sitting in the tub, he noticed that his penis was gripped nervously in his fist, and let it go, and it fell to one side, as if it had just passed out.

"Do the girl a favor, Mickey," Ma said. "Call it off. She's too big for you. You'll never stick with her. You never stick with anyone. You couldn't even stick with Ellen Wiest, for crying out loud, who was so wonderful, you honestly think you're going to stick with this Tabby or Zippy or whatever?"

Of course Ma had to bring up Ellen Wiest. Ma had loved Ellen, who had a regal face and great manners and was always kissing up to Ma by saying what a great mother Ma was. He remembered the time he and Ellen had hiked up to Butternut Falls and stood getting wet in the mist, holding hands, smiling sweetly at each other, which had really been fun, and she'd said she thought she loved him, which was nice, except wow she was tall. You could only hold hands with her for so long before your back started to hurt. He remembered his back sort of hurting in the mist. Plus they'd had that fight on the way down. Well, there were a lot of things about Ellen that Ma wasn't aware of, such as her nasty temper, and he remembered Ellen storming ahead of him on the trail, glaring back now and then, just because he'd made a funny remark about her height, about her blocking out the sun, and hadn't he also said something about her being able to eat leaves from the tallest of the trees they were passing under? Well, that had been funny, it had all been in fun, why did she have to get so mad about it? Where was Ellen now? Hadn't she married Ed Trott? Well, Trott could have her. Trott was probably suffering the consequences of being married to Miss Thin Skin even now, and he remembered having recently seen Ed and Ellen at the ValueWay, Ellen pregnant and looking so odd, with her big belly pressing against the cart as she craned that giraffelike neck down to nuzzle Ed, who had a big stupid happy grin on his face like he was the luckiest guy in the world.

The barber stood up angrily from the tub. Here in the mirror were his age-spotted deltoids and his age-spotted roundish pecs and his strange pale love handles.

Ma resettled against the door with a big whump.

"So what's the conclusion, lover boy?" she said. "Are you canceling? Are you calling up and canceling?"

"No I'm not," he said.

"Well, poor her," Ma said.

8.

Every morning of his life he'd walked out between Ma's twin rose trellises. When he went to grade school, when he went to junior high, when he went to high school, when he went to barber college, he'd always walked out between the twin trellises. He walked out between them now, in his brown cords and the blue button-down, and considered plucking a rose for Gabby, although that was pretty corny, he might seem sort of doddering, and instead, using the hand with which he'd been about to pluck the rose, he flicked the rose, then in his mind apologized to the rose for ripping its skin.

Oh, this whole thing made him tense, very tense, he wished he was back in bed.

"Mickey, a word," Ma called out from the door, but he only waved to her over his shoulder.

South Street was an old wagon road. Cars took the bend too fast. Often he scowled at the speeding cars on his way to work, imagining the drivers laughing to themselves about the way he walked. Because on days when his special shoes hurt he sort of minced. They hurt today. He shouldn't have worn the thin gray socks. He was mincing a bit but trying not to, because what if Gabby drove up South on her way to meet him at the shop and saw him mincing?

On Fullerton were three consecutive houses with swing sets. Under each swing was a grassless place. At the last of the three houses a baby sat in the grassless place, smacking a swing with a spoon. He turned up Lincoln Ave, and passed the Liquor Mart, which smelled like liquor, and La Belle Époque, the antique store with the joyful dog inside, and as always the joyful dog sprang over the white settee and threw itself against the glass, and then there was Gabby, down the block, peering into his locked shop, and he corrected his mincing and began walking normally though it killed.

Did she like the shop? He took big bold steps with his head thrown back so he'd look happy. Happy and strong, with all his toes. With all his toes, in the prime of his life. Did she notice how neat the shop was? How professional? Or did she notice that four of the chairs were of one type and the fifth was totally different? Did it seem to her that the shop was geared to old blue-hairs, which was something he'd once heard a young woman say as he took out the trash?

How did she look? Did she look good?

It was still too far to tell.

Now she saw. Now she saw him. Her face brightened, she waved like a little girl. Oh, she was pretty. It was as if he'd known her forever. She looked so hopeful. But oops. Oh my God she was big. She'd dressed all wrong, tight jeans and a tight shirt. As if testing him. Jesus, this was the biggest he'd ever seen her look. What was she doing, testing him by trying to look her worst? Here was an alley, should he swerve into the alley and call her later? Or not? Not call her later? Forget the whole thing? Pretend last night had never happened? Although now she'd seen him. And he didn't want to forget the whole thing. Last night for the first time in a long time he'd felt like someone other than a guy who wanks it on the milking stool in his mother's pantry. Last night he'd bought a pitcher for the Driving School group and Jenks had called him a sport. Last night she'd said he was a sexy kisser.

Thinking about forgetting last night gave him a pit in his stomach. Forgetting last night was not an option. What were the options? Well, she could trim down. That was an option. That was a good option. Maybe all she needed was someone to tell her the simple truth, someone to sit her down and say: Look, you have an incredibly beautiful, intelligent face, but from the neck down, sweetie, wow, we've got some serious work to do. And after their frank talk, she'd send him flowers with a card that said *Thanks for your honesty, let's get this thing done.* And every night as she stood at the mirror in her panties and bra he'd point out places that needed improvement, and the next day she'd energetically address those areas in the gym, and soon the head–bod discrepancy would be eliminated, and he imagined her in a fancy dress at a little table on a veranda, a veranda by the sea, thanking him for the honeymoon trip, she came from a poor family and had never even been on a vacation, much less a six-week tour of Europe, and then she said, Honey why not put down that boring report on how much your international chain of barbershops earned us this month and join me in the bedroom so I can show you how grateful I am, and in the bedroom she started stripping, and was good at it, not that she'd ever done it before, no, she hadn't, she was just naturally good at it, and when she was done, there she was, with her perfect face and the Daisy Mae body, smiling at him with unconditional love.

It wouldn't be easy. It would take hard work. He knew a little about hard work, having made a barbershop out of a former pet store. Tearing out a counter he'd found a dead mouse. From a sump pump he'd pulled three hardened snakes. But he'd never quit. Because he was a worker. He wasn't afraid of hard work. Was she a worker? He didn't know. He'd have to find out.

They'd find out together.

She stood beside his wooden bench, under his shop awning, and the shadow of her dark mane fell at his feet.

What a wild ride this had been, how much he had learned about himself already!

"Here I am," she said, with a shy, pretty smile.

"I'm so glad you are," he said, and bent to unlock the door of the shop.

I CAN SPEAK!™

Mrs. Ruth Faniglia
210 Lester Street
Rochester, N.Y. 14623

Dear Mrs. Faniglia,

We were very sorry to receive your letter of 23 Feb., which accompanied the I CAN SPEAK!™ you returned, much to our disappointment. We here at KidLuv believe that the I CAN SPEAK!™ is an innovative and essential educational tool that, used with proper parental guidance, offers a rare early-development opportunity for babies and toddlers alike. And so I thought I would take some of my personal time (I am on lunch) and try to address the questions you raised in your letter, which is here in front of me on my (cluttered!) desk.

First, may I be so bold as to suggest that your disappointment may stem from your own, perhaps unreasonable, expectations? Because in your letter, what you indicated, when I read it, was that you think and/or thought that somehow the product can read your baby's mind? Our product cannot read your baby's mind, Mrs. Faniglia. No one can read a baby's mind, at least not yet. Although believe me, we are probably working on it! All the I CAN SPEAK!™ can do, however, is respond to aural patterns in a way that makes baby seem older. Say baby sees a peach. If you or Mr. Faniglia (I hope I do not presume) were to loudly say something like "What a delicious peach!" the I CAN SPEAK!™, hearing this, through that little slotted hole near the neck, would respond by saying something like "I LIKE PEACH." Or "I WANT PEACH." Or, if you had chosen the ICS2000 (you chose the ICS1900, which is fine, perfectly good for most babies), the I CAN SPEAK!™ might even respond by saying something like "FRUIT, ISN'T THAT ONE OF THE MAJOR FOOD GROUPS?" Which would be pretty good, for a six-month-old like Derek, your son, don't you think?

But here I must reiterate: That would not in reality be Derek speaking. Derek would not in reality know that a peach is fruit, or that fruit is a major food group. The I CAN SPEAK!™ knows, however, and, from its position on Derek's face, it will give the illusion that Derek knows, by giving the illusion that Derek is speaking out of the twin moving SimuLips. But that is it. That is all we claim.

Furthermore, in your letter, Mrs. Faniglia, you state that the I CAN SPEAK!™ "mask" (your terminology) takes on a "stressed-out look when talking that is not what a real baby's talking face appears like but is more like some nervous middle-aged woman." Well, maybe that is so, but, with all due respect, you try it! You try making a latex face look and talk and move like the real face of an actual live baby! Inside are over 5000 separate circuits and 390 moving parts. And as far as looking like a middle-aged woman, we beg to differ: we do not feel that a middle-aged stressed-out woman has (1) no hair on head and (2) chubby cheeks and (3) fine downy facial hair. The ICS1900 unit is definitely the face of a baby, Mrs. Faniglia. We took over twenty-five hundred photos of different babies and using a computer combined them to make this face, this face we call Male Composite 37 or, affectionately, Little Roger. But what you possibly seem to be unhappy about is that Little Roger's face is not Derek's face? To be frank, Mrs. Faniglia, many of you, our customers, have found it disconcerting that their baby looks different with the I CAN SPEAK!™ on. Which we find so surprising. Did you, we often wonder, not look at the cover of the box? On that cover the ICS1900 is very plainly shown, situated on a sort of rack, looking facewise like Little Roger, albeit Little Roger is a bit crumpled and has a forehead furrow of sorts.

But this is why we came up with the ICS2100. With the ICS2100, your baby looks just like your baby. And, because we do not want anyone to be unhappy with us, we would like to give you a complimentary ICS2100 upgrade! We would like to come to your house on Lester Street and make a personalized plaster cast of Derek's real, actual face! And soon, via FedEx, here will come Derek's face in a box, and when you slip that ICS2100 over Derek's head and Velcro the Velcro, he will look so very much like himself! Plus we have another free surprise, which is that, while at your house, we will tape his actual voice and use it to make our phrases, the phrases Derek will subsequently say. So not only will he look like himself, he will sound like himself, as he crawls around your house appearing to speak!

Plus we will throw in several other personalizing options. Say you call Derek "Lovemeister." (I am using this example from my own personal home, as my wife, Ann, and I call our son Billy "Lovemeister," because he is so sweet.) With the ICS2100, you might choose to have Derek say, upon crawling into a room, "HERE COMES THE LOVEMEISTER!" or "STOP TALKING DIRTY, THE LOVEMEISTER HAS ARRIVED!" How we do this is, laser beams coming out of the earlobes, which sense the doorframe. So the I CAN SPEAK!™ knows it has just entered a room, from its position on Derek's head! And also you will have over one hundred Discretionary Phrases to more highly personalize Derek. For instance, you might choose to have him say, on his birthday, "MOMMY AND DADDY, REMEMBER THAT TIME YOU CONCEIVED ME IN ARUBA?" Although probably you did not in fact conceive Derek in Aruba. That we do not know. (Our research is not that extensive!) Or say your dog comes up and gives Derek a lick. You could make Derek say (if your dog's name is Queenie), "QUEENIE, GIVE IT A REST!" Which, you know what? It makes you love him more. Because suddenly he is articulate. Suddenly he is not just sitting there going glub glub glub while examining a piece of his own feces on his own thumb, which is something we recently found Billy doing! Sometimes we have felt that our childless friends think badly of us for having a kid who just goes glub glub glub in the corner while looking at his feces on his thumb. But now when childless friends are over, what we have found, my wife, Ann, and I, is that it's great to have your kid say something witty and self-possessed years before he or she would actually in reality be able to say something witty or self-possessed. The bottom line is that it's just *fun* when you and your childless friends are playing cards, and your baby suddenly blurts out (in his *very own probable future voice*), "IT IS LIKELY THAT WE STILL DON'T FULLY UNDERSTAND THE IMPORT OF ALL OF EINSTEIN'S FINDINGS!"

Here I must admit that we have several times seen a sort of softening in the eyes of our resolute childless friends, as if they, too, would suddenly like to have a baby.

And as far as Derek flinching whenever that voice issues forth from him? When that speaker near his mouth sort of buzzes his lips? May I say this is not unusual? What I suggest? Try putting the ICS on Derek for a short time at first, maybe ten minutes a day, then gradually building up his Wearing Time. That is what we did. And it worked super. Now Billy wears his even while sleeping. In fact, if we forget to put it back on after his bath, he pitches a fit. Kind of begs for it! He starts to say, you know, "Mak! Mak!" Which we think is his word for mask. And when we put the mask on and Velcro the Velcro, he says, or rather it says, "GUTEN MORGEN, PAPA!" because we are trying to teach him German, and have installed the German Learning module in our ICS2100. Or for example, if his pants are not yet on, he'll say, "HOW ABOUT SLAPPING ON MY ROMPERS SO I CAN GET ON WITH MY DAY!" (I wrote that one.)

My point is, with the ICS2100 Billy is much, much cleverer than he ever was with the ICS1900. He has recently learned, for example, that if he spills a little milk on his chin, his SimuLips will issue a MOO sound. Which he really seems to get a kick out of! I'll be in the living room doing a little evening paperwork and from the kitchen I'll hear, you know, "MOO! MOO! MOO!" And I'll rush in, and there'll be this sort of lake of milk on the floor. And there'll be Billy, pouring milk on his chin until I yank the milk away, at which point he bellows, "DON'T FENCE ME IN." (Ann's contribution — she was raised in Wyoming!)

I, for one, Mrs. Faniglia, do not believe that any baby wants to sit around all day going glub glub glub. My feeling is that a baby, sitting in its diaper, looking around at the world, thinks to itself, albeit in some crude nonverbal way, What the heck is wrong with me, why am I the only one going glub glub glub while all these other folks are talking in whole complete sentences? And hence, possibly, lifelong psychological damage may result. Now, am I saying that your Derek runs the risk of feeling bad about himself as a grownup because as a baby he felt he didn't know how to talk right? No, it is not for me to say that, Mrs. Faniglia, I am only in Sales. But I will say that I am certainly not taking any chances with our Billy. My belief is that when Billy hears a competent, intelligent voice issuing from the area near his mouth, he feels excellent about himself. And I feel excellent about him. Not that I didn't feel excellent about him before. But now we can actually have a sort of conversation! And also — and most importantly — when that voice issues from his SimuLips he learns something invaluable; namely, that when he finally does begin speaking, he will be speaking via using his mouth.

Now, Mrs. Faniglia, you may be thinking, Hold on a sec, of course this guy loves his I CAN SPEAK!™ He probably gets his for free! But not so, Mrs. Faniglia, I get mine for two grand, just like you. We get no discounts, so much in demand is the I CAN SPEAK!™, and in addition we are strongly encouraged by our management to purchase and use the I CAN SPEAK!™ at home, on our own kids. (Or even, in one case, on an elderly senile mom! Suffice it to say that, though she looks sort of funny with the Little Roger head on her somewhat frail frame, the family takes great comfort in hearing all the witty things she has to say. Just like her old self!) Not that I wouldn't use it otherwise. Believe me, I would. Since we upgraded to the ICS2100, things have been great, Billy looks almost identical to himself; and is not nearly so, you know, boring as before, when we had the ICS1900, which (frankly) says some rather predictable things, which I expect is partly why you were so unhappy with it, Mrs. Faniglia, you seem like a very intelligent woman. When people come over now, sometimes we just gather around Billy and wait for his next howler, and last weekend my supervisor, Mr. Ted Ames, stopped by (a super guy, he has really given me support, please let him know if you've found this letter at all helpful) and boy did we all crack up laughing when Billy began rubbing his face very rapidly across the carpet in order to make his ICS2100 shout, "FRICTION IS A COMMON AND USEFUL SOURCE OF HEAT!"

Mrs. Faniglia, it is nearing the end of my lunch, and so I must wrap this up, but I hope I have been of service. On a personal note, I did not have the greatest of pasts when I came here, having been in a few scrapes and even rehab situations, but now, wow, the commissions roll in, and I have made a nice life for me and Ann and Billy. Not that the possible loss of my commission is the reason for my concern. Please do not think so. While it is true that, if you decline my upgrade offer and persist in your desire to return your ICS1900, my commission must be refunded, by me, to Mr. Ames, it is no big deal, I have certainly refunded commissions to Mr. Ames before, especially lately. I don't quite know what I'm doing wrong. But that is not your concern, Mrs. Faniglia. Your concern is Derek. My real reason for writing this letter, on my lunch break, is that, hard as we all work at KidLuv to provide innovative and essential development tools for families like yours, Mrs. Faniglia, it is always sort of a heartbreak when our products are misapprehended. Please do accept our offer of a free ICS2100 upgrade. We at KidLuv really love what kids are, Mrs. Faniglia, which is why we want them to become something better as soon as possible! Baby's early years are so precious, and must not be wasted, as we are finding out, as our Billy grows and grows, learning new skills every day.

Sincerely yours,
Rick Sminks
Product Service Representative
KidLuv, Inc.

David Foster Wallace

The fiction of David Foster Wallace is complex, convoluted, beautifully wrought. His work is formally experimental in a way that brings Coover and Barthelme to mind, but he is less interested in surfaces than Barthelme, and his stories are concerned with revealing more about the psychology of the times than the aesthetics. Borges is another obvious influence, in that Wallace stretches fictional boundaries by employing the form of essays, interviews, and scholarly notes, as if his stories are found objects. He is endlessly inventive. "The Depressed Person," for instance, uses clinical language and a growing body of footnotes to suggest the dynamic between patient and therapist, and the several pieces that make up the interviews with hideous men are presented as monologues interrupted by deleted questions, which give the revelations an intense dramatic emphasis. In addition to *Brief Interviews with Hideous Men,* from which the two stories in this volume have been excerpted, Wallace is the author of the novels *The Broom of the System* and *Infinite Jest,* as well as another collection, *Girl with Curious Hair.*

"Forever Overhead," reproduced here, is an intoxicatingly sensuous piece, in which the concrete details of a remembered experience — going off the high dive on the day of the (second-person) narrator's thirteenth birthday — become the story. It reminds me of the work of Robbe-Grillet and the *nouveau roman* or, more recently, of Nicholson Baker's intense meditations on his material environment. What distinguishes Wallace's piece from the work of either of them is the exquisite language that makes the story sing, especially the lyrical closing lines. The second piece, one of the "Brief Interviews with Hideous Men," reveals character in a naked and unsettling way. Because of the device of inserting the Q. to indicate that a question has been put to the narrator or a response has been made, the story becomes a dramatic monologue, which is significant in that it makes the crudeness of the narrator's observations stand out in relief. In this case, he uses his deformity in the most casually manipulative way, and yet, one wonders all the while about the depth of hurt and shame his braggadocio is meant to conceal.

Forever Overhead

Happy Birthday. Your thirteenth is important. Maybe your first really public day. Your thirteenth is the chance for people to recognize that important things are happening to you.

Things have been happening to you for the past half year. You have seven hairs in your left armpit now. Twelve in your right. Hard dangerous spirals of brittle black hair. Crunchy, animal hair. There are now more of the hard curled hairs around your privates than you can count without losing track. Other things. Your voice is rich and scratchy and moves between octaves without any warning. Your face has begun to get shiny when you don't wash it. And two weeks of a deep and frightening ache this past spring left you with something dropped down from inside: your sack is now full and vulnerable, a commodity to be protected. Hefted and strapped in tight supporters that stripe your buttocks red. You have grown into a new fragility.

And dreams. For months there have been dreams like nothing before: moist and busy and distant, full of yielding curves, frantic pistons, warmth and a great falling; and you have awakened through fluttering lids to a rush and a gush and a toe-curling scalp-snapping jolt of feeling from an inside deeper than you knew you had, spasms of a deep sweet hurt, the streetlights through your window blinds cracking into sharp stars against the black bedroom ceiling, and on you a dense white jam that lisps between legs, trickles and sticks, cools on you, hardens and clears until there is nothing but gnarled knots of pale solid animal hair in the morning shower, and in the wet tangle a clean sweet smell you can't believe comes from anything you made inside you.

The smell is, more than anything, like this swimming pool: a bleached sweet salt, a flower with chemical petals. The pool has a strong clear blue smell, though you know the smell is never as strong when you are actually in the blue water, as you are now, all swum out, resting back along the shallow end, the hip-high water lapping at where it's all changed.

Around the deck of this old public pool on the western edge of Tucson is a Cyclone fence the color of pewter, decorated with a bright tangle of locked bicycles. Beyond this a hot black parking lot full of white lines and glittering cars. A dull field of dry grass and hard weeds, old dandelions' downy heads exploding and snowing up in a rising wind. And past all this, reddened by a round slow September sun, are mountains, jagged, their tops' sharp angles darkening into definition against a deep red tired light. Against the red their sharp connected tops form a spiked line, an EKG of the dying day.

The clouds are taking on color by the rim of the sky. The water is spangles of soft blue, five o'clock warm, and the pool's smell, like the other smell, connects with a chemical haze inside you, an interior dimness that bends light to its own ends, softens the difference between what leaves off and what begins.

Your party is tonight. This afternoon, on your birthday, you have asked to come to the pool. You wanted to come alone, but a birthday is a family day, your family wants to be with you. This is nice, and you can't talk about why you wanted to come alone, and really truly maybe you didn't want to come alone, so they are here. Sunning. Both your parents sun. Their deck chairs have been marking time all afternoon, rotating, tracking the sun's curve across a desert sky heated to an eggy film. Your sister plays Marco Polo near you in the shallows with a group of thin girls from her grade. She is being blind now, her Marco's being Polo'd. She is shut-eyed and twirling to different cries, spinning at the hub of a wheel of shrill girls in bathing caps. Her cap has raised rubber flowers. There are limp old pink petals that shake as she lunges at blind sound.

There at the other end of the pool is the diving tank and the high board's tower. Back on the deck behind is the SN CK BAR, and on either side, bolted above the cement entrances to dark wet showers and lockers, are gray metal bullhorn speakers that send out the pool's radio music, the jangle flat and tinny thin.

Your family likes you. You are bright and quiet, respectful to elders — though you are not without spine. You are largely good. You look out for your little sister. You are her ally. You were six when she was zero and you had the mumps when they brought her home in a very soft yellow blanket; you kissed her hello on her feet out of concern that she not catch your mumps. Your parents say that this augured well. That it set the tone. They now feel they were right. In all things they are proud of you, satisfied, and they have retreated to the warm distance from which pride and satisfaction travel. You all get along well.

Happy Birthday. It is a big day, big as the roof of the whole southwest sky. You have thought it over. There is the high board. They will want to leave soon. Climb out and do the thing.

Shake off the blue clean. You're half-bleached, loose and soft, tenderized, pads of fingers wrinkled. The mist of the pool's too-clean smell is in your eyes; it breaks light into gentle color. Knock your head with the heel of your hand. One side has a flabby echo. Cock your head to the side and hop — sudden heat in your ear, delicious, and brain-warmed water turns cold on the nautilus of your ear's outside. You can hear harder tinnier music, closer shouts, much movement in much water.

The pool is crowded for this late. Here are thin children, hairy animal men. Disproportionate boys, all necks and legs and knobby joints, shallow-chested, vaguely birdlike. Like you. Here are old people moving tentatively through shallows on stick legs, feeling at the water with their hands, out of every element at once.

And girl-women, women, curved like instruments or fruit, skin burnished brown-bright, suit tops held by delicate knots of fragile colored string against the pull of mysterious weights, suit bottoms riding low over the gentle juts of hips totally unlike your own, immoderate swells and swivels that melt in light into a surrounding space that cups and accommodates the soft curves as things precious. You almost understand.

The pool is a system of movement. Here now there are: laps, splash fights, dives, corner tag, cannonballs, Sharks and Minnows, high fallings, Marco Polo (your sister still It, halfway to tears, too long to be It, the game teetering on the edge of cruelty, not your business to save or embarrass). Two clean little bright-white boys caped in cotton towels run along the poolside until the guard stops them dead with a shout through his bullhorn. The guard is brown as a tree, blond hair in a vertical line on his stomach, his head in a jungle explorer hat, his nose a white triangle of cream. A girl has an arm around a leg of his little tower. He's bored.

Get out now and go past your parents, who are sunning and reading, not looking up. Forget your towel. Stopping for the towel means talking and talking means thinking. You have decided being scared is caused mostly by thinking. Go right by, toward the tank at the deep end. Over the tank is a great iron tower of dirty white. A board protrudes from the top of the tower like a tongue. The pool's concrete deck is rough and hot against your bleached feet. Each of your footprints is thinner and fainter. Each shrinks behind you on the hot stone and disappears.

Lines of plastic wieners bob around the tank, which is entirely its own thing, empty of the rest of the pool's convulsive ballet of heads and arms. The tank is blue as energy, small and deep and perfectly square, flanked by lap lanes and SN CK BAR and rough hot deck and the bent late shadow of the tower and board. The tank is quiet and still and healed smooth between fallings.

There is a rhythm to it. Like breathing. Like a machine. The line for the board curves back from the tower's ladder. The line moves in its curve, straightens as it nears the ladder. One by one, people reach the ladder and climb. One by one, spaced by the beat of hearts, they reach the tongue of the board at the top. And once on the board, they pause, each exactly the same tiny heartbeat pause. And their legs take them to the end, where they all give the same sort of stomping hop, arms curving out as if to describe something circular, total; they come down heavy on the edge of the board and make it throw them up and out.

It's a swooping machine, lines of stuttered movement in a sweet late bleach mist. You can watch from the deck as they hit the cold blue sheet of the tank. Each fall makes a white that plumes and falls into itself and spreads and fizzes. Then blue clean comes up in the middle of the white and spreads like pudding, making it all new. The tank heals itself. Three times as you go by.

You are in line. Look around. Look bored. Few talk in the line. Everyone seems by himself. Most look at the ladder, look bored. You almost all have crossed arms, chilled by a late dry rising wind on the constellations of blue-clean chlorine beads that cover your backs and shoulders. It seems impossible that everybody could really be this bored. Beside you is the edge of the tower's shadow, the tilted black tongue of the board's image. The system of shadow is huge, long, off to the side, joined to the tower's base at a sharp late angle.

Almost everyone in line for the board watches the ladder. Older boys watch older girls' bottoms as they go up. The bottoms are in soft thin cloth, tight nylon stretch. The good bottoms move up the ladder like pendulums in liquid, a gentle uncrackable code. The girls' legs make you think of deer. Look bored.

Look out past it. Look across. You can see so well. Your mother is in her deck chair, reading, squinting, her face tilted up to get light on her cheeks. She hasn't looked to see where you are. She sips something sweet out of a bright can. Your father is on his big stomach, back like the hint of a hump of a whale, shoulders curling with animal spirals, skin oiled and soaked red-brown with too much sun. Your towel is hanging off your chair and a corner of the cloth now moves — your mother hit it as she waved away a sweat bee that likes what she has in the can. The bee is back right away, seeming to hang motionless over the can in a sweet blur. Your towel is one big face of Yogi Bear.

At some point there has gotten to be more line behind you than in front of you. Now no one in front except three on the slender ladder. The woman right before you is on the low rungs, looking up, wearing a tight black nylon suit that is all one piece. She climbs. From above there is a rumble, then a great falling, then a plume and the tank re-heals. Now two on the ladder. The pool rules say one on the ladder at a time, but the guard never shouts about it. The guard makes the real rules by shouting or not shouting.

This woman above you should not wear a suit as tight as the suit she is wearing. She is as old as your mother, and as big. She is too big and too white. Her suit is full of her. The backs of her thighs are squeezed by the suit and look like cheese. Her legs have abrupt little squiggles of cold blue shattered vein under the white skin, as if some-thing were broken, hurt, in her legs. Her legs look like they hurt to be squeezed, full of curled Arabic lines of cold broken blue. Her legs make you feel like your own legs hurt.

The rungs are very thin. It's unexpected. Thin round iron rungs laced in slick wet Safe-T felt. You taste metal from the smell of wet iron in shadow. Each rung presses into the bottoms of your feet and dents them. The dents feel deep and they hurt. You feel heavy. How the big woman over you must feel. The handrails along the ladder's sides are also very thin. It's like you might not hold on. You've got to hope the woman holds on, too. And of course it looked like fewer rungs from far away. You are not stupid.

Get halfway up, up in the open, big woman placed above you, a solid bald muscular man on the ladder underneath your feet. The board is still high overhead, invisible from here. But it rumbles and makes a heavy flapping sound, and a boy you can see for a few contained feet through the thin rungs falls in a flash of a line, a knee held to his chest, doing a splasher. There is a huge exclamation point of foam up into your field of sight, then scattered claps into a great fizzing. Then the silent sound of the tank healing to new blue all over again.

More thin rungs. Hold on tight. The radio is loudest here, one speaker at ear-level over a concrete locker room entrance. A cool dank whiff of the locker room inside. Grab the iron bars tight and twist and look down behind you and you can see people buying snacks and refresh-ments below. You can see down into it: the clean white top of the ven-dor's cap, tubs of ice cream, steaming brass freezers, scuba tanks of soft drink syrup, snakes of soda hose, bulging boxes of salty popcorn kept hot in the sun. Now that you're overhead you can see the whole thing.

There's wind. It's windier the higher you get. The wind is thin; through the shadow it's cold on your wet skin. On the ladder in the shadow your skin looks very white. The wind makes a thin whistle in your ears. Four more rungs to the top of the tower. The rungs hurt your feet. They are thin and let you know just how much you weigh. You have real weight on the ladder. The ground wants you back.

Now you can see just over the top of the ladder. You can see the board. The woman is there. There are two ridges of red, hurt-looking callus on the backs of her ankles. She stands at the start of the board, your eyes on her ankles. Now you're up above the tower's shadow. The solid man under you is looking through the rungs into the contained space the woman's fall will pass through.

She pauses for just that beat of a pause. There's nothing slow about it at all. It makes you cold. In no time she's at the end of the board, up, down on it, it bends low like it doesn't want her. Then it nods and flaps and throws her violently up and out, her arms opening out to inscribe that circle, and gone. She disappears in a dark blink. And there's time before you hear the hit below.

Listen. It does not seem good, the way she disappears into a time that passes before she sounds. Like a stone down a well. But you think she did not think so. She was part of a rhythm that excludes thinking. And now you have made yourself part of it, too. The rhythm seems blind. Like ants. Like a machine.

You decide this needs to be thought about. It may, after all, be all right to do something scary without thinking, but not when the scariness is the not thinking itself. Not when not thinking turns out to be wrong. At some point the wrongnesses have piled up blind: pretend-boredom, weight, thin rungs, hurt feet, space cut into laddered parts that melt together only in a disappearance that takes time. The wind on the ladder not what anyone would have expected. The way the board protrudes from shadow into light and you can't see past the end. When it all turns out to be different you should get to think. It should be required.

The ladder is full beneath you. Stacked up, everyone a few rungs apart. The ladder is fed by a solid line that stretches back and curves into the dark of the tower's canted shadow. People's arms are crossed in the line. Those on the ladder's feet hurt and they are all looking up. It is a machine that moves only forward.

Climb up onto the tower's tongue. The board turns out to be long. As long as the time you stand there. Time slows. It thickens around you as your heart gets more and more beats out of every second, every movement in the system of the pool below.

The board is long. From where you stand it seems to stretch off into nothing. It's going to send you someplace which its own length keeps you from seeing, which seems wrong to submit to without even thinking.

Looked at another way, the same board is just a long thin flat thing covered with a rough white plastic stuff. The white surface is very rough and is freckled and lined with a pale watered red that is nevertheless still red and not yet pink — drops of old pool water that are catching the light of the late sun over sharp mountains. The rough white stuff of the board is wet. And cold. Your feet are hurt from the thin rungs and have a great ability to feel. They feel your weight. There are handrails running above the beginning of the board. They are not like the ladder's handrails just were. They are thick and set very low, so you almost have to bend over to hold on to them. They are just for show, no one holds them. Holding on takes time and alters the rhythm of the machine.

It is a long cold rough white plastic or fiberglass board, veined with the sad near-pink color of bad candy.

But at the end of the white board, the edge, where you'll come down with your weight to make it send you off, there are two areas of darkness. Two flat shadows in the broad light. Two vague black ovals. The end of the board has two dirty spots.

They are from all the people who've gone before you. Your feet as you stand here are tender and dented, hurt by the rough wet surface, and you see that the two dark spots are from people's skin. They are skin abraded from feet by the violence of the disappearance of people with real weight. More people than you could count without losing track. The weight and abrasion of their disappearance leaves little bits of soft tender feet behind, bits and shards and curls of skin that dirty and darken and tan as they lie tiny and smeared in the sun at the end of the board. They pile up and get smeared and mixed together. They darken in two circles.

No time is passing outside you at all. It is amazing. The late ballet below is slow motion, the overbroad movements of mimes in blue jelly. If you wanted you could really stay here forever, vibrating inside so fast you float motionless in time, like a bee over something sweet.

But they should clean the board. Anybody who thought about it for even a second would see that they should clean the end of the board of people's skin, of two black collections of what's left of before, spots that from back here look like eyes, like blind and cross-eyed eyes.

Where you are now is still and quiet. Wind radio shouting splashing not here. No time and no real sound but your blood squeaking in your head.

Overhead here means sight and smell. The smells are intimate, newly clear. The smell of bleach's special flower, but out of it other things rise to you like a weed's seeded snow. You smell deep yellow popcorn. Sweet tan oil like hot coconut. Either hot dogs or corn dogs. A thin cruel hint of very dark Pepsi in paper cups. And the special smell of tons of water coming off tons of skin, rising like steam off a new bath. Animal heat. From overhead it is more real than anything.

Look at it. You can see the whole complicated thing, blue and white and brown and white, soaked in a watery spangle of deepening red. Everybody. This is what people call a view. And you knew that from below you wouldn't look nearly so high overhead. You see now how high overhead you are. You knew from down there no one could tell.

He says it behind you, his eyes on your ankles, the solid bald man, Hey kid. They want to know. Do your plans up here involve the whole day or what exactly is the story. Hey kid are you okay.

There's been time this whole time. You can't kill time with your heart. Everything takes time. Bees have to move very fast to stay still.

Hey kid he says Hey kid are you okay.

Metal flowers bloom on your tongue. No more time for thinking. Now that there is time you don't have time.

Hey.

Slowly now, out across everything, there's a watching that spreads like hit water's rings. Watch it spread out from the ladder. Your sighted sister and her thin white pack, pointing. Your mother looks to the shallows where you used to be, then makes a visor of her hand. The whale stirs and jiggles. The guard looks up, the girl around his leg looks up, he reaches for his horn.

Forever below is rough deck, snacks, thin metal music, down where you once used to be; the line is solid and has no reverse gear; and the water, of course, is only soft when you're inside it. Look down. Now it moves in the sun, full of hard coins of light that shimmer red as they stretch away into a mist that is your own sweet salt. The coins crack into new moons, long shards of light from the hearts of sad stars. The square tank is a cold blue sheet. Cold is just a kind of hard. A kind of blind. You have been taken off guard. Happy Birthday. Did you think it over. Yes and no. Hey kid.

Two black spots, violence, and disappear into a well of time. Height is not the problem. It all changes when you get back down. When you hit, with your weight.

So which is the lie? Hard or soft? Silence or time?

The lie is that it's one or the other. A still, floating bee is moving faster than it can think. From overhead the sweetness drives it crazy.

The board will nod and you will go, and eyes of skin can cross blind into a cloud-blotched sky, punctured light emptying behind sharp stone that is forever. That is forever. Step into the skin and disappear.

Hello.

DAVID FOSTER WALLACE

Brief Interviews with Hideous Men

B.I. #40 06-97
BENTON RIDGE OH

'It's the arm. You wouldn't think of it as a asset like that would you. But it's the arm. You want to see it? You won't get disgusted? Well here it is. Here's the arm. This is why I go by the name Johnny One-Arm. I made it up, not anybody being, like, hardhearted — me. I see how you're trying to be polite and not look at it. Go ahead and look though. It don't bother me. Inside my head I don't call it the arm I call it the Asset. How all would you describe it? Go on. You think it'll hurt my feelings? You want to hear me describe it? It looks like a arm that changed its mind early on in the game when it was in Mama's stomach with the rest of me. It's more like a itty tiny little flipper, it's little and wet-looking and darker than the rest of me is. It looks wet even when it's dry. It's not a pretty sight at all. I usually keep it in the sleeve until it's time to haul it out and use it for the Asset. Notice the shoulder's normal, it's just like the other shoulder. It's just the arm. It'll only go down to like the titty-nipple of my chest here, see? It's a little sucker. It ain't pretty. It moves fine, I can move it around fine. If you look close here at the end there's these little majiggers you can tell started out wanting to be fingers but didn't form. When I was in her stomach. The other arm — see? It's a normal arm, a little muscley on account of using it all the time. It's normal and long and the right color, that's the arm I show all the time, most times I keep the other sleeve pinned up so it don't look to be even anything like a arm in there at all. It's strong though. The arm is. It's hard on the eyes but it's strong, sometimes I'll try and get them to armwrestle it to see how strong it is. It's a strong little flippery sucker. If they think they can stand to touch it. I always say if they don't think they can stand touching it why that's OK, it don't hurt my feelings. You want to touch it?'

Q.

'That's all right. That is all right.'

Q.

'What it is is — well first there's always some girls around. You know what I mean? At the foundry there, at the Lanes. There's a tavern

626

right down by the bus stop there. Jackpot — that's my best friend — Jackpot and Kenny Kirk — Kenny Kirk's his cousin, Jackpot's, that are both over me at the foundry cause I finished school and didn't get in the union till after — they're real good-looking and normal-looking and Good With The Ladies if you know what I mean, and there's always girls hanging back around. Like in a group, a bunch or group of all of us, we'll all just hang back, drink some beers. Jackpot and Kenny're always going with one of them or the other and then the ones they're going with got friends. You know. A whole, say, group of us there. You follow the picture here? And I'll start hanging back with this one or that one, and after a while the first stage is I'll start in to telling them how I got the name Johnny One-Arm and about the arm. That's a stage of the thing. Of getting some pussy using the Asset. I'll describe the arm while it's still up in the sleeve and make it sound like just about the ugliest thing you ever did see. They'll get this look on their face like Oh You Poor Little Fella You're Being Too Hard On Yourself You Shouldn't Be Shameful Of The Arm. So on. How I'm such a nice young fella and it breaks their heart to see me talk about my own part of me that way especially since it weren't any fault of mine to get born with the arm. At which time when they start with that stage of it the next stage is I ask them do they want to see it. I say how I'm shameful of the arm but somehow I trust them and they seem real nice and if they want I'll unpin the sleeve and let the arm out and let them look at the arm if they think they could stand it. I'll go on about the arm until they can't hardly stand to hear no more about it. Sometimes it's a ex of Jackpot's that's the one that starts hanging back with me down at Frame Eleven over to the Lanes and saying how I'm such a good listener and sensitive not like Jackpot or Kenny and she can't believe there's any way the arm's as bad as I'm making out and like that. Or we'll be hanging back at her place in the kitchenette or some such and I'll go It's So Hot I Feel Like Taking My Shirt Off But I Don't Want To On Account Of I'm Shameful Of The Arm. Like that. There's numerous, like, stages. I never out loud call it the Asset believe you me. Go on and touch it whenever you get a mind to. One of the stages is I know after some time I really am starting to come off creepy to the girl, I can tell, cause all I can talk about is the arm and how wet and flippery it is but how it's strong but how I'd just about up and die if a girl as nice and pretty and perfect as I think she is saw it and got disgusted, and I can tell all the talk starts creeping them up inside and they start to secretly think I'm kind of a loser but they can't back out on me cause after all here they been all this time saying all this nice shit about what a sensitive young fella I am and how I shouldn't be shameful and there's no way the arm can be that bad. In this stage it's like they're committed into a corner and if they quit hanging back with me now why they know I can go It Was Because Of The Arm.'

Q.

'Usually long about two weeks, like that. The next is your critical-type stage where I show them the arm. I wait till it's just her and me alone someplace and I haul the sucker out. I make it seem like they talked me into it and now I trust them and they're who I finally feel like I can let it out of the sleeve and show it. And I show it to her just like I just did you. There's some additional things too I can do with it that look even worse, make it look — see that? See this right here? It's cause there ain't even really a elbow bone, it's just a — '

Q.

'Or some of your ointments or Vaseline-type jelly on it to make it look even wetter and shinier. The arm's not a pretty sight at all when I up and haul it out on them I'm telling you right now. It just about makes them puke, the sight of it the way I get it. Oh and a couple run out, some skedoodle right out the door. But your majority? Your majority of them'll swallow hard a time or two and go Oh It's It's It's Not Too Bad At All but they're looking over all away and try and not look at my face which I've got this totally shy and scared and trusting face on at the time like this one thing I can do where I can make my lip even tremble a little. Ee? Ee anh? And ever time sooner or later within inside, like, five minutes of it they'll up and start crying. They're in way over their head, see. They're, like, committed into a corner of saying how it can't be that ugly and I shouldn't be shameful and then they see it and I see to it it is ugly, ugly ugly ugly and now what do they do? Pretend? Shit girl most of these girls around here think Elvis is alive someplace. These are not girl wonders of the brain. It breaks them down ever time. They get even worse if I ask them Oh Golly What's Wrong, how come they're crying, Is It The Arm and they have to say It Ain't The Arm, they have to, they have to try and pretend it ain't the arm that it's how they feel so sad for me being so shameful of something that ain't a big deal at all they have to say. Oftentimes with their face in their hands and crying. Your climatic stage then is then I up and come over to where she's at and sit down and now I'm the one that's comforting them. A, like, factor here I found out the hard way is when I go in to hold them and comfort them I hold them with the good side. I don't give them no more of the Asset. The Asset's wrapped back up safe out of sight in the sleeve now. They're broke down crying and I'm the one holding them with the good arm and go It's OK Don't Cry Don't Be Sad Being Able To Trust You Not To Get Disgusted By The Arm Means So Very Very Much To Me Don't You See

You Have Set Me Free Of Being Shameful Of The Arm Thank You Thank You and so on while they put their face in my neck and just cry and cry. Sometimes they get me crying too. You following all this?'

Q. . . .

'More pussy than a toilet seat, man. I shit you not. Go on and ask Jackpot and Kenny if you want about it. Kenny Kirk's the one named it the Asset. You go on.'

John Edgar Wideman

John Edgar Wideman has been compared to Faulkner, both for his lyrical gift and for the fact that so much of his work centers around a single region — the inner-city neighborhood of Homewood in Pittsburgh. Wideman's 1981 collection, *Damballah,* was the first of his Homewood books, which include the novel *Sent for You Yesterday,* the memoir *Brothers and Keepers,* and the bulk of his short stories. Notable among his other titles is *Philadelphia Fire,* a novel based on the 1985 police bombing of a West Philadelphia row house owned by Move, an Afrocentric cult. What I admire most in Wideman's work is the way he integrates the speech patterns of African-American slang into his stories without sacrificing narrative authority. So many writers — especially beginners — limit their stories to the consciousness of an often uneducated young colloquial speaker, whether that speaker be African-American, Latino, Asian-American, or one of the endless variants on Holden Caulfield. In contrast, Wideman' s stories move effortlessly between authorial narration and the dialect of the streets.

"Doc's Story" is a prime example. We get this neatly realized description: "In summer fine grit hangs in the air. Five minutes on the court and you're coughing. City dirt and park dust blowing off bald patches from which green is long gone, and deadly ash blowing over from New Jersey. You can taste it some days, bitter in your spit." And then, one of the characters takes over, telling the story of Doc, the purblind basketball legend: "Doc bounce the ball, one, two, three times like he does. Then he raise it. Sift it in his fingers. You know he's a ballplayer, a shooter already way the ball spin in them long fingers way he raises it and cocks his wrist." The effect is dynamic and bears comparison to the use of dialect in Saunders and Díaz. The second piece, excerpted, like "Doc's Story," from *Fever,* is also about the need and uses of storytelling ("The story has more skins than an onion. And like an onion it can cause a grown man to cry when he starts to peeling it."). The language is what carries the piece, achieving a grim beauty and poignancy in the final lines. Who is that man lying in the street? we ask, averting our eyes. Now we know.

Doc's Story

He thinks of her small, white hands, blue veined, gaunt, awkwardly knuckled. He'd teased her about the smallness of her hands, hers lost in the shadow of his when they pressed them together palm to palm to measure. The heavy drops of color on her nails barely reached the middle joints of his fingers. He'd teased her about her dwarf's hands but he'd also said to her one night when the wind was rattling the windows of the apartment on Cedar and they lay listening and shivering though it was summer on the brass bed she'd found in a junk store on Haverford Avenue, near the Woolworth's five-and-dime they'd picketed for two years, that God made little things closer to perfect than he ever made big things. Small, compact women like her could be perfectly formed, proportioned, and he'd smiled out loud running his hand up and down the just-right fine lines of her body, celebrating how good she felt to him.

She'd left him in May, when the shadows and green of the park had started to deepen. Hanging out, becoming a regular at the basketball court across the street in Regent Park was how he'd coped. No questions asked. Just the circle of stories. If you didn't want to miss anything good you came early and stayed late. He learned to wait, be patient. Long hours waiting were not time lost but time doing nothing because there was nothing better to do. Basking in sunshine on a stone bench, too beat to play any longer, nowhere to go but an empty apartment, he'd watch the afternoon traffic in Regent Park, dog strollers, baby carriages, winos, kids, gays, students with blankets they'd spread out on the grassy banks of the hollow and books they'd pretend to read, the black men from the neighborhood who'd search the park for braless young mothers and white girls on blankets who didn't care or didn't know any better than to sit with their crotches exposed. When he'd sit for hours like that, cooking like that, he'd feel himself empty out, see himself seep away and hover in the air, a fine mist, a little, flattened-out gray cloud of something wavering in the heat, a presence as visible as the steam on the window as he stares for hours at winter.

He's waiting for summer. For the guys to begin gathering on the court again. They'll sit in the shade with their backs against the Cyclone fencing or lean on cars parked at the roller-coaster curb or lounge in the sun on low, stone benches catty-corner from the basketball court. Some older ones still drink wine, but most everybody cools out on reefer, when there's reefer passed along, while they bullshit and wait for winners. He collects the stories they tell. He needs a story now. The right one now to get him through this long winter because she's gone and won't leave him alone.

In summer fine grit hangs in the air. Five minutes on the court and you're coughing. City dirt and park dust blowing off bald patches from which green is long gone, and deadly ash blowing over from New Jersey. You can taste it some days, bitter in your spit. Chunks pepper your skin, burn your eyes. Early fall while it's still warm enough to run outdoors the worst time of all. Leaves pile up against the fence, higher and higher, piles that explode and jitterbug across the court in the middle of a game, then sweep up again, slamming back where they blew from. After a while the leaves are ground into coarse, choking powder. You eat leaf trying to get in a little hoop before the weather turns, before those days when nobody's home from work yet but it's dark already and too cold to run again till spring. Fall's the only time sweet syrupy wine beats reefer. Ripple, Manischewitz, Taylor's Tawny Port coat your throat. He takes a hit when the jug comes round. He licks the sweetness from his lips, listens for his favorite stories one more time before everybody gives it up till next season.

His favorite stories made him giggle and laugh and hug the others, like they hugged him when a story got so good nobody's legs could hold them up. Some stories got under his skin in peculiar ways. Some he liked to hear because they made the one performing them do crazy stuff with his voice and body. He learned to be patient, learned his favorites would be repeated, get a turn just like he got a turn on the joints and wine bottles circulating the edges of the court.

Of all the stories, the one about Doc had bothered him most. Its orbit was unpredictable. Twice in one week, then only once more last summer. He'd only heard Doc's story three times, but that was enough to establish Doc behind and between the words of all the other stories. In a strange way Doc presided over the court. You didn't need to mention him. He was just there. Regent Park stories began with Doc and ended with Doc and everything in between was preparation, proof the circle was unbroken.

They say Doc lived on Regent Square, one of the streets like Cedar, dead-ending at the park. On the hottest afternoons the guys from the court would head for Doc's stoop. Jars of ice water, the good feeling and good talk they'd share in the shade of Doc's little front yard was what drew them. Sometimes they'd spray Doc's hose on one another.

Get drenched like when they were kids and the city used to turn on fire hydrants in the summer. Some of Doc's neighbors would give them dirty looks. Didn't like a whole bunch of loud, sweaty, half-naked niggers backed up in their nice street where Doc was the only colored on the block. They say Doc didn't care. He was just out there like everybody else having a good time.

Doc had played at the University. Same one where Doc taught for a while. They say Doc used to laugh when white people asked him if he was in the Athletic Department. No reason for niggers to be at the University if they weren't playing ball or coaching ball. At least that's what white people thought, and since they thought that way, that's the way it was. Never more than a sprinkle of black faces in the white sea of the University. Doc used to laugh till the joke got old. People freedom-marching and freedom-dying, Doc said, but some dumb stuff never changed.

He first heard Doc's story late one day, after the yellow streetlights had popped on. Pooner was finishing the one about gang warring in North Philly: Yeah. They sure nuff lynched this dude they caught on their turf. Hung him up on the goddamn poles behind the backboard. Little kids found the sucker in the morning with his tongue all black and shit down his legs, and the cops had to come cut him down. Worst part is them little kids finding a dead body swinging up there. Kids don't be needing to find nothing like that. But those North Philly gangs don't play. They don't even let the dead rest in peace. Run in a funeral parlor and fuck up the funeral. Dumping over the casket and tearing up the flowers. Scaring people and turning the joint out. It's some mean shit. But them gangs don't play. They kill you they ain't finished yet. Mess with your people, your house, your sorry-ass dead body to get even. Pooner finished telling it and he looked round at the fellows and people were shaking their heads and then there was a chorus of You got that right, man. It's a bitch out there, man. Them niggers crazy, boy, and Pooner holds out his hand and somebody passes the joint. Pooner pinches it in two fingers and takes a deep drag. Everybody knows he's finished, it's somebody else's turn.

One of the fellows says, I wonder what happened to old Doc. I always be thinking about Doc, wondering where the cat is, what he be doing now . . .

Don't nobody know why Doc's eyes start to going bad. It just happen. Doc never even wore glasses. Eyes good as anybody's far as anybody knew till one day he come round he got goggles on. Like Kareem. And people kinda joking, you know. Doc got him some goggles. Watch out, youall. Doc be skyhooking youall to death today. Funning, you know. Cause Doc like to joke and play. Doc one the fellas like I said, so when he come round in goggles he subject to some teasing and one another thing like that cause nobody thought nothing serious wrong. Doc's eyes just as good as yours or mine, far as anybody knew.

Doc been playing all his life. That's why you could stand him on the foul line and point him at the hoop and more times than not, Doc could sink it. See he be remembering. His muscles know just what to do. You get his feet aimed right, line him up so he's on target, and Doc would swish one for you. Was a game kinda. Sometimes you get a sucker and Doc win you some money. Swish. Then the cat lost the dough start crying. He ain't blind. Can't no blind man shoot no pill. Is you really blind, brother? You niggers trying to steal my money, trying to play me for a fool. When a dude start crying the blues like that Doc wouldn't like it. He'd walk away. Wouldn't answer.

Leave the man lone. You lost fair and square. Doc made the basket so shut up and pay up, chump.

Doc practiced. Remember how you'd hear him out here at night when people sleeping. It's dark but what dark mean to Doc? Blacker than the rentman's heart but don't make no nevermind to Doc, he be steady shooting fouls. Always be somebody out there to chase the ball and throw it back. But shit, man. When Doc into his rhythm, didn't need nobody chase the ball. Ball be swishing with that good backspin, that good arch bring it back blip, blip, blip, three bounces and it's coming right back to Doc's hands like he got a string on the pill. Spooky if you didn't know Doc or know about foul shooting and understand when you got your shit together don't matter if you blindfolded. You put the motherfucker up and you know it's spozed to come running back just like a dog with a stick in his mouth.

Doc always be hanging at the court. Blind as wood but you couldn't fool Doc. Eyes in his ears. Know you by your walk. He could tell if you wearing new sneaks, tell you if your old ones is laced or not. Know you by your breath. The holes you make in the air when you jump. Doc was hip to who fucking who and who was getting fucked. Who could play ball and who was jiving. Doc use to be out here every weekend, steady rapping with the fellows and doing his foul-shot thing between games. Every once in a while somebody tease him, Hey, Doc. You want to run winners next go? Doc laugh and say, No, Dupree . . . I'm tired today, Dupree. Besides which you ain't been on a winning team in a week have you, Du? And everybody laugh. You know, just funning cause Doc one the fellas.

But one Sunday the shit got stone serious. Sunday I'm telling youall about, the action was real nice. If you wasn't ready, get back cause the brothers was cooking. Sixteen points, rise and fly. Next. Who got next? . . . Come on out here and take your ass kicking. One them good days when it's hot and everybody's juices is high and you feel you could play till next week. One them kind of days and a run's just over. Doc gets up and he goes with Billy Moon to the foul line. Fellas hanging under the basket for the rebound. Ain't hardly gon be a rebound Doc get hisself lined up right. But see, when the ball drop through the net you want to be the one grab it and throw it back to Billy. You want to be out there part of Doc shooting fouls just like you want to run when the running's good.

Doc bounce the ball, one, two, three times like he does. Then he raise it. Sift it in his fingers. You know he's a ballplayer, a shooter already way the ball spin in them long fingers way he raises it and cocks his wrist. You know Doc can't see a damn thing through his sunglasses but swear to God you'd think he was looking at the hoop way he study and measure. Then he shoots and ain't a sound in whole Johnson. Seems like everybody's heart stops. Everybody's breath behind that ball pushing it and steadying it so it drops through clean as new money.

But that Sunday something went wrong. Couldna been wind cause wasn't no wind. I was there. I know. Maybe Doc had playing on his mind. Couldn't help have playing on his mind cause it was one those days wasn't nothing better to do in the world than play. Whatever it was, soon as the ball left his hands, you could see Doc was missing, missing real bad. Way short and way off to the left. Might hit the backboard if everybody blew on it real hard.

A young boy, one them skinny, jumping-jack young boys got pogo sticks for legs, one them kids go up and don't come back down till they ready, he was standing on the left side the lane and leap up all the sudden catch the pill out the air and jams it through. Blam. A monster dunk and everybody break out in Goddamn. Do it, Sky, and Did you see that nigger get up? People slapping five and all that mess. Then Sky, the young boy they call Sky, grinning like a Chessy cat and strutting out with the ball squeezed in one hand to give it to Doc. In his glory. Grinning and strutting.

Gave you a little help, Doc.

Didn't ask for no help, Sky. Why'd you fuck with my shot, Sky?

Well, up jumped the Devil. The joint gets real quiet again real quick. Doc ain't cracked smile the first. He ain't playing.

Sorry, Doc. Didn't mean no harm, Doc.

You must think I'm some kind of chump fucking with my shot that way.

People start to feeling bad. Doc is steady getting on Sky's case. Sky just a young, light-in-the-ass kid. Jump to the moon but he's just a silly kid. Don't mean no harm. He just out there like everybody else trying to do his thing. No harm in Sky but Doc ain't playing and nobody else says shit. It's quiet like when Doc's shooting. Quiet as death and Sky don't know what to do. Can't wipe that lame look off his face and can't back off and can't hand the pill to Doc neither. He just stands there with his arm stretched out and his rusty fingers wrapped round the ball. Can't hold it much longer, can't let it go.

Seems like I coulda strolled over to Doc's stoop for a drinka water and strolled back and those two still be standing there. Doc and Sky. Billy Moon off to one side so it's just Doc and Sky.

Everybody holding they breath. Everybody want it over with and finally Doc says, Forget it, Sky. Just don't play with my shots anymore. And then Doc say, Who has next winners?

If Doc was joking nobody took it for no joke. His voice still hard. Doc ain't kidding around.

Who's next? I want to run.

Now Doc knows who's next. Leroy got next winners and Doc knows Leroy always saves a spot so he can pick up a big man from the losers. Leroy tell you to your face, I got my five, man, but everybody know Leroy saving a place so he can build him a winner and stay on the court. Leroy's a cold dude that way, been that way since he first started coming round and ain't never gon change and Doc knows that, everybody knows that but even Leroy ain't cold enough to say no to Doc.

I got it, Doc.

You got your five yet?

You know you got a spot with me, Doc. Always did.

Then I'ma run.

Say to myself, Shit . . . Good God Almighty. Great Googa-Mooga. What is happening here? Doc can't see shit. Doc blind as this bench I'm sitting on. What Doc gon do out there?

Well, it ain't my game. If it was, I'd a lied and said I had five. Or maybe not. Don't know what I'da done, to tell the truth. But Leroy didn't have no choice. Doc caught him good. Course Doc knew all that before he asked.

Did Doc play? What kinda question is that? What you think I been talking about all this time, man? Course he played. Why the fuck he be asking for winners less he was gon play? Helluva run as I remember. Overtime and shit. Don't remember who won. Somebody did, sure nuff. Leroy had him a strong unit. You know how he is. And Doc? Doc ain't been out on the court for a while but Doc is Doc, you know. Held his own . . .

If he had tried to tell her about Doc, would it have made a difference? Would the idea of a blind man playing basketball get her attention or would she have listened the way she listened when he told her stories he'd read about slavery days when Africans could fly, change themselves to cats and hummingbirds, when black hoodoo priests and conjure queens were feared by powerful whites even though ordinary black lives weren't worth a penny. To her it was folklore, superstition. Interesting because it revealed the psychology, the pathology of the oppressed. She listened intently, not because she thought she'd hear truth. For her, belief in magic was like belief in God. Nice work if you could get it. Her skepticism, her hardheaded practicality, like the smallness of her hands, appealed to him. Opposites attracting. But more and more as the years went by, he'd wanted her with him, wanted them to be together . . .

They were walking in Regent Park. It was clear to both of them that things weren't going to work out. He'd never seen her so beautiful, perfect.

There should have been stars. Stars at least, and perhaps a sickle moon. Instead the edge of the world was on fire. They were walking in Regent Park and dusk had turned the tree trunks black. Beyond them in the distance, below the fading blue of sky, the colors of sunset were pinched into a narrow, radiant band. Perhaps he had listened too long. Perhaps he had listened too intently for his own voice to fill the emptiness. When he turned back to her, his eyes were glazed, stinging. Grit, chemicals, whatever it was coloring, poisoning the sky, blurred his vision. Before he could blink her into focus, before he could speak, she was gone.

If he'd known Doc's story he would have said: *There's still a chance. There's always a chance. I mean this guy, Doc. Christ. He was stone blind. But he got out on the court and played. Over there. Right over there. On that very court across the hollow from us. It happened. I've talked to people about it many times. If Doc could do that, then anything's possible. We're possible . . .*

If a blind man could play basketball, surely we . . . If he had known Doc's story, would it have saved them? He hears himself saying the words. The ball arches from Doc's fingertips, the miracle of it sinking. Would she have believed any of it?

Presents

I stood on the bank . . .

Oh yes, she said. Oh yes and I did not know what she was yessing any more than I know how her voice, her yes reaches from wherever she is to wherever I am now, except it's like the ships seen from the bank of Jordan in that song sailing on, sailing on from there to here quietly as dream.

Big Mama. Big Mama. Doubling her not because she is not real enough once but because her life takes up so much space. I stare at her afraid to look away. Scared she'll be gone if I do. Scared I'll be gone.

Baby, you listen to your Big Mama now. Listen cause I ain't got nothing but mouth and time and hardly none that left.

He is saucer-eyed. Awkward. A big, nappy head.

She pats each nap and each awakes. A multitude stirring as she passes her old hand once in the air over the crown his skull.

Love Jesus and love yourself and love those who love you, sugar. Those who don't love you don't love theyselves and shame on them. Nobody but Jesus can save their sorry souls.

She purses her lips. Her tongue pushes that hard-as-the-world bitter lemon into one cheek. She sucks on it. All the sour of it smears her old lips. She is Big Mama. No bones in her body. Even now, even this Christmas so close to death the bones cannot claim her. Nothing will crack or snap or buckle in her. In her lap he will curl and sleep and always find soft room to snuggle deeper. To fall. To sleep.

He remembers being big enough to crawl alone under her bed and little enough, little sweet doodlebug, you come on over here gimme some sugar, to sit upright and his head just grazes the beehive network of springs. Hiding under her bed and playing with the dust and light he raises and the tasseled knots of fringed chenille bedspread. Bed so high so you had to *climb* up on it. Mind you don't roll off, boy. He did not think *throne* but he knew her bed was raised high to be a special place, to be his Big Mama's bed.

So when she kneels beside the bed he hears the sigh of the room rushing together again over her head, sigh as the fist of her heart, the apron pocket of her chest empties and fills, the grunt and wheeze of his

Big Mama dropping to one knee and lifts the spread and her arm disappears as if she's fishing for him under there. Come out, you little doodlebug rascal. I know you hiding in there. Boogeyman get you you don't come from under there. Her arm sweeps and he can see her fingers under the edge of the bed, inside the cave, though he is outside now and it's like being two places at once, hiding and looking for his ownself, watching her old hand, the fingers hooked, beckoning. C'mon out, you monkey you, sweeping a half inch off the floor, precisely at the level of the unfailing, fringed spread hanging off the side of the bed.

What she drags forth this Christmas Eve afternoon as he watches her kneeling beside the bed is wrapped in a blanket. Not him this time, but something covered with a sheet and swaddled in a woolly blanket. Shapeless. Then Big Mama digs into folds and flaps, uncovers woman curves, the taut shaft. There are long strings and a hole in the center. Gently as she goes she cannot help accidents that trick stirrings from the instrument. A bowl of jelly quivering. Perhaps all it needs is the play of her breath as she bends over it, serious and quiet as a child undressing a doll. Or the air all by its ownself is enough to agitate the strings when Big Mama finally has it laid bare across her bed.

The story as he's preached it so many times since is simple. A seven-year-old boy makes his grandmother a song. He intends to sing it for her Christmas Day but Christmas Eve afternoon she calls him into her bedroom and kneels and pulls a guitar wrapped in rags and blankets from under her bed. He is mesmerized and happy. He hugs his Big Mama and can't help telling her about the love song he's made up for her Christmas present. She says you better sing it for me now, baby, and he does and she smiles the whole time he sings. Then she lays out the sad tale of his life as a man. He'll rise in the world, sing for kings and queens but his gift for music will also drag him down to the depths of hell. She tells it gently, he is only a boy, with her eyes fixed on the ceiling and they fill up with tears. Oh yes. Oh yes, yes. Yes, Jesus. The life he must lead a secret pouring out of her. Emptying her. Already she's paying for the good and evil in him. Yes. Yes. She's quiet then. Still. They sit together on the side of her high bed till it's dark outside the window. He can't see snow but smells it, hears how silently it falls. She asks him, Sing my song one more time. His little Christmas gift song because he loves to sing and make rhymes and loves his Big Mama and the grace of sweet Jesus is heavy in this season of his birth. By the next morning his Big Mama is dead. The others come for Christmas Day, discover her. He's been awake since dawn, learning to pick out her song quietly on his new guitar. His mother and the rest of them bust in, stomp their snowy shoes in the hallway and Merry Christmas and where's Big Mama? They find her dead in bed and he's been playing ever since. Everything she prophesied right on the money, honey. To this very day. He's been up and he's been down and that's the way she told him it would be all the days of his life. Amen.

Each time in the middle of the story he thinks he won't ever need to tell it again. Scooted up under the skirt of Big Mama's bed. His mother comes over to visit and she fusses at him. You're too big a boy to be hiding go seek under Mama's bed. Don't let him play under there, Mama. Don't baby him. Time he start growing up.

His mother visits and takes a bath in Big Mama's iron tub. He sees her bare feet and bare ankles, her bare butt as he holds his breath and quiet as a spider slides to the edge and peeks up through the fringy spread. He lifts the covering to see better. Inch by inch. Quiet as snow. She has a big round behind with hairs at the bottom. He thinks of watermelons and can't eat that fruit without guilt ever after. He watches her as she stands in front of the mirror of his grandmother's chiffonier. His heart beats fast as it can. He's afraid she'll hear it, afraid she'll turn quickly and find his eye peeking up from under the covers at her. But when she does turn, it's slowly, slowly so he hears the rub of her bare heel on the linoleum where the rug doesn't stretch to where she's standing. He drops the window of his hiding place. He's spared a vision of the front of her. Titties. Pussycat between her legs. Just ankles and bare feet till she's finished and wrapped in one Big Mama's housecoats and asking for him in the other room.

You been in here all this time? You been hiding under there while I was dressing? Why didn't you say something, boy?

The story has more skins than an onion. And like an onion it can cause a grown man to cry when he starts to peeling it.

Or else it can go quick. Big Mama said, That's the most beautiful song in the world. Thank you, precious. Thank you and thank Jesus for bringing such a sweet boy to this old woman.

Will you teach me how to play?

Your old grandmama don't know nothing bout such things. She's tired besides. You learn your ownself. Just beat on it like a drum till something come out sound good to you.

The music's in the box like the sword in the stone. Beat it. Pound it. Chisel away. Then one day it gon sound good. Gon slide loose easy as it slided in. Then it's smooth as butter. Then it sings God's praise. Oh yes. Oh yes.

She gave him the guitar in Jesus' name. Amened it. Prayed over it with him that Christmas Eve afternoon how many years ago. Well, let's see. I was seven then and I'm an old man now so that's how long it's been, that's how many times I've preached the story.

My grandmother believed in raising a joyful noise unto the Lord. Tambourines and foot stomping and gut-bucket piano rolls and drums and shouts and yes if you could find one a mean guitar rocking like the ark in heavy seas till it gets good to everybody past the point of foot patting and finger popping in your chair past that till the whole congregation out they seats dancing in the air.

Something born that day and something died. His fate cooked up for him like a mess of blackeyed peas and ham hocks and he's been eating at the table of it ever since. Lean days and fat days.

Where did she find a guitar? Who'd played the instrument before it was his? Could it ever be his if other fingers had plucked the strings, run up and down the long neck? Grease and sweat ground into its wood, its metal strings. When he was at last alone with the gift she'd given him and told him not to play till Christmas, he'd peered into the hole in its belly. Held it by its fat hips and shook it to hear if anybody'd left money in there. If the right sound won't come out plucking it, there was always the meaty palm of his hand to knock sense in it.

How long did he hide in the church before he carried his box out on the street corner? How long for the Lord, how many licks for the Devil? How long before you couldn't tell one from the other? Him the last to know. Always.

A boy wonder. An evil hot blood Buddy Bolden Willie the Lion Robert Johnson wild man boy playing the fool and playing the cowboy fool shit out that thang, man. Yes. Oh yes.

And one day Praise God I said, Huh uh. No more. Thank you Jesus and broke it over my knee and cried cause I'd lost my Big Mama.

Atlantic City. Niggers pulling rickshaws up and down the Boardwalk. Naw. If I'm lying, I'm flying. They did, boy. Yes they did. Drugging white folks around behind them in these big carts. Like in China, man. Or wherever they keep them things. Saw that shit on the Boardwalk in Atlantic City, U.S. of A. Yeah. And niggers happy to be doing it. Collecting fabulous tips, they say. Hauling peckerwoods around. Not me. See, I knew better. I'd seen the world. Had me a gig in one those little splib clubs on Arctic Avenue. Enough to keep me in whiskey. Didn't need no pad. It was summer. Sleep on the beach. Or sleep with one the ladies dig my playing. A real bed, a shower every few days to scald the sand out my asshole. Living the life, partner. Till I woke up one morning in the gutter. Stone gutter, man. Like a dead rat. Head busted. Vomit all on my clothes. In broad daylight I'm lolling in the gutter, man. Said, Huh uh. No indeed. These the bonds of hell. Done fell clean off the ladder and I'm down in the pit. The goddamn gutter floor of the pit's bottom. I'm lost. Don't a living soul give one dime fuck about me and I don't neither.

That's when I hollered, Get me up from here, Big Mama. You said I'd rise and I did. You prophesied I'd fall and here I am. Now reach down and help me up. Gimme your soft silk purse old woman's hand and lift this crusty burden off the street. Take me back to your bosom. Rise and fall, you said. Well, I can't fall no further so carry me on up again. Please. Please, Big Mama. Reach down off the high side of your bed and bring me back.

Her fingers hooked like a eagle's beak. Holding a cloak of feathers fashioned from wings of fallen angels. Where you find this, Big Mama? How'm I spozed to play this thing? Beat it, you say. Pound it like a drum. Just step out in the air with it round your shoulders. Let the air take you and fly you on home. Squeeze it till it sound like you need it to sound. Good. Giant steps ain't nothing if they ain't falling up and falling down and carrying you far from this place to another.

Sailing. To meet me in the morning. On Jordan one day. Singing, Yes. Oh yes.

I stood on the bank . . .

And my neck ached like I'd been lynched. Like I'd been laid out for dead and hard rock was my pillow and cold ground my bed.

Hard rock my pillow and help me today, Lord. Help me tell it. I scrambled to my feet and shook the sooty graveclothes and sand and scales and dust and feathers and morning blood off my shoulders. Skinny as a scarecrow. Funky as toejam. My mouth dry and my eyes scored by rusty razors, my tongue like a turtle forgot how to poke his head out his shell. Scrambled to my aching feet and there it was spread out over me the city of my dreams, Philadelphia all misbegotten and burnt crisp and sour sour at the roots as all my bad teefs.

Play it, son.

Bucka do. Bucka do little dee.

Black as sugar burnt to the bottom of a pan. And Big Mama told me. She said, Squeeze it to the last drop.

A simple story. Easy to tell to a stranger at the bar who will buy you a drink. Young boy and old woman. Christmastime. Reading each other's minds. Exchanging gifts of song. His fortune told. The brief, bright time of his music. How far it took him, how quickly gone. The candle flaring up, guttering, gone. He'd told it many times. Risen. Fallen. Up. Down. Rubs his crusty eyes and peers into a honey-colored room with no walls, feet scurry past his head, busy going every which way, sandals and brogans and sneakers and shiny Stacy-Adamses and pitter-pat of high-stepper high heels on the pavement as he lifts his head and goes over the whole business again, trying to settle once and for all who he must be and why it always ends this way his head on the hard rock of curbstone, the ships sailing on, sailing on.

The river is brass or blood or mud depending on the day, the season, the hour. Big Mama is where she is. He is here. Her voice plain as day in his ear. He wishes someone would pat him on his head and say everything's gon be all right.

Tobias Wolff

Tobias Wolff, who was a colleague of Raymond Carver at Syracuse University, has produced a body of short fiction as resonant and original as Carver's. Like Carver, he is a realist, and he is particularly adept at the elliptical, understated ending and in investing his characters with a deep humanity and psychological complexity few can match within the confines of a short story. He has said that he admires the Russian masters of the form, and his intense, character-driven pieces bring Chekhov to mind. His first collection, *In the Garden of the North American Martyrs,* was published in 1981 and won the St. Lawrence Award. Since then, he has published three other collections, *The Barracks Thief and Selected Stories, Back in the World,* and *The Night in Question,* from which the two stories included here were selected. He is also the author of two memoirs, *This Boy's Life* and *In Pharaoh's Army,* an account of his service in Vietnam. The comparisons to Tim O'Brien are obvious, as both have written penetrating memoirs of Vietnam and both have excelled in the short story, but Wolff is more a minimalist than O'Brien and sticks closer to the bare bones of realism and the telling moment.

"Powder" is a memory piece, a shining example of how a writer can manipulate experience to discover its meaning. The story is a mere four pages in length, and yet both characters — the teenaged narrator and his glamorous daredevil of a father — come vividly to life, even as the narrator, so obsessed with order, opens up to his epiphany in the chaos of that wild and liberating drive with his father at the wheel ("My father in his forty-eighth year, rumpled, kind, bankrupt of honor, flushed with certainty. He was a great driver. All persuasion, no coercion. Such subtlety at the wheel, such tactful pedalwork. I actually trusted him."). The second piece, "Bullet in the Brain," is a tour de force that manages to be both wickedly satiric on the nature of criticism and deeply moving at the same time. The final phrases, with the oddness and illegitimacy of their grammar, question the nature of beauty and whether it can ever be subject to the strictures of criticism.

Powder

Just before Christmas my father took me skiing at Mount Baker. He'd had to fight for the privilege of my company, because my mother was still angry with him for sneaking me into a nightclub during his last visit, to see Thelonious Monk.

He wouldn't give up. He promised, hand on heart, to take good care of me and have me home for dinner on Christmas Eve, and she relented. But as we were checking out of the lodge that morning it began to snow, and in this snow he observed some rare quality that made it necessary for us to get in one last run. We got in several last runs. He was indifferent to my fretting. Snow whirled around us in bitter, blinding squalls, hissing like sand, and still we skied. As the lift bore us to the peak yet again, my father looked at his watch and said, "Criminy. This'll have to be a fast one."

By now I couldn't see the trail. There was no point in trying. I stuck to him like white on rice and did what he did and somehow made it to the bottom without sailing off a cliff. We returned our skis and my father put chains on the Austin-Healey while I swayed from foot to foot, clapping my mittens and wishing I was home. I could see everything. The green tablecloth, the plates with the holly pattern, the red candles waiting to be lit.

We passed a diner on our way out. "You want some soup?" my father asked. I shook my head. "Buck up," he said. "I'll get you there. Right, doctor?"

I was supposed to say, "Right, doctor," but I didn't say anything.

A state trooper waved us down outside the resort. A pair of sawhorses were blocking the road. The trooper came up to our car and bent down to my father's window. His face was bleached by the cold. Snowflakes clung to his eyebrows and to the fur trim of his jacket and cap.

"Don't tell me," my father said.

The trooper told him. The road was closed. It might get cleared, it might not. Storm took everyone by surprise. So much, so fast. Hard to get people moving. Christmas Eve. What can you do.

My father said, "Look. We're talking about five, six inches. I've taken this car through worse than that."

The trooper straightened up. His face was out of sight but I could hear him. "The road is closed."

My father sat with both hands on the wheel, rubbing the wood with his thumbs. He looked at the barricade for a long time. He seemed to be trying to master the idea of it. Then he thanked the trooper, and with a weird, old-maidy show of caution turned the car around. "Your mother will never forgive me for this," he said.

"We should have left before," I said. "Doctor."

He didn't speak to me again until we were in a booth at the diner, waiting for our burgers. "She won't forgive me," he said. "Do you understand? Never."

"I guess," I said, but no guesswork was required; she wouldn't forgive him.

"I can't let that happen." He bent toward me. "I'll tell you what I want. I want us all to be together again. Is that what you want?"

"Yes, sir."

He bumped my chin with his knuckles. "That's all I needed to hear."

When we finished eating he went to the pay phone in the back of the diner, then joined me in the booth again. I figured he'd called my mother, but he didn't give a report. He sipped at his coffee and stared out the window at the empty road. "Come on, come on," he said, though not to me. A little while later he said it again. When the trooper's car went past, lights flashing, he got up and dropped some money on the check. "Okay. Vamanos."

The wind had died. The snow was falling straight down, less of it now and lighter. We drove away from the resort, right up to the barricade. "Move it," my father told me. When I looked at him he said, "What are you waiting for?" I got out and dragged one of the saw-horses aside, then put it back after he drove through. He pushed the door open for me. "Now you're an accomplice," he said. "We go down together." He put the car into gear and gave me a look. "Joke, son."

Down the first long stretch I watched the road behind us, to see if the trooper was on our tail. The barricade vanished. Then there was nothing but snow: snow on the road, snow kicking up from the chains, snow on the trees, snow in the sky; and our trail in the snow. Then I faced forward and had a shock. The lay of the road behind us had been marked by our own tracks, but there were no tracks ahead of us. My father was breaking virgin snow between a line of tall trees. He was humming "Stars Fell on Alabama." I felt snow brush along the floorboards under my feet. To keep my hands from shaking I clamped them between my knees.

My father grunted in a thoughtful way and said, "Don't ever try this yourself."

"I won't."

"That's what you say now, but someday you'll get your license and then you'll think you can do anything. Only you won't be able to do this. You need, I don't know — a certain instinct."

"Maybe I have it."

"You don't. You have your strong points, but not this. I only mention it because I don't want you to get the idea this is something just anybody can do. I'm a great driver. That's not a virtue, okay? It's just a fact, and one you should be aware of. Of course you have to give the old heap some credit, too. There aren't many cars I'd try this with. Listen!"

I did listen. I heard the slap of the chains, the stiff, jerky rasp of the wipers, the purr of the engine. It really did purr. The old heap was almost new. My father couldn't afford it, and kept promising to sell it, but here it was.

I said, "Where do you think that policeman went to?"

"Are you warm enough?" He reached over and cranked up the blower. Then he turned off the wipers. We didn't need them. The clouds had brightened. A few sparse, feathery flakes drifted into our slipstream and were swept away. We left the trees and entered a broad field of snow that ran level for a while and then tilted sharply downward. Orange stakes had been planted at intervals in two parallel lines and my father steered a course between them, though they were far enough apart to leave considerable doubt in my mind as to exactly where the road lay. He was humming again, doing little scat riffs around the melody.

"Okay then. What are my strong points?"

"Don't get me started," he said. "It'd take all day."

"Oh, right. Name one."

"Easy. You always think ahead."

True. I always thought ahead. I was a boy who kept his clothes on numbered hangers to insure proper rotation. I bothered my teachers for homework assignments far ahead of their due dates so I could draw up schedules. I thought ahead, and that was why I knew that there would be other troopers waiting for us at the end of our ride, if we even got there. What I did not know was that my father would wheedle and plead his way past them — he didn't sing "O Tannenbaum," but just about — and get me home for dinner, buying a little more time before my mother decided to make the split final. I knew we'd get caught; I was resigned to it. And maybe for this reason I stopped moping and began to enjoy myself.

Why not? This was one for the books. Like being in a speedboat, only better. You can't go downhill in a boat. And it was all ours. And it kept coming, the laden trees, the unbroken surface of snow, the sudden white vistas. Here and there I saw hints of the road, ditches, fences, stakes, but not so many that I could have found my way. But then I didn't have to. My father was driving. My father in his forty-eighth year, rumpled, kind, bankrupt of honor, flushed with certainty. He was a great driver. All persuasion, no coercion. Such subtlety at the wheel, such tactful pedalwork. I actually trusted him. And the best was yet to come — switchbacks and hairpins impossible to describe. Except maybe to say this: if you haven't driven fresh powder, you haven't driven.

Bullet in the Brain

Anders couldn't get to the bank until just before it closed, so of course the line was endless and he got stuck behind two women whose loud, stupid conversation put him in a murderous temper. He was never in the best of tempers anyway, Anders — a book critic known for the weary, elegant savagery with which he dispatched almost everything he reviewed.

With the line still doubled around the rope, one of the tellers stuck a "POSITION CLOSED" sign in her window and walked to the back of the bank, where she leaned against a desk and began to pass the time with a man shuffling papers. The women in front of Anders broke off their conversation and watched the teller with hatred. "Oh, that's nice," one of them said. She turned to Anders and added, confident of his accord, "One of those little human touches that keep us coming back for more."

Anders had conceived his own towering hatred of the teller, but he immediately turned it on the presumptuous crybaby in front of him. "Damned unfair," he said. "Tragic, really. If they're not chopping off the wrong leg, or bombing your ancestral village, they're closing their positions."

She stood her ground. "I didn't say it was tragic," she said. "I just think it's a pretty lousy way to treat your customers."

"Unforgivable," Anders said. "Heaven will take note."

She sucked in her cheeks but stared past him and said nothing. Anders saw that the other woman, her friend, was looking in the same direction. And then the tellers stopped what they were doing, and the customers slowly turned, and silence came over the bank. Two men wearing black ski masks and blue business suits were standing to the side of the door. One of them had a pistol pressed against the guard's neck. The guard's eyes were closed, and his lips were moving. The other man had a sawed-off shotgun. "Keep your big mouth shut," the man with the pistol said, though no one had spoken a word. "One of you tellers hits the alarm, you're all dead meat. Got it?"

The tellers nodded.

"Oh, bravo," Anders said. *"Dead meat."* He turned to the woman in front of him. "Great script, eh? The stern, brass-knuckled poetry of the dangerous classes."

She looked at him with drowning eyes.

The man with the shotgun pushed the guard to his knees. He handed the shotgun to his partner and yanked the guard's wrists up behind his back and locked them together with a pair of handcuffs. He toppled him onto the floor with a kick between the shoulder blades. Then he took his shotgun back and went over to the security gate at the end of the counter. He was short and heavy and moved with peculiar slowness, even torpor. "Buzz him in," his partner said. The man with the shotgun opened the gate and sauntered along the line of tellers, handing each of them a Hefty bag. When he came to the empty position he looked over at the man with the pistol, who said, "Whose slot is that?"

Anders watched the teller. She put her hand to her throat and turned to the man she'd been talking to. He nodded. "Mine," she said.

"Then get your ugly ass in gear and fill that bag."

"There you go," Anders said to the woman in front of him. "Justice is done."

"Hey! Bright boy! Did I tell you to talk?"

"No," Anders said.

"Then shut your trap."

"Did you hear that?" Anders said. "'Bright boy.' Right out of 'The Killers.'"

"Please be quiet," the woman said.

"Hey, you deaf or what?" The man with the pistol walked over to Anders. He poked the weapon into Anders' gut. "You think I'm playing games?"

"No," Anders said, but the barrel tickled like a stiff finger and he had to fight back the titters. He did this by making himself stare into the man's eyes, which were clearly visible behind the holes in the mask: pale blue and rawly red-rimmed. The man's left eyelid kept twitching. He breathed out a piercing, ammoniac smell that shocked Anders more than anything that had happened, and he was beginning to develop a sense of unease when the man prodded him again with the pistol.

"You like me, bright boy?" he said. "You want to suck my dick?"

"No," Anders said.

"Then stop looking at me."

Anders fixed his gaze on the man's shiny wing-tip shoes.

"Not down there. Up there." He stuck the pistol under Anders' chin and pushed it upward until Anders was looking at the ceiling.

Anders had never paid much attention to that part of the bank, a pompous old building with marble floors and counters and pillars, and gilt scrollwork over the tellers' cages. The domed ceiling had been decorated with mythological figures whose fleshy, toga-draped ugliness

Anders had taken in at a glance many years earlier and afterward declined to notice. Now he had no choice but to scrutinize the painter's
work. It was even worse than he remembered, and all of it executed
with the utmost gravity. The artist had a few tricks up his sleeve and
used them again and again — a certain rosy blush on the underside of
the clouds, a coy backward glance on the faces of the cupids and fauns.
The ceiling was crowded with various dramas, but the one that caught
Anders' eye was Zeus and Europa — portrayed, in this rendition, as a
bull ogling a cow from behind a haystack. To make the cow sexy, the
painter had canted her hips suggestively and given her long, droopy
eyelashes through which she gazed back at the bull with sultry welcome. The bull wore a smirk and his eyebrows were arched. If there'd
been a bubble coming out of his mouth, it would have said, "Hubba
hubba."

"What's so funny, bright boy?"

"Nothing."

"You think I'm comical? You think I'm some kind of clown?"

"No."

"You think you can fuck with me?"

"No."

"Fuck with me again, you're history. *Capiche?*"

Anders burst out laughing. He covered his mouth with both hands
and said, "I'm sorry, I'm sorry," then snorted helplessly through his fingers and said, "*Capiche* — oh, God, *capiche,*" and at that the man with
the pistol raised the pistol and shot Anders right in the head.

The bullet smashed Anders' skull and ploughed through his brain and
exited behind his right ear, scattering shards of bone into the cerebral
cortex, the corpus callosum, back toward the basal ganglia, and down
into the thalamus. But before all this occurred, the first appearance of
the bullet in the cerebrum set off a crackling chain of ion transports
and neuro-transmissions. Because of their peculiar origin these traced a
peculiar pattern, flukishly calling to life a summer afternoon some forty
years past, and long since lost to memory. After striking the cranium
the bullet was moving at 900 feet per second, a pathetically sluggish,
glacial pace compared to the synaptic lightning that flashed around it.
Once in the brain, that is, the bullet came under the mediation of brain
time, which gave Anders plenty of leisure to contemplate the scene
that, in a phrase he would have abhorred, "passed before his eyes."

It is worth noting what Anders did not remember, given what he
did remember. He did not remember his first lover, Sherry, or what he
had most madly loved about her, before it came to irritate him — her
unembarrassed carnality, and especially the cordial way she had with

his unit, which she called Mr. Mole, as in, "Uh-oh, looks like Mr. Mole wants to play," and, "Let's hide Mr. Mole!" Anders did not remember his wife, whom he had also loved before she exhausted him with her predictability, or his daughter, now a sullen professor of economics at Dartmouth. He did not remember standing just outside his daughter's door as she lectured her bear about his naughtiness and described the truly appalling punishments Paws would receive unless he changed his ways. He did not remember a single line of the hundreds of poems he had committed to memory in his youth so that he could give himself the shivers at will — not "Silent, upon a peak in Darien," or "My God, I heard this day," or "All my pretty ones? Did you say all? O hell-kite! All?" None of these did he remember; not one. Anders did not remember his dying mother saying of his father, "I should have stabbed him in his sleep."

He did not remember Professor Josephs telling his class how Athenian prisoners in Sicily had been released if they could recite Aeschylus, and then reciting Aeschylus himself, right there, in the Greek. Anders did not remember how his eyes had burned at those sounds. He did not remember the surprise of seeing a college classmate's name on the jacket of a novel not long after they graduated, or the respect he had felt after reading the book. He did not remember the pleasure of giving respect.

Nor did Anders remember seeing a woman leap to her death from the building opposite his own just days after his daughter was born. He did not remember shouting, "Lord have mercy!" He did not remember deliberately crashing his father's car into a tree, or having his ribs kicked in by three policemen at an anti-war rally, or waking himself up with laughter. He did not remember when he began to regard the heap of books on his desk with boredom and dread, or when he grew angry at writers for writing them. He did not remember when everything began to remind him of something else.

This is what he remembered. Heat. A baseball field. Yellow grass, the whirr of insects, himself leaning against a tree as the boys of the neighborhood gather for a pickup game. He looks on as the others argue the relative genius of Mantle and Mays. They have been worrying this subject all summer, and it has become tedious to Anders: an oppression, like the heat.

Then the last two boys arrive, Coyle and a cousin of his from Mississippi. Anders has never met Coyle's cousin before and will never see him again. He says hi with the rest but takes no further notice of him until they've chosen sides and someone asks the cousin what position he wants to play. "Shortstop," the boy says. "Short's the best position they is." Anders turns and looks at him. He wants to hear Coyle's cousin repeat what he's just said, but he knows better than to ask. The others will think he's being a jerk, ragging the kid for his grammar. But that isn't it, not at all — it's that Anders is strangely roused, elated, by those final two words, their pure unexpectedness and their music. He takes the field in a trance, repeating them to himself.

The bullet is already in the brain; it won't be outrun forever, or charmed to a halt. In the end it will do its work and leave the troubled skull behind, dragging its comet's tail of memory and hope and talent and love into the marble hall of commerce. That can't be helped. But for now Anders can still make time. Time for the shadows to lengthen on the grass, time for the tethered dog to bark at the flying ball, time for the boy in right field to smack his sweat-blackened mitt and softly chant, *They is, they is, they is.*

Credits

Authors and Titles Index